THE LOAN OFFICER'S
HANDBOOK FOR SUCCESS

Steven W. Driscoll

COPYRIGHT

TABLE OF CONTENTS

TABLE OF CONTENTS

ACKNOWLEDGMENTS

I would like to thank the many people who helped me make this book possible since its first edition in 2003. Many of those are Mortgage Branch Managers, Loan Processors, and Mortgage loan originators I have worked with and know. To name a few they are: Tim Swartout, Terry Jo Carter, Ed Latscha, Michael Schneiderman, and Gary Wisben. My many thanks to those who have reviewed and edited this book, in whole or in part, prior to first publishing it in 2003. They are: Ernie Kroll, Debbie Herman, Steven Johnson, Tiffany Ipock, Barney Barnhart, Leslie Wilson, and Robert Van Hemel. Their comments and recommendations (which I have included) made this book better than it would have been otherwise.

I would be remiss if I didn't thank Gary Grahn for patiently teaching me how to effectively write business reports and memos in my early years in banking. On too many occasions to recount he mercilessly showed me, by using his red marker pen, how to reduce a multi-paged business report summary into one small paragraph. Also, thanks to Gary, I learned to express and state information in business memos the same way as if I were speaking to that person in the same room. And I hope, dear reader, that as you read this book you get a sense of that as well: Like I am speaking to you personally.

I also thank those of you who have previously purchased this book and emailed me with requests and suggestions of subjects to expound upon and/or include certain lending subjects in this book. I listened to you and have followed up as you requested. You know who you are and, again, I thank you.

And finally, to all of my family, friends, and working associates who have influenced and stood behind me throughout the years. I thank you all.

INTRODUCTION

This mortgage-training manual is the 2021 edition of *The Loan Officer's Handbook for Success*. Whenever I update this book, I research the mortgage lending business and market as much as I can. That means reviewing the latest version of Fannie Mae's Selling Guide and Eligibility Matrix, what new mortgage lending laws have become effective (since the previous year), and any new originating and processing documents, forms, and maximum loan amounts that are now required. Thus, a lot of time is spent reviewing Fannie Mae's and the Consumer Financial Protection Bureau (CFPB) website. And, sometimes I contact my friends, who are Escrow Officers, Mortgage Branch Managers, Appraisers, Loan Processors, and Underwriters and ask them what, if any, changes have occurred within the past year and in their particular area of mortgage lending that should be included in this book. I take their suggestions, along with what I feel needs to be included, and the revised 2021 edition of *The Loan Officer's Handbook for Success* is what you are now reading.

It seems that after the mortgage meltdown and crash of 2008 the "Powers that Be" were very busy burning the midnight oil in researching and implementing changes for originating and processing mortgage loans - so that the mortgage lending industry does not have (hopefully) another mortgage meltdown and crisis that we all went through. This mortgage loan originator's training manual contains those changes that have been implemented and are required that you now need to be familiar with and employ in loan origination and processing for 2021. That includes regulatory requirements from the Consumer Financial Protection Bureau (CFPB) for the mortgage industry and mortgage loan originators. For example, included within this revised and updated mortgage loan originator's manual are:

- Ability-To-Repay Rule
- Qualified Mortgage Rule
- High-Cost Mortgage Rule
- The Loan Origination Compensation Rule
- The new and revised Uniform Residential Loan Application (effective 2/1/2020)
- The Loan Estimate (replaced the Good Faith Estimate and Truth-In-Lending Statement)
- The Closing Disclosure (replaced the HUD-1 Settlement Statement)
- The Appraisal Rule
- New Home Loan Underwriting guidelines from Fannie Mae's *Eligibility Matrix* and *Selling Guide,* for the year 2021.
- Fannie Mae's *Lender Letter LL-2020-14*, dated November 24, 2020 showing the new maximum loan limits for 2021 that become effective on January 1, 2021.

The information in this book is also from actual trainings I have given to mortgage loan originators (when I was a mortgage Branch Manager), from seminars I have given to first-time homebuyers, and from my own personal experiences as a mortgage loan originator. I have structured this book with the new mortgage loan originators in mind and doing it this way I felt I could be more certain that "no stone would be unturned". And, after you have read this book I felt I could rest assured that you have the information you need to go forward and do your job professionally and hopefully make some good money while doing it. The sequence of subjects presented within this book also follows very closely the way I have trained mortgage loan originators.

It's kind of a funny thing that when the opportunity for me to become a mortgage loan originator first presented itself, in early 1995, I wanted to obtain and read a book that wrote about being a mortgage loan originator and about all the steps in originating mortgage loans. Or, more importantly, a book that would introduce me to this profession and train me on what I needed to know and how to do the things mortgage loan originators do in originating loans. At that time I could not find one book on this subject. I looked in books stores and libraries and found zilch! I thought perhaps knowing the ins and outs of this profession might be like knowing the secrets of magic. However, I must say that today, on the Internet, there are many mortgage training materials and resources that were not available when I first wrote this book. If you are thinking about getting into this profession, are just starting out as a mortgage loan originator, or have been in this profession for a while but would like to have a good reference guide then this is the book for you.

I have tried to present the information in this book as if you were in one of my training classes. I have also tried to make it as interesting as possible, throw in a story here and there, and go beyond what any technical book might discuss. I will be presenting the information contained within this book in my own words and in a way that (I hope) will be easily understandable to you. Also, because this is a training manual you will find that throughout this book I have capitalized, highlighted, and underlined certain words. I have done this because I believe that word or phrase deserves capitalizing and/or I wish to bring attention to that word or phrase. If I have made any grammatical errors in doing this (or any others) I apologize for that.

I was in the banking business for many years as an internal consultant and provided training seminars to employees and managers. For me, training was both exciting and gave me a great deal of personal satisfaction. Especially when I saw how that training improved an individual's job performance. As a manager, within the banking and mortgage lending areas, I have found that 80% of an employee's problems, with his or her job (often referred to as non-performance), could usually be attributed to the employee not knowing what they were supposed to do or were unaware of what they were not supposed to do. I learned, at that time, how important it is for managers to provide or see to it that their new employees received that all-important thing called training. Training, that gives new employees the necessary informational tools that can enhance their chances of realizing success in their new job and career.

I bring this up because after I had been a mortgage loan originator for only about a year I began attending some parties and gatherings that title and escrow companies give on holidays and special occasions for people in the mortgage lending business. When I first started attending those events I felt somewhat conscious of myself because I felt I was still "wet behind the ears." However, when I spoke with some other mortgage loan originators, who had been in the mortgage business longer than I had (with some of them having quite a few more years), I found that some of them did not know, understand, or had been trained in some very basic things regarding originating and processing of mortgage loans. Some of those mortgage loan originators told me that when they first started - their manager showed them to their desk and said, "There's the telephone, the phone book, and your telephone script. Call me if you have any questions." I could hardly believe it! But I have heard this story (or something similar to it) more than once. So, what happened to their training? There really wasn't any.

When I first got into the mortgage lending business, as a mortgage loan originator, my manager didn't have a structured training program but gave me the information he felt I needed to do the best job possible. For example, on my first morning as a new mortgage loan originator he put on my desk a stack of papers three inches thick, covering subjects such as FHA, VA, and conventional conforming loan processing and lending regulations. When I finished with that stack then he tested me and gave me another stack to read. After that he did the same. This went on for about four weeks. I hadn't taken a call or met with any loan customers yet. It was his mortgage company and I'm sure he wanted me to be knowledgeable and professional when I finally did meet with loan customers. Since I was representing his mortgage company, I'm sure he wanted me to know what I was doing and to be able to provide the best customer service possible to them. Into my fifth week I told him, "Look, I have demonstrated that I know the lending information (he had given me). I think it's time for me to begin applying this." He agreed and that's when all the material I had read really started to come together and make sense.

On reflection, there was a lot of information he gave me to read that I really didn't need to know or read at that time. But that will not happen here. I have specifically designed this book to contain just the nuts and bolts and real-world information of mortgage lending that you need to know, as a new mortgage loan originator, to be knowledgeable, professional, and provide the best customer service to your prospective borrowing customers. And, of course, make a good living while doing it. I realize that this training manual now contains 519 pages - but let me assure you: Everything in this training manual is the "meat and potatoes" of what every mortgage loan originator should be familiar with. I absolutely refuse to put any fluff in any of my training manuals.

As I mentioned previously, I have designed this book pretty much the way I have trained mortgage loan originators in the past. Thus, the subjects being covered are presented in a sequential order that goes from the simple to the more complex, while building on the information previously discussed. And, the flow of the chapters, within each section of this book and what they cover, follows very closely the sequence of originating and processing home loans by a mortgage loan originator (if that is possible):

1. How to Setup Your Work Station to make your time more productive.
2. Understanding the Basic Concepts and Terms of mortgage lending.
3. Qualifying Customers: When they call-in and/or you meet with them.
4. The different Types of Mortgage Loans and their Underwriting Guidelines.
5. Completing the Loan Application and Packaging the Loan for Submission.

6. Reading and Understanding the various Reports that can affect your loans and are required.
7. Processing Loans from Start (loan application) to Finish (loan closing).
8. Lending Regulations you need to be familiar with and apply.
9. Marketing Your Services as a mortgage loan originator.

Also, I wanted to make this book as self-contained as possible. I did this because some of you may not be currently working at a mortgage or lending company and may either not be aware of these forms or have them available to you. I therefore have included some exhibits of those forms and reports discussed in this book. And, where available, I also show the website addresses of those forms so you can download them in PDF format to your computer.

And, I have included a comprehensive Index to make it easy for you to find the subject matter you are researching or working on. Thus, I have composed this book to be not only a training manual for mortgage loan originators but also a reference guide for new and experienced mortgage loan originators as well. It is my hope that I have done this in a way that enables you to obtain the information you need easily and quickly.

In writing this mortgage loan originator's training manual I wanted it to be as complete and comprehensive as possible. Therefore, the training material in this book is primarily for mortgage loan professionals that work for a mortgage company. If you work for a bank, credit union, financial institution, or correspondent lender then some of the lending procedures, stated in this book may not apply to you. For example:

1. **Shopping your mortgage loans to Wholesale Lenders:**
   Your bank or financial institution may require you to submit all your mortgage loans to your bank or financial institution versus shopping the Wholesale Lender Market for the right loan program with the best interest rates and terms for your loan customers.

2. **Loan Disclosures to your Loan Customers:**
   Working for a bank or financial institution may require you to provide more or less mortgage Loan Disclosures, given to your loan customers, than what a mortgage loan originator working for a mortgage company may be required to provide.

3. **Processing of your mortgage loans:**
   This training manual was written for mortgage loan originators who process their own loans as well as for those who pass their home loan files over to their Loan Processor. If you work for a bank or financial institution then you would most likely pass your home loan files over to your Loan Processor after you have originated that loan.

There may be a few more minor differences that may exist but those would most likely depend on what bank or financial institution you work for. However, although these small differences may exist for you - that would not affect the rest of the other 98% of the material within this training manual. It has been my experience that most banks and financial institutions have an in-house mortgage loan originator training program - which should enable you to make those distinctions and differences in what is expected of you as a mortgage loan originator for that bank or financial institution and what is stated in this book. If you are uncertain of this then please contact me at: StevenD@MortgageTrainingLibrary.com

I love the mortgage lending business because it allows me to do many of the things I enjoy doing: Meeting with customers - sometimes in their home, doing the financial stuff that needs to be done, and interacting with all the different mortgage lending related professionals necessary to make a home loan happen. There are times when I felt I have really helped some folks financially by savings them hundreds of dollars per month on their monthly bills or helped some young couple get a mortgage loan for their first home. Sometimes these types of loans give you what I call a "warm fuzzy" - it just makes you feel good to be in a profession you enjoy and can truly help people. I hope that once you have read the information in this book, get your feet wet with a few loans, then you too will love this business.

And finally, I wish to include in this Introduction something I would rather not have to - but have been advised that I should: A Disclaimer. First, let me say that the information in this book has been well researched and, as I previously mentioned, much of it is based on my personal experiences as a branch manager, mortgage loan originator, and trainer of mortgage loan professionals.

Now, when I first told other experienced mortgage professionals, back in 2003, that I was writing a training book for new mortgage loan originators, some of them asked me if I was including a chapter on mortgage lending regulations. I told them that, of course, I was. After hearing my reply some of them looked startled and looked at me like I had two heads. When this occurred, I just asked them, "How can I write a book for training new mortgage loan originators on mortgage lending if I do not include a chapter on lending regulations? Many of the very things we must do in originating and processing loans is influenced and dictated by lending regulations that determine if our home loans and we are "In Compliance". And, the consequences for being out of compliance can be quite severe. Besides, a mortgage lending training manual without a discussion on lending regulations and laws would just not be complete." On these points they did agree.

However, one thing is for sure: I am not an Attorney and do not have the legal right and/or capacity to advice on any legal matters. And yet, many of the required procedures for processing mortgage loans presented in this book are based on lending regulations and laws, within the Real Estate Settlement Procedures Act (RESPA) and the Truth-In-Lending Act (TILA), and by the Consumer Financial Protection Bureau (CFPB) for example. I, therefore, respectfully submit my Disclaimer on the following page:

DISCLAIMER:

The Loan Officer's Handbook for Success is published in recognition of the great need for mortgage lending information for new and experienced mortgage loan originators regarding the origination and processing of mortgage loans. Reasonable care and research has been taken in preparation of this text. However, the material presented in this book is for training purposes only and is not intended to provide legal advice. If you have any questions regarding any loan procedures, regulations, and/or laws presented in this book then please consult your attorney. Use of the information and material in this book is done without recourse.

OK. With that said, let's get started now and go on to the first Section and begin at the beginning – with some Basic Stuff You Should Know.

Section I

BASIC STUFF

I felt that the title of "Basic Stuff" for the first Section of this book was the most appropriate because in the first two chapters of this book that's exactly what we are going to talk about. Within the first chapter I'll begin by discussing how to use your calculator - to determine those amounts and figures related to mortgage loans, how mortgage branches are usually set up and arranged, and how mortgages loans generally flow in a branch from loan origination to closing. And, how to setup your desk and workstation when you show up for your first day of work as a mortgage loan originator.

The second chapter presents and defines many of the mortgage lending terms you'll hear that are commonly used in your profession as a mortgage loan originator. The following two chapters present those subjects:

> ➤ Basic Stuff You Should Know
> ➤ Common Mortgage Lending Terms

Let's get started and go to the first chapter and begin at the beginning with Basic Stuff You Should Know.

Chapter 1

BASIC STUFF YOU SHOULD KNOW

When you show up for your first day of work, as a new mortgage loan originator, for a mortgage branch or company, you should bring with you some basic tools of the trade and have a plan of action of what you intend to accomplish that day. This chapter is designed to assist you in achieving exactly that. To begin, let's talk about some of the tools you should bring with you when you arrive at your new mortgage company.

I. Tools of the Trade:

One of the most important tools you need as a mortgage loan originator is a good financial calculator. I am not endorsing any but my thinking is that the best ones out there are the HP-12C or the HP-10B. However, the HP-12C is historically looked upon as 'The Financial Man's Calculator'. When I first bought mine in 1983 it cost me all of about $135.00. Today, you can buy one of these for about $65.00 - that's technology for you. However, the newer HP financial calculators seem to come with turbo speed and this is very apparent when you are doing a complicated financial calculation. For example, the HP-12C displays the word "running" while it's calculating - while the newer HPs give you the answer right away. I can tell you that it was like parting with an old friend when I retired my HP-12C and bought my new HP-10B. Whether you get an HP calculator or not - the important thing is to get a good financial calculator that you can use and depend on.

For those of you who have never used a financial calculator before - this is for you. Otherwise, feel free to skip over this.

If you have a financial calculator then the top row of all the keys on your calculator will most likely have four of the most important keys you will use as a Mortgage loan originator. Because I cannot see your particular calculator - I will guess what the top of those Keys have written on them:

N   I/YR   PV   PMT

N = Stands for the Term of the Loan. For example, if the loan has a term of 30 years then you would enter 360 (months). For a 15 year term = 180 months and so on.

I/YR = This represents the Interest Rate Per Year. Thus, if the annual interest rate is 7.50% you would enter 7.5 here. I should note that some calculators are designed for you to enter the interest rate converted into the monthly rate (if this Key is labeled "I" only then that is probably the case). If you have a calculator like that then divide the annual rate by 12 and enter that figure into the "I" Key. For example, with an annual interest rate of 7.50% - the monthly interest rate of 0.625 should be entered into that Key (for exactness - enter the interest rate with 3 digits to the right of the decimal point = for thousandths of a point).

PV = Enter here the Present Value (outstanding balance) of the mortgage - or the Total Amount of the Loan.

PMT = This Key gives you the Monthly Payment Amount. I should mention here that some calculators always display this figure as a Negative. This is because that calculator, being a financial calculator, interprets amounts (entered and displayed) in terms of cash flows. And, Payments are interpreted (by that calculator) as outgoing cash flows and therefore presented as a negative. If your calculator does this then remember this when you are entering the Payment Amount into this Key: Always enter the number as a Negative (with a minus sign). Otherwise, that calculator will give you some goofy numbers - and that's not what you want. However, if your calculator displays the PMT figure as a positive number then please disregard my comments regarding this and any future reference to this as well.

How can we use this information in our jobs as Mortgage loan originators? Well, say you are working on a loan and want to know what the monthly payment is on that loan. Let's say the Loan amount is $150,000, the Interest Rate is 7 or 7.0%, and the term is 30 years. OK, then we would enter 150,000 into the **PV** Key (always enter these without the dollar sign or commas) then 7.0 in the **I/YR** Key and finally enter 360 into the **N** Key. After you have done that - then press the **PMT** Key and that will give you the monthly payment of -997.95 or 997.95 for $997.95.

The beauty of these four keys is that you can enter information into any three (regardless of the order in which you entered them) and it will give you the correct answer in the 4th Key. For instance, using the same numbers, as in our example above, let's say you are trying to figure out what the interest rate is on an outstanding loan. You know the original amount of that loan (when it first closed) was $150,000 on a 30 Year fixed rate loan with a P&I payment of $997.95 (don't forget to enter this number as a negative if required). What is the Interest Rate on that Loan? You already know the answer but just press the Interest Rate key and you will see for yourself. Pretty cool, huh?

Just like we did above, to determine what the interest rate was, you could do the same if you were looking for the Principal Loan Amount, the Term of the loan, or the Monthly Payment. All you have to do is enter the loan's information you know for three of these four Keys and it will accurately figure out the 4th Key's information for you.

Now here's a little additional tidbit of information that many Mortgage loan originators don't know about. Looking at this same row of financial keys on your calculator - look to the right of that **PMT** (payment) Key. You should see a Key labeled **FV**. The **FV** on this Key stands for Future Value and many times, in doing financial calculations, this key is used to determine the value of an investment sometime in the future.

However, you can also use this key to determine what the outstanding balance of a loan will be after so many months and years of payments having been made. This is a question you may get every once in a while and if you can show your customers the answer to this question then they will be even more impressed with you than they already were. So, let's see how we do this. Using the numbers in our example above let's say your customer asked you what the balance on their loan will be after 3 years of making payments. You give a thoughtful expression and say something like, "Hmmm, I believe I can calculate that for you." OK, stay with me on this:

1. First you enter the numbers of the customer's current or possible loan. Taking those numbers from our example above:

   360   = **N**
   7.0   = **I/YR**
   150,000 = **PV**
   Now Press the PMT Key => -997.95 (or shows it as a positive number: 997.75)

2. Next (without changing any of the numbers in the registers on that calculator) enter now the number of months representing the time period (in the future) you are looking at - into that **N** Key. Thus, we are looking at a time horizon of 3 years - or 36 months (I should note that those months represent months that the customers have actually made payments on that loan). So you enter:

   36 = into **N**

3. And finally, all you now need to do is press the **FV** Key and it will give you the outstanding balance of that loan after 36 payments have been made.

   FV = $145,090.44

   Pretty neat don't you think? If you want to have a little fun - to test out what I told you about most Mortgage loan originators not knowing how to do this then check it out for yourself. Now please, don't be arrogant about it. But do have fun and, show them how to do it as well - so they can have the opportunity to impress their customers too. Who knows, they may need this information to work out an important but difficult loan one day.

Before I leave this discussion on calculators I do want to mention that each time you are doing a new calculation on your calculator be sure to clear it (the registers) out before you begin a new financial problem. Otherwise, the calculator may use the information, of the previous calculation, in calculating the solution to your current problem or calculation. So, be sure to clear your calculator or registers before beginning a new calculation. Got it? Good.

The next thing I would recommend you have is a **good blue ink pen**. You would be surprised how often customers have complemented me on my pens - how nice it was or how good it felt in their hand. But beyond that - you always want to have a pen with you in case you need it. Also, when I am working, I always carry a standard sized yellow pad with me as well. That's because I do not like to rely on my memory for those things that are important to recall later. I write it down.

And finally, a **good briefcase**. I still have my leather briefcase I bought myself when I graduated from college. I was in banking then so it was more or less expected of me. But even in the mortgage lending business - you are carrying around important papers and that's one of the purposes of a briefcase.

II. Composition of Most Mortgage Branch Offices:
When you show up for your first day of work, as a mortgage loan originator, you may be wondering what it will look like and the layout of that branch office. I have been in many mortgage branch offices and although the shape may change the actual layout (of that shape) seems to change very little. For starters, there are usually about 5 main areas you will become familiar with: 1. The manager's office - usually at one end of the branch's office, 2. The Loan Processor's office - usually not too far away from the manager's office, 3. The Utility Room - where the fax, the copy machine, loan files and documents, interest rate pricing sheets (more on this later) are located (usually tacked to a corkboard on the wall), 4. The Receptionist - at the front of the office (if you are lucky enough to have one), and 5. The mortgage loan originators' desks and offices. If you are a new mortgage loan originator (a trainee) and you have your own office – wow, you are a lucky person.

This is generally how you will find the layout of your mortgage branch office. The way it is actually laid out usually alludes to how loans flow through that branch. I will speak more about this later.

III. Dress For Success:
Some people may consider this to be somewhat snobbish but I have found that people treat you differently depending upon how they perceive you. John T. Molloy who wrote the book *Dress for Success* also wrote an excellent book titled *Live for Success*. In his book (*Live for Success*) John Molloy empirically proved (and I am paraphrasing here since it has been years since I read it) that people react differently to others depending upon the way they are dressed, walk, carry themselves, and the way they speak. Molloy found, through his personal experiments that if someone was perceived as professional and what Molloy coined as "upper class" then most people would respond favorably to that person and give them their attention. However, if they did not perceive in that person those qualities - then they most likely would respond otherwise or without any enthusiasm. My point here is: No matter how you dress to work - dress well. If you wear jeans - wear clean jeans. If you wear ties - wear a fashionable tie. Whatever you

wear should have the appearance of someone professional and whom your customers will feel comfortable talking with. Where your business is located will usually dictate your dress code. For example, if you are a mortgage loan originator in the city of San Francisco, Seattle, Los Angeles, New York, or Boston you most likely would wear a suit and tie. In outlying areas - perhaps a more casual dress is appropriate. Rule of Thumb: Wear what your boss wears (same gender) or what other successful mortgage loan originators in your branch or office wear.

IV. Know Your Loan Products:

Certainly, one of the most important things you should know as a mortgage loan originator are the various loan products. While one could say, sure - knowing a company's products could be true with any job or profession, it's even truer when you are in sales. This is because in sales you are usually meeting with your customers face to face or on the telephone and primarily selling them on two things: Yourself and your product(s). You are first selling them on yourself because in doing this you are answering the question: Why should they go with you versus all the other mortgage companies or mortgage loan originators who sell the same thing? And, you are selling them on your loan products.

And, there is another reason why it is so important to know your loan products: Not only so you can talk intelligently about them but also because you don't know what a customer knows – when you do talk about a loan product. Because you don't know what your customer knows it is very important to not try to BS your way through a sales presentation. If you try to do this and your prospect knows you are BSing them then you will have lost integrity and credibility in their eyes and no sale will take place. However, if they ask a question that you don't know the answer to and you say something like, "You know, that's a good question and if you will allow me to, I'd like to: 1. Talk to my manager about that, or 2. Look that up and get back to you. Would that be acceptable?" If that prospect knows the answer (or even if they didn't) they will respect you for admitting that (that you don't know it all) and perhaps appreciate the extra effort you said you would make to get that answer back to them. I have made many sales just this way.

But for now, don't worry about your loan product knowledge. That's what this book is for. For now, just make it a goal to acquaint yourself with most of the basic and most often requested loan products. We will get into the Loan Products in detail in a later chapter. So hang in there.

V. Know the Mortgage Loan Originator's responsibilities in Originating and Processing Home Loans:

As a mortgage loan originator it is your responsibility to originate, package, and follow-up to oversee each (of your) loans to closing and funding. I have found that each mortgage branch office has slightly different expectations of their mortgage loan originators. However, most mortgage loan originators are expected to:

1. Originate the Loan: This means you obtain the loan by answering incoming telephone calls from interested prospects, market your services through mail, flyers, obtain loans on the Internet, etc.

2. Complete an Application on Your Customers: This could be done in person at your office or their home, over the telephone, or by mail.

3. Research the Loan Request to find the best loan product that meets the needs and goals of your customers.

4. Complete the Paperwork on Your Customers: This includes getting a completed and signed Loan Application and Loan Disclosures and sending them a completed Loan Estimate.

5. Maintain an ongoing Comments Sheet of what has transpired on each loan and your conversations with your customers and any third-party providers (or any parties connected to that loan). And, obtain the supporting documents required for that type of loan.

6. Prepare a Shadow File containing copies of those loan documents that you absolutely need, after you have passed your loan file to the Loan Processor, so you can continue to move that loan file towards the closing table, and then…

7. Package your loan (usually in a loan stacking order requested by your Loan Processor) and submit it to a Wholesale Lender or your Loan Processor (many times your Loan Processor will do this).

8. Keep in touch with your customers while the loan is in Loan Processing and obtain the information and loan documents as requested by the Loan Processor or as required to fully approve and close that loan.

9. Upon Approval of your Loan, order the Appraisal and Title report. Review the Appraisal and Title Report when they are received.

10. In concert with the Loan Processor - seek to satisfy all Prior-To-Doc and Prior-To-Funding conditions on your loans.

11. Upon satisfaction of all Prior-To-Doc requirements orchestrate the closing of that loan with your customers and the Title & Escrow Company, Attorney, or Closing Office. Again, your Loan Processor may do this for you.

12. Attend the closing of your loans (if the distance from you is not too far away).

13. And finally, after your loans have funded then package each loan in a folder (usually in a loan stacking order) to be stored in the Closed Loans section. This is another step which Loan Processors also usually do.

I know, it sounds like a lot to learn and it is - but this is exactly why training is so important. And, you can be sure that we are going to talk about each one of these. And, when we are done you will see that it really isn't as difficult or insurmountable as it appears. And, don't worry about the terminology and acronyms I used or will use. I will later talk more about these in the next chapter. And, after you have read that chapter then you will be talking like an "old pro". Now that I think about it this may be the first time I have ever seen a sequential list of the duties of a mortgage loan originator in originating and processing loans. But again, that's one of the reasons I wrote this book.

VI. Understand the Flow of a Loan in a Mortgage Branch Office:

While this ties in with what we have discussed above, it differs because here we are focusing on the flow of a loan as it is being processed and progressing through the mortgage office towards closing. Listed below are the usual steps a loan goes through as it is processed through the Branch Office:

1. Loan Application is completed and a loan file (folder) is prepared by the mortgage loan originator.

2. Loan File is submitted to the Loan Processor – either by receiving a borrower's home loan file folder or directly through the Loan Processor's underwriting software – from what is on the MLO's loan originator's software.

3. Copy of the Loan File is submitted to the targeted Wholesale Lender. Or, the loan file is emailed to the targeted Wholesale Lender.

4. The Loan File is worked on by the Loan Processor and mortgage loan originator to satisfy all PTD and PTF Conditions (assuming the loan has been approved).

5. After loan closing, documents from the Loan Processor and mortgage loan originator are combined and stored away in a Closed or Declined file section (usually in a labeled box stored in some closet).

VII. Know How to Read Prior-To-Doc (PTD) and Prior-To-Funding (PTF) Loan Conditions & How to Satisfy Them:

Once you have put together a loan file and identified what Wholesale Lender you wish to send your loan to (more on this later) then you or your Loan Processor will submit your loan request to that Wholesale Lender. About 48 hours later (24 if you are lucky) that Wholesale Lender will email and/or fax back to you one of two things: An Approval Sheet (or Conditional Approval) or Denial Sheet. They look the same except one says Approved and the other Denied. If it says Approved, at the top of that sheet, then it will also show the approved loan amount, the interest rate, and term.

It's important to always review this because sometimes Wholesale Lenders change things - in order to approve a loan. This usually falls around the loan amount or interest rate. Below, on that sheet, you will also find a list of the Prior-To-Doc conditions that need to be satisfied before the Closing Docs will be wired (or mailed) to the closing office - where your customers sign their closing loan documents. On this approval sheet may also be listed some Prior-To-Funding conditions. These are conditions that must be satisfied before Funding of that loan takes place. The important point here is that it's important for you to know how to read this sheet and how to satisfy the PTD and PTF conditions - so no time is lost in this phase of processing your loan. We will go over this later so you are familiar with this statement and confident on how to proceed.

VIII. Become (Personally) Acquainted with Wholesale Lenders & Their Loan Products:

It can be quite common that on a daily basis that Wholesale Lender Reps (who represent their Lenders) will drop by your branch office and leave you a flyer of their latest and greatest loan programs and products. This is an excellent opportunity to acquaint yourself with what that Lender has to offer. Some of those Wholesale Reps used to be mortgage loan originators and they appreciate what you're going through - in terms of learning the business. If you are working on a loan most Wholesale Reps will be happy to talk to you about it. If they (their Lender) are unable to do that loan then they may even suggest one or more (other) Lenders who possibly could.

I therefore suggest introducing yourself to every Wholesale Rep that comes into your branch office and find out what you can about their loan programs and products. Doing this you'll learn the nuances of packaging loans a lot quicker and who knows - they might just have the loan program you are looking for at that time or will need tomorrow or next week.

Later in this book we will talk about reading a Wholesale Lender's product sheet (what they call a matrix - nothing to do with the movie) as well as reading the Lender's pricing sheet (showing their interest rates for each type of loan).

IX. Understand How to Qualify Your Customers:

If you have been in sales then you understand what I mean by qualifying your customers. When we are qualifying a customer in mortgage lending we are asking questions to determine (and this is most important) - what is the Customer's Goal in obtaining their loan (i.e. lower their interest rate with a lower monthly mortgage payment, home improvements, cash-out to take a vacation, consolidate debts - to also lower their monthly debt servicing, etc.)? Once we know this then it is your job, as mortgage loan originator, to ask addition questions to see if the customer qualifies for that loan (or provides you with information so you can research that possibility).

When I first became a mortgage loan originator, I admit it, I was a little nervous about talking to folks who first called in for a loan. But after a while I got pretty comfortable with it. I figured, hey, they don't know I'm new. I will just ask those questions and try to provide the best customer service I can. And that's exactly what I recommend you do. Like an experienced mortgage loan originator I knew once told me, "Just like being a medical doctor - you are the Mortgage Doctor. When you go see a medical doctor that doctor asks you where does it hurt and might pock you here and there. As a Mortgage Doctor find out where it hurts your customers and/or what their financial needs are. They might say that their interest rate is too high with too high a mortgage payment. Or, need more room in the house (home improvement) or all their monthly payments are too much (debt consolidation). You get the idea. Once you have diagnosed their problem or need - then you need to ask further to see if you can prescribe a cure (a loan that will solve their problem)."

So, see yourself as the Mortgage Doctor. In doing so and in qualifying your customers remember: The most important thing you should initially find out is what's troubling that customer or what their loan need and goal is. Later on I will show you a customer-qualifying worksheet you can use so you will know what questions to ask. This should help you to feel more comfortable about qualifying your customers. After you do this once or twice you'll see there's nothing to it.

X. Stay in Touch with Your Customers:
I cannot over emphasize how important it is to stay on top of your loans and stay in touch with your loan customers. What I mean by staying in touch with your loan customers is to call your customers at least once a week and let them know how their loan is progressing, what your current loan needs are (waiting for the appraisal, title report, employment verification, etc.), what you are still needing from them, and when you estimate their loan closing will occur. I cannot tell you how many times I have met with customers who wanted a loan who told me that they previously met with a mortgage loan originator (with another company) and after that they either never heard back from him or her again or rarely called them (and/or they were unable to contact him or her and they didn't return their calls). Don't let this happen to you.

Regarding this: One of your goals should be to provide the best customer service possible to your customers. You do that by: 1. Calling your customers at least once a week and updating them on the progress of their loan, 2. When something important comes up in the loan (e.g. it's approved, need a PTD condition from them, appraisal came in lower than expected, and/or need to adjust the loan amount, etc.) then call your customers at once and inform them, 3. Make yourself accessible to your customers so they can call or contact you if they want or need to, and 4. Follow-up with all calls (customer or loan related calls) immediately, or at least the same day or within 24 hours.

You should be aware that there are plenty of mortgage loan originators or lenders out there who would love to take (or as we say in the business – steal) your customers away from you and take your loan. If you stay in touch with your customers then it improves your chances that you won't lose that customer and at the very least they won't be sitting at the desk of another mortgage loan originator telling them about how they met with you but they never heard back from you after that. Stay in touch with your customers.

XI. Stay on Top of Your Loans in Your Loan Pipeline:
The term "Pipeline" is a term used in sales that refers to the number of sales you are currently working on (and completed) for a specific period of time (usually the current month). In the field of lending this refers to how many loans you are currently working on (and I mean that you have also completed a home loan application on) and loan(s) closed (or expect to) for that month. For example, your manager may ask you "How many loans do you have in your pipeline this month?"

When you are first starting out or when things are slow and you are working on only one or two loans then it's not too difficult to stay on top of them. However, as your pipeline begins to increase (usually around 3 or more) then it begins to get increasingly difficult to remember the details of each loan and what remains to be done for each and what each customer and other third-party provider (e.g. Appraisers, Title Officers, etc.) said to you. Because of this, it is even more important that you maintain a record of what's going on with each loan and what yet needs to be done for each.

To facilitate that and help you along here you should be maintaining a Comments Sheet on each loan you are working on (item #5 in Know the mortgage loan originator's Responsibility in Originating/Processing a Loan above). Also, years ago I designed a form that I complete on a weekly basis (Monday mornings) that includes all loans I am working on and what needs to be done that week for each. This helps me stay on top of my loans and at a glance I can tell what my loan priorities are and what I need to accomplish that week for each loan. You will find a copy of this form in Exhibit I. While this Exhibit shows you what the Weekly Loan Status Worksheet looks like - if you wish to use this type of form then I suggest entering this form on either MS Excel (or any worksheet) and setup the page size as Legal and Landscape orientation. Doing that will provide you with more space to enter more data for each loan you are working on.

When I was a mortgage branch manager one of my responsibilities was to make sure that my Mortgage loan originators were on top of their loans. If I walked up to a mortgage loan originator and asked them, "How's it going on that Davis file and what's the status of it?" If that mortgage loan originator said, "I don't know or I'm not sure." My response would be, "That's not good enough. Review your loan file and get back to me within the hour." If a Mortgage loan originator is not on top of his or her loans and doesn't know the status of their loan(s) and what needs to be done then they either can't or won't progress that loan towards closing in a timely manner - as they should be doing. In other words, they are not doing their job. So please, Stay on Top of Your Loans.

XII. Setting Up Your Work Station:

After you have been shown your desk, where you will be working, and got settled in then one of the first things I suggest you do is get your Work Station setup to do loans. Your Work Station is your desk and if you are lucky enough would include an office. The thing you want to do is setup your work area so those things you need, in researching and processing loans, will be at your fingertips. Doing this, will result in the time you are working on loans to be more effective, efficient, and productive. It also will save you the time you would otherwise spend in running around trying to find those documents or files you need to research and/or process your loans. So, with that said, here are the things I suggest you do to setup and prepare your Work Station for the time when you start to GET BUSY:

Prepare File Folders Containing the Following:
  A. Documents Directly Related to Taking a Loan:
    Prepare separate File Folders containing the following:

1. Blank Qualifying Analysis Worksheets (Copied from this Book)
2. Uniform Residential Loan Applications (1003)
3. Loan Estimates
4. Comment Sheets
5. About 3 complete sets of Loan Disclosures
6. Loan Document Needs List (Copied from this Book)
7. Flowchart on Processing a Loan (Copied from this Book)
8. Title Insurance Fee Schedule, Private Mortgage Insurance (PMI) Fee Booklet, any notes you have made regarding completing the 1003, and Loan Estimate. And, any other notes regarding taking and preparing a loan application.

  B. Lender Rate Sheets:
    1. Approved Lender List:
      If you are working for a mortgage company then your branch office should have an Approved Lenders List. This is a list of those Wholesales Lenders that your company is currently approved with and can submit loans to. This list may have as many as 50 Lenders or more!

    2. Conforming Lender Rate Sheets:
      Out of all those Lenders, on the above approved Lenders List, your office will most likely have selected a handful of Lenders (on that list) who they normally send their Conforming loans to. Talk with your Branch Manager or other mortgage loan originators in your office and find out who those Lenders are. Then take a copy of those Lenders' rate and matrix sheets and put those in this file folder. And, when you have time, become familiar with what those Lenders have to offer – in terms of interest rates, loan products, etc. Doing this, when you do get a Conventional Conforming Loan application then you won't be running around wondering what Lender you should sent that loan to.

    3. Non-Conforming Lender Rate Sheets:
      Do the same thing here you did with Conforming Lenders, but here you are preparing a file folder for Non-Conforming Lenders. Try to limit the number of Lenders in this folder to no more than two Non-Conforming Lenders.

    4. Government Loan Lender Rate Sheets:
      If your mortgage company does FHA and VA loans then who is the best Lender to send those to? Because govie loans require different and additional loan documents and processing steps it wouldn't hurt to include those here (in this folder) and any processing notes to do these types of loans.

As time goes on you may decide to create separate file folders for each individual Lender. But for now a separate folder based on loan type should be fine.

C. Third-Party Provider File Folder or Folders:

When you start working on a loan you will sooner or later need to order an Appraisal, Title Report, and make arrangements for the Closing or Escrow of a loan. Who is going to do that? Don't wait until that time comes. Find out now who is a good Conforming, FHA, and VA Appraiser. Get at least 3 appraiser names for each. What Title Company does your office usually order Title Insurance from and why? Who does most of the Closings for your office? Sometimes your purchasing customers may want to have the home inspected. Who will do that? You get my point. The idea here is to create file folders that have the information you need when you need it.

Also, within each Third-Party Provider File Folder you should have current pricing sheets that show you how much that provider charges for different properties, loan amounts, and locations. When we get to Chapter 12, that discusses the Loan Estimate, you will see how important it is for you to have this pricing information available and at your fingertips.

D. Index Card File:

Just as you have done in creating file folders for the above items - begin filling up your Card File Index with everybody you do business with. Thus, when you want to call someone to setup a meeting, order an Appraisal or Title Insurance, or schedule a Closing – you will have the telephone numbers and ways of contacting that person right there in front of you.

E. Marketing Your Services as a Mortgage Loan Originator:

This book discusses Marketing Your Services, within Chapter 27, but you should also talk with the other mortgage loan originators in your office and find out what has worked for them. Did they create a mail flyer that really brought in the business for them? See if you can get a copy of it and put that in this file folder for Marketing. Not to copy that Flyer but to give you some ideas when you create your own. As you encounter and see creative and new marketing ideas that bring loan leads in - write them down and/or get a copy of them and put them in this folder. When you are trying to come up with a new marketing approach then take out this file folder and go through it. Doing that might be just what you need to get the cobwebs out of the way and get those creative juices flowing.

F. Office Equipment on Your Desk:
   Have those office equipment items that you need and use throughout the day either on top of your desk or in one of your top desk drawers (e.g. Stapler, standard size or legal note pad, blue ink pens, and paper clips). And don't forget your calculator.

XIII. Get Organized:

I cannot overemphasize how important it is to be organized in our business. As I have said, sometimes it can get quite crazy in our mortgage lending business, especially around the end of the month and when you are processing about 3 or more loans that hopefully will close before month-end. Many of the things I have suggested should keep you in good shape when things do get a little frantic and other mortgage loan originators are running around trying to find a Lender's Rate sheet and Loan Processors are starting to pull the hair out of their heads. Besides what I have said, one thing that I learned many years ago when I was a young bank executive was - **Plan Your Day and Work Your Plan**.

That is often referred to as one of the aspects of Time Management. One of the things that I did every day and still do is - that the very first thing I did in the morning when I got to work (and after getting a cup of coffee) was to make a list of all the important things I needed to do that day to stay on track and make the most productive use of my time. I'd list the folks I needed to call that day and their phone numbers, the various people I had to see, and meetings planned for that day. And, what tasks must be done that day as well. And, I would place that list on top of my desk, so I could easily see it when I needed to. After I completed each task I would then checked off that task and then focused on the next remaining high priority task or objective. When I got into a management position I really appreciated the habit of doing this every day. Because when you are in a management position then interruptions are part of your job and it's easy to get sidetracked. But if you have your Daily To-Do List then you can glance at your list and remind yourself of what yet you need to do to achieve the goals you have set for yourself for that day.

If you do what I have suggested above then you will find that you will be well organized and have those loan documents, telephone numbers, and contact names right there in front of you when you need them the most. And, this very thing becomes increasingly more important when you are under the pressure of time – like putting together a loan proposal. Sure, you will most likely have to go get a copy of a Lender's current rate sheet (or look it up on your computer) but most everything else you will need should be right there at your fingertips. Believe me, it gets crazy sometimes in our business but the more organized you are then the less running around and less pressure you will feel. And that is a very good thing.

Now that we have talked about some of the basic stuff you should be aware of and know in your ongoing activities as a mortgage loan originator let's now go over the common terms and acronyms you will encounter in the mortgage lending business. It's important to know these not only to be able to speak the language and jargon of lending but also to avoid any misunderstandings between you and other mortgage loan originators, Loan Processors, and any Third-Party Providers. In presenting these I will try not to sound like Webster's Dictionary or like some boring list of definitions. With that said, let us now go on to the next chapter - which talks about Common Mortgage Lending Terms.

Chapter 2

COMMON MORTGAGE LENDING TERMS

𝕷ike most professions, when you first get into the mortgage lending business, people are using jargon, terms, and acronyms that you most likely are not familiar with. In anticipation of that I have included this chapter to address that very thing. Once you have gone through this chapter then you too will be speaking just like the rest of us.

ABILITY-TO-REPAY RULE (ATR):
According to the Ability-To-Repay rule a creditor shall not make a loan unless the creditor makes a reasonable and good faith determination at or before loan consummation that the consumer will have a reasonable ability to repay the loan according to the terms of that loan. The effective date for the Ability-To-Repay Rule was January 1, 2014. The basis for determining a consumer's ability to repay their loan should be based upon:

- Current or reasonably expected income
- Current employment status
- Monthly mortgage payment
- Monthly payment on any simultaneous loans
- Monthly payment for mortgage-related obligations
- Current debt obligations (e.g. alimony and child-support)
- Monthly debt-to-income ratio or residual income
- Credit History

I discuss the Ability-To-Repay Rule in much more detail within Chapter 6. I should note that these two rules are also referred to as the Government-Sponsored Enterprises Patch (GSE Patch). These two rules (ATR/QM) were originally considered temporary and are expected to expire in January 2021.

ACCELERATION CLAUSE:
This is a clause seen in trust deeds and/or mortgages that allows the lender to demand full payment of the outstanding loan at once if the regular loan payments are not paid when due. This can also occur if there was a breach in the conditions of the mortgage.

ACRE:
This is not a real estate book but since you are dealing with property and land it's good to know this. An acre equals 160 square rods or 4840 square yards or (now we're getting to what I understand) 43,560 square feet.

ACT vs. REGULATION:

I often hear mortgage-lending folks refer to mortgage lending Acts and Regulations like they are the same thing. Although they may be the same thing there are differences between these two terms: Under federal law, the Act identifies what the law covers and may provide broad rules related to it while the Regulation interprets the Act and explains how that Act will be administered.

I have to admit it; this was somewhat confusing to me when I first got into the mortgage lending business. For example, my branch manager would sometimes state the Truth-In-Lending Act or say TILA, and at other times might say Regulation Z. My thinking at that time was, "Which one is she talking about: TILA or Regulation Z?" Of course, she was talking about the same thing. And, this is how mortgage lending folks talk when they are referring to mortgage lending Regulations: Either referring to the Act, as in the Real Estate Settlement Procedures Act (RESPA), or referring to it as Regulation X.

I should also note, that when parts of a Regulation are being discussed or mentioned it is often referred to as a numbered Section. For example, Section 226.62 of Regulation Z. This makes it easier to find the information you are looking for when researching various lending regulations and laws.

ADJUSTABLE RATE MORTAGE (ARM):

This is a mortgage loan whereby the interest rate can adjust up or down in accordance with its existing interest rate, its Index and Margin. Most ARM loans you come in contact with will have an initial fixed rate period before the adjustable rate period begins. For example, an ARM with an initial fixed rate period of 3 years and then adjusts yearly thereafter for the rest of the life of the loan would be referred to as a 3/27 or 3/1 ARM. An ARM with the initial fixed rate period of 2 years and adjusts annually thereafter - could be referred to as a 2/28 or 2/1 ARM.

AMORTIZATION:

This is a term that refers to how the principal of a loan will be retired. With an amortization loan part of each (monthly) payment goes towards the interest on that loan and the other part (of that payment) goes towards the outstanding principal of that loan. Hence, with each payment made - the principal is reduced and at the end of the amortization period (e.g. 30 years or 15 Years) the loan will be paid off in full.

ANNUAL PERCENTAGE RATE (APR):

The Annual Percentage Rate or APR of a loan represents the note rate plus specific identified finance charges on that loan – as shown on the Loan Estimate. The Annual Percentage Rate or APR is a measure of the Cost of Credit for a loan and is expressed as an Annual Interest Rate and is shown (and disclosed) on the Loan Estimate and Closing Disclosure. This area (regarding the APR) is probably one of the most esoteric concepts in the lending industry and certainly one of the least understood by customers and many Mortgage loan originators. The APR of a home loan is presented is now presented on page 3 of the Loan Estimate. This used to shown on the first page of the previously required Truth-In-Lending Statement. Because of one of the main reasons for the displaying the

APR of a home loan, I do feel that it is better presented on the Loan Estimate. To view how to calculate the APR of a loan please refer to APR Calculation.

APPLICATION FEE:
Sometimes referred to as an upfront deposit. An application fee represents any money initially paid by prospective loan customers (usually at the time of loan application) to cover loan processing and credit report expenses and/or third-party provider expenses such as the title insurance and/or the appraisal. The policy of your mortgage company will dictate whether this is initially required and how much is needed. When I first started in this business it was my boss's policy that if I did not get an application fee covering the Credit Report and Appraisal, when I first met with my customers, then there was no loan and I was not to do any more work on that loan until I received it. This usually required the customers to give me (our company) a deposit check of about $385.00. The deposit amount given by the customers is later applied to all costs on their loan (more on this later).

Competition and our desire to make it as easy as possible for the customers to meet with us and allow us the opportunity to explore lending options for them compels most mortgage companies out there to not require this (up-front) deposit. However, I always recommend that you do get some money at the time of application if you can - even if it's only about $15.00 for the Credit Report. I recommend this because some customers do shop around - even after they have met with you. But if a customer gives you a deposit (no matter how small) then that is a tacit signal that they are going to do the loan with you. So always try to get a deposit (no matter how small) at the time of loan application.

APPRAISAL:
An appraisal is an estimate of a property's value determined by a licensed appraiser. Most loans you do will require an appraisal as a Prior-To-Doc (PTD) condition. The highest amount of the loan for your customer (if they are requesting this) weighs very heavily on what the appraised value of their property is. This is what they call Loan-To-Value or LTV (another common acronym). Be aware that after you have ordered an appraisal that it could take as long as 2 or more weeks before you receive it. This waiting period, for your ordered appraisal, usually depends on whether the interest rates are low and whether the lending market is busy (and so are appraisers) and/or if the subject property (another term I'll talk about later here) is in another city or state. Once you have been in this business for a while and get on personal terms with some appraisers then you can sometimes get appraisals back within the same week. Just like wholesale lending reps, sometimes appraisers come into your mortgage office to get their business (from you). Here's another reason (and opportunity) to introduce yourself to them.

When it comes to appraisals, one common question is: When do I order the appraisal? My response to that is - either when you have loan approval or you have a very strong "green light" that this loan is going to close (or what I refer to sometimes as "going to the closing (signing) table." You do this because: 1. You don't want your customers to pay for an appraisal if the loan is not doable, and 2. If the loan doesn't close (or is denied) then many mortgage companies will expect you to pay for the appraisal if your customers don't. So be smart: Order the appraisal when the time is appropriate and right. I discuss the subject of appraisals in more detail when discussing the Appraisal Rule within Chapter 25

APPRECIATION:
This is a common term referring to the increase in the value of a property. It's usually used in reference to a time period. For example, it could be said that the subject property at 1234 Monroe Street seems to have appreciated by $10,000 over the past 5 years. Or, the appreciation of those homes in the city's valley area has only been 2% per year in the past 3-4 years.

ASSESSED VALUE:
This is the value placed on a property by a public officer or tax board - as a basis for taxation. Most refer to this as the Tax Assessed Value. When you first begin researching a loan, on a customer's property, you can find the tax-assessed value of that property through a Property Profile or Metroscan (more on this later). This gives you some idea of what an appraisal will come in at. Unless the homeowner has made valued improvements to that property then I generally consider the tax-assessed value at about 80% to 90% of what an appraisal would come in at. Using this and when and how much the customers paid for that property will temper what you come up with. But let's say your customers bought their home about three years ago for $90,000 but haven't made any significant home improvements since and the tax-assessed value is about $85,000. You could surmise, based on only this that an appraisal could come in at about $106,250 ($85,000 / 80%). We'll talk more about this when we discuss ordering a Property Profile.

AUTOMATED VALUATION MODEL (AVM):
Automated Valuation Models are statistically based computer programs that use real estate information, such as comparable sales, property characteristics, tax assessments, and price trends, to provide an estimate of value for a specific property.

AVERAGE PRIME OFFER RATE (APOR):
The Average Prime Offer Rate (APOR) is a survey-based estimate of Annual Percentage Rates (APRs) currently offered on prime mortgage loans. The rates are calculated and published weekly for Fixed Rate Mortgages and Adjustable Rate Mortgages. You can research the current APOR by going to the Federal Financial Institutions Examination Council's website at: https://www.ffiec.gov/ratespread/aportables.htm.

APOR is used to calculate Rate Spread for HMDA reporting purposes and to determine whether the loan is a High-Risk Mortgage Loan (HRML) and/or a Higher-Priced Mortgage Loan (HPML) under Regulation Z.

BALLOON MORTGAGE & BALLOON PAYMENT:
First, a Balloon Mortgage is a loan whereby the amortization period is longer than the Term (actual length of Time of Repayment) of the loan. Balloon Loans are usually referred to as "15 due in 5." The first number (15) refers to the amortization period - 15 years or 180 months and the second number refers to when the Balloon (or outstanding principal balance) of that loan will be due - in 5 years. If it is an amortized loan then all payments

made for the initial 5 years will have reduced (somewhat) the principal of that loan and at the end of its 5-year period the borrower pays off whatever is remaining (the Balloon Payment). If the loan is an Interest Only Loan then the borrower's monthly payments then pays for only the outstanding interest on that loan and does not reduce the amount of the loan's principal. Here the Balloon Payment would be the same as the original amount of that loan being paid off after the 5th year.

BANKRUPTCY:

I'm sure you are familiar with what a Bankruptcy is. But to review, there are generally three types of Bankruptcies: 1. Chapter 7: Whereby a court declares the person(s) free of all or most of their debts (they don't have to pay back their creditors), and 2. Chapter 13: whereby a court reduces and consolidates all their debts into one monthly payment, and finally 3. Chapter 11. This is a Bankruptcy for small businesses, sole proprietors, and partnerships. You won't see this (Chapter 11) very often in residential mortgage lending.

It used to be (in the old days) that if a prospective customer had a Bankruptcy within the last 3-4 years then you couldn't help him (within the Conforming lending area). However, according to Fannie Mae Selling Guide dated 10/07/2020 a four-year waiting period is required - starting from the discharge or dismissal date of the bankruptcy action.

However, exceptions for this four-year period could be for Extenuating Circumstances. For example, a two-year waiting period is permitted if extenuating circumstances (e.g. medical bills) can be documented, and is measured from the discharge or dismissal date of the bankruptcy action. Also, a distinction is made between Chapter 13 bankruptcies that were discharged and those that were dismissed. The waiting period required for Chapter 13 bankruptcy actions is as follows:

- Two years from the discharge date, or
- Four years from the dismissal date.

For now, the important thing here to know is to find out when that customer's Bankruptcy was first filed and discharged and what type of Bankruptcy it was (e.g. 7, 13, or 11).

You should know that if your prospective customers were still paying on their Chapter 13 then you would need the signed approval of that customer's Bankruptcy court appointed Judge to do that loan. And, the only type of loan (I have heard of) that a Judge would approve would be a Rate/Term Refinance loan. This is a loan that refinances only the outstanding principal of that loan (loan goal usually being to obtain a lower interest rate with lower monthly mortgage payments). To obtain an approval from the Bankruptcy appointed judge would require you to clearly show that this loan would significantly (or noticeably) lower their monthly mortgage payments and improve their financial situation. Conversely, no Judge (on a Chapter 13) would approve a Cash-Out refinance loan - for any reason that I know of. The logic here (and I am projecting) is that if the customer could get cash out from their home then the Judge would want them to pay off their creditors first.

And lastly, you should be aware that if your customers went to an attorney and filed Bankruptcy and later decided (before going to court) that they didn't want to do it and had it dismissed - it will still show up on their Credit Report and some Lenders would look at it the same way - as if they went through with it! Frankly, this is one I can't figure out myself. This is also true if a foreclosure was filed and the customers subsequently sold their house before it went to the "courthouse steps" for sale.

Also, be aware of those customers who have gone to the Consumer's Credit Counseling Services (or whatever they are called) that lowers and consolidates their debts. Many people have gone through this type of debt counseling and servicing because they didn't want to file bankruptcy. The irony is: That many Conforming Lenders look upon this (filing or working with a debt consolidating service) as a Bankruptcy and treat it as the same thing. So, look out for this when you are first meeting with and talking to your customers and when you first read their Credit Report (more on this later).

BINDER:
This term usually refers to an Insurance Binder. Whenever you do a home loan one of the PTD or PTF conditions will be to order and receive an Insurance Binder - showing the amount of coverage (enough to protect that Lender). And, to have the Lender (of that new loan) shown on it as the new Loss Payee or Mortgagee - the Lender who will receive the benefits of that insurance policy in case of a total or substantial loss to the home (more on this later).

BI-WEEKLY MORTGAGE:
Sometimes you will get an inquiry from a customer who is considering doing a Bi-weekly Mortgage. A Bi-weekly Mortgage is a mortgage payment plan whereby the mortgage payments are due every two weeks. Thus, instead of the homeowners making one monthly mortgage payment, here they make their mortgage payments every other week. Hence, each payment made would be about ½ of a full-month's payment. Now the thing about Bi-weekly Mortgages - is that the homeowner is actually making 26 mortgage payments each year. This results in the homeowner making about one full month's P&I payment each year - that plows directly into the principal of that loan. As a result, a 30-year fixed amortized mortgage loan could be paid off in 20 – 22 years. That's a reduction in paying off their mortgage by almost 27% and what makes the Bi-weekly Mortgage so popular. Well worth doing if the homeowners plan to keep their home (and/or the home mortgage) long enough to fully pay it off. Therefore, when folks ask you about a Bi-weekly Mortgage make sure you ask them about this in qualifying them. Hence, if your loan prospects are purchasing or refinancing a home and tell you they will most likely be selling their home within the next 10 years then I would not recommend this.

Bi-Weekly Mortgages work especially well for folks who get paid on a bi-weekly basis. I have found that people who work for banks, the U.S. Post Office, and hospitals generally get paid on a bi-weekly basis and could be excellent candidates for this type of mortgage payment plan - if it meets their home goals as stated previously.

BLANKET MORTGAGE:

A Blanket Mortgage is a mortgage that includes more than one parcel of property. For example, let us say you are doing a loan on a property we will call Parcel A (or property A). On the loan application you indicated that your customer not only own this property A (which has a mortgage on it) but also own free and clear (owns outright) another piece of property (which we will call Property B). You submit your loan to a lender (it's a tough loan though) and because of their credit, or lack of equity in the subject property (property A) or whatever - that lender comes back with an approval - conditioned upon Blanketing Property B. In other words, in structuring this loan that lender will have (additional security) - a lien position on the second property (Property B) as well. Hence, if the borrower doesn't make his mortgage payments and home foreclosure ensues then that lender can also take possession of that second property as well.

BORROWER CONTRIBUTION:

According to Fannie Mae's recent *Selling Guide*, a minimum required Borrower Contribution for purchase home loans, that are principal residences and second homes, and which contains Gifts is dependent on three things: 1. whether the purchase home loan has an LTV, CLTV, or HCLTV of less than or greater than 80%, 2. the type of occupancy, and 3. the number of units being purchased. The matrix below shows you what I mean:

Borrower Contribution Matrix

LTV, CLTV or HCTV Ratios	Occupancy Type	Number of Units	Minimum Borrower Contribution Requirement from Borrower's Own Funds
80% or Less	Principal Residence	1-4	A minimum Borrower Contribution from the Borrower's own funds is not required. All funds needed to complete this purchase transaction can come from a Gift.
	Second Home	1	
Greater than 80%	Principal Residence	1	A minimum Borrower Contribution from the Borrower's own funds is not required. All funds needed to complete this purchase transaction can come from a Gift.
	Principal Residence	2 - 4	The Borrower must make a 5% minimum Borrower Contribution from his or her own funds. After the minimum Borrower Contribution has been met then Gifts can be used To supplement the down payment, closing costs, and reserves.
	Second Home	1	

I should also mention here that if the borrower is receiving a Gift from a relative or domestic partner who has lived with the borrower for the last 12 months, or from a fiancé, then the Gift is considered the borrower's own funds and may be used to satisfy the minimum Borrower Contribution requirement as long as both individuals will use the home being purchased as their principal residence.

BRIDGE LOAN:

This type of loan is usually used in home purchase type of scenarios. As the name implies this type of financing provides loan funds – "a Bridge" for the borrower - from his current home (which he or she is selling) towards the down payment and loan costs for the home they are interested in purchasing. This is generally used when the borrowers don't have enough time to sell their currently owned home - before purchasing their new home. A slow home sales market, in that area, could be the reason for that. At any rate, in doing this, the borrowers will need to be qualified based on those two mortgages. The goal of a bridge loan is to provide temporary financing and is looked upon as a short-term type of loan providing the needed funds to purchase the new home. Once their house is sold (for which the Bridge Loan was created and based upon) the Bridge Loan is then paid off. A Bridge Loan may also be referred to as a Swing Loan, Gap or Interim Financing.

BUYDOWN:
This refers to the Buying Down of an interest rate, on a loan, to something lower. As you will see, when we discuss the Lender's Rate Sheets, at a certain point there is an inverse relationship to the interest rate a borrower can obtain and what the cost would be to obtain that rate. For example, let's say that at today's rates the interest rate at par (no cost) is 4.0%. You are doing a loan for $200,000 here and your customer tells you he is willing to Buydown (pay for) a lower interest rate to 3.5% - if it makes financial sense. You say OK and begin your research.

First, you look at the Rate Sheet and see that the cost to Buydown that rate to 6.5% is ½ point or 0.50%. You know (or we will discuss this later) that this percent is a function of the total loan amount. Therefore, the cost is ($200,000 x 0.50%) $1,000.00. So, it will cost your customer $1,000 to Buydown that Rate to 3.5%. Now the next question is: Does this make financial sense? Let's see. To do this we need to calculate the monthly mortgage payment based on the first interest rate of 4.0% and then based on the Buydown Rate of 3.5%. Assume here a 30-Year fixed rate mortgage.

- Monthly payment at 4.0% = $954.83
- Monthly payment at 3.5% = $898.09

Next, we subtract the two monthly payments to show the financial monthly benefit of going with that lower interest rate. Benefit = $56.74 per month. Next, we calculate the Payback Period it will take your customer to payoff that Buydown. In other words, how many months or years will it take for this monthly savings of $56.74 to payback that Buydown - whereby he is truly enjoying that Buydown rate? Although this is a moot point, I always like to have my customer's payback period within 24 to 30 months. So, let's see what we have here: If we divide the Buydown cost of $898.09 by $56.74 (benefit per month) that equals = 15.83 or about 16 months. I'd say that was a good Buydown and would recommend it to my customer.

CALL OPTION:
A provision in a loan that gives the lender the right to accelerate the debt and require full payment of the loan immediately at the end of a specified period or for a specified reason.

CHATTEL MORTGAGE:
A Chattel Mortgage is any document offering property as security for payment of a debt. This term is not used very often in the lending area but it's good to be aware of what it means.

CHURNING:

This is a Wall Street stock investment term that refers to when stockbrokers are excessively buying and selling stock securities in a customer's account. This practice of Churning results in those stockbrokers making more commissions since they make money only when they execute trades for their clients. Now, regarding real estate mortgage loans, I have heard this term used quite often when referring to the illegal practice of Flipping. When mortgage-lending folks talk about Churning of real estate they are usually referring to the practice of unscrupulous investors who are Flipping properties more than once to continue to increase the selling price of that property. This is normally done with the assistance of an insider appraiser who is inflating the value of that property (more than what it is actually worth), with the investor selling that property to some straw buyers. And, having an insider closing agent or closing attorney pretty much completes the circle of the persons necessary to make a Churning scheme successful.

Once this has been done a number of times (Churning) then that Flipped property is put on the market to be sold to some honest and unsuspecting buyers. Unfortunately, those buyers, who do purchase that property, end up paying much more than that property is actually worth. This practice of Flipping and Churning is illegal.

CLOSING:

The Closing is where all the respected parties to a loan come together for the purpose of signing the loan closing documents. Attending this Closing are the Escrow closing folks, closing attorney, owners of the home being refinance and/or buyers and sellers of a property. In a mortgage refinance loan only the homeowners will usually attend with the Escrow folks or attorney presiding. However, I do recommend that you also attend all your loan closings – if you can.

I should note and I bring this up only because a Real Estate agent "smacked my chops around" when I used the term Loan Closing for the signing of a purchase home loan. I found out then that Realtors refer to this (when the Buyers and Sellers come together to sign and complete the closing documents) as The Signing and after those documents have been recorded and the Sellers have been paid - as The Closing.

Generally, however, in the lending area mortgage loan originators refer to the signing of the loan documents as The Closing and when funds are later disbursed as The Funding.

CLOSING DISCLOSURE:

The Closing Disclosure is a statement (form) that the Closing Agent prepares - that summaries all the costs of the loan, the loan amount, and the amount the borrowers will receive (or amount of money they need to bring to loan closing) after the funding of their loan. On October 3, 2015 the Closing Disclosure replaced the HUD-1 Settlement Statement.

Now, when the loan is ready to close and all Prior-To-Doc conditions have been satisfied then the loan documents "will be drawn" and either mailed or wired (emailed) to the Closing Agent's office. Once the Closing Agent receives those Closing Loan Documents (with their closing instructions) then he or she prepares the Closing Disclosure. This is a very important document as you can see from the paragraph above. Because of its importance you want to be sure all the loan costs on this document are correct. Make sure you ask the Closing Agent to fax or email to you a copy of the Closing Disclosure just as soon as he or she completes it - so you can review it to ensure it is complete and correct. You will want to be sure that all the closing costs are correct. Remember that the Closing Agent is not normally privy to all the loan facts that you are. So, if you see something that is not included in the Closing Disclosure that should be (or should not be) just inform him or her of this. They will be happy to make those change(s) if possible.

CONSUMER FINANCIAL PROTECTION BUREAU (CFPB):
In the fall of 2010 President Obama appointed Dr. Elizabeth Warren to begin exploring and building an independent organization that would "help empower consumers with the information they need to make financial decisions that are best for them and their families." The result of this was the Consumer Financial Protection Bureau (CFPB). The CFPB is within and a part of the Federal Reserve System. I should also mention, that even though the CFPB is within the Federal Reserve System it is independent of the Federal Reserve System.

The CFPB is also a result of the Dodd-Frank Wall Street Reform and Consumer Protection Act. One of the goals of the CFPB is to promote fairness and transparency for mortgages, credit cards, and other financial products and services. Its other main goal is to set and enforce consistent rules for banks and consumer service providers (like mortgage companies). In doing this the CFPB seeks to create a level playing field between depository financial institutions and mortgage companies. Thus, the CFPB creates rules and regulations that impact what all loan originators need to know, in order that they and their mortgage loans be "In Compliance". The CFPB also acts as the enforcer of those rules and regulations.

Since the CFPB first began its operations on July 21, 2011 regulatory and enforcements authority were transferred to the CFPB for all of the following consumer protection laws:

- Alternative Mortgage Transaction Parity Act (AMTP)
- Consumer Leasing Act (CLA)
- Equal Credit Opportunity Act (ECOA)
- Fair Credit Billing Act (FCB)
- Fair Credit Reporting Act (FCRA)
- Fair Debt Collection Practices Act (FDCP)
- Home Mortgage Disclosure Act (HMDA)
- Home Owners Protection Act (HOPA)
- Home Ownership and Equity Protection Act (HOEPA)
- Mortgage Acts and Practices (MAP)
- Mortgage Assistance Relief Services (MARS)
- Gramm-Leach-Bliley Act (GLBA)
- Real Estate Settlement Protection Act (RESPA)
- S.A.F.E. Mortgage Licensing Act (SAFE)

- Truth-In-Lending Act (TILA)
- Truth-in-Savings Act (TISA)

COMBINED LOAN-TO-VALUE (CLTV):
When there are (or you are doing research for) two or more mortgage loans on a property then we use the term Combined Loan-To-Value or CLTV to represent the total loan amounts in relation to the (appraised) value of the subject property. For example, if your customer has an existing 1st mortgage of $80,000 on a property worth $100,000 and wants a 2nd mortgage of $15,000 then together these two loans would result in a CLTV of 95%.

CONVENTIONAL CONFORMING LOANS:
First, Conventional Conforming Loans are loans that satisfy the underwriting guidelines stipulated by FNMA and FHLMC and are oftentimes referred to as "A" paper loans. Conforming loans are also sometimes referred to as Prime loans. I should also note that some conforming wholesale lenders might also have broader underwriting guidelines than what FNMA or FHLMC have. This is due in large part to what that lender's conforming loan investors will allow and accept.

OK, now for a little history: When the mortgage bubble finally burst, in late 2008, and we went into the so-called Mortgage Meltdown and Mortgage Crisis, it became increasingly clear that Fannie Mae's maximum loan amounts needed to be adjusted upward for certain "High-Cost" areas. In response to this, on February 13, 2008 President Bush signed into law The Economic Stimulus Act of 2008 which identified those metropolitan statistical areas and rural counties that were classified by HUD as "High-Cost Areas" and increased the maximum Conforming loan limits for each up to (or times) 1.75% (or $729,750) of the maximum Conforming loan limit. This enabled those mortgage loans, where the subject property was located in a "High-Cost Area", to continue to enjoy the benefits that Conforming loans offer in terms of lower rates and fees.

The Economic Stimulus Act of 2008 also resulted in a new mortgage lending term: Jumbo-Conforming or Mini-Jumbo. A Jumbo-Conforming or Mini-Jumbo mortgage loan represented a mortgage loan in which the subject property was located within a High-Cost area, as classified by HUD, and the loan amount was greater than the Conforming Loan limit for that type of property (1-Unit). Otherwise, if the total loan amount was $417,000 or less, for a 1-Unit property, than that loan would be considered a Conforming loan. At that time this was considered to be a temporary program for loans originated from July 1, 2007 to December 31, 2008.

Then, for 2009 the term Jumbo-Conforming and its program was phased out and was replaced by what was called "High-Balance Loans". However, the basic concept of Jumbo-Conforming was and is the same for High-Balance loans but the maximum loan amounts and underwriting for High-Balance loans are different. We are now into 2021 and the term "High-Balance" loans remains.

Today, we still find that there are two sets of loan limits that are provided for mortgage loans:

1. General Loan Limits
2. High-Cost Area Loan Limits

For a more detailed discussion on the loan underwriting guidelines for General Conforming and High-Cost Area Loans Limits please refer to Chapter 4 titled "Loan Underwriting". And, the loan-to-value acronym for High-Cost loans is referred to as HCLTV.

CONVERTIBLE MORTGAGE OR FEATURE:

A Convertible Feature allows the borrower of an ARM loan to convert it to a fixed rate loan after a specified period of time. Usually this is just prior to when that ARM reaches its adjustable rate period (after its initial fixed rate period). This is a great feature because borrowers do not have to go through the normal mortgage loan refinancing costs and steps again. However, there is usually a conversion fee to exercise this privilege (e.g. $50.00 - $250.00) but still - quite a savings. The interest rate that the loan will adjust to (for the converted fixed rate loan) is usually the prevailing FNMA rate (at conversion time) plus 0.375 – 0.625% depending on that loan's program and Lender.

CONVEYANCE:

This is term you will hear quite often. It refers to the transfer of ownership of real property from one person to another. If someone asks you "When did conveyance last take place on that property?" They are asking when that property last sold and changed owners.

DEBT SERVICE:

You usually see this term used as "Monthly Debt Service" which refers to all of a customer's monthly payments paid to creditors. You would use this most often when considering a Debt Consolidation Loan whereby you combine all or some of the monthly payments (towards creditors) within the mortgage payment (on that new loan) - enabling your customers to realize a lower or reduction in their Monthly Debt Servicing.

DECLARATION PAGE:

The Declaration Page is the first or front page of the Homeowner's Hazard Insurance policy – sometimes referred to as the Insurance Binder. This page has all the important information regarding that insurance policy: Names of insures, address of subject property, coverage amount, annual premium, and renewal date on that policy. Also included will be the Loss Payee or Mortgagee of the current Lender (usually at the bottom of that page). When you call the homeowner's insurance company (and you don't need the entire policy) just ask them to fax you the Declaration Page. They'll know what you are talking about.

DEED:

The Deed or Deed of Trust is also sometimes called (depending on the state of origin) Mortgage, Contract for Sale, and Security Instrument. The Deed is one of the most important documents of a home financing (the other is The Note). The Deed pledges the subject property as collateral on the Note. The Deed of Trust also identifies the three parties to a home purchase transaction. They are the Trustor, Trustee, and the Beneficiary:

1. The Trustor: Writes the Note to the benefit of the Lender and is the Payor (your customer) of the Note and is referred to sometimes as the Mortgagor.

2. The Trustee: Is like an escrow company or intermediary, if you will, between the Trustor and Beneficiary who holds title to that property until the agreement or loan between the Trustor and Beneficiary is no longer in force (e.g. the loan is paid off).

3. The Beneficiary is the Lender. Sometimes referred to as the Mortgagee.

I bring this up because sometimes you'll get in the company of lending folks who will start saying words like mortgagee, mortgagor, and beneficiary. Many Mortgage loan originators out there don't know the difference between a mortgagee and a mortgagor. But you do.

DEED-IN-LIEU OF FORECLOSURE:

The Deed-in-Lieu of Foreclosure is a transaction type that is completed as an alternative to foreclosure. Also included here are Preforeclosure Sales and Charge-off of a Mortgage Account. Below gives you a little more detail on these:

- A Deed-in-Lieu of Foreclosure is a transaction in which the Deed to the real property is transferred back to the servicer. These are typically identified on the credit report through Remarks Codes such as "Forfeit deed-in-lieu of foreclosure.

- A Preforeclosure Sale or Short Sale is the sale of a property in lieu of a Foreclosure resulting in a payoff of less than the total amount owed, which was pre-approved by the servicer. These are typically identified on the credit report through Remarks Codes such as "Settled for less than full balance.

- A Charge-off of a Mortgage Account occurs when a creditor has determined that there is little (or no) likelihood that the mortgage debt will be collected. A charge-off is typically reported after an account reaches a certain delinquency status, and is identified on the credit report with a manner of payment (MOP) code of "9."

A four-year waiting period is required from the completion date of the Deed-in-Lieu of Foreclosure, Preforeclosure Sale, or Charge-off as reported on the credit report or other documents provided by the borrower. However, there are Exceptions for Extenuating Circumstances (e.g. Medical Bills) whereby a two-year waiting period is permitted if extenuating circumstances can be documented.

DISCOUNT POINTS:

This is an amount expressed as a percent of the total loan amount that is usually charged to the Borrower for the purpose of Buying Down the interest rate. We will talk more about this when we get to the Chapter 12 on the Loan Estimate.

DODD-FRANK WALL STREET REFORM AND CONSUMER PROTECTION ACT:

The Dodd-Frank Wall Street Reform and Consumer Protection Act was signed into law by the President Barack Obama on July 21, 2010. This Act was in part designed with the intent of promoting financial stability through improved accountability and transparency in the financial system. The two primary architects of this Act are Senator Chris Dodd and

Representative Barney Frank. Due to their involvement with this Act – this Bill and Act was named after these two members of Congress.

Within the Dodd-Frank Wall Street Reform and Consumer Protection Act there are sixteen main financial areas addressed with new regulations and laws for each. Each one of those areas, presented within this Act, is referred to as a "Title". The Mortgage Lending area was addressed under Title XIV. Title XIV is called the Mortgage Reform and Anti-Predatory Lending Act, whose subtitles A, B, C, and E are designated as Enumerated Consumer Law, which will be administered by the Consumer Financial Protection Bureau. Within Title XIV there are 8 Subtitles:

Subtitle A - Residential Mortgage Loan Organization Standards
Subtitle B - Minimum Standards for Mortgages
Subtitle C - High-Cost Mortgages
Subtitle D - Office of Housing Counseling
Subtitle E - Mortgage Servicing
Subtitle F - Appraisal Activities: Property Appraisal Requirements
Subtitle G - Mortgage Resolution and Modification
Subtitle H - Miscellaneous Provisions

The Dodd-Frank Wall Street Reform and Consumer Protection Act was passed as a response to the 2008 recession and is considered by many to be the most sweeping change to financial regulation in the United States since the Great Depression and represents a significant change in the American financial regulatory environment affecting all Federal financial regulatory agencies and affecting almost every aspect of the nation's financial services industry.

DOWN PAYMENT ASSISTANCE PROGRAMS (DAPs):

Down Payment Assistance Programs provide funds that are donated to third parties which are then applied toward some or all of the borrower's closing costs for a specific transaction. As long as the DAP allows such uses, these funds may also be used to pay for energy-related improvements - that meet acceptable requirements. Interested Party Contribution funds that flow through a DAP may be used for allowable closing costs, prepaids, and energy-related expenses in compliance with Fannie Mae's IPC limits.

DRAWING THE DOCS:

This is a common term in lending and refers to the Lender preparing the loan closing documents to be "wired" or sent to the closing agent. When the Loan Docs "are drawn" all Prior-to-Doc conditions have been satisfied for that loan and those closing docs are prepared. Once those docs have actually been sent to the closing agent then the Lender will state, "Docs have gone out."

EARNEST MONEY:

This term is usually stated as the Earnest Money Deposit (EMD) and represents the amount of money that an interested home Buyer gives to a home Seller when he or she makes an offer (and it is accepted) to purchase a property. This Earnest Money Deposit is also shown on the Purchase and Sales Contract, which is drawn up (usually) by the representing

Realtors, and should also be shown on your Loan Estimate - for that purchase loan. On the Loan Estimate it should be shown as a negative since it will be applied against all loan costs.

END LOAN:
You won't see this type of loan until you get into home construction type of loans. In home construction financing there are sometimes two loans involved. The first one is called the Construction or Interim Loan. This is the loan that pays for the actual construction of that home. Once construction of that home is completely finished then the owners can refinance their home with an End Loan or as some refer to it as the "Take Out Loan". The reason for having two loans is because the Risks for each loan are so different. Any type of construction loan is looked upon as being very risky. As such, the interest rate is higher. But remember, because it's a construction loan its actual term may be between 6 months to a year (or shorter). Once the home is completely built then the loan's risk dramatically decreases. And, after the home has been built then the Take-Out loan is a normal refinance loan.

You will also hear the term "All-In-One loan." This just means that the lender provides financing for both the Interim and End Loan (All-In-One). In doing two loans the customer has to put up with the loan costs for each. However, the Take-Out Loan (the 2nd loan) usually provides the customer with a much better interest rate (then would have been available with an All-In-One type of construction loan).

I should note that the Interim Loan (first) and the End (take out) Loans work hand-in-hand. Some lenders who only provide financing for home construction (Interim Loans only) will not do that loan without a firm commitment from another lender who will provide the End or Take-Out Loan.

EQUAL CREDIT OPPORTUNITY ACT (ECOA):
The Equal Credit Opportunity Act was enacted on October 28, 1974 and is also referred to as Regulation B. One of the main purposes of The Equal Credit Opportunity Act is to promote the availability of credit to all creditworthy applicants without regard as to whether they are a member of a Protected Class. Nor may creditors consider any factor(s), of a home loan applicant, that they are or may be a member of a Protected Class. There are nine Protected Class members within the Equal Credit Opportunity Act.

- Race
- Color
- National Origin
- Sex
- Religion
- Marital Status
- Age
- Income derived from Public Assistance
- Exercising rights under any Consumer Credit Protection law.

The Equal Credit Opportunity Act also requires Creditors to:

- Notify applicants of action taken on their home loan applications,
- Report credit history in the names of both spouses on an account,
- Retain records of credit applications,
- Collect information about the applicant's race and other personal characteristics in applications for certain dwelling-related loans, and
- Provide home loan applicants with copies of appraisal reports used in connection with credit transactions.

EQUITY:

Equity in property is the actual ownership a homeowner has above the outstanding mortgages and liens on that property. For example, if a property is appraised at or is valued at $100,000, and there is only a 1st mortgage of $80,000 on that property, then we could say that homeowner has $20,000 in equity in their property.

ESCROW HOLDBACKS:

When that time of year rolls into the fall and winter months then this is when Escrow Holdbacks are sometimes required and accepted by most Lenders. As the name implies an Escrow Holdback is essentially funds that are set-aside (held back or reserved) in an escrow account to be used towards payments for the required (minor) repairs on the subject property – after the loan closes. Although the funds for the Escrow Holdback usually come from the mortgage loan being funded they could come from the borrower's own funds (if they are able and choose to provide their own funds). But this is rare when that happens.

For an example of an Escrow Holdback - let us say that you are doing a refinance loan on a single-family residence (SFR). The appraiser goes out to the subject property and finds that the back of that house is in need of a new paint job (the paint on the back of the house is peeling away – exposing the wood to the elements). This would be noted in that appraisal and, of course, you could expect the Lender on that loan to require this to be taken care of before loan closing. Unfortunately, it is the month of November and the average outside temperature is about 45 degrees - too cold for paint to properly dry.

Assuming this loan is approvable, with this exception, that Lender may approve this loan with an Escrow Holdback - to have the back of the house painted as soon as possible (when the temperature warms up again). Also, with an Escrow Holdback there are a couple of things that most Lenders require - that you should be aware of:

1. The unfinished work that needs to be done (resulting in the Escrow Holdback) does not (at that time) in any way affect the safety, occupancy, or significantly have an adverse effect on the value of that property. For example, an Escrow Holdback is generally not accepted for foundation work and replacement of the roof.

2. Most Lenders do not like the Escrow Holdback to extend beyond 90 days from the date of loan closing.

3. Lenders also generally required at least 2 bids to do the work from licensed contractors. And each bid, to do the required work, should be signed and dated by that contractor. And, you can expect the Lender to also require a copy of the contractor's business license – which should accompany their bid.

4. And, it has been my experience that most Lenders will accept and use the highest bid.

5. Your loan customers will need to have in their escrow account, at loan closing, the same amount or as much as one and a half times the licensed contractor's bid (the one accepted by that Lender). These Escrow Holdback funds can be taken from the (refinance) loan if your customers wish to do that.

6. Once the work is completed (for the Escrow Holdback) a Certificate of Completion – a form called the 442 is usually required. This certifies that the work has been fully completed – as certified by a licensed real estate appraiser (usually the appraiser who did the original appraisal on that loan).

7. And finally, some Lenders have a maximum Escrow Holdback amount that can be held in that escrow account. This figure equals the contractor's bid times 1.5% - or whatever the Lender requires (#4 above). My experience has been Lenders do not like to see an Escrow Holdback amount greater than $10,000.

ET AL & ET UX:
I just wanted to throw these two in because sometimes you may see these on a Title Report or Property Profile. ET AL means: And others. ET UX means: And wife.

FANNIE MAE MAXIMUM LOAN LIMITS:
Listed below, according to Fannie Mae's *Lender Letter* (LL-2020-14) dated November 24, 2020, are the maximum loan limits that are to become effective for whole loans delivered, and mortgage loans delivered into MBS with pool issue dates, on or after January 1, 2021.

Prior to 2006 the maximum loan limits, for Conforming loans, were applied for all States of our great nation. Since 2006 the maximum loan amount, for a 1-unit property conforming loans, has gone up from $417,000 to its current loan limit of $548,250: That's 31.47% increase since 2006. And, it is the Federal Housing Finance Agency (FHFA) that decides what the maximum Conforming Loan amount limits will be for each year. The FHFA's decision and announcement to change (or not change) the maximum loan amount limits usually occurs sometime around Thanksgiving of every year. We went through some years, from 2006 – 2016, whereby the maximum loan limits did not change. Then, on November 28, 2017, the FHFA increased the maximum loan amounts for the year 2018 and also did so for the year 2019. And then, on November 24, 2020 Fannie Mae announced, within its *Lender Letter LL-2020-14*, the maximum loan limits 2021.

The current Loan Limits for General Conforming and High-Cost area mortgage loans, for the Contiguous United States, District of Columbia, and Puerto Rico, for 2021 are listed below. Now, if the loan amount, for a property and loan type, is larger than listed below then it is usually referred to as a Jumbo loan and becomes a Non-Conforming loan as well. The new maximum loan limits, listed below, are to become effective for whole loans delivered, and mortgage loans delivered into MBS with pool issue dates, on or after January 1, 2021. The maximum loan limits, for General Loans and High-Cost Areas, has increased, since 2020, by 7.42%

MAXIMUM LOAN LIMITS FOR 2021
General Loan Limits

Units	Contiguous U. States, District of Columbia, Puerto Rico	Alaska, Guam, Hawaii, & U.S. Virgin Islands
1-Unit	$548,250	$822,375
2-Units	$702,000	$1,053,000
3-Units	$848,500	$1,272,750
4-Units	$1,054,500	$1,581,750

If you would like to see a Map representing the maximum loan limits, for General Loan Limits, for the contiguous United States as well as Alaska and Hawaii, then checkout the Federal Housing Finance Agency's (FHFA) site at:
https://www.fhfa.gov/DataTools/Tools/Pages/Conforming-Loan-Limits-Map.aspx

Below are the maximum loan limits for High-Cost Areas for the year 2021.

MAXIMUM LOAN LIMITS FOR 2021
High-Cost Areas

Units	Contiguous U. States, District of Columbia, Puerto Rico	Alaska, Guam, Hawaii, & U.S. Virgin Islands
1-Unit	$822,375	Not Applicable
2-Units	$1,053,000	Not Applicable
3-Units	$1,272,750	Not Applicable
4-Units	$1,581,750	Not Applicable

Now, I know, when you are looking at the far-right column above you see the maximum loan limits, for High-Cost Areas, as "Not Applicable". What the heck does that mean? Well, that is a very good question and my response to that is - what was first stated on the FHFA announcement for maximum loan limits for 2019: "Special statutory provisions establish different loan limit calculations for Alaska, Hawaii, Guam, and the U.S. Virgin Islands". In other words, the maximum loan limits, for these High-Cost Areas, is based upon the specific county within each U.S. State and/or Territory.

However, once you identify the county, within a High-Cost Area, then you will be able to determine its maximum loan limit. Simply click the link below to see the maximum loan limits based upon the counties within each U.S. State and/or Territory.
https://www.fhfa.gov/DataTools/Downloads/Documents/Conforming-Loan-Limits/FullCountyLoanLimitList2021_HERA-BASED_FINAL_FLAT.pdf

FEDERAL HOUSING ADMINISTRATION (FHA):

The FHA is a division under the US Department of Housing and Urban Development (HUD). I am sure you have heard of FHA loans. However, it's important to know that FHA does not actually lend money to borrowers or lenders but does insure those FHA loans made by (private) Lenders. Having those loans insured by the FHA reduces the perceived risk by a Lender. FHA, like FHLMC and FNMA below, also set underwriting standards and guidelines for these types of loans. FHA loans (like VA loans) are often referred to as govies (government loans). With an FHA Loan your customers can obtain a 98% LTV purchase loan. Of course, they need to have good credit and other required standards stated by the FHA. Years ago, if a prospective buying customer didn't have 10% or 20% of the selling price of the property saved up then FHA was the way to go.

FEDERAL HOME LOAN MORTGAGE CORPORATION (FHLMC):

The Federal Home Loan Mortgage Corporation (FHLMC, referred to as Freddie Mac) is a publicly owned corporation established in 1970 to support the secondary mortgage market and is one of the Government-Sponsored Enterprises (GSEs). It is a major player in the buying and selling of Conforming residential mortgages in the secondary market. Besides providing a secondary mortgage market resource FHLMC also dictates policies and guidelines for qualifying for FHLMC Conforming Residential Loans (e.g. maximum loan amounts and underwriting guidelines). The five main programs that FHLMC is involved in are: Conforming fixed rate home loans (15 and 30 year), Multi-Family home securities, Adjustable Rate Mortgages (ARMs), Second Mortgages (e.g. Home Improvement Loans), and Mortgage-back Securities.

The Financial Institutions Reform, Recovery and Enforcement Act of 1989 (FIRREA) revised and standardized the regulation of both Fannie Mae and Freddie Mac. Prior to this act, Freddie Mac was owned by the Federal Home Loan Bank System and governed by the Federal Home Loan Bank Board, which was reorganized into the Office of Thrift Supervision by the Act. The Financial Institutions Reform, Recovery and Enforcement Act severed Freddie Mac's ties to the Federal Home Loan Bank System and subjected it to oversight by the U.S. Department of Housing and Urban Development (HUD).

However, on September 7, 2008, the U.S. Government, under the Federal Housing Finance Agency (FHFA), took control of both Fannie Mae and Freddie Mac. Both CEOs, of Freddie Mac as well as Fannie Mae were replaced at that time. Although it was discussed there currently appears to be no plans to liquidate either Freddie Mac or Fannie Mae.

FEDERAL NATIONAL MORTGAGE ASSOCIATION (FNMA):

The Federal National Mortgage Association (FNMA, referred to as Fannie Mae) was first established in 1938 as a wholly owned government corporation. However, in 1954 it was restructured into a mixed-ownership corporation. Like the Federal Home Loan Mortgage Corporation it was established to support the secondary mortgage market. When it was first established its main focus was on government type of loans (e.g. FHA and later VA loans). In 1970 Congress expanded Fannie Mae's purchasing authority (in supporting the secondary market) to include conventional mortgages. Today, although FNMA still purchases govie loans, its primary focus of acquisitions is with conventional type of mortgages. You hear the term FNMA and FHLMC referred to quite often in our business. Like FHLMC, FNMA also dictates policies and loan underwriting guidelines for qualifying for FNMA Conforming Residential Loans.

However, just as with Freddie Mae (above), the Financial Institutions Reform, Recovery and Enforcement Act of 1989 (FIRREA) revised and standardized the regulation of both Fannie Mae. And also, as with Freddie Mac, on September 7, 2008, the U.S. Government, under the Federal Housing Finance Agency (FHFA), took control of Fannie Mae. Currently, The Federal National Mortgage Association is one of the Government-Sponsored Enterprises (GSEs) and operates under the conservatorship or receivership of the Federal Housing Finance Agency (FHFA). GSEs are currently under Federal conservatorship.

FEDERAL FINANCIAL INSTITUTIONS EXAMINATION COUNCIL (FFIEC):
The Federal Financial Institutions Examination Council is a formal interagency body empowered to prescribe uniform principles, standards, and report forms for the federal examination of financial institutions by the Board of Governors of the Federal Reserve System (FRB), the Federal Deposit Insurance Corporation (FDIC), the National Credit Union Administration (NCUA), the Office of the Comptroller of the Currency (OCC), and the Consumer Financial Protection Bureau (CFPB), and to make recommendations to promote uniformity in the supervision of financial institutions.

FIRST-TIME HOMEBUYER:
There are home loan programs that are available to First-time Homebuyers. But what is a First-time homebuyer? Well, according to the Fannie Mae Selling Guide, a First-time Homebuyer is an individual that:

- Is purchasing the security property;
- Will reside in the security property as a principal residence;
- Had no ownership interest (sole or joint) in a residential property during the three-year period preceding the date of the purchase of the security property, and
- Additionally, an individual who is a displaced homemaker or single parent also will be considered a first-time home buyer if he or she had no ownership interest in.

FLIPPING:
Flipping real estate occurs when real property is purchased and then sold shortly thereafter. While this practice can be totally above board it becomes illegal when investors, working with other (insider) real estate appraisers (and/or lenders), conspire to over-value or inflate the value of a property for the purpose of selling it at a higher price than what its actual market value would be. This results in the Flipping person(s) making more money and the buyers of that flipped property paying more for that property than it is actually worth. This is an illegal practice. See Churning in regards to Flipping.

FORECLOSURE:
This is a term and procedure that takes place to sell the Foreclosed property "at the courthouse steps" in order to payoff the outstanding debt (on the subject property) in the event that there is a default in payment or terms. I guess I don't have to tell you that

Lenders do not like to see Home Foreclosures on a prospective borrower's the credit report. Many Conforming Lenders will not lend to borrowers who have a history of home foreclosure or at the very least 7 years out (from when the Foreclosure occurred), and - have a darn good reason or explanation for it. Remember also what I said above about Bankruptcies - which are subsequently dismissed. This applies to Foreclosures filed but later dismissed as well. They continue to show up on the Credit Report.

According to the Fannie Mae *Selling Guide* dated 10/07/2020, a seven-year waiting period is required, and that waiting period begins from the completion date of the Foreclosure action as reported on the credit report or other foreclosure documents provided by the borrower. There are, however, Exceptions for Extenuating Circumstances (e.g. Medical bills): A three-year waiting period is permitted if extenuating circumstances can be documented, and that time begins from the completion date of the foreclosure action. Additional requirements apply between three and seven years, which include:

- Maximum LTV, CLTV, or HCLTV ratios of the lesser of 90% or the maximum LTV, CLTV, or HCLTV ratios for the transaction per the Eligibility Matrix.
- The purchase of a principal residence is permitted.
- Limited cash-out refinances are permitted for all occupancy types pursuant to the eligibility requirements in effect at that time.

However, I should note here that the purchase of second homes or investment properties and cash-out refinances (any occupancy type) are not permitted until a seven-year waiting period has elapsed.

GIFT OF EQUITY:
A "Gift of Equity" refers to a gift provided by the seller of a property to the buyer of that property. The gift represents a portion of the Seller's Equity in the property, and is transferred to the buyer as a credit in the purchase loan transaction. A gift of equity is:

- Permitted for principal residence and second home purchase transactions;
- Can be used to fund all or part of the down payment and closing costs (including prepaid items); and
- Cannot be used towards financial reserves.

The acceptable donor and minimum Borrower Contribution requirements for gifts also apply to Gifts of Equity. When a Gift of Equity is provided by an acceptable donor, the donor is not considered to be an interested party and the Gift of Equity is not subject to Fannie Mae's Interested Party Contribution requirements.

For Gifts of Equity, the following documents must be retained in the purchase loan file:

- A signed Gift Letter and
- The Settlement Statement listing the gift of equity.

GOOD FAITH ESTIMATE (replaced by the Loan Estimate):
The Good Faith Estimate was and is a loan disclosure and statement that presents and summarizes all the costs of the home loan and includes the loan amount, monthly mortgage

payment, and the loan's interest rate. The revised Good Faith Estimate, that became effective in 2010, was replaced by the Loan Estimate loan disclosure, on October 3, 2015, for all close-end home loans. However, according to the CFPB, the previous Good Faith Estimate form and disclosure can still be used on open-end home loans.

When referring to the Loan Estimate in written form you can generally just write it as LE. The Loan Estimate is one of the most important documents for you to have a good handle on as a Mortgage loan originator. I will go into much more detail on the Loan Estimate within Chapter 12. But for now, just be aware that the LE (Loan Estimate) presents all the important costs and fees of a loan: Loan amount, monthly payment, interest rate, term, amortization period, loan costs, pre-pays (see below), sales price, and amount refinanced (if a refinance loan), and the amount the borrowers may need to bring to their closing or will receive at loan funding.

GOVERNMENT SPONSORED ENTERPRISE (GSE):

The Government Sponsored Enterprise (GSE) is a quasi-governmental entity established to enhance the flow of credit to specific sectors of the American economy. It was created by the U.S. Congress to purchase mortgage loans in the secondary market, thereby providing money to lenders and financial institutions. Today, the GSE is primarily made up of two organizations under the Government National Mortgage Association (Ginnie Mae):

- The Federal National Mortgage Association (Fannie Mae) and
- The Federal Home Loan Mortgage Corporation (Freddie Mac)

These two organizations purchase mortgages on the secondary mortgage markets from Lenders. When these mortgages are sold then Lenders use those funds to provide credit to homebuyers. Thus, the GSEs provide liquidity in the secondary mortgage market.

It's important to note here that GSEs do not lend money directly to the public – such as homebuyers. Besides purchasing secondary mortgage loans, GSEs guarantee third party loans and issue agency bonds, which are either short or long-term bonds. These bonds are exempt from state and local taxes.

I should mention that while some believe that the Government Sponsored Enterprise was created by Congress for the purpose of expanding home ownership for lower and middle-income members of the public – that apparently is not the case. However, Congress did establish the GSEs "to improve the efficiency of capital markets" and to overcome "statutory and other market imperfections which otherwise prevent funds from moving easily from suppliers of funds to areas of high loan demand". Thereby making the flow of these funds more efficient.

GRACE PERIOD:

This is a term we hear a lot of in the lending business. You may hear prospective home borrowers tell you they were told there is a Grace Period on their monthly mortgage payment - up to the 15th of the month. While it is true that generally after the 15th of the month most Lenders will charge a late fee of 5% of the monthly payment (P&I) amount -

you should tell your customers the following: Monthly Mortgage Payments (for 1st Mortgages) are due on the First of the Month. Period.

HAZARD INSURANCE:

All homeowners should and will be required to carry Hazard Insurance. This is oftentimes referred to as Fire Insurance. One of the Prior-To-Doc (PTD) conditions you will usually see is the Hazard Insurance Policy having adequate insurance (in relation to the loan amount) and the new Lender shown on that Declaration page (of the Hazard Insurance Policy for that subject property) as the Loss Payee. Loss Payee, as the name implies, is the name of the Lender who the insurance company will pay in the event of a major loss to the subject property. You make sure it is shown on the Declaration Page. It will generally read as:

Lender's Name, It's assessors and/or assigns, The Lender's (main) Corporate address

HIGH-BALANCE MORTGAGE LOANS:

A High-Balance Mortgage Loan represents a mortgage loan in which the subject property is located within an area classified as "High-Cost Area". High-Balance Mortgage Loans are loans with original principal balances that exceed the 'General loan limit" amounts but meet the High-Cost Area loan limits. Otherwise, if the total loan amount, for a 1-unit property, is at or less than $548,250 that loan would be considered a Conforming loan. Please refer to the term "Fannie Mae Maximum Loan Limits", within this chapter for the 2021 loan limits for General Loans and High-Cost Area Loans. And, that distinction is important because when a loan becomes a High-Balance Loan then there are different originating and processing restrictions and underwriting guidelines that apply to these that do not apply to "General" conforming Loans. Please also refer to Chapter 4 titled "Loan Underwriting" for loan underwriting guidelines on High-Balance Loans. These types of home loans can be underwritten manually or with Direct Underwriting (DU).

Also, for clarification purposes, even though these types of mortgages (High-Balance Mortgage Loans) are based on properties located within what has been classified as a High-Cost Area these are not High-Cost Loans. High-Cost Loans are those that because of their higher-cost fall under Section 32 or HOEPA loans. Which leads us to our next definition.

HIGH-COST MORTGAGE LOANS (Section 32, HOEPA Loans):

While there may be a number of definitions as to what a "High-Cost" mortgage loan is, the Consumer Financial Protection Bureau (CFPB) has laid out some very specific descriptions of what this is, and what "Triggers" cause a loan to be covered under HOEPA. This falls under the "High-Cost Mortgages" rule and became effective on January 10, 2014.

The following types of mortgages apply to the special protections afforded by HOEPA:

- Purchase-money mortgages
- Refinances
- Close-end home equity loans, and
- Open-end home-equity loans (HELOCs).

However, HOEPA does not apply when:

- Obtaining the initial financing for a construction home loan.
- A home loan is obtained directly from a Housing Finance Authority.
- The home loan borrower uses the U.S. Department of Agriculture's Rural Housing Service (Section 502) Direct Loan Program. And,
- Reverse Mortgages.

According to the CFPB, under the High-Cost Mortgage Rule (which started in January 2014) the maximum points and fees as well as the maximum APR allowed also depends on whether the home loan is a 1st or 2nd mortgage. The following are the revised HOEPA coverage tests under the High-Cost Mortgage Rule that became effective on January 10, 2014:

First Mortgage Loans:

- The APR exceeds the Average Prime Offer Rate (APOR) by 6.5% for 1st lien mortgages.
- However, if the home loan is less than $50,000, for a personal property dwelling (e.g. Manufactured home) then the APR exceeds 8.5 percentage points higher than the APOR.
- The Creditor is permitted to charge or collect a prepayment penalty that extends more than 36 months after closing or permits such fees or penalties to exceed (in the aggregate) more than 2% of the amount prepaid.

Second or Junior Mortgages:

- The APR exceeds 8.5 percentage points higher than the Average Prime Offer Rate (APOR) for a similar second mortgage.
- However, is that home loan is $20,000 or more and the total points and fees exceed 5% of the total home loan amount then it is a High-Cost Mortgage Loan. Or,
  - If the home loan amount is less than $20,000 and the total points and fees exceed the lesser of 8% of the loan or $1,000 then it becomes a High-Cost Mortgage Loan.
- And, like First Mortgage Loans above, The Creditor is permitted to charge or collect a prepayment penalty that extends more than 36 months after closing or permits such fees or penalties to exceed (in the aggregate) more than 2% of the amount prepaid.

And, whether the loan is for a first or second mortgage loan, all creditors that are originating HELOCs must assess the consumer's ability to repay.

In addition to the above, the High-Cost Mortgage Rule bans:

- Balloon Payments, except for those that account for seasonal or irregular borrower income, short-term bridge loans, made by specialized and approved creditors that may operate in rural or underserved areas.
- Prepayment penalties and financing points and fees.

- Charging late fees larger than 4% of the regular payment amount.
- Charging fees for a payoff statement.
- Changing fees for loan modification – if the home loan borrower runs into financial trouble and cannot pay their mortgage.
- Creditor or brokers from advising homeowners refinancing into high-cost mortgage to not make their payments on their existing mortgage loan.

And finally, when a home loan becomes a High-Cost Mortgage Loan and falls under HOEPA then the Lender must follow the below Counseling requirements:

- Lenders must provide a list of homeownership counseling organizations to consumers within 3 business days after they apply for a mortgage loan.
- The lender must obtain a list from a website that has been developed by the CFPB or data that will be made available by the CFPB and HUD.
- Provide the home loan borrower with information in advance that explains that they are getting a high-cost mortgage loan and which also states the terms, costs, and fees associated with that loan.
- Certify that the home loan borrowers have completed the homeownership counseling about that particular high-cost mortgage loan that Lender is offering that consumer and that the counseling service completed was done by a federally certified or approved homeownership counselor or organization.

HIGH-RATIO LOAN:
This is a term that is not used these days very often but generally refers to any loans whose Loan-to-Value (LTV) is greater than 80%. Historically, Lenders preferred to see the homeowner have equity in their property - of at least 20%. Less than that - it is perceived by Conventional Lenders as a higher risk loan and that's when we see Private Mortgage Insurance (PMI) required on Conventional and Conforming loans. We'll talk more about PMI later.

HIGH-RISK MORTGAGE LOANS (HRML):
The Dodd-Frank Wall Street and Consumer Protections Act, within Title XIV, added an additional section For the Truth-In-Lending Act which established new appraisal requirements that apply to "Higher-Risk Mortgages". According to this new section of TILA, a Creditor is prohibited from extending credit for a Higher-Risk Mortgage loan to any consumer without first:

- Providing the home loan prospect, at the time of the initial mortgage application, with a statement or disclosure stating that any appraisal prepared for that home loan is for the sole use of the creditor. And that the applicant may choose to have a separate appraisal conducted at their own expense.
- Provide that home loan prospect with one copy of each appraisal completed, without charge, at least 3 days prior to their home loan closing date.

The Truth-In-Lending Act, Section 129H(f), defines a "Higher-Risk Mortgage" that is secured by a principal dwelling with an Annual Percentage Rate (APR) that exceeds the Average Prime Offer Rate (APOR) for a comparable transaction as of the date the interest rate is set:

- By 1.5 or more percentage points, for a first lien residential mortgage loan with an original principal obligation amount that does not exceed the amount for the maximum limitation on the original principal obligation of a mortgage in effect for a residence of the applicable size, as of the date of the interest rate set.

- By 2.5 or more percentage points, for a first lien residential mortgage loan having an original principal obligation amount that exceeds the amount for the maximum limitation on the original principal obligation of a mortgage in effect for a residence of the applicable size, as of the date of the interest rate set. Also, Non-conforming/Jumbo Loans. And...

- By 3.5 or more percentage points, for a subordinate lien residential mortgage loan.

Now when it comes to appraising the subject property of a High-Risk Loan then the following requirements need to be done:

- The first appraisal needs to be performed by a certified or licensed appraiser who conducts a physical property visit of the interior of the property, and

- The 2nd and additional appraisal needs to be performed by a different certified and licensed appraiser - if the Higher-Risk Mortgage finances the purchase or acquisition of a property from a seller at a higher price than the seller paid, within 180 days of the seller's purchase or acquisition. This additional appraisal must also include an analysis of the difference in sale prices, changes in market conditions, and any improvements made to the property between the date of the previous sale and the current sale.
  And get this, the cost for this 2nd appraisal is done at no cost to the borrower, when the "Higher-Risk Mortgage" will finance the purchase of that consumer's principal dwelling and there has been an increase in the purchase price from a prior sale that took place within 180 days of the current sale (the Creditor pays for this 2nd appraisal).

However, the definition of "Higher-Risk Mortgage" excludes "Qualified Mortgages," as defined by TILA and also excludes transactions:

- Secured by a new Manufactured Home,
- Secured by a Mobile Home, Boat, or Trailer,
- To finance the initial Construction of a Dwelling,
- With maturities of 12 months or less, if the purpose of the loan is a "Bridge Loan" connected with the acquisition of a dwelling intended to become the consumer's principal dwelling, and
- That are Reverse Mortgage Loans

And finally, I would like to mention here that prior to the Dodd-Frank Act there was the term "Higher-Priced Mortgage Loan (HPML) used within Regulation Z and had a meaning that was substantially similar to the meaning of the "Higher-Risk Mortgage Loan" described above.

HOME MORTGAGE DISCLOSURE ACT (HMDA):
The Home Mortgage Disclosure Act oftentimes referred to as HMDA (that's pronounced like HOMDA – like Honda but with an "M" in there) was first enacted by Congress in 1975 and was updated and expanded in 1989. The Home Mortgage Disclosure Act is also referred to as Regulation C. The main purpose of HMDA is to provide additional (and required) information and data about the loan application, location of the subject property, and characteristics of your loan applicants. It also relates to the types of loan applications received by your mortgage company and the credit decisions for each.

Primarily, HMDA focuses on detecting lending discrimination by home mortgage lenders. These are what is referred to as Government Monitoring questions. Therefore, when you are completing the 1003 with your borrowers and get to an area on that form that asks about personal characteristics of your borrowers, the location of the subject property, and some features of the loan for those borrowers, then it is a good chance that you are asking questions related to HMDA.

HMDA was enacted in 1975. Then on July 21, 2011, the Dodd-Frank Act transferred HMDA rulemaking authority from the Federal Reserve Board to the CFPB. In October 2015, the CFPB finalized changes to Regulation C implementing HMDA that, among other things, expanded the number of data fields reported.

And, with the HMDA data that is collected on the Uniform Residential Loan Application (1003), each year the public has access to home mortgage application and loan information from thousands of financial institutions. In recent years, HMDA public data have contained roughly between 12 to 19 million records per year. The data includes loan-level information about the lender, loan, property, and applicant. The purposes of HMDA data are to:

- Help show whether lenders are serving the housing needs of their communities
- Provides public officials with information that helps them make certain housing-related decisions, and
- Shows (or indicates) whether lenders could be discriminatory in their lending patterns.

The following page lists those important areas that you, as a mortgage loan originator, need to be aware of that relates to the subject of HMDA:

1. Personal Characteristics of the Borrowers:
   As you complete the loan application (the 1003) on your customers you will need to include, on that application, important personal information that relates to your borrower(s):
   - **Date of Birth** of all Borrowers (Found on Page 1 of the 1003)
   - **Years of Schooling** of the Borrowers (Found on Page 1 of the 1003)
   - **Annual Income** of the Borrowers (Found on Page 2 of the 1003)

- **Applicants' National Race, Ethnicity and Sex** (Found on Page 4 of the 1003)

2. Date the Loan Application was Completed and/or Received:

The Date you completed that application with your customer or when you received that completed application in the mail. Now, when I said completed that application with your customer, I mean either face-to-face or completed it over the telephone. If you mailed the application to the customer, then you sign and date it when you receive it back from that customer. Therefore, to summarize:

- **Face-to-Face Application**: Date Application was personally completed with Customer.
- **Telephone Application**: Date Application was completed over the Telephone.
- **Mailed Application**: Date you received the Application from your Customer.

3. Important Information Regarding that Loan Application:

Here you enter information that relates to that specific type of mortgage loan. Examples of this would be:

- **Loan Number** Assigned on that Application
- **Date the Application was Received** (see #2 above)
- **Purpose** of that Loan (i.e. home purchase, refinance)
- **Type of Property** (SFR, 3-Unit, Manufactured Home)
- **Address and Location of the Subject Property**
- **Type of Occupancy** (O/O, NOO)
- **Amount of the Loan**

4. Disposition and/or Credit Decision on that Loan:

What was the final credit decision on that loan? If the loan was denied then what was the reason for that? You, as a Mortgage loan originator, won't normally get involved with this particular piece of information but I just wanted you to know it anyway.

Many times your Loan Processor may say that a particular item on a loan application (the 1003) is HMDA related or required. When he or she says that – this is what she is referring to. As we go through the chapter on completing The Uniform Residential Loan Application (the 1003) I will note when we have come to a HMDA related item.

HUD-1 SETTLEMENT STATEMENT (replaced by the Closing Disclosure):

Referred to as the HUD-1 (HUD stands for the Housing and Urban Development). This was a statement (form) that Closing Agents used to prepare - that summarized all the costs of the loan, the loan amount, and the amount the borrowers will receive after the funding of their loan (or amount of money they need to bring to loan closing). On October 3, 2015 the HUD-1 Settlement Statement was replaced by the Closing Disclosure.

Now, when the loan is ready to close and all Prior-To-Doc conditions have been satisfied then the loan documents "will be drawn" and either mailed or wired (emailed) to the Closing Agent's office. Once the Closing Agent receives those Closing Loan Documents (and their closing instructions) then he or she now prepares the Closing Disclosure. This is a very important home loan closing document. Because of its importance you want to be sure all the loan costs on this document are correct. Make sure you ask the Closing Agent to email or fax you a copy of the Closing Disclosure just as soon as he or she completes it - so you can review it to ensure it is complete and correct. You will want to be sure that all the closing costs are correct. Remember, that the Closing Agent is not normally privy to all the loan facts that you are. So, if you see something that is not included in the Closing Disclosure that should be (or should not be) just inform him or her of this. They will usually be happy to make those change(s) if possible.

INDEXES – FOR ARM LOANS:
The interest rate on an Adjustable-Rate Mortgage or ARM, unlike Fixed Rate Loans, does change or varies over the life or term of an ARM. And that's why they call it an Adjustable-Rate Mortgage. In Chapter 8, titled "Types of Mortgage Loans", I talk about ARM loans and what influences the existing interest rate on an ARM loan resulting in its newly adjusted rate at its adjustment period. One of the things that cause the interest rate on an ARM to change, at each adjustment rate period, is the Index for that interest rate on an ARM. And, there are many different types of Indexes, so let's talk about those Indexes now:

- **Certificate of Deposit (CD):**
  The Indexes from Certificate of Deposit, or CDs, are averages of the secondary market interest rates on nationally traded Certificates of Deposit. There are a number of different types of maturities that come with these types of CDs: 1, 3, and 6-months as well as the 1-year maturity CD.

- **Certificate of Deposit Index (CODI):**
  The Certificate of Deposit Index is commonly referred to as "CODI". It represents the 12-month average of the monthly yields on the national 3-Month Certificate of Deposit interest rates.

- **Cost of Funds Index (COFI):**
  Like the above Index, this Index is referred to as "COFI" – which is pronounced just like the word 'coffee'. And, COFI stands for the 11th District Cost Of Funds Index. This Index primarily represents the weighted-average of the interest rates paid by the 11th Federal Home Loan Bank District savings institutions for checking and savings accounts, and advances from the Federal Home Loan Bank. I should note here that the 11th District represents those financial institutions (e.g. banks and savings & loans) that are headquartered within the three states of Arizona, California, and Nevada. These COFI ARM loans can offer very low initial interest rates (what we sometimes refer to as teaser rates).

- **Constant Maturity Treasury (CMT):**
  These Indexes, referred to as "CMT", can be either a weekly or monthly average yield on U.S. Treasury securities that are adjusted to constant maturities.

- **Cost of Savings Index (COSI):**
  This Index has recently undergone some changes and today is referred to as the Wachovia Cost of Savings Index or W-COSI.

- **Treasury Bill (T-Bill):**
  This is a commonly used Index and is based on the results of the auctions of Treasury Bills by the U.S. Treasury.

- **London Inter-Bank Offering Rate (LIBOR):**
  This is an international indexed rate and is calculated using the interest rates of six major European banks (to their largest and best customers). When you refer to this Index pronounced it as LYE-BORE.

- **12-Month Treasury Average (MTA):**
  Our final Index listed here is the Monthly Treasury Average or "MTA". I should note that it is also known as the 12-Month Moving Average Treasury index and that is referred to as "MAT".

I can tell you that when you are talking with other Mortgage loan originators and refer to any of these Indexes, in their abbreviated way, such as, "Did you see how today's LIBOR compares to the T-Bill rate? Then you will sound pretty smooth.

INTEREST ADJUSTMENT:
Interest Adjustment, also referred to as Daily Interest Charges, is shown on the Loan Estimate and represents the Interest paid for the new loan from the day of funding of that loan to the end of that month. Hence, Interest Adjustment is made up of three items: 1. The number of days from the date of loan funding to the end of that month, 2. The monthly Interest on that loan translated (or broken down) into a per-day cost, and 3. Multiplying these two figures together to arrive at the total Interest Adjustment for that loan.

Thus, if the loan funded on the 15th of the month in a 30-day month then the number of days shown on the LE for Interest Adjustment would be 15. And, the easiest way I have found to manually calculate the Interest cost per day is to take the total loan amount and multiply that times the (annual) Note Rate and then divide that by 366 (days in the year). To show you what I mean let's say the total loan amount is $100,000 with an Interest Rate of 7.0%. Using the above here ($100,000 X 7.0% = $7,000). Then we divide that $7,000 by 366 to give us = $19.99 Interest per day. Any actual difference or variance of this calculated Interest per day cost to what your LP software program may come up with should be negligible I believe.

Another nice thing to tell your customers is that Interest Adjustment pays for the loan up to the end of that month (their loan closed and funded) and that their first mortgage payment (for their new 1st mortgage) won't be due until the 1st of the following month. Thus, it looks like they will skip a month. Hence, if your customers funded their loan on July 15th (or any day in July) then their first mortgage payment (on this new loan) would not be due until September 1st. This is because when borrowers make monthly payments on a mortgage - they are paying in arrears. In other words, they are paying for the time they have had that loan. This departs from when you are renting or leasing a property. Here you are paying in advance - for the time you will occupy that residence.

This is really a cool thing - especially for First-Time Homeowners. I remember when my wife and I bought our first house: When the first of the month came up, following our loan closing, I said to my Wife, "Hey, I'm ready to make our first mortgage payment." She replied "Don't you remember, we don't have to pay that until next month." I paused and said, "Great, let's have a house warming party!" And we did. My point here is that whether you are setting up a refinance loan or a home purchase loan – to remind or inform your customers of this. I'm sure they can think of something to do with that money they thought they would have to pay – on the first of the month following the closing of their home purchase or refinance loan. I should mention here that as of October 3, 2015, Interest Adjustment will be shown as "Prepaid Interest" on the new Loan Estimate and Closing Disclosure statements and disclosures.

INTEREST-ONLY LOANS (I/O):
Interest-Only loans, as the name implies, are loans whereby the monthly mortgage payments includes and pays only for the Interest on that loan. Hence, there is no pay down of the principal on that loan. Usually with these types of loans there is a shorter term (say 3 - 10 years) with a balloon payment at the end of that term. Interest-only loans can be abbreviated and referred to as I/O.

INTERESTED PARTY CONTRIBUTIONS (IPCs)
Interested Party Contributions are costs that are normally the responsibility of the property purchaser that are paid directly or indirectly by someone else who has a financial interest in, or can influence the Terms and the Sale or Transfer of, the subject property. Interested parties to a transaction include, but are not limited to, the property seller, the builder/developer, the real estate agent or broker, or an affiliate who may benefit from the sale of the property and/or the sale of the property at the highest price possible.

A Lender or employer is not considered an interested party to a sales transaction unless it is the property seller or is affiliated with the property seller or another interested party to the transaction. Interested Party Contributions are either financing concessions or sales concessions. Fannie Mae considers the following to be IPCs:

- Funds that are paid directly from the interested party to the borrower;
- Funds that flow from an interested party through a third-party organization, including non-profit entities, to the borrower;
- Funds that flow to the transaction on the borrower's behalf from an interested party, including a third-party organization or nonprofit agency; and
- Funds that are donated to a third party, which then provides the money to pay some or all of the closing costs for a specific transaction.

A Lender credit derived from premium pricing is not considered an IPC even if the lender is an interested party to the transaction. Fannie Mae does not permit IPCs to be used to make the borrower's down payment, meet financial reserve requirements, or meet minimum borrower contribution requirements.

Having said that, let's take a look at the table below which shows the maximum Interested Party Contributions for conventional mortgage loans:

Occupancy Type	LTV/CLTV	Max. IPC Ratio
Principle Residence or 2nd Home	Greater than 90%	3%
	75.01% - 90%	6%
	75% or Less	9%
Investment Property	All CLTV Ratios	2%

I should also mention that when the Interested Party Contributions exceed these limits then those (above the acceptable IPC ratios) are then considered Sales Concessions. When that happens then the property's sales price must be adjusted downward to reflect the amount of contribution that exceeds the maximum acceptable IPC. And, the Maximum LTV/CLTV ratios must be recalculated using the reduced sales price or appraised value of the subject property.

JUMBO LOANS:
This is a common term used in lending and refers to a loan amount larger than the loan limits that have been set by FNMA and FHLMC for General Conforming and High-Cost Loans. At present, for an owner-occupied SFR, if the total loan amount is greater than $548,250 for a General Conforming loan or $822,375 for a High-Cost Area, where the subject property is located in a HUD classified High-Cost Area, then that loan is considered a Jumbo and Jumbo Non-conforming loan in most States.

JUMBO-CONFORMING LOANS:
A Jumbo-Conforming or Mini-Jumbo mortgage loan represents a mortgage loan in which the subject property was within a High-Cost Area, and the loan amount was greater than $822,375 for a 1-unit property.

Let me just say, for historical purposes only, that when the mortgage bubble finally burst, in early 2007, and we then went into the so-called Mortgage Meltdown and Mortgage Crisis. Prior to and during that period it became increasingly clear that Fannie Mae's maximum loan amounts needed to be adjusted upward for certain "High-Cost Areas". This made sense to me because in my "neck of the woods" in Spokane, Washington, the average selling price of a home, at that time, was around $200,000. However, in San Francisco and San Diego, California the average selling price of a home could have been around $500,000. That meant that many homebuyers and homeowners in San Francisco and San Diego had to obtain a Jumbo Loan when purchasing or refinancing a home. And, that usually meant having a higher interest on their home loan with perhaps higher loan fees as well.

In response to this, on February 13, 2008 the President Bush signed into law The Economic Stimulus Act of 2008 which identified those metropolitan statistical areas and rural counties that were classified by HUD as "High-Cost Areas" and increased the maximum Conforming loan limits for each up to (or times) 1.75% (or $729,750) of the maximum Conforming loan limit and still enjoy the benefits that Conforming loans offer in terms of lower rates and fees. The Economic Stimulus Act of 2008 also resulted in a new mortgage lending term: Jumbo-Conforming or Mini-Jumbo. A Jumbo-Conforming or Mini-Jumbo mortgage loan represented a mortgage loan in which the subject property was located within a High-Cost area, as classified by HUD, and the loan amount was greater than the Conforming loan limit for that type of property (1-Unit). Otherwise, if the total loan amount was $417,000 or less, for a 1-Unit property, then that loan would be considered a Conforming loan. And, that distinction was important because when a loan becomes Jumbo-Conforming then there are different originating and processing restrictions and underwriting guidelines that apply to these that do not apply to General Conforming Loans. For example, at that time all Jumbo-Conforming loans must have been manually underwritten, have lower minimum required credit scores as well as lower maximum LTVs (per loan type). This too has changed.

However, each metropolitan area or county, of each contiguous state of the United States, could have a different maximum Conforming loan limit – depending upon whether that area is classified as a High-Cost Area or not. For example, the maximum Jumbo-Conforming amount for San Francisco, California (High-Cost area), for a 1-unit SFR was (at that time) $636,150 – and yet, for Spokane, Washington was at $425,100. HUD initially considered lowering this maximum Conforming loan limit of $417,000 for what it considered "Low-Cost" areas and counties but decided against that. I should also mention that these increased loan limits for Jumbo-Conforming loans, for properties located in HUD classified High-Cost Areas, was originally intended as a temporary adjustment for loans originated from July 1, 2007 to December 31, 2008. Because of this the term Jumbo-Conforming loans was phased out (during 2009) and was replaced with what is called "High-Cost Area" loans.

LAND SALES CONTRACT:
This is a personal sales contract between a buyer and seller for the purpose of purchasing a home or property. In this case title is usually not passed on to the buyer until the contract is paid in full.

LEGAL DESCRIPTION:
A legal description of a property is the location of that property referenced by government surveys and approved recorded maps. The Uniform Residential Loan Application (1003) asks for this information. You can find this (Legal Description) on a Metroscan for a property or a Property Profile. Legal descriptions are generally written as:

The North Half of Lot 5, Block 10, in the Adams Addition.

All properties with a legal description also usually have a parcel number whereby it can be referenced as well.

LESSEE & LESSOR:
Here are a couple of those jargon terms you may hear now and then. The Lessee is the person who rents or pays for the lease on a property. The Lessor is the person who owns and rents (leases) a property and receives payment for the lease.

LIEN:

A Lien is an encumbrance which a person or company has on a property of another person as security for a debt. For example, sometimes you will see a "Mechanic's Lien" on a property. This could happen when a home painter (the mechanic) has painted a house and the homeowner never paid him for the job of painting his home. The Painter can then put (record) a lien on that property (and any other properties that homeowner owns) for the amount of the (originally) agreed home paint job (plus any additional expenses that contractor may have incurred). The significance of this is: Before that homeowner can refinance or sell his or her house (or any other of their properties that have this lien on it) then he or she will have to first payoff that lien to that painter (or any others) either prior to or at loan closing.

Liens, on the subject property (that you are doing a loan on), can be found on the Preliminary Title Report that will be ordered during the processing of that loan.

LIQUID ASSETS:

If you have taken an accounting course then you know that Liquid Assets are assets that can be converted into cash quite readily and quickly. On the Uniform Residential Loan Application (1003) the prospective borrower is asked about their Liquid Assists. This amount can be important if the Lender is asking for a certain number of months of Reserves on the borrower's loan. Liquid Assets can usually be used for this purpose. See below regarding definition of Reserves.

LOAN ESTIMATE:

The Loan Estimate is a loan disclosure and statement that presents and summarizes all the costs of a home loan and includes the loan amount, monthly mortgage payment, and the loan's interest rate. The Loan Estimate replaced the Good Faith Estimate on October 3, 2015. When referring to it in abbreviated form you can generally just write it as LE. The Loan Estimate is one of the most important documents for you to have a good handle on as a Mortgage loan originator. I will go into much more detail on this form in a later chapter. But for now, just be aware that the Loan Estimate presents all the important costs and fees of a loan: Loan amount, monthly payment, interest rate, term, amortization period, loan costs, pre-pays (see below), sales price, and amount refinanced (if a refinance loan), and the amount the borrowers may need to bring to their closing or will receive at loan funding. According to the CFPB, the Loan Estimate, as of October 3, 2015, is to be used on all close-end home loans. The existing revised Good Faith Estimate, that became effective in 2010, can still to be used on open-end home loans.

MORTGAGE LOAN ORIGINATOR COMPENSATION:

First, let me say that April 1, 2011 changed how all mortgage loan originators got compensated for their loans - from the way they have been paid in the past. The Federal Reserve Board amended the Truth-In-Lending Act and in doing that implemented new rulings regarding a Loan Originator's Compensation. According to the Federal Reserve Board's final rulings, as it impacted Loan Originators' Compensation, the following three prohibitions first went into effect on April 1, 2011 and then was expanded as of June, 1 2013.

1. Loan Originators can no longer be compensated based upon the Terms and Conditions of a mortgage loan.

2. Loan Originators can be compensated directly or indirectly by the loan consumer or Creditor – but not from both for the same loan transaction.

3. Steering a Customer towards a Loan with Higher Compensation is in violation.

The CFPB also implemented the Loan Originator Rule which became effective on January 10, 2014. This Loan Originator Rule continues to maintain much of what was required under the Loan Originator's Compensation rules and requirements that began on April 1, 2011, but does make some changes and additions to it.

For a more in-depth discussion on this subject – please go to the Loan Originator Rule discussion within Chapter 25 on Mortgage Lending Regulations.

LOAN ORIGINATOR – DEFINED:

To be sure that everyone is on the same page and wavelength, in terms who is impacted by the Fed's new rulings, the amended Truth-In-Lending Act dated September 24, 2010, also defines what it considers as Loan Originators, Mortgage Brokers, Creditors, and Managers and Administrative Staff. So, let's go over these so we are all singing along with the TILA and on the same key. This also follows the CFPB's definition of a Loan Originator:

Loan Originators:

TILA defines a Loan Originator as "any person who for compensation or other monetary gain arranges, negotiates, or otherwise obtains an extension of consumer credit for another person". The two main points of this statement, I believe, are "for compensation" and "obtains credit for another person".

TILA goes on to include, as a Loan Originator, employees of a creditor, as well as employees of a mortgage broker that "that satisfy this definition". TILA also makes the distinction that a consumer that arranges and negotiates a loan for themselves would not be considered a Loan Originator – because of the two main points I noted above. And, of course, writing it in legalese, it makes the statement that the term "person" means a natural person or an organization".

Mortgage Brokers:

The amended Truth-In-Lending Act first clarifies that a Mortgage Broker is a Loan Originator who is not an employee of the Creditor. It further states that a Mortgage Broker can include companies that engage in the activities stated in the definition of Loan Originator above.

And, the prohibitions that were discussed above (within Loan Originator Compensation) also applies to payments to Mortgage Brokers and payments made by a company acting as a Mortgage Broker to its employee, who are also Loan Originators.

Creditors:
The amended Truth-In-Lending Act defines a Creditor as:

- Not deemed to be a Loan Originator on a loan transaction according to the above definitions of Mortgage Broker and Loan Originator.

- TILA goes on to clarify (if I may say that) that a person that closes a loan in its own name (but another person provides the funds for the transaction at loan closing and receives an immediate assignment of the Note, Loan Contract, or other evidence of the debt obligation) is deemed a Loan Originator, not a Creditor. However, that person is still a Creditor for all other purposes of Regulation Z. Got it? If you are like me you might have to read that one more time. But that's legalese for you.

Managers and Administrative Staff:
It appears that the "Powers That Be" wanted to be sure to exclude those who are not considered Loan Originators – as defined within TILA and stated above. Therefore, TILA states that managers, administrative staff, and similar individuals who are employed by a Creditor or Loan Originator (e.g. Mortgage Broker) – but do not arrange, negotiate, or otherwise obtain an extension of credit for a consumer <u>and</u> whose compensation is not based on whether any particular loan is originated - are not Loan Originators. This seems pretty clear from the definitions of Loan Originator above.

LOAN-TO-VALUE RATIO (LTV):
This is probably one of the most commonly used terms in our industry and is generally referred to as the LTV. As the name implies - it represents the percent of the loan amount to the (appraised) value of a property. For example, if the loan amount is $80,000 and the property is valued at $100,000 then the LTV (on that loan) is 80%. Conversely, the homeowner has or will have 20% equity on their property. Also see Combined Loan-To-Value (CLTV).

MANUFACTURED HOME:
I throw this one in here because I think it's important to know the definition of a Manufactured Home (versus a Modular Home). When I first started out in this business I didn't know the difference between the two. A Manufactured Home is built at a factory in sections (usually) and then transported to a permanent site and has a metal foundation. While a Modular Home has the same construction features it does not have a metal foundation (usually wood) and is generally treated the same as a stick-built home. If you need more information regarding Manufactured Homes then please refer to the term Property Types in this chapter.

MAXIMUM DEBT-TO-INCOME RATIOS:
Within Chapter 4 I go into the details of Manually Underwritten and Automated Underwritten (DU) home loans. As you will see there are underwriting requirements and distinctions between these two types of underwriting loans. According to Fannie Mae's recent Selling Guide one area of distinction between these two is the Maximum DTI ratios allowed for each underwriting type:

- For Manually Underwritten loans, Fannie Mae's maximum total DTI ratio is 36% of the borrower's stable monthly income. However, if the borrower meets the credit score and reserve requirements reflected in the Eligibility Matrix then the maximum can be exceeded up to 45%.

- For Loan Casefiles underwritten through DU, the maximum allowable DTI ratio could be high as 50%.

MORTGAGE INDUSTRY STANDARDS MAINTENANCE ORGANIZATION:

The Mortgage Industry Standards Maintenance Organization or MISMO® is the standards development body for the mortgage industry. These were the folks who were involved in the development of the new 1003 to be fully utilized for manual and AUS underwritten mortgage loans.

- MISMO developed a common data language for exchanging information for the residential finance industry. Today, MISMO standards are accepted and deployed by every type of entity involved in creating mortgages, and they are required by most regulators, housing agencies and the GSEs that participate in the industry. Use of MISMO's standards has been found to lower per loan costs, improve margins, reduce errors and speed up the loan process by reducing manual, paper-based processes while creating cost savings for the consumer. MISMO is a wholly owned subsidiary of the Mortgage Bankers Association.

- MISMO provides specification for residential, commercial, and eMortgage areas of mortgage finance. Residential standards are available for the entire lifecycle of a mortgage loan – from start to finish.

You can obtain more information about MISMO and how it relates to the mortgage industry by going to their website at: https://www.mismo.org/

MIXED-USE PROPERTY:

Mixed-Use property is any property that has a combination of residential and commercial use. An example of this could be a retail store where the storeowners live on the second floor above that store. Another example might be a single-family unit home whereby the owner conducts commercial business in their home (i.e. an Attorney who has legal customers visit him at his place of business – his home).

MODIFIED HOME LOANS:

A Modified Home Loan is a loan that was legally modified after loan closing in a way that changed any of the loan terms or attributes reflected in the original Note. In general, loans with material modifications, such as changes to the original loan amount, interest rate, final maturity, or product structure, are not eligible for delivery to Fannie Mae.

A loan that was modified to effect technical or typographical corrections is permitted for delivery, provided that all of the changes correct errors in the executed documents, which reflect the terms of the original loan transaction. None of the changes can be the result of a subsequent modification or amendment to the original loan amount, interest rate, or other material loan term. The correction may not result in a change to, or create any inconsistencies with, other legal documents. However, Fannie Mae does permit the delivery of certain other modified loans based primarily on whether the loan was owned or securitized by Fannie Mae prior to the modification, or the modification of the loan was done in accordance with a standard product or is common and customary in a certain area.

I should also mention that loan Limits for Modified Loans are based on the original loan amount of the loan and not on the unpaid principal balance of the loan - at the time of modification or acquisition by Fannie Mae. A Modified Loan with an original loan amount exceeding the current loan limit is not eligible for purchase by Fannie Mae, even though the balance, at the time of the modification, may be at or below the current applicable loan limit.

MONTHLY MORTGAGE PAYMENT:
Monthly Mortgage Payments are usually expressed as PITI meaning: Principal, Interest, (property) Taxes, and (hazard) Homeowner's Insurance paid each month on a mortgage loan. A monthly mortgage payment having PITI means that the monthly property taxes and homeowner's insurance payments have been impounded (or escrowed) in with that loan's P&I payment. If you are looking strictly at the monthly mortgage loan payment then you would refer to it as the P&I: Principal and Interest.

There are also Interest-Only loans in which each monthly mortgage payment pays only for the outstanding interest on that loan. If that is the case then it could be written as IO. And, if Taxes and Homeowner's Insurance are included in that monthly mortgage payment then it is written as ITI.

MORTGAGE:
Quite simply a mortgage is a legal instrument by which property is hypothecated to secure the payment of a debt or obligation. That big word "hypothecated" just means that the homeowners are giving their home as security (for the loan) without giving up possession of it.

As you may know, within lending there are 1st and 2nd mortgages. And, on rare occasions you might even see a 3rd mortgage. The important thing to know is that the position of a mortgage (whether it is a 1st or 2nd mortgage) doesn't have anything to do with the amount of that mortgage (although you will usually see the 1st mortgage being the greater amount of the two). It has to do with when (or put another way) the timing of the recording of the mortgages. Hence, the 1st mortgage was recorded prior to the 2nd mortgage.

NATIONWIDE MORTGAGE LICENSING SYSTEM AND REGISTRY (NMLS):
This is the organization that assigns to mortgage loan originators their NMLSR ID number. This system of each mortgage loan originator having their own NMLSR ID number facilitates electronic tracking and uniform identification of loan originators and public access to loan originators' employment, disciplinary, and enforcement-action history.

According to the Loan Originator Rule all mortgage loan originators must be licensed and registered if required under the SAFE Act or other state or federal law. However, if a state does not require mortgage loan originators to be licensed (according to the SAFE Act) then the Loan Originator Rule lays out legal requirements that apply to their required training and loan origination activities.

NEGATIVE AMORTIZATION:

This is a term you will hear every once in a while. Negative Amortization occurs on a loan when the required monthly mortgage payment (P&I or Interest Only) is not enough to pay for all the interest due (at that time) on that loan. When this happens then the unpaid interest is then (usually) added onto the outstanding balance of that loan. As a result, the homeowner can end up owing more than the original amount of their loan.

Within the past couple of years there has been a number of ARM loan programs that offer home loan borrowers and investors a number of monthly payment options. The choice of a particular type of ARM and its monthly payment options may result in a much lower monthly mortgage payment - but not be enough to service the outstanding interest on that loan. In that case Negative Amortization would then occur with the result that the Deferred Interest on that loan (not paid by that monthly payment) would be added onto the principal of that loan.

NET LEASE:

If you get into commercial loans (which I cover very little in this book) or non-owner occupied (NOO) residential property - you will encounter the subject of leases. If the subject of leases comes up then the question may arise as to what type of lease does the Lessee's pay on. A Net Lease is a lease whereby, in addition to paying the monthly rent, the Lessee also pays for all operating expenses, real estate taxes, and may also pay for the hazard insurance on that property. This ends up being a sweet deal for the Lessor because his gross monthly payments received are also his net monthly payments received.

This is important when you are trying to show as much income for your customer who is a Lessor as well. On the 1003 it asks for how much the Lessor gets in rent per month. It also asks for the Net Rental Income. This is generally arrived at by multiplying the Gross Rental Income by 75%. This is a common practice in lending. This reduction (by 25%) of the Gross Rental Income received - is for the taxes, operating expenses, etc., to maintain that property. If your customer has a Net Lease then you have a good case to not have to reduce his Gross Rental Income.

At this point, when discussing Rental Income, please also refer to my discussion on Fannie Mae's current policy on Rental Income Qualifying Requirements.

NICHE (LOAN PRODUCTS):

A Niche Loan Product is a term that usually refers to a loan program or product that a particular Wholesale Lender offers – that other lenders may not offer. It could also refer to the fact that a Wholesale Lender specializes in a particular market (e.g. 4-plexes or Mixed-Use Properties) and because of that they may offer much better Pricing (lower interest rates) and also may offer loan programs with lower LTVs on their Niche Loan Products - than what other lenders offer.

NO-COST LOAN:

This is a term that you will hear every once in a while. I find that few borrowers out there are familiar with this type of loan. In previous years, a No-Cost Loan was a loan whereby the loan costs, shown on a LE, were paid by the originating Mortgage loan originator (through their rebate they were to earn on that loan). For more information on this see Premium Pricing below. Over the years I have found that lending folks (and some customers) use this term and mean that they pay no loan costs (i.e. for the appraisal, credit report, loan processing, flood certification, etc.). However, for this type of loan some customers have told me that it <u>does</u> include Interest Adjustment and Prepays. Others I have discussed this with consider a No-Cost Loan to include <u>all</u> costs of the loan. So, be sure you understand what they are referring to and are on the same "wavelength" as they are when you discuss this with a customer.

Although some folks think a "No-Cost" loan is the way to go, in my opinion it is a moot point. A No-Cost Loan is a misnomer. There are very real costs in putting together a loan and with a No-Cost Loan that customer is actually paying for those loan costs with a higher interest rate – with those loan costs being paid through the (additional) points charged on their loan or with a higher interest rate. This is often referred to as Premium Pricing. The interest rate you would have to offer (on one of these types of loans) would be one that has rebate points that not only covers the actual costs of that loan but also any origination fee you would charge on that loan.

Personally, I don't think No-Cost Loans are that good of a thing. I would much more prefer to offer my customers the benefits of a lower or "At par pricing "interest rate. However, sometimes it just gets down to what your customer wants. As I said, you most likely won't see this very often but I wanted to go over it with you - so you have an idea of this type of loan and what to do if you ever get a request for one.

NON–U.S. CITIZEN BORROWER ELIGIBILITY REQUIREMENTS:

Originating mortgage loans for Non-U.S. Citizens can sometimes get confusing – wondering what is needed or if the mortgage loan can even be done. However, Fannie Mae does purchases and securitizes mortgages made to non–U.S. citizens who are lawfully permanent or non-permanent residents of the United States under the same terms that are available to U.S. citizens. On the other hand, Fannie Mae does not specify the precise documentation the Lender must obtain to verify that a non–U.S. citizen borrower is legally present in the United States. The Lender must make a determination of the non–U.S. citizen's status based on the circumstances of the individual case and using documentation it deems appropriate. By delivering the mortgage to Fannie Mae, the Lender represents and warrants that the non–U.S. citizen borrower is legally present in this country.

So, if you are working on one of these types of loans then be sure to contact the prospective Lender, for that loan, and ask them what their document requirements are.

NOTE (MORTGAGE):

The Note is evidence of a debt. It also usually references the Deed of Trust (see Deed above). Within real estate there are generally two types of Notes:

1. **The Straight Note**:
   This is a Note whereby the borrowers pay interest-only payments during the term (see Interest-Only Loans above).

2. **The Fully Amortized Note**:
   This is the more common type of Note whereby every loan payment applies part of it to the loan's principal and interest.

In lending you will sometimes get requests, from the Lender, who wants to see a copy of The Note. This is because the Note contains within it a description of the conditions of the borrower's current mortgage loan and how it is to be repaid. For example, it contains and shows the interest rate, when payments are due, and if there is a Prepayment Penalty feature on that loan. When I am doing 2nd mortgages, refinancing an ARM loan, or refinancing an unseasoned 1st mortgage – then I definitely like to get a copy of that homeowner's Mortgage Note.

NOTICE OF DEFAULT:
If a mortgage loan customer has been making late payments on their mortgage and their mortgage payment is late up to or beyond 120 days then usually the Lender on that loan will send to that homeowner a Notice of Default (referred to as an NOD). Receiving an NOD generally sets into the motion the first steps towards home foreclosure. And, for many a Lender's standpoint, if a customer wishes to refinance their existing mortgage and a Lender's Underwriter, in reviewing that loan, sees an NOD issued and filed on that mortgage then that is like the 'kiss of death' and that loan could subsequently be denied. This might be true even if that mortgage has been bought current (after receiving that NOD).

OCCUPANCY:
When you are qualifying your customers you definitely want to know what type of occupancy they are talking about or what your customers are interested in doing. This will significantly affect the loan program and interest rate you can offer them. Within residential lending there are basically two types of occupancy:

1. **Owner-Occupied**. Written as O/O. Here the borrowers have lived or wish to live in and occupy that residence.

2. **Non-Owner Occupied**. Written as NOO. Here the borrowers do not or are not planning to occupy that property as their primary residence. NOO properties are generally investment type of properties with the purpose of being rented or leased by their owners.

I should note here that sometimes you might have an opportunity to do a refinance or purchase loan on a Second Home. This is also usually considered O/O.

ORIGINATION FEE:
The Origination Fee, sometimes referred to as the "Up-Front Fee" is expressed as a percent of the total loan amount and is also the dollar amount a mortgage broker or lending

institution charges the borrower to cover the expenses of originating and processing a home loan. This represents what you and your mortgage company will make on that loan. How much should you charge? That depends on the policy of your mortgage branch office and the total amount of the home loan.

For a $200,000 loan it is common practice to charge a 1.0% loan origination fee. I should mention here that there is an inverse relationship here to what a Lender charges for a particular interest rate: As the offered interest rate decreases then the cost (or rebate) to obtain that interest rate increases. I have also found that, in many cases, that this principle also applies to the total work to complete a home loan: As the total amount of a home loan decreases (e.g. $125,000 or less) then the amount of work to originate and process that loan increases. The converse to this seems to also be true.

PAR PRICING:

Par Pricing refers to what a particular interest rate is at "O" rebate (no cost or credit for your loan customer). The at Par Pricing interest rate might be the ideal rate for your loan customer – if they qualify for that rate and it fulfills their financial needs and goals for that loan. However, your loan customer may request for you to obtain a lower or higher rate than what is available at Par Pricing.

Using the interest rate at "Par" as a starting point, your loan customer may want to "Buydown the Rate" (obtain a lower interest rate than what is offered at Par Pricing). Doing this, your loan customer would incur a cost to obtain that lower interest and that cost would be with what is referred to as Discount Points. The percent and amount for Discount Points is shown within Line (box) Item #2 at the top of page 2 of the LE.

On the other hand, let's say your loan customer is willing to obtain a higher interest rate (than what is shown on the Rate Sheets at Par Pricing) and wants to apply credits, in doing this, towards their total loan costs. Doing this is referred to as Premium Pricing and the percent and amount for this is also shown within Line (box) Item #2 at the top of page 2 of the Loan Estimate.

PAYMENT SHOCK:

This is a term that refers to what sometimes happens when homebuyers go from paying rent (i.e. for an apartment) to paying a monthly mortgage payment. In other words, the increase in the monthly housing expense (e.g. monthly rental payment to the new mortgage payment). Payment Shock could also represent the increase from a borrower's previous monthly mortgage payments to their new and proposed mortgage payments. Most Lenders consider any increase in monthly housing expense of 30% or greater to fall under Payment Shock. For example, if your borrowers currently have a monthly mortgage (or rental payment) of $500 and this new mortgage loan would result in their new monthly mortgage payment (PITI) of $650 or greater - then this is considered Payment Shock.

The above is true for what are considered Fixed Rate Loans. But what about ARM home loans? There is also a term referred to as "ARM Payment Shock". This can be a consideration especially if an ARM provides for low initial payments - based on a fixed introductory rate that expires, after a short period of time, and then adjusts to a variable rate for the remaining term of the mortgage loan. These have the potential for ARM Payment Shock. After the interest rate and payments increase, the borrower could be subsequently faced with a large increase in monthly PITI. Lenders must limit the impact of any potential Payment Shock on an ARM with an initial fixed-rate period of five years or less by qualifying borrowers based on the greater of either:

- The Note rate plus 2%, or
- The Fully Indexed Rate with a fully amortizing repayment schedule (including taxes and insurance). The Fully Indexed Rate equals the sum of the value of the applicable index and the mortgage margin.

If a Lender sees Payment Shock, as a result of the new proposed loan, then they may be concerned about the borrower's ability to continue to service that loan. Although the Ratios (Housing & Total Debt) may be in line many Lenders will request from those borrowers: 1. A Letter from them stating that they are aware of this increase and that it will not financially overburden them, and sometimes, 2. A monthly budget showing their income and monthly expenses, including utilities and things like food, auto gas, etc.

POINTS:

Points, like the origination fee above, represent a percentage of the total loan amount that is being charged or credited to the borrower on a loan. In lending, Points are expressed in 8 parts or eighths of a point (when they are less than a full point). For example, an interest rate may be expressed as 6& 7/8ths. Thus, the rate here would be 6&7/8% or written as 6.875%.

In written form, each eighth of a point equals 0.125 of a point. Below breaks it down for you:

Parts of a Point:

1/8%	=	0.125	= Eighth of a Point
2/8%	=	0.250	= A Quarter of a Point
3/8%	=	0.375	= Three-Eighths of a Point
4/8%	=	0.500	= Half a Point
5/8%	=	0.625	= Five-Eighths of a Point
6/8%	=	0.750	= Three-Quarters of a Point
7/8%	=	0.875	= Seven-Eighths of a Point
1.0%	=	1.000	= A Full Point

As a mortgage loan originator you need to be familiar with these and comfortable in speaking in those terms. An eighth of a point can sometimes make a big difference in, for example, what your customer would have to pay on his or her monthly mortgage payments as well as using Discount Points or Premium Pricing for an interest rate for their loan.

Since I am talking about Points I should also mention the term "Basis Points". It has been my experience that you see the use of Basis Points more in investment type of products. For example, a Basis Point equals 1/100th of a percentage point. For example, if an investment fee were 50 basis points (which equals ½ of a point) of $100,000 then that translates into a fee of $500.00 ($100,000 x .005).

PRE-QUALIFICATION VS. PRE-APPROVAL LETTER:

Sometimes a prospective homebuyer may approach you that is looking to do a home loan but has not yet identified the home "of their dreams" they wish to purchase. Those prospective homebuyers may also be first-time homebuyers as well and they may not even know what they can afford or the maximum home loan amount that they would qualify for. The question you may ask, at that time, (as well as any realtor might ask) is - are those folks serious about buying a house or are they just "kicking the tires" and browsing? This is where a Pre-Qualification or Pre-Approval Letter can come into play. So, let's now talk about the difference between a Pre-Qualification (referred to as a Pre-Qual) and a Pre-Approval Letter.

Pre-Qualification Letter:

Now, a Pre-Qual Letter merely states that the prospective homebuyer have visited with a home lender (as shown on the Lender's letterhead) and based on that prospective borrower's qualifying features that the mortgage loan originator has quickly reviewed (e.g. their income, savings, and current debts) that they could be eligible for a home loan up and within a maximum loan amount range. It's important to note here that a Pre-Qual Letter is not an official offer or guarantee, by the Lender, to finance a home loan amount (or within a loan amount range). That Pre-Qual Letter is merely an estimate, by the mortgage loan originator, of what the borrower could be approved for based upon what they told that mortgage loan originator. And that's because, at that point in time, none of those items (their credit, income, savings, and debts) have been verified. And, for that reason I have heard some loan officers say that a Pre-Qual Letter is not worth the paper it is written on. However, home sellers oftentimes do ask for these because it shows that those looking to buy a home could be serious homebuyers who have identified a Lender and provided them with a Pre-Qual Letter. That could be just what those homebuyers need to begin serious negotiations with the home seller to purchase a property.

Pre-Approval Letter:

A Pre-Approval Letter from a Lender, on the other hand, carries much more weight because it is a conditional commitment from a mortgage company or Lender stating that the prospective home loan borrower(s) are pre-approved for a mortgage loan within a certain loan amount range (e.g. $200,000 - $250,000). A maximum home loan range is usually presented, on the Pre-Approval Letter, because the subject property (home they wish to purchase) has not yet been identified. And, the main reason a Pre-Approval carries more weight, with a realtor and seller of a property, is because those qualifying aspects for a home loan, for those homebuyer(s), and has been verified:

- Their Credit Report was pulled:
    - Borrower's credit scores have been identified
    - Their debt obligations can be verified
- Income & Assets have been verified
- The prospective borrowers have gone through an in-depth eligibility process
- Their Debt-to-Income Ratios have be calculated

- Their eligibility may even have been reviewed by the MLO's Loan Processor

Thus, as you can see, a Pre-Approval Letter, is more robust and representative of what a prospective homebuyer can afford and be qualified for when shopping for a home and obtaining a home loan. And, that could be just what a homebuyer needs when they are seriously negotiating with a home seller.

PREDATORY LENDING:

This is a term you will hear every so often and usually is used in reference to a possible violation of a RESPA rule or law. Predatory Lending generally refers to abusive practices by a mortgage loan originator or lender to a home loan borrower. If a lender is using any form of deceptive, fraudulent, or even discriminatory lending practices, in their interactions with their mortgage loan borrowers, then you can safely assume that they are guilty of Predatory Lending. This practice of Predatory Lending, by a mortgage loan originator or Lender, can result in locking in high or exorbitant interest rates and charging excessive loan settlement fees. This victimizes loan borrowers and creates a higher monthly P&I mortgage payment, for that mortgage loan borrower, and puts additional and undo pressure on a homeowner's total monthly debt servicing. And, can cause erosion of a homeowner's equity. All these factors can contribute towards an increase in mortgage delinquencies, defaults, and foreclosures. Because of this, The Housing and Urban Development (HUD), since 1999, has been actively involved in monitoring Lenders' practices and submitting and passing regulations that address these types of (Predatory Lending) concerns. This has also resulted in those changes on a Mortgage loan originator's Compensation (which began on April 1, 2011) and the Dodd-Frank Wall Street Reform and Consumer Protection Act (specifically Title XIV of this Act).

The most common forms of Predatory Lending, I believe, are: 1. Charging borrowers excessive loan fees – than are normally charged in that area, 2. Not fully disclosing or disclosing (e.g. the Loan Estimate and Loan Disclosures) within the time periods required by RESPA, 3. Bait and Switch practices whereby Lenders initially offer low interest rates and/or fees (to motivate the borrowers to meet with them and/or complete a loan application) and subsequently (and intentionally) increase the interest rate and/or loan fees, and 4. Convincing a borrower to refinance his or her property when it is not in their best financial interest to do so (at that time). Or, to convince a borrower to refinance their home - with the sole purpose of charging that borrower a high interest rate and fees (which benefits that loan originator but not the borrower), and 5. Paying kickbacks and/or referral fees on a loan (these may be shown and included on a loan or not).

While this list is not all-inclusive it does give you an idea of what is involved in Predatory Lending. Although I do not have statistics to support this, my feeling is that most likely about 1% - 5% of the lenders out there have done or currently practice some form of Predatory Lending. Unfortunately, it's that percentage of lenders that has hurt the rest of us honest and ethical lending folks and has caused such policing and regulations by HUD and the CFPB to protect mortgage loan borrowers.

PRELIMINARY TITLE REPORT:

The Preliminary Title Report is something you order, in processing your loan, from a Title Company. This report is the results of a title search by that title company before they issue a new title insurance policy. Understand that each time a property is refinanced or changes hands or ownership - a new title insurance policy is usually required. This ensures that each time title changes it is a clear title.

You will also want to look this over to make sure that 1. The borrowers refinancing the subject property are the actual owners, and 2. That there exist no other liens or mortgages on that property (other than what those borrowers told you). For more information on this subject please go to Chapter 20 on Title Insurance.

PREMIUM PRICING:

Premium Pricing refers to quoting and/or locking in your customer with a higher interest rate (above Par Pricing) in order to pay for part or all of the loan fees and/or funds to close - from the rebate points charged by the Lender for a higher interest rate. This credit amount is shown within the 2nd Box, item #2, on the second page of the new LE.

Also, recall when we discussed a "No Cost Loan?" If a customer wants a No Cost Loan, who is going to pay for all those loan costs that are required to make that loan happen? That customer will – with a higher interest rate than if they included those costs in their loan and/or paid (upfront) for it prior to or at loan closing. This amount would also be shown within the 2nd Box, item #3, on the second page of the new LE.

PREPAYMENT PENALTY:

A Prepayment Penalty refers to the fee (a penalty) that a loan customer would have to pay if they paid off the full amount of their loan within a loan's Prepayment Penalty period. A rule of thumb, and quick way to figure the Prepayment Penalty, is to calculate about 6 months of the P&I payment on that loan. This is only a conservative rule of thumb and the actual Prepayment Penalty calculation may be different with each Lender and/or loan program. For example, these days I am also seeing some ARM loans with Prepayment Penalties amounting to 2–3% of the original loan amount. Here, the actual percent used in calculating that loan's Prepayment Penalty seems to be determined when the full amount of that loan is paid off (before the end of that loan's Prepayment Penalty period).
So, it can get rather expensive for your borrowers to get out of that loan during their Prepayment Penalty Period (and that's the reason for it).

I should note here that even though a Prepayment Penalty is charged when the outstanding amount of a loan is paid off, during that Prepayment Penalty period, this normally doesn't apply when that borrower is making only an additional partial payment (which is greater than the minimum required monthly payment) on their loan.

And finally, when discussing the subject of Prepayment Penalty there are two types of Prepayment Penalty options you can offer your customers:

1. **Hard Prepayment Penalty**:
   This is the conventional form of Prepayment Penalty as I have discussed above.

2. **Soft Prepayment Penalty**:
    The Soft Prepayment Penalty has an added feature to it that allows the borrower (on their loan) to sell their home, during the Prepayment Penalty Period, without incurring that Prepayment Penalty expense. The Pricing is also better with this feature - than on a mortgage loan with No Prepayment Penalty feature. Depending on your borrowers' loan goals - that may very well be their only concern regarding their loan having a Prepayment Penalty feature: To have the freedom to sell their home if they so choose - without incurring any Prepayment Penalty costs.

Also, check out the new requirements for including a Prepayment Penalty feature onto a Qualified Mortgage Loans.

Since I am talking about the Prepayment Penalty of a loan I thought it might be a good time to also mention a loan feature somewhat related to this. It's called the "Lock-in Clause". Including a Lock-in Clause, within a home loan agreement means that the home loan borrower cannot repay that home loan prior to a specified date.

PREPAYS:
As the name implies this refers to Prepayment of certain costs included in a loan. Generally speaking, Prepays relate to setting up reserves in a loan for property taxes and homeowners insurance (hazard insurance). In some cases, where required, Private Mortgage Insurance (PMI) as well. Those Prepays are shown on the borrower's LE. We will talk more about Prepays when we discuss the Loan Estimate statement in a later chapter.

PRICING:
This is a term you will use and hear quite often in the lending area. Pricing has a number of references in which it is used - but basically, it is always in relation to mortgage interest rates and related loan programs. For example, a Mortgage loan originator may ask you, "How's the pricing going on the Jone's loan file?" Basically, that Mortgage loan originator is asking you if you have found a loan program and selected an interest rate on that loan yet. Another use of this term could be in reference to the interest rate matrix that are put out by Lenders each day (e.g. Conforming Lenders). For example, a Mortgage loan originator may ask you, "Have you taken a look at the pricing sheets from XYZ Lender today?" Here the Mortgage loan originator is asking if you have looked at the Interest Rate matrix that came out, on their website, today from that Lender. Also, much like the first example here, if someone asks you if you have priced that loan yet they are asking if you have selected an interest rate for that loan. And finally, if someone asks you what the pricing is on an interest rate you have selected for a loan they are referring to the basis points charged by a Lender for that interest rate.

PRINCIPAL, INTEREST, TAXES, AND INSURANCE (PITI):
This refers to what is contained in a loan customer's monthly mortgage loan in which that loan is fully amortizing (pays down the principal) and includes that homeowner's monthly escrows for property taxes and homeowner's insurance. Most mortgage folks just refer to this as PITI. If they are referring to only the principal payments then it is usually referred to as P&I.

However, if a customer's loan is an 'Interest Only' loan then that is referred to as IO. And, if escrows for monthly property taxes and homeowner's insurance are included in that monthly mortgage payment then it is referred to as ITI.

PRIOR-TO-DOC (PTD) CONDITIONS:
On approved loans these are conditions that must be satisfied prior to the Lender sending the final closing loan documents to the Closing Agent, Closing Company, Attorney, or Title Company (doing the closing on that home loan).

PRIOR-TO-FUNDING (PTF) CONDITIONS:
Once the loan has closed or put another way - the borrowers have signed the closing loan documents then The Prior-to-Funding conditions are those conditions that must be satisfied before the Lender will wire the closing loan funds to the closing agent.

Sometimes things get a little crazy in processing a loan towards closing. Things come up at the last minute that we didn't see previously or we are having difficulty getting a Prior-To-Doc condition within the needed time to close a loan. In this case sometimes you can request that a Lender make a Prior-To-Doc condition a Prior-To-Funding condition. Depending on the relative importance of that condition and other aspects regarding the loan and your loan customer - the Lender just might consent to this. This could save you perhaps 3 days to a week on funding that loan.

PRIVATE MORTGAGE INSURANCE (PMI):
I am sure you have heard of homeowner's insurance or hazard insurance (discussed above) oftentimes referred to as home fire insurance. As I have mentioned above, this type of insurance protects (and insures) the homeowners (and indirectly) the home Lender(s) if there is damage to the subject property.

Private Mortgage Insurance, on the other hand, is an insurance policy that is designed to protect the Lender only - in the event that the borrower of the loan, on the subject property, defaults on that loan. This type of insurance is often referred to as PMI or just MI for short (mortgage insurance). For Conforming type of loans it is generally required on loans whenever the LTV is 80% or greater.

Historically speaking, when the LTV of a loan was greater than 80% then bankers and lenders perceived an increased risk on that loan to justify and require PMI (on that loan). The thinking here is that loans with less equity (than 20% for example) carry a greater risk because it is believed (by Lenders) that the borrowing homeowners, during financially difficult times, would more likely walk away (from their home) and default on their loan if they had little or no equity on that subject property. Hence, this PMI compensates the Lender for the additional risk they are accepting in granting that type of loan.

If you have ever read a book or taken a course in investments then you know that there is a corresponding relationship to Risk and Reward. In other words, as the perceived risk of an investment increases then the interest rate or return increases. You can easily see this when you compare savings bonds (safe and lower risk) with a corresponding lower rate of return (interest rate) - to stocks in the stock market: More risky but does have a higher rate of return. You will see this also in interest rates on loans. As Lenders perceive greater risk of borrowers (bad credit, lack of job stability, home located in rural areas or out in the country) then the interest rate will generally increase in some proportion to that perceived risk. And, as we have discussed above, beyond a certain LTV percent - PMI will be required.

Also keep in mind that as the LTV gets higher, beyond which point PMI is required (increased perceived Risk) then the amount of PMI required on that loan gets larger as well. This can get to be rather expensive sometimes for your borrowers. For example, if you were structuring a 95% LTV Purchase loan with an amount of $100,000, then that loan might have a PMI of about 0.85% (or more) of the total loan amount. Or, put another way, an initial annual premium of $850.00 - or $70.83 per month! So, you see it can get rather expensive for your borrowers. But it does enable them to purchase a home with a lower down payment. I recently did a small purchase loan having an LTV of 100% with the loan amount of $72,100. The PMI was about 0.96% making my customer's monthly PMI payment $57.63. Of course, the PMI reduces over time as the outstanding balance on the loan decreases. So, don't forget about PMI when structuring your loans and drawing up your Loan Estimates: When the LTV goes beyond 80% on a Conforming Loan. Also keep in mind that different Lenders may require different percentages of PMI to the loan amount. So check it out to be sure.

Years ago it used to be that companies offering PMI required the first year's premium up-front - at loan closing. Fortunately, it is rare that we see that today. What I see today is that Lenders generally require 1 maybe 2 months of PMI payments in reserves and shown on the LE.

Now, will your customers always have to pay that PMI on their home loan? No. The Homeowner's Protection Act of 1998 (this is also referred to as the PMI Act) addresses this very issue. Essentially, within this Act it states three situations in which a borrower's PMI may be cancelled:

1. **By Request:** When the LTV on a customer's home loan reaches 80% (or less) through a combination of reduction of their outstanding loan balance and/or appreciation of the value of their home then that customer can request their Lender to cancel the PMI on their loan. It has been my experience that when this option is used then the Lender will generally require a minimum of a Drive-by appraisal (to verify the current value of that home).

2. **Automatic:** When the LTV on their home loan reaches 78%. This would be due to the reduction of their outstanding loan balance through the borrower's monthly mortgage payments. Here the Lender would automatically cancel their PMI when the borrower's equity position reaches at least 22%.

3. **Final Termination:** If the PMI on a mortgage has not been terminated through numbers 1 and 2 above, then it is required, by this Act, that following the first day of the month immediately following the date that is the midpoint of the amortization

period of that loan – that the PMI be eliminated from that homeowner's monthly mortgage payments.

I should also mention here that in order for a homeowner to eliminate the PMI on their mortgage, either through options 1, 2, or 3 above, that the homeowner's monthly mortgage payments must be current (at that time) according to the terms of that mortgage.

And, I should further add that the above PMI Act relates only to those home loans - which originated after July 29, 1999. However, I believe you will find that even for those loans older than that most Lenders would be agreeable to eliminating the borrower's PMI if those conditions as stated in numbers 1 & 2 above are or could be realized.

And finally, some wholesale lenders and banks are now offering Conforming Loan programs whereby they pay for the PMI on a loan – when the LTV is 80% or greater (those borrowers would not then incur or pay for PMI on their home loan). These types of mortgage loans are referred to as Lender Paid MI and/or No MI loans. Of course, you can expect that the interest rates on these types of loans will be higher (than those with PMI) to compensate the lender for paying for that borrower's PMI.

PROPERTIES -TYPES:
As a mortgage loan originator you will be asked to see if you can do a loan on someone's property and one of the most important questions you should ask is: What type or kind of property does your prospective customers have? On the following page is a list of some of the more common types of residential properties you will be seeking financing for:

1. **Stick-Built House:**
   This is your normal wooden built house with wooden frames and infrastructure: Just your common everyday house.

2. **Manufactured Home on Land**:
   Some people still refer to manufactured homes as mobile homes, but they are definitely not mobile. The important question here is whether a Manufactured Home includes the land on which it is attached. This is oftentimes referred to as Land/Home. I won't go into too much detail here regarding manufactured homes but you should know that four of the most important qualifying questions you should ask customers regarding these are:

   • When was the Manufactured Home built? Most Lenders will not loan on Manufactured Homes built before 1976. This is because those Manufactured Homes built prior to June 15, 1976 have not been built according to HUD's quality requirements. Those Manufactured Homes built after this date will have a "HUD tag" affixed on the outside of that Manufactured Home. This HUD tag verifies that that Manufactured home was built after 1976. I have usually found this HUD tag to be near the front entrance door of that home.

   • What size is it? Single, double, or triple-wide. Here again, you will find fewer and fewer Lenders today who loan on a Singlewide Manufactured Home. And, if it is a Singlewide then what is its size in square feet. Conforming guidelines generally require the Singlewide home to have at least 400 square feet.

- Is the Manufactured Home permanently attached to the property (land)? Permanently attached generally means that the Manufactured Home is on a permanent chassis and resting on metal piers supported by cement blocks and with a metal cable tying the chassis of that home to those cement blocks (referred to as tie-downs). And, have the Axles and Wheels been removed?

- Is the Manufactured Home Real or Personal property? Usually when Manufactured Homes are first built then they are registered just like a car – being personal property. However, after the Manufactured Home has been permanently attached to the land (upon which it rests) it can then be registered on Title as Real Property. If your customers are not sure about this then pull a Property Profile on the subject's address and see what it says there (See the chapter called The Property Profile). For Mortgage Lenders to loan on a Manufactured Home it must be Real Property.

3. Manufactured Homes in Parks.
Here the customers own the Manufactured Home but do not own the land upon which it rests (they lease the land or parcel it is on - as in a Manufactured Home Park). This is oftentimes referred to "Manufactured Home only." Even fewer Mortgage Lenders these days loan on these.

4. Condos:
These are separate living units in a building. In some cases they may be separate units on community property. Lenders generally like to know how old the building is and how many units are in the building. Sometimes Lenders also want to know the percent of occupancy of that building and where the Condo is located.

5. Duplex:
This is a home with two separate living units.

6. Triplex and Four-Plex:
Just as the names implies, these are units (generally rental units) and have 3 (Triplex) or 4 Units in them. However, the Duplex above, as well as the Triplex and 4 Units residences, could be rental units and also be Owner-occupied (O/O). This means that the owner (your borrower) lives in one of the units there. This works to the borrower's advantage because many times, with the subject property being rental as well as Owner-Occupied, this could make the difference between a lender doing the loan or not. And, usually results in a better interest rate for that borrower (than if the property was Non-owner Occupied - NOO).

PROTECTED CLASS MEMBERS:
According to the Equal Credit Opportunity Act (ECOA) anyone within the mortgage lending process may not discriminate, in any way, towards a home loan applicant because they are a member of a Protected Class. Nor may they consider any factor(s), of a home

loan applicant, that they are or may be a member of a Protected Class. There are nine Protected Class members within the Equal Credit Opportunity Act.

- Race
- Color
- National Origin
- Sex
- Religion
- Marital Status
- Age
- Income derived from Public Assistance
- Exercising rights under any Consumer Credit Protection law.

PURCHASE MONEY LOAN:
In the mortgage lending business this term refers to a loan for the purpose of purchasing a home and/or commercial property.

QUALIFIED MORTGAGE:
a "Qualified Mortgage", as defined by The Dodd-Frank Wall Street Reform and Consumer Protection Act, is any residential mortgage loan that the regular periodic payments for that loan do not increase the principal balance or allow the consumer to defer repayment of principal (with some exceptions), and has points and fees being less than 3% of the loan amount. And, the Term cannot exceed 30 years. For more information on this subject of what a Qualified Mortgage is and the requirements and regulations for it - please refer to the Qualified Mortgage Rules within Chapter 6.

RATE SHEETS:
Rate Sheets were very often referred to as Pricing Sheets. These showed the scale or range of interest rates with the basis points for each - and for each (or most popular) loan programs that Lender offers. Most Mortgage Companies received these Rate Sheets daily either emailed to them or on their fax machines, generally from those Lenders they use most often. Today, a lender's interest rates are shown on their website. However, much of the important features, explained below, still apply.

The important features of a Rate Sheet were:

1. **Name of the Lender, Their Telephone, Fax Number,** and **Email Address**.

2. **Who their Wholesale Rep. Is:** This is whom you can call and talk to about your Loan you are working on and thinking about submitting to them.

3. **Their Most Popular Loan Programs:** With each loan program shown in a separate section. For example, for Conforming Lenders you will see a section for 30-Year Fixed rate loans, 15-Year Fixed, Jumbo, 15 and 30-year fixed, and sometimes a section for govie loans (FHA & VA).

4. **Interest Rates and Basis Points:** Of course, this is why they call it a Rate Sheet. Because for each Loan Program shown, on that Rate Sheet, there are ranges of Interest Rates and Basis Points that are available for the Qualified Borrower.

5. **Adjustments**: This is something you definitively always want to look out for: If there are any Adjustments. Adjustments generally affect (negatively or positively) the Basis Points in relation to the interest rate you are looking at. For example, you may look at the rate sheet and see the interest rate of 5.5% (on a particular loan program) with <1.0%> rebate. As we discussed previously (and will go into more detail within Chapter 19 on Reading the Rate Sheets) this means that if you lock your customer's interest rate in at 5.5%, for that loan program, then your loan customer could receive a credit of 100 Basis Points of the total loan amount (which could help them pay for their loan costs).

   OK, now say you are doing a Cash-Out Refinance Loan. Looking at the Adjustments shown in that section it shows that for Cash-Out Refinance Loans there is an Adjustment of +0.25% to the Rebate. This means that at the rate of 5.5% your loan customer could incur a cost of 25 Basis Points. For a $100,000 that could mean a cost of $250.00! So look out for those Adjustments.

6. **Loan Program Requirements**: Are also shown within each section (for each type of loan). Loan Program Requirements, unlike those Adjustments (we discussed above), don't necessarily impact the interest rate or Basis Points but instead relate to requirements or features for doing that type of loan (e.g. maximum LTV on a type of loan). For example, it may say: Min. FICO 620. What it is saying here is that the minimum (middle) credit score of that borrower for this type of loan (e.g. 30-Year Fixed) needs to be 620 or greater. Another example could be: Max. C/O LTV = 80%. You probably figured this one out for yourself, and that's good because you're beginning to understand the jargon of all this. But just to be sure, this means that the maximum acceptable LTV (for that loan program) for a Cash-Out Refinance loan is 80%. Again, lookout for those Loan Program Requirements.

7. **The Wholesale Lender's Fees:** These are usually shown on the bottom of the Rate Sheets. Items that are usually included in the Lender's fees are: Underwriting, Tax Service, Flood Certification, and sometimes a Document and Wire fee. The total of these fees can range from $450 to $800 (or greater). These fees do change with every Lender so make sure you are aware of what a particular Lender charges for their fees if you are seriously considering submitting a loan to them.

Off-Sheet Pricing:
This term relates to the Rate Sheets - so I'm going to throw it in here. Off-Sheet Pricing refers to pricing (interest rates and Basis Points) that are not shown on the daily Rate Sheets sent out by a Lender. If you are wondering what the Basis Points (fees) for a specific interest rate (that is not shown on that day's Rate Sheet) you would need to call that Lender's Representative (Rep) or that Lender's Wholesale Rep. Department or Underwriting Department and tell them you want to inquire about Off-Sheet Pricing on

whatever type of loan program you are looking at. They will know what you are talking about.

When would you have a need to do this? Well, perhaps your customer is thinking about Buying Down the (obtaining a lower) interest rate on their loan you are working on. You look on the rate sheet to see what it will cost your borrower for that rate and it is not shown. You then call that Lender for the Off-Sheet Pricing for that rate. Another example could be that you have a customer who is sold on a "No-Cost" loan (see No-Cost Loans above).

So, you just call up that Lender and ask them for Off-Sheet Pricing on whatever loan program you are looking at. You then ask them what the rate is today for this loan program and what the Net Basis Points will be. Make sure you ask for the Net Basis Points. This relates to our discussion of Adjustments above. Otherwise, you may later find out that after the Adjustments are included (if any) that the actual (Net) Basis Points are more. This means that what is charged to that customer, to obtain that interest rate, will be more to either pay for that interest rate or (with a "No-Cost" loan) all the related loan costs for that loan. Unfortunately, when this happens it has been my experience that the originating Mortgage loan originator then pays for whatever amount is yet required from their Origination Fee they were to earn on that loan. So, always ask for the Net Basis Points.

REAL PROPERTY:
If you ever took a course in real estate then you already know what Real Property is (versus Personal Property). If not, then Real Property is anything that is permanently attached to the subject property. Sometimes Personal Property can become Real Property. For example, let us say that the homeowners' bought and installed a beautiful chandelier in their dining room. The weight of it required the installer to make some heavy-duty attachments - to make sure it could be safely held over the years. As a result, if those homeowners later wanted to sell their house and to take out that chandelier would damage or disfigure that house in its removal - that chandelier would then become Real Property (attached) to that house.

REBATE (POINTS):
Rebate is also has been referred to as the Yield Spread Premium and what a particular Lender is offering for their range of interest rates – shown on their daily Rate Sheets. Pricing a mortgage loan or selecting an interest rate, for a home loan borrower's loan, is a process of considering a number of factors related to the home loan borrower and the targeted Lender's rates and rebates for each interest rate.

However, when it comes to what Mortgage loan originators could make on the "Back End" of a loan, the Federal Reserve Board has ruled that since April 1, 2011, mortgage companies and banks are no longer allowed to charge Rebates and Yield Spread Premiums on any of their residential mortgage loans that would directly or indirectly benefit either the originating Mortgage loan originator or their mortgage company – based upon the Terms of a home loan.

However, Mortgage loan originators and mortgage companies can still charge customers "basis points" (or rebates) for a particular interest rate (Buydown and Discount Points). The ideal interest rate you would offer your loan customers is at "Par Pricing". This means that at Par Pricing there is no charge by that Lender for a particular interest rate. However, if your loan customer wants a lower interest rate then what a Lender offers at "Par Pricing" then most likely that customer will incur the cost of those basis points to obtain that lower interest rate. Or, if the customer wants a "No-Cost" loan or wanted some of their loan costs paid for by accepting a higher interest rate – then the basis points for that higher interest rate (and its translated dollar amount) would be a credit, and could be applied towards that customer's home loan costs. So, let's talk about pricing a loan here.

When you are researching interest rates for your customers then one significant influencing factor is what we call the rebate or points to get a particular interest rate. We will go into more detail on this when we get to Chapter 19 called Reading the Rate Sheets. But for now, let me just give you a cursory overview of this term. Basis Points for an interest rate (or, as some call it: Rebate) is what a Lender either charges (for a lower interest rate) or credits the loan customer (for a higher interest rate). For our discussion here I'll refer to the basis points as Rebates – but this term is in no way used as a cost or income to the originating Mortgage loan originator. All Rebates charged to a home loan customer is done with their full knowledge and consent. OK, having said that....

For example, if your loan customer wanted a lower interest than at Par Pricing then that loan customer might incur a cost of +0.25% (for example) of their total loan amount. Let's assume that the "At Par Pricing" interest rate is 5.0%. And, for our example here, the total loan amount is $200,000. Then, according to the Rate Sheet, obtaining a rate of 4.5% would cost your customer $500.00 ($200,000 x 0.25%}. This cost would be shown within Line (box) Item #2 at the top of the 2nd page of the LE. Doing this is usually referred to as "buying down the rate" and it is with, what is referred to as, Discount Points that the loan customer pays for their lower interest rate.

On the other hand, if the interest rate, shown on a Rate Sheet, is expressed as a negative or in brackets then this represents credits that your loan customer could apply towards their loan costs. Let's now say your loan customer is willing to obtain a higher interest rate (than at Par Pricing) in order to pay for some of their loan costs. You look at the Rate Sheet and for an interest rate of 6.0% the rebate is <0.50%>. For a $200,000 loan amount that loan customer would be able to apply $1,000 ($200,000 x 0.50%} towards their loan cost. Doing this is referred to as Premium Pricing.

In lending, as I have mentioned above (in Points), the Origination Fee, Interest Rate, Rebates, and loan Interest Rates are generally expressed in 1/8ths of a Point (if less than a full point). For example, an interest rate may be expressed as 4&5/8ths%. This, of course, is greater than 4.50% by 1/8 of a point. 1/8 of a point may not sound like much but depending on your loan amount it could make the difference between you paying or reducing their loan costs by $200 or more. Get familiar with this because this is how lenders will express their interest rates and rebates.

RECAST:

Here's a term that refers to the restructuring of a mortgage loan – by the current mortgage servicer. When I first heard of this word I thought of someone molding something in clay - like the face of a famous person. When that artist was done then they took a good look at that cast of what they had created and perhaps thought the nose was too big or too small. So they changed the face of that mold and recast it to more match what they had in mind for that face.

Recasting of a mortgage loan is pretty much the same thing. For example, a mortgage loan may be an ARM loan with the understanding that after 5 years it will convert to a fixed rate loan (see Convertible Mortgage). At that time that ARM converts to a Fixed Rate Loan it is Recast (or restructured) based on the Outstanding Balance of that loan, the prevailing or converted Interest Rate, and the remaining Term on that loan. A mortgage loan could also be Recast if the outstanding balance of a mortgage loan increases, above its original loan amount, up to a certain amount or percent. For example, let's say an ARM loan may have Negative Amortization. When and if that occurs then that part of the Negative Amortization is added onto the principal of that loan. If this occurs enough times to cause the outstanding balance of that loan to increase to 110% of that loan's original loan amount then that loan may be Recast at its Current Loan Balance, the Prevailing (or agreed upon) Interest Rate, and the remaining Term on that loan. This is, of course, all written into and agreed upon in that mortgage loan.

RECORDING:

Recording is the filing in the Public Records of a new mortgage - usually in the County Recorder's Office. This is usually done by the Title Insurance Company (or Attorney) that performed the closing on that loan and is generally done within 24 to 48 hours after loan funding.

REFINANCE LOANS:

A Refinance Loan is a loan that pays off an existing mortgage loan and replaces it with a new mortgage loan. It's important to understand that a refinance loan is exactly that. It refinances an existing loan. However, if your customer calls you and tells you that he wishes to refinance his home and he now owns the property free and clear then this is also usually referred to as a Refinance Loan.

When we talk about Refinance Loans there are really only two types: 1. Rate/Term Refinance and 2. Cash-Out Refinance. Let's go over each type:

1. Rate/Term Refinance:

A Rate/Term Refinance loan seeks to only refinance the outstanding balance of the existing loan. Its goal, as the name implies, is either to obtain a better interest rate (Rate) or to change the term of the loan (Term). In this type of loan - there is little, if any, cash-out to the borrower. Rate/Term Refinance loans are also referred to as Limited Cash-Out Refinance loans and its loan-to-value acronym is represented by LCLTV.

You'll see a lot of Rate/Term Refinance loan requests when interest rates have fallen and folks wish to refinance and get a lower interest rate on their loan with an accompanying reduction in their monthly mortgage payment. Depending on the loan amount - I usually suggest a benefit of at least 1.0% or better in interest rate reduction to make it worthwhile - when you consider the cost to do a loan (Refer to Payback period in my discussion of Buydown above).

You'll also get requests from time-to-time from customers who wish to refinance and change the Term of their loan. Usually, they're thinking about going from a 30-year fixed rate loan to a 15-year fixed rate loan. I tell my customers who wish to do this that in going from a 30-year to a 15-year loan that even though they will realize a better interest rate (rates on 15-year loans are generally better than 30-year loans by about anywhere from 25 to 50 basis points). And, because they are squeezing the time period (term) of their loan from 30 to 15 years this would significantly reduce the amount of interest they would otherwise pay over the entire life of their loan. But also, in doing this - it will increase their P&I payment by about 28%. But many times this will result in their monthly mortgage payment (P&I) increasing by about $250 or more (depending on the total loan amount). That's fine - if they can afford it. And certainly, with this loan, they will payoff their mortgage in 15 years.

2. Cash-Out Refinance:

As the name implies here the customer is taking cash-out with their refinance loan. They are usually using their home equity to achieve this. Now, most lenders consider a loan "Cash-Out" anytime a refinance loan is not a Rate/Term Refinance loan. For example, your customers may want to consolidate and payoff all of their outstanding credit cards but don't wish to obtain any extra cash at costing. This would still be considered a Cash-Out Refinance loan.

Sometimes you will also get requests to consolidate the 1st and 2nd mortgages on the subject property. It used to be that Lenders generally considered any financing beyond refinancing the existing 1st mortgage to be a "Cash Out" Refinance Loan. However, I am finding many Non-Conforming Lenders out there today who still view a refinance loan that consolidates the existing 1st and 2nd mortgages only as a Rate/Term refinance loan. So check this out with the Lender you are targeting to submit your loan to. It can sometimes make a (big) difference in the PTD conditions and the (better) interest rate you can offer your customers.

RESERVES:

In setting up a loan your Lender may tell you that the borrower will need to have so many months of Reserves for the loan prior to closing. What the Lender is saying is that the borrower will need to show enough funds saved or set aside (many times this can be Liquid Assets) for those number of months - times the monthly PITI payment. For example, let's say your targeted Lender wants your borrower to have 3 months of Reserves. If your borrower's new monthly PITI payment will be $350.00 then your borrower will need to have available $1,050.00 in Reserves - prior to loan closing. This would be considered a Prior-To-Doc condition.

The reasons why a Lender may require Reserves can depend on the type of mortgage loan: Second home loan, a piggyback second mortgage, and jumbo loans greater than $500,000 to name a few. And, the number of months of required Reserves differs with each type of loan. However, the most common reason requiring Reserves is:

- The Type of Loan Transaction
- The Occupancy Status & Amortization type of the Subject Property
- The Number of Units in the Subject Property
- The Number of other Financed Properties the borrower currently owns, and
- The Loan-To-Value (LTV) of a loan. Most Conforming loans with a LTV of 90% or greater (especially Purchase Loans) will usually be required to have 2 or more months of Reserves.

So, be aware of this when qualifying your borrowers and look for this when completing the Loan Application (1003) on your customers.

Also, sometimes some lending folks refer to Reserves as Prepays on the LE. To determine the number of months of Reserves for Fannie Mae loans please refer to Chapter 4 on Loan Underwriting.

REAL ESTATE SETTLEMENT PROCEDURES ACT (RESPA):
This is a common acronym used in lending and stands for Real Estate Settlement Procedures Act. This is one of the most important federal laws that you need to be familiar with as a Mortgage loan originator. RESPA requires Lenders (mortgage brokers, Mortgage loan originator, etc.) to provide mortgage home borrowers with information and Disclosures on their loan and settlement costs. And, to provide this information, within a certain period of time, to their mortgage loan customers. It also dictates when that "clock starts ticking" as to when a loan customer should receive those documents and Disclosures. The Real Estate Settlement Procedures Act was also recently amended by the Dodd-Frank Wall Street Reform and Consumer Protection Act. Because of its importance I will cover RESPA in more detail within Chapter 25 on Mortgage Lending Regulations and Laws.

SALES CONCESSIONS:
Sales Concessions are Interested Party Contributions that take the form of non-realty items. They include cash, furniture, automobiles, decorator allowances, moving costs, and other giveaways, as well as financing concessions that exceed Fannie Mae limits. Consequently, the value of sales concessions must be deducted from the sales price when calculating LTV and combined LTV ratios for underwriting and eligibility purposes.

SEASONED LOANS:
A Seasoned Loan refers to how long that mortgage has been in existence and how long the borrowers (homeowners) have made payments on their mortgage. In lending, a seasoned loan generally means that the borrowers have made at least 12 monthly payments on their mortgage loan. This is important, because if your borrowers want to refinance their home then whether their mortgage is Seasoned or not can affect the loan programs available (to them) as well as the interest rates you can offer them. This is true for 1st and 2nd mortgages as well.

I should note here that if you are talking to a customer who wants to refinance and consolidate their 1st and 2nd mortgages then you should always ask what kind of a second mortgage they have. In other words, do they have a HELOC (home equity line of credit) as a 2nd mortgage? If they do then you will want to ask them if they have made any withdrawals (or draws) on their HELOC in the past year. This is important because Conforming guidelines in the past have stated that the homeowner (of the HELOC) could take out up to $2,000 worth of withdrawals in the past 12 months (for whatever purpose) - and still be considered Seasoned. However, as of December 15, 2002 this has changed. Conforming guidelines now dictate that if any withdrawals have been taken out of a customer's HELOC in the past 12 months then those funds must have gone only towards improvement(s) of their home (on which the loan is secured). Otherwise, that HELOC is not seasoned.

I mentioned this because if you are working on a refinance loan to consolidate the 1st and 2nd mortgages and want the new loan to be considered a Rate/Term Refinance loan then both existing 1st and 2nd mortgages need to be Seasoned. If they are not then the loan will usually be considered a Cash-Out Refinance loan.

Regarding the value of the subject property, on an Unseasoned Loan, be aware that most Conforming Lenders will generally only use the lower of the last appraised value or purchase price of that subject property – to assess the subject property's value. However, documented improvements can usually be added to this value. So, this can definitely affect the LTV on your unseasoned loans.

SECONDARY FINANCING (SECOND MORTGAGE):
Often referred to as a 2nd mortgage and sometimes a Junior Mortgage (under the Senior 1st mortgage) - which is secured by a Deed of Trust on Real Property. See all these words and terms are starting to make sense.

So, be aware that if a borrower of yours has an existing 1st and 2nd mortgage, on his property, and wishes to refinance only the 1st mortgage then you would need to obtain an approved and signed Subordination Agreement from that Lender holding the 2nd mortgage. Remember what I said before about the timing of recordation of mortgages in discussing Mortgages above? The reason you need to obtain an approved Subordination Agreement from the Lender holding that 2nd mortgage is to protect the 1st position of the loan you are refinancing (the existing 1st mortgage). Otherwise, without that approved Subordination Agreement the older 2nd mortgage would then move into first position (it was recorded prior to the recent 1st mortgage).

SECURE AND FAIR ENFORCEMENT FOR MORTGAGE LICENSING ACT: (SAFE ACT):
The President of the United States, during July 2008, signed into law the Housing and Economic Recovery Act of 2008 (HERA). Title V of HERA entitled The Secure and Fair Enforcement for Mortgage Licensing Act of 2008 (S.A.F.E Mortgage Licensing Act with

the purpose of enhancing consumer protection and reduce fraud by requiring all mortgage loan originators to be either state-licensed or federally licensed.

Under the S.A.F.E. Mortgage Licensing Act all states must implement a Mortgage loan originator (MLO) licensing process that meets certain standards through the Nationwide Mortgage Licensing System & Registry (NMLS). This Act requires all MLOs seeking state-licensure, or currently holding a state license, to pass the NMLS-developed S.A.F.E. Mortgage loan originator Test. That test includes both state and national components and those taking the test must obtain a score of 75% or better on each component. I discuss the Safe Act in more detail within the Chapter 25 on Mortgage lending Regulations.

To obtain information, guidance, and assistance on state participation, testing, pre-licensing, continuing education, and system updates visit the Nationwide Mortgage Licensing System & Registry's online resource center at:
http://mortgage.nationwidelicensingsystem.org/Pages/default.aspx

SUBJECT PROPERTY:
This is a term that is used quite often in the mortgage lending industry. Subject Property refers to the property on which the loan is being made - or being discussed. Sometimes you will be discussing two or more separate properties but are lending on only one of those. You would then refer to that property, for which you are lending on, as the Subject or Subject Property. Knowing this reduces confusion when discussing loans and properties with other Lenders, Mortgage loan originators, Loan Processors, and Third Party Providers.

SUB-PRIME LOANS:
As the name implies these types of loans were originally designed for borrowers who had less than prefect credit: -A or B credit or worse. Some lending folks just refer to this lending area as B/C, some as Sub-prime, and folks like me join the two together and call it B/C Sub-prime. I should also note that a couple of years ago a Branch Manager told me that it is "politically correct" to refer to Sub-prime loans as Non-prime Loans when discussing these with your loan customers. Today these types of loans are often referred to as Non-Qualified Mortgage loans (Non-QM). However, I believe you will find that most Mortgage loan originators, when discussing these types of loans, still refer to these as Sub-prime loans. Therefore, throughout this book I will refer to these types of loans as Sub-prime as well.

I should also mention here that following the mortgage crisis, and during the year 2008, many of the Sub-prime Lenders fell to the "wayside" and/or closed their doors. Today, in 2021, we still find that there are few Sub-prime lenders for your B/C credit customers. However, I believe, that as the mortgage crisis wanes and the number of mortgage loan requests increases then we will again see the need for Lenders who will fund loans for home loan customers who don't qualify for a Conforming or a Non-Conforming Loan. For more information on Sub-prime loans please refer to Chapter 8 which discusses Sub-prime loans in more detail.

SUSPENSION:

This is the response you may see sometimes from the Underwriter of a Lender you have submitted your loan to. It sounds kind of negative but actually what the Underwriter is stating is that they do not have enough information (or documents) to make a final decision on that loan. It sure beats being declined! When you receive this type of response then discuss that loan with your Loan Processor and/or call that Underwriter (of that Lender) and find out what is needed so they can make a decision on that loan. Oftentimes the Underwriter will state what they need (conditions) on the Suspension Notice in order to further review that loan file – and possibly get that loan approved.

SWEAT EQUITY:

Every once in a while, while discussing home purchase transactions, you may hear this term. I should mention however that you will find that generally Sweat Equity is not an acceptable source of funds for the down payment, closing costs, and reserves, since it is difficult to accurately assess the contributory value of Sweat Equity work. Only for specific transactions and if all eligibility requirements are met does Fannie Mae consider sweat equity to be an acceptable source of funds.

TABLE FUNDING:

Within the amended Truth-In-Lending Act, dated September 24, 2010, TILA also wanted to further clarify its definition of a Loan Originator when Table Funding occurs. Therefore, its states that Table Funding "occurs when the creditor does not provide the funds for the transaction at consummation out of the creditor's own resources, including drawing on a bona fide warehouse line of credit, or out of deposits held by the creditor".

TILA further states that a Table Funding transaction is consummated with the debt obligation initially payable by its terms to one person, but another person provides the funds for the transaction at consummation and receives an immediate assignment of the Note, loan contract, or other evidence of debt obligation.

TILA also, for clarification here, provides two examples of what is or not a Creditor or Loan Originator when Table Funding occurs:

1. If a person closes a loan in its own name but does not fund the loan from its own resources or deposits held by it - because it assigns the loan consummation then it is considered a Creditor for purposes of Regulation Z and a Loan Originator.

2. However, if a person closes a loan in its one name and draws on a bona fide warehouse line of credit to fund the loan at consummation then it is considered a Creditor, not a Loan Originator, for purposes of Regulation Z.

For our purposes of definition and common usage, Table Funding occurs when a Mortgage Broker (person) closes the mortgage loan in their own company's name and then at the time of settlement transfers that loan to a Lender who then advances the funds for that loan. After the loan has funded that Mortgage Broker then delivers the entire loan package to the funding Lender - including the new promissory note, mortgage deed of trust, and releases all rights on that loan to that Lender.

TERM:
The Term of a loan is the length of time over which a loan is repaid. Sometimes referred to as the amortized period when the Term and the amortized period of a loan are the same (e.g. 30-Year or 15-Year loans). However, sometimes the Term of a loan may be shorter than the amortized period of a loan. A balloon loan, for example, may be stated as 20 due in 5. The "20" represents the amortized period of that loan (20 years) and the 5 (the Term of that loan) represents when the outstanding loan balance will become due (in 5 years).

THIRD-PARTY PROVIDERS:
Third Party Providers refer to the type of individuals or companies that provide professional services related to home loans - you are working on. Examples of these are: Appraisers, Title Insurance Companies, Home Inspectors (for home inspections), and Credit Reporting Agencies for the Credit Report

THREE-DAY RIGHT OF RESCISSION:
This is a loan term you will hear quite often and one that can impact when your customer's home loan "Funds" and when you get paid. The Three-Day Right of Rescission gives your refinance home loan borrowers, of owner-occupied properties, 3 business days following the signing of their closing loan documents to rescind their loan. Or, to put it another way, cancel their loan if they wish to do so. HUD wants to give home loan borrowers, of O/O properties, enough time to think about their loan (after signing their loan docs) and cancel it (within this 3-day period) if they wish to do so.

This Three-Day Right of Rescission is also an important consideration in planning when your refinance home loans will close or sign and when they will fund. This very feature of O/O home loans sometimes creates a frenzy in mortgage branch offices around the end of the month period because Mortgage loan originators are trying to get all their PTD conditions satisfied, loan docs out, and their borrowers to the signing table - in time so the loan funds (after 3 business days) within that month's period. According to Regulation Z, and their definition of what is a business day for this rescission period, you would include all calendar days (including Saturdays) except Sundays and federal legal holidays. Hence, if your home loan borrowers signed their loan docs on Monday then funding would take place on Friday.

Your mortgage company (and we as mortgage loan originators) does not get paid until funding takes place. Also, watch out for those weeks that have a federal holiday between Monday and Friday. So, keep this in mind when you are planning the closing of your loans.

Exception of the 3-Day Rule due to the COVID-19 Pandemic:
During January 2020 the COVID-19 virus hit America. Shortly thereafter people in our great country started to make contact with this virus which caused then to get ill with a percentage of them dying. This became one of the worst pandemics our country has ever seen. As I recall, during the latter part of February to early March 2020 those businesses that had the public enter their business (e.g. restaurants, movie theaters, etc.) were told to (temporarily) lockdown or shut their doors. Thus, businesses closed, people lost their jobs as well as the income from those jobs. This set into motion a downward spiral for our

economy with the greatest numbers of unemployment since the great depression. People, affected by this, were beginning to have difficulty paying their monthly bills.

Therefore, on April 29, 2020 the Consumer Financial Protection Bureau issued a Ruling that will waive certain provisions in the TILA-RESPA Integrated Disclosures Rule and Regulation Z Right of Rescission Rules - caused by the COVId-19 pandemic.

It is understood, by the CFPB, that the COVId-19 pandemic could create temporary business disruptions and challenges for these covered persons. Also, the CFPB, recognizes that (some) consumers may have acute needs for proceeds from mortgage transactions and uncertainty about the origination process. Therefore, the CFPB issued this Ruling that if a consumer determines that his or her need to obtain funds, from a mortgage transaction, is due to the pandemic that:

- Necessitates consummating the home loan transaction before the end of a TRID Rule waiting period, or
- Must be met before the end of the Regulation Z Rescission Rules waiting period,

Then that home loan consumer would have a bona fide personal financial emergency that would permit that consumer to utilize the modification and waiver provisions, subject to the TRID and Regulation Z Rescissions Rules' applicable procedures.

The CFPB also recognized that the pandemic is a "changed circumstance" for purposes of the TRID Rule, allowing Lenders to use revised estimates reflecting changes in settlement charges for purposes of determining good faith. The goal of this interpretive rule is to help expedite consumers' access to credit under the TRID and Regulation Z Rescission Rules.

TRADE EQUITY:
Trade Equity is an acceptable source of funds to supplement the borrower's minimum borrower contribution provided the following requirements are met:

- The seller's equity contribution for the traded property must be a true-value consideration supported by a current appraisal.
- The borrower must make the minimum required contribution from his or her own funds unless - the LTV or CLTV ratio is less than or equal to 80%; or - the borrower is purchasing a one-unit principal residence and meets the requirements to use gifts, donated grant funds, or funds received from an employer to pay for some or all of the borrower's minimum contribution.

These requirements apply to all purchase transactions that involve property trades, including those that are evidenced by two separate contracts

TRAILING SPOUSE:
When folks move to a new location then sometimes one of the spouses will stay behind (at their current residence) for a while. The spouse that stays temporarily behind is known as the Trailing Spouse. The reason for this could be (for example) that the Trailing Spouse will stay behind until the school year ends for their children. Or, until that other spouse,

who moved to the new location, has set up a new residence. You see this quite often in military folks and those who accepted a new employment position at a new and different location.

Since Fannie Mae's *Selling Guide* of 2010, I am not seeing any references to the use of a Trailing Spouse's income in qualifying for a home loan. However, your assessment of the borrower's ability to repay their home loan, based on "Future Income" seems to be acceptable - according to the ATR Rule.

Although the current FNMA *Selling Guide*, dated October 2, 2020, does not specifically address qualifying income for Trailing Spouses I believe an argument could be made for qualifying this income source if it satisfies FNMA requirements under Employment Offers and Contracts.

TRANSMITTAL SUMMARY (1008):
The Transmittal Summary is usually referred to as the 1008 and is pronounced as "Ten – Oh 8." Like the 1003 this number is located at the lower right-hand corner of this form. The 1008 summarizes, pretty much, all the important features regarding a loan. As such, it enables the Lender's Underwriter to get the main points of that loan at a glance. When you (or your Loan Processor) submit a loan to a Lender you will usually include a 1008 as well. We will discuss this report in more detail when we get to Chapter 13 titled The Transmittal Summary.

TRUTH-IN-LENDING ACT (TILA):
This is an important federal law that requires disclosure of credit terms using a standard format. The Truth-In-Lending Act, referred to as TILA, was first enacted by Congress in 1968. The Truth-In-Lending Act is amended from time-to-time and its most recent amended time was during 2014 in which the CFPB implemented new changes, rulings, and prohibitions to Loan Originator Compensation. Those new LO Compensation rulings and prohibitions went into effect on January 10, 2014.

As previously mentioned, effective July 21, 2011, TILA's general rule-making authority was transferred to the Consumer Financial Protection Bureau (CFPB), whose authority was established according to the provisions enacted by the passage of the Dodd–Frank Wall Street Reform and Consumer Protection Act in July 2010. This transference of rule-making authority also occurred to most of the mortgage regulations and laws presented in this chapter.

Now, another one of the requirements of this Act is providing your customers with the Annual Percentage Rate (APR) on their loan as well as other important features of their loan. This APR is calculated using the interest rate on your LE and considers certain identified loan costs that are referred to as the Prepaid Finance Charges on that loan. Really, the main purpose of the APR is to give your prospective borrowing customers the information (or index) they need to shop around and compare - to find the least cost home loan. I will explain more about this and how to calculate the APR on a loan when we get to the Chapter 17 which also discusses the new Closing Disclosure.

UNDERWRITING:

Underwriting, in the lending area, refers to the analysis of the submitted loan by a Wholesale Lender's Underwriter. If you have submitted a loan to a Lender and you are talking to them (or someone there) about your loan then you most likely are talking to one of that lender's Underwriters. Also, when you complete the LE, the Lender's fees are included within "Our Originations Charges" (Line item #1) on page 2 of the LE. Here is where you would enter that lender's Underwriting fees. Be aware that different lenders have different Underwriting fees.

UNIFORM CLOSING DATASET (UCD):

The Uniform Closing Dataset is a common industry dataset that allows information on the Consumer Financial Protection Bureau's (CFPB's) Closing Disclosure to be communicated electronically. It was developed by Freddie Mac and Fannie Mae (the GSEs) at the direction of the Federal Housing Finance Agency (FHFA).

UNIFORM MORTGAGE DATE PROGRAM (UMDP):

Uniform Mortgage Data Program (UMDP) is an effort undertaken jointly by Fannie Mae and Freddie Mac at the direction of the Federal Housing Finance Agency to enhance mortgage data quality and standardization.

UMDP is composed of several initiatives, and in concert with UCD (above), supports standardization of appraisal data, loan application data, closing disclosure data, and loan delivery data.

UNIFORM RESIDENTIAL LOAN APPLICATION (1003):

This is the loan application form you will complete (or have completed) to gather all the information on your loan borrowers so that you can properly and timely research your customer's loan request and (hopefully) provide them with the best loan program that best meets their financial needs. This form is usually referred to as the 1003 and that's the number you see when you look at the lower right-hand corner of this form. That term "1003" is pronounced 10 – Oh-3. If you pronounce it as "one thousand and 3" then lending folks may look at you like you have two heads. Also, when you are referring to a form by its number and the form's number has 3 digits (e.g. 442) then lending folks will generally state that form's number by saying the first digit then the next one or two digits together (i.e. 442 is stated as 4 – 42 or 4 – forty-two). The latest designed 1003, began being used in 2020, is a multi-page document and because of its importance I will cover the 1003 in detail within Chapter 10.

VENDEE & VENDOR:

Here are a couple of terms, that again, you won't see very often - but I still want you to know what they mean (you will probably be the only one in your office who does). Vendee refers to the Buyer and Vendor refers to the Seller. OK, enough of that.

VETERANS ADMINISTRATION (VA):

The Veteran's Administration guarantees home loan programs for Veterans of the United States Armed Forces. A VA loan is oftentimes referred to as a govie (government) loan. One of the great things about VA loans is that with them the Veteran can finance the purchase of a home with an LTV of 100% of the sale price or appraised value (whichever is less) of a property. I think VA loans are one of the best loan programs out there - if the Veteran doesn't have much of a down payment saved up.

It's important to realize that the Veteran's Administration actually Guarantees the VA loan. This differs from an FHA loan (discussed above) where FHA insures the loan. These two types of govie loans definitely have their time and place for your borrowers. However, because of the many details peculiar to processing and packaging these loans I don't go into much discussion of these in this book.

YIELD-SPREAD PREMIUM (YSP):
First, a bit of history: Yield Spread Premium is another name for what we used to call the Interest Rate Rebate (see Rebates discussed above) and oftentimes was referred to as the Back-End income of a loan. It was called the "Back-end" income for a loan because it was the income (in dollar amount) that the originating mortgage loan originator made on a loan – in addition to their Origination Fee. Thus, prior to April 1, 2011, mortgage loan originators could obtain two income sources on a home loan: The Origination Fee and the Yield Spread Premium offered by a Lender for a particular interest rate offered on home loan.

According to HUD, Yield Spread Premium was also referred to as Indirect Compensation by a Lender. The subject of Yield Spread Premium, over the years, has been one of the most controversial subjects in the field of lending and brokering loans. While it was often debated and questioned as to whether the Yield Spread Premium paid to Mortgage Brokers was legal or not – HUD, in years prior to 2010, did not consider the payment of Yield Spread Premiums to Mortgage Brokers to be legal or illegal. However, the debating by the "Powers that Be" is now over - regarding the subject of Yield Spread Premiums. As of April 1, 2011, and according to the Truth-In-Lending Act (TILA) and the current Loan Origination Compensation rules - mortgage loan originators will now be able to only obtain their compensation, for origination a home loan, from one source: Either the loan customer or the Creditor – but not from both for the same loan transaction. For greater detail on this discussion please refer to the discussion on Loan Originator Rule within Chapter 25. Yield Spread Premium, however, can be used as a credit for the loan customer that they can apply towards reducing their total loan cost (e.g. Premium Pricing).

ZONING:
Zoning describes the type of allowable building use of a property in a specified area. This is usually decided upon and drawn up by the city or county authorities that the subject property is located in. When you are refinancing a property or someone is interested in purchasing a property then this is something you definitely want to check out as soon as you can. Obtaining a Metroscan or Property Profile will usually reveal this. For example, if you are working on a refinance loan for a home and you pull a Metroscan on that subject property and the Zoning states: Residential - you are OK. However, if it states: Commercial, then this could be a problem for your Lender(s) – and your borrowers. How can a residence (home) be in a commercially zoned area? This could happen whereby the home was built many years ago and the surrounding area has developed into and became

commercially Zoned. Conforming Lenders generally do not like to lend on homes located in a commercially Zoned area. And, since I am now talking about Zoning I'd also like to throw in another term you may not have hear of:

INCLUSIONARY ZONING:
This is a practice by a state or local governments in which zoning restrictions are imposed that require a specified percentage of new development in a designated area to be set aside to provide housing for low- and moderate-income persons.

Now that you have become acquainted with some of the more common lending terms that you will find in speaking mortgage loan originator jargon, let's begin to use this information and now take a look at one of the most important things you first do as a mortgage loan originator – Qualify Your Customers.

Section II

LOAN QUALIFYING

At this point in this book I hope that you are beginning to get comfortable with the terms and jargon used in our mortgage profession and have a better idea of what Mortgage loan originators do. In mortgage loan origination training presentations I have given, as well as in writing this book, it was frustrating for me sometimes to decide on what lending subject I should talk about next. It would be great if I could touch the heads of each one of you and give you a "mind link" that Spock does in the Star Trek movies - whereby you could see and understand all the important aspects of mortgage lending and being a mortgage loan originator all at once. But since I cannot do that I must then decide on the proper sequence of the subjects to be covered - so that it all comes together for you in a nice orderly manner. This makes it tough sometimes because I might mention or talk about an area, idea, or loan program we haven't covered yet. But hang-in there and we will get through this with shining colors.

In this section of the book I'll initially discuss one of the most important areas you need to be familiar with when first making contact with a loan-inquiring customer as well as during the initial stages of originating a mortgage loan: Qualifying the customer. If you have been in sales then you know how important this initial phase of selling is. Because if you don't properly qualify the customer then you most likely will not match up the customer with the product that best meets their expressed need or want. And, that's what you should be doing as a Mortgage loan originator: Presenting and proposing mortgage loan products that best meets the home financial needs and goals of your customers.

Within this section, I also discussed the Consumer Financial Protection Bureau's regulations regarding the Ability-to-Repay and Qualified Mortgage Rules. Then, within Chapter 7, I'll discuss most of the common Subject Property Concerns you should be aware of when you first begin working on a mortgage loan and Chapter 8 answers the question of what type of mortgage loans are available for your loan-inquiring customers. And finally, Chapter 9 discusses the documents you will need to obtain in originating your mortgage loans. The following seven chapters present these important subjects for you:

> Qualifying Your Borrowers
> Loan Underwriting
> Qualifying Documents
> Ability-to-Repay & Qualified Mortgage Rules
> Subject Property Concerns
> Types of Mortgage Loans
> Types of Loan Documentation

So, let's begin Section II with Chapter 3.

Chapter 3

<u>QUALIFYING YOUR BORROWERS</u>

In talking about Qualifying Your Borrowers I am going to break it up into two parts:

1. What Lenders look for when Underwriting Borrowers
2. How you, as a mortgage loan originator, should qualify prospective Home Loan Customers

In talking about what Lenders look for I will primarily be looking at what Conventional Conforming Lenders generally focus on as well as those guidelines for Conforming loans stipulated by Fannie Mae and Freddie Mac. Conventional Conforming Lenders is a term generally given to those lenders who provide mortgage loans (conventional – conforming loans) for those borrowers who have good to excellent credit, adequate income (to their qualifying standards), and a home (to be purchased or refinanced) that is acceptable to that Lender. Also, Conventional Conforming loans offer your qualifying customers the best interest rates and loan programs.

If a customer doesn't qualify under Conventional/Conforming guidelines and standards (and those standards sometimes differ with different lenders) then they may qualify under Non-conforming loan standards. As you move away from Conventional Conforming loans to Non-conforming loans then the interest rate increases and the maximum allowable LTV changes (increases) as well.

I want you to know that standards and guidelines required for Conforming loans and Non-conforming loans change over time and are not written in stone. This is even more true since the beginning of the mortgage crisis and meltdown in late 2006. Believe me when I tell you that just prior to this period mortgage loans that were qualified, approved, and funded for a Conforming loan would not be approved for a Fannie Mae Conforming loan today. Why is this? Because Conforming-qualifying guidelines have become more stringent – making it more challenging for the average homeowner to get approved for a Conforming loan. That's especially true with the implementation of the Consumer Financial Protections Bureau's (CFPS) underwriting guidelines for a "Qualified Mortgage" and their "Ability-to-Repay" (ATR) rules.

But that just goes to show how dynamic the mortgage industry can be. Things do change in the mortgage business. So, because of this and because qualifying your customers does change, within the mortgage lending area, I will present the traditional ways of qualifying your customers and borrowers. That will give you a good foundation to build upon and guide you towards steering your loan requests towards the best loan program that meets the financial needs and goals of your customers. And that truly is what we want and should be doing as mortgage loan originators.

I. What Conventional/Conforming Lenders Look For In Qualifying Borrowers:
When I was in college I took a course in Consumer Finance and I remember today what those guidelines were, that I was taught, what lenders look for when evaluating the credit worthiness of a customer. Those general guidelines were (and are) called The Five C's of Credit. They are:

1. Credit
2. Capacity
3. Collateral
4. Cash
5. Character

Let's talk about each one of these separately and how each applies to what we do as mortgage loan originators.

1. CREDIT:
Quite simply, Credit today applies to what we will see when we "pull" a Credit Report on a customer. What are lenders really looking for? They are looking for the payment patterns of the customer over a stated period of time - usually the most recent two-year period. Have they established credit? Do they pay their bills and creditors on time and as agreed? Do they continue to pay despite temporary financial hardships (this alludes to the Character of the borrower)? Are they overextended on their credit?

Most Conforming lenders will require that you pull a 3-bureau Credit Report on your borrowers. This is oftentimes referred to as a "Tri-Merge" and generally includes Credit Reporting and credit scores from: TRW, Equifax, and TransUnion. Conforming lenders will be most interested in what they see on this report for the last 2 years and are generally looking for at least 24 months of good credit.

Evaluating the credit worthiness of a borrower has evolved over the years whereby today it seems that Lenders are looking almost solely at the Credit Scores of the borrowers. If the credit score is below a Lender's guidelines then they won't even look at that loan. Each credit-reporting bureau on that Credit Report will summarize what they calculate as the credit worthiness of that customer into a credit score. Because each credit bureau (it seems) is focusing (and weighing) the importance of different credit aspects of the borrowers differently (and the way they calculate their credit scores) it is rare when you will find any one of them coming up with the same credit score as the other. You will usually find these credit scores on the first or last page of the Credit Report. Conforming Lenders generally accept the middle credit score of all three - for the primary income-earning Borrower.

Prior to the mortgage crisis, during mid-2006 a borrower could have a middle credit score 680 with no add-on to the rate. Also, at that time I saw Conforming loans being approved with credit scores as low as 580. However, since early 2007 this too has changed. What I am generally seeing today is that most home Conforming loan customers (assuming everything else is acceptable) need to have a middle credit score of at least 700 - 720 to not incur any add-on to the interest rate. And, today, the minimum credit score of a Conforming loan borrower generally needs to be at least 620.

However, I should mention that the minimum and maximum required credit scores can vary –depending upon the Lender and their loan investors. The important point of mentioning this is to look at the credit scores and identify the middle credit score and compare that to the minimum required credit score of the loan program and Lender you wish to submit that loan to.

Also, Conforming lenders generally want to see at least 24 - 36 months since a bankruptcy was first filed or discharged (depending on the lender) and also want to see credit re-established with perhaps 3 or more creditor accounts shown and no late payments since the bankruptcy.

Let's say that you are working with a young couple that wants to buy a home but haven't really established any credit yet. You pull a Credit Report and sure enough there is nothing there and no credit scores either. Are you dead in the water? Not really. There is another means of measuring credit and that is called the Non-Traditional means of credit. Because your customers have probably been paying rent, paying electric and heating bills, and perhaps some medical bills - you get the picture, you now have a means (payment history) available to you. Anyway, with Non-Traditional credit you (or your Loan Processor) can contact those utilities companies and individuals leasing the property or apartment manager and determine if your borrowers have been paying their monthly bills on time and as agreed. If they have been paying their monthly bills (rent and utilities) on time and you have a two-year history then this could very well satisfy a Lender's credit requirements or at least provide a means to determine their credit worthiness. Please refer to Non-traditional requirements for more information on this.

The Credit Report gives you a pretty good idea of what you most likely can do for your customers with a loan and possibly what Lender you should send it to. We will discuss the Credit Report in more detail when we get to Chapter 18 on Reading the Credit Reports. And, it does seem today that the credit of a customer is the most important thing in evaluating the lending options for a loan customer. If your customer has excellent or outstanding credit then it is rare that you would not be able to help that customer.

Customers with "less than perfect" credit will probably not qualify for a Conforming or Non-conforming loan and, quite frankly, you may not be able to get them a loan program with an interest rate that makes financial sense in doing or benefits them. But keep in mind we also need to look at the other aspects of the borrower.

2. CAPACITY:
Capacity refers to the borrower's ability to repay the loan. In evaluating a customer's Capacity we are first looking at all the income the borrower and co-borrower make and earn each month. These income figures are expressed as "Gross Monthly Income" - before taxes and other deductions are taken out. Next, you list (in qualifying) all their monthly creditor payments. Here, you are not including utility type of payments. Just payments they are making each month to creditors (auto loan, credit cards, store cards,

medical expenses, etc.). Once you have totaled up the Gross Monthly Income of your borrowers and their total monthly expenses then we do a little calculating with these figures called Ratio Analysis.

Ratio Analysis is a two-step process that compares the Gross Monthly Income of your borrower(s) to:

1. Housing Ratio: The Borrowers' monthly rent or monthly PITI on their home, and/or total of their 1st and 2nd mortgages, and

2. Total Debt Ratio: Their total monthly expenses - including their housing expenses.

Let's now talk about these two ratios.

1. Housing Ratio:
This is oftentimes referred to as the Front-End Ratio and is arrived at by dividing the total monthly housing expenses by the total Gross Monthly Income of the borrowers. This gives us a percent representing the Housing Ratio. For example, if a borrower and co-borrower's monthly gross income is $3,500 and their current monthly mortgage payment (PITI) is $950.00 then their Housing Ratio would be about 27%. Conforming (FNMA) guidelines generally like the Housing Ratio on a 1st Mortgage to be no greater than 28%. But keep in mind that this 28% is only a guide.

2. Total Debt Ratio:
This is often referred to as the Back-End Ratio. This also is expressed as a percent and is arrived at by dividing the total monthly debts of the borrowers by the Gross Monthly Income of the Borrowers. For example, if the total monthly payments made to creditors, including their current monthly rent or mortgage payment, is $1,200 and their Gross Monthly Income is $3,500 then their Total Debt Ratio would be about 34%. Conforming (FNMA) guidelines generally like the Total Debt Ratio for 1st Mortgages to be no greater than 36%. However, since the release of the new Fannie Mae *Selling Guide* dated October 2, 2020, the Total Debt Ratio for manually underwritten loans can now go up to 45% with strong Compensating Factors. But again, keep in mind that these (Housing and Total Debt Ratio percentages) are guidelines.

When you write the Housing and Total debt ratios you can write them as 28%/36%. Folks in lending know that the first ratio represents the Housing (Front-End) Ratio and the second represents the Total Debt (Back-End) Ratio. And, if that wasn't enough, sometimes these ratios are referred to as The First and Second Ratios. I am sure you can figure out which is which.

Once you have calculated those two ratios then you compare those to what the minimum acceptable qualifying ratios are for your targeted lender or lenders. It used to be that Conforming Lenders generally wished to see a borrower's ratios no greater than: 1. Housing Ratio = 28% and 2. Total Debt Ratio = 36%. This has changed over the years and I am seeing more today are that Conforming Lenders seem to be conservative in what they are willing to accept. This, no doubt, is a result of CFPB's anticipated and implemented definition of a "Qualified Mortgage".

You may also find that as the LTV of a loan gets lower then Conforming Lenders may allow the Back-End Ratio of the customer to get higher (up to a point). The LTV of a loan is an important influencing factor in the level of Risk perceived by the Targeted Lender. As the LTV gets higher then the Risk of the loan is also perceived to be higher. And this is why loans with higher LTVs (i.e. greater than 80%) have higher interest rates, sometimes are more expensive, harder to qualify for, and usually require Private Mortgage Insurance.

Again, the ratios you come up with and what different Lenders require are not written in stone. They too change over time. But here is where the total picture of the borrower(s) can begin to develop. For example, perhaps the ratios are high but your customer has excellent credit. Also, perhaps they have owned their home for the past 5 years with no late payments. Lenders look very closely at the payment history of current and previous mortgages of the borrowers (or their rent payments).

You do a Ratio Analysis on the Borrowers to see where they are financially now and what it will look like after the new loan. As I said, these days it does seem that the 2nd ratio (Total Debt) is the one that most Lenders now are focusing more on.

In looking at the income of the borrowers keep in mind that the Lenders will want to see what the borrowers have made in income within the last two years and prefer that they have been in the same line of work or profession continuously for the past two years or at least been in the same type of profession for two years or more. We will talk more about this within Chapter 10 on completing the Uniform Residential Loan Application (the 1003).

When you do a Ratio Analysis on your borrowers you will clearly see how much debt they have in relation to their total gross monthly income and whether they are overextended and the benefits of doing the new proposed loan.

3. COLLATERAL:

Collateral really refers to the subject property. And, while the total property is considered in the value of the subject property you should know that most Conforming Lenders like to maintain a relationship of about 70/30 of the total appraised value of the subject property. By that I mean: Of the total appraised value of a property - at least 70% of that total value should represent the actual value of the home in relation to the value of that home's surrounding land and outbuildings.

Given the above and the fact that lenders are really lending on the home (what they refer to sometimes as "The Dwelling") the next question you should be asking, when qualifying your customers is: What kind of a house are we talking about here? Are you talking about a Stick-built, Single Family Residence (SFR), or are we talking about a Manufactured Home or whatever? The loan programs that you can offer your customers can be influenced by (and possibly limited by) what kind of home your customer is applying for or wish to refinance. Also, the interest rates available on a particular type of home loan could be very different - depending upon what kind of a home the borrowers are interested in obtaining a loan on. So, you need to be sure and ask.

The Type of Home you are seeking financing on will also be one of the determining factors as to what Lender or Lenders you are thinking about submitting your loan to. For example, not all Lenders do loans on manufactured homes, or log cabin type of homes.

Another consideration, when looking at the borrower's Collateral, is where is the property located? Is it in the suburbs? OK, that's good. What about in a rural area or 10 miles or more from town where each neighbor is about a quarter of a mile away? Many Conforming Lenders do not like to lend in rural areas or those "out in the sticks." So you need to know where the property is located.

Another important question, regarding the home of the subject property, is: What is the condition of that home? If the home is in good shape with no need of any (major) repairs, with good siding or outside paint, and the roof is in good condition then you probably have no concerns here (refer to Subject Property Concerns). Sometimes, however, you just don't know the true condition of a house until an appraisal is done. An appraisal may reveal that the roof is in disrepair or the back of the house or balcony is in need of a paint job. Or, there is a crack in the foundation or there exist earth-to-wood contact. These are all examples of concerns a Lender would have. So you need to find out what the condition of the property is in. Lenders look closely at this because the home will be what that loan is secured on and what the Lender will assume if the loan is defaulted on. Lenders don't like or want to be homeowners. They want to be Lenders. A repossessed home is a non-performing (income) asset - which doesn't make them any money until it is sold. So the type of home, its condition, and where it is located is very important to Lenders.

And finally, another very important question to ask your customers here is: What is the property worth or valued today? This is a very important question because this can strongly influence and perhaps dictate what the Loan-To-Value (LTV) will be - depending on the amount of that new loan. Today, most Conforming Lenders (we will discuss this within Chapter 8 on Types of Mortgage Loans) generally will not lend on a prospective loan when the LTV goes above 95% for refinance and home purchase loans. Beyond that it tends to go into the Non-Conforming lending area. Again, we will talk more about this in the chapter on Mortgage Loans.

So, when you are qualifying a customer then be sure you have a good idea of what the LTV will be for that loan. Depending on the financial needs and goals of your borrowers and what those borrowers need - to make the loan work and doable, the LTV of that loan will greatly influence what type of loan program you will most likely be structuring the loan as, as well as what type of Lender you will be submitting that loan to (e.g. Conforming or Non-Conforming).

4. CASH:

Cash generally refers to what Cash is in that borrower's bank account(s) and/or Liquid Assets (investments) are available to your borrowers. Lenders like to see customers who have a savings account and have saved money over the years. To Lenders this alludes to the Character (item #5) of the borrowers and shows that the customers have a habit of saving part of their income. This could be considered a strong Compensating Factor if there are weak areas in the loan. But Cash or Cash available becomes even more important when your customers are interested in purchasing a house. With this type of loan we know that there could be a Down Payment required and certainly some closing costs that will need to be paid at loan closing. So, where are those funds coming from? You need to ask.

Remember what I said in the beginning of this book - where I asked you to look at yourself as being the "Mortgage Doctor"? Sometimes we have to change our "hat" and be the "Mortgage Detective". This is ever so true when we are completing the Loan Application with our customers. We need to ask questions and if something doesn't make sense then we need to follow-up and inquire further. We will cover this in more detail when we get to Chapter 10 on completing the Loan Application.

So, you need to ask: How much have they saved up? Are they anticipating receiving any money before loan closing (tax return, inheritance, etc.)? Can they obtain or are they anticipating receiving Gift Funds towards the Down Payment or Loan Costs? If yes, then who will be providing those Gift Funds and where will they (the folks providing the Gift Funds) be obtaining it from? When it comes to Gift Funds Lenders like to see what we call an Audit Trail, sometimes referred to as a Paper Trail, showing where the Gift Funds are coming from and to where they are going.

Another source of funds could be the Liquidation of an Investment or Asset. An example of this, as well as how a Paper Trail works is: Years ago I had a customer who said they were planning to sell their motorcycle to obtain funds for the loan closing. As a Prior-To-Doc condition that customer had to bring to me a fully signed Bill of Sale showing the amount that motorcycle was sold for and a bank deposit statement showing those funds (from the sale) were deposited into their bank account. Also, some Underwriters like to see a copy of a page from the latest Blue Book showing that vehicle's value (to make sure the value you told them was a realistic and perhaps true value). This should give you an idea of the details of a Paper Trail: Documents showing exactly where those funds came from and where they went.

So basically, in considering the subject of Cash here, your interest or concern should be: Does the customer need to bring some money to "the closing table?" And if so, how much is it and where is it coming from? If you are doing a refinance or purchase loan and the customers need to bring money to the loan closing and you don't see anywhere on the loan application where that source might be and the customers have no idea where it is or how they are going to get it then "Houston, we have a problem!" In this type of situation, it sometimes is best to suggest to your customers that they hold off doing their home loan at this time, save up some money for the down payment (for example), and come back and see you when they do. This usually works to their benefit as well.

5. CHARACTER:

In discussing the above 4 Cs of qualifying your customers I have sometimes referred to the Character of the customer. The Character of a customer or customers cannot be objectively arrived at. It is highly subjective. However, from looking at all the factors regarding the loan (the loan application, the Credit Report, your personal meeting with them) you most certainly will derive an idea of the Character of your prospective borrowers.

In the old days (if I may refer to it as that) a man or woman might be able to walk into a bank or savings & loan association and get a loan - perhaps right there on the spot. The borrower could be going through a rough financial period in their life but that banker knew that that customer had good character and would repay the loan regardless of any setbacks or unforeseen hardships. Today, getting a mortgage loan "right on the spot" rarely happens. Of course, Lenders want borrowers who will repay their loans and repay them on time and as agreed. If a Lender is "on the fence" regarding the decision to approve a loan then their "gut feelings" about the Character of the borrower may sometimes determine which way they go. The Lender, in doing this, will review all aspects of the loan application, the Credit Report, any letters of explanation from the borrowers, their job history, purpose of the loan, etc. But remember that assessing Character is a subjective thing. It can work for or against a prospective borrower depending on how a Lender assesses all the paperwork of a loan.

Let's turn now to what you, as a mortgage loan originator, should do when you first make contact with your customers.

II. Qualifying Your Customers:

When I was training new mortgage loan originators one of the more common questions asked me when I got to this point is, "What do I ask the customer if he or she calls on the phone for a loan?" Or, "What do I ask the customer if they walk into the office and want to talk about doing a Loan?" After hearing this question a number of times I decided to put together something that could be a guide for those new mortgage loan originators. If you will refer to Exhibit II you will see my Customer Pre-Qual Sheet I designed for those mortgage loan originators and I too sometimes used this form when first talking to customers about a loan. As you can see, it covers most of the important questions we need to ask in first qualifying a customer and using it also helps to keep you on track - in terms of what to ask, so you don't forget.

This form is pretty much self-explanatory but let's go over it together because there are a number of points I haven't discussed yet and this will give me an opportunity to do just that. Also, please feel free to copy this form and use it for yourself and/or any other mortgage loan originators you work with that you feel would benefit from its use.

First, this form was really designed for mortgage loan originators when customers first call in to inquiry about obtaining a home loan. Although it's important to gain as much information as you can from a customer, while they are on the telephone, you should always remember that one of the main goals of talking to your customers (when they first call in to inquiry about a loan) is to setup an appointment with them. Unless that customer lives way out of town, if you don't meet with that customer or complete an application on that customer (over the telephone) then you probably don't have a loan. So try to setup an appointment with them or at the very least obtain the information on this form, put together a loan proposal, and then call them back to setup a time to meet with them to present it to them.

While I'm talking about answering the telephone for customers who first call in - let me say one more thing: When I first became a mortgage loan originator it seemed I'd get a lot of incoming calls from customers who wanted to know what the interest rate was that day. Now, this is something you cannot answer unless you have some information regarding that customer (recall our 4 Cs of Credit). Customers usually don't know this and shop around calling mortgage companies to see who has the best interest rate or rates. Actually, while most of the mortgage companies have pretty much the same rates it really comes down to who provides the best customer service and knows what they are doing.

Years ago I had a Loan Sales Manager who had been in the lending business for many years. There is not much "under the sun" he hasn't done in mortgage lending. At one of our weekly branch meetings he told us that if a customer calls in and asks you what the interest rate is today - don't tell them. How can you without getting more information from that customer? Besides, if you do tell them a certain interest rate then the next sound you will hear on that phone will most likely be the click (on the other end of that line) when that customer hangs up and is now calling another mortgage company for their rates. So, don't just spew out an interest rate. You may find out later you could have offered a better rate to that customer or not been able to do a loan with them after all. Talk to your customers who call in, ask them questions, and try to develop a rapport with them and gain their trust. If you do then you will have a much better chance of meeting with that customer and having them do their loan with you.

It was, at first, hard for me to do this. Especially when a customer was insistent on knowing what the interest rates were. But over the years I have learned that my manager was right. Today, if a customer asks me what the interest rate is - I tell him, "I don't know, I need more information." I then go into a questioning mode. I'll ask them a question like, "Can you tell me what you would like to accomplish with your loan?" It's funny, but this seems to mess them up - maybe because no previous mortgage loan originator has asked them that question. They sometimes responded with, "What do you mean?" I then asked them, "Well, what are the goals of your loan? What is it you want to achieve with this loan?" If that customer is still on the line then I can usually get them to start talking. And that's what we really want: For them to start talking to us - telling us what their loan goals are and what's been troubling them or what their needs are (remember being The Mortgage Doctor).

Okay, I think I made my point here. Let's go now to my Customer Pre-Qual Sheet.

~ THE CUSTOMER PRE-QUAL SHEET ~

After you have entered that day's date, the **Borrower and Co-Borrower's name, telephone numbers,** and **their address** - it then next asks you, **"How did you hear about us?"** Branch Managers who are actively promoting your branch office, through the newspaper, flyers, and mailings to "farming lists," generally like to know the answer to this question. This lets them know what promotions are working and worth paying for.

Below this is - the **Purpose of the Loan.** I designed this so you can quickly circle which one applies to your customers.

Below that are questions for - either a **Purchase loan** or **Refinance loan**. If it's a **Purchase loan** request then ask them what the sales price of that property is and its address. However, they may not have identified a property yet. In that case ask them if they have a sale price or range in mind. Of course, they may not know that either and that could be why they are calling you now - to get pre-qualified and find out what they would qualify for. In the Down Payment Amount enter here any amount they have either saved up or have for the Down Payment.

If it's a **Refinance loan** then ask them what they think the Outstanding Balance is on their 1st mortgage and if they have a 2nd mortgage. If they do have a 2nd mortgage - what is its outstanding balance as well? Also, ask them what their monthly payment is for each. And, ask them what they think their property is worth or what it could be appraised for. If they are not sure then ask them if they sold their home today what would they sell it for? This may give you a ballpark figure - at least something to work with. If this is a Cash-Out Refinance Loan then ask your customers how much money do they need to accomplish the goals of their refinance loan.

If your loan-inquiring customer wishes to refinance their property then you also need to know if there is an existing **Prepayment Penalty** on that loan (see Prepayment Penalty). If that customer is refinancing a Conforming fixed rate loan then it is highly unlikely that there is a Prepayment Penalty on it. However, if they are refinancing an ARM loan then there is a good chance that there is (or was) a Prepayment Penalty when that loan was originally written up and closed. You need to be sure. If that customer wishes to refinance their loan during their Prepayment Penalty period then it is possible that that penalty fee (the Prepayment Penalty) could nullify the financial benefits of doing that loan. This is something you want to find out early on in qualifying a borrower and doing a loan. I have heard of mortgage loan originators who showed up to their customer's loan closing only to find out then that their loan customer had to pay a Prepayment Penalty in order to refinance their existing mortgage. That can be embarrassing and makes a mortgage loan originator look unprofessional.

Now, if you suspect that a loan-inquiring customer may have a Prepayment Penalty on their loan and/or that customer cannot recall whether they do or not then ask them to get a copy of their loan's Note (see Note). The Note document, on that loan, will state whether it has a Prepayment Penalty and the terms and costs of it.

Below that is - the **Property Type**. First, circle here what type of occupancy exists with this property – which the customers wish to obtain financing on. Next, indicate what kind of property are we talking about here: A stick-built house, manufactured home, or commercial property? If it is a manufactured home - is it a singlewide, doublewide, or triple-wide. Another very important question you definitely want to ask regarding manufactured homes is - when was that home first built? If you are talking to a customer who wishes to refinance a duplex then enter 2 in Units, for Triplex enter 3, and so on.

Below that is the **Credit Rating**. When I was a "new and green" mortgage loan originator I usually felt somewhat nervous and hesitate whenever I had to ask someone about his or her credit. I don't know why. Maybe it was because I felt that the credit history of a person or customer was (and is) a very personal thing. And, for sure, it is. However, as mortgage loan originators, in order to do our job - we need to ask this question and find out what their credit is. Over the years I have developed a credit inquiry question that is presented on this form. What I do is ask the customer, "Now, Mr. Customer, regarding your credit - on a scale of 1 to 10, with 10 being excellent, how would you rate your credit?"

If the customer responds by saying, "It's an 11! My credit is outstanding. I make all my payments on time and take my credit very seriously." Then that customer most likely has good credit. Conversely, if they say, "Oh, it's about a 7." Then you should explore this response further - because your customer might actually be a 10 and not know it. On the other hand they may be a 3! So, I ask them, "Mr. Customer, why do you believe you are a 7 or a 6 or whatever?" You may be surprised with the answers you get. One gentleman I asked where he felt he was on this credit scale told me he thought he was a 6. I then asked him why he felt he was that. He told me that his wife and he had filed Bankruptcy about 6 years ago because of medical reasons and that he was so embarrassed by having to file a Chapter 7. I then asked him if he had re-established any credit since then. He said yes and that they watch their credit very closely. I then asked him if he has had any late payments in the past 2 years. He said, "No." I said, "Well Mr. Customer, it looks to me like you may be a 10." He couldn't believe it but when I pulled his Credit Report - I saw that he had outstanding credit scores. So, that just goes to show you how important it is for us to ask questions.

Below that credit scale question - it asks if the customers ever had a **Bankruptcy**. If they did then was it a Chapter 7 or 13 and what month and year was it discharged?

If you have gotten this far with your prospect then I would go right into their **Employment** information. Because you are looking for the last 2 years with their employer or working within the same profession - for at least 2 years (it doesn't have to be continuous) I have an area to write in that information. Also, of great importance, is their gross monthly income. And, I always like to ask if there are any other sources of income that they receive. In qualifying loan customers I usually try to show as much income as I can. The more income that you can show (that can be verified) then the better the Housing and Total Debt Ratios will be. And finally, what's the total minimum amount they must pay to their creditors each month? That will tell you what their monthly debt service is and with that and the above income figures you should be able to calculate those customer's current

Housing and Total Debt Ratios. That will also assist you when you start putting together a proposed loan (prior to actually meeting with them).

And lastly, you can see that this form is asking for the Borrower and Co-Borrower's **Social Security Numbers (SSN)**. This is, of course, to enable you to pull a Credit Report. I purposely put this in the last section of this form because some folks, when you first bring up the subject of their Credit Report and you ask them for their Social Security number(s), sometimes start to clam up on you. However, if you have gotten this far then you should have a pretty good idea if your customers will be receptive and open to this. When I get to this point then I usually say something like, "Mr. Customer, in order to do a professional job for you and provide a loan proposal with fairly firm numbers I will need to pull a Credit Report. Do I have your permission to do that?" By that time most folks will grant you permission to pull their Credit Report and will give you their Social Security numbers. However, be aware that there are some folks out there who are very nervous about giving that kind of information over the phone - especially to someone they didn't know existed until about 10 minutes ago. That's OK. Just tell them you will put together a loan proposal based on the information they have given you. Or, perhaps that (their Credit Report information) can be taken care of when you meet with them.

At that point setup a time to meet with them - to complete a loan application or setup a time to call them back with your loan proposal. Like I said above, your prime objective on the telephone should be to setup a meeting with your prospective customers - to complete a home loan application.

After completing the above Customer Pre-Qual Sheet you should then have a pretty good idea of most of the important influencing factors that will determine what you can do for that prospective loan customer and perhaps how to structure that loan and where to submit it to. And, you have the basic information (regarding that customer) that should enable you to put together a loan proposal for that customer and enter most of the required information on the Uniform Residential Loan Application (the 1003) and Accompanying Disclosures. Doing this - you will look quite professional and could result in your meeting with your customers probably taking up less time than it would otherwise (and customers like that too).

So, to recap: In completing the Customer Pre-Qual Sheet here's what you can assess and derive from your follow-up before you actually meet with your customers:

1. The Names of the Borrower(s) and how to contact them.
2. The Address of the Subject Property.
3. What is it that they want to do here - Purchase a Home or Refinance?
4. Whether there is a Prepayment Penalty on that loan. And if there is, has the Prepayment Penalty period passed?
5. What is the Subject Property's Worth? This alludes to the LTV on that loan.
6. If they want to Refinance - Why? Do they need money - How Much?
7. What type of Subject Property are you looking at? SFR, Manufactured Home, Duplex, log cabin, or whatever.

8. What kind of Credit do those folks have? They said it was Excellent but what will the Credit Report show (if you have their SSNs)? What will their Credit Scores look like?
9. Where they work and what their Gross Monthly Income is. This helps you in the area of Ratio Analysis.

With all this information you should be able to assess and determine what loan program would best meet their financial needs (or what loan program you will need in order to do this loan). Or, in the end, perhaps you cannot help them at all. This could be because their credit scores are too low, there is no equity in the property, and/or they just don't make enough income (Housing and Total Debt Ratio are too high). Having this information puts you in the position whereby you can immediately begin working on this proposed loan and determine, at the very least, if it is doable. If you can help these folks then when you do meet with them and you show them what you have and they like it then you are on the road towards processing and closing a loan and, of course, making good money.

As I mentioned above, sometimes you just can't help your customers with a loan. Some of the reasons I noted above. One of the first (and painful) things you need to learn, as a new mortgage loan originator, is knowing when a prospective loan is not doable or when to just let a loan go. What I mean when I say the loan is not doable, I mean - after you have obtained all the information you can (on that loan), calculated all the ratios, looked at different types of loans programs and their LTVs, and reviewed their Credit Report, sometimes the loan just cannot be done or doesn't make financial sense (or benefits the customer) in doing it. In that case you should stop working on that loan and inform the customers, as soon as you can, of what you have come up with and why. Sometimes that's all customers want to know anyway - whether the loan can be done or not. And, if it can't, then why not?

Secondly, on rare occasions, after you have met with your customer, completed the loan application and all the paperwork, put together a loan proposal (and they liked it) then maybe that customer asks you to hold off awhile or he wants to wait a bit to think about it. This could be a loan for $450,000 and you are really excited about doing it. So you continue to follow-up and contact that customer only to have them keep telling you to hold off or wait just a bit longer, just a bit longer, just a little bit longer. This happened to me when I was a relatively new mortgage loan originator. It was becoming very frustrating for me because that customer kept putting off doing that loan. But I really wanted to do that loan because of the benefits my customer would realize with it (as well as the money I would make on it).

After this went on for about six weeks then I finally had to own up to the fact that this loan most likely wasn't going to happen. But before writing it off I wanted to be sure - so this is what I did: I called up that customer and said, "Mr. Customer, I just wanted you to know that the interest rate that we can offer you on that loan today would enable you to achieve the goals of this loan and significantly reduce your monthly debt servicing by about $500.00. I think this is a good loan and I would really like to do this for you. However, you seem to be putting off doing this loan. I have spent a lot of time working on this loan for you and I would appreciate it very much if you would tell me now whether you want to do this loan or not. Please be honest with me and just let me know whether you really want to do it or not - and I will be happy with whatever you decide or tell me." Unfortunately, in that case, the customer told me that both his wife and he had decided to not refinance their home at that time.

However, in other loans I have worked on - just asking this question has sometimes gotten them "off the fence" towards doing the loan. In other cases (as above) they let me know that they have decided to not do the loan. Of course, that's too bad. But you know what? I'm not wasting my time on that loan anymore and/or having false expectations about it either. And that brings me back to my main point here: You need to learn when to let a loan go. If a loan cannot be done then contact that customer and put it away. If the customer is putting off deciding on whether to do that loan or not then call them up and ask them if they really want to do it. If they do - Great! If not, then put it away. Next! Doing this will help contribute towards making your working time, as a mortgage loan originator, more productive and profitable.

Okay, let's now go on to the next chapter - which explores further the subject of qualifying your borrowers – The Underwriting of your customers' home loans.

Chapter 4

LOAN UNDERWRITING

This chapter was not written for a Loan Processor or Wholesale Underwriter but for you, the mortgage loan originator. And, this chapter primarily discusses underwriting guidelines for conventional conforming mortgage loans. Knowing the underwriting guidelines that the Underwriters of wholesale Lenders (that you broker your loans to) use in reviewing your home loan files will enable you to better consult and advise your loan customers as well as anticipate the document and informational needs of the mortgage loans you are working on.

Besides doing the many things that Underwriters do in reviewing your submitted loan files an important goal of underwriting is to determine the likelihood of mortgage loan delinquency and/or default. If, after reviewing a loan file and based on the applied underwriting rules and what is contained within a loan file, the Underwriter feels that the probability of default is high then that loan will most likely be declined. On the other hand, if it seems that the likelihood of default is minimal then that loan has a good chance of being approved.

Underwriting mortgage loans today can be done using two methods:

1. **Manual Underwriting**:
   This is the traditional means of underwriting mortgage loans. Manual Underwriting is also sometimes referred to as "Rules Based Underwriting."

2. **Automated Underwriting**:
   This is sometimes called AU and is also referred to as the "Risk Assessment Approach" to mortgage loan Underwriting.

As I mentioned, within Chapter 2, since the passage of The Economic Stimulus Act of 2008 a new conforming loan category came into existence called Jumbo-Conforming loans. Those Jumbo-Conforming loans were designed for properties that were located in High-Cost Areas, as classified by HUD, and have higher maximum loan limits then the "normal" conforming loan amounts. For example, a SFR property in a High-Cost Area could have a maximum loan amount of up to $636,150 and still be considered a conforming type of loan (enjoying the lower rates offered by conforming loans versus being a Jumbo loan). These Jumbo-Conforming loans were for 1st Lien position mortgage loans only and must have been Full-Doc and at that time - Manually Underwritten. Also, according to The Economic Stimulus Act of 2008 those Jumbo-Conforming loans were for those High-Cost Area loans written from July 1, 2007 to December 31, 2008.

Then, according to Fannie Mae Announcement 2008-27, dated October 3, 2008, and the Federal Housing Finance Agency (FHFA) news released, dated November 7, 2008, the

Jumbo-Conforming loans were then being phased out and replaced by what is still referred to as "High-Cost Area" loans. While the main idea behind Jumbo-Conforming loans was the same as High-Cost Area loans - the 2009 loan limit amounts and underwriting guidelines for High-Cost Area loans were different (this was also true for 2015). And then, on December 3, 2009 the term "High-Cost Area" Loans was apparently replaced with the term "Super Conforming" loans. However, I should mention that most of the material I have read (for 2013 - 2019) refers to these types of loans as "High-Balance" loans. Therefore, I too will refer to these types of loans as "High-Balance" loans.

Now, as I discuss the various Processing and Underwriting guidelines and categories that follow, I will separate and explain the "General" Conforming and "High-Balance" guidelines, for each listed category, when applicable and required.

So, let's begin our discussion here with the good ole' traditional way of underwriting – Manual Underwriting.

I. MANUAL UNDERWRITING:

As the name implies Underwriters are manually reviewing your submitted loans and determining if they qualify to be approved. To determine this Underwriters are using their manual underwriting guidelines, which are generally based on Fannie Mae and Freddie Mac's rules and guidelines as well. Manual underwriting is also referred to as "Rules Based Underwriting" because underwriters are comparing their rules and guidelines to what they are seeing in your loan customers' files. For example, Manual Underwriting, for Conforming loans, may state that the middle credit score or FICO score be no less than 680. If the borrower's middle credit score were below that then the Underwriter would most likely not qualify and approve that loan. Also, in reviewing the housing and total debt ratios of your borrowers the guidelines may state that the housing ratio should be no greater than 28% of their total gross monthly income. And, the total debt ratio should be no greater than 36%. If it does then this creates a "red flag" on that loan file for the Underwriter as he or she further reviews that loan.

I should also mention here that although, High-Balance loans were previously allowed to be manually underwritten, High-Balance loans must since 2016, are to be underwritten with Automated Underwriter® (AU®). With that said, let's take a quick look, on the following page, at some of the more important rules and guidelines that underwriters may use in Manually Underwriting your submitted loans.

ALLOWABLE LOAN TERMS:
General Conforming:
- Minimum Loan Term is generally 10 Years. I have not found many Wholesale Lenders who offer a mortgage loan with this short of a loan Term.

- Loan Term of 15-Years. This is the favorite amongst those homebuyers and owners who wish to payoff their mortgage before they retire. Also, amortizing a mortgage loan over a 15-year period highly reduces the interest paid (over the life of that loan) compared to a 30-year fixed rate loan.

- Maximum Loan Term of 30-Years. This seems to be the all-time favorite for fixed-rate mortgage loans.

CREDIT AND MAXIMUM LTV, CLTV, AND HCLTV:

On Fannie Mae Loans and according to Fannie Mae's *Eligibility Matrix*, dated December 16, 2020, you see that 'ole relationship between the maximum LTV offered for the type of loan transaction and the primary borrower's minimum required FICO or credit score: If the borrower does not have the minimum required credit score then the LTV, CLTV, and HCLTV on their loan is reduced. For this year again, Fannie Mae's *Eligibility Matrix* includes additional columns, for manually underwritten mortgage loans showing the minimum number of months of reserves required for each type of loan. As you will see below, that minimum number of required months of reserves (for each type of loan) is influenced by a combination of the borrower's DTI, credit score, and LTV on their loan.

So, to properly read the loan underwriting matrices, presented within this chapter, below is an example of how to property read and interpret the data within it.

Maximum LTV, CLTV, HCLTV	Maximum DTI $\leq 36\%$		Maximum DTI $\leq 45\%$	
	Credit Score / LTV	Minimum Reserves	Credit Score / LTV	Minimum Reserves
FRM: 75%	680	6	700	6
ARM: 75%	680	6	680	12

Ok, starting with the column on the far left-hand side:

- **Maximum LTV, CLTV, and HCLTV:**
  This presents the maximum LTV, CLTV, and HCLTV for that type of loan with a Fixed Rate Mortgage (FRM) and an Adjustment Rate Mortgage (ARM). As you can see above, the maximum LTV, CLTV, and HCLTV for a FRM is 75% and for ARMs 75%.

- **Maximum DTI $\leq 36\%$ and Maximum DTI $\leq 45\%$**
  This began showing up within the *Eligibility Matrix* (dated July 25, 2017) which shows the minimum Reserve Requirements for a loan borrower – based first, upon their DTI with their new loan. Here you can see that this matrix first considers if their DTI is equal to or less than 36%. If it is than the minimum credit score required as well as the minimum months of Reserves required is shown. You can also see that the minimum credit score as well as the minimum required reserves may differ depending upon whether the loan is a FRM or an ARM.

  However, if the borrower's DTI, with their new loan, is equal to or less than 45% (less than would mean between 36.1 to less than 45% - then if it is than the minimum credit score required as well as the minimum months of Reserves required is shown. And, again, you can also see that the minimum credit score as well as the minimum required reserves differ depending upon whether the loan is a FRM or an ARM. For example, in this case, for a FRM the minimum credit score is 700 with minimum monthly Reserves of 6. However, for an ARM loan the minimum credit score is lower at 680, but the minimum monthly Reserves is twice that as a FRM with 12 months of Reserves required.

Alrighty then. Having gone over that I think that you now have a pretty good idea of how to properly read these matrices. You probably already knew how to read these but I just wanted to be sure.

First, Fannie Mae separates the loan transactions types, for Manual Underwriting, into four main categories:

1. Standard Eligibility Requirements
2. HomeStyle Renovation® Mortgage
3. HomeReady Mortgage
4. High LTV Refinance

And, in each one of the above two categories Fannie Mae provides underwriting guidelines for Purchase, Limited Cash-out Refinance (LCOR), Second Home, and Investment Property transactions.

So, let' begin, on the following page, with the first category, for Manually Underwritten mortgage loans, under Standard Eligibility Requirements: Principal Residences. And, as you will see, there have been no changes for 2021 – from the previous year of 2020 (using Fannie Mae's *Eligibility Matrix* guidelines dated December 16, 2020).

I. Standard Eligibility Requirements:

1. Principal Residence: Purchase and Limited Cash-out Refinance (LCOR) Loans:

1 Unit:

Maximum LTV, CLTV, HCLTV	Maximum DTI ≤ 36%		Maximum DTI ≤ 45%	
	Credit Score / LTV	Minimum Reserves	Credit Score / LTV	Minimum Reserves
FRM: 95% ARM: 95%	680 if > 75% FRM: 620 if ≤ 75% 640 if ≤ 75%	0 2 0	720 if > 75% 680 if ≤ 75%	0 0
	660 if > 75%	6	700 if > 75% 660 if ≤ 75%	6 6

2 Units:

Maximum LTV, CLTV, HCLTV	Maximum DTI ≤ 36%		Maximum DTI ≤ 45%	
	Credit Score / LTV	Minimum Reserves	Credit Score / LTV	Minimum Reserves
FRM: 85% ARM: 85%	680 if > 75% 640 if ≤ 75%	6 6	700 if > 75% 680 if ≤ 75%	6 6

3-4 Units:

Maximum LTV, CLTV, HCLTV	Maximum DTI ≤ 36%		Maximum DTI ≤ 45%	
	Credit Score / LTV	Minimum Reserves	Credit Score / LTV	Minimum Reserves
FRM: 75% ARM: 75%	660 660	6 6	680 680	6 6

Cash-Out Refinance for Principal Residence:

1 Unit:

Maximum LTV, CLTV, HCLTV	Maximum DTI ≤ 36%		Maximum DTI ≤ 45%	
	Credit Score / LTV	Minimum Reserves	Credit Score / LTV	Minimum Reserves
FRM: 80% ARM: 80%	680 if > 75% 660 if ≤ 75%	0 0	700 if > 75% 680 if ≤ 75%	2 2
	660 if > 75% 640 if ≤ 75%	6 6		

I. Standard Eligibility Requirements (continued):

Cash-Out Refinance

2-4 Units:

Maximum LTV, CLTV, HCLTV	Maximum DTI ≤ 36%		Maximum DTI ≤ 45%	
	Credit Score / LTV	Minimum Reserves	Credit Score / LTV	Minimum Reserves
FRM: 75%	680	6	700	6
ARM: 75%	680	6	680	12

2. Second Home on Principal Residence:

Purchase and Limited Cash-out Refinance (LCOR) Loans:

1 Unit:

Maximum LTV, CLTV, HCLTV	Maximum DTI ≤ 36%		Maximum DTI ≤ 45%	
	Credit Score / LTV	Minimum Reserves	Credit Score / LTV	Minimum Reserves
FRM: 90% ARM: 90%	680 if > 75% 640 if ≤ 75%	2 2	720 if > 75% 680 if ≤ 75%	2 2
			700 if > 75% 660 if ≤ 75%	12 12

Second Home – Cash-Out Refinance Loans:

1 Unit:

Maximum LTV, CLTV, HCLTV	Maximum DTI ≤ 36%		Maximum DTI ≤ 45%	
	Credit Score / LTV	Minimum Reserves	Credit Score / LTV	Minimum Reserves
FRM: 75%	680	2	700	2
ARM: 75%	680	2	680	12

I. Standard Eligibility Requirements (continued):

3. Investment Property:

Purchase Transactions on Investment Property:

1 Unit:

Maximum LTV, CLTV, HCLTV	Maximum DTI ≤ 36%		Maximum DTI ≤ 45%	
	Credit Score / LTV	Minimum Reserves	Credit Score / LTV	Minimum Reserves
FRM: 85% ARM: 85%	680 if > 75% 640 if ≤ 75%	6 6	700 if > 75% 680 if ≤ 75%	6 6

Purchase Transactions on Investment Property:

2-4 Units:

Maximum LTV, CLTV, HCLTV	Maximum DTI ≤ 36%		Maximum DTI ≤ 45%	
	Credit Score / LTV	Minimum Reserves	Credit Score / LTV	Minimum Reserves
FRM: 75% ARM: 75%	660 660	6 6	680 680	6 6

Limited Cash-Out Refinance on Investment Property:

1 Unit:

Maximum LTV, CLTV, HCLTV	Maximum DTI ≤ 36%		Maximum DTI ≤ 45%	
	Credit Score / LTV	Minimum Reserves	Credit Score / LTV	Minimum Reserves
FRM: 75% ARM: 75%	660 660	6 6	680 680	6 6

2-4 Units:

Maximum LTV, CLTV, HCLTV	Maximum DTI ≤ 36%		Maximum DTI ≤ 45%	
	Credit Score / LTV	Minimum Reserves	Credit Score / LTV	Minimum Reserves
FRM: 75% ARM: 75%	680 680	6 6	700 700	6 6

3. Standard Eligibility Requirements - Investment Property (continued):

Cash-Out Refinance on Investment Property:

1 Unit:

Maximum LTV, CLTV, HCLTV	Maximum DTI ≤ 36%		Maximum DTI ≤ 45%	
	Credit Score / LTV	Minimum Reserves	Credit Score / LTV	Minimum Reserves
FRM: 75%	700	6	720	6
ARM: 75%	700	6	700	12

2-4 Units:

Maximum LTV, CLTV, HCLTV	Maximum DTI ≤ 36%		Maximum DTI ≤ 45%	
	Credit Score / LTV	Minimum Reserves	Credit Score / LTV	Minimum Reserves
FRM: 70%	700	6	720	6
ARM: 70%	700	6	700	12

II. HomeStyle®Renovation Mortgages:

Fannie Mae accepts, for Manual Underwriting mortgage loans, under the HomeStyle® Renovation Mortgage loan programs for Principal Residences, Second Homes, and Investment properties. Also, if all borrowers are first-time homebuyers, then at least one borrower is required to take homeownership education, regardless of LTV.

1. Purchase and LCOR Transactions for Principal Residence:

1 Unit:

Maximum LTV, CLTV, HCLTV	Maximum DTI < 36%		Maximum DTI < 45%	
	Credit Score / LTV	Minimum Reserves	Credit Score / LTV	Minimum Reserves
FRM: 95%	680 if > 75%	0	720 if > 75%	
	640 if ≤ 75%	0	680 if ≤ 75%	0
ARM: 95%	620 if ≤ 75%	2	700 if > 75% 660 if ≤ 75%	6
	660 if > 75%	6		

II. HomeStyle®Renovation Mortgages (continued):

1. Purchase and LCOR Transactions for Principal Residence:

2 Units:

Maximum LTV, CLTV, HCLTV	Maximum DTI < 36%		Maximum DTI < 45%	
	Credit Score / LTV	Minimum Reserves	Credit Score / LTV	Minimum Reserves
FRM: 85%	680 if > 75%	6	700 if > 75%	6
ARM: 85%	640 if < 75%	6	680 if < 75%	6

3-4 Units:

Maximum LTV, CLTV, HCLTV	Maximum DTI < 36%		Maximum DTI < 45%	
	Credit Score / LTV	Minimum Reserves	Credit Score / LTV	Minimum Reserves
FRM: 75%	660	6	680	6
ARM: 75%	660	6	680	6

2. Second Home for HomeStyle Renovation Mortgages:

Purchase and LCOR Transactions:

1 Unit:

Maximum LTV, CLTV, HCLTV	Maximum DTI < 36%		Maximum DTI < 45%	
	Credit Score / LTV	Minimum Reserves	Credit Score / LTV	Minimum Reserves
FRM: 90%	680 if > 75%	2	720 if > 75%	2
			680 if < 75%	2
ARM: 90%	640 if < 75%	2	700 if > 75%	12
			660 if < 75%	12

3. Investment Property under HomeStyle Renovation Mortgages:

Purchase Transactions:

1 Unit:

Maximum LTV, CLTV, HCLTV	Maximum DTI < 36%		Maximum DTI < 45%	
	Credit Score / LTV	Minimum Reserves	Credit Score / LTV	Minimum Reserves
FRM: 85%	680 if > 75%	6	700 if > 75%	6
ARM: 85%	640 if < 75%	6	680 if < 75%	6

2. Second Home for HomeStyle Renovation Mortgages (continued):

Limited Cash-Out Refinance Transactions:

1 Unit:

Maximum LTV, CLTV, HCLTV	Maximum DTI ≤ 36%		Maximum DTI ≤ 45%	
	Credit Score / LTV	Minimum Reserves	Credit Score / LTV	Minimum Reserves
FRM: 75%	660	6	680	6
ARM: 75%	660	6	680	6

III. HomeReady Mortgages:

Fannie Mae accepts, for Manually Underwritten mortgage loans, under the HomeReady Mortgage loan programs for Purchases and Limited Cash-Out Refinance loans for 1, 2, and 3-4 Units. However, these all needed to be Principal Residences. And, if all borrowers are first-time homebuyers, then at least one borrower is required to take homeownership education, regardless of LTV.

1. Purchase and LCOR Transactions:

1 Unit:

Maximum LTV, CLTV, HCLTV	Maximum DTI ≤ 36%		Maximum DTI ≤ 45%	
	Credit Score / LTV	Minimum Reserves	Credit Score / LTV	Minimum Reserves
FRM: 95% ARM: 95%	680 if > 75%	0	720 if > 75%	0
	640 if ≤ 75%	0	680 if ≤ 75%	0
	FRM: 620 if ≤ 75%	2	700 if > 75%	6
			660 if ≤ 75%	6
	660 if > 75%	6		

2 Units:

Maximum LTV, CLTV, HCLTV	Maximum DTI ≤ 36%		Maximum DTI ≤ 45%	
	Credit Score / LTV	Minimum Reserves	Credit Score / LTV	Minimum Reserves
FRM: 85% ARM: 85%	680 if > 75%	6	700 if > 75%	6
	640 if ≤ 75%	6	680 if ≤ 75%	6

3-4 Units:

Maximum LTV, CLTV, HCLTV	Maximum DTI ≤ 36%		Maximum DTI ≤ 45%	
	Credit Score / LTV	Minimum Reserves	Credit Score / LTV	Minimum Reserves
FRM: 75%	660	6	680	6
ARM: 75%	660	6	680	6

IV. High LTV Refinance (Manual Underwriting):

Before I leave Manual Underwriting Transactions I would like to lastly mention the High LTV Refinance loan. The High LTV Refinance loan is a Fannie Mae loan product that came out about two years ago. As you can see below it is a little different from the others matrices above.

Types of Transactions	Number of Units	Minimum LTV	Maximum LTV	Minimum Credit Score	Maximum DTI
Purchase Residence	1 Unit	97.01%	FRM: No Limit ARM: 105%	620	45%
	2 Units	85.01%			
	3-4 Units	75.01%			
Second Home	1 Unit	90.01%			
Investment Property	1-4 Units	75.01%			

I should mention here that, according to Fannie Mae's *Eligibility Matrix* dated December 16, 2020, DU should first be used to underwrite this loan product. However, if an 'Alternative Qualification Path' is needed, for loan approval, then Manual Underwriting it is then offered as an option.

The High LTV Refinance loan provides opportunities for homeowners who have an existing Fannie Mae mortgage to refinance their home. It also offers home loan borrowers an opportunity to refinance their home loan when their LTV ratio would exceed the maximum allowed for a Standard Limited Cash-out Refinance transaction.

However, Fannie Mae does require that in order to qualify for a High LTV Refinance loan that homeowners must realize at least one of the following benefits:

- Reduced monthly principal and interest payment.
- Lower interest rate.
- Shorter amortization term.
- More stable mortgage product, such as moving from an adjustable-rate mortgage to a fixed-rate mortgage.

The following requirements and options are also included with obtaining a High LTV Refinance loan:

- If there is Mortgage Insurance on the existing home loan then that must be transferred to the new High LTV Refinance loan.
- **Simplified Documentation** requirements can be used for the borrower's employment, income and assets.
- In underwriting the new High LTV Refinance loan both DU and Manual Underwriting options may be used whether this new loan is for the same or

new servicer. However, Manual Underwriting may be necessary in certain situations.

CREDIT:
High-Balance Loans:
- All borrowers must have a minimum FICO score 620. However, if it's a purchase mortgage loan and the LTV is greater than 80% then the minimum FICO score is raised to 700.

CREDIT REPORTS:
General Conforming:
- All Credit Reports must not be older than 90 days from when it was first pulled to the date your borrower's new loan funds or the new loan's Note date. However, I should note that for Construction Loans this time period is increased to 180 days. Order a Tri-Merge Credit Report and use the middle credit score of the primary (income) borrower. If there are only two credit scores showing on the Credit Report then use the lower of those two scores.

- Minimum of 3 trade lines showing - with a payment history of 12 months each. Some lenders also want to see a minimum outstanding balance on a creditor account with a payment history of at least 12 months (i.e. with a balance or high credit of $3,000).

- Bankruptcy: For Primary Residences, Fannie Mae guidelines generally required a minimum of 4 years since the discharge of a Chapter 7 BK. This also includes a Home Foreclosure. However, this time period can be shortened to 2 years if the borrowers can demonstrate through documentation that the BK (and/or Foreclosure) was due to extenuating circumstances and/or medical reasons. The Underwriter on that loan may also expect, since the time of discharge of a Bankruptcy, the following:

  - Must have re-established credit with a minimum of 4 credit references. One of the 4 credit references must be housing related (rent) with a minimum of 12 months payment history. The other 3 credit references should have a minimum payment history of 24 months.

  - No 30-day lates in the past 2 years including payments of rent.

  - No Unpaid Collections or Judgments or garnishments since the discharge of the Bankruptcy.

FANNIE MAE MAXIMUM DTI RATIOS:

The maximum DTI for a home loan depends on the type of Underwriting Type used to processed that home loan (Manual or DU). Below shows you what I mean.

Underwriting Type	Maximum DTI
Manual	36%
Manual*	45%
DU	50%

> * Note: However, the maximum loan amount can be exceeded up to 45% if the borrower has the credit score and reserve requirements reflected within the current *Eligibility Matrix*.

I should note here that although Underwriters do want to see the borrower's Qualifying Ratios fall within their guidelines, it should be remembered that in many cases these are primarily used as guidelines. If a borrower's ratios are higher than the Underwriter's guidelines, but that borrower has some strong Compensating Factors then that very thing may enable the Underwriter to continue to review that loan file towards approval.

FANNIE MAE MAXIMUM LOAN LIMITS:

Listed below, according to Fannie Mae's *Lender Letter (LL-2020-14)* dated November 24, 2020, are the maximum loan limits that are to become effective for whole loans delivered, and mortgage loans delivered into MBS with pool issue dates, on or after January 1, 2021.

The maximum loan limits, for General Loans and High-Cost Areas Loans has increased, since 2020, by 7.42%

MAXIMUM LOAN LIMITS FOR 2021
General Loan Limits

Units	Contiguous U. States, District of Columbia, Puerto Rico	Alaska, Guam, Hawaii, & U.S. Virgin Islands
1-Unit	$548,250	$822,375
2-Units	$702,000	$1,053,000
3-Units	$848,500	$1,272,750
4-Units	$1,054,500	$1,581,750

If you would like to see a Map representing the maximum loan limits, for General Loan Limits, for the contiguous United States as well as Alaska and Hawaii, then checkout the Federal Housing Finance Agency's (FHFA) site at:
https://www.fhfa.gov/DataTools/Tools/Pages/Conforming-Loan-Limits-Map.aspx

On the following page is a matrix that displays how often the maximum loan limits for General Conforming Home Loan Limits have changed from the years 2000 – 2020. As you can see, from this matrix, there were no maximum loan limit changes during the 11- year period from 2006 – 2016.

HISTORY OF MAXIMUM GENERAL LOAN LIMITS
Years: 2000 – 2020

Year	1 Unit	2 Units	3 Units	4 Units
2020	$510,400	$653,550	$789,950	$981,700
2019	484,350	620,200	749,650	931,600
2018	453,100	580,150	701,250	871,450
2017	424,100	543,000	656,350	815,650
2016	417,000	533,850	645,300	801,950
2015	417,000	533,850	645,300	801,950
2014	417,000	533,850	645,300	801,950
2013	417,000	533,850	645,300	801,950
2012	417,000	533,850	645,300	801,950
2011	417,000	533,850	645,300	801,950
2010	417,000	533,850	645,300	801,950
2009	417,000	533,850	645,300	801,950
2008	417,000	533,850	645,300	801,950
2007	417,000	533,850	645,300	801,950
2006	417,000	533,850	645,300	801,950
2005	359,650	460,400	556,500	691,600
2004	333,700	427,150	516,300	641,650
2003	322,700	413,100	499,300	620,500
2002	300,700	384,900	465,200	578,150
2001	275,000	351,950	425,400	528,700
2000	252,700	323,400	390,900	485,800

Below are the Maximum Loan Limits for High-Cost Areas for the year 2021.

MAXIMUM LOAN LIMITS FOR 2021
High-Cost Areas

Units	Contiguous U. States, District of Columbia, Puerto Rico	Alaska, Guam, Hawaii, & U.S. Virgin Islands
1-Unit	$822,375	Not Applicable
2-Units	$1,053,000	Not Applicable
3-Units	$1,272,750	Not Applicable
4-Units	$1,581,750	Not Applicable

Now, I know, when you are looking at the far-right column above you see the maximum loan limits, for High-Cost Areas, as "Not Applicable". What the heck does that mean? Well, that is a very good question and my response to that is - what was first stated on the FHFA announcement for maximum loan limits for 2019: "Special statutory provisions establish different loan limit calculations for Alaska, Hawaii, Guam, and the U.S. Virgin Islands". In other words, the maximum loan limits, for these High-Cost Areas, is based upon the specific county within each U.S. State and/or Territory.

However, if you can identify the county, within a High-Cost Area and/or General Loan Area, then you will be able to determine its maximum loan limit. Simply click the link below to see the maximum loan limits based upon the counties within each U.S. State and/or Territory:
https://www.fhfa.gov/DataTools/Downloads/Documents/Conforming-Loan-Limits/FullCountyLoanLimitList2021_HERA-BASED_FINAL_FLAT.pdf

LOAN ELIGIBILITY FOR HIGH-BALANCE LOANS:

I should also mention here that the loan limits shown above for High-Cost areas, as stated by HERA, reflect an expansion of what is defined as a "Conforming" mortgage loans. Thus, Fannie Mae is broadly integrating High-Balance mortgage loans by applying General Conforming loan eligibility requirements with a few exceptions as shown below. Fannie Mae now treats High-Balance mortgage loans as a separate loan product. The following page guidelines apply to all High-Balance mortgage loans.

- 1-to-4 unit properties, for Purchases, LCOR, and Investment Property, are now eligible.
- High-Balance mortgage loans must meet all standard Fannie Mae eligibility and delivery requirements, as outlined in Fannie Mae's *Selling Guide*, October 2, 2020.
- High-Balance mortgage loans, depending on the type of loan and subject property, must be underwritten with Desktop Underwriter® (DU®) Version 10.0.

EMPLOYMENT:

Borrowers should have a minimum of 2 years in their current job or have a minimum of 2 years in their (current) profession. Their time spent in other jobs (or training and school courses) that relates to their current profession could be added together to the time spent in their current job – adding up to two years.

RESERVES:

Fannie Mae's new *Eligibility Matrix*, dated December 16, 2020, for Manually Underwritten mortgage loans, now shows what the minimum required reserves will be based upon two primary factors on a borrower's mortgage loan: The LTV on their loan and the borrower's credit score. If the mortgage loan is being underwritten using Desktop Underwriter then the DU will determine what the minimum required reserves will be (if any are required).

PRIVATE MORTGAGE INSURANCE (PMI):

When the LTV on a Conforming or High-Cost mortgage loan gets greater than 80% then Private Mortgage Insurance will be required on that loan. As we will discuss later in this book, as the loan's LTV increases above this 80% point then the amount of PMI increases as well.

RULING REGARDING RATE/TERM REFINANCE LOANS.

Some time ago Fannie Mae changed a ruling of theirs that relates to Rate/Term refinance loans. Previously, if you were structuring a Conforming refinance loan to combine the existing 1st and 2nd mortgages, with no cash-out to the borrower, then this could be considered a Rate/Term refinance loan. However, Fannie Mae has changed that ruling whereby it now states that if you are combining the 1st and 2nd mortgages together then in order for that refinance loan to be considered a Rate/Term loan - the 2nd mortgage must have been used in the actual purchase of that home. Therefore, if the funds, from the existing 2nd mortgage, were used for home improvement, debt consolidation, or simply cash-out then today that consolidation loan would be considered a Cash-Out Refinance loan.

Keep this in mind because this could (adversely) affect the pricing on your Conforming loan and the maximum LTV you could offer on this type of refinance loan. Also, keep in mind that while this is a Conforming Loan guideline, there may be some Non-Conforming Wholesale lenders (and Investors) who still consider consolidating the 1st and 2nd mortgages (regardless of the 2nd loan's original purpose) as a Rate/Term refinance loan.

ACCEPTABLE APPRAISAL TYPES FOR PRIMARY RESIDENCE:

When it comes to the type of Appraisal for Conforming loans then that is usually dictated by the type of mortgage loan (e.g. Purchase or Streamline Refinance) and/or what the Lender requires and/or is willing to accept.

However, for High-Cost loans a Full Appraisal is always required with the appraiser inspecting the interior and exterior of the subject property. And, if the value of the subject property is $1,000,000 or greater then a Field Review is also required.

TYPE OF HOME AND ITS LOCATION – ACCEPTABLE TO LENDER:

Although this may not be a Fannie Mae rule or guideline it certainly is something that an Underwriter will consider – as it relates to his or her Wholesale Lender that he or she works for. For example, not all Conforming Lenders lend on manufactured homes - some do. Some Conforming Lenders do not like to lend on homes in rural areas - some do. But that's all part of our job as mortgage loan originators: To try to find a Wholesale Lender who will lend on your customer's property. Another important point, in evaluating the subject property (the Collateral), is what is the size of the lot surrounding the home? Many Conforming lenders do not like to lend on property having more than 10 acres. If they do then the appraiser on that property will most likely discount the land surrounding the home that is beyond 10 acres. Usually the biggest challenge, when working on a loan with sizable acreage, is getting similar and acceptable home comparables (called Comps) in the appraisal. As a general rule, most Conforming Lenders do not want more than 30% - 35% of the total value of the subject property to be in the surrounding land and outbuildings of the main home.

The above should give you a pretty good idea of what Underwriters are looking for when reviewing your submitted loans. Keep in mind that the above guidelines are Fannie Mae guidelines and some Wholesale Lenders may not apply all the above guidelines rigidly. For example, on a Conforming loan a Wholesale Lender may accept a minimum credit score of 620 for an owner-occupied single-family residence. One of the reasons for this may be that that Wholesale Lender's investor for that type of loan program will allow a lower credit score than what the stricter Fannie Mae guidelines would allow. But these (Fannie Mae) rules and guidelines should give you a good idea of what is required, in Manual Underwriting, when qualifying your borrowers and structuring your borrowers' home loans.

Let's now move on to the second Underwriting method which is my favorite one and that I generally request my Processor to use when I am submitting a Conforming type of loan: Automated Underwriting.

II. AUTOMATED UNDERWRITING® (AU®):

Automated Underwriting or Desktop Underwriter (DU) is an online way of Underwriting submitted Conforming and Non-conforming loans. I have heard mortgage loan originators refer to this way of loan submission as DU® or LP® and used these two terms interchangeably. But this is not entirely correct. DU® stands for Desktop Underwriter® and represents the automated underwriting "program" based on Fannie Mae guidelines. LP® stands for Loan Prospector® and this represents the automated underwriting "program" based on Freddie Mac guidelines. However, since mid-2016 Loan Prospector® was changed to Loan Product Advisor.

Although the Automated Underwriting guidelines for DU® and LPA® are very similar LPA® does offer an automated underwriting option when a home loan cannot be approved through Fannie Mae's DU. For example, the following list two differences allowed in LPA® that are not allowed in DU®:

- LPA® allows non-occupying co-signers and the use of their income in qualifying for a home loan. DU®, on the other hand, does not allow the use of income from a co-signer not living in the home.

- DU® generally requires minimum employment and income standards of a 2 year history, with variable incomes, such as overtime, bonuses, and commission income averaged over 24 months. However, LPA® will, in some cases, only require a 1 year of employment and income history.

It has also been my experience, in the past, that Fannie Mae DU® loans offered the best pricing for your loans. LP® or Loan Prospector® (Freddie Mac) type of automated underwriting seemed to me to be more geared towards the A to A- credit borrower and with loans that have a higher LTV. It used to be that when you went from a Fannie Mae DU® submission to a Freddie Mac LP® submission there usually was an adjustment to the pricing (to the worst) by as much as +0.25 to +0.50. Today, however, that may not be the case.

If, however, you do have a choice between submitting your loans either through DU® or LPA® then I suggest you try to first submit all you Conforming Loans via DU® - if you can. If you cannot obtain loan approval there then submit it via LPA® underwriting.

For our purposes here, I will be discussing Desktop Underwriter® as it is represented by Fannie Mae's DU® Version 10.3 program, as well as their new and current *Selling Guide*.

Desktop Underwriting is also referred to as the "Risk Assessment Approach" to loan underwriting. Recall what I said above when first discussing Underwriting - where I said that one of the main goals of Underwriting is to determine the likelihood of mortgage loan delinquency and/or default. Well, it seems that Fannie Mae, during the latter 1980s to the mid-1990s, did an analysis on those loan factors (e.g. credit, loan LTV, mortgage term, debt ratios, etc.) called Risk Factors (or Layers of Risk) and measured the effect that each of those Risk Factors had on each loan's performance (delinquency, default rate, or excellent payment history). Each Risk Factor was then analyzed to determine its risk impact and importance in contributing towards a mortgage loan's default rate.

At the end of this analysis Fannie Mae identified two main risk factors that they concluded strongly influences the performance of mortgage loans (its repayment and payoff versus delinquency and default). They are:

1. Primary Risk Factors
2. Contributory Risk Factors

1. Primary Risk Factors:
These Risk Factors are made up of two of a loan's features:

1. The Loan's LTV and/or CLTV, and
2. The FICO score and credit history of the borrower.

Fannie Mae found that borrowers who had high credit scores (above 740) had very low percentages of defaults – even with LTVs over 90%. And, borrowers with low credit scores (ranging from less than 620 to 580) seem to indicate that as the LTV increased from 60% to about 90% that there was a general corresponding increase in the default rate. Especially for borrowers having a credit score of 580 or less. When the LTV went from 81-91% or more then the default rate just about doubled. This study seemed to clearly show that as a borrower's credit score got lower (from 800 to 580) and the LTV was increased (from 50% to 100%) then there was a corresponding increase in default rates. Thus, as a result of this study the DU looks very closely at the credit score of the borrower in relation to the LTV of the loan.
I should note here, that with Fannie Mae's DU® there is now No Minimum (upfront) credit score required. The DU® will determine what the credit score should be for a borrower's loan file – after considering all the Risk Factors on that loan. This is another important distinction between Manual Underwriting and the Risk Assessment Approach used in DU® and LP® Underwriting.

2. Contributory Risk Factors:

Contributory Risk Factors are made up of a number of Risk Factors and each of those has been studied as to their impact on loan delinquency and default. Following are eight major Contributory Risk Factors:

1. Employment Classification:

Here Fannie Mae compared salaried workers to self-employed borrowers and found that Self-Employed borrowers had a noticeably higher default rate over the Salaried paid workers.

2. Total Debt-to-Income Ratio (DTI):

As you would expect, as the DTI ratio increased the default rate increased as well. For example, going from a DTI Ratio range of 33 - 42% to 55% or more increased the default rate by about 55%.

3. Co-Borrowers on the Loan:

This showed that when there were Co-Borrowers on the loan (I am assuming income earning Co-borrowers) that this reduced the default rate by as much as 47% over those loans that had only a single borrower.

4. Reserves:

Fannie Mae found here that when borrowers had available 2 – 4 months of reserves (PITI) that this reduced the rate of default by almost 31%.

5. Previous Bankruptcy and/or Foreclosure:

Here Fannie Mae compared the default rate of home loans of those borrowers who had a bankruptcy within the past 3 years to those borrowers who had no history of bankruptcy or home foreclosure. What they found is that those with a history of bankruptcy or foreclosure, within the past 2 years, had a default rate almost twice that of those without any history of bankruptcy or home foreclosure.

6. Previous Mortgage Delinquency:

Here Fannie Mae measured the rate of defaults on those who had a mortgage delinquency to those who never have had a delinquency. What they found was that if the mortgage delinquency was between 7-12 months prior to the new loan closing then the default rate was 43% greater than those borrowers with no prior delinquency. But check this out: If the prior mortgage delinquency was within the last 6 months of the new loan closing then this increased the default rate by a little over twice that realized by those borrowers with no prior mortgage delinquencies.

7. Mortgage Term:

I found this one pretty interesting. This compared 30-year fixed rate loans to loans with Terms less than 30 years (e.g. 20 or 15 years). According to this study those mortgages that had a Term of less than 30 years had a default rate of almost one half of those with 30 years!

8. Property Type:

This study showed that as the number of units increased (SFR to 4 units) that there was a corresponding increased relationship to the default rate. For example, 2 units had a default rate of about 60% over a 1 unit. But 4 units had a default rate of almost 320% over the 1-unit home!

The results of this study developed into what we have today called DU® and LP® Underwriting which focuses on the cumulative effect that these key Risk Factors or Layers of Risk (Primary and Contributory) have on a loan's payment performance and the likelihood of default. This differs from Manual Underwriting, which is "Rules Based." With DU® and LP® it is Risk Assessment Based. In other words, the DU "program" looks at all the Risk Factors or Layers of Risk of the loan that were submitted with it. When the DU® program analyzes all these Risk Factors that we have discussed above (and perhaps more), it then considers all of those Risk Factors (i.e. weighing the importance of each) and develops them into a Comprehensive Risk Assessment. A loan "decision" is then made for approval or decline.

As you can see, submitting your loans through DU® or LP® allows you to possibly obtain loan approval on loans that would not or may not be approved by Manual Underwriting. For example, as I mentioned above, DU® automated underwriting does not have a minimum required credit score. However, after the DU® "program" reviews a loan file and its Layers of Risk it then will determine what the minimum credit score should be.

Most of the Underwriting Fannie Mae guidelines for previously discussed Manual Underwriting section apply to DU® and LP® as well. However, here DU® and LP® looks at and considers all the Risk Factors or Layers of Risk in evaluating the loan file for approval or not. For example, the loan borrower may have a low credit score (e.g. 620) but has other very positive Primary and Contributory Risk factors (e.g. money in the bank, low DTI, job stability, wife as co-borrower who also has good income and job stability, and loan LTV is about 88% or less). And, they have owned their home for four years - with no late payments.

See what I mean here? This loan might not pass and be approved by a (Conforming) Manual Underwriter because of the low credit score. But I believe it would have a very good chance with DU® - especially when you consider all the positive Risk Factors. Why decline a loan via Manual Underwriting because one or two "Risk Factors" don't pass an Underwriting rule when the other Risk Factors are positive and shining through and through? This is why for me DU® and LP® Underwriting is "make sense" Underwriting.

Since we previously talked about Fannie Mae's underwriting guidelines, from their new *Selling Guide* and *Eligibility Matrix* (for 2021), for Manual Underwritten mortgage loans, let's now take a look at the guidelines for loans submitted through Desktop Underwriter® (DU® Version 10.3). Now, in the guidelines below you won't see any minimum credit scores because the DU® determines what the borrower's minimum credit score should be based upon each borrower's Layers of Risk. However, you should know that DU® Version 10.3 requires that all borrowers (using DU®) have a minimum credit score of at least 620. The exception to this requirement is, however, those loans using DU® Refi Plus. And, as you will see, Fannie Mae has made quite a few changes, for Interest-Only loans, that are submitted via DU®.

In our discussion that follows I'll present Fannie Mae's current Underwriting Guidelines based on its *Eligibility Matrix*, dated December 16, 2020 (for the year 2021). Fannie Mae's *Eligibility Matrix* presents its allowable loan products into five main loan products or categories with a discussion of Principle, Second Home, and Investment properties for each (if any of these loan products are allowed for that category). These underwriting guidelines are based using Desktop Underwriter Version 10.3. And, for each possible loan product it provides underwriting guidelines for doing Purchase, Limited Cash-Out Refinance, and Cash-Out Refinance type of loans. And, just as we saw, with Manual Underwriting, there have been few, if any, changes here since 2020.

1. Standard Eligibility Requirements
2. HomeStyle® Renovation Mortgages
3. Manufactured Housing
4. HomeReady Mortgages
5. High LTV Refinance

So, let's get started here beginning with Standard Eligibility Requirements for Automated or Desktop Underwritten loans:

1. Standard Eligibility Requirements:

Within this category, for Standard loans, there are three areas that Fannie Mae allows and focuses on: Principal Residences, Second Home, and Investment Property. So, let's start with Principal Residences for Standard Eligibility Requirements:

1. Principal Residences:

Purchase, Limited Cash-Out Refinance:

Transactions Type	Number of Units	Maximum LTV, CLTV, HCLTV
Purchase Limited Cash-Out Refinance	1 Unit	FRM: 97% ARM: 95%
	2 Units	FRM: 85% ARM: 85%
	3-4 Units	FRM: 75% ARM: 75%

1. Standard Eligibility Requirements (continued):

Cash-Out Refinance:

Transactions Type	Number of Units	Maximum LTV, CLTV, HCLTV
Cash-Out Refinance	1 Unit	FRM: 80% ARM: 80%
	2-4 Units	FRM: 75% ARM: 75%

2. Second Homes:

Purchase, Limited Cash-Out Refinance:

Transactions Type	Number of Units	Maximum LTV, CLTV, HCLTV
Purchase Limited Cash-Out Refinance	1 Unit	FRM: 90% ARM: 90%

Cash-Out Refinance:

Transactions Type	Number of Units	Maximum LTV, CLTV, HCLTV
Cash-Out Refinance	1 Unit	FRM: 75% ARM: 75%

3. Investment Property:

Purchase:

Transactions Type	Number of Units	Maximum LTV, CLTV, HCLTV
Purchase	1 Unit	FRM: 85% ARM: 85%
	2-4 Units	FRM: 75% ARM: 75%

I. Standard Eligibility Requirements (continued)

Limited Cash-Out Refinance:

Transaction Type	Number of Units	Maximum LTV, CLTV, HCLTV
Limited Cash-Out Refinance	1 Unit	FRM: 75% ARM: 75%
	1-4 Units	FRM: 75% ARM: 75%

Cash-Out Refinance:

Transactions Type	Number of Units	Maximum LTV, CLTV, HCLTV
Cash-Out Refinance	2-4 Units	FRM: 70% ARM: 70%

II. HomeStyle® Renovation Mortgages:

HomeStyle® Renovation Mortgages, using DU®, permits 1-4 Unit properties for Principal loan transactions only. However, only 1-Unit properties are allowed for Second Homes, and Investment Properties. I should also mention here that Interest-Only loans are not allowed on any of the HomeStyle® Renovation Mortgages for DU® loan submissions. And, if all borrowers are first-time homebuyers, then at least one borrower is required to take homeownership education, regardless of LTV.

No changes here since 2020 for the maximum LTV, CLTV, and HCLTV for Fixed Rate Mortgages and ARM loans.

1. Principal Residences for HomeStyle® Renovation Mortgages:

Purchase, Limited Cash-Out Refinance:

Transactions Type	Number of Units	Maximum LTV, CLTV, HCLTV
Purchase Limited Cash-Out Refinance	1 Unit	FRM: 97% ARM: 95%
	2 Units	FRM: 85% ARM: 85%
	3-4 Units	FRM: 75% ARM: 75%

II. HomeStyle® Renovation Mortgages (continued):

2. Second Homes HomeStyle® Renovation Mortgages:
For Second Homes, under HomeStyle® Renovation for DU, only 1 Unit properties are allowed (but you knew that anyway).

Purchase, Limited Cash-out Refinance:

Transactions Type	Number of Units	Maximum LTV, CLTV, HCLTV
Purchase Limited Cash-Out Refinance	1 Units	FRM: 90% ARM: 90%

3. Investment Property:
As with Second Homes above, only 1 Unit properties are allowed under HomeStyle® Renovation loans for DU® for Investment Property.

Purchase for Investment Property:

Transactions Type	Number of Units	Maximum LTV, CLTV, HCLTV
Purchase	1 Unit	FRM: 85% ARM: 85%

Limited Cash-Out Refinance for Investment Property:

Transactions Type	Number of Units	Maximum LTV, CLTV, HCLTV
Limited Cash-Out Refinance	1 Unit	FRM: 75% ARM: 75%

III. Manufactured Housing:

I should mention here, if I haven't already, that according to Fannie Mae's *Eligibility Matrix*, dated December 16, 2020 that Manufactured Housing can now only be underwritten using Desktop Underwriter.

1. Principal Residences:

Purchase and Limited Cash-Out Refinance:

1 Unit:

Transactions Type	Number of Units	Maximum LTV, CLTV, HCLTV
Purchase Limited Cash-Out Refinance	1 Unit	FRM: 97% ARM: 95%

Cash-Out Refinance:

Cash-Out Refinance loans for manufactured housing must have amortizing Terms of 20 years or less.

1 Unit:

Transactions Type	Number of Units	Maximum LTV, CLTV, HCLTV
Cash-Out Refinance	1 Unit Term ≤ 20 Years	FRM: 65% ARM: 65%

B. Second Homes:

Transactions Type	Number of Units	Maximum LTV, CLTV, HCLTV
Purchase Limited Cash-Out Refinance	1 Unit	FRM: 90% ARM: 90%

IV. HomeReady Mortgages:

Just as you saw above, with Manual Underwriting, HomeReady Mortgages are for Principal Residences only. And, if all borrowers are first-time homebuyers, then at least one borrower is required to take homeownership education, regardless of LTV.

Purchase, Limited Cash-Out Refinance:

I Unit:

Transactions Type	Number of Units	Maximum LTV, CLTV, HCLTV
Purchase Limited Cash-Out Refinance	1 Unit	FRM: 97% ARM: 95%

Purchase and Limited Cash-Out Refinance:

For 2 and 3-4 Units:

Transactions Type	Number of Units	Maximum LTV, CLTV, HCLTV
Purchase Limited Cash-Out Refinance	2 Units	FRM: 85% ARM: 85%
	3-4 Units	FRM: 75% ARM: 75%

V. High LTV Refinance (DU):

This transaction type that came out about two years ago and because of that I have saved it for the last listed matrix. As you can see, it is a little different from the other matrices above.

Types of Transactions	Number of Units	Minimum LTV	Maximum LTV	Minimum Credit Score	Maximum DTI
Purchase Residence	1 Unit	97.01%	FRM: No Limit ARM: 105%	No Minimum	No Maximum
	2 Units	85.01%			
	3-4 Units	75.01%			
Second Home	I Unit	90.01%			
Investment Property	1-4 Units	75.01%			

Also, according to Fannie Mae's *Eligibility Matrix* dated December 16, 2020, DU should first be used to underwrite the High LTV Refinance loan. However, if an 'Alternative Qualification Path' is needed (for approval) then using Manual Underwriting it is then offered as an option.

The High LTV Refinance loan provides opportunities for homeowners who have an existing Fannie Mae mortgage to refinance their home. It also offers home loan borrowers an opportunity to refinance their home loan when their LTV ratio would exceed the maximum allowed for a Standard Limited Cash-out Refinance transaction.

However, Fannie Mae does require that in order to qualify for a High LTV Refinance loan that homeowners must realize at least one of the following benefits:

- Reduced monthly principal and interest payment.
- Lower interest rate.
- Shorter amortization term.
- More stable mortgage product, such as moving from an adjustable-rate mortgage to a fixed-rate mortgage.

The following requirements and options are also included with obtaining a High LTV Refinance loan:

- If there is Mortgage Insurance on the existing home loan then that must be transferred to the new High LTV Refinance loan.
- **Simplified Documentation** requirements can be used for the borrower's employment, income and assets.
- In underwriting the new High LTV Refinance loan both DU and Manual Underwriting options may be used whether this new loan is for the same or new servicer. However, Manual Underwriting may be necessary in certain situations.

Exceptions:

Within Fannie Mae's *Eligibility Matrix* there are exceptions applicable to some of the above matrices. Therefore, I would also like to also include the following notes that were also contained within Fannie Mae's *Eligibility Matrix* dated December 16, 2020.

105% CLTV Ratio/Community Seconds:

The CLTV ratio may exceed the limits stated in the above matrices up to 105% only if the mortgage is part of a Community Seconds transaction. Manufactured housing that is not MH Advantage that have Community Seconds are limited to the LTV, CLTV, and HCLTV ratios as stated in the above matrices.

Cash-out refinances:

If the property was purchased within the prior six months, then the borrower is ineligible for a cash-out transaction unless the loan meets the delayed financing exception as stated within the *Selling Guide*, Cash-Out Refinance Transactions. If the property was listed for sale within the past six months then the LTV/CLTV/HCLTV ratios for a cash-out transaction are limited to the lower of 70% or the maximum allowed per the matrices (as shown above). Minimum reserves apply to DU loan casefiles with DTI ratios exceeding

45%.

Condos:
It appears that lower LTV/CLTV/HCLTV ratios may be required for certain mortgage loans, for condos, depending on the type of project review the lender performs for properties in condo projects - as in Florida. For more information on this refer to the *Selling Guide* under Geographic-Specific Condo Project Considerations.

Construction-to-Permanent:
These transactions are subject to the applicable eligibility requirements based on loan purpose. Single-closing transactions are processed as purchases or limited cash-out refinances, and two-closing transactions are processed as limited cash-out or cash-out transactions. However, mortgage loans secured by units in a co-op project or attached units in a condo project are not eligible for construction-to-permanent financing.

Co-op Properties:
The following are not permitted with co-op share loans: Subordinate financing, investment properties, and cash-out refinances on second home properties.

HomeStyle Energy:
For manually underwritten loans, the criteria that applies to DTI ratios of 36% may apply up to 38% for HomeStyle Energy Loans (DTI ratios up to 45% are also permitted in accordance with this matrix. However, loans with energy-related improvements are still subject to the applicable LTV, CLTV, and HCLTV ratios for purchase and limited cash-out refinance transactions.

High-Balance Loans:
High-Balance loans must be underwritten with DU. All Borrowers on the loan must have a credit score.

Manufactured Housing:
Manufactured Housing loans (including MH Advantage) must be underwritten with DU.

Multiple Financed Properties:
Borrowers of second homes or investment properties with multiple financed properties are subject to additional reserve requirements. Borrowers with 7 – 10 financed properties are subject to a minimum credit score requirement (only permitted in DU).

Non-occupant Co-borrowers:
If the income of a non-occupant borrower is used for qualifying purposes then lower LTV/CLTV/HCLTV ratios are now required and exceptions apply if there is a subordinate lien that is a Community Second.

Non-Traditional Credit:
Exceptions to the eligibility requirements apply to all transactions when one or more borrowers are relying on non-traditional credit to apply.

In closing, on this chapter on Underwriting loans, I believe that the only thing about using DU® Underwriting that some new mortgage loan originators out there may not like is that the Risk Assessment Approach of Underwriting is not "cut and dry" – like Manual Underwriting for Conforming loans. Sometimes in evaluating a loan I just didn't know if it would be approved via DU®. I could see weak points in the loan and yet see some very strong points (Contributory Risk Factors) as well. I have submitted loans for DU® and quite frankly had no idea what the loan decision would be. Oftentimes, however, I have been pleasantly surprised with a loan approval. So, this is a lending area you may need to get some experience in - before you get comfortable with it. However, the more you become familiar with and use DU® for your loans then the more you will most likely agree with me – that this is the way to have your loans underwritten – if you can.

Now, with all that loan underwriting information floating around in your head - let's go on to the next chapter that talks about the Qualifying Documents you will need to obtain in processing your customers' mortgage loans.

Chapter 5

QUALIFYING DOCUMENTS

𝕴 have designed this book to be not only a manual for new and experienced mortgage loan originators but also as a quick reference guide as well. With this in mind I have presented the main subjects or ideas of importance in bold letters (below) accompanied by an explanation of what document or documents you will need in reference to that subject matter. These loan needs are based on what Conforming Lenders will generally require. As you go towards a Non-Conforming Loan or even a Sub-prime loan or Lender then the actual document needs may change or in some circumstances require less documentation. However, as I said before, if you go into the meeting with your borrowers assuming you are doing a Conforming loan then you won't go wrong. You may later find out that you have obtained more loan documents than you actually needed. However, something later has come up on that loan (or whatever) that has caused that loan to now go Non-conforming or Sub-prime (requiring less docs). But at least you have what you needed then or need now to go forward with your loan without delay.

The purpose of obtaining the needed and required documents on your loans is to: 1. Verify the information the customer told you (and that you wrote on the 1003), and 2. Provide the information the Loan Processor needs to send out (what we call) Verifications. Regarding this, there are primarily four types of Verifications:

1. **Verification of Employment (VOE):**
    Referred to as the VOE. This form is sent to the borrower's current and past employers (within the last 2 years). Once sent, that employer completes this form. Some of the main points on this VOE for the borrower's current employer are: When that employee first began work there, what their current income is and has been (since beginning work), and the likelihood of the employee's continuance with that company.

2. **Verification of Mortgage (VOM):**
    Referred to as the VOM. This form is sent to the current Mortgage Servicer (mortgage company that receives the mortgage payments) or Escrow Company. This VOM inquires: What is their current monthly mortgage payment, is the mortgage current and has it been paid on time and as agreed, and has there been any history of late payments?

3. **Verification of Rent (VOR):**
    Referred to as the VOR. This form is sent to landlords and/or apartment managers of residences your borrowers have lived in within the past two years. When completed this form verifies the dates that your borrowers lived at that residence,

what their monthly rent is or was, and whether they paid their monthly rent payments on time.

4. **Verification of Deposit (VOD):**
Referred to as the VOD. This form is usually sent to the borrower's bank (or investment company) verifying the amount of funds in their account(s). Primarily used to determine if the borrowers have Adequate Reserves and/or sufficient "Funds to Close."

5. **Verification of Loan (VOL):**
Referred to as the VOL. You most likely won't see this one very often but I thought I'd throw it in anyway. This form is usually sent to the borrower's creditor(s) to assess the borrower's payment history balance and terms of the debt. Again, we are looking to see if the borrowers have paid on time and as agreed.

So, the information you obtain on your customers will not only assist you in qualifying your prospective borrowers but will also assist your Loan Processor in her efforts to do her job for you and your home loan customers. Let's now focus on those documents you should be asking your customers for when they mention or inform you of the following items I have listed below:

I. Employment:
Employment and Income are probably the areas where most of the documentation and qualification of a loan will weigh on. For these reasons I have grouped them together.

What Lenders really want to see is the monthly Effective Income for the borrower as well as the proper document(s) that supports that Effective Income. By Effective Income I mean that income that can be used in qualifying a customer for a loan. The customer may have other sources of income but because you may not be able to use that income – that income would not be considered Effective Income. And, the amount of Effective Income is always translated into monthly terms. So, sometimes you have to do a little calculating, called income averaging, to arrive at the correct monthly amount to use to qualify your customers.

Therefore, in our discussion that follows, I will first state the classification of employment, employment situation or income source, its required supporting documents, and the calculation used to arrive at the proper monthly Effective Income.

1. **Works for an Employer (Full-Time):**
When customers work for an employer and earn a salary then usually the salary they make will not normally change from month-to-month. The question is - how often do they get paid: Every week, bi-weekly, semi-weekly? When the customer gets paid determines how you will calculate their monthly Effective Income. And, Effective Income is what is used in qualifying your loan customers.

⇨ **Recent Paystub:** Covering a 30-day period with Year-to-Date Income figures. In calculating the effective monthly income figure for your borrowers first determine how often they get paid each month and use the following formulas to calculate their monthly Effective Income:

- Customer Receives a Salary:
  - **(Weekly Salary** X 52) / 12
  - **(Bi-Weekly Salary** X 26) / 12
  - **(Semi-Monthly Salary** X 2) /12
  - **Annual Salary** / 12

- Customer gets paid by the hour then:
  - (Hourly Rate Paid X Hrs. Worked per Week X 52) / 12
    Be aware that for Hourly Paid Employees some Lenders will average the hourly income received over the last 2 years.

⇨ **Last 2 Years of W2's**

2. Employment Offers or Contracts:

According to Fannie Mae Selling Guide, date October 2, 2020, if the loan borrower has an employment offer or contract (but has not started in that job yet) you would be able to qualify him or her based on the salary of that new employment – provided that the employment offer or contract to start that job is at some point after the Loan Application date but no later than 90 days after the Note Date of that new mortgage loan. And, with the following requirements as well:

- For 1-Unit, Principal Residence, Purchase Transactions;
- The Borrower is not employed by a family member or by an interested party to the transaction; and
- The Borrower is qualified using only fixed base income;

⇨ **Letter of Employment Offer or Contract**: Showing date of starting employment and monthly or annual salary printed on company's letterhead paper. And, signed by those with authority to make that employment offer.

3. Different Employers in the Last 2 Years:

⇨ **Recent Paystub:** For their current employer covering a 30-day period with Year-to-Date Income figures.

⇨ **Letter of Explanation**: From Borrower explaining the commonality of what they are doing now to what they have done in the past - if on the surface it appears that the borrower is doing something different than what they previously were doing. This requirement depends on the Lender.

⇨ **Last 2 Years of W2's**

Lenders like to see continuous employment with the same employer over the last 2 years. This isn't always possible. If they've changed employers within the past 2 years and it appears that they are now not in the same profession - then you should try to show some sort of commonality in what they are currently doing to what they have done in the past (if this is possible). For example, does their current position relate to management or sales or whatever that they have done in the past?

But maybe you can't do that. Then try to show that even though they have been working for their current employer for less than 2 years and in a position different from their previous position (in the last 2 years) - that your customer has been in that type of profession (over the past years) for 2 or more years. In other words even though your borrower has been in their current position for less than 2 years – that over the working life of your borrower you can show that they have 2 or more years of experience in that profession.

4. **Part-Time Employment (Primary Source of Income):**
   ⇨ **Recent Paystub:** Covering a 30-day period with Year-to-Date Income figures. In calculating the effective monthly income figure for your borrowers first determine how often they get paid each month and use the formulas in item #1 above to calculate their monthly Effective Income:

   ⇨ **Last 2 Years of W2's**

If the loan customer works Part-Time and that is their primary employment (and source of income) then the document requirements are very much like I discussed above regarding working Full-time employment. But when it comes to Part-time work Lenders like to see 2-years of work history without any interruptions – for it to be considered Effective Income. However, I should mention that some Lenders might allow a minimum of one year's work history (of Part-time work) if there is a strong indication that their Part-time work will continue. If the customer has worked, in that Part-time job for less than two years but at least one year then a VOE will most likely need to be sent to that customer's employer - to verify that fact (of the customer's future continuance with that employer).

5. **Seasonal/2nd Job Income:**
   ⇨ **Recent Paystub:** Covering a 30-day period with Year-to-Date Income figures. In calculating the effective monthly income figure for your borrowers first determine how often they get paid each month and use the formulas in item # 1 above to calculate their monthly Effective Income.

   ⇨ **Last 2 Years of W2's**

As you can see the qualifying documents for Seasonal and/or a 2nd Job are the same as Full-time or Part-time work. However, when considering Seasonal or a 2nd Job - Lenders generally like to see a two-year history of that work and without any interruptions. However, if it can be shown that the loan customer took the Seasonal or 2nd Job to compensate for a loss or lower hours (i.e. less overtime hours) and they have worked at that Seasonal or 2nd Job for at least a year then that (additional) income could be considered Effective Income.

6. Military Types of Income:

U.S. Military folks may receive additional types of income – in additional to their normal base salary. Examples of these are:

- Hazardous Duty Pay
- Flight Pay
- Housing and/or Quarters Allowance

A Verification of Employment will usually need to be sent - with the objective of not only verifying that the military home loan customer receives that additional income but of the continuance of that income.

Because many of these types of additional military income sources are not taxed I'd like to introduce you to another term you may not have heard before: It's called "Gross Up." This term doesn't refer to getting sick or disgusted. It refers to increasing a non-taxable income source by about 15% to 25% (depending on the Lender). Because these military income sources may not be taxed and because you want the Gross Income amount received for your borrowers (Gross Income represents Income before taxes) you may be able to increase that military customer's income source by as much as 25%. That could make a big difference in qualifying some of your loan customers.

For example, if your customer receives military housing allowance payments of $250 each month and, if you can Gross-Up this amount by 25% it could mean increasing their income source to $312.50 = ($250 X 1.25)! See what I mean? You can do this (Gross-Up) also with any other types of income earned or received by your loan customers that is not taxed. However, whenever you are considering this - first check with the Lender to determine if they will allow you to do this and what Gross-Up percent they will allow you to use.

7. Gap in Employment - within the Last 2 years:

⇨ **Letter of Explanation**: From the Borrower. If there was a time within the last two years when the borrower was unemployed for a period of 30 days or more then a letter of explanation from the borrower may be required - explaining what happened and why this unemployment period extended beyond 30 days.

8. Attended Related Courses, Seminars, or Study of Current Vocation:

⇨ **Copy of Diploma or Transcripts of Course, Seminar, or Related Area of Study:** Because you want to show at least 2 years, within the same profession (as noted in #2 above), Lenders sometimes give credit for the time spent in studying towards a particular profession or vocation. For example, let's say your customer has been an employed mechanic for the past year and a half. Just prior to that he attended Mechanics School (or studied or majored in mechanics) at a private school for 6 months or greater. His diploma or transcripts demonstrating this might satisfy that Lender's 2-year employment history requirement.

9. Borrower Receives "Straight" Commission as Income:

⇨ **Recent Paystub**: Covering a 30-day period with Year-to-Date Income figures.

⇨ **Last 2 Years of Tax Returns**: And with <u>all</u> Schedules.

⇨ **Last 2 Years of W2's:**

Because Commission Income can increase or decrease over time Conforming Lenders will take the average of the customer's Commissioned Income over the last 2 years. Lenders also like to see an increase in Commissioned Income over that 2-year period. And, you could also include, the customer's Commissioned Income from the beginning of that current year. For example:

(Annual Commission Income for 2 years ago + Annual Commission Income for Last Year + Year-To-Date Commission Income) / Number of Months of Commission Income considered

For example, let's say your home loan customer earns Straight Commission Income and has been working for an employer for the past 4 years. You look over that customer's tax returns and it shows the following (the current year is 2021):

Year 2019: $60,500
Year 2020:   70,200
YTD Income: 21,000   * 3 Months Commission
Total Comm.: $151,700

Therefore: $151,700 / 27 Months = $5,618.52 per month of Effective Income

The unfortunate thing about income averaging is that the customer's calculated monthly Effective Income is usually going to be lower than what they are actually currently earning. And, that's because the current or more recent income figures are being weighted down by the previous year's income (which is usually lower). You can see that above. The customer (in our example here) is actually currently earning about $7,000 each month and yet his Effective Income that you will be able to use in qualifying him or her is only $5,618.51.

10. Borrower Receives Base + Commission as Income:

⇨ **Recent Paystub**: Covering a 30-day period with Year-to-Date Income figures.

⇨ **Last 2 years of Tax Returns**: With all Schedules.

⇨ **Last 2 Years of W2's**.

In evaluating this type of income, Conforming Lenders will generally take the current Base Income figure (like any salaried employee) plus the average of the last 2 years of the Commissioned Income (as discussed above in Commissioned Income) and combine those two income figures together.

11. Bonus (Monthly or Yearly):

Sometimes you will get borrowers who, in addition to their monthly income, (whether part of items #1, #8, or #9 above) receive a Bonus as part of or in addition to their normal (Base and/or Commission) income. This is usually tied to some type of job performance done or reached (sales completed, goals achieved, etc.).

Bonuses are calculated just like Commissioned Income: By averaging it out over the past two years. If your borrower cannot show a two-year track record of Bonuses received over the past 2 years then the Lender may not accept this income source in qualifying your borrower. This is also true with regards to Commissioned Income.

A VOE may need to be sent to that customer's employer because all income shown on their W2s may have their Bonuses combined with their Base Salary and/or Commissioned income. Sending a VOE to the customer's employer will answer three questions regarding that home loan customer's Bonus income that a Lender will be most interested in:

1. What was the amount of the previous two years' Bonuses?
2. Are these Bonuses expected to Continue?
3. What is the expected Bonus (to be received) for the current year?

If you can show a strong track record of Bonuses received in previous years (and they have increased with each subsequent year) then you should have a good chance of including their expected Bonus to be received for that current year – and use that amount in your averaging of the Bonus amount you will use in qualifying them.

12. Overtime Income:

Sometimes Conforming Lenders can be so detailed - it can drive you crazy sometimes. If a Lender wants to separate any Overtime Income received by your borrower then you will need to average the Overtime Income received over the last 2 years - just like we discussed with Bonuses (in item #10 above). Again, like Bonuses above, a VOE may need to be sent out - so you can see the separated overtime hours and income from their other income earned.

13. Child Support and/or Spousal Support:
⇨ **Divorce Decree or Separation Settlement Agreement**

⇨ **Documents Showing This Income** is received consistently and on time for the past 2 years and will continue for the next 3 years. To show this part - bank statements or canceled checks can usually demonstrate this. Sometimes (e.g. Child Support) payments are "escrowed" and taken care of through a government or special agency that receives the monthly payments from the paying spouse and makes those payments available to the receiving spouse. If this is the case (and this is the easiest way for you to go) then just get a statement from that agency showing that spouse's account for the last 2 years.

And, don't forget to check the ages of the children that the Child Support income is based on. Remember, in order to be able to use that income source, in qualifying your customers, it should continue for the next 3 years. Child Support is usually no longer required to be paid to the receiving Spouse after that child becomes 18 years old. For example, if the receiving Spouse is receiving Child Support payments on a son or daughter 17 years old then you may not be able to use that as a source of income in qualifying your borrower.

14. **Receives Public Assistance Income:**
   ⇨ **Copy of their Annual Award Letter**: If the prospective home loan borrower is disabled, for example, and is using any form of Public Assistance Income (e.g. SSA, SSDI) and wishes to use that income in income-qualifying for a home loan then you will need to request from them their Annual Award Letter that they receive January or February of every year showing how much they will be receiving each month for that year. The Social Security Administration, within the past couple of years, has gone 'green' and those receiving this form of income can receive their Annual Award Letter online.

   And the good news is, that since the release of HUD's Mortgage Letter 12-18, dated 08/17/2012: Fannie Mae's underwriting guidelines state that if there is no expiration date shown on an Annual Award Letter – then that income amount, shown on that Award Letter, is expected to continue for at least the next 3 years. Therefore, regarding this income source, if there is no expiration date shown on a recipient's Annual Award Letter then lenders can use that income document in income-qualifying them for their home loan. Because of this - lenders no longer need to obtain additional documentation, like a physician's letter, stating that the individual's disability income will continue for at least the next 3 years.

15. **Receives Social Security:**
   ⇨ **Copy of their Annual Social Security Award Letter**: All Social Security recipients receive this Annual Award Letter, from the Social Security Administration, each year (usually about January or February) showing how much they will be receiving that year (for each month).

   And, as I discussed within #14 above, if there is no expiration date shown on a recipient's Annual Award Letter then lenders can use that income document in income-qualifying them for their home loan.

   And, because Social Security is not taxed you could explore the option of Grossing Up that income source – as I discussed above.

16. **Temporary Leave Income:**
   If a prospective home loan borrower is working (as we went over above) and they are going on a 'short-term or long-term' leave following the closing of their home

loan then Fannie Mae underwriting guidelines state that you could still possibly income-qualify them for a home loan. A woman who is currently on or planning on going on maternity leave after her home loan closing is an example of this.

Now, the questions that you will need answers for when someone is taking Temporary Leave are:

- When will he or she be returning from their Temporary Leave: Before or after her new home loan's first mortgage payment?
- Will he or she be receiving any income from their employer while on Temporary Leave?
- Has he or she saved up any documented liquid assets that could be used while they are on Temporary Leave?
- If they will be returning from their Temporary Leave after their first mortgage payment, of their new home loan, then how many months will they be on Temporary Leave before they return to work for their employer?

Once you have the answers to the above questions then this is how you would income-qualify them (or use their income in qualifying him or her if there are two borrowers on that home loan).

1. **He or She will be returning from their Temporary Leave <u>before</u> their 1st mortgage Payment:**
   In this case you could use his or her normal monthly employment income in income-qualifying him or her for their home loan.

2. **He or She will be returning from their Temporary Leave <u>after</u> their 1st mortgage Payment:**
   In this case you could still income-qualify them but you will need to use Fannie-Mae's formula to determine what their Temporary Income Amount you could use in qualifying that person for their home loan. Please refer to Exhibit V that shows you a Temporary Income Calculation Worksheet I developed for this purpose. You can use that worksheet as you follow the steps below:
   - First, you list his or her monthly income that he or she may be receiving from their employer during their Temporary Leave.
   - Then you take their documented Liquid Assets and subtract from that the amount of funds, for their home loan costs, that they need to bring to the closing table for their home loan (if any). That shows you their calculated 'Net Liquid Assets'.
   - Then you divide their Net Liquid Assets by the number of months that they will be on Temporary Leave. That shows you what their 'Available Liquid Assets per Month' will be.

- And finally, you add their 'Monthly Temporary Income' to their 'Available Liquid Assets per Month'. And that shows you what their 'Temporary Income per Month' is.

That calculated "Temporary Income per Month" figure is the amount you can use in income-qualifying him or her for their home loan. The two caveats that you should be aware of, regarding the borrower's calculated "Temporary Income per Month" are:

1. That income amount cannot be greater than their normal monthly employment income.

2. The Lender must reduce the amount of the borrower's total liquid assets by the amount of reserves used to supplement the temporary income. Thereby, avoiding the borrower's reserves being used for both income and assets.

17. Rental Income:

⇨ **Copy of Lease Agreement.**

If your borrower has property or properties that he or she rents out then here's another source of income for your borrower. Now, when you were completing the loan application on your customer, that customer mostly likely told you the amount of their Gross Rental Income that they receive each month for renting that property. For example, let's say this was the case and on that customer's loan application you entered that your loan customer receives a monthly rental check from the couple that leases their property for $1,250. Be aware that this is not the amount that you would use in qualifying that customer. What you need to determine is the Net Rental Income of their rental property in qualifying that customer. And, the way you calculate the Net Rental Income, for rental properties, depends on whether that rental property is Owner-Occupied or Non-Owner-Occupied. Let's first discuss how to calculate the Net Rental Income on NOO rental properties:

NOO Rental Property:

1. Determine the total monthly rental income from that rental property.

2. Multiply that monthly gross rental income by 75%. This 25% reduction, from the gross rental income, is for the maintenance, vacancies, and any other expenses on that investment property.

3. Subtract from the above figure in #2 the existing or proposed new monthly mortgage payment.

If, after doing the calculation of #3 above, the result is positive then that loan customer is realizing a positive cash flow on that property and that amount would be entered onto the Net Rental Income line, for that property, on their loan application. And, it also represents additional income that customer realizes and is added on to their other income sources. However, if the result was a negative amount then that amount becomes a liability and is shown as such on their loan application. Since the property, in the above NOO rental property, is not the customer's primary residence the proposed monthly payment, on that property, would not be used in their housing and total debt ratios.

Continuing with our example above: If we knew that the monthly gross rental income was $1,250 and the proposed new monthly mortgage payment would be $750 then you would calculate the customer's Net Rental Income as:

1. $1,250 X 75% = $937.50
2. $937.50 - $750.00 = <u>$187.50</u>

Because this $187.50 is a positive cash flow then that amount is another income source for your customer and what is entered as the Net Rental Income, for that property, on that loan application. And, that positive income amount is also added to the employment and other income sources that customer may have.

If, on the other hand, subtracting the monthly mortgage payment from the amount you arrived at after step #1 above - results in a negative cash flow then this is shown as an expense in qualifying your customer and that amount would be entered as a negative amount on the Net Rental Income line, on their loan application. And, also shown as a liability on their loan application.

If your loan customer has more than one rental property then you would do the above for each additional NOO rental property shown on that customer's loan application. When you are done calculating the Net Rental Income for each property then total all the Net Rental Incomes on that loan application. Again, if that final amount is positive then it is an income source for your loan customer. Otherwise, if it is a negative then it is shown as a liability.

As I mentioned, there is a difference in calculating the Net Rental Income for Owner-Occupied Rental Properties and those that are Non-owner Occupied. Let's now discuss how to calculate Net Rental Income for O/O rental properties.

O/O Rental Property:
Calculating the Net Rental Income for Owner-Occupied Rental Properties is a little different than with NOO Rental Properties. With O/O rental properties you would: Total all the monthly rents from the NOO units and then multiply the sum of those rents by 75% (not including the unit occupied by your customer). For example, if there were 5 common units and all NOO units pay $1,200 each month (with your loan customer living in one of those units) then that property's Net Rental Income amount is calculated as:

1. $1,200 X 4 = $4,800
2. $4,800 X 75% = $3,600

That $3,600 calculated above is what you use as the Net Rental Income because, in this case (O/O rental property), the rent from that property is considered income for that loan customer. And, that Net Rental Income amount should also be added to that customer's other employment and income sources. Also, in this case, that loan customer's proposed new monthly mortgage payment should be used in calculating that customer's proposed qualifying housing and total debt ratios.

18. **Dividend or Interest Income:**
   ⇨ **Last 2 years of Tax Returns**: With all Schedules.

   ⇨ **Last 3 years of Account Statements**

   When it comes to Dividend or Interest Income Lenders will generally require a two-year history of receiving that income source and will use the average of the last two years in calculating the amount of Effective Income from either of those two income sources.

19. **Trust Income:**
   ⇨ **Copy of Trust Agreement, or**

   ⇨ **Letter from Trustee confirming amount, when received, and continuance of payments.**

   When it comes to Trust Income then one of the questions here is how long will that Trust Income continue to be received? For Trust Income to be considered Effective Income it must be shown that it will continue for at least the next 3 years.

20. **Self-Employed:**
   First of all, when you become aware that a customer of yours is Self-Employed then you need to determine which type of business structure that customer has. This is important, because the type of business structure your customer has will determine what qualifying and supporting documentation will be needed from them. And, when I say qualifying documentation, I am usually referring to the type of tax returns and schedules that the wholesale lender, for that customer's loan, will be requesting. And, just like I mentioned before, when talking about the number of years Lenders look at – yes, it's usually the last 2 years. That's two years if you're submitting that loan via Manual Underwriting. However, if you plan on submitting your Self-Employed borrower's loan via Automated Underwriting (AU) and your customer has excellent credit (for example) then the AU program will determine whether a full two years of tax returns is necessary (or qualify your Self-Employed borrowers with at least one year in business but less than the normally required two years).

   Sole Proprietorship:
   As this name implies this is a business that is owned by a single individual. In this type of business structure there is no legal separation between the business (itself) and the owner of that business. Those income-supporting documents that would normally be expected for a Sole Proprietor type of business are:

⇨ Full Personal Tax Returns for the past two years. This would include the following with a files Tax Form 1040:

    A. Supporting Tax Schedules:
- Schedule C
- Schedule F (if income is from Farming)
- Schedule SE
- Form 4562: Depreciation and Amortization (if applicable)

⇨ If you are doing that loan sometime during the midyear period then you could also expect the Wholesale Lender to ask for a Year-To-Date Profit & Loss Statement. This is normally just referred to as a (Year-To-Date) P&L statement.

⇨ In some cases the Lender may also require that a CPA certify the borrower's tax returns. Some of the reasons for requiring this are:

1. The company is a relatively new company and in reviewing the last two years of tax returns (it shows that) the income earned, during the most recently year is significantly higher than its previous year.

2. Although the company is profitable, the borrower is showing no reserves within his or her accounts.

Once I have gathered all the requested tax returns from my customer (as noted above) I then spread them out on my desk, grab a note pad and pen, and do the following:

1. Looking on page one of the 1040 (for the most recent year), within the Income section, and on line #12 for Business Income (or loss) I write the total income on my note pad that he or she wrote. That's the financial figure we use to begin this calculating process.

2. Next, I grab the Schedule C and look at the lower right-hand corner (line #31) where it shows the calculated Net Profit (or Loss) for that business and for that year. The financial figure there should match what was entered for the Business Income on line #12 (on the first page of the 1040).

3. Again, looking at the first page of Schedule C I look at Part II. This is the section where that individual listed all of their business expenses. Some of those business expenses may also be listed on the second page of Schedule C. Then, looking at the first page of the Schedule C and within Part II – look for those types of deductions that could be considered Non-cash items. The place I first look here is line #13 for Depreciation. If my customer has claimed any Depreciation, for business assets that have been purchased, then I write that down on my note pad and add the total amount of that Depreciation claimed to that Business Income figure shown on page one of the 1040.

4. If your borrower is also claiming deductions for Amortization(s) then this too would be found on Schedule C. Then list those Amortization deductions on your note pad and add those to that Business Income figure as well.

5. Then look on the second page of Schedule C and see if there are any other claimed expenses that could be considered Non-cash items. If there are then write those Non-cash item or items down and add those also to the Business Income figure shown on page one of the 1040.

6. And, don't forget to check to see if you borrower has also filed a Form 4562.

The result of doing the above usually gives you what your customer's Net Income before Taxes is for his Sole Proprietor business for that year. After doing the above, for that customer's tax returns for the most recent year, then you do the same for their previous year's tax returns. Once you have calculated their Net Income before Taxes, for both years then take the average of those two years and that gives you the income figure of what you will most likely use in qualifying that customer – unless, of course, they have other sources of income. In that case those other sources of income would be added onto the average income figure from your customer's business.

The other types of business ownerships are Partnership, Corporation, and Limited Liability. However, if you are doing any type of loans, with these types of business ownerships, then I suggest working with your Loan Processing in properly and completely originating and processing these types of loans.

II. Cash:
Cash or the amount of Cash (in the bank, investments, and liquid assets) becomes an increasing subject of concern and importance when you are working on a Purchase Home Loan. When this is the case and you are completing the 1003 then this is when you need to be in the Mortgage Detective mode and determine where the Down Payment is coming from – inquiring whether the prospective homebuyers (and borrowers) have sufficient funds to cover the Down Payment and all loan closing costs (if needed). If, while completing the 1003, you are not seeing it in their savings or checking account, some type of investment (preferably a liquid asset), or cash received from the sale of an asset they own (Motorcycle - Harley - Oh Yeah), or sale of their existing Home - then where is it coming from?

The borrowers, in purchasing a home, may be able to get the Home Seller to make some concessions (what we call Seller Contributions) and offer to pay for a percent of the Down Payment and Loan Costs. However, the borrowers usually do have to come up with some funds of their own. Even if you have set them up with a 100% LTV loan there could still (generally) be funds required from the borrowers for loan closing costs. (see Borrower Contributions). However, your borrowers may have a Parent or Grandmother who will provide a nice Gift of Funds. This can be very helpful in paying for the loan costs but is it enough? So we need to ask and be sure our borrowers have what we call - sufficient "Funds to Close."

You should be aware (and look out for) what the Lender requires from the borrower - as "Their Own Funds." What this means is that most (Conforming & Non-Conforming) Lenders want the Borrowers to contribute a certain percent of their own money towards the Down Payment and Loan Costs. Depending on the loan program you are setting them up on this could mean that the borrowers may need to bring to the Closing Table a minimum of 3% - 5% of their own funds. So, check this out and be sure what your Lender requires for that loan program you plan on setting up your borrowers on.

Regarding the area of Cash, once your Loan Processor receives the loan file, on your customers, she then will generally send out a **VOD**. With that said, let's now take a look at some of the more common types of Down Payment and Loan Costs assistance or sources that a borrower may use or be receiving and what Lenders will generally require in terms of Documentation for each:

1. **Borrower's Own Funds:**
   As I mentioned above, for purchase home loans, most Conforming Lenders will expect the borrower to contribute 3 - 5% of their own funds for the loan. As you probably have guessed that's 3 - 5% of the sales price of the subject property. What the Lender will require is proof, in the form of documentation that shows that the borrowers do indeed have those funds. Normally Lenders like to see that the borrowers had those funds available for the last 90 days (seasoned funds). Thus, those funds will usually be shown on:

   - Last 3 months Bank Statements

   - Stock Certificates or Investments (that could be sold & are Liquid Assets)

2. **Cash Received from Sale of their Home:**
   - Copy of the Closing Disclosure of the Home Sold.

   - Statement or Transcript from their Bank of where those funds were deposited: Showing those funds were deposited and are available (to the borrowers) there.

3. **Gift Funds:**
   As I mentioned above, when talking about Purchase Loans, Gift Funds allow the buyer (your borrower) to obtain Gift Funds from a relative, close friend, and sometimes an employer - to be applied towards their down payment and closing costs. There is usually a maximum amount that can be Gifted (e.g. 3% of the sales price) and applied to the Loan Costs. When it comes to Gift Funds - Lenders like to see what we call an Audit Trail. This is sometimes referred to as a Paper Trail - showing where the Gift Funds are coming from and where they are going. With Gift Funds you will generally need:

   - A letter from the Gifting Person stating that they intend to give a certain amount of Gift funds to your borrowers and that they do not expect repayment of this Gifted amount. Of course, that's because it's a Gift and not a loan.

- Bank Statement (or other funds source) from the person gifting the funds, showing that they have had and have the funds available to Gift to your borrowers.

- Bank Statement showing Funds were taken out or withdrawn from the Bank Account above – from the person providing those Gift funds.

- Bank Statement showing that those Gift funds were deposited into your borrower's bank account.

This can be quite tedious sometimes but be aware that most Conforming Lenders are not very flexible when it comes to Gift Funds or other sources of funds outside of the borrower's own funds that will be applied towards the Total Loan Costs. Lenders will want to see documentation showing where those funds are coming from and where they are going or have gone. As I said above, this is referred to as the Audit Trail of those funds. See Borrower Contribution for more information.

4. **Liquidation of Investments (Stocks, IRA, and Keogh Accounts):**
Here the borrower is selling their interest in an investment to obtain funds for their loan. Just as we discussed with Gift Funds above we will need to show an Audit Trail of where those funds are coming from and where they went and are now located. So you will need:

- Copy of Statement showing Ownership of the Stock and its current worth.

- Statement showing Stock(s) were sold for a certain sum amount.

- Bank Statement showing that the funds, from the sale of that investment, were deposited into your borrower's bank account.

5. **Selling an Asset:**
Here your borrowers may own an Asset (be it a Motorcycle, antique, or whatever) and plan to sell that asset prior to loan closing to obtain funds for their loan. Like item # 4 above you will need:

- Document showing ownership of that Asset.

- A document showing the (estimated) value of that Asset (i.e. Blue Book showing the value of that asset).

- Statement showing that the Asset was sold for a certain sum amount (bill of sale).

- Bank Statement showing that the funds from that sale were deposited in your borrower's bank account.

I think you are getting the picture here as to what I mean when I refer to an Audit Trail. Yeah, it's a hassle sometimes but it's what your Conforming Lenders will usually require - so be prepared for this.

6. Seller Contributions:

Sometimes when homebuyers are in their negotiations a home seller they may be able to work out an agreement whereby the Seller will help the Buyers with their home loan costs. Perhaps in this case the Seller has agreed to help out by paying as much as 3 - 6% of the Sales Price of their Property. If this is the case then those costs or amount of funds (Seller Contribution) will be taken out of the total amount of money the Seller receives at Loan Closing or Funding. The Document that will show the Seller's agreement to do this will be on "The Purchase and Sales Agreement" - the contract to sell and purchase the subject property.

Before you start working on a Purchase Loan - make sure you have a copy of this document => The Purchase and Sales Agreement. Otherwise, you most likely don't have a purchase loan here - you have some folks who are looking to be Pre-Qualified for a home loan. Or, your borrowers do not have the sale of that home they are talking about - firmly set into a contract with the Seller. So, get a copy of this before you seriously begin working on a Purchase Home Loan. We will talk more about this within Chapter 15 on The Purchase and Sales Agreement.

In discussing Seller Contributions you should know that different purchase loan programs (and Lenders) offer and allow the Seller to make their Contributions up to a certain maximum percent (e.g. 3-6%). So, you want to be sure to check with your Lender (that you are submitting that loan to) as to what is the maximum percent the Seller can contribute towards the loan costs - for the loan program you are talking about and wish to submit your customers on.

Another influencing factor, as to what the Seller can contribute (the maximum Seller Contribution) is whether that purchase home loan is for a primary residence or an investment property. The flip-side of any type of the Seller Contribution, for a purchase loan, is what is required of the borrower on that loan. To see what is currently required of home purchasers – please see Borrower Contribution.

III. Credit:

When I have trained mortgage loan originators in the past, I have tried to indelibly imprint in their minds the numbers = 2,2,2, & 2. The reason I do that is because - for most Qualifying items of importance on your borrowers (employment and residence) most lenders are looking at what has happened in the LAST 2 YEARS. And, when reviewing the Credit History of a prospective borrower it is no different. Lenders look very closely at what is shown on the Credit Report within the last 2 years. With this in mind let's go over some of the more common things we might encounter here and need to know:

1. Credit Scores:

As I may have previously mentioned, the "Art" of reading a Credit Report is all but lost - to now focusing mainly on the Credit Score of the borrowers. And when I say Credit Score I am generally referring to the middle of the three credit scores (of the primary income-earning Borrower on that loan) you will find on a 3-bureau Credit Report. What is oftentimes referred to as a Tri-Merge.

Within different types of loan programs (e.g. Conforming, Non-Conforming, and Sub-prime) and for different types of loan programs, in each of the above categories (e.g. Conforming), different Lenders require different minimum (middle) Credit Scores in order to be (credit) qualified for a loan. If your borrower doesn't have that minimum (middle) credit score (it is lower than the lender requires) they won't even look at it. The exception to this is when you are submitting your Conforming loan via DU and/or LP Underwriting (as we discussed in the last chapter on Loan Underwriting). So, the Credit Score of your borrower is one of the very first hurdles that your customer needs to get over and what Lenders use to "filter" what loans they will receive loan submissions on. This is one of the most important areas you will first want to concentrate on and get comfortable with - Credit Scoring of your Borrowers.

It used to be that Conforming Lenders required the Middle Credit Score to be no lower than 680. This changed over the last few years. Today I am seeing a lot of conforming lenders wanting to see a minimum credit score of at least 700. But, the important point here is: Be aware of this fact and try to stay on top of those changes and checkout the Rate Sheet of your targeted Lender or contact them to see what they will accept.

We will talk more about this and the Credit Report when we get to the chapter on Reading the Credit Report.

2. Late Payments Shown on the Credit Report:
If your borrowers have some late payments shown on the Credit Report, within the past 2 years, then the Lender will be very interested as to why those lates occurred - especially if it was a late mortgage payment. Many Conforming Lenders will ask for a letter of explanation from your borrowers as to why those lates occurred. What they really want to hear is that those lates were a one-time, unforeseen thing, and will not happen again. Medical reasons could be an example of this.

3. Bankruptcy:
Bankruptcy is often referred to as a BK and written as such. It used to be that if a borrower had a Bankruptcy within the past 7 years then the Lender would want to see a copy of the Full Bankruptcy Papers. However, if the Bankruptcy (e.g. Chapter 7) was discharged 3 or more years ago I am increasingly seeing that Lenders today are not knee-jerking and asking for this as often. However, if you pull a Credit Report and see that there are creditor accounts and/or charge-offs showing up on the Credit Report that were included in a Bankruptcy - then you can be pretty sure that the Lender will want to get a copy of those Bankruptcy Papers to be sure that those accounts were indeed included in that BK.

When a borrower has had a Bankruptcy then Conforming Lenders like (and generally require) the borrower to have re-established their credit and have at least 3 current and outstanding creditor accounts that they have been paying on for at least a year now. And, the Lenders definitely do not want to see any lates (late payments) since the Bankruptcy.

Depending on the Lender and when the Bankruptcy took place and was discharged a letter of explanation from the borrower may be required - explaining the circumstances causing the Bankruptcy. Again, just as I mentioned above, regarding customer's explanations for late payments, what Lenders really want to hear is: That their Bankruptcy was caused by a one-time, unforeseen thing, and will not happen again. Again, medical reasons could be an example of this.

4. **Foreclosure - Home:**
Conforming Lenders want to see a Home Foreclosure at least 3 years out. With a history of Home Foreclosure you can expect that the Lender will ask for a letter of explanation from that borrower as to why this occurred (much like Bankruptcy discussed above). However, you should know that with some Lenders a Home Foreclosure is like the "kiss of death:" They would not do a loan with a customer who has had a Home Foreclosure - no matter what the reason. So, if your customer has had a Home Foreclosure then make sure you check this one out with the Lender who you may want to submit their loan to, and see if this is the case with that Lender.

5. **Tax Liens - on the Subject Property:**
Some Lenders will allow an outstanding Tax Lien or Property Taxes, that are past due, to be paid off (and made current) within their Refinance Loan (e.g. Cash-Out Refinance). Other Lenders will not allow this and will require the borrower to bring those past due taxes current before a refinance loan will be closed and funded. Here again, you need to check it out with your targeted Lender (the lender you wish to submit your loan to).

6. **No Credit History:**
This can happen sometimes when a young couple calls you and say they want to be Pre-Qualified to buy a home. Employment looks good and they make enough income but guess what - they don't have any Credit to speak of! Are you "dead in the water?" Not really. As I explained, in the section on Qualifying Your Borrowers, there is another way of measuring credit and that is called the Non-Traditional means of Credit. Because those customers have probably been renting, paying electric and heating bills, perhaps some medical bills, you have a means of measuring their credit that is available to you. By using Non-Traditional Credit, you (or the Loan Processor) could contact those utility companies, individuals leasing the property or apartment manager, and a doctor, to determine and verify (document) if your borrowers have been paying their monthly bills on time and as agreed. If they have been paying their monthly bills on time and there are four references you can obtain verifications on, and you have a 12-month payment history on each, then this could very well satisfy any Lender's concerns and requirements about their credit.

For 2019 and 2020, what I saw was that Non-traditional credit could be used for most General Account type of loans. However, if you are working on a Purchase Fannie Mae Conforming loan and all borrowers on that loan are relying solely on Non-Traditional Credit to qualify for that loan, then today those borrowers will need to complete the Pre-purchase Homebuyer Education and Counseling. For more information on using Non-traditional credit please refer to requirements for Non-traditional credit.

However, when you get into High-Balance or High-Cost Loans then your borrower will need to have credit scores from a currently ordered credit report.

7. **Outstanding Judgments:**
   If there is an actual outstanding judgment that is showing up on your customer's Credit Report then it is highly probable that a Conforming lender may require that that Judgment either be settled prior to loan closing or may allow your customer to pay this off with (cash-out) funds from that refinance home loan. Either way, that Judgment will most likely need to be settled and paid off. Here again, you need to check this out with your targeted Lender to see what their requirements are.

IV. Current and Past Residence:

In completing the 1003, on your prospective borrowers, you will need to find out where your customers have lived in the past two years. If your customers have lived in their current residence for the past 2-3 years then this can be quite simple. However, if they have moved around a lot and lived in 6 different residences, within the past two years, then you will need to list every one of those places they lived at in the past two years.

So let's take a look at what (documents) we need in this area.

1. **Own Their Home:**
   Here the customers have owned their home and make monthly mortgage payments either to their current mortgage servicer or an escrow company.

   - Copy of mortgage payment coupon.
   - Copy of Escrow Statement or Name & Telephone No.# of Escrow Company
   - Copy of Note - they signed at their home loan closing (Optional)
   - Copy of the Declaration Page of their homeowner's hazard insurance policy
   - Name & Telephone Number of their homeowner's insurance agent

Some of the information above can be used by your Loan Processor to send out a **VOM -** if needed.

2. Rented in the Past Two Years:

Here your customers are currently renting or have rented or leased an apartment or home in the last 2 years:

- Name, Address, and Telephone No.# of Landlord(s) and/or Apt. Manager(s) for the past 2 years.

- Rental/Lease Agreement signed (this is not required very often).

Some of the information above can be used by your Loan Processor to send out a **VOR** - if needed.

V. Liabilities:

Within the Assets and Liabilities Section of the 1003 (specifically the area of Liabilities) you will list all of your customer's current liabilities, including their existing mortgage.

- Mortgage Statement: Showing the O/S balance on their mortgage (If they own a home).

- Recent Credit Card statements (that will be paid off with this loan)

- Any Statements showing current outstanding balances on those accounts that will also be paid off with this loan.

- Statement showing any Judgments and/or Collection accounts showing up on the Credit Report that shows that those Judgments and/or Collections have been paid and/or are now satisfied.

In closing, on this discussion of Qualifying Documentation, let me say that as a mortgage loan originator it is your responsibility to review all documents you have asked for, ordered, and received regarding your home loan file. And, it is always wise to do this as soon as you get them. I have seen too many times when a mortgage loan originator didn't review a certain document received, on a loan file they were working on, only to find out near closing time that there was a problem with that loan - a problem that was clearly shown on one of those documents. That problem could be a loan killer or something that might take some time to resolve. When you are preparing to close a loan the next day, for example, it doesn't give you much time to react to problems (that should have been addressed sooner - when you could have).

An example of this could be that during your meeting with your customers they told you that their Gross Monthly Income was $3,000. You entered that on their 1003. And, at that meeting you asked your customers for a current Paystub (covering a 30-day period) and for the last 2 years of W2's. A few days later you receive those and look them over. You discover that the Borrower's Gross Monthly Income is actually only $2,700! The last two years of W2's also seem to confirm this. Do we have a problem here? Perhaps. Recalculating the Housing & Total Debt Ratios may indicate this. But that's a $300 a month difference! I would call my customer up right then and (gently) try to find out what's happening here. Maybe there's some income here he forgot to tell you about. My

Point here is: Be sure to review all documents you receive on your loan file as soon as you get them.

That pretty much covers the important stuff you need to be aware of and obtain or ask for when you first meet with your customers. If your customers are meeting you in your office then ask them to bring those items you know (at that time) you will need. This will help you to "package" the loan file a lot quicker and reduce the number of documents you might later request from your borrowers.

I believe you are starting to get the general idea here as far as loan document needs are concerned. When you first meet with your customers and you are completing the 1003 you should be in your Mortgage Detective Mode. You are like the television detective Columbo, asking questions and sometimes trying to make sense of the information you are getting. As you go through and complete the 1003 some of the answers your customers tell you should cause your ears to peak up (like Spock in the Star Trek movies) reminding you to not forget to ask your customers if they have that particular document - that relates to that subject of inquiry. Or, during the meeting, your customers tell you something, and because of that you now know that you need to inform them of a required procedure that needs to be followed. An example of this could be your customers are purchasing a home and they tell you that they are expecting a relative to provide Gift Funds to help them with their loan costs. Most folks out there don't know much or anything about what we have discussed regarding the Audit Trail of Gift Funds. You will want to inform them of this so that they can properly and timely provide you with all the documents you need here - to move that loan along quickly and without delay.

And finally, as you know, the COVID-19 pandemic has currently affected how many businesses, and our society as a whole, should conduct themselves. The mortgage lending business has also been affected by this pandemic. So, I thought I'd list some of those changes that are currently taking place.

COVID-19 Pandemic: Impact on the (American) Mortgage Market:
The COVID-19 Pandemic has adversely affected virtually all areas of American life: Our businesses and society as well. Below is a list of some of the effects of the COVID-19 pandemic on our mortgage lending business during 2020 – that will most likely continue into 2021.

- **Mortgage Interest Rates:**
  Prior to the pandemic, mortgage interest rates were already historically low. In order to influence and maintain strong home loan buyer demand the Federal Reserve appears to continue to maintain mortgage interest rates at a low level. However, I should mention (as we all know), that should the economy and unemployment rates improve then the mortgage interest rates would, no doubt, increase as well.

- **Increased Mortgage Forbearance Requests:**
  Concurrently, with businesses (temporarily) locking down and closing and affected people losing their jobs and income sources, caused by the pandemic, those and

many folks are having problems paying their monthly bills. As a result of this the national mortgage forbearance requests are currently at about 8%: That translates into over 4.0 million U.S. homes.

- **Mortgage Loan Origination, Processing, and Underwriting Standards**:
  As a result of the pandemic and in order to reduce their risk exposure, some banks and mortgage companies, across our great nation, have tightened and changed some of their loan origination, processing, and underwriting requirements by implementing the following:

  - Are now requiring Income and Employment Verification documents being closer to the date of home loan closing than previously. Many Lenders now may require updated documents, from borrowers, just before their home loan closing.

  - Discontinued certain home loan products that they previously offered (e.g. Non-conforming and Jumbo home loans).

  - Raised the Down Payment for Jumbo home loans.

  - Raised their minimum FICO score requirements and lowered the acceptable LTV ratios for certain home loan products.

  - No longer accept applications for Home Equity Lines of Credit.

  - Where permissible and possible, Lenders are increasingly utilizing Automatic Valuations, Desktop Appraisals, and Exterior Updates. For refinance home loans, Lenders are increasingly using Drive-by, Desktop, and Exterior Only Appraisals, and

  - Reduced the currently required time-period for those documents and processes affected by the 3-Day Right of Rescission (This is allowed for all Lenders).

Hopefully, these loan processing changes, listed above, for some banks and mortgage companies, will only be temporary, while the COVID-19 pandemic continues to be a major concern for our country.

- **Fannie Mae & Freddy Mac's FAQs :**
  Fannie Mae and Freddy Mac have also been observing and responding to the COVID-19 national emergency. Both Fannie Mae and Freddie Mac have provided temporary guidance to lenders on several policy areas to support mortgage originations. As a result, they have prepared a document titled "*COVID-19 Frequently Asked Questions – Selling*" that provides answers to frequently asked questions on any temporary policies during the COVID-19 pandemic period. This document, in PDF format, is at:
  https://singlefamily.fanniemae.com/media/22326/display.

Questions on various origination and processing areas are addressed, within this document, such as:

- Underwriting
- Income – Self-Employed
- Income – Variable
- Employment
- Desktop Underwriter® (DU®) Validation Service
- Temporary Purchase and Refinance Eligibility
- Appraisals
- Power of Attorney (POA
- Notarization
- Closing and Title
- Quality Control
- Selling Loans in Forbearance

In reviewing this FAQ document I did have a question that was addressed and answered:

> **Question:** Do Fannie Mae's existing disaster policies in the *Selling Guide* apply to the COVID-19 pandemic?
>
> **Answer:** No, Fannie Mae's existing policies related to disasters do not apply to loans impacted by COVID-19. Instead, lenders can follow the guidance in *Lender Letters* LL-2020-03, Impact of COVID-19 on Originations and LL-2020-04, © 2020 Fannie Mae dated November 30, 2020.

Also, Fannie Mae and Freddy Mac will be adding more frequently asked questions to this document, as time goes on, so they encourage you to checkout this document frequently for updates.

Having finished the previous chapters on qualifying your home loan borrowers, loan underwriting, and the proper documentation of your prospective home loan borrower's loan let's now move on to the next chapter that discusses the topics that everybody within mortgage lending industry has been and is talking about: The Ability-to-Repay and Qualified Mortgage Rules.

Chapter 6

ABILITY-TO-REPAY
&
QUALIFIED MORTGAGE RULES

Since the mortgage crash and crisis of 2008 and with the passing of the Dodd-Frank Wall Street Reform and Consumer Protection Act of 2010 the Consumer Financial Protection Bureau (CFPB) has been very busy with its mortgage lending rule-making and enforcement responsibilities. During the latter part of 2012 up to 2014 I gave seminars on fair lending laws to bankers and mortgage loan originators. And, during those presentations, I often spoke about two terms that seemed to come up quite often when I was reading the latest editorial about what is and will be happening in the mortgage lending market: The Ability-to-Repay and Qualified Mortgages Rules. Some respected financial analysts stated that the implementation of these two areas (ATR & QM rules) would change the entire landscape of the mortgage lending market. That seemed like a profound statement to me and perhaps an extreme envision of the mortgage market. Yes, things have changed within the mortgage market: There are less conventional (Fannie Mae loan products); and Lenders have tightened-up their qualifying standards in anticipation of and following the implemented ATR and QM Rules in early January, 2014.

But, you know what? The Ability-to-Repay is nothing new and has been and is written within the Truth-In-Lending Act (Regulation Z). However, today, the consequences for not following the Ability-to-Repay rule, as amended in TILA by the CFPB, can be quite severe - not only to mortgage lenders but also to originating mortgage loan originators. So, having said that, I thought it just would not be appropriate to update this mortgage loan originator's manual and handbook, without having a chapter specifically addressing these two items. So, let's get started.

First, let me say that when I first heard about the Ability-to-Repay Rule and what a Qualified Mortgage will be it always sounded like these were two separate subjects to be considered. However, although these two subjects are separate - they are inter-connected. And that's why today you see the written acronym ATR/QM Rule. Or, sometimes they just refer to it as the "Rule". For example, if a Qualified Mortgage, and its QM requirements, is ever questioned or rebutted - but it can be demonstrated that mortgage loan (and mortgage loan originator) satisfied the Ability-to Repay Rule requirements then that should provide a safe harbor for the originating Lender and/or mortgage loan originator. I also would like to mention that the ATR/QM Rule generally applies to fixed-rate loans (closed-end) mortgage loans for mortgage loan applications after January 10, 2014.

Now, in presenting this chapter on the ATR/QM Rule I first would like to discuss in detail the Ability-to-Repay & Qualified Mortgage Rules and then finish off this discussion with the subject of the Government Sponsored Enterprises Patch (GSE Patch.

So, to begin here, I will discuss each part of the ATR/QM Rule, but discuss each one separately:

- Ability-to-Repay Rule
- Qualified Mortgage Rule

Ability-to-Repay Rules:
First, let me say here that according to the CFPB the ATR/QM Rule applies to almost all closed-end consumer credit transactions that are secured by a dwelling – including any real property attached to the dwelling such as 1-4 units, condominiums, and co-ops. And, unlike some other mortgage types, the ATR/QM Rule is not limited to 1st liens or to loans on primary residences.

In determining whether a reasonable and good-faith evaluation of a prospective home loan borrower's capacity and ability to repay has been done, the Ability-to-Rule requires that you satisfactorily considered eight ATR underwriting factors:

1. Current and reasonably expected income or assets that the consumer will rely upon in order to qualify and repay their mortgage loan.
2. The borrower's current employment status (if this is needed to qualify for their mortgage loan).
3. Their new monthly mortgage payment.
4. The new monthly mortgage payment, which may include any simultaneous loans on the same subject property.
5. Consideration of the borrower's new PITI and any assessments.
6. The borrower's debts that they pay and are responsible for (e.g. Alimony, child support, etc.).
7. The home loan borrower's monthly DTI that considers all of their mortgage and non-mortgage obligations – as a ratio of their gross monthly income.
8. That the home loan borrower's credit history is fully considered.

You could, of course, consider other additional factors, regarding a home loan borrower, but the Ability-to-Repay Rule requires that you at least consider the above eight factors.

Now, when you look at these eight ATR Rule requirements you may be thinking, "Hey, this is nothing new, I always check for these things". If you do, then your thinking is just like mine. However, to not consider any one of these factors and not have documentation, within that loan file, that shows that you did consider these factors could result in a mortgage loan being classified as a non-qualified mortgage. However, if you always consider the above eight underwriting qualifying ATR Rule factors and properly document your evaluation of each factor (as we discussed within Chapter 6) then you should not have any problems regarding this Rule with any of your mortgage loans.

One important question you should always ask yourself, after going through this process and prior to submitting a home loan to a Lender is: If this home loan borrower (of that home loan file) defaulted on their home loan shortly after consummation or whether the ATR Rule was fully satisfied for all 8 factors, have I properly and fully documented that home loan file to show and prove that all 8 factors were considered in qualifying that borrower?

You can't foresee the future (home loan borrower subsequently losses their job after their home loan closing) but you are responsible, as a mortgage loan originator, to ensure that home loan borrowers qualify for their home loans according to the ATR Rule (at the time you are qualifying them for their home loan).

And, if you are submitting your mortgage loans via DU then whether your loan is approved or not does not determined if that loan satisfied the ATR Rule. Satisfaction of the ATR Rule is based upon whether the originating MLO fully satisfied all the 8 factors listed above for a home mortgage loan. Remember that 'ole adage: Garage In – Garage Out (GIGO).

OK, enough preface about this, let's get into

The Ability-to-Repay Rules:

I. Type of Home Loan:

In considering the above listed 8 factors, of the ATR Rule, the type of home loan product is also important in calculating a home loan borrower's monthly P&I mortgage payment. For example, the following are some important things you should be aware of when doing this:

- **For an ARM loans:**
  The calculated borrower's P&I monthly mortgage payment should be based upon the home loan's introductory or _fully-indexed interest rate, whichever is higher, and monthly, fully-amortizing payments that are substantially equal.

  And, using a fully-amortizing schedule, with the maximum interest rate permitted during the first 5 years after the date of the first periodic payment.

- **For Balloon Home Loans:**
  The calculation of the monthly P&I mortgage payment is determined by whether the home loan is a Higher-priced loan or what they refer to as Non-higher priced home loans. Higher-Priced home loans are those having an APR, as of the date that loan's interest rate is set, that exceeds the Average Prime Offer Rate (APOR) by 1.5% or more for 1st Lien loans. However, for subordinate mortgage loans (e.g. 2nd mortgages) that loan's APR exceeds the Average Prime Offer Rate (APOR) by

3.5% or more. You can check the weekly published Average Prime Offer Rate at: https://www.ffiec.gov/ratespread. OK, to calculate the monthly

P&I mortgage payment for each of these two types of mortgage loans you do the following:

- **Non-Higher Priced Balloon Loans:**
  Use the maximum payment scheduled during the first five years after the first regular periodic payment comes due.
- **Higher-Priced Balloon Loans:**
  Use the maximum payment in the payment schedule, including any balloon payment.

- **For Interest-Only Loans:**
  Use the greater of the fully-indexed or introductory interest rate and equal, monthly payments of P&I that will repay the outstanding home loan on the date the loan recasts over the remaining term of that home loan.

- **Home Loans with Negative-Amortization:**
  First, you calculate the maximum loan amount that will include the potential added principal that assumes that the borrower makes the minimum required payments until the date that loan recasts. Then use the greater of the fully-indexed or introductory interest rate and equal, monthly payments of P&I that will repay that maximum loan amount on the date the loan recast over the remaining term of that home loan.

- **Home Loan paid Quarterly or Annually:**
  These types of mortgage payments need to be converted into monthly payments and no two monthly payments should vary by more than 1%.

- **Simultaneous Home Loans:**
  Simultaneous home loans need to be considered regardless of whether you are closing that loan or not. If you are aware that a simultaneous loan will occur for your home loan borrower then the required payment for that loan needs to be considered in that borrower's DTI. However, if a simultaneous home loan is a HELOC then:
  - **Simultaneous HELOC:**
    Your ATR assessment should include that HELOC loan's monthly payment based on the amount of credit to be drawn down at or before the consummation of the main (1st mortgage) loan.

II. Borrower's DTI Considerations:

First, I would like to mention that the CFPB requires Lenders to follow a list of technical requirements known as Appendix Q - for how they document a mortgage applicant's income and liabilities. Those guidelines are a key factor in calculating a borrower's Debt-to-Income ratio. Secondly, Effective Income may only be used in calculating the home loan borrower's Debt-to-Income ratio if it comes from a source that can be verified, is stable, or will continue. Okay, having said that, let's begin here.

- **Recurrent Monthly Debts:**
  Your ATR Rule assessment should also consider the following typical recurring monthly debts such as:
  - Student Loans
  - Auto Loans
  - Revolving Debt
  - Existing mortgages that are not being paid off at or before consummation of the borrower's home loan.

  Although the ATR Rule doesn't seem to address the use of the "10-Month Rule" I would suggest being very careful if you do use this. Before you do, you should carefully consider the borrower's credit history and how much money they will have left over after they make all of their monthly debt payments. In other words, the home loan borrower's monthly residual income.

- **Future Income:**
  If you can properly document that a home loan borrower will be receiving a certain income amount (within the near future) then that amount may be considered in qualifying him or her for their home loan. Of course, what their current DTI will be prior to that income increase needs to be consider – along with any other borrower qualifying factors you need to consider. Although the ATR Rule does not seem to specifically address Trailing Spouses, I believe that this could be consider here as well – if you are able to get the proper documents to verify that future income source.

- **Non-Traditional Credit:**
  The ATR Rule does allow you to use Non-Traditional Credit if you find that the prospective home loan borrower has not developed any traditional credit at the time of their home loan application.

Having discussed the Ability-to-Repay Rule let's now go on and discuss the rules regarding Qualified Mortgages.

Qualified Mortgage Rules:
To begin here, let's first define what a Qualified Mortgage is. According to the CFPB a Qualified Mortgage is one that (the originating MLO) has complied with the ATR requirements for that type of mortgage. And, the protection afforded you is based on what type of Qualified Mortgage you originated. So, let's then start with the types of Qualified Mortgages:

I. Types of Qualified Mortgages:

There are four types of Qualified Mortgages and the type of Creditor can determine what types of Qualified Mortgages a Creditor may originate. First, I'll briefly list the four types of Qualified Mortgages and then below I'll define each:

1. General Qualified Mortgage,

2. Temporary Qualified Mortgage:
   These two types of Qualified Mortgages can be originated by all types of Creditors.

3. Small Creditor Qualified Mortgage, and

4. Balloon-Payment Qualified Mortgage:

These last two types of Qualified Mortgages can only be originated by Small Creditors. I'll define what Small Creditors are in a moment.

However, the following requirements apply to each one of the four listed Qualified Mortgages above:

- Interest Only Payments and Negative Amortization are not allowed.

- Mortgage loan Terms can be no longer than 30 years.

- Limitation on Points and Fees. The threshold is generally 3.0% of the loan balance. However, larger amounts are allowed when the total loan amount is less than $100,000. For example, total loan amounts of:
    - ➤ $60,000 - $99,999: Total fees can be up to $3,000.
    - ➤ $20,000 - $59,999: Total fees can be 5% of the total loan amount.
    - ➤ $12,500 - $19,999: Total fees can be up to $1,000.
    - ➤ $12,499 or less: Total fees can be up to 8% of the total loan amount.

Let's now talk about the compliance protection afforded you for a Qualified Mortgage.

II. Types of Compliance Protection:

According to the CFPB the type of presumption of compliance (ATR Rule) for a Qualified Mortgage depends on whether or not it is a Higher-Priced Qualified Mortgage. In other words, a court will treat a case differently depending upon whether a Qualified Mortgage is a higher-priced QM or not. For example:

- **Not Higher-Priced Qualified Mortgages:**
  If a mortgage loan is not Higher-priced and satisfies the QM criteria (which I will go into more detail in a moment) then a court will conclusively presume that, in originating that mortgage loan, you complied with the ATR Rule. Thus, if a Qualified Mortgage in not Higher-priced then this affords you a Safe Harbor – which means that the court will conclusively presume that you complied with the ATR requirements in originating that mortgage loan. I think you can begin to see what I meant by the interconnectedness of the ATR and Qualified Mortgage Rules (ATR/QM Rules).

- **Higher-Priced Qualified Mortgages:**
  However, if a Qualified Mortgage is Higher-priced then it falls under what the CFPB refers to as a Rebuttable Presumption. Rebuttable Presumption means that if you originated a Higher-Priced Qualified Mortgage then the court will allow a consumer to argue that you may have violated the ATR Rule in some manner. However, for that consumer to win their case they must conclusively show, that based on the information that was available to you when their mortgage loan was made, that they did not have enough residual income left, within their monthly budget, to meet their living expenses after paying their monthly mortgage payment and their other debts.

  This ties in with what I mentioned above about being cautious about using the "10-Month Rule".

In considering both types of compliance protection, the CFPB states that the Rebuttable Presumption provides more legal protection and certainty to you than the general ATR requirements, but less protection and certainty than the Safe Harbor.

I should mention here, as I may have previously mentioned, that mortgage companies that I have worked for in the past all had a loan origination policy of not doing any Section 32 – higher-priced mortgage loans. That was fine with me and, quite frankly today, for me, I somehow prefer to be protected under the Safe Harbor status rather than the Rebuttable Presumption status.

Before finishing this Section I should also mention that the CFPB does have exceptions to either of these two types of Qualified Mortgages. Examples of those are any extensions of credit made by the following organizations:

- U.S. Department of the Treasury as Community Development Financial Institutions
- Creditor designated as exempt by HUD as either the Community Housing Development Organization or a Down-payment Assistance Provider of Secondary Financing.
- Creditors designated as non-profit organizations as stated under section 501(c)(3) of the Internal Code of 1986.
- Extensions of credit made by housing finance agencies made directly to consumers. And,
- Extensions of credit made pursuant to an Emergency Economic Stabilization Act program.

And, because these home loan financings are exempt the ATR requirements do not apply to these types of loans. Additionally (and this ties in with what I discussed above), consumers who obtained a loan that is exempt from the ATR requirements would have no ability-to-repay claim under the ATR/QM Rule.

III. Types of Qualified Mortgages Defined:

Previously I listed the four types of Qualified Mortgages. Now, I would like to go into a little more detail regarding each one of those.

1. **General Qualified Mortgage:**

    Quite simply, General Qualified Mortgages may not have interest-only loan features, negative amortization, balloon-payment features, and Terms that exceed 30 years. They also may not have total points and fees that exceed what I listed above for the various total loan amounts.

    Additionally, the creditor, of the General Qualified Mortgage must have:

    - Underwritten that mortgage loan using a fully-amortizing schedule and used the maximum interest rate permitted during the first 5 years after the date of the first periodic payment (for ARM mortgage loans).

    - Qualified that mortgage loan according to the ATR Rule (that I discussed previously within the ATR Rule section above).

    - Determined that the home loan borrower's total monthly DTI is not greater than 43%.

2. **Temporary Qualified Mortgage:**

    The term 'Temporary Qualified Mortgage' refers to time periods, of Qualified Mortgages, that are eligible for purchase or guarantee by the GSEs, certain agencies in order to be considered, as well as extend the Qualified Mortgage loan status. I won't go into detail regarding this aspect of Temporary Qualified Mortgages because this information is primarily for mortgage lenders and creditors. However, if you are interested in researching this information then please refer to CFPB's website at: http://www.consumerfinance.gov/regulations/

    Now, as far as originating Temporary Qualified Mortgages goes, their underwriting guidelines are very much like those required for General Qualified Mortgages (no interest-only loan features, negative amortization, balloon-payment features, and Terms that exceed 30 years). And, they also may not have total points and fees that exceed what I listed above for the various total loan amounts. However, Temporary Qualified Mortgages do not have to meet the 43% DTI ratio requirement that applies to General Qualified Mortgages. This is true as long as the mortgage loan is still eligible to be purchased or guaranteed by either of the GSEs.

3. **Small Creditor Qualified Mortgage:**

    According to the CFPB, the requirements for Small Creditor Qualified Mortgages are the following:

    - Small Creditor Qualified Mortgages are not allowed to have interest-only features, negative amortization, and must comply with the maximum points and fee limits listed above for Qualified Mortgages.

    - The Term of this type of QM cannot exceed 30 years.

- This QM must not be subject to a Forward Commitment. A forward commitment is a written agreement by a Lender to advance a loan on a future date at a specified interest rate.

- Must qualify the home loan customer using the ATR Rules.

- You must also consider (but apparently not rigidly adhere to) the home loan borrower's DTI or their residual income. Although the Rule sets no specific threshold for DTI or residual income for this type of Qualified Mortgage.

- I would also like to mention that (although this too is lender and creditor information) any Balloon-Payment Qualified Mortgages that are sold or otherwise transferred prior than 3 years after their consummation will lose their Qualified Mortgage status. The exception to this (minimum 3-year period) is if that Balloon-Payment Qualified Mortgage is transferred as part of a merger or acquisition of or by the creditor.

4. **Balloon-Payment Qualified Mortgage**:
   As I mentioned above, only Small Creditors are allowed to originate Balloon-Payment Qualified Mortgages. The requirements for origination of these types of Qualified Mortgages are:

   - These types of QMs are not allowed to have interest-only features, negative amortization, and must comply with the maximum points and fee limits listed above for Qualified Mortgages.

   - This Balloon-Payment Qualified Mortgage must have a fixed interest rate and periodic payments that would fully amortize that loan over a Term of 30 years or less (this excludes the balloon payment).

   - This QM must have a Term of at least 5 years prior to the balloon payment.

   - This QM must not be subject to a Forward Commitment.

   - The originating MLO must qualify the home loan borrower's ATR for the schedule periodic payments up to the balloon payment.

   - Must qualify the home loan customer using the ATR Rules.

   - You must also consider (but apparently not rigidly adhere to) the home loan borrower's DTI or their residual income. Although the Rule sets no specific threshold for DTI or residual income for this type of Qualified Mortgage.

   - And, as I mentioned above, that (although this too is lender and creditor information) any Balloon-Payment Qualified Mortgages that are sold or otherwise transferred prior than 3 years after their consummation will lose their Qualified Mortgage status. The exception to this (minimum 3-year period) is if that Balloon-Payment Qualified Mortgage is transferred as part of a merger or acquisition of or by the creditor.

IV. Small Creditors Defined:

Since I have talked about Small Creditors and what Qualified Mortgages they are able to originate I'd now like to define what a Small Creditor is according to the CFPB:

- That lending organization (the Small Creditor) must have Assets no greater than $2 billion at the end of the last calendar year. That amount can be adjusted annually for inflation by the CFPB.

  And, according to the CFPB, this Asset size limitation considers only the Assets of the main lending organization and not the Assets of any of its affiliates (if it does have affiliates).

- The main lending organization and its affiliates (combined) originated no more than 500 first-lien, closed-end residential mortgages that were subject to the ATR requirements in the preceding calendar year.

  Now, in counting the total of mortgages, as stated above, do not include in that count the following types of mortgage loans:

  - Subordinate-Lien mortgages
  - Any mortgages that are not subject to the ATR/QM Rule:
    - HELOCs
    - Time-share plans
    - Reverse Mortgages
    - Temporary or Bridge loans with Terms of 12 months or less

V. Debt-to-Income (DTI) Ratio Requirements:

As you read above, not all Qualified Mortgage need to rigidly adhere to the DTI rule of not exceeding 43%. However, you do know that this DTI rule (of 43%) does apply to General Qualified Mortgages. Therefore, because of this you do need to be aware that different DTI rules apply to loans complying with the ATR standard and to the other Qualified Mortgages. For example:

- To satisfy the general ATR standard you must not only consider the home loan borrower's DTI but also their residual income.

- To originate a Qualified Mortgage under the Temporary definition you must meet the relevant entity's applicable DTI and other requirements. An example of this could be the eligibility for sale or guarantee by a GSE or insured or guaranteed by a specified federal agency. Thus, if you are going to originate any one of these then you should research that organization's DTI and other underwriting requirements.

- When originating a Small Creditor or Balloon-Payment Qualified Mortgage you must consider not only the borrower's DTI but also their residual income. But get this: The CFPB provides no specific threshold requirements for these types of loans. Therefore, when originating either one of these loans I suggest being very conservative in determining if the prospective borrower has adequate monthly residual income left over after paying their mortgage payment(s) and other debts.

VI. Points and Fees Cap for Qualified Mortgages:

For a loan to be classified as a Qualified Mortgage the Points and Fees must not exceed the maximum points and fees for that type of loan. As previously presented, if the loan amount is equal to or greater than $100,000 then the maximum points and fees can be no greater than 3%. However, as you previously saw, as a loan's total amount gets lower than $100,000 then the maximum points and fees are increased as well. To repeat, total loan amounts of:

- ➢ $60,000 - $99,999: Total fees can be up to $3,000.
- ➢ $20,000 - $59,999: Total fees can be 5% of the total loan amount.
- ➢ $12,500 - $19,999: Total fees can be up to $1,000.
- ➢ $12,499 or less: Total fees can be up to 8% of the total loan amount.

Okay, once you have identified what the maximum points and fees will be for a particular Qualified Mortgage then the next question you might ask is, "What loan costs do I need to include in that maximum loan amount?" That's a very good question and the only way I know how to answer that is to give you CFPB's cryptic and complex answer and then try to simplify it for you. First, let me give you CFPB response to that question:

"To calculate points and fees for the Qualified Mortgage points and fees you would use the same approach that you use for calculating points and fees for closed-end loans under HOEPA thresholds in the CFPB's High-Cost Mortgage and Homeownership Counseling Amendments to the Truth-In-Lending Act (Regulation Z) and Homeownership Counseling Amendments to the RESPA (Regulation X) rulemakings. Those rules are available online at: http://www.consumerfinance.gov/regulations/"

See what I mean? This is the kind of stuff I read all the time. OK, not to worry. Let me simplified it for you here. First, for those of you who have been originating mortgage loans for some time this will not be so much of a challenge. However, for those of you who are just starting out you will perhaps need to read Chapter 6 before this all comes together for you.

First, the CFPB states that unless specified otherwise, you should include those loan amounts and costs that are known at or before consummation of the loan, even if the borrower pays for them after consummation by rolling them into the loan amount. Also, unless specified otherwise, closing costs that you pay and recoup from the home loan borrower over time through the interest rate are not to be counted in this points and fees calculation.

Having said that, include in your calculation of points and fees those amounts paid in connection with the loan transaction for the following 6 categories of charges:

1. **Finance Charges:**
   Within Chapter 12, where I talk about the calculation of a mortgage loan's Annual Percentage Rate (APR), I present what a mortgage loan's Finance Charges are and to be included in calculating the loan's APR. Those Finance Charges are included in your loan's calculated Points and Fees.

   However, and I know you saw this coming, there are exceptions to this. The following you would not include in your Points and Fees calculation:

   - **Interest or the time-price differential.**

   - **Mortgage Insurance Premiums (MIPs):**
     - Federal or state government-sponsored MIPs.
       Here, you would exclude any upfront and annual FHA premiums, VA funding fees, and USDA guarantee fees.

     - Private Mortgage Insurance (PMI) premiums:
       Here, you would exclude any monthly or annual PMI premiums. You can also exclude upfront PMI premiums if that premium is refundable on a prorated basis and a refund is automatically issued upon loan satisfaction (mortgage loan is paid-off). However, and you saw this coming, even if the premium is excludable, you must include any portion that exceeds the upfront MIP for FHA loans.

   - **Bona Fide Third-party Charges:**
     Bona Fide third-party charges that are not retained by the creditor, loan originator, or an affiliate (if there is an affiliate). As presented, within Chapter 12, these are considered Non-Finance charges and are not considered in calculating a loan's APR. Examples of these are:

     Credit Report Fee
     Flood Certification
     Appraisal
     Title Insurance
     Hazard (Property) Insurance
     Property Taxes (paid or impounds for reserves)
     Recording Fees

   - **Bona Fide Discount Points:**
     Okay, now here is another exception. Normally you would include all Discount Points that the borrower pays to get a lower interest rate. But here, the CFPB makes an exception to this. For example:

     - You can exclude up to 2.0 Bona Fide Discount Points if the interest rate, before the discount, does not exceed the APOR for a comparable loan transaction by more than 1 percentage point; or

     - You can exclude up to 1.0 Bona Fide Discount Point if the interest rate, before the discount, does not exceed the APOR for a comparable loan transaction by more than 2 percentage points.

2. **Loan Originator Compensation:**

You would include any compensation that the loan originator received that is or was paid directly or indirectly by a consumer for a mortgage loan – other than an employee of a creditor or of a mortgage broker. For more information on this, please refer to the discussion on Mortgage Loan Originator Compensation.

Included in this amount would be any amounts the creditor has paid to the mortgage broker for the loan transaction.

3. **Real Estate-Related Fees:**

In referring to 'Real Estate-Related Fees' this normally means services such as the costs for the loan closing by a title company, Notary, or Attorney, title insurance, and settlement documents and services. This could also refer to Prior-to-Doc (PTD) property requirements such as pest-infestation or flood-hazard determination, property survey, and similar purpose services and inspections for the subject property.

Some of these services are normally considered as a Finance Charge and considered in calculating the APR of a home loan. However, the CFPB is looking at all of these services and allows you to exclude the costs for these services from your points and fees if and only if:

- The charge for that service is reasonable. Thus, if that service charges a unreasonable fee then it would be included.

- The creditor receives no direct or indirect compensation in connection with that charge, and

- The charge is not paid to an affiliate of the creditor (if they have an affiliate).

Now, if one or more of these three conditions (listed above) is not satisfied then you must include those charges in your points and fees calculation – even if those costs are normally excluded from the Finance Charge. Examples of those that would fall under here would be:

- Fees for Title Examination, Abstract of Title, Title Insurance, Property Survey, and similar purposes (these are normally not considered a Finance Charge).

- Fees for preparing loan-related documents, such as deeds, mortgages, and reconveyance or settlement documents (Again, not normally considered a Finance Charge).

- Notary and credit-report fees.

- Property Appraisal and home inspection fees.

Amounts paid into escrow or trustee accounts that are not otherwise included in the Finance Charge (except amounts held for future payment of taxes).

4. **Premiums for Various Types of Insurances**:
   Include within your calculation of points and fees the premiums paid to these types of insurance policies (other than homeowner's insurance). Examples of these types of insurance are:

   ➢ Credit Insurance

   ➢ Credit Property Insurance

   ➢ Life, Accident, Health or Loss-of-Income Insurance where the creditor is the beneficiary – and not the homeowner. However, if the borrower is the sole beneficiary of this type of insurance policy then you could exclude it from your points and fees calculation. The key question here is: Who benefits from that insurance policy? The creditor or the home loan borrower?

   ➢ And, any Debt Cancellation or Suspension Coverage payments.

   You should include the premiums, for these types of insurances, that are payable at or before consummation of the borrower's loan even if such premiums are rolled into the loan amount (if that is permitted by law). However, you do not need to include these charges if they are paid for after the consummation of the borrower's home loan. For example, if there is no upfront premium required but only monthly premiums are required. However, even though you might not include that 'monthly premium' cost into your calculation of your points and fees – you would certainly include that in that borrower's DTI as a required monthly debt payment.

5. **Maximum Prepayment Penalty**:
   If your home loan customer must pay a prepayment penalty for prepaying their mortgage loan then you would include the maximum prepayment penalty amount that they will need to pay in with your calculation of points and fees.

6. **Prepayment Penalty Paid in a Refinance Mortgage Loan**:
   However, let's say that you are doing a refinance loan for a prospective home loan borrower whose mortgage loan is held by the creditor you work for or an affiliate of the company your work for. Or, either one of these is currently servicing that home loan. In that case you include any penalties you charge that borrower for prepaying their home loan.

VII. Prepayment Penalty:
First, let me say that if you wish to include a prepayment penalty option, within a home loan, then you may only do so for fixed-rate or Step-rate Qualified Mortgages that are not Higher-priced and, of course, when permissible by law. Unfortunately, when a prepayment penalty feature is included with a loan then you must also include the maximum prepayment penalty amount that the borrower could pay when you calculate that loan's points and fees. In my

opinion, doing this could push the total points and fees amount above what is allowed for that type of Qualified Mortgage.

However, if one is considering including a prepayment penalty into a home loan then the following are required by the CFPB:

- The Prepayment Penalty cannot extend beyond the initial three years of the home loan.
- A Prepayment Penalty also cannot be greater than:
  - 2% of the outstanding mortgage loan balance prepaid during the first two years of the loan.
  - 1% of the outstanding mortgage loan balance prepaid during the third year of the loan.

- You must also offer that home loan borrower an alternative loan transaction that you believe he or she would also qualify for. Also, that alternative cannot have a prepayment penalty feature. That alternative home loan must be similar to the home loan with a prepayment penalty feature. And, finally, that alternative home loan:
  - Must be a fixed-rate or graduated-payment loan and must match the rate type from the loan with the prepayment penalty.
  - Must have the same Term as the mortgage with the prepayment penalty.
  - Cannot have deferred principal, balloon or interest-only payments, or negative amortization.

VIII. Broker or Table-Funded Mortgage Loans:

And finally, when your organization is a broker and/or does table-funded loans and you want to use the Safe Harbor for compliance with anti-steering rules for MLOs, in accordance with Regulation Z, then you must show your prospective home loan customers:

- The home loan with the lowest interest rate overall.
- The loan with the lowest interest rate with a prepayment penalty feature.
- The mortgage loan with the lowest total origination points and fees and discount points.

Okay, you should now have a pretty good idea regarding what the ATR/QM Rules are all about. I know, it is a lot of information to consider with originating mortgage loans. Let's now move into the latter part of this chapter and talk about some of the upcoming changes that the CFPB is proposing that will impact ATR/QM Rules during 2021.

Government Sponsored Enterprises Patch (GSE Patch) :
Having presented the ATR/QM Rules I'd like to now discuss the Government Sponsored Enterprises Patch (GSE Patch). What is referred to as the GSE Patch or simply the "Patch".

When the CFPB amended the Truth-in-Lending Act (TILA) to establish the ATR requirements in 2010, they also created the Government Sponsored Enterprises Patch (GSE Patch). The GSE Patch is an important provision of the mortgage lending reforms imposed by the 2010 Dodd-Frank Act, which aimed to prevent the predatory lending practices, which it is believed, contributed to the 2008 financial crisis. However, this was created as a Temporary Qualified Mortgage definition that also provides a Qualified Mortgage status to certain mortgage loans eligible for purchase and guarantee by either of the GSEs (Temporary GSE QM loans). Now, as I previously discussed, these Temporary GSE QM loans are eligible for Qualified Mortgage status even if their DTI ratio exceeds 43%.

Now, here's the important point of all this: The GSE Patch, for Temporary QM Loans, was scheduled to expire in January 10, 2021 or when the GSEs (Fannie Mae & Freddie Mac) exit their conservatorship, whichever comes first. As I understand it, the expiration of the GSE Patch would eliminate this Qualified Mortgage loan status, for Temporary GSE QM loans, if and when a loan's DTI exceeds 43%.

Now you may ask, "Why is that important"? Well, the Consumer Financial Protection Bureau estimated that approximately 957,000 mortgage loans would be (adversely) affected by the expiration of this GSE Patch. As a result, CFPB further estimated that after the GSE Patch expires then many of these mortgage loans would either not be made or would be made at a higher price (and possibly become unaffordable). Because of this the CFPB is proposing that at the time the GSE Patch expires, that it be replaced with a Price-based Approach to Qualified Mortgage loans. It is hoped that doing this would prevent any significant reduction in the size and numbers of Qualified Mortgages and continue to provide access to responsible and affordable credit.

Thus, the CFPB is proposing to amend its Qualified Mortgage definition by removing a previous Debt-to-Income (DTI) limit that home buyers were required to meet, replacing it with a Price-based Approach that would account for the difference between the loan's Annual Percentage Rate (APR) and the Average Prime Offer Rate (APOR) for comparable home loan transactions.

In preparation for this transition, from the GSE Patch to the Price-based Approach, the CFPB released in 2020 two **Notices** of Proposed Rulemaking – what they refer to as NPRMs. The purpose of these NPRMs was to inform mortgage professionals and Lenders of what the CFPB is proposing, regarding this, and enabling Lenders to comment on those proposed changes.

So, now I would like to highlight the main proposed points, by the CFPB, for each of these two NPRMs):

NPRM #1:

- The CFPB proposes to amend the General QM definition, in Regulation Z, to remove the 43% DTI limit and adopt a Price-based approach for the General QM loan definition.

- For eligibility for Qualified Mortgage status, under the General QM definition, the CFPB is also proposing a Price Threshold for most mortgage loans as well as higher price thresholds for smaller loans – which strongly affects manufactured homes and loans for minority consumers.

- The CFPB also proposed the removal of Appendix Q – which currently provides the qualifying requirements for Qualified Mortgages: (i.e. obtaining the home loan borrower's income, debt, and DTI or residual income as well as verifying the borrower's income and debts). However, this proposal would clarify and continue the requirements to consider and verify a home loan borrower's income, assets, debt obligations, alimony, and child support.

- The current threshold separating Safe Harbor from Rebuttal Presumption QMs would be preserved.

NPRM #2:

- The CFPB proposes to amend Regulation Z to also replace the "Sunset Date" of the Temporary GSE QM loan definition with a provision that extends the Temporary GSE QM loan definition to expire upon the effective date of final amendments to the General QM loan definition. This proposal is meant to extend the Temporary GSE QM loan definition for home loan borrowers who may be affected if the Temporary GSE QM loan definition expires before the amendments to the General QM loan definition takes effect.

  Now you may be wondering, "What the heck is a "Sunset Date". A Sunset Date is the expiration date (e.g. Sun going down – get it?). This type of QM has a Sunset Date of January 10, 2021. Okay, now to continue;

- Again, as above, the CFPB proposes to amend the General QM definition, in Regulation Z, to remove the 43% DTI limit and adopt a Price-based approach for the General QM loan definition.

CFPB's Final Ruling:

And finally, to bring you up to date following the above comment period, on October 20, 2020 the CFPB issued a Final Ruling that amended Regulation Z to replace the January 10, 2021 Sunset Date, of the Temporary GSE QM loan definition, with a provision stating => that the Temporary GSE QM loan definition will be available only for covered transactions for which the creditor receives the consumer's application before the mandatory compliance date of final amendments to the General QM loan definition in Regulation Z. The effective date of this Ruling was December 28, 2020.

Also, following this comments period the CFPB then published their Final Ruling in the Federal Register on October 26, 2020. So, look for this ATR/QM Rules change in early 2021.

OK, enough of the ATR/QM Rules. Let's now talk about some of those things you need to lookout for regarding the subject property - when you initially start working on a home loan. This takes us to the next chapter where we talk about Subject Property Concerns.

Chapter 7

SUBJECT PROPERTY CONCERNS

One of the things you should be thinking about, in the back of your mind, when you are getting ready to setup an appointment with your customers to complete an application is: Are there any concerns about the subject property? Sure, you have identified the type of subject property your customers wish to purchase or refinance and may have a pretty good idea that their home would be acceptable to a number of Lenders you are thinking about. But, could there be some characteristics or conditions of that property that will need to be addressed prior to the closing of that loan? I originally wanted to title this chapter "Things to Lookout For" but afterwards felt that title was too nebulous. So, I settled for the shorter one you see above. But that is what this chapter is all about: Things to lookout for and enquire about when you see and/or suspect certain conditions may exist regarding a subject property - of a loan you working on. In this chapter I will talk about some of the more common property concerns that may come up when you first start working on a mortgage loan, some of the questions you should ask regarding these, and what you should do when you encounter some of those.

Understand, that from a Lender's standpoint that home (the subject property) could become an income-producing asset – if they do fund the loan on that property. Therefore, from a Lender's perspective they most likely will be concerned about the livability, safety, and condition of that home as well as its resale value. So, with that in mind, let's take a look at some of the things you may encounter when doing a home loan and what questions to ask when you do see these. Now, let me say here that if an appraiser goes out to the subject property then they will certainly note some of these items if they exist. But, by the time you receive that appraisal report you may not have much time to respond to that area of concern. And, some of those items of concern, as noted by the appraiser, may turn out to be difficult and/or insurmountable problems that could prevent you from taking that loan to the closing table. This is one of the reasons I prefer to meet with my customers at their home, if I can, to give me an opportunity to take a look at their home and see if there are any (obvious) concerns and/or items (listed below) that will need to be addressed. So, let's now go over some of the more common Subject Property Concerns you may encounter and should lookout for.

I. The Structure of the Home:
1. The Roof:
If you are meeting your customers at their home (the subject property) then check out the condition of the roof - as you approach their house. Does it look in good shape or in need of repair or replacement? Is there moss growing on the roof - like those homes in hobbit land? You don't need to be an expert to know or suspect that the roof is in good condition or that there may be a (obvious) concern here regarding the customer's roof. Also, when you are inside the house

do you see any water stains on the ceiling or ceiling tiles? This could be an indication of possible roof leakage. If and when you do see these types of adverse roof symptoms then be sure to ask your customers about this when you first meet with them.

2. **Painting on the House and Patio/Balcony:**
    Also, as you approach the house how does the paint look on that home? Does it appear to be in good condition or does it looked faded and/or peeling in some areas. If this is the case, then you will usually see this happening on the south and west sides of the house. The roof also takes a beating from the sun on those sides as well. Maybe the paint on that house looks great but the paint on the balcony or patio in the backyard is old and faded and possibly peeling away. This might be something the Lender will want corrected before loan closing. Of course, if it's wintertime and the Lender wants that balcony painted before loan closing then you might be able to setup an Escrow Holdback - to have that balcony or patio painted after that loan closes (For more information on this please refer to the term Escrow Holdbacks.

3. **Interior of the House:**
    Once you are inside your customer's home then check out the condition of the interior of that house. I have gone to customers' homes and found that one or more entire wall coverings were missing – showing the wood frames of those walls. On other occasions, ceiling tiles in some rooms were missing with electrical wires exposed and hanging down. This may be the very reason those customers are meeting with you: To obtain funds to finish and/or repair those types of things – with a home improvement loan. However, you should be asking yourself: Will a Lender loan on this property before those types of improvements or repairs are completed? If the condition of the subject property does not satisfy that Lender's definition of Livability and Safety then chances are they will not. However, if the home is considered Livable and there are no Safety concerns there then it is possible that an Escrow Holdback might be an option here.

    However, know that the option of an Escrow Holdback is not always available. An example of this might be cases in which there exist major damage to the foundation of the home. This leads us to our next item:

4. **Foundation of the House:**
    Usually when you are meeting with your customers you won't have an opportunity to check out the foundation of their house. And, if there are any concerns here then you most likely will not find that out until you receive the completed Appraisal Report. Some of the more common concerns you will encounter here are:

    -   **Crack or cracks in the cement foundation** – possibly indicating that there is movement in the foundation of that home and/or that the foundation is starting to deteriorate and fall apart. Most Lenders I have worked with will require this (the foundation) to be examined, addressed, and repaired as a PTD condition.

- **Earth-to-Wood Contact**. Sometimes, for example, one or all of the wooden beams holding up the balcony of a home are now making contact with the ground. Or, one or more of the wooden beams supporting the house (e.g. in the basement) is making contact with the ground. Having Earth-To-Wood contact can cause wood rot and insect infestation. If there is earth-to-wood contact then you can expect that the Lender will want to have this corrected (so that the wood no longer makes contact with the ground) as a PTD condition.

II. Location of Subject Property:
1. Location of Home:

Prior to visiting your customer's home did you order a Property Profile to find out how that property is currently zoned in that county? In the chapters on the Property Profile and Reading the Appraisal Report I talk more about this. But for now, how is that property zoned? Is it residentially zone? Then good. However, if you discover that that property is located in a commercially zoned area then you most likely will have a problem here with most Conforming Lenders. This concern could also exist when the subject property is not actually on commercially zoned property but is adjacent to and/or backed up right next to commercially zoned property. This is where you can encounter those types of things listed below.

- ➢ Homes located near an Airport and/or Underneath the Landing Path of airplanes.
- ➢ Located near the (city) Dump and/or Sewer (e.g. it smells).
- ➢ Near Freeways.
- ➢ Near (active) Railroad Tracks.
- ➢ Subject Property is located in an area that has been declared potentially hazardous to the health of those living there (i.e. Home is next door to a nuclear reactor, the surrounding area has excessive emissions of radon there, etc.).

The above conditions could create a challenge for you in terms of finding a Conforming Lender who will loan on a home located near the above listed areas. Although this list is not all-inclusive, it does give you a general idea of some of the things to lookout for when initially working on a mortgage loan for a customer. And, I should add that these types of concerns also create added challenges for the appraiser in trying to find valid comps for that property.

2. Neighborhood Surrounding the Subject Property:

As you are driving to your customer's home - observe how the subject property's surrounding neighborhood looks like. Does the value of your customer's home look more or less the same as their neighbors? Is your customer's home more modern, much larger, custom built, or clearly worth much more (or less) than the surrounding homes? Is your customer's home a stick-built home and yet surrounded by manufactured homes? Okay, enough questions. My point of asking these is: How does your customer's home compared to those in their neighborhood and surrounding nearby areas?

If the subject property is significantly different than those homes around it then this may create another added challenge for the appraiser in coming up with valid appraisal comps. This also holds true if the subject property is unusually designed and built (e.g. dome shaped house or looks like the Seattle Space Needle!) Here again, the uniqueness of that home might make it extremely difficult for the appraiser to find valid comps for that property.

3. Size of the Lot and/or Property Surrounding the Home:

Remember what I previously discussed - regarding the value distribution of the home to the surrounding land that Conforming Lenders like to stay within? Yes, you remember, it's within about 65%/35%. That's 65% of the appraised value for the actual home with a maximum of about 35% of the total (appraised) value for the surrounding land and outbuildings of the property. And, we also talked about the preference that most Conforming Lenders have - to keep the surrounding acreage of the home to within 10 – 15 acres. Okay. You got that. But what do you do when your customers wish to purchase or refinance a home and the home has about 20 – 25 acres (or more)? First, you can safely assume that those acres beyond 10 – 15 acres will be highly discounted in value (if given any value at all) and secondly: And this is probably the most important question you should ask yourself when you encounter this is: What Is Common for that area?

For example, let's say your customers have a home on about 20 acres of land. What are the sizes (in acres) of the property homes that surround that subject property? Here, a plat map should be able to answer this question for you. If the surrounding homes have comparably sized land lots, as the subject property, then usually that will address the size concerns with most Conforming Lenders. However, if the subject property is much smaller or larger than the neighboring and surrounding homes and/or properties then this can create a concern for a Conforming Lender.

Again, one of the main concerns and challenges with these types of properties is finding valid comps by the appraiser. Now, I am not saying that a loan (on these types of properties) cannot be done by a Conforming Lender: What I am saying is - that properties that are not comparatively sized to their neighboring and surrounding properties creates a real challenge in finding valid (appraisal) comps that will show and demonstrate the current (and Lender accepted) value of that property. So, keep this in mind when considering doing a home loan with sizeable acreage.

III. Utilities of Home:

1. Septic Tank:

If you are working on a mortgage loan whereby the subject property is located within the city limits (or close to town) then that home is most likely using the Public Sewer System. However, if the subject property is in a suburban or rural area then there could be a good chance that that house has and is using a Septic Tank connected to it. So, if you are getting out into the rural areas (or further out) then be sure to ask if your customers are using a Septic Tank. If they are then you should ask them when was the last time it was pumped? It has been my experience that if that Septic Tank has been pumped within the last year or two then most Conforming Lenders will be happy with that. However, you should know that some Lenders might ask for and want to see the contractor's receipt or statement of work completion showing when that Septic Tank was last pumped and showing it was (at that time) operating satisfactorily. So I suggest, that if your customers are using a Septic Tank then ask them when it was last pumped and if they still have the receipt from that contractor who last pumped it.

Also, some states require that if the number of residents in a home has increased, whereby the existing Septic Tank's treatment disposal capability has been exceeded, then that Septic Tank and/or treatment system may (or will) need to be upgraded. And, some Conforming Lenders require that whenever the ownership of a home changes (a purchase transaction) then the Septic Tank should be pumped (or have records showing it was recently pumped).

Now, if the Lender has no requirements or concerns regarding when that Septic Tank, to the subject property, was last pumped then usually their only concern would be whether that Septic Tank is typical for that area. That bit of information is normally shown on an appraiser's report.

2. Private Water Well:

Also, when you get out into the suburban and rural areas you may find some folks who have their own Private Water Well. While this is not a concern, the Lender may want to know when was the last time that Well was checked and/or tested (Purity Test) to make sure that it meets with that State's drinking water standards and that the well is properly connected and the water of that well is flowing according to their minimum required standards. An example of this (e.g. minimum required water flow) could be: That well is capable of producing 5 gallons per minute for 4 hours without any serious draw down.

As above, the Lender may require a document showing when that well was last inspected and the results of that contractor's survey and water tests. If a Well survey and test is required and you (and/or your customers) are not sure who to contact to do this then I suggest contacting the City Health Department in the county in which that subject property is located and ask them for a list of approved and licensed engineers who do this type of work.

3. **Electrical System of the Home:**

If you are doing a mortgage loan on a very old house then ask your customers what the voltage output of their electrical system is. Most Conforming Lenders prefer (or require) that the minimum voltage output of a home be 120 amps or greater.

IV. Access to Home:

1. **Main Road Fronting Property of Home:**

What kind of road is fronting that subject property? Is it a paved or gravel road? Again, as above, if the subject property is within the city limits or near the town then the road fronting that home will most likely be paved. However, as you get out into rural areas you may find that the fronting road is gravel and in some cases dirt and rock. As I mention, within Chapter 8 on Types of Mortgage Loans, some Conforming Lenders prefer to not to loan to homes in rural areas. And, if they do then sometimes you will see an adjustment to the interest rate fee and/or maximum loan LTV for homes located in rural areas. So, keep this in mind when you are working on and shopping your loans.

2. **Access Road to Home:**

How far away is the home from the main street fronting it? And, what kind of driveway does that subject property have for access to that home? A prime concern of any Lender is the ease and ability of emergency vehicles to get to a house quickly if the need arises. For example, if that house caught fire would fire trucks be able to quickly get to it - to put out the fire? Of course, this deals with not only the condition but also the width of that access road.

V. Miscellaneous Stuff:

Fireplace & Wood-burning Stove:

If your customers have a Fireplace or (stand-alone) Wood-burning Stove in their home, then ask them when was the last time they cleaned the chimney of that Fireplace and/or Wood-burning stove. Most Conforming Lenders I have worked with have not made it an issue with Fireplaces. However, Wood- burning Stoves can be another issue here. Especially if that stovetop (or pipe), on that Wood-burning Stove, is "L" shaped and enters the side of a wall. If that type of stove is used often and is not cleaned yearly then creosote can build-up in that chimney pipe - creating a fire hazard. Creosote, if you are not familiar with that term, is a flammable black or brown tar substance that sticks to the insides of chimneys (and/or stovetop pipes) and can come from wood burning smoke. Here again, if your customers do have a Wood-burning Stove with an "L" shaped stovetop chimney pipe then ask them when they last cleaned that chimney and stove and if they have any records showing that.

Also, if it is a stand-alone Wood-burning Stove or a Pellet Burning Stove (that usually was purchased and installed after that home was first built) then underneath that stove does it have a solid (blocked of) foundation built specifically for it? This insulates the home from the heat of that burning stove – which could get quite hot at times. If it doesn't then that will surely be a problem with any Lender.

VI. Environmental Concerns:

1. Auto/Vehicle Repairs:

It has been my experience that residential Conforming Lenders will not loan on any properties where there exist any Environmental Concerns. Environmental Concerns could exist, for example, where engines and/or vehicles are being worked on – with the possibility of oil (and/or other toxins) spilling on the ground. This could result in contaminating that and the surrounding grounds of that site.

For example, let's say that your new loan customers some time ago converted the garage of their home into an Auto Repair Shop – whereby they work part-time repairing, tuning up, and working on cars and other various types of vehicles. Now this changes things. First, you now know that that property will be considered Mixed-Use Property (remember that mixed-use property is any property that has a combination of residential and commercial use). And secondly, that type of business being done there could be a real Environmental Concern for a Conforming Leader (as well as any type of Lender). Of course, your customers could get an Environmental Test done on their property to verify and show that there are no Environmental Concerns that exist there. However, a test of this nature (referred to as a Level I or Level II test) could cost anywhere from $2,000 - $4,000 or more. Would they be willing to pay for that test?

Environmental Concerns, of a Lender, can exist anytime there is a possibility of spillage or leakage – thereby polluting and/or contaminating the subject property, the surrounding grounds, air, and underground water systems. Of course, there are other types of Environmental Concerns than what we have discussed above but usually it will be those activities or operations that can create the possibility of polluting the surrounding grounds and water systems near the subject property that you will encounter (if at all).

2. Aspects of the Subject Property Creating a Hazard:

This is an area that you, in most cases, will not become aware of until you receive the Appraisal on that subject property. However, if you have a chance (before the Appraisal is done) to inspect that property then here are a few things to look for in this category:

- Items or objects surrounding, near, or on the subject property that could be a Hazard and potentially harm someone. Examples of this could be junk, sharp metal objects, beat-up cars (being worked on), and large holes in the ground.

- Unsafe walkways, from the subject property to a floating dock, across a crevice, or large hole in the ground.

- Sharp cliff or drop-off near the subject property with no fence or barrier separating it from your customer's home.

This list should give you an idea of what I am talking about here when I am referring to existing Hazards on the subject property. If you are inspecting a property and wondering if a particular aspect or item on that property is a potential Hazard (that could create a concern for a Lender) then ask yourself: Would I let my child run freely on this property? If you could see your child (or any child) accidentally falling down that cliff or hole, or seriously hurting herself on that stuff or junk surrounding that property – then you may (most likely) have a Hazard concern there.

Hazard Concern: Now what does that mean? Does that mean you will now be unable to do the loan on that property? Not necessarily – if those causes of potential Hazard can be removed and/or made safe according to the Lender's guidelines. And usually, this (removal of the source creating the Hazard) will need to be done as a Prior-To-Doc condition. Sometimes it doesn't take much (in terms of effort and money) to address (or cure) a Hazard concern. On the other hand, the cost to remove and/or get rid of the source creating that Hazard may be so expensive – it just may not make any sense, to your loan customer, to now do that loan. Or, in some cases, your customer may not want to remove that Hazardous source (i.e. he sculptures metal art and loves to have pieces of sharp, metal objects surrounding his property). In that case, that loan is most likely not going to happen.

Remember when I talked about being in the Mortgage Detective Mode? Here you should go into that same mode when you encounter, suspect, and/or believe that any of those concerns listed above exist (or any others that may be related to the subject property). Being in the Mortgage Detective Mode you ask your customers questions to get a clearer idea of the condition, characteristics, and/or location of the subject property. For example, let's say you are first talking to your customer on the telephone about a home loan. He or she may say that they can hear the sounds of the trains from their home every once in a while (or you hear the train in the background while you are talking to them). You then should ask them how far away are they from the train tracks. If they say the tracks are a couple of blocks away then you probably have nothing to worry about. However, if they say that those train tracks are across the street then I would say that you definitely have an issue here that will need to be addressed. And, if you begin shopping for a Lender, for that loan, then one of the first questions you should ask a prospective Wholesale Lender is: Would you lend on a home near railroad tracks?

The purpose of this chapter has been to introduce you to some things you should be aware of and lookout for when you first begin working on a home loan. If you initially follow-up and order a Property Profile then some of those areas of concern (if they exist) will be on that report and/or can be seen on the accompanying plat map (e.g. railroad tracks to the subject property). Doing this and/or following up on something the customer initially told you (that may be a concern) is all part of doing our jobs as mortgage loan originators. And, it enables us to be better prepared when we do meet with our customers and subsequently begin shopping the loan for the best Lender who can do the loan for that customer.

When you are first qualifying your customers and/or meeting them at their home then you can get a heads-up on any Subject Property Concerns (if there are any) by asking your customers the following questions regarding their property:

1. Tell me about your property: Type, size of lot, where it is located?

2. What kind of neighborhood is the home located in? Are the homes similar to yours?

3. How's the condition of that home? The roof, outside paint, the foundation of that home?

4. Is there anything unusual about that house that I should know?

Just asking these questions can confirm to you that there are (probably) no Subject Property Concerns there or their answers may lead you to ask additional questions regarding a Subject Property Concern that may exist with that property.

Now, sometimes you just don't know what the value of a property could be (because of an existing Property Concern) or how to proceed with a loan, and perhaps are wondering if that loan is even doable. That's when it is a good time to talk to some of the more experienced mortgage loan originators in your branch (e.g. Senior mortgage loan originators and/or Branch Manager) and ask them what they think. And, they will (or should) respect the fact that you have done your homework (e.g. ordered a Property Profile) and are aware of and believe that a particular aspect of that subject property could be a concern in the initial origination of that loan. They will probably be thinking to themselves that most new mortgage loan originators would have overlooked that very thing you are now talking with them about. I can tell you that some of those Subject Property Concerns, we discussed above, have tripped up many new and even experienced mortgage loan originators. So, it's understandable if you wish to discuss this with your Branch Manager or a senior mortgage loan originator in your branch. It is also highly likely that one of those folks has done a loan or experienced that very thing in the past and may have some suggestions for you on how to proceed with that loan and what Lender or Lenders to submit that loan to. And, if you have established relationships with any third-party providers (e.g. Appraisers) then this could be the time to call them and see what they think as well.

I should also mention that when you first begin working on a home loan and strongly suspect that there exist some concerns regarding a subject property, that makes the ability to do that loan highly suspect, then I suggest holding off on ordering the appraisal and title report (on that property) until you are fairly certain that you will be able to do that loan. Doing this shows that you know what you are doing and have the wherewithal to order the services of those third-party providers when the time is right. And, this can save you the aggravation and possibly the personal expense of paying for an appraisal and/or title report in the event that home loan is eventually denied and/or cannot be done.

To give you an example of what I am talking about here – let me tell you a story about a home loan I was working on, some time ago, and had some subject property concerns that, in the end, resulted in not being able to do that loan. This also shows you how we (me in this case) can make an erroneous assumption – only to later find out my assumption was totally incorrect.

I met with a gentleman, in a bank branch, to complete a loan application to refinance his home to obtain a better interest rate on his first mortgage and payoff one of his credit cards. As we will discuss, in the next chapter on Types of Mortgage Loans, this loan would be a Cash-Out Refinance Loan. As I completed the 1003, with that customer, I asked him what type of property he had? He replied that he has an "A" frame house, fronting a lake. I have done loans on "A" frame homes before so I wasn't overly concerned at that time. I then asked him who the original Lender was on that loan and he said it was one of our local (and well-known) nationwide banks. He also said that his Lender did the last appraisal on his property and everything seemed to come out OK. That was four years ago when he first purchased that property.

Now, here's my assumption: I figured that since that bank inspected and appraised that property that that property should still be in pretty good shape. At least, it should pass an appraisal for a Conforming loan. And, I should note here, that bank provided a 100% LTV loan to him in purchasing that property. Banks are generally pretty conservative, in doing home loans, so I thought there should be no Subject Property Concerns here (that was an assumption that eventually ended up biting me on the bottom).

Okay, so I completed that application and began processing that refinance home loan request. I originally tried to submit that loan, as a Conforming, 30-year fixed rate loan but the qualifying ratios were just too high. I then submitted it, via LP, for an FHA loan with an LTV of 85%. It then was approved. By that time I had spent some time on that loan and wanted to take it to the closing table as soon as possible (and so did my customer). I then ordered the appraisal. The appraiser said he could be out to that property, within the next couple of days, at around 2:00 in the afternoon (that's unusual to be out there that soon, but I love it when that happens). I told him that I would meet him there, at that property, because I still had some FHA docs that I now needed my customer to sign.

Driving to that property, near the lake that afternoon, I recall that it was sunny outside and I thought how nice it would be to own a home near the lake. As I took the last turn, to go to my customer's house, I noticed that the road went from being asphalt to dirt. Still, I wasn't concerned. However, as I turned the corner and saw that "A" frame house - I then knew I just might have some challenges to address. I parked my car, got out, and saw that the appraiser had already arrived there and was in the process of inspecting that property as my loan customer accompanied him. After I said "hello" to everyone there I began doing my own inspection of that "A" frame house and this is what I saw:

- The balcony, on the back of that "A" frame house, was built of wood and had never been painted or coated with any protective sealant.

- Paint, on the outside of the house, was fading and chipping (in some areas) exposing the home to nature's elements.

- And get this: The entire foundation of that "A" frame house was suffering from Earth-To-Wood contact. Now, when I saw that I knew then that that loan was in trouble.

- At that point I pretty much felt that that loan was not going to happen. So, I thought I'd walk out to the small floating dock, in front of that house, and get my thoughts together. As I went in that direction I noticed that there were two 12 inch X 8 feet footboards from the edge of the land, of his property, to that floating dock. Underneath those 2 boards was a pile of large and small rocks. Not something you would want to fall onto. Now I was really discouraged and decided to talk to that appraiser about what I was seeing.

- I then walked back to that house and went inside to join the appraiser and my loan customer. After I walked in - I saw something I had never seen before. Just to my right, as I walked in, was a pellet stove resting on a square strip of vinyl flooring. No foundation block (for that pellet stove), just a strip of vinyl flooring.

Now, I may not be the smartest guy around but I knew then that loan wasn't going to happen (unless that customer was willing to spend a lot of money to cure all those subject property concerns). At that point I asked the appraiser if he could step outside for a minute because I wanted to show him something (I really just wanted to talk to him in private). We walked outside the house and across those 2 boards to the floating dock. Once we were both standing on the dock I then commented on how beautiful it was out here. Then I look at him and ask him if he felt there was a snowball's chance (in blankadi-blank) that this house would pass an FHA or any type of Conforming loan appraisal. He replied, "Well, there are many challenges here and it does appear that it would entail a lot of money to cure those – in order to finally pass any type of FHA or Conforming loan type of appraisal."

Shortly thereafter I then said, "Okay, I think we are done here." I thanked him for taking the time to come out and inspect this property and asked him if he would just tell our customer that he was done there. And, I told him that I would talk to him later about this. He said, "Okay," and prepared to leave (fortunately, I have done enough business with that appraiser – otherwise he might have charged me for him coming out there).

I then met with my loan customer and discussed with him all the subject property concerns that appraiser and I had seen. I then told him that those would (most likely) need to be cured before proceeding on his loan. Things like addressing the Earth-To-Wood contact and the peeling paint would entail spending a good amount of money to take care of and correct. He said he couldn't understand it since the bank (of his existing 1ˢᵗ mortgage) saw this when he first purchased this property. That is something I just couldn't understand myself: How could that "A" frame house have passed a Conforming loan appraisal?

Anyway, to make a long story short (if that is possible) I then tried to do that loan by doing a Streamline Refinance loan (refinancing only the 1ˢᵗ mortgage). As you will read in the next chapter, a Streamline Refinance loan normally does not require an appraisal (See Streamline Refinance Loans). However, because of the other requirements of doing a Streamline Refinance Loan (i.e. the new home loan amount cannot be greater than the original loan amount) I just couldn't make that loan happen. Because, if an appraisal needed to be done, in order to do that loan, then it just wasn't going to happen. And that's what happened here, I just wasn't able to do that loan for that customer because of all the subject property concerns. In the end, working on that loan request taught me some important lessons that I'd like to share with you: Make no assumptions about the subject property and/or what the original or current mortgage servicer did to prepare that loan for approval. And, when you are first inquiring about the subject property and you think there is anything unusual about that property then put on your Mortgage Detective Hat and start asking those questions related to those subject property concerns listed above. Doing this, will help you stay on track by spending your time on those loans that are doable and will (or can) go to the closing table. And, this will also contribute towards making your working time more productive.

In closing here, I am happy to say that most of the home loans you will be working on will most likely not encounter any subject property concerns. And that's good. However, knowing what you have learned in this chapter will enhance your Mortgage Loan Detective ability and your loan processing skills as a mortgage loan originator.

Let's now go to the next chapter that talks about the various types of Loan Programs and Products available - that you can offer your home loan customers. Given the knowledge that you have acquired in this and the previous chapters I believe we are now ready to get into the subject matter that lies at the very heart of lending and being a mortgage loan originator: Knowing the different types of loan programs. After that we will talk about what I call "The Paperwork". But for now, let's move on to the next chapter that talks about the different Types of Mortgage Loans.

Chapter 8

TYPES OF MORTGAGE LOANS

At this point in the book it is my hope that you are getting comfortable with the language and jargon used in residential mortgage lending and how we can apply those terms, concepts, and principles. Now that we have talked about that let's now start to get into the real stuff of lending. By that I mean - talk about mortgage loans.

In this chapter we'll discuss the three main areas of Mortgage Loans that you should be familiar with. Those are the areas of:

1. Mortgage Loans
2. Loan Transactions
3. Loan Products

Let's begin with the first one on…

I. Types of Mortgage Loans:

Within the home lending profession there are basically five types of home loans that are available through most Wholesale Lenders - Lenders that you "broker" and submit your loans to. Those six primary types of mortgage loan programs are:

1. Government loans (FHA & VA)
2. Conforming Loans
3. High-Cost and High-Balance Loans
4. Non-conforming Loans
5. Jumbo Loans
6. Sub-prime Loans

Let's talk about each one of these now.

I. Government Loans - FHA & VA:

As I mentioned, within Chapter 2 on Common Mortgage Lending Terms, these types of loans are often referred to as govies. Govie loans include FHA (Federal Housing Administration) loans and VA (Veterans Administration) loans. These two types of loans (FHA and VA) have very specific requirements and guidelines peculiar to them. Because of the complexity and uniqueness of these I will not be discussing in detail these types of loans in this book. But I do want you to be familiar with FHA loans - loans that can offer your customers home purchase loans with an LTV up to about 97.75%. The FHA was the first to offer this type of high LTV loan to prospective home purchasers. Of course, good credit was and usually is required to obtain an FHA loan. Years ago if a prospective home buying customer didn't have 10% or 20% of the selling price of the property saved up then FHA was the way to go. Today however, we have available Conforming and Non-conforming loans offering 95%, 97%, 100%, and even 105% LTV financing for home purchase loans. Today, having both of these types of loans (govie and conventional loans) you have many options that you can offer your qualified borrowers today that did not exist years ago.

FHA Loans:

FHA actually insures their (FHA) loans and because of this the borrower of an FHA loan pays for what is called an Upfront Mortgage Insurance Premium. This Upfront Mortgage Insurance Premium (UFMIP) can be as much as 1.75% of the original loan amount or what is called the "Base Loan Amount" and is added on to the Base Loan Amount to make the Gross Loan Amount. Thus, if the base loan amount was $100,000 then the Upfront Mortgage Insurance Premium could be $1,750. This amount would be added onto the base loan amount of $100,000 for a total loan amount of 101,750. In addition to this the borrower pays monthly MIP (mortgage insurance premium) to the tune of about 0.80% - 85% of the Base Loan Amount translated into a monthly figure (depending on whether their down payment is 5% or 3.5% respectively, of the Base Loan Amount). Using our example here, if the home loan borrower is planning on coming up with a 5% down payment then annual MI would be ($100,000 X 0.80%) = $800 per year and then divide the annual amount by 12 = $66.67 per month for that FHA loan's monthly MI.

VA Loans:

The VA or Veteran's Administration provides home loan programs for veterans and active members of the United States Armed Forces. One of the great things about VA loans is that with them the veteran can finance the purchase of a home with an LTV of up to 100% of the sale price or appraised value (whichever is lower) of a property. The VA loan, I believe, was the first to offer this type of high LTV financing (a 100% LTV purchase loan). I think VA loans are one of the best (purchase) loans out there - if the veteran doesn't have much of a down payment saved up.

It's important to realize that the Veteran's Administration actually Guarantees the VA loan. This differs from an FHA loan (discussed above) whereby the FHA insures the loan. Because of this distinction VA loans do not include an UFMIP but does include a one-time VA Funding fee (which is added on to the base loan amount) but has no monthly MIP. Today, that one-time VA Funding is 2.5% of the Base Loan Amount. Thus, as above, if the based loan amount is $100,000 then $2,500 is then added on to it to result in a total loan amount of $102,500. But again, VA loans have no monthly MIP payments. To learn more about VA home loans online go to: http://www.homeloans.va.gov.

I also suggest contacting one of your wholesale lenders who does VA loans and ask them if they can send you their loan processing guidelines for VA loans. You can also obtain some information as well as loan documents on VA loans through the Internet via the website mentioned above.

2. Conventional Conforming Home Loans:

These two terms are very often used interchangeably. Also, these types of loans are sometimes referred to as Prime loans. Although you don't hear that term used very often these days. But if you say a Conforming Loan then lending folks know what you are talking about. Also, if you said Conventional Loans then lending folks also would know what you talking about as well: The same type of home loans. For our discussion here, I will refer to these types of loans as Conforming. Both of these types of loans use the same type of Conforming Loan Standards and Guidelines.

For a residential mortgage loan to be considered a Conforming/Conventional loan it must satisfy the underwriting guidelines of the Federal National Mortgage Association (FNMA) and/or the Federal Home Loan Mortgage Corporation (FHLMC) – these two are often referred to as Fannie-Freddie guidelines. I should also note that a Wholesale Lender might have an Investor and/or Investors, for their Conforming Loans, whose underwriting guidelines may be more lenient than what FNMA or FHLMC require (I mentioned this previously when we discussed Loan Underwriting). Conforming Lenders offer loan programs with the best interest rates and terms. For this reason alone it should be your initial objective to make every attempt to place your borrowers in a Conforming Loan program first - if that is possible.

Also, when processing Conforming Loans, many of these can be submitted either through Fannie Mae's <u>DU</u> or Freddie Mac's <u>LP</u> and this enables you to quickly see whether your customer's loan will be approved as submitted – before it is sent to the Wholesale Lender's Underwriter. Of course, there may be a small number of Conforming Loan Programs, of that lender, that may need to be <u>Manually Underwritten,</u> but for most you should be able submit their loans via DU or LP.

Recall our discussion on Qualifying Your Borrowers: When you are reviewing all the facts and documents on your borrower then you should be asking yourself: Now do I have a Conforming loan borrower here or not? As you become more experienced then your ability to determine this may improve to the point that while you are talking to a prospective home loan customer on the telephone you will know (or strongly suspect) whether this is a Conforming loan borrower or not. The most important thing you should initially focus on, when you are evaluating a customer for a Conforming Loan, is the Credit of that Borrower. As I mentioned, in Qualifying Your Borrowers, if your customer has outstanding credit then that may make up for any deficiencies or shortfalls in that borrower's other areas.

The most common loan programs you will receive requests for, in the Conforming Lending area, are:

- 30-Year Fixed Rate loans. A fixed interest rate over the entire term of the loan - 360 months. This is the all-time favorite.

- 40-Year Fixed Rate Loans. A fixed interest rate amortized over a 480-month period (I should mention here that even though, in previous years, that we thought this would become the mortgage Term of choice, it is now not allowed according to the Qualified Mortgage Rule).

- 15-Year Fixed Rate loans. A fixed interest rate over the entire term of the loan - 180 months.

- Adjustable-Rate Mortgages (ARMs). ARMs are home loans whose initial interest rate is lower than a fixed rate loan (main benefit) and then after a specified initial period of time (whereby it has been fixed) the interest rate then adjusts periodically at a pre-determined period or cycle and that adjustment is based on a particular market rate (interest rate), index, and margin. Later I will talk more about ARMs and why anyone would prefer or need to go this route in lending.

- Second Mortgages: Usually with a maximum LTV or CLTV of 95%. CLTV stands for Combined Loan-To-Value. It represents the combined amounts of the 1st and 2nd mortgages to the value of the subject property.

3. High-Balance Loans:

First, a bit of history: This term and loan product is the result the Home Economic Recovery Act of 2008 and was preceded by what was referred to as Jumbo-Conforming loans during 2008. For example, in preparing The Economic Stimulus Act of 2008 HUD identified and classified certain metropolitan areas and counties they considered "High-Cost areas" and increased the maximum Conforming loan limits for each up to (or times) 1.75% of the maximum Conforming loan limit of $417,000, for 1-Unit properties, while still enabling them to enjoy the benefits and features that Conforming loans offer in terms of lower rates and fees. A Jumbo-Conforming or Mini-Jumbo mortgage loan represented a mortgage loan in which the subject property was located within a High-Cost area, as classified by Federal Housing Finance Agency (FHFA), and the loan amount was greater than $417,000 (for a 1-Unit property). Otherwise, if the total loan amount was $417,000 or less (for a 1-Unit) than that loan was considered a Conforming loan. And, that distinction was important because when a loan became a Jumbo-Conforming then there were different originating and processing restrictions and underwriting guidelines that applied to those that did not apply to "normal" Conforming Loans.

I should also mention here that these increased loan limits for Jumbo-Conforming loans, for properties located in HUD classified High-Cost areas, was a temporary adjustment for loans originated from April 1, 2008 to December 31, 2008. In other words, these increased loan limits for Jumbo-Conforming loans, in their classified High-Cost areas, ended after December 31, 2008. Thus, this "Jumbo-Conforming" term and program ended and was phased out as of December 31, 2008.

However, with the enactment of The Housing and Economic Recovery of 2008, on July 30, came a new loan term and type of mortgage loan called "High-Cost" and "High-Balance" loans. Although the basic concept of High-Balance loans is the same as the Jumbo-Conforming loans, the loan limits and loan processing is a little different. For example, All Jumbo-Conforming loans had to be manually underwritten. This, however, has changed and for 2021 most High-Balance loans can be processed either manually or using DU. The exception to this requirement is with "Refi Plus" High-Balance loans. Please refer to Chapter 4 titled "Loan Underwriting" for Underwriting guidelines for High-Balance loans.

Now, those areas and counties not classified as High-Cost areas will continue with their maximum Conforming loan limit amounts. For the maximum Conforming Loan Limits for 2021 please refer to the definition of Conforming Loans within Chapter 2. Thus, each metropolitan area or county could have a different maximum Conforming loan limit – depending upon whether that area is classified as a High-Cost area or not. To view the maximum loan limits and Underwriting guidelines for High-Balance loans please also refer to Chapter 4 titled "Loan Underwriting". And, to view the various and many Metropolitan and Metropolitan Areas and Rural Counties classified as High-Cost areas, with their specific maximum High-Balance loan limits for 1, 2, 3, and 4-Units, please visit Fannie Mae's website at: https://www.efanniemae.com.

4. Non-Conforming Loans:

Non-conforming Loans are also often referred to as Alt-A Loans. Years ago when I first heard of someone referring to a Non-Conforming Loan I thought that was somehow a bad thing – or there was a problem with that loan. Possibly the credit of that borrower was "less than perfect." However, that is not always the case at all. Quite frankly, Non-conforming (loans) simply means that some of those loans (Non-conforming) do not conform to Fannie-Freddie Underwriting Guidelines. Because those Underwriting guidelines, of Non-conforming loans, are outside of Fannie-Freddie's required guidelines, there tends to be a lot more loan program options you could offer to your prospective loan customers. There are many reasons why your loan customer may need to go Non-conforming: Credit, Income, Collateral, or LTV on a loan. The amount of the loan can also result in a loan becoming Non-Conforming. For example, today if the total loan amount, for a single-family residence (SFR), is greater than the maximum Conforming amount of $510,400 it then becomes a Jumbo loan and is referred to as a Non-conforming Loan as well. The interest rates on these types of loans are usually slightly higher than what Conforming Loans offer.

Okay, so let's talk about some of the features of Non-conforming loans in comparison to Conforming Loans:

- The customer's Credit may be "less than perfect" (but still very good), what could be called –A. With some late payments in the last 2 years with the middle credit score in the 600's. A Chapter 7 Bankruptcy usually still needs to be discharged for at least 2 - 3 years.

- Job History or Job Stability: Less than 2 years with the same Employer or Less than 2 years in the same profession.

- Income that results in acceptable ratios (Housing and Total Debt Ratios) within the Non-conforming Lender's guidelines.

- The Type of home and its Location needs to be acceptable to the Non-conforming Lenders. Here again, what does the Non-conforming Lender loan on? There are usually more options available to borrowers as far as the Collateral goes within the Non-conforming area. For example, maybe your borrower wants a loan on a cabin by the lake. This may not be a loan for a Conforming Lender, but perhaps a Non-conforming Lender might be willing to do that loan.

- Also the maximum allowable LTV (per loan product) could be higher in Non-conforming loans as compared to Conforming loans (i.e. LTV up to 100% for refinance and purchase loans).

- Non-conforming Loan amounts, for SFRs , can be greater than $510,400. Here again, we are talking about Jumbo Loans – which as the name implies, the loan amount is larger than the maximum amount a Conforming loan allows.

Again, keep in mind what I previously mentioned about the Risk-Reward Relationship. As the Risk of a loan is perceived to be higher then the interest rate, on that loan, generally gets higher in some relationship to that level of perceived Risk. For example, a cabin by the lake may be located some distance from the main road. This would make it difficult for Fire Fighters and Fire Trucks to get to that cabin if they had to. Just this creates an added risk to the point whereby no Conforming Lender may loan on this type of property. But perhaps a Non-conforming Lender might. Yes, the interest rate will be higher (than a Conforming loan) but you may still be able to do that home loan and possibly achieve the goals of your customer.

A point I haven't made previously is that some Conforming Lenders also have Non-conforming loan programs. If this is the case then this makes your job a lot easier. I have had the experience whereby I submitted a loan to a Conforming Lender and after the Underwriter of that Lender examined that loan file she then called me and told me that the borrower did not qualified for their Conforming Loan Program I had submitted it for. However, she told me that she felt she could get it approved with one of her Non-conforming Loan Programs. She reviewed it in that new light and then passed that loan on to the Non-Conforming Underwriting Department and that loan was subsequently approved. Granted, we didn't get the interest rate we were initially targeting for but we were able to get an interest rate acceptable to that borrower and whereby he was able to achieve the goals he had set for his home loan.

If you have submitted a loan to a Conforming Lender and it is denied and they don't have a Non-conforming Loan Program then you will need to do some additional research on that loan (to find another Wholesale Lender who might do it), repackage your loan, and submit it to another Conforming or Non-conforming Lender. But that's what we do as mortgage loan originators.

Many times the reasons you have to go the Non-conforming route has nothing to do with the Credit of your borrowers. They may have very good credit, but the LTV on that loan may be higher than what a Conforming Lender would accept (for that type of loan program) and/or it is a Jumbo Loan (loan amount is greater than $510,400 for a 1-

Unit property in a non-High-Cost area). The need to go Non-conforming could also deal with the income of the borrowers or the type of property (Collateral) the borrowers wish to obtain a loan on. But as I have said time and time again, the lending area is very dynamic and is changing all the time. Just when you think you've got it all figured out - it changes on you. For example, it seems like just a short while ago there were a number of different types of mortgage loans that no Conforming Lender would even look at. Today, not only are they looking at those types of loans but approving them (if qualified) as well. So, things change and that can be a good thing for you and your borrowers.

Just as with the Conforming Lending area, the loan programs that are available within the Non-Conforming Lending areas are pretty much the same. The most common loan programs that you will receive requests for, in the Non-conforming Lending area, are: 30-Year Fixed Rate loans, 15-Year Fixed Rate loans, and Adjustable-Rate Mortgages (ARMs).

5. Jumbo Loans:
A mortgage loan is considered a Jumbo Loan when its total loan amount is greater than the maximum loan limit for General Conforming loans and, in HUD classified High-Cost areas, High-Cost loans. And, as previously discussed above, Jumbo Loans are also referred to as Non-conforming loans. When a loan becomes Jumbo then there are usually additional adjustments to the rate and fee. Also, the available loan programs for Jumbos are usually less than Conforming loans and the borrowers, of Jumbo loans, usually need to have higher credit scores. Because of the rate and fee adjustments to Jumbo loans many borrowers, of these types of loans, are willing to go with an ARM type of loan in order to obtain a lower interest rate (than would be available with a Jumbo fixed rate loan).

Our next and sixth Type of Loan program is in an area that has undergone significant changes during its initial first 15 years. That type of loan program is commonly referred to by mortgage lending folks (like you and me) and Wholesale Lenders as Sub-prime Loans. Now, before I discuss these types of loans – please allow me to say that prior to the mortgage meltdown and crisis, that began to show its ugly head in the latter part of 2006, there were many Lenders that offered Sub-prime loans (Conforming, Non-conforming, and Sub-prime Lenders). However, since the subsequent years when the mortgage crisis began that has changed. Today, in 2021 we still see few, if any, lenders in mortgage lending land offering Sub-prime loans. But that too, I believe, could and will change.

Therefore, in my efforts to provide you with a comprehensive summary on Mortgage Loans I will discuss the subject of Sub-prime loans. And, I also believe, that in the near future, when our USA economy improves, the unemployment rate gets lower, that many more folks will, again, be looking to either refinance their home or purchase a home. Unfortunately, many of those folks will have gone through some tough times (been laid off, loss their job, or whatever) and their credit will have suffered. Because of that (their credit) many of those folks will not be qualified for a Conforming or Non-conforming loan. So, who will do the loans for these folks? That's when, I believe, we will again see Sub-prime loans being offered. However, I also believe that those newly offered Sub-prime loans will have more stringent guidelines, than in the past, for those loan customers as well as for the respective mortgage loan originators offering these.

Anyway, enough about my mortgage theories. And, finally, if you hear anyone use the term Sub-prime loans or Lender then you will at least have an idea of what they are talking about. OK, having said that, the following discusses the conventional definition and guidelines for Sub-prime loans:

6. Sub-Prime Loans:

As this name implies these types of loans were originally designed for borrowers who had less than prefect credit: A- or B credit or worse. Some lending folks just refer to this lending area as B/C, some as Sub-prime, and folks like me join the two together and call it B/C Sub-prime. As I mentioned previously - a Branch Manager told me that it was "politically correct" to refer to Sub-prime loans as Non-prime Loans when discussing these when your loan customers.

Before I proceed any further here, let say here that the following discussion is for historical and informative purposes only and does not represent so-called "Sub-prime Loans" that might be in existence today (if there are any). After the mortgage crisis began most of the Sub-prime lenders left the market and today I still see little if any Sub-prime lenders. However, I do believe, that in the near future many prospective home loan customers will be looking to either refinance their home or purchase a home. Unfortunately, many of those folks may not be qualified for a conventional mortgage loan. Since "need is the mother of invention" I believe Sub-prime loans will then reappear. If that occurs then Sub-prime lending, I believe, will look very different than what we have experienced in the past. OK. Having said that, let's now talk about Sub-prime loans – as we used to know them.

Prior to the common use of Sub-prime loans many lenders referred to these types of loans as Non-conforming. However, I believe, as time went on it became increasingly clear that Sub-prime Lenders, who did those types of loans, were getting the loan business that Non-conforming Lenders were unwilling to accept (or loan on). For our discussion and simplicity here I have separated Sub-prime loans from Non-conforming loans.

As I mentioned, when processing Non-conforming Loans, when it comes to processing Sub-prime Loans - these types of loans usually needed to be Manually Underwritten (versus being submitted via DU or LPA).

Primarily, Sub-prime Lenders offered loan customers, who had what we called "less than perfect credit", an opportunity to obtain a purchase or refinance loan that they otherwise would not have been able to obtain. Less than perfect credit generally means that the borrower(s):

1. Had a middle credit score that was lower than what Conforming and Non-conforming lenders would accept, and/or

2. There were many late payments showing up on the credit report: Some out to 60 or more days late, and/or

3. There were outstanding collections showing, and/or

4. There is a bankruptcy (e.g. Chapter 7) showing on the report within the last 2 years.

While these reasons are not all-inclusive of what could be showing up on a customer's credit report, (bad) credit is usually one of the main reasons why they could not go Conforming or Non-conforming. When you are first qualifying your borrowers then this is something you first want to determine: Do you have a Conforming or Non-conforming loan or is it Sub-prime? But remember, even though this is true, today with DU and LP Underwriting, the actual credit scores of the borrowers are less restrictive because these Underwriting programs (DU and LP) usually determine what the minimum credit scores of the borrowers should be – after analyzing all their Layers of Risk.

I should note here that there is usually a corresponding relationship to the (middle) credit score of a borrower and the maximum allowed LTV on a (their) loan: As a borrower's middle credit score gets lower then Lenders generally lower the maximum LTV that they will lend on (more on this when we get to Chapter 19 on Reading the Rate Sheets). And, this is also true for Conforming and Non-conforming Loan Programs as well. Another reason a home loan borrower might have to go Sub-prime could be that the Total Debt Ratio is too high for a Conforming or Non-conforming Loan Program (e.g. their Capacity). I have seen Sub-prime loans approved with a Total Debt Ratio as high as 65%! Another reason could deal with the Collateral or Subject Property on a prospective loan. Given the nature, condition, location, and/or type of property that the borrowers wish to obtain a home loan on may require them to have to go Sub-prime or Non-conforming on their loan.

Recall when we discussed the 5 Cs of Credit in Qualifying Your Borrowers? In Qualifying borrowers for Conforming Loans you will usually see the number one "C" being Credit. This is because if your customer doesn't have good Credit, that is required for Conforming Loans, then you can pretty much forget about that loan and borrower going Conforming. On the other hand, with Sub-prime loans an interesting thing happens: The sequence of importance of the 5 Cs of Credit changes. Because (it is assumed) that the credit could already be bad, damaged, or less than perfect - Credit here is no longer the prime candidate in the number one slot in the 5 Cs of Credit. Collateral (value of the subject property and type) becomes #1, with Capacity as #2, and then Credit as #3.

I should also note here, that while the above is generally true, Sub-prime Lenders usually required the customer to have a minimum (middle) credit score in order to qualify and, as with Conforming and Non-Conforming loans, that middle credit score will usually determine the maximum LTV on that loan as well. Most Sub-prime lenders, I have seen in the past, would not accept a loan file with the customer's middle credit score below 500. So, this is something you want to keep in mind when qualifying your borrowers. If your loan can't go Conforming then do you have a Non-conforming or Sub-prime loan here? And, if you do then will structuring it and packaging it as a Non-conforming or Sub-prime loan still enable the borrowers to achieve the goals of their loan and financially benefit them? These are the questions you need to ask in Qualifying and finding the best home loan for your customers.

Also, remember what I said about interest rates increasing with the perceived increase risk of the loan by Lenders. And, as you have probably guessed, Sub-prime loans, by their very nature, carry with them greater risk and hence higher interest rates (I've seen rates as high as 15%!). Also, the LTV on Sub-prime Loans often tends to be lower as well. The types of loan programs that are available through Sub-prime lenders are also different. The most common types of loans that Sub-prime Lenders offered were the 2, 3, 4, and 5-Year ARM loans. The 2-Year ARM used to be a popular Sub-prime loan product. But since the Sub-prime Mortgage Crisis period, beginning in early 2007, many Sub-prime wholesale lenders discontinued offering that ARM loan product.

With a 3-Year ARM the interest rate is fixed for the first 3 years and then becomes adjustable and usually adjust each year thereafter. With a 4-Year ARM the initial fixed interest rate period is 4 years. Some Lenders charged a slightly higher interest rate on a 4-Year ARM over a 3-Year ARM loan. Thus, as the fixed interest rate period gets shorter then the interest rate, on that loan program, usually improves and gets lower. These types of loans (ARMs) are written as 3/27 (3-Year ARM), 4/26 (4-Year ARM), and the 5/25 (5-Year ARM). Adding together those two numbers (3 & 27) or (4 & 26) results in 30 (years). That represents the term of those loans.

And, those types of Sub-prime ARM loans usually came with a Prepayment Penalty feature. A Prepayment Penalty refers to the fee (a penalty) that a loan customer would have to pay if they paid off the full amount of their loan within a loan's Prepayment Penalty period. A rule of thumb, and quick way to figure the amount of the Prepayment Penalty, is to calculate about 6 months of the P&I payment on that loan. This is only a conservative rule of thumb and the actual Prepayment Penalty calculation may be different with each Lender and/or loan program. For example, some ARM loans with Prepayment Penalties amounted to 2–3% of the original loan amount. Thus, the actual percent used, in calculating that loan's Prepayment Penalty, seemed to be determined when the full amount of that loan is paid off (before the end of that loan's Prepayment Penalty period). So, it could get rather expensive for borrowers to get out of their loan during their Prepayment Penalty Period (and that's the reason for it).

On Sub-prime loans, with 3-Year ARMs, having a Prepayment Penalty feature, I always tried to match the Prepayment Penalty period to the fixed rate period on the home loan borrower's ARM. In other words, you should always try not to have the Prepayment Penalty period extend beyond the fixed rate period of that ARM loan. For example, if the loan is a 3-Year ARM then the Prepayment Period should be no longer than 3 years. You would want to do this because your (Sub-prime) loan customers will usually want to refinance out of their ARM loan when it gets into the Adjustable-Rate Period.

Now why, you may ask, would we want to setup a customer on a 2-Year ARM loan (if you could find a Lender who offers this ARM product these days) when you might be able to set them up with a 30-Year Fixed Rate loan offered by a Sub-prime lender? First, the interest rate on a 2-Year ARM loan is lower than a 30-year fixed rate loan. And second, the reasons that a borrower may have to go Sub-prime could be because of a one-time thing in the past or of a temporary nature. It occurred, but is in the past (job layoff, medical bills, divorce, bankruptcy, etc.). This occurrence may have resulted in an adverse effect on their Credit. As time goes on, and assuming the borrowers continue to pay their bills on time and as agreed (after you have set them up on a 2/28 ARM loan), then after two years of paying on their Sub-prime loan they may then qualify for a Conforming Loan. It just so happens that Conforming Lenders like to see 2 years of good credit. So, if you have set up your customers on a 2-Year ARM and they subsequently take care of their credit and pay their mortgage payments and creditors as agreed - then after 2 years they should have good credit that could enable them to refinance their 2-Year ARM (for example) - into a Conforming Loan with a lower interest rate and with a corresponding lower monthly mortgage payment.

If you have the opportunity to do any Sub-prime loans it may surprise you to see how high the interest rates are for some borrowers on these types of loans. But, always keep in mind the goals of your borrowers and the benefits of your proposed home loan. In being the Mortgage Doctor your customers may tell you that they have too many debts and would like to consolidate them into their new mortgage. You then know the loan prognosis and that the customer's loan goal is to obtain a new loan that will enable them to consolidate all, most, or some of their outstanding debts - resulting in an appreciable reduction in their monthly debt servicing.

For example, many years ago, I did a home loan for a customer whereby the interest rate was 9.75%! I know, today that sounds like a very high interest rate (and I wish I could have gotten him a better rate too) - but with that loan (and at that rate) I was able to reduce that customer's monthly debt servicing by $525. That translated into an annual savings of $6,300 hard dollars for that customer. Well worth doing that loan for. That home loan was structured as a 2-Year ARM I set him up with and after 2 years (assuming he took care of his credit) he could then refinance into a 30-Year Fixed Rate Conforming Loan. My point here is: Sometimes when you present your (Sub-prime) loan program to your home loan customers they may balk or complain about the high interest rate. When this happens then try to get them to focus instead on the benefits of that loan: Their monthly savings or whatever benefits that loan will enable them to achieve (that they wanted in the first place).

I cannot stress this enough when it comes to "selling" your loans to your customers – whether it's a Conforming, Non-conforming, or Sub-prime loan. Focus on the benefits (i.e. the reduced monthly payment) that the loan provides instead of the higher interest rate. And, always keep in mind that the amount of a monthly mortgage payment is a function of the interest rate (as well as the loan amount and amortization period). Knowing this, you could say to your customers (if they balk at that rate), "I understand what you are saying about the interest rate being high but look at the monthly savings you'll realize with this loan. Isn't that what you really wanted to achieve with this loan?" If you fully researched this loan and finally submitted it to a Lender with the best interest rate (and term) for that type of loan program - then you also probably know that no other Lender (or mortgage company) would be able to offer them any better (loan program) than what you are offering them. In other words - you did your homework. Researching the home loan for the best rate and terms for your prospective borrowers - that's one of the most important parts of being a good, professional mortgage loan originator.

An important point I should not forget to mention is that although Sub-prime loans did have higher interest rates, they did not have PMI (private mortgage insurance) - regardless of the LTV. You may sometimes see this also in some Non-conforming loans. When you consider the Sub-prime's loan's monthly payment, with the higher interest rate and absence of PMI, to a Conforming Loan's lower rate (with a loan having a high LTV – greater than 80%) and with PMI - then the total monthly payment on that Sub-prime loan doesn't look so bad. For an example of this - please refer to Exhibit III showing a letter I wrote to one of my customers explaining this to him. After he read this letter he agreed.

Now that we have talked about the six types of loan programs, let's now talk about the different types of what are called Loan Transactions that are available.

II. Types of Loan Transactions:
There are basically two types of Loan Transactions that you will find within one or more of the Loan Programs above. They are Purchase or Refinance loans. Let's now go over each of these.

1. Purchase Loans
2. Refinance Loans

1. Purchase Loans:
Purchase loans are pretty straightforward in that the purpose of this type of loan is to Purchase a home or property. Depending upon what Type of Loan Program you are submitting your Purchase Loan through, the following are the more common loan features that may be available to your home buying customers in their Home Purchase Loan:

- Purchase Loans with LTVs as high as 95%, 97%, and 100%. There are even purchase loans with LTVs of 105% - to assist the purchase loan customer in the down payment and closing costs.

- Seller Contributions. Many purchase loans enable the Home Seller (if they so choose) to assist in paying for part of the Buyer's loan closing costs. Depending on the Purchase Loan program and whether that purchase is for primary residence or investment property, Seller Contributions can be from 3% up to 6% of the sales price of that property.

- Gift Funds: Depending on the Lender and loan program, Gift Funds allow the homebuyer to obtain gift funds from a relative, close friend, and sometimes their employer - to be applied towards the down payment and/or closing costs. For more information regarding Gift Funds please refer to Borrower Contributions.

Also, it has been my experience that for certain types of Purchase Loans many Conforming Loan Programs like the purchasers to have 3% - 5% (of the sales price of the property) of their own funds saved up for the down payment. Many times you might find that these funds need to be "seasoned." In other words, the purchasers (your loan customers) must demonstrate that they have had those funds (i.e. in their checking or savings account) for a minimum of 90 days or more. This is why it is so important to ask, while qualifying your home purchase customers, if they have saved up any money for the down payment. I will talk more on this subject when we get to Chapter 10, which covers The Uniform Residential Loan Application (the 1003). Because if those home buying customers haven't saved up any money for the down payment and/or loan closing costs (and there are no Gift Funds forthcoming) then you can safely assume that you are looking at a high LTV purchase loan. Most Non-Conforming Lenders, who offer these types of high LTV home purchase loan programs (that I am seeing today) require a minimum credit score of 700 to qualify for these.

Therefore, when you know that you are looking at a high LTV purchase loan program then the very next thing you want to know is – how is their credit? Next, of course, is do they income qualify for the amount of home loan they are requesting?

Also, keep in mind, while qualifying your home purchase customers that one of your prime objectives, as a mortgage loan originator, is to "get them in the door." By that I mean, your goal, in structuring a loan program for your customers, should be to put together a loan program that will enable them to qualify for that home they wish to purchase. For example, let's say your customers don't income qualify based on the interest rates for a 30-year fixed loan. But they might qualify for a home loan with an ARM loan having a lower initial (and fixed) interest rate. I know, your customer's may not like the idea of having an ARM loan. But hey, if it can get them the home of their dreams, even if it's an ARM loan - then that is something they should seriously consider. Just explain to them the features and benefits of your proposed ARM loan program. Most home purchase and refinance customers don't fully understand how ARM loans work – as well as the financial benefits they offer. But explaining that to them is all part of that excellent customer service you provide to your customers.

Homeownership Education Requirements:
Before I leave this section on Purchase Loans I would also like to mention Fannie Mae's policy on Homeownership Education Requirements. Fannie Mae now requires at least one borrower to complete homebuyer education prior to closing when:

- If all borrowers on the loan are relying solely on Non-traditional Credit to qualify, or
- For all HomeReady® purchase transactions.

According to Fannie Mae current policy, at least one borrower must complete homebuyer education for the following transactions:

- If all borrowers on the loan are relying solely on Non-traditional Credit to qualify, regardless of the loan product or whether the borrowers are first-time home buyers (no change to current requirement);
- HomeReady purchase transactions when all occupying borrowers are first-time homebuyers, regardless of the LTV ratio; or
- Purchase transactions with LTV, CLTV, or HCLTV ratios greater than 95% when all borrowers are first-time homebuyers.

And, as of October 23, 2019 Fannie Mae waives the fee for the Framework Homeownership, LLC (Framework®) course for lenders, removing the cost burden for borrowers.

2. Refinance Loans:

A Refinance Loan is a loan that pays off an existing mortgage loan, replacing it with a new mortgage loan. It's important to understand that a refinance loan is exactly that: It refinances an existing mortgage (or land contract) loan. However, if your customer tells you that he wishes to refinance his home and he now owns the property free and clear - then this too is usually considered a refinance loan.

In talking about refinance loans there are basically two types:

- Rate/Term Refinance loans
- Cash-Out Refinance loans

Rate/Term Refinance:
A Rate/Term Refinance loan seeks to refinance only the outstanding balance of the existing mortgage loan and/or loans. Its goal, as the name implies, is either to obtain a better interest rate (Rate) or to change the term of the loan (Term). In this type of loan there is little, if any, cash-out to the borrower. The maximum LTV you will see on a Fannie Mae Conforming Refinance Rate/Term loans these days, for a SFR that is the homeowner's primary residence, is 95%. Rate/Term Refinance loans are also

referred to as Limited Cash-Out Refinance loans and its loan-to-value acronym is represented by LCLTV.

Also, if a customer wishes to obtain a Refinance loan, to consolidate their existing 1st and 2nd mortgages (only), then this too is considered by Conforming Lenders, as a Rate/Term Refinance loan. However, I should note, for historical purposes only, that Fannie Mae a number of years ago changed a ruling (and LTV limitation) on what could be considered a Rate/Term refinance loan – when consolidating the 1st and 2nd mortgages. To be considered a Rate/Term Refinance Loan (in this case) the 2nd mortgage, being consolidated (into that loan) must have been used solely to assist in the financial purchase of that subject property. Otherwise, that refinance loan would then be considered a Cash-Out Refinance loan (see below). An example of this could be that the purpose of the existing 2nd mortgage loan was to consolidate debts, obtain cash-out (for whatever reason), and/or for home improvements.

Having a loan go from a Rate/Term refinance loan to a Cash-Out Refinance Loan will usually result in lowering the maximum LTV on that loan. For an O/O SFR Conforming loan, it lowers the maximum LTV from 95% to 80%.

This requirement (in consolidating the 1st and 2nd mortgages) with the goal of calling it a Rate/Term Refinance loan is a Fannie/Freddie guideline for Conforming loans. If you are researching a loan to be submitted towards the Non-Conforming or Sub-prime lending areas then this requirement might not apply.

I should also mention that some Lenders will consider a refinance loan as a Rate/Term Refinance loan when the purpose of that loan is solely to buyout an ex-spouse as a result of a loan customer's divorce. The subject property, when considering this option, needs to be owner-occupied.

You'll see a lot of Rate/Term refinance loan requests when interest rates have fallen and folks wish to refinance and get a lower interest rate on their loan with an accompanying reduction in their monthly mortgage payments. Depending on the loan amount, I usually suggest a benefit (rate reduction) of at least 1.0% or better in the new interest rate to make it worthwhile - when you consider all the costs to do that loan (please refer to Payback Period in my previous discussion on Buydowns).

You'll also get requests, from time-to-time, from customers who wish to Refinance and change the Term of their loan. Usually, they're thinking about going from a 30-year fixed interest rate loan to a 15-year fixed rate loan. I tell my customers who wish to do this that in going from a 30-year to a 15-year fixed rate loan that even though they would realize a better interest rate (rates on 15-year loans are generally better than 30-Year loans by about anywhere from 25 to 50 basis points) that they can anticipate their new monthly P&I payment increasing by about 28%. This is because they are squeezing the time period (Term) of their loan from 30 to 15 years. Many times this will result in their monthly mortgage payment (P&I) increasing by as much as $250 or more. That's fine - if they can afford it. And certainly, with this type of loan, they will payoff their new mortgage in 15 years. Another big benefit in going from a 30-year to a 15-year loan is that doing this will significantly reduce the amount of interest they would otherwise pay - over the entire term of that 30-Year loan.

It's not uncommon for a husband and wife that I am doing a home loan for, to inquire about doing a 15-year mortgage. Over the years this is exactly what I do: First, I explain to them what I just said above. Then I take a piece of paper and write on it what their new monthly mortgage loan payment would be with the proposed 30-year fixed rate loan and beside that - what their new mortgage payment would be with a 15-year fixed rate mortgage. I subtract the difference between the two, underline it, and turn the page around so my customers can see it. Then I explain to them those figures they see on that paper. I don't want to sound like a chauvinistic person - but during the time I am doing this - I first look at the husband and then (most importantly) I look at the wife. If she looks at the figures and says, "That's great, we can handle that" then I'd say something like, "Terrific, let me look into this for you." If, however, she says nothing and/or frowns in any way – then I will back away from this idea and say something like, "I tell you what, if you would like, I could set you up on this 30-year fixed rate loan and provide you with a 15-year amortization schedule based on this loan. Then, if you follow that payment schedule then you'll have that loan paid off in 15 years. And, if you get caught short a month or you need to buy new tires or shoes for the kids – then you won't be under the gun to make that mortgage payment (of about $250 more)." Most that I have suggested this to decided to go with the 30-year fixed rate home loan.

Now, why do I look at the wife for a sign? I guess it's because, in many cases (of my own personal experiences), it's the wife who is doing the budget for the family. If that's the case then she knows where just about every dollar goes. If it will put a strain on their family's finances then she usually will say so and/or show it in some way. And that's what I look for. So, that's what I do and it has worked for me.

As mortgage loan originators we have an ethical (and maybe moral) obligation to provide the best home loan program possible that will enable our customers to achieve the goals of their Purchase or Refinance loan. The worst thing that could happen to me here is that I get a call from one of my customers, about 6 months later (after their home loan's closing) telling me that they now need to refinance again because they are having difficulty making their monthly mortgage payments - on that 15-Year Fixed rate loan. That has never happened yet. But if it did I would know then - that I did not do My Job as a mortgage loan originator for those folks. Don't let this happen to you. Take care of your customers.

In structuring your Rate/Term Refinance loans the total loan amount would include:
- Payoff Amount of the Outstanding Mortgage or Mortgages, and
- All the Loans Costs included in that Loan

Hence, if the outstanding mortgage payoff amount is $100,000 and the loan costs amount to about $3,000 then the new loan amount will be about $103,000. Although Rate/Term Loans are not designed to provide any Cash-Out to the borrowers, most Conforming Lenders will allow a small cash-out amount of up to 2.0% of the total loan amount or $2,000 - whichever is less. If I can I like to provide at least about $300 for my customers on Rate/Term Refinance loans for some "walking around" money - to take the wife or husband out to dinner or whatever. However, prior to structuring your loan for this, do discuss this with your customers to make sure this meets with their approval.

Streamline Refinance:

Another and unique type of Rate/Term Refinance Loan is the Streamline Refinance loan. A Streamline Refinance loan seeks to refinance the existing 1st mortgage only. Like the Rate/Term Refinance loan a Streamline Refinance loan seeks only to obtain a better interest rate or change the term of the loan. I love Streamline Refinance loans because they can be so simple and easy to process and package. And, those that I have done in the past didn't require me to order a new appraisal or needed to pull a full Credit Report to credit or income qualify those borrowers. I just needed to show that they had made their existing mortgage payments on time.

There are, however, a couple of Fannie Mae and Freddie Mac guidelines you should be aware of - if you are planning on doing any of these:

- The new Streamline Refinance loan can include closing costs and points but only up to a maximum of 2.5% of the total loan amount.
- The new Loan Amount cannot exceed the Original Loan Amount.
- The Maximum LTV on this New Loan cannot exceed the LTV on the Original Loan.
- If there is an existing 2nd Mortgage then that will need to be re-subordinated (see Subordination Agreement). However, I should note that the 2nd Mortgage cannot be changed in doing this Streamline Refinance loan.
- And, of course, with this Streamline Refinance loan there is no cash back to the Borrower. But, I know you knew that.

Remember also, that Conforming Lenders will require PMI on Rate/Term loans with an LTV greater than 80%. Rate/Term Refinance loans are written and abbreviated as: Refi. R/T.

Cash-out Refinance:

As the name implies here, your loan customers are Refinancing their existing mortgage and taking Cash-Out with a Refinance Loan. They are using the equity in their home to achieve this. Now, most Lenders consider a loan "Cash-Out" anytime the loan is not a Rate/Term refinance loan. For example, your customers may want to consolidate and payoff all of their outstanding credit cards but don't wish to obtain any extra cash at loan closing. Today, this would still be considered a Cash-Out Refinance loan. This is also true if your customers want to Refinance in order to obtain funds for home improvements - but want no additional funds for themselves. Conforming Cash-Out Refinance loans for O/O SFR, according to Fannie Mae, now have a maximum LTV of 80%.

Cash-Out Refinance loans can also be used to consolidate the existing 1st and 2nd mortgages. However, as I mentioned above, when discussing Rate/Term Refinance loans, a Refinance Loan that seeks to consolidate both the 1st and 2nd mortgages would be considered a Cash-Out Refinance loan – if the existing 2nd mortgage's funds were not used in its entirety for providing the additional funds needed to purchase that home. This is an important distinction - because just this fact could reduce the maximum LTV on that Conforming Refinance Loan from 95% (Rate/Term) to 80% (Cash-Out).

In structuring your Cash-Out Refinance loans the total loan amount needed would include:

- Payoff Amount of the Outstanding Mortgage or Mortgages.
- All the Loans Costs included in that Loan, and
- The Additional Funds needed to achieve the goals of that loan

Remember that the maximum amount of that loan will be tempered or possibly limited by the LTV that is available for this Type of Loan Program - that offers the range of interest rates you are looking at. And, don't forget that once the LTV of a Conforming loan goes beyond 80% then PMI will also be required. So, that is certainly a consideration. But just as we discussed, when I was talking about Sub-prime loans, the resulting benefits of a loan (reduced monthly payment) needs to be considered in relation to the additional monthly PMI costs.

While within this area of Cash-out Refinance loans I'd like to also mention one of the newer Fannie Mae refinance loan transactions that came out last year in 2019. As a mortgage loan originator you will sometimes have the opportunity, after you have completed a home loan for someone, to experience what I call "a warm fuzzy." This can happen when you do a home loan for a customer and it makes them so happy and/or you saved them from losing their home or from bankruptcy and/or has really improved their financial situation. When this happens then it can make you feel like you are in one of the greatest professions in the world. And you know what? You are. To give you an example of what I am talking about, about 10 years ago I got a call from some nice older folks who were thinking about doing a debt consolidation home loan (Cash-Out Refinance). I first met with them in their home. After arriving there I talked with them for a while in their living room. It was snowing outside but very warm and comfortable in their living room. Their fireplace was crackling away and I could feel the warmth from the fireplace on my face. I looked around and could see the pictures of their family on their living room walls - their sons and daughters and grandchildren. After talking with them for a short while I suggested we go to the dining table (to do the paperwork). There I began completing their home loan application (the 1003).

While completing the Employment Section, of the 1003, they told me they were both retired and had modest fixed incomes (retirement & Social Security) coming in each month. However, when we got to the Liabilities Section of the 1003 they then told me of all their outstanding monthly payments they paid to their creditors. I couldn't believe it. Those folks had virtually every credit card and store card in existence! I needed to use the 4th page of the 1003 to list them all! Later, when I completed a Qualifying Analysis Worksheet on those folks, I saw that they had only a few hundred dollars left over each month after they paid all their creditors. And yet, they had excellent credit and always paid on time. Wow!

Fortunately, those folks did have enough equity in their home for me to help them. Well, to make a long story short (as I can), I put together a Cash-Out Refinance loan that paid off all of their outstanding creditors and also structured it so they could maybe take a vacation and also so the Husband could get some new dentures. When I was all done that loan resulted in those folks making one monthly mortgage payment and enabled them to realize a monthly savings of about $1,100! They (and I) were amazed. That loan actually increased what they would have in their monthly budget by about $1,100. Now $1,100 is a lot of savings, but for folks who are on a fixed income - well it's unbelievable. Anyway, doing that loan really gave me a warm fuzzy. Afterwards, I couldn't wait to do another loan like that - whereby I could again offer a benefit like that to another customer. Yeah, the ole warm fuzzy. It's really cool when it happens to you. When it does you know you are in one of the greatest professions in the world.

I also should mention that many Lenders have a maximum amount of actual cash that the borrower can receive on a Cash-Out Refinance loan (e.g. $200,000). This maximum limit on the actual cash that can be received does seem to vary with different Lenders – so check with your targeted Lender if this is a concern of yours. A Lender's maximum cash-out amount is usually shown on their Rate Sheets. Cash-Out Refinance loans are written and abbreviated as: Refi. C/O.

Bridge Loan:
This is another type of Cash-Out Refinance home loan that is usually used in home purchase type of scenarios. As the name implies this type of financing provides loan funds – "a Bridge" for the borrower - from his current home (which he or she is selling) towards the down payment and loan costs for the home they are interested in purchasing. In doing this type of home loan the borrowers will need to be qualified based on those two mortgages. The goal of a bridge loan is to provide temporary financing and is looked upon as a short-term type of loan providing the needed funds to purchase the new home. Once their house is sold (for which the Bridge Loan was created and based upon) the Bridge Loan is then paid off. A Bridge Loan may also be referred to as a Swing Loan, Gap or Interim Financing.

Within these loan Transactions are what we call Loan Products. For example, in doing a Refinance Loan you might setup a loan as a 30-Year Fixed Rate loan or a 15-Year Fixed Rate loan. With that said, let's turn now turn the page to. . . .

III. Types of Loan Products:

In this section, where I discuss the Types of Loan Products, I'll be presenting the following seven types of Loan Products:

1. Fixed Rate Loans
2. Adjustable-Rate Mortgages (ARMs)
3. Second Mortgages
4. Balloon Mortgages
5. Home Equity Line of Credit (HELOC)
6. Reverse Mortgages
7. Investment Property (Loans)

1. Fixed Rate Loans:

With Fixed Rate Loans you will usually be originating a 30-year fixed rate loan or the 15-year fixed rate loan. As both names imply, the monthly P&I payment is fixed (with the loan's interest rate not changing) over the Term of those loans. For 30-year fixed rate loans we are looking at a 360-month Term and with 15-year fixed rate loans - a 180-month Term. I should note that many Conforming Lenders today also offer 10, 20, and 40-year fixed rate loans. Fixed Rate loans are also referred to as Close End loans.

Adjustable Rate Mortgages (ARMs) are our next discussion and for simplicity (and perhaps technically) I have separated my coverage of ARMs loans into what I call Short and Long ARMs. I hope my doing so helps you to better understand these types of mortgage loans.

2. Adjustable Rate Mortgages (ARMs):

First, let me say that <u>any</u> loan that has an Adjustable Rate Feature is called an ARM (Adjustable Rate Mortgage). As I mentioned above, with ARM Loans there are what I call Short ARMs and Long ARMs.

Also, many lending folks refer to ARM loans that have a fixed and adjustable feature as Hybrid ARMs. In this discussion of ARMs I'd like to talk about three types of ARMs:

- Long ARMs
- Short ARMs
- Step Interest-Rate Loan

Long ARMs:

"Long" ARMs, as I refer to them here, are ARM loans that have a noticeably long initial fixed rate period and then it (the interest rate) begins to adjust - usually every year thereafter. An example of this is the 3/1 ARM: So written because with this ARM it has a fixed interest rate period for the first 3 years and then begins its adjustment period, whereby it adjusts every year thereafter - for the rest of the Term of that loan (usually amortized over 30 years).

Other popular types of Long ARMs are the 5/1, 7/1, and 10/1. As far as the interest rates on these are concerned - the shorter the initial fixed rate period then the lower the interest rate. If the ARM program (you are evaluating) is a Conforming type of loan then it is rare that that ARM will have a Prepayment Penalty with it. However, if an ARM is a Non-Conforming or Sub-prime loan type product then you can generally assume that those ARMs come with a Prepayment Penalty feature - which continues (on that ARM) for a certain time period (i.e. first 2 – 5 years of that loan). But, many times, your customer could have the option to "buy-out" part or all of that Prepayment Penalty Period if they wanted to, either by paying a Loan Discount or with a slightly higher interest rate (than would be available with the full Prepayment Penalty period included. See Premium Pricing). For example, on a 5/1 ARM, that has a Prepayment Penalty period (written as P/P) of 5 years, your customer might be able to Buy-Out that Prepayment Penalty Period down to 3 years. I suggest you do this only if your customer requests this or doing it would more enable your customers to meet the goals of their loan.

I should also note here that there is another type of Prepayment Penalty called a "Soft Prepayment." A Soft Prepayment has an added feature to it that allows the borrower (on that loan) to sell their home during the Prepayment Penalty Period without incurring that Prepayment Penalty expense. The interest rate is also better with this feature - than on an ARM loan with No Prepayment Penalty feature. Depending on your borrower's loan goals - that may very well be their only concern regarding any Prepayment Penalty feature: To have the freedom to sell their home if they so choose to without incurring any Prepayment Penalty costs. So, look for this when structuring your ARM loans.

When might you consider suggesting a "Long" ARM to a customer? Let's say that you get a call from a customer who is interested in doing a Refinance Loan and wants the best interest rate possible or that they can get => customer's loan goal. You say, "OK," and then ask him additional questions. You might ask, "Mr. Customer, how long do you and your family plan on living in your current home? I mean, do you plan on staying there for the next 10, 20, or 30 years or perhaps sell your property before then?" Your customer may reply, "You know, my wife and I have discussed that and with the kids getting older (to around 11 and 12 years old) and maybe another one in a couple of years, we feel very strongly that we will be moving out of this house in about 4-5 years." Now here's when you could research and present that 5/1 ARM to him. It would offer him a lower interest rate (than a 30-year fixed rate loan would) and provides a fixed interest rate for that time period he and his family intend to live in their current home. And, when the loan goes into the Adjustable-Rate Period then your borrowers could either sell their home (just as they intended) or Refinance that loan.

Also, keep in mind that as the interest rate gets lower then the monthly mortgage payment (P&I) gets lower as well and this in turn can enable your customers to Qualify for a larger loan amount. As I mentioned previously, this could be an important consideration (in suggesting an ARM) when you are working on a Home Purchase Loan and your customers do not qualify (based on their current income) for a selected fixed-rate loan amount. With an ARM (having a lower interest rate) they may then qualify for that higher loan amount. We call that - getting more house with a lower interest rate. Or, having a lower initial interest rate, with a lower monthly mortgage payment, might also just qualify them now for that house they wish to purchase. This can also enhance their chances of getting their Housing and Total Debt Ratios in line and of being approved on their loan.

You should know, however, that many homeowners have an aversion to ARM loans and don't like or want any home loan that has an adjustable-rate feature to it. Some of those folks had home loans during the latter 1970's and early 80's when mortgage interest rates went as high as 18%! Their common argument (or concern) is that the future is uncertain and who knows what the interest rates will be when the adjustable-rate period gets here? They're right. Who knows? I certainly don't. But I would be extremely surprised if, in my lifetime, we again see interest rates getting that high. I sure hope not.

I remember, while working for a bank in San Francisco, California in 1980, I was walking down the hallway when I overheard one gentleman (who worked for that bank) ask another man he was walking with, "What's the rate now?" The other man replied with an interest rate and the first man said, "Darn, it has increased another quarter of a point in just the last 30 minutes!" Understand, prior to that period, mortgage interest rates generally changed about 2 maybe 3 times a year. So, a lot of those (home-buying and home refinancing) folks understandably have an affinity with fixed rate mortgages and like to stay on the safe side: Like always knowing what their interest rate will be and knowing how much their next monthly mortgage payment will be - the same as it was last month.

However, after saying all of that I should note that recently there has been a number of surveys that have found that today young homebuyers and owners are increasingly open to the idea of doing an ARM loan - if it better enables them to achieve their goals of homeownership. So, keep that in mind when suggesting and structuring home loan proposals for new and existing homeowners.

Short ARMs:
With these types of "Short" ARMs the initial fixed interest rate period, before its first adjustable-rate period begins, is significantly shorter than those discussed above. For example, this initial fixed rate period could be anywhere from 1 to 6

months to a year - from the date of loan funding. Once this type of ARM loan hits its first Adjustable-Rate Period (anniversary date) then its interest rate will continue to adjust at the next and subsequent designated adjustable time periods (i.e. every 3 months).

Another common well-known ARM is the ARM based on the 6-Month CD. This ARM first adjusts 6 months after the funding of this ARM loan. It then subsequently adjusts every 6 months thereafter, for the entire Term of that loan. The interest rate it adjusts to is a function of its existing rate, the indexed CD rate, and the margin on that ARM loan.

Another example of this type of ARM is the 1-Year ARM based on the Treasury Bill (T-Bill) rate referred to as 1/1. Here, the ARM adjusts on its first anniversary date (1 year after funding of that loan) and adjusts each year thereafter. The interest rate that it will adjust to will be a function of where that ARM's current interest rate is, where the T-Bill Index is at that time, and the margin on that ARM (we'll talk more about that in a minute).

There are also some LIBOR (index) ARMs that are offered as a 3 or 6 month LIBOR ARMs. That index "LIBOR" is pronounced like LYE-BORE. For example, on the 3-Month LIBOR ARM the interest rate will first adjust 3 months after loan funding and adjusts every 3 months thereafter. There are also the 3/6, 5/6, 7/6 month LIBOR ARM loans. And, there are the 3/1, 5/1, 7/1 LIBOR ARMs. The first group here (e.g. 3/6-month LIBOR ARM) adjusts every 6 months – after its initial fixed rate period (depending on which one you go with). The second group here is LIBOR ARMs that adjust after their initial first fixed-rate period (i.e. 3, 5, and 7 years respectfully) and adjust every year thereafter for the entire Term of that loan.

The 5/6-month LIBOR ARM is fixed for the first five years and then begins its adjustment period - adjusting every 6 months thereafter. Some of these LIBOR ARMs, because of their longer initial fixed interest rate periods, could also be considered Long ARMs (as I am referring to them here). At the adjustment period the interest rate will adjust to whatever is the current interest rate on that loan, plus the LIBOR index rate at that time, plus the margin on that loan.

For a review of the common Indexes used for ARM loans please refer to the term Indexes, within Chapter 2 titled "Common Mortgage Lending Terms".

3. **Step Interest-Rate Mortgage Loan:**
The Step Interest-Rate Mortgage Loan is sometimes referred to as a Graduated Payment Mortgage (GPM). And the GPM was fairly popular during the 1980s. With this type of mortgage loan the initial Interest Rate is usually lower than what is normally offered for a Fixed Rate Loan. Then, on the anniversary of that

mortgage loan's closing, the Interest Rate adjusts and increases – usually by about 0.50% each year.

With this Step Interest-Rate Loan the initial Interest Rate is lower and then the loan's Interest Rate is adjusted upward in incremental steps - usually every year at the anniversary date of that loan's closing. And then, on the final adjustment (if there is one) the Interest Rate becomes fixed for the remaining Term of that home loan.

This type of ARM differs from the others discussed above because the Fixed-Rate Period begins at the end of the adjustment periods. In the example below you see a Step Interest-Rate Loan with an initial Rate of 3.0%, with incremental increases of 0.50% per year and then on the 5th year the interest rate is increased to 5.0% where it remains for the remaining Term of that loan. Now, depending on the type Step Interest-Rate Loan you are working on the incremental interest rate adjustments (or increases) can be assigned or could be dependent upon the market rate at the time of the loan's interest rate adjustment.

The previously mentioned Step Interest-Rate Mortgage Loan (with a pre-assigned interest rate adjustment increases on its anniversary date of its loan closing) is the one that is used in the Home Affordable Modification Program (HMP) that became available to homeowners on March 4, 2009. This Step Interest-Rate Mortgage Loan Program gives a homeowner, who is experiencing a financial hardship, financial relief by immediately reducing their monthly mortgage payments. And, this program also allows years for the homeowner to financially get back on their feet.

The example below should give you an idea of what I'm talking about:

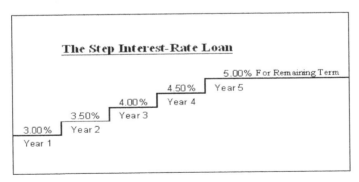

Qualifying Your Borrowers on an ARM:
Qualifying your borrowers on an ARM loan can sometimes be significantly different than doing so on a Fixed Rate Loan. Because the ARM's interest rate can (and usually will) increase at the Anniversary Dates (with a corresponding increase in that borrower's monthly mortgage P&I payment) the Lender might be concerned as to whether the borrowers will have the capacity to adequately service their loan (as the loan's interest rate increases). For this reason many Lenders require that the borrowers qualify for an ARM loan based on the maximum allowable newly Indexed Rate on the

first, second, or third adjustment period. At what period your borrowers need to qualify for depends on that ARM's loan program and the Lender's ARM Underwriting loan guidelines.

Also, according to the new Qualified Mortgage Rule, if an ARM's interest rate will adjust within the first five years of home closing then that home loan borrower will need to be qualified on the P&I payment based on the highest interest rate it could adjust to within that initial five-year period. This is also true for step-rate home loans.

So, just be aware of this when considering an ARM loan for your customers. Also be aware, as I said, that different Lenders have different Underwriting Guidelines for determining how they Qualify and Underwrite borrowers on ARM loans submitted to them. Some may require the borrowers to qualify based on that loan's initial interest rate, or based on its first year's adjustment, or perhaps in later years. Therefore, I suggest that you check it out with your targeted Lender to be sure of what their Qualifying and Underwriting Guidelines are on their ARM loans. And, don't forget the rules regarding this according the Qualified Mortgage Rule.

Before leaving this subject of ARM loans I'd like to introduce you to some terms peculiar to ARM loans that you need to be familiar with if you intend to do any of these types of loans.

ARM Loan Terms:

Start Rate:
The Start Rate, sometimes referred to as the Initial Rate, is the interest rate that an ARM loan begins with.

Anniversary Date:
As I mentioned previously above, this term refers to the date that the ARM's interest rate will adjust. When it does is a function of what kind of ARM it is: 6-month, 1 year, etc.

Floor Rate:
The Floor Rate (if there is one) is the lowest interest rate that an ARM's loan rate may go at the Anniversary Date.

Index:
This is that feature of an ARM that most influences what its new interest rate will be when its Anniversary Date comes around. The Index Rate on an ARM will be determined by: 1. What Index is being used for that ARM (e.g. LIBOR, T-Bill, or Certificate of Deposit), and 2. What that Index is at the Anniversary Date. Between the two (the Index and Margin) it is the ARM's Index that moves up or down over the life of an ARM loan.

Margin:

The margin on an ARM is represented by a percentage that is added onto the ARM's specified index rate at the anniversary date. Together, or the sum of these two percentages (margin + index rate), plus the existing interest rate, become the new adjusted interest rate for that ARM (unless it is limited by a Periodic Cap). Here again, when you look at our first example above, whereby the existing rate was 7.5% at the first Anniversary Date - the Index was 6.5% and the Margin was 2.5% equaling 9.0%. Together this represents the Fully Indexed Rate. However, because of the Periodic Cap that interest rate can be adjusted only up to 8.5%. I should also note that on an ARM loan - even though the interest rate may change over the life of that type of loan, the margin (on that ARM loan) does not change.

Periodic Interest Rate Cap:

Many ARMs have what is called a Periodic Cap or what some call an Interim Cap. This refers to the maximum interest rate increase (or decrease) that an ARM's interest rate can adjust to at the Anniversary Date. For example, if we are talking about a 1-year ARM that adjusts every year - based on the T-Bill rate (Index) and the Periodic Cap on this ARM is 1.0% then that means that the new adjusted interest rate can be increased no greater than 1.0% over what it previously was. For example, let's say an ARM, that is indexed to the T-Bill rate, first started out with an interest rate of 7.5% and has a Margin of 2.5% with a 1.0% Periodic Cap. At the time of the first Anniversary date the T-Bill rate is 6.5%. When we add this to the Margin of 2.5% - then this equals 9.0%. However, because this ARM has a Periodic Cap of 1.0% then the newly adjusted rate will adjust only up to 8.5%. These caps are often referred to as Ceilings - because the newly adjusted interest rate can only go so high and is limited by the Periodic Cap.

Life Time Caps:

Just as there are Periodic Caps (or Ceilings) on ARMs, you will find that most have a Life Time Cap as well. A Life (time) Cap refers to the fact that the interest rate on an ARM cannot be increased beyond a pre-specified percent over the Term (or life) of that loan. For example, let's again look at the ARM discussed above with a Periodic Cap of 1.0%. If this ARM had a Life Cap of 12% then that would mean that this ARM's interest rate would never adjust over and above 12% - no matter how high the interest rates were in the market. In our example above (with a Periodic Cap of 1.0%) if this ARM here adjusted upward each time to the full 1.0% then after 5 years (from loan funding) that ARM would reach 12% and would stay there (unless an adjustment would result in reducing its interest rate).

ARM Loan Caps Displayed:

On Rate Sheets you will sometimes see an ARM's Caps displayed or written (for example) as = **3/2/5**. When you see this then you know that the first number (3) is the maximum percent that the Interest Rate can adjustment to at the First Anniversary period. Following that period then the second number (2) refers to the maximum Periodic Interest Rate Cap. And, the third number (5) represents – yeah, you guessed it, the Maximum Life Time Cap (the maximum increase in percent from the initial interest rate over the life of that ARM loan).

Interest Rate Movement:

What I mean by Interest Rate Movement is that interest rates, in the lending market, generally move in 1/8 of a point (increments) either up or down to a full point. Whenever the interest rate is somewhere in-between (of an 1/8 of a point) it is rounded up to the next 1/8 of a point. For example, if the Indexed Rate, in the example above, came out to 8.20% then this would be rounded up 8.25%.

III. SECOND MORTGAGES:

Often referred to as a 2nd Mortgage and sometimes a Junior Mortgage. These mortgages are under the Senior 1st mortgage - which is secured by a Deed of Trust on Real Property. A 2nd Mortgage, depending on the type of loan program, could be used at the time of originating a 1st mortgage loan for the purpose of a home Purchase (Combo loan) or for Refinancing. A 2nd mortgage loan could also be used as a Combo loan (with a 1st mortgage loan) or as a stand-alone 2nd mortgage loan.

One of the important things that makes a 2nd Mortgage loan (versus a 1st Mortgage loan) has to do with when (the date and time) that mortgage was recorded. It's funny, but some folks think this has to do with the amount of the mortgage (the 1st mortgage loan being larger than the 2nd mortgage loan). But this is not the case. It's the time when that mortgage was first recorded. Because of this you should know that if a borrower of yours has an existing 1st and 2nd mortgage on his property and wishes to refinance only the 1st mortgage then you will need to obtain an approved and signed Subordination Agreement from that Lender holding the 2nd mortgage.

This Subordination Agreement states that the 2nd mortgage lien holder (the Lender on that loan) agrees to stay in 2nd position following the refinancing of that existing 1st mortgage (I know I mentioned this previously, however because of its importance I believe it's worth repeating). The need for this Subordination Agreement relates to the timing of Recordation of mortgages. The reason you need to obtain an approved Subordination Agreement, from the Lender holding the 2nd mortgage, is to protect the 1st position of that new refinance loan. Otherwise, without that approved Subordination Agreement the 2nd mortgage would then move into first position (it was recorded prior to the new 1st mortgage) – at that time that new 1st mortgage is funded and recorded.

Second Mortgage Loans can be at or under 100% CLTV or be greater than 100% CLTV – I've seen up to 125% (or greater). For example, for a 125% CLTV loan the total loan amount (1st and 2nd mortgages) on the subject property can be no greater than 25% over the appraised value of that property. For example, let's say that your borrower wants to obtain a 125% CLTV 2nd Mortgage. His home recently was appraised at $90,000. The outstanding balance on his 1st Mortgage is $75,000. Now multiply the appraised value of his property by 125% ($90,000 X 1.25) equals $112,500. We then subtract from that the amount of the outstanding balance on his existing 1st Mortgage and that equals your borrower's maximum loan amount on that 2nd Mortgage loan ($112,500 - $75,000 = $37,500). Your borrower may not need that much. That's OK. You can just lower that loan amount to the point you see that he would achieve the goals of his loan after paying all loan costs - which are generally included in a Refinance Loan.

When discussing 2nd Mortgages just remember that anytime a 2nd Mortgage Loan goes above a CLTV of 100% some Lenders today consider those a 125% 2nd Mortgage loan. However, there are some Non-Conforming Lenders who offer 105% and 107% LTV (all in one loan) and CLTV Purchase and Refinance loans.

A 125% 2nd Mortgage Loan is considered a Non-Conforming loan and because this type of loan, I believe, is certainly not secured by any equity in that property (beyond 100% LTV) it really is a "signature loan" secured by the owner of that property. For this reason I am increasingly seeing Lenders, who provide this type of loan, requiring borrowers to have middle credit scores of at least 700, and with no history of bankruptcy or home foreclosure - no matter what the reason. Interest rates on these types of 2nd Mortgages do tend to be higher (less equity in the property = increased perceived risk). But again, the benefit of providing this type of loan to your customers' needs to be considered against that higher interest rate.

When you are doing a Ratio Analysis on customers for a Second Mortgage and the CLTV is within FNMA guidelines (at or under 95%) then the Housing and Total Debt Ratios should be no greater than 45/50 respectively. But again, this is a guideline and some Conforming Investors may be more flexible regarding this guideline and may allow those ratios to go above 45/50 if there exists some positive Compensating Factors on your borrowing customers to justify and compensate for those higher than normally accepted qualifying ratios.

COMBO LOANS:
Since we are talking about Second Mortgages I now would like to briefly discuss another way of structuring your Purchase and Refinance loans – especially when the LTV on any of your Conforming loans is greater than 80%. As I have mentioned above, when talking about Private Mortgage Insurance (PMI), when the LTV on a Conforming loan is greater than 80% then PMI will usually be required. In structuring your customers' home loans you should always try to avoid having PMI on their loans - if you can. This isn't always possible. However, one common way of avoiding PMI, when the LTV is greater than 80%, is to split the loan into two parts or loans with the 1st mortgage having an LTV of 80% and with a piggyback 2nd mortgage having the remaining loan amount needed to achieve the goals of that loan. Doing this, your customers will not incur PMI in the 1st mortgage and this should also enable you to offer them a better interest rate on the 1st mortgage as well (with the LTV now at or under 80%).

For example, let's say that you are looking at a Conforming Refinance loan with an LTV of 90%. This would require PMI. To avoid this you decide to split this loan into two parts (or loans) - what we would call in this case as an 80/10 Combo. With the 1st mortgage under 80% no PMI would be required and now you can offer your customers a better interest rate on that loan as well. The interest rate on that second mortgage would be higher (than the first) but together these two loans (Combo) should result in a monthly P&I mortgage payment savings to your customers - compared to the single loan with PMI. This savings is the result of realizing those two benefits (no PMI and better interest rate on the 1st mortgage).

This can also result in what we call an improved Blended Rate: The combined interest rates on the 1st and piggyback 2nd mortgages - compared to the interest rate of a single mortgage loan with an LTV greater than 80% and having PMI. Doing Combos on loans, with LTVs above 80%, usually results in a lower Blended Rate over the interest rate on a single loan with an LTV greater than 80% and having PMI. You can calculate the Blended Rate (on a Combo loan) by adding together the two P&I monthly (Combo) P&I payments (the 1st mortgage payment with an LTV of 80% and the P&I monthly payment on that piggyback 2nd mortgage). Then enter the total of these two (P&I) payments into your financial calculator in the PMT key (don't forget the minus sign if that applies to your calculator). Then enter the Term period in N and the total loan amounts for both loans in PV. Then press the Interest Rate button and that gives you the Blended Rate on your 1st and 2nd loans.

Now compare that Blended Rate to that same loan's interest rate requiring PMI. To do this, first enter the loan amount (of that single loan) in PV Key on your financial calculator. Then enter the sum of the monthly P&I payment on that loan plus its monthly PMI payment into your PMT Key. Now enter that loan's Term into the N Key, and then hit the I/YR (Interest Rate) Key. You now compare the interest rate of that single loan, with PMI, to the Blended Rate you previously calculated on that Combo loan. Usually you will see that the Blended Rate (on that Combo loan) is lower than the interest rate you just calculated - which included the monthly PMI payment (on that single loan). So, consider structuring your loans as a Combo when you have Purchase and Refinance Conforming loans with LTVs greater than 80%.

For Purchase loans you will also see a number of "Loan Combos." Two of the more common Purchase Loan Combos are the 80/15/5 and the 80/10/10. The first loan Combo (80/15/5) has a 1st mortgage with an LTV of 80%, a 2nd mortgage with a loan amount of 15% of the home sales price (total CLTV of 95%), and with the purchase borrowers coming in with 5% of their own funds. As you most likely have already figured out, the 80/10/10 Combo has a 1st mortgage with an LTV of 80%, a 2nd mortgage with a loan amount of 10% of the home sales price (loan CLTV of 90%), and the purchasing customers coming in with 10% of their own funds. The main purpose of these loan Combo packages is to avoid PMI in the customer's 1st mortgage while structuring it (the Combo) in such a way so as to reduce the borrower's total P&I monthly mortgage payment (compared to what a single 1st mortgage with PMI would require). And sometimes, that's all your customers are really looking for: Which mortgage loan option offers the lowest P&I monthly mortgage payment.

Also, it used to be argued that another benefit of obtaining a Combo loan, with a Piggyback 2nd mortgage, is that the interest paid on that Piggyback loan was tax deductible - compared to a single mortgage loan, with PMI, in which payments made towards that PMI were not tax deductible. However, beginning in 2007 that argument may not always be true. In December of 2006 President Bush signed the Tax Relief and Health Care Act of 2006 that enabled (certain) American homeowners the right to claim their PMI payments made on their tax returns. This option to claim those PMI payments, on their tax returns, applies to those home loans closed (purchased or refinanced) after January 1, 2007.

Above I stated *"certain* American homeowners" and please allow me to explain what I mean by that. This ability to claim, for tax purposes, the PMI payments made on a homeowner's mortgage loan is not available to everyone. The biggest limitation seems to be the annual income of the homeowners. For example, if a homeowner's annual adjusted gross income was greater than $110,000 then this tax-deductibility privilege may not be available to them.

Of course, there are other things that should be considered when calculating the financial benefit of a single mortgage loan with PMI versus going the Combo route. But one thing is for sure: I am not an accountant or CPA and you probably are not either. Therefore, always preface your comments regarding this (tax deductibility feature) with the fact that you are not an accountant or CPA and that your customers should consult their accountant if they so choose to explore this option.

IV. BALLOON MORGAGES:

A Balloon Mortgage is a loan whereby the Amortization Period is longer than the Maturity or Term of that loan. In other words, a loan may be amortized over a 30-year period (360 months) but may become due in 5 years. Balloon Loans are usually referred to (for example) as "15 due in 5." The first number (15) refers to the amortized period of that loan - 15 years or 180 months. And the second number refers to when the Balloon on that loan will become due (its Term) - in 5 years. If it is an Amortized Loan then all payments made for the initial 5 years will have reduced (somewhat) the principal on that loan and at the end of the 5th year period the borrow needs to payoff whatever is remaining (the Balloon Payment). And, the date when the balloon payment is due is referred to as the "Stop Date". Balloon Loans are generally requested by the financially astute who are familiar with these and want to enjoy the lower interest rate that these loans offer.

If the Balloon loan is an Interest-Only loan then that borrower's monthly P&I mortgage payments only pay for the outstanding interest on that loan. With an Interest-Only loan the borrower's monthly payments do not reduce the amount of that loan's principal. Here the Balloon Payment (paid at the end of that loan's Term) would be the original amount of that loan - being paid off after the 5th year period (as in our example above). The usual Balloon Loans you will see will be with amortization periods of 30 or 15 years and with the payoff or maturity (of the Balloon on that loan) occurring at the end of the 5th or 7th year. For example: 30 due in 7. This is a 30-year amortized loan due in 7 years.

V. HOME EQUITY LINE OF CREDIT (HELOC):

Home Equity Line of Credit or HELOC (that's pronounced He-Lock) is generally a Second Mortgage that provides a Line of Credit for the Borrowers. I said Second Mortgage loan because most HELOCs, that you get requests for, will be Second Mortgages. However, you should know that some Lenders offer HELOCs as a Stand Alone loan product - as a 1st Mortgage. HELOCs and Line of Credit type of loans are also referred to as Open-End loans.

Now, because it is a Line of Credit those borrowers may not be receiving a certain amount of money at loan funding (like a Cash-Out Refinance Loan) but will have the right to take funds from their HELOC up to a maximum loan amount when they wish to do so. So that you are familiar with these, here are the most important points and features of HELOCs (as a 2nd Mortgage loan):

> You prepare this loan just like any 2nd mortgage or C/O Refinance Loan.

> The Loan Amount would be the maximum loan amount the borrower Qualifies for and/or maximum amount they have requested.

> Although there are different types of HELOCs, generally though, your customer won't start paying on their HELOC until he or she starts taking money out of it. Or, taking out what is referred to as "Draws".

> The interest rates on HELOC loans tend to be Variable - in that they change based on an interest rate, index, and margin that it is tied to.

> Not all Lenders offer this type of loan (HELOCs) and those that do are usually Conforming Lenders. Because of this, and the nature of this type of loan, your prospective borrowers (who want to do this) need to have very good Credit and Capacity (Income).

I also should note that HELOCs could make an excellent Second Mortgage as a temporary means of financing a home purchase or possibly as a stand-alone Second Mortgage. One of the advantages of going this route is that once the HELOC is paid off then the borrower will still have that HELOC, at their convenience, to use if they wish to take funds out – sometime later.

Clearly, the HELOC is not for everyone. The only ones I have received requests from, for these, are business owners (although today HELOCs are offered for employed and W2s as well). With HELOCs, as with other types of loan programs, as the Borrower's credit score increases – the maximum CLTV on their HELOC can increase as well. I have found (and it seems to me) that HELOCs tend to be more for the more financially astute person whose money needs increase and decrease over time.

VI. REVERSE MORTGAGES:

Kind of sounds like something is going backwards here doesn't it? In actuality things are going backwards here. With Reverse Mortgages, instead of the Borrower making monthly payments to the Lender, here it is the Lender making monthly payments to the Borrower. This type of mortgage is designed for Senior Homeowners (who are at least 62 years or older) who wish to use the equity they have built up in their home and convert it into cash. Reverse Mortgages generally guarantee what is called "life tenure" with no payments due to the Lender until the borrower moves, sells their home, or dies. At the time that occurs then the outstanding loan balance (which represents all the payments made to the homeowner of that loan plus the interest - over the life of that loan) becomes due. Also, with Reverse Mortgages, income and credit qualifying are generally not required.

At this time the two most popular Reverse Mortgage programs out there are:

1. The Home Equity Conversion Mortgage (HECM): This is an FHA-insured Reverse Mortgage.

2. The Home Keeper Mortgage: This is a type of Fannie Mae Reverse Mortgage.

There are a couple of important points regarding Reverse Mortgages that you may find interesting and may be asked by customers who are considering getting one of these:

➢ All Reverse Mortgages have Private Mortgage Insurance. This insurance protects the Lender in the event that the subject home is subsequently sold and the sales price (sold) is less than the outstanding balance on that Reverse Mortgage (which includes payments made to that homeowner).

➢ Once the Reverse Mortgage is closed and funded, and as long as the homeowners (borrowers) live in that home as their primary residence they are not obligated to make payments on that loan. However, if they move away, sell their home, or the borrowers (both if two are on title) die then the outstanding balance of their Reverse Mortgage becomes due.

Now, it isn't necessary to sell that home. Just payoff the outstanding balance on that Reverse Mortgage. For example, let's say that the homeowners (who originally obtained a Reverse Mortgage) later wish to payoff the outstanding balance on their loan. They could do that either by paying cash or refinancing their home and paying off the existing Reverse Mortgage's outstanding balance. Or, in the case where both homeowners have died and their children (sons and daughters - their heirs) wish to keep the home in the family: They too could either payoff the outstanding balance on their parent's Reverse Mortgage by either paying cash or refinancing that home. However, the amount due, on that Reverse Mortgage, will never be greater than the value of the home.

➢ There are a number of payment plan options available with Reverse Mortgages:

- **Term**: Here the homeowners receive a fixed cash payment (each month) for a set period of time.

- **Tenure**: this is also a fixed cash amount received (each month) but continues as long as the homeowners occupy the home as their primary residence.

- **Line of Credit**: Here the homeowners establish a credit line in which they can draw upon as they wish (up to a maximum amount).

- **Cash-Out:** Another option is for the homeowners to take out a lump sum amount at closing (this could also be considered a line-of–credit).

- **A Combination of the Above:** The Reverse Mortgage loan customers could also take out a combination of the above options.

➤ At this time it is my understanding that all Reverse Mortgages have an interest rate that is Adjustable (ARM).

➤ All applicants for a Reverse Mortgage also need to attend a consumer counseling session with a HUD-approved counseling agency. This is to educate those homeowners of the financial consequences of doing this type of mortgage loan and helps them determine if this is right for them.

A common question you will be asked, when discussing Reverse Mortgages, is how much (equity) does a homeowner need and how much can they obtain? That's a good question. I don't know all the answers here - but I can tell you some things you can use to determine if they have enough equity in their home to qualify them for one of these.

1. First, ask them what county their home is located in and what do they believe is the appraised value of their property. Reverse Mortgages, like FHA loans, have a maximum loan amount based on the county that property is located in. The Reverse Mortgage program will take the lesser of the maximum loan amount for that county or the appraised value of the subject property.

2. Next, the youngest age of the borrowers (on their loan) is used to determine the percent applied - towards the amount arrived at in step #1 above. As the age of the borrower (or youngest borrower) increases (above 62 years old) the percentage factor that is applied increases as well. For example, with a homeowner of 62 years old we might use a percentage factor of about 60% to be applied towards the amount arrived at in step #1 above. If the (youngest) homeowner were 75 years old then perhaps a percentage factor of about 70% would be used. Are you following me here? Good.

3. Now we deduct from that figure, after our calculations in step #2 above, all the loan costs involved in doing this Reverse Mortgage. Let's say that adds up to about $5,200.

4. If the homeowners own their property free and clear then the amount left over, after step #3 above, is the amount that is available for those homeowners. However, if the homeowners have a 1ˢᵗ and/or 2ⁿᵈ mortgage on

their home then those mortgage loans will need to be paid off: This could be done either through the homeowner's own funds (or other means) or with the funds from this Reverse Mortgage. If those mortgages were paid off with their Reverse Mortgage then you would subtract from that amount (you arrived at in step #3 above) all the outstanding liens (mortgages) on that homeowner's property.

5. Now, if the homeowners <u>do</u> have a mortgage or mortgages on their property and the sum of these is greater than the amount you ended up with in step #3 above then those homeowners do not have enough equity for a Reverse Mortgage. However, if the sum of their existing mortgage is less than the amount you arrived at, during step #3 above, then those homeowners could obtain a Reverse Mortgage and at the very least they will no longer have to make monthly P&I mortgage payments – with their new Reverse Mortgage.

Okay. Let's apply the above to an example. Remember, this is only an example, but going through this should give you a better idea of how this process works. OK, your prospective loan customer is 63 years old and wants a Reverse Mortgage. His home is located in Spokane County.

1. You look up the Reverse Mortgage loan amount for Spokane County and see that the maximum loan amount is $154,000. The borrower says his home is worth $200,000. That's great, but we know that the maximum we could apply here would be $154,000 (lesser of the two).

2. Next, you see that the percentage factor for someone 63 years old (he is the only homeowner on title) is about 60%. You therefore multiply $154,000 X 60% = $92,400.

3. You estimate all the loan costs for this Reverse Mortgage will add up to about $5,200. This leaves the homeowner with $87,200.

4. If the homeowner owns the property free and clear then that's what that homeowner could use in his Reverse Mortgage (in choosing his payment plan options). However, if the homeowner has an existing mortgage on his property then the amount of that mortgage would be subtracted (assuming the existing 1st is paid off with this Reverse Mortgage) from the $87,200 above. And then, whatever is the amount left over, after doing this, would be the amount that homeowner could use towards whichever payment plan they decide to go on.

If you followed me along, in my explanation of Reverse Mortgages above, then you probably know more than most mortgage loan originators out there about this subject. This is an area where, I believe, we will be getting increasing requests for in the future.

VII. INVESTMENT PROPERTY LOANS:

And finally, I'd like to briefly discuss loans on Investment Properties. If someone is doing a Purchase or Refinance loan on a SFR and they do not occupy that property, as their primary residence and it is not a second home of theirs, then we are talking about an Investment Type of Property. Investment Properties are properties that are either a NOO (non-owner occupied) SFR or NOO 2 to 4-unit properties (see Occupancy) and are income generating for that property's owner. When you are initially qualifying a borrower for a loan on an Investment Property then you can safely expect that the interest rate on that loan will be higher than for a loan on an Owner-Occupied, SFR property (whether it's a Conforming, Non-Conforming, or Sub-prime loan). And, you should also expect that the LTV, on that Investment Property loan, will be lower than what an Owner-Occupied Purchase or Refinance loan would offer.

Traditionally, if someone was interested in Purchasing or Refinancing an Investment Property then you could expect that the maximum LTV on that loan would be about 75 – 90%. That, however, has changed. Recently I am seeing some Wholesale Lenders offering Combo and single loans with CLTV and LTVs, respectively, of up to 95%! And, as you would expect, the credit scores of those borrowers who wish to do a loan on Investment Type of Properties, needs to be very good. And, you can also expect that those borrowers will need to have at least 4 – 6 months of reserves (PITI) saved up. And, in some cases, the customer may need up to 12 months of PITI reserves saved up. And, when it comes to Investment Type of Properties, here are a few questions that most Wholesale Lenders might be wondering regarding your borrower. The answers to these questions can sometimes influence what interest rate and LTV you can offer them or whether you can even do a loan for them (that benefits or makes financial sense):

- Do they have any renting and/or landlord experience? If so, for how long?

- How far away do they live from that investment property? Lenders like it when borrowers, for investment properties, are close enough to be able to easily visit that property and keep an eye on it.

- How much money have they have saved up for the Reserves on that loan (PITI) and for the maintenance on that property? Remember, they will become the landlord and it will be their responsibility to fix, repair, and maintain that property.

- What is the expected monthly Rental Income for that investment property – in relationship to the monthly PITI (income) payments for the loan (on that investment property)? Remember, that for most (NOO) Investment Properties - Conforming Lenders will take the total monthly rental income received and multiply that by 75% - to arrive at the Monthly Net Rental Income (operating income) for that property and use that figure (income or loss) in qualifying those borrowers. When an Appraisal is completed on that investment property, then the appraiser on that appraisal will state what is a reasonable rent (to pay) for investment properties in that area and properties with those amenities as the subject property (see Income Approach within Chapter 21 on Appraisals).

- If the borrowers are currently renting the subject property then the Lender may want to see a completed and fully signed rental/lease agreement on all those who currently live or plan to live in the subject property – as a PTD condition.

- How many Investment Properties do they currently own?

When you work on loans for Investment Type of Properties then you will generally find that the loan goals of your borrowers are usually different than those who are buying or Refinancing O/O homes: Now, it's the Bottom Line. Or, put more succinctly, Positive Cash Flow. Therefore, when you are working on a loan, for an Investment Property, consider suggesting and structuring loans that are ARMs (with lower initial interest rates) and possibly with Interest-Only features. Of course, as always, the loan goals of your borrowers should determine what loan program or programs you suggest that would best enable them to meet their financial needs.

Now that we've discussed the various Types of Mortgage Loans Programs, Transactions, and Products let's move on to the next chapter that talks about the various Types of Loan Documentation.

Chapter 9

TYPES OF LOAN DOCUMENTATION

This chapter presents the different types of documentation required on mortgage loans and what kind of supporting documents you will need in properly qualifying your borrowers and processing your loans without delay towards the loan closing. Knowing what I will cover in this chapter will enable you to anticipate the document needs of your loans and put you in a position whereby you can inform your customers of those needs when you first meet with them and thereafter.

When you do this then you are and have the appearance of being a professional mortgage loan originator. One thing I have learned over the years is that customers do not like you to keep calling them back and asking for additional things (documents). Many of these documents (they may think) could and should have been asked for initially. And many times that could be true. Also, when you know what the document needs of your loans are, ask for and get them, then your loans move along a lot smoother and quicker. And quicker also means you get paid sooner.

Although there are subcategories of different types of loan documentation that a Loan Processor may use (which are presented in this chapter) the four main types of loan documentation are:

1. Full Doc
2. Alt-Doc
3. Lite Doc
4. Reduced Doc

I. Full Doc:
This is a term you will hear quite often and refers to the fact that this loan will require all documents that a Conforming Loan typically requires. Simply put, this will usually require from all borrowers on that loan:

1. 2 years of Job History (preferably in the same profession).

2. Employed (Base Salary) = 2 Years of W2's with a recent Paystub covering a recent 30-day period.

3. Employed (Commissioned Income) = 2 Years of Tax Returns with a recent Paystub covering a recent 30-day period.

4. If Self-Employed = Last 2 years of Tax Returns with Business License.

5. Bank Statements (full) covering recent 1-3 months.

6. Alimony/Child Support Payments => Divorce Decree or Property Settlement Statement (if either husband or wife pays and/or receives child and/or separation payments).

7. Documents showing above payments (item #6) are paid or received on time and continuous. And, will continue for the next 3 years.

8. Filed Bankruptcy => Bankruptcy Papers (Full) - if a BK occurred within the past 2 - 4 years.

9. Landlord's Name & Address - If borrowers have rented in the past 2 years.

Unless you definitely know otherwise then I suggest you always assume you are going to do a Full-Doc loan and ask for those (related and required) items when you first meet with your customers. Or, just ask them to bring those documents and/or information with them to your first meeting.

II. Alt-Doc:

This is a term you hear sometimes but is not well understood. So, let's go over this and be very clear here. Alt-Doc, as its name implies, means that you are using Alternative Documentation (that is required on Full-Doc loans) in qualifying your borrowers for the loan you are submitting it for. When Loan Processors refer to using Alt-Docs on a loan they are usually referring to an alternative way of showing income for that borrower in order to qualify them for their loan.

An example of this might be - look above at Items # 2 & 3. We can see that Lenders (in Full-Doc loans) want to see 2 years of income on the borrower. For an employed borrower - 2 years of W2's with a recent paystub. For a self-employed borrower, 2 years of Tax Returns. Let's say, for example, you are working on a loan and may have difficulty in either coming up with those required income documents or those documents don't show the true and total income picture of your borrowers. With Alt-Doc the borrowers may be able to satisfy this document requirement by providing recent bank statements over the last 12 - 24 months - showing a definite pattern of income going into his or her bank accounts (using the last 12 months banks statements instead of using paystubs and W-2's is also referred to as Limited Documentation). Or, copies of checks that have been received showing income received. In other words, Alt-Doc allows us to move away from the more traditional way of documenting the income of borrowers and allows us other (and sometimes imaginative) ways of showing their income.

III. Lite Doc (Simplified Documentation):

Here's a term you will hear sometimes from your Loan Processor. She may start processing your loan and after her review she may say something like, "With this borrower we can use Lite Doc." Or, she may refer to that as using Simplified Documentation instead (both these refer to the same thing). What she means is the borrower doesn't need to bring in all the documentation normally required. It's still technically a Full-Doc loan but because of the borrower's income (ratios are very low) and/or their credit is excellent the Loan Processor is in a position to submit the loan with less documentation than is normally required (Lite = Lesser Docs. get it?). After you've been a mortgage loan originator for a while and seen how thick and heavy some of these loan files can get then you'll agree that less documentation means a lighter loan file.

IV. Reduced Documentation:

I thought I'd throw in this term even though you probably won't hear this one very often. This is a loan documentation method that is used to determine the income of the home loan borrower. However, and get this, no verification documentation is generally done with this method.

And finally, I would like to provide for you a "Loan Application Needs Sheet" that lists for you the more common loan documents you will need when you are qualifying your borrowers and processing your loans. When you first meet with your customers you (usually) will be completing the 1003 with them. As you do so you sometimes will need to be in the Mortgage Detective Mode - asking questions and sometimes trying to make sense of what they are telling you. As you complete the 1003 (which we will go into more detail in the chapter on completing The Uniform Residential Loan Application – the 1003) the answers that your customers give you alludes to and lets you know that you have (specific) document needs that will most likely be required on that loan. This is an ideal time, while meeting with them, to list those loan documents or items needed as you complete their 1003. If they are interested in doing that loan then they will usually get those docs to you as soon as they can. To see what this document looks like please refer to Exhibit IV.

We've covered quite a bit of information in this chapter and in the previous sections as well. I have tried to structure this book in a kind of building block sort of way - in which information that is presented (with each step) builds on information previously discussed. This isn't always possible but I hope this is what you are generally experiencing as we move forward in this book

I believe we are now ready to move on into another very important section of this book that contains those chapters that discuss the various loan documents you prepare prior to meeting with a loan customer and in preparing their mortgage loan file. So, let's now move on to the next Section and get into what I call The Paperwork.

Section III

THE PAPERWORK

$\mathfrak{I}$ titled this section "The Paperwork" because within the next eight chapters we are going to cover those loan forms you will actually need to complete yourself in order to have what is called a "working loan file." When I say "working loan file" I mean that you have met with the customers, have a fully completed and signed 1003 (by the borrowers), all required loan disclosures have been signed, and you also have a completed Loan Estimate (LE). Having these in your loan file you then can truly say that you have a working loan file and can put that loan in your Loan Pipeline. Pipeline refers to the loans you are currently working on and/or have closed and funded that month.

Within Section III you will begin to learn how to apply all the material and information you have read so far when doing one of the first things you do when originating a mortgage loan: Completing the loan application on a loan-inquiring customer. Therefore, the first chapter, within this Section, presents how to properly and fully complete The Uniform Residential Loan Application and following that the chapter on Loan Disclosures. Also, within this Section, we'll talk about completing the Loan Estimate. I am really looking forward to getting into these loan documents because they are so important in giving you the information you need to properly qualify your customers for a home loan and in preparing the loan file for loan submission. I have seen mortgage loan originators who have been in the mortgage lending business for a number of years now and still don't know how to properly and fully prepare and complete these forms. After you have learned the information that we will cover in this Section I know you will not be one of those.

I am going to cover these loan forms in the sequence that you would normally complete these. At this point in the book you've learned the process by which you qualify loan customers for mortgage loans and the thinking, or logic, behind Automated Underwriting as well as Manual Underwriting. You've learned many of the common concerns regarding the subject property of mortgage loans as well as the different types of mortgage loan products and programs you can offer you loan customers. Now, you are ready to begin Section III.

Also, within this section, I will talk about a report you should order and use in preparing the Uniform Residential Loan Application: A Property Profile. And finally, this section includes some suggestions on how to originate mortgage loans for those loan customers living out of your area.

The eight chapters, within this Section, that discuss these subjects are:

- ➤ The Uniform Residential Loan Application
- ➤ Mortgage Loan Disclosures
- ➤ The Loan Estimate
- ➤ The Transmittal Summary
- ➤ The Property Profile
- ➤ The Purchase and Sales Agreement
- ➤ Out of Town Customers
- ➤ The Closing Disclosure

So, let's begin this Section with the discussion on The Uniform Residential Loan Application.

Chapter 10

THE UNIFORM RESIDENTIAL LOAN
APPLICATION

The first thing that you should do, before you seriously begin working on a loan (or spend a lot of time on it), is complete a Uniform Residential Loan Application on your home loan-inquiring customer. What we affectionately refer to as the 10-0-3. I should mention here that refers to the Fannie Mae form (1003). These are the Fannie Mae (and Freddie Mac) form numbers that you see at of the bottom left-hand corner of this form. It can also be referred to as the Freddie Mac Form 65. It is also called a U.R.L.A. or URLA within the mortgage lending industry. But most mortgage professionals simply refer to this form as the 1003. The purpose of the 1003 was and is to provide an industry standard home loan application form to be used by all Lenders within the United States.

For historical purposes, I would like note here, that in late 2005 the Federal Housing Finance Agency (FHFA) came out with a revised 1003. This was the first time any revisions to the original 1003 had been made - since it first came out. And then, the Federal Home Loan Mortgage Corporation and the Federal National Mortgage Association, under the conservatorship of the Federal Housing Finance Agency, issued a revised and redesigned Uniform Residential Loan Application on August 23, 2016. This revised version of the 1003 became a required document for Lenders and mortgage loan originations as of January 1, 2018.

And then the Federal Home Loan Mortgage Corporation and the Federal National Mortgage Association, under the conservatorship of the Federal Housing Finance Agency, again issued a revised and redesigned Uniform Residential Loan Application for the third time. This new (and redesigned version of the) 1003 was approved by the Consumer Financial Protections Bureau (CFPB) during November, 2019.

Now, even though Lenders, for all new home loan applications commencing February 1, 2020, could begin using this new Uniform Residential Loan Application – Fannie Mae, during 2020, designed a new timetable for implementation and required utilization of this new 1003. According to the Desktop Underwriter/Desktop Originator Release Notes, date November 18, 2020, Lenders must use the newly redesigned Form 1003 for all new home loan applications received on or after Mar. 1, 2021.

Now, when I first read this, in the later part of 2020, I thought, "Huh, did I miss something here? Did Fannie Mae come out with an even newer 1003 for the year 2021?" I then printed out the 1003 designed in 2019 and compared it to what they now referred to as the "New 1003". After comparing the content of both 1003s I found that they were the same. Whew, what a relief! So, I can only assume that this Implementation Timeline was designed to allow Lenders more time to bring their loan origination and underwriting systems into compliance with this "newly redesigned" 1003.

Below is the Implementation Timeline for this newly redesigned Uniform Residential Loan Application (form 1003):

- **August 1, 2020:**
  Limited Production Period Began: The Limited Production Period can be thought of as an early adopter period. Fannie Mae began accepting the MISMO v3.4 loan application submission files in production on a limited basis. Lenders have controlled access to the DU production environment based upon validation of eligibility requirements and completion of a Partner Readiness Questionnaire. Only participants who have completed the prerequisites and received Fannie Mae approval will be allowed to submit loans using the redesigned Form 1003 prior to its new effective date of January 1, 2021.

- **January 1, 2021:**
  Open Production Period Begins: All Lenders may submit the MISMO v3.4 loan application submission files to the Fannie Mae DU production environment using the redesigned Form 1003 and based on the DU Spec.

- **March 1, 2021:**
  Mandate and Pipeline Transition Period Begins: All Lenders are required to submit the MISMO v3.4 loan application submission files to the DU production environment using the redesigned Form 1003 beginning March 1, 2021.

Additionally, I would like to note that Fannie Mae will continue to process applications received prior to the mandate date (March 1, 2021) within the AUS format on which they were initially submitted. If a legacy AUS file was submitted prior to the mandate, the submitted file may remain in the legacy format and the lender may complete the loan using the 07/05 (Rev. 06/09) URLA, even after the mandate date.

Okay, now when I was a mortgage branch manager and reviewed a loan file, from a mortgage loan originator for the first time, I could pretty much tell if that mortgage loan originator had received any training when he or she first got into this business. If the 1003 was not completely done or completed incorrectly then it was a sure sign to me that mortgage loan originator had most likely received little, if any, training. You would be amazed how many mortgage loan originators out there have not had someone take the time with them, when they first entered this profession, and showed them some of the basic and correct ways of doing things in our business. And, you can be sure that drives a lot of Loan Processors crazy! Because when the loan file (including the 1003) is not complete or completed incorrectly then the Loan Processor has to try to figure out what that mortgage loan originator wants or is doing. This wastes her time. She could be spending her time more productively following up on those things that need to be done (and that mortgage loan originator wants her to do) to move that loan file along without delay.

And, that is one of the main reasons I wrote this book: To provide a manual and reference for those mortgage loan originators, like you maybe, that would like to have that information available - to help you do your job professionally and completely. When you do this then you will see this having a positive effect on your business as a mortgage loan originator and your income as well. So, with that said, let's get started and take a look at what this 1003 business is all about.

The Uniform Residential Loan Application:

If you have a copy of all 9 pages of the **URLA: Borrower Information** form - then please get a hold of it now. Otherwise, you can obtain a copy of all pages of the 1003, in pdf form, by going to: https://singlefamily.fanniemae.com/media/7896/display. In going to this site, I suggest using Google Chrome as the browser.

I should also note that there are three other additional Uniform Residential Application forms, in additional to the main URLA: Borrower Information form that may also need to be completed – depending on the circumstances of the primary borrower. For example, if the primary borrower is "Unmarried", and/or there is or are Co-borrowers on that home loan, and if you need additional space to write the borrower's or co-borrower(s)' information that the source URLA form does not provide. In those cases you may need to also complete one or more of the following URLAs:

- URLA: Unmarried Addendum
- URLA: Additional Borrower Information
- URLA: Continuation Sheet

But don't worry about all that for now. I will talk more about these three forms later on within this chapter - so you will be very clear on this.

Now, when someone refers to the Uniform Residential Loan Application (the 1003) they are primarily referring to the URLA: Borrower Information – which contains 8 pages. However, as mentioned above, circumstances regarding the primary borrower could be such that additional URLA forms are required. And those additional URLA forms become part of that home loan customer's loan application file.

As you can see, when you look over the URLA: Borrower Information form, it is made up of seven Sections. And, each Section has a particular purpose to it: Each is usually addressing one of the four "Cs" of credit qualifying we discussed within chapter 3 on "Characteristics of Borrowers." As you may recall four of those "Cs" of credit are:

1. Credit
2. Capacity
3. Collateral
4. Cash

For our purposes of discussion here I will cover each page, of the URLA: Borrower Information form, in the order that you would normally complete it when meeting with your customers. Also, as we discuss each section, I will talk about why that page and sections of that page are important and what we, as mortgage loan originators, need to be looking for and what questions to ask.

As I mentioned before, when we are completing the 1003, we should have our Mortgage Detective hat on: Asking questions, getting answers, and always asking ourselves:

- Do the answers I am getting regarding this area of inquiry make sense?
- Am I missing anything here or need to explore further (in asking questions) to gain more information that might be helpful in doing this home loan?
- Given the answers I am getting, for this area of inquiry, do I need any additional supporting documents for this home loan?

Now, when I first got into this business my manager, who was training me, told me that the 1003 is the most important mortgage loan document that you will initially complete and once completed it should tell you most of what you need to know regarding your prospective loan customer(s). When he first told me this - I was skeptical. But after a while (and it didn't take me too long) I saw that he was right. After we are done discussing this form then I believe you too will see its importance as well. So, let's begin now and take a look at this new 1003 and see what it is all about.

The new 1003 is made up of 8 pages and is referred to as the **URLA: Borrower Information**. And, this may be the only 1003 that you need to complete – if there is only one borrower on that home loan and you can enter all the required information on him or her within those eight pages. However, if there is an additional borrower, and/or those borrowers are unmarried, or you need additional space to enter information for a particular section then an additional page of the 1003 may be needed. We will talk about those as we go along here.

Now, the **URLA: Borrower Information** form contains 9 pages with 8 Sections:
1. Borrower Information:
   - Page One – Borrower's Personal Information
   - Page Two – Borrower's Employment & Other Income Sources
2. Financial Information - Assets & Liabilities
3. Financial Information – Real Estate
4. Loan and Property Information
5. Declarations
6. Acknowledgments and Agreements
7. Demographic Information
8. Loan Originator Information

So, let's begin at the top of this new 1003:

URLA: Borrower Information:
At the top of page one of the **URLA: Borrower Information** form is a shaded area with small print stating, "To be completed by the Lender: Lender Loan No.# / Universal Loan

Identifier and to its right "Agency Case No." Don't worry about this – your loan processor will complete this area after you have submitted this URLA to her or him.

Then below that it states, "**Verify and complete the information on this application**. If you are applying for this loan with others, each additional Borrower must provide information as directed by your lender.

Now, what does that mean? That means that if the Borrower is purchasing or refinancing the subject property on their own (without any co-borrowers) then no other URLA (1003s) may need to be completed. However, if there are co-borrowers, for the loan (on the subject property) then each co-borrower will need to complete a separate 1003 as it relates to them. Following that, then you and/or your loan processor will combine the information from those 1003s to form a complete financial picture for that home loan for those borrowers. Immediately below that is our first actual section of this 1003. So, let's begin now and take a look at completing the 1003 for your home loan customer.

As I previously mentioned, this new 1003 (first available in 2020) is made up of 8 pages and contains 8 Sections. And, each one of those sections also have sub-sections within them.

Section One: Borrower Information
Section 1 for Borrower Information is made up of two pages and has with it 5 sub-sections:
- 1a: Personal Information
- 1b: Current Employment/Self Employment & Income
- 1c: (If Applicable): Additional Employment/Self Employment & Income
- 1d: Previous Employment/Self Employment & Income (If Current Employment is less than 2 years)
- 1e. Income from Other Sources

So, let's begin with page one of Section 1: Borrower Information…

Section 1: Borrower Information – Page One:

1a: Personal Information:

Name:
Within this area you first enter the borrower's full name, and below that enter any **Alternate name(s)** they might have used in the past. At the right of this enter their **Social Security Number**, and below that enter their **Date of Birth**. To the right of that you then enter a check for their **Citizenship**: a U.S. Citizen, a Permanent Resident Alien, or a Non-Permanent Resident Alien.

I should note here that when entering the customer's **DOB** on the 1003 that it is expected you that will write their exact date of birth in **MM/DD/YYYY** format (i.e. as 01/02/1960). Please do not enter here just their age. Enter their date of birth in the format that is requested. This was one of the requirements of the previously revised 1003 that came out in January 2004. Prior to that version of the 1003 it asked for just the numerical Age of the borrower. This has changed, so please enter the borrower's exact date of birth.

Type of Credit:

Below that you check off whether that borrower is applying for **Individual Credit** or for **Joint Credit** (i.e. there are co-borrowers on that loan). If there are co-borrowers on that loan then enter the number of co-borrowers and obtain the primary Borrower's initials for that. To the right of that you **List Name(s) of Other Borrower(s) Applying for this Loan**. Here you enter the full names of all the co-borrowers that will be on that loan. This information gives you and the loan processor a heads-up notice that there will be co-borrowers on that loan. And, it lets you know who you will be completing additional 1003s on for that home loan.

Marital Status:

Below that it asks for the Marital Status of that Borrower and whether they have any Dependents. For **Marital Status**, enter a check in which marital status applies to that Borrower. Now, if the borrower is unmarried then enter a check at "Unmarried". When the borrower states that they are unmarried then this indicates that the **URLA – Unmarried Addendum** will also need to be completed for that borrower.

To the right of Marital Status enter the number of **Dependent**s <u>actually living in that household</u> and the Age of each. I should mention here that in asking for the number of Dependents – this is not necessarily focusing only on the borrower's children (if any). By Dependents, it is asking for <u>any</u> Dependent(s) that are currently living in their home. So, when you get to this area then ask your customers, "Do you have any Dependents that are currently living in your home?" If they answer "yes", then complete this area. If they say "no" then move on to the next area of inquiry. To the right of this is…

Contact Information:

Enter within this area the various ways that they may be contacted: Home phone, Cell phone, Work Phone, and Email. This information is not only for you but also your loan processor (and perhaps the lender on that loan) who will be following up on information disclosed or further needed for their home loan. When I have gotten to this area I always like to also ask the Borrower which way that would they prefer to be contacted by and when (time during the day) would be best to contact them. You can note that information within that area.

Current Address:

Enter here their current (full) **Street Address**. No P.O. Box addresses allow here folks (unless it cannot be avoided). Also, check the box that relates to whether they own or rent and how many years they have lived at that address. Or, No primary housing expenses (e.g. still living with their parents).

If at Current Address for LESS than 2 years, list Former Address:
Now, recall what I said previously about 2, 2, 2, & 2? We need to obtain 2 years of residency. If they have lived in their current address for less than 2 years then you will need to know the (full) address of every one of those places they have lived at - within the last 2 years. If your borrowers have been renting for the past 2 years then what is it that you also want to ask your customers? That's Right! We need to ask them the name, address, and telephone number of their landlord or apartment manager. And, we need this information for every different address they have lived at for the last 2 years. Now, this is something that you do not see provided for on this 1003 but you can be sure that your Loan Processor will need that information so she or he can send out any VORs (if required) to each of their current and previous landlords or apartment managers in the past 2 years. I suggest entering that additional information on the **URLA – Continuation Sheet**.

Regarding the borrowers' residency, I have actually completed 1003s on customers who have lived at 5 or 6 different places in the past two years! As you can see, after 2 entered residences - you will run out of space with this area. If that happens then use the **URLA – Continuation Sheet** for entering those additional addresses. Enter on that Continuation Sheet the 3rd or more places your customers have lived, as well as whether or not they rented (most likely) and the time period that they lived there and their monthly rent or lease expense. Altogether, all current and previous residence addresses shown and the time spent in each should add up to 2 years or more. However, if the borrower has lived at their current address for two or more years then just enter a check at – **Does Not Apply**.

Mailing Address - if different from Current Address:
Now, within this area, and after you entered your borrower's current residence address(es), there is an area for their Mailing Address, if different from Present Address. If your customers receive their mail at a different address than where they live (e.g. P.O. Box) then enter that address here. Otherwise, enter a check in the box "Does not apply" and leave this area blank.

Military Service:
Within this area it asks if the Borrower (or their deceased spouse) ever served, or is currently serving, in the United States Armed Forces. Enter a check for "Yes" or "No". If you checked "Yes" then place a check for that sentence that applies to them. Now, if the borrower replies that they are retired from the military or receiving some sort of income from the armed forces (e.g. military disability) you know then that you will need additional documentation for that income source – if they wish to include that income in qualifying for their home loan.

Language Preference – Your loan transaction is likely to be conducted in English.
This is an optional area for the home loan borrower to respond to. What this is really asking is if the borrower wishes the language (in completing their home loan application) be in a different language other than English for them. Knowing this information at that time, or beforehand, gives you a heads up that an interpreter may be

necessary in order to properly complete their home loan application. As you can see, besides the option of **English**, it offers the options of: **Chinese, Korean, Spanish, Tagalog, Vietnamese**, and **Other** (where they can state another preferred language). And, finally, it provides an option of "**I do not wish to respond**".

The vast majority of your loan originations will most likely be in English. However, this could change depending upon where you are originating your home loans (e.g. Southern California and Texas). If the borrower lets you know before your loan application process and/or during the loan application period (of a preferred language other than English) then this lets you know that you will need to make every (reasonable) accommodation you can to take their loan application in their preferred language (e.g. a translator). For example, if a home loan applicant walks into your mortgage lending office and they speak only Spanish and prefer to be spoken to in Spanish, and you have no one, in your mortgage office who speaks Spanish: Then you cannot just point them out the door to another mortgage company who you know (or may suspect) has a Spanish speaking loan originator. No, you need to do better than that if you can: like obtaining a telephone translator.

On the other hand, like most of your originations in English, just enter a check within the circle "**English**" and move on to page 2 of this 1003.

Okay, let's move on to…

Section 1: Borrower Information – Page Two:

1b: Current Employment/Self-Employment and Income:

First, you enter the employer's name and below that the address of the employer that borrower works for. If your customer is **Self-Employed** then enter the name of their business and its address. To the right of that enter the **business (company's) Phone Number.** What you are looking for here is the telephone number (of the person) that your Loan Processor may call to verify your customer's employment information. Below that enter what his **Position/Title** is at work or what he does. If he is Self-Employed then you would usually enter here: Owner/President.

Below that enter the **Start Date** that the borrower first began working for that company. Enter their Start Date as the month and year they started working for that company. And just below that you enter **How long in this line of work? Total Years and Months**. For example, your customer said he has worked for his current employer for only 6 months, but he has been in this type of profession for over 10 years. Years ago Lenders wanted to see 2 years of continuous employment with the same employer or company. That has changed over the years and now Lenders are really looking at the total number of years' experience (in the same profession or line of work) of whatever they are currently employed as. This alludes to Capacity and stability of employment in qualifying a borrower.

To the right of that is a sectioned-off area titled: **Check if this statement applies:** I am employed by a family member, property seller, real estate agent, or other party to the (this) transaction. If this does not apply then leave it blank.

And below that you see: **Check if you are the Business Owner or Self-Employed.** If you entered a check here then it asks if they have an ownership share in that company of more or less of 25%. To the right of that it asks for any **Monthly Income (or loss)** from that company. Enter that respective amount here. If the borrower is realizing a monthly income from that company then that is additional income you can use in qualifying them for their home loan. If they are realizing a monthly loss then that amount could be used to reduce their Gross Monthly income stated on the right of that area.

To the far-right, of this sub-section, you see an area for **Gross Monthly Income**. There you enter all the monthly gross income sources from their current employer. After you have entered all of their income sources there you then add those up and enter their **Total** (gross) monthly income.

As you can see, the working income for the Borrower is broken down (separated) into **Base salary, Overtime, Bonuses, Commissions, Military Entitlements, and Other**. Based upon what your borrower does for a living will determine what you enter here. If they are in a job where they get paid a straight salary (e.g. $30,000 per year) then you would enter here their gross annual salary divided by 12 (e.g. $2,500). Remember, we want the **Gross Monthly Income figure** (before the tax man gets his share and all the other payroll deductions). And, as you may recall, this is a HMDA related question. Sometimes base salary folks also have overtime. Unless that overtime is significant - don't worry about it. If your borrower is in sales then he or she is most likely on straight commission or a base and commission. In that case you will need to separate the two (please refer to Qualifying Documents for a discussion on this). If they also receive a monthly or annual **Bonus** then you will need to separate it and enter that here as well. As I have mentioned previously, Conforming Lenders generally want to see two years of Commissioned Income received and/or two years of Bonuses received. Conforming Lenders will generally take the average of these incomes received, over the past two years, and use that figure in qualifying your borrowers.

1c: IF APPLICABLE, Complete Information for Additional Employment/Self-Employment and Income:

This sub–section may not need to be completed by you – if you don't need it. As I mentioned above lenders are looking for at least 2 years of employment (within the same profession). If your borrower has worked for the same company (or been self-employed) for less than two years then complete this sub-section, as you did in the previous sub-section. However, if completing this sub-section still does not add up to two years of employment then move on down to the next sub-section (1d) and complete that sub-section. If you have entered two or more years in the previous (first sub-section) then enter a check at the top-right of this sub-section (**Does not apply**) and leave this sub-section blank.

1d: IF APPLICABLE, Complete Information for Previous Employment/Self-Employment and Income:

Just as with sub–section 1c, you may not need to complete this area – if you don't need it. Again, Lenders are looking for at least 2 years of employment (within the same profession). If after completing sub-sections 1b & 1c and you still do not have at least two years of employment then complete this sub-section as well.

I would also like to mention here that Lenders do like to see a borrower's (monthly) income increasing over time. Sometimes a borrower may leave a company to come on board with another firm because it has greater opportunities for advancement and/or to learn new and additional skills within that profession, a nicer office, or whatever. However, the income that borrower now earns, with this subsequent job, may be less than the previous job. A Lender in that case may ask for a letter of explanation regarding this. Explaining why they took another job with less income. You will get few requests for this - but expect this when their current income is less than what they were earning in their previous job.

As you can see, you have enough space there for 2 additional employers within this 2-year period. But what do you do if any of your Borrowers have worked for more than 2 employers (besides their current employer) within the past 2 years? That's when you obtain a **URLA – Continuation Sheet** and enter that additional information – just as it asks within sub-section 1d. Quite Frankly, I doubt if you would ever need this page. But if you did, man, that person has moved around quite a bit!

Also, I should note, that if your customer was unemployed or out of work, during this 2-year period for 30 days or more, then that (time period) will need to be noted as well. Try to put that (unemployment period) on a **URLA – Continuation Sheet** as well. If this is a conforming loan you are working on here and that customer was out of work for 30 days or more during the last 2 years then it is not uncommon for a Lender to request the borrower to provide a letter of explanation regarding this (we talked about this in Qualifying Documentation).

However, if you have entered two or more years within the first or second sub-sections above then enter a check at the top-right of this sub-section (**Does not apply**) and leave this sub-section blank.

1e. Income from Other Sources:

If your Borrower has other sources of income that they wish to include, to qualify for their home loan, then that is what this sub-section is for. If not, then just enter a check within the box on the right: **Does not apply**. And, if you Borrower does not have any other income sources then I would suggest drawing a line through this entire sub-section

However, if the Borrower does have other sources of income and they wish to include it then at the top of this sub-section is a list of numerous income sources and below that are 3 blank rows for listing those income sources. First, in completing this area, I would suggest underlining which applicable **Income Source(s)** the Borrower wishes to list and then below also write the name of that income source. To the right of each listed income source enter the gross **Monthly Income** the Borrower is receiving from that income source. If you can Gross-Up their income then enter that Gross-Up income figure here. If you are Grossing Up an income source then I find it's a good practice to write that on the description line with the percentage you are Grossing-Up that income source. For example, your borrower receives Social Security each month for $1,000. You call the Lender and ask them if you can Gross-Up this income source and by how much. They say, "Yes" and that you can Gross-Up that income source by 25%. You would then enter $1,250 under income and next to its description (Social Security) you would write - Grossed-Up by 25%. The Lender (and your Loan Processor) will know what you are talking about.

As you can see here, there are lines for only 3 additional income sources. So, what do you do if your customers have more than 3 additional sources of income? You would, again, go to the **URLA– Continuation Sheet** and enter those additional income sources noting its description, and its monthly (gross) amount.

After you have completed this "**Other Income**" sub-section then total all the incomes in this section (don't forget to include the additional amounts on the URLA – Continuation Sheet if you needed it) and write that totaled figure in the line called "**Provide TOTAL Amount Here**." This Total Amount will be added onto the Borrower's employment income amounts in qualifying that Borrower.

And finally, if your Borrower is including additional income sources then you know that you will need the proper documentations, from that Borrower, to support each listed income source.

And finally, at the bottom left-hand side of this 2nd page you enter the **Borrower's Name**.

Thus far, we have inquired into the Borrower's personal information, their income from employment, and any other income sources that they would like included within their loan. Let's now move on to the next section and find out about their financial information regarding any Assets they own and any Liabilities that they owe.

After completing the first two pages of this 1003 we then move on to the 2nd page for…

Section 2: Financial Information – Assets and Liabilities:

Section 2 is made up of one page with 4 sub-sections and it shows what the borrower owns that is worth money and could be considered in qualifying them for their loan and their liabilities (or debts) that they pay each month (or transacted into a monthly debt). Those sub-sections are:

2a: Assets – Bank Accounts, Retirement, and Other Account You Have
2b: Other Assets You Have
2c: Liabilities – Credit Cards, Other Debts, and Leases that You Owe

2d: Other Liabilities and Expenses

The purpose of this section is to assist the Lender in calculating the net worth of the borrower. Quite simply, net worth is calculated by adding up all the Cash and Assets of the borrower and subtracting from that all of their Liabilities. The result is their net worth. So, let's begin here with the borrower's Assets.

2a. Assets – Bank Accounts, Retirements, and Other Accounts You Have:

At the top of this sub-section are listed the various types of assets that should be listed here. Below that are four columns with each column containing five rows whereby you can list (for each Asset) the Account Type, the Financial Institution of that Asset, and that Asset's Account Number. And, at the far-right column you enter the Cash or Market Value for each corresponding Asset.

This sub-section and any applicable supporting schedules may be completed jointly by both married and unmarried co-borrowers if their assets and liabilities are sufficiently joined so that this area can be meaningfully and fairly presented on a combined basis. Otherwise, if Assets are to be listed separately then completion of a **URLA – Additional Borrower Information** would then be required for that co-borrower.

For clarification, I'd like to go over some of those Assets you might list for your Borrowers. Okay, let's begin with…

Checking and Savings Accounts:

Here you list all the borrower's checking and savings accounts that they currently have. If your Borrower have a checking and savings account with a single Bank or financial institution then list each on a separate row. For each account you enter that **Account's Type** (e.g. Checking or Savings), **Financial Institution** (e.g. Name of the bank or credit union), and its **Account Number**.

Now, when you get to the far-right column you enter each **Account's Cash or Market Value**. Here, I usually phrase my question like, "For your checking account, about how much do you think you have in that account today?" And I enter there whatever they tell me. I do the same for their savings account and any other accounts where there is a checking and/or savings feature. But what do you do if your customers have more than 4 checking and/or savings accounts? That's when you would list those additional accounts on a **URLA – Continuation Sheet**. And, you would do the same for the rest of any other Assets listed within this sub-section.

Stocks & Bonds:

Then, you list any stocks and/or bonds that the borrower may own. When you get to this point then ask your loan customer, "Do you have any Stocks, Bonds, Mutual Funds, or any forms of Investment?" If they say, "Yes" then I ask them what type it is (stocks, mutual funds, or whatever) and write it in there. Then I ask them the name of the Financial Institution those investments are with and each investments' Account Number.

Next, I ask them what they think their investments are worth today. I write that figure on the corresponding row within the column Cash or Market Value. That's great if you can get the company's name, the account number, and its full description. If your customer's Investments become a material and important aspect of their loan, in qualifying them, then the Lender on that loan may request a "Stock Certificate" or a current Statement of their Investment. This will generally tell the Lender all the information they need on those. Yes, we do want to do a thorough job in completing the 1003 but, on the other hand, you don't want to wear out your welcome at your customer's home (if that's where you are meeting with them) and have them running all over their place looking for Stock Certificates and such. You won't get out of there until 1:00 AM in the morning. So, just try to keep it as simple as you can.

Life Insurance Net Cash Value:

If your Borrower has a Life Insurance policy then list it here as well. First, let me say that within the area of Life Insurance there is a type of policy called "Whole Life Insurance." A Whole Life Insurance policy has within it an investment feature and/or a potential loan feature. After the policyholder (your customers) have paid on that policy for a certain number of years, whereby they have built up a small investment, then they may (in some cases) be able take out a loan on that investment amount if they so choose. Applying what I have said here, to what the 1003 is asking for, I first enter the amount of what the customers tell me is the total investment amount of their Whole Life Insurance policy (Face Amount) and how much they could take out as a loan or take out of that investment if they decided to do so. I enter that amount within the column **Cash or Market Value**. Whole Life Insurance policies were quite popular during the eighties. Today however, you will probably find few people out there who still have this type of insurance product. If your customers tell you that they have Term Insurance then leave this space blank (there is no investment or savings feature in those).

Bridge Loan Proceeds:

If your customer is doing a home purchase loan and is or will be taking out a Bridge Loan for that purpose then the proceeds from that loan would be listed here. As the name implies this type of financing provides loan funds – "a Bridge" for the borrower - from his current home (which he or she is selling) towards the down payment and loan costs for the home they are interested in purchasing. This is generally used when the borrowers don't have enough time to sell their currently owned home - before purchasing their new home. A slow home sales market, in that area, could be the reason for that. At any rate, in doing this the borrowers will need to be qualified based on those two mortgages. The goal of a bridge loan is to provide temporary financing and is looked upon as a short-term type of loan providing the needed funds to purchase the new home. Once their house is sold (for which the Bridge Loan was created and based upon) the Bridge Loan is then paid off. If your Borrowers are taking out a Bridge Loan then enter the respective information within this sub-section and enter the net proceeds that they will be receiving within the column **Cash or Market Value**.

Once you have entered all of their Assets, within sub-section 2a, that are to be considered for their loan, then add up the amounts within the Cash or Market Value column and enter the total within the row **Provide TOTAL Amount Here**. I usually leave this blank until I get back to the office. Now, if you have listed more than five Assets and entered those on a **URLA – Continuation Sheet** then I suggest you write on the left side of this row "Also refer to the URLA – Continuation Sheet for additional Assets". That gives your Loan Processor a heads-up that there are additional **Assets** to be considered for that loan customer.

After you have completed sub-section 2a then move on down and begin completing the next sub-section which shows the types of any other Assets that the loan customer wishes to be considered in qualifying for their home loan.

2b. Other Assets You Have:

Just as you saw, within sub-section 2a, at the top of sub-section 2b are listed the various types of assets that should be listed there. This sub-section only has two columns: the first column you enter the name of the **Asset Type** (e.g. Earnest Money Deposit) and the **Cash or Market Value** for each listed Asset.

And, just as you did within sub-section 2a, if your loan customer is listing more than four **Other Assets** then you would list those additional Assets on a **URLA – Continuation Sheet**. Also, as above, if you have listed more than four Other Assets and entered those on a separate **URLA – Continuation Sheet** then I suggest you write on the left side of bottom row "Also refer to the URLA – Continuation Sheet for additional Other Assets".

Once you have entered all of their Other Assets, within sub-section 2b, that are to be considered for their loan, then add up those amounts within the Cash or Market Value column and enter the total within the row **Provide TOTAL Amount Here**.

Up to this point, within the **Assets** side of calculating the Net Worth of your Borrowers, we have been primarily focusing on what are called Liquid Assets. These are assets of the borrowers that can be readily converted into cash. Cash, which the borrowers may need - to pay for the down payment and/or closing costs of their loan. When you have gotten to this point, in completing the 1003, then here's where you might have to put on your Mortgage Detective Hat again and see if this loan is making sense to you so far. For example, let's say you are working on a purchase loan. You know your customers are probably going to need to have some money for the down payment and closing costs. You haven't figured out exactly what that amount will be yet but you are pretty sure it's going to be at least around $2,500. When you first discussed this home loan with your customers they told you that they have saved up about $3,300 for this home purchase.

Okay, you thought, that's great. But now you are looking at what that customer's Earnest Money Deposit is - plus all the balances in their checking and savings accounts. Your customers here don't have any stocks, bonds, or any investments and the Life

Insurance area is blank. In your mind you total it all up and it comes to about $1,800. So, where's the rest of it? Many a mortgage loan originator has been in just this position. At that point you may feel like you want to stand up and ask, "Show me the money or where's the money?" - just like that football player in one of Tom Cruise's movies. But you don't and you shouldn't, because we still have a few more questions to ask on the Asset side that might reveal where some more money might be coming from and shown on other Sections that you will additionally cover with your loan customer.

Now that you have discussed your loan customer's Assets side of their net worth let's now move to the **Liabilities** side. That brings us to the next sub-section.

Before I get into the Liabilities sub-section here I'd like to first go over some points regarding the listing of Liabilities that Loan Processors (and Lenders) like to see. First, Underwriters of Lenders (Loan Processors too) like to see all outstanding debts that are shown on the Credit Report, to be listed on the 1003. They also like to see the monthly payments and outstanding balances that are shown on the Credit Report - to match what is shown on your 1003. Now, when you first meet with your customers this may not be possible. But when you return to your office and pull a Credit Report then you will need to ensure that this takes place. Usually, when you get back to the office you will also type out a new 1003, using your company's loan processing software. Most mortgage loan originators do these types of corrections and additions at that time. We're talk more about the Credit Report later. Alrighty then. With that said, let's look at the first sub-section of Liabilities.

2c. Liabilities – Credit Cards, Other Debts, and Leases that You Owe:

Within this sub-section you will list all of your loan customer's Liabilities except those related to Real Estate as well as any Liabilities that fall under Alimony, Child Support, Separate Maintenance, and Job-Related Expenses. And again, just as you saw above, for sub-section 2b, at the top of Sub-section 2c are listed the various types of Liabilities that should be listed here. Sub-section 2c is comprised of five columns:

1.) **Account Type:** Select the name of that account from those listed above.

2.) **Company Name:** The name of the company your customer is indebted to and makes monthly payments to.

3.) **Account Number:** Here, it is asking for the account number on that account. When you are meeting with your customers and asking them about their monthly creditor debts - they most likely will not remember each of their creditor's account numbers (unless they have a photographic memory). Don't worry about it. When you get back to the office and order a Credit Report then that account will most likely be on that customer's Credit Report and show you the information you need here: (Company-Creditor Name, Account Number, Monthly Payment, and Outstanding Balance on that account). If your customers do have it then write the account numbers in at that time. Otherwise, wait until you get back to the office.

236

4.) **Unpaid Balance**: Enter here the outstanding balance on that account. Now, if any listed Liability here **will be paid off either before or at the closing of this loan** then enter a check within the box "**To be paid off at or before closing**" on the row for that Liability.

5.) **Monthly Payments:** This, of course, is for the monthly payment on that account. Now, sometimes your customers may have forgotten to tell you about a particular creditor account that they have been paying on and you later see it now on their Credit Report. However, although the Credit Report shows an outstanding balance on that account it may not show any amount for minimum monthly payments due. You may then call up your customers and ask them about this and they may say, "Oh yeah, sorry about that. We do have that and we just pay whatever we can on that." Now, from a Lender's (and Loan Processor's) standpoint - that's not good enough. Lenders like exact figures. In that case, most lenders may require you to take 5% of the outstanding balance on that account and use that figure as the minimum monthly payment amount (in qualifying them). Thus, if they had a creditor account with an outstanding balance of $2,000 then their minimum monthly payment would be shown as $100.00 (calculated as $2,000 X 0.05).

Now, if your customers have 5 or more Liability accounts that you need to list, what do you do then? That's right; you would list those additional Liabilities on a separate **URLA – Continuation Sheet**.

Before I leave this sub-section of the Liabilities I'd like to introduce you to what is called the '10-Month Rule'. Although this is referred to as a 'rule' it is actually a 'practice' that many Lenders will allow you to use in qualifying your home loan customers. According to this rule, if an installment account (a liability) will be paid off within the next 10 months then you could exclude that monthly payment in qualifying your customers (e.g. Total Debt Ratio). However, I have always been told to use common sense when doing this. For example, if that monthly payment is $100 or more then I usually include it in qualifying those customers - even though they will be paying that account off within the next 10 months. But you need to temper this by also considering that customer's gross monthly income. If their combined gross monthly income is about $2,500 then I would include it. However, if their combined gross monthly income is about $8,000 or more then I would apply this 10-month rule and exclude that monthly payment: Because that $100 monthly payment isn't really going to impact their ability to service their new loan. But do use common sense when applying this 10-Month Rule. And, if you do use this '10-Month Rule' then be sure to inform your Loan Processor about that.

Let's now talk about the borrower's monthly obligations that are not included within the Liabilities section. Some obligations, often identified on a borrower's paystub, are not considered a liability and will not be included as a debt or deducted from the borrower's gross income when calculating the borrower's debt-to-income ratio. These obligations include items such as:

- Federal, State, and local taxes

- Federal Insurance Contributions Act (FICA) or other retirement contributions, such as 401(k) accounts (including repayment of debt secured by these funds);
- Commuting costs
- Union dues; and
- Voluntary deductions
- Open 30-Day Charge Accounts:
  Open 30–day charge accounts require the balance to be paid in full every month. Therefore, Fannie Mae does not require open 30– day charge accounts to be included in the debt-to-income ratio.

Now, the next sub-section is listed for those Liabilities that you loan customer owes, that were not listed above in 2c. However, Real Estate Liabilities are again not listed here.

2d. Other Liabilities and Expenses:

Within this sub-section you will list all of your loan customer's **Other Liabilities** related to **Alimony, Child Support, Separate Maintenance, and Job-Related Expenses**. Sub-section 2d is comprised of only two columns. Within the first column you enter the Type of Liability and a short description of that. And, within the far-right column you enter the Monthly Payment for each listed Liability. If your customers have more than 3 Liability accounts that you need to list here then you would list those additional Liabilities on a separate **URLA – Continuation Sheet**.

And again, at the bottom left-hand side of this 3rd page you enter the **Borrower's Name.**

At this point you have pretty much summed up the Assets and Liabilities of your Borrower. However, there could be some more major Assets and Liabilities of your borrower – and that is any Real Estate that they may own. Thus, that takes us to the next page and section of this 1003…

Section 3: Financial Information – Real Estate:

Although this section is a separate from the previous Section 2 information, this section is really a continuation of the loan customers Assets and Liabilities: For any real estate that they may own. Now, if your loan customer is doing a purchase loan and does not own any real estate or properties then enter a check in the box above "I do not own any real estate" and draw a diagonal line across this section. You can see that this section enables you to provide the loan customer's real estate information for three properties. If they own more than three properties than each of those additional properties would be listed on a separate **URLA – Continuation Sheet**.

The sub-sections with Section 3: Financial Information – Real Estate are:

3a. Property You Own
3b. IF APPLICABLE, Complete Information for Additional Property
3c. IF APPLICABLE, Complete Information for Additional Property

So, let's begin here with the first sub-section on the following page...

3a. Property You Own:

If your loan customer is doing a home refinance loan then that property's real estate information would be listed first. Otherwise, if this is a purchase loan, and they own more than one property, then enter the loan customer's property that has the largest appraised value first and then list subsequent properties in descending appraised value order.

You begin completing sub-Section 3a by entering the **street address, Unit # (if it's a condo), City, State, and Zip**. Then below that line, and starting on the left, enter that **Property's Value**. In completing this, just ask your loan customer what they think their property is worth. You know that if it's a refinance loan that property will need to be appraised anyway, so just enter in there (for now) what your customer tells you.

Next, it asks what the **Status** is of that property: has it been **Sold**, is there a **Pending Sale** on that property, or is it **Retained**.

Then enter the total of what the monthly escrows are for that property: **Monthly Insurance, Taxes,** any **Association Dues**, plus any **Other Monthly Fees** that the loan customer pays for that property. I should note here that these are monthly fees that are not included in the loan customer monthly payments for that property. So, if these fees are included in the loan customer's monthly PITI payments for this property then leave this information blank. That information will be listed below. However, if the loan customer owns that property free and clear then you would enter the amounts for whatever Insurance, Taxes, any Association Dues, plus any Other Monthly Fees that they pay on that property.

Next, if that property is owned for investment purposes and he or she rents out that property then enter the **Monthly Rental Income** for that property. To the right of that it states: **For Lender to Calculate: Net Monthly Rental Income**. Just leave that boxed area blank for now. The Lender will fill that in. However, I can tell you that in the past we normally considered the Net Monthly Rental Income to be 75% of the gross Rental Income received by the property owner.

Then, below the above you would list **all the Mortgages** that your loan customer has on that property. You list those mortgage(s) in order of the first mortgage and then any second mortgages on that property. In completing this area, for each mortgage, you first enter the **Creditor's Name** for that mortgage. Then that mortgage's **Account Number**. Now, if you loan customer doesn't readily have that number available then just move on to the next area. You can get that information later when you pull a credit report on that loan customer. Then enter the **Monthly Mortgage Payment** for that mortgage loan and to the right of that enter the **Unpaid Balance** on that mortgage. Again, if your loan customer is unsure of the outstanding balance on that mortgage then the credit report on that loan customer will show that.

To the right of **Unpaid Balance** is a box to be checked off if that mortgage is to be paid off at or before closing. If that property is being refinanced then you know that mortgage will be paid off at loan closing – so you would enter a check within that box.

To the right of that enter what **Type** of mortgage loan is on that property: **FHA, VA, Conventional, USDA-RD,** or any **Other**.

And, to the right of that is **Credit Limit**. Within this area box you would enter the maximum amount that that home loan customer is permitted to borrower – if they have a line of equity on that subject property. Otherwise, leave this area blank.

3b. IF APPLICABLE, Complete Information for Additional Property:

Now, if your loan customer owns more than one property then you would complete this area just as you did in sub-section 3a above. Remember, that if your loan customer owns two properties then you list each property in descending order. The exception to this is if this loan if a refinance loan then you enter the subject property first in sub-section 3a. If this area doesn't apply to your loan customer then enter a check in the box for "**Does not apply here**" and I suggest drawing a diagonal line through this sub-section.

3c. IF APPLICABLE, Complete Information for Additional Property:

Here again, if your loan customer owns more than two properties then you would complete this area just as you did in sub-sections 3a & 3b above. As mentioned above, if your loan customer owns more than two properties then you list each property in descending order. The exception to this is if this loan if a refinance loan then you enter the subject property first in sub-section 3a. And, if this area also does not apply to your loan customer then enter a check in the box for "**Does not apply here**" and I suggest drawing a diagonal line through this sub-section.

And, if the loan customer owns more than three properties then enter that or those properties within a separate **URLA – Continuation Sheet,** including all those properties information shown within sub-sections 3b & 3c.

And again, at the bottom left-hand side of this 4th page you enter the **Borrower's Name.**

Next, we move on to the fifth page of this 1003 which talks about what this Uniform Residential Loan Application is all about: the home loan information and the subject property for that home loan. This takes us to…

Section 4: Loan and Property Information:

Within this Section we finally get around to entering information about this home loan and property information on that subject property and the purpose of this home loan (e.g. purchase or refinance). Section 4 has within it four sub-sections:

4a: Loan and Property Information
4b: Other New Mortgage Loans on the Property You are Buying or Refinancing
4c: Rental Income on the Property You Want to Purchase
4d: Gifts or Grants You Have Been Given or Will Receive for this Loan

Okay, let's begin here with the first sub-section…

4a. Loan and Property Information:

The first thing it asks here is what is the total **Loan Amount**? When you are first meeting with your customers it is sometimes difficult to assess, with any certainty, what the amount of their loan will be (or its interest rate, or loan term). However, you should know that - that is exactly what HUD is expecting of you. The thinking here is that after you have completed the 1003 then the customers will sign it. Once your customers have signed it then there should be no changes on this form after that. So, to satisfied HUD's requirement here, enter in the closest loan amount you believe you could offer your customers. You will need to explain to your customers that those figures are only estimates and that you will be providing to them more firmer numbers after you get back to your office and sort this all out. The irony of this is that many Wholesale Underwriters that I have worked with on loans in the past want your Loan Estimate (and its loan amount) to match with what is on the original 1003. But this rarely happens. As a result, I find many mortgage loan originators completing this sub-section after they get back to the office and figure out what it takes to make that loan happen (e.g. loan amount, interest rate, and term).

To the right of that **Loan's Amount** – enter a check in the circle for the **Loan's Purpose** (Purchase, Refinance, or Other).

Below that you enter the subject's **Property Address.** Enter here the complete Address of the Subject Property (Street, Unit #m City, State, Zip, County, and Number of Units). No P.O. Boxes please. I should note here that this is a HMDA related question. Now, you might ask, "Why is that"? Well, recall my previous discussion on the purposes of HMDA (you can refer to HMDA). This question relates to the location of the subject property. Many years ago there were some Lenders who choose to lend in only certain parts of the city (for example) and avoided lending to other parts of that city (i.e. it could be a slum area or have a high rate of crime). This type of lending practice is referred to as "Red Lining" because some lenders would outline those areas on a map, of the city, that they would not do home loans on with a red marker. If a customer wanted to obtain a home loan and that home was within that area, outlined in red, then they would not help that customer with their home loan. Today, this practice of Red Lining is unlawful and one of the reasons HMDA looks at this question on the 1003 (along with the other HMDA questions).

To the bottom- right of that it is asking for **Property Value.** Just ask your loan customer what they think that property is worth and enter that information in here. Again, you know that property will need to be appraised so most likely that number will change.

Below that it is asking for the type of **Occupancy** for the proposed subject property: **Primary Residence** (borrowers live or will live there), **Secondary Residence** (the home will be their Second Home - still O/O), **Investment Property** (i.e. borrowers do not live there and plan to rent out that property). Or, **FHA Secondary Residence**. Enter a check in the circle with the proper occupancy type.

And below that it asks additional information regarding the type of subject property. First, it asks if the subject property will be a **Mixed-Used Property**. Recall that a Mixed-Used Property is a combination of Primary Residence with an accompanying business. For example, the owners live upstairs and own have (or will have) a business or retail outlet on the first floor. Enter a check in the circle "No" or "Yes" for this.

Below that it enquires whether the subject property is a **Manufactured Home**. Enter a check in the circle "No" or "Yes" for this. Another question you might ask, regarding this, is what year that manufactured home was built. This could be a critical question because many Lenders do not wish to loan on manufactured homes that were built before 1976. Then enter the year that manufactured home was built to the right of the "Yes" answer.

4b. Other New Mortgage Loans on the Property You are Buying or Refinancing:

This sub-section is where you would enter any new or existing 2nd mortgage loan (that will not be refinanced) on the subject property. For example, if it is known, at the time of completing this 1003 with your loan customer, that they will also be obtaining a 2nd mortgage loan (for the purchase or refinancing of the subject property) then complete as much of this area as you can. The key words above, in the description of this sub-section, is "**New Mortgage Loans**...". However, if the borrower is not obtaining any new mortgage loans then enter a check within the box "Does not apply" and leave this sub-section blank.

First, if there is to be "new" secondary financing to fulfill any financial requirements of the borrower for this home loan (e.g. down payment, closing costs, etc.) then enter the **Creditor's Name** or names.

To the right of that and under "**Lien Type**" you can see that there are two options there: **First Lien and Subordinate Lien**. To tell you the truth, I am not sure why there are two options here because if the loan were a "First Lien" then that information would have been entered in sub-section 4a above (you can't have two First Liens on a property). Of course, if they are obtaining a new 2nd mortgage loan then that would be subordinate to the first mortgage loan. Therefore, I would conclude that in all cases, if this area applies, then enter a check within the "**Subordinate Lien**" option under Lien Type.

To the right of that you see **Monthly Payment**. Enter there the amount of the monthly payment the borrower will be paying for that secondary financing loan.

To the far-right of this sub-section you see a column named "**Credit Limit** (if applicable)". This would only apply if your customer was also obtaining a HELOC type of loan. If he or she is - then enter the maximum amount of that HELOC here. Otherwise, leave this area blank.

Again, this is an area that you may not be able to complete (because of the unknowns) at the time you are completing this area with your loan customer. Therefore, I suggest do the best you can and get some firmer numbers when you return to your mortgage office.

4c. Rental Income on the Property You Want to Purchase:

If your loan customer is purchasing the subject property for investment purposes then complete the first row of this area: **Expected Monthly Rental Income**. Otherwise, enter a check within the box "Does not apply" and leave this sub-section blank.

If you are completing this sub-section then under the "**Amount**" column enter the Gross Rental Income (total amount) that they plan to receive each month from their renter(s).

Just below that is a row stating "**For Lenders to Calculate: Expected Net Monthly Rental Income**". Leave that blank and your Loan Processor or Underwriter will determine what the Net Rental Income will be from their Gross Rental Income you entered above.

4d. Gifts or Grants You Have Been Given or Will Receive for this Loan:

Now, here is where things can get a little complicated – especially is someone is gifting them some money to help them with the financing of their mortgage loan. If that is the case then here is also where you will most likely need to coach and advise your customers on the requirements of **Gift Funds**. And that's because most loan customers are not aware of all of the stringent and detailed requirements of Gift Funds. However, if the borrower will not be receiving any additional funds from these sources then simply enter a check within the box "Does not apply" and leave this sub-section blank.

For a brief review of this subject please refer to the previous discussion on Gift Funds.

On the other hand, if the source of funds (for this purpose) is from a Grant then enter that information here. And, if the source of funds is a combination of Gift Funds and a Grant then you would enter the information for both here.

To assist you in completing this sub-section (if applicable) you see a list of sources of Gift Funds and Grants. Use this list in completing the rows below.

Under **Asset Type**, list each type of source funds here (e.g. Cash Gift, Gift of Equity, or Grant). For each type of listed source funds enter a check within the proper circle for "**Deposited**" or "**Not Deposited**". If it's a Gifted Fund then most likely you will find that that Gifted Fund has not yet been deposited at that time. So, in that case simply enter a check in "Not Deposited" for that line item. If it is a Grant of some kind then enter "Grant", for **Asset Type** for that line item.

To the right of that is the column **Source**. Use the list above in describing the source of those funds. I should mention here that if the source of those funds is from a Grant then enter the name of that Grant here – if it is known at that time.

And, to the right of that is the column **Cash or Market Value**. If your loan customer is receiving Gifted Funds, in Cash, from a relative or employer (for example) then enter the total amount of those funds that are expected to be received. Or, let's say that a relative of your loan customer will be receiving cash from the liquidation of some stock of bonds – then enter the current Market Value of those investments. Again, here is where you will need to advise your loan customer on what supporting documentation will be needed to verify those Gifted Funds.

However, if that source of funds will be from a Grant then enter here the total amount of funds that is expected to be received from that Grant.

And, as you previously have done, at the bottom left-hand side of this 5th page you enter the **Borrower's Name.**

Let's now move on to the 6th page of this 1003 that is titled…

Section 5: Declarations:
With Section 5 there are two sub-sections:

5a: About the Property and Your Money for this Loan
5b: About Your Finances

Within this Section there are 13 questions you ask your borrowers. Five of those thirteen questions are within the first sub-section (5a) and the other 8 are below those – within sub-section 5b. Depending on the borrower(s) answers (No or Yes) you check the appropriate circle to the right of that question.

When I was a new mortgage loan originator, I didn't like getting to this section of the 1003 and asking my customers if they had any bankruptcies in the past 7 years or had any history of home foreclosures. There have been times when I have asked those questions and my customers looked at me like I had insulted them - for asking. So, over the years I've learned to "lighten it up" as much as possible and throw some humor in there if I can. What I do, when I get to this section and before I ask any of these questions, is I usually say the following, "Now folks, I need to ask you a couple of goofy questions I ask everyone at this point in the application. I'm sure you have heard these before" (if your customers are refinancing then you know that they have). At this point, they look at me and probably know the questions I am about to ask them.

When I have asked those questions - I ask them in a very calm and matter-of-fact way and I try to get through this as quickly as I can (without loss of detail). If the customer answers "Yes" to questions "A" – "M" then you may need to stop, ask about that, and make notes regarding that.

A "Yes" answer could also indicate that there may be a Qualifying Document needed or something that may need to be done during the processing of that loan. As you can see this entire Section is made up of two sub-sections.

The first sub-section (5a) contains questions that relate to information regarding the subject property as well as the borrower's money for this loan. The second sub-section (5b) has questions regarding the borrower's current and past financial situation. These questions, within this entire Section, are listed in alphanumerical order from "A" to "M". Okay, let's begin with the first sub-section...

5a. About this Property and Your Money for this Loan:

Subsection 5a contains five questions in alphanumerical order beginning with...

A. Will you occupy the property as your primary residence?

If you are doing a home loan that is to be owner-occupied then the answer to this question should be "Yes." If it's a loan for Investment property that will not be owner-occupied then you would expect the answer to be "No".

If the answer is "Yes" then it further asks: **Have you had an ownership interest in another property in the last three years?**

If you are doing a Refinance loan then you know what the question to this is. However, if you are doing a purchase loan then the answer to this question may not be so clear. If the loan customer answers "Yes" to this question then enter the type of property they owned in the right-hand column for questions 1 and 2 below.

(1.) What type of property did you own?
- For Primary Residence – enter "PR"
- For Second Home – enter "SH" and
- For Investment Property – enter "IV"

(2.) How did you hold title to the home?
- For Solely by Yourself – enter "S"
- For Jointly with your spouse – enter "SP" and
- For Jointly with another person – enter "O"

B. If this is a Purchase Transaction: Do you have a family relationship or business affiliation with the seller of the property?

C. Are you borrowing any money for this real estate transaction (e.g. money for your closing costs or down payment) or obtaining any money from another party, such as the seller or realtor that you have not disclosed on this loan application?

This question is reserved for purchase money transactions and the purpose of this question is to make sure that all monies for the purchase of the subject property will be recognized. This is not referring to Gift funds but money obtained by the borrower that is expected to be paid back. And, most certainly could affect the borrower's Total Debt Ratio.

If YES, what is the amount of this money?
If the borrower is obtaining additional funds, for this purchase transaction, then enter that total amount in the far-right column.

D. 1. Have you or will you be applying for a mortgage loan on another property (not the property securing this loan) on or before closing this transaction that is not disclosed on the loan application?

Quite frankly, I have never originated a purchase or refinance loan where a borrower replies "Yes" to this question. But you never know. If the borrower does reply "Yes" then you know you will need to obtain all the information regarding that loan and that loan will certainly affect that borrower's Total Debt Ratio.

2. Have you or will you be applying for any new credit (e.g. installment loan, credit card, etc.) on or before closing of this loan that is not disclosed on this application?

Now, this is a question that is a slippery beast and can drive mortgage loan originators and loan processors crazy: like when borrowers incur additional debt just before their loan's closing. A common example is borrowers purchasing a new car just before their home loan closing. These days, it is not uncommon for auto loans to have monthly payments from $300 to $500 a month. So, that definitely will adversely affect their Total Debt Ratio and possibly disqualify them for the loan you have set them up on. However, when you are first completing this 1003 on your borrower - he or she may not even be aware that they will be incurring new debt before their loan's closing. So, after asking this question (and the answer is "No") then I suggest you advise your home loan borrower not to incur any new additional debt and the reasons why.

E. Will this property be subject to a lien that could take priority over the first mortgage lien, such as a clean energy lien paid through your property taxes (e.g. the Property Assessed Clean Energy Program)?

This question refers to any lien(s), on the subject property, that could place that lien in first position and subordinate the new first mortgage loan. A mechanic's lien is a common example of this. This is another reason why it is a good idea to take a look at the Metroscan or property profile of the subject property. That document should show any liens on that property. Regarding this question, you should know that if there are any liens on the subject property then you will need to obtain the documentation for that lien and proof that lien has or will be paid off before the closing of that home loan (no Lender that I know of would lend on a property that could put their primary home loan in a subordinate position).

However, if there is a lien on the property and paying it off is not possible, before the closing of that loan, then you might consider obtaining a Subordination Agreement from that lien holder.

Okay, having obtained the answers to questions A-E, within subsection 5a, let's move on down to...

5b. About Your Finances:

F. Are you a co-signer or guarantor on any debt or loan that is not disclosed on this application?

Whenever I have trained on the 1003 and I get to this question then it is not uncommon for new mortgage loan originators to ask me what a co-signor, guarantor, or endorser is on a Note. Customers also ask me about this. A co-signer or endorser on a Note is someone who (in addition to the primary signor) also signs on a Note (usually referred to as a co-signer) who agrees to make the required monthly payments or repay the entire outstanding debt (on that Note) if the primary signer defaults or for whatever reason does not, will not, or cannot make payments on that Note. This is not Webster's or a real estate dictionary's definition but stated in my own words - words that I think you can understand. Hence, if the primary signer on that Note can't make the required payments then the Lender (of that Note) will then look to your borrower who is the co-signer, co-maker, or endorser on that Note to make those payments.

Now, if your borrower is a co-signor on a Note then the Lender (of the loan we are working on) will want to know if there are any concerns regarding this. In other words, what are the chances that your borrower will be asked and/or be required to fulfill his or her obligation as a co-maker and co-signer? For this reason Lenders like to see a track record of payments made, by the Primary Signer, on that Note showing that they have made their payments on time and as agreed. The amount of time over which they wish to see those payments made may depend on the Lender but you can expect at least a year or more. To satisfy this requirement (or document needed) you will generally need: Canceled checks or bank statements, from the primary signer, showing payments made and date payments were made for the last 12 months.

On the downside of this - is where the Primary Signer, on that Note, has not paid on time or has missed payments or payments are delinquent. If this is the case then you can expect the Lender to require you to include this monthly (co-signer) obligation in with their other monthly expenses in qualifying them for their home loan (you are working on).

G. Are there any outstanding judgements against you?

If your customer replies "Yes" to this question then what are those judgments and what is the outstanding balance (if any) on those. If there is an outstanding judgment amount - then will that amount need to be paid off prior to loan closing? Does the customer have any documentation regarding that judgment?

H. Are you currently delinquent or in default on a federal debt?

If your loan customer replies "Yes" to this question then what are the circumstances of that? If the customer wishes to do a VA loan and they are in default on any Federal debt then that can be like the "kiss of death" regarding doing that VA loan. On the other hand, this loan that the customer wishes to do, like a cash-out refinance loan, may be just what they need to assist them in paying off some debts that have been troubling them.

I. Are you a party to a lawsuit in which you potentially have any personal financial liability?

If your loan customer replies "Yes" to this question then is the customer suing or are they being sued? Lenders get nervous when a prospective loan customer is being sued. The Lender may be concerned whether that loan customer will lose that lawsuit and the damages that they might have to pay could impact the subject property and/or the customer's ability to continue to service that loan. You can expect that the Lender will want to see any documentation regarding that lawsuit.

J. Have you conveyed title to any property in lieu of foreclosure in the past 7 years?

This and the next two questions below relate to the borrower having any history of foreclosure. If a foreclosure has occurred within the last 7 years then you could expect that a letter of explanation may be requested by the Lender – asking them to explain why that home foreclosure occurred. Also, you can expect that the Lender will want to see the full documentation surrounding that property in lieu of foreclosure

K. Within the past 7 years, have you completed a pre-foreclosure sale or short sale, whereby the property was sold to a third party and the Lender agreed to accept less than the outstanding mortgage balance due?

If your loan customer replies "Yes" to this question then, here again, you could expect that a letter of explanation may be requested by the Lender – asking them to explain what were the circumstances that caused that(e.g. pre-foreclosure sale) to occur. Also, you can expect that the Lender will want to see the full documentation surrounding that property for pre-foreclosure or short sale. The concern that a Lender may have, regarding this, is whether that property (and its debt servicing) could later impact that borrower's finances and negatively affect the borrower's ability to service this new mortgage loan.

L. Have you had property foreclosed upon in the last 7 years?
If your loan customer replies "Yes" to this question then, here again, you could expect that a letter of explanation may be requested by the Lender – asking them to explain why the foreclosure occurred. Also, you can expect that the Lender will want to see the full documentation on their foreclosure.

M. Have you declared bankruptcy with the past 7 years?
If YES, identify the type(s) of bankruptcy: O Chapter 7   O Chapter 11
O Chapter 12   O Chapter 13.

If your loan customer replies "Yes" to this question and that Bankruptcy occurred within the past 7 years then you could expect that your Loan Processor and the Lender will want to see those customer's full Bankruptcy Papers. Please refer to the discussion on Bankruptcy to help you checkoff the proper type of Bankruptcy it asks here.

And, as you previously have done, at the bottom left-hand side of this 6th page you enter the **Borrower's Name.**

Once you have done that then it's time to get into the technical and legal details of loan customers doing a home loan. And that's where you go to page 7 of this 1003 which presents…

Section 6: Acknowledgments and Agreements:

Section 6 is made up six fairly large sized paragraphs that contain important statements that the borrowers should and needs to be aware of in completing their application for a loan:

1. The Complete Information for this Application
2. The Property's Security
3. The Property's Appraisal Value, and Condition
4. Electronic Records and Signatures
5. Delinquency
6. Use and Sharing of Information

Succinctly, these small printed and wordy paragraphs essentially state and inform the prospective home loan borrower:

*   That all the information on this application, provided by the borrower(s), is true to the best of their abilities. As you can read here, there can be quite serious consequences for borrowers who lie and give us false or misleading information on their home loan application for the purposes of obtaining a mortgage loan.
*   This loan will be secured by a deed of trust and real property.
*   The property will not be used for any illegal purposes.
*   All statements made and information obtained in this application is for the purpose of obtaining a residential mortgage loan.

- The property will be occupied as indicated on this application.
- The lender, its successor or assigns may retain the original and/or electronic record of this application.
- The broker and lender may rely on the information on this application and the borrower must inform the broker and/or lender if any material facts change prior to the loan closing.
- If the borrower becomes delinquent in their payments then the lender, its servicers, and/or assigns may take whatever (legal) steps to remedy that as well as inform the various credit reporting agencies.
- Their loan may be transferred to another lender and/or mortgage servicer.
- The lender, its agencies, brokers, insurers have made any representation or warranty, expressed or implied as to the condition and/or value of their property.
- An electronic transmission of this application with the borrower's "electronic signature" shall be effective, enforceable and valid as if a paper version of this application were delivered containing the original application with the borrower's written signature.

When I've completed this part of the 1003, with my home loan customers, I first placed this page in front of them and then I turn it around and move that page closer to my customer - so they can clearly see it. Doing this enables them to read it if they wish. I then say something like, "These six paragraphs basically state that all the information you have given me is true to the best of your abilities and that you are not making it up as we go along here" (I try to keep it light). I then say, "That you will occupy the subject property, as you have indicated, in this application (if it is owner-occupied). And, if any material facts come up that relate to this loan and the property, prior to your loan closing, then you must inform us of that at once. And, that this (or your) property cannot be used for any illegal purposes".

I then give them time to read every word of this Section if they wish to do so.

As a mortgage loan originator you should read this entire Section and be very familiar with what it says and what is in it. I say this because you never know when a customer may ask you about something in this Section. You want to be professional as well as appear and be knowledgeable. If you can answer their questions correctly and casually then they will most likely just say, "Fine" and then sign their names at the bottom of that page. Of course, you should be intimately familiar with all Sections of this application as well as all documents you use in putting together a home loan.

After you have gone through Acknowledges and Agreements on this page and/or finished answering any questions your home loan customer may have then ask them to sign and date at the bottom of this page.

HUD wants you to do this (obtain the customer's signatures and date) because they (and the Lender) want to be sure that the information on this loan application was disclosed and obtained from them personally. Their signature and date confirms this.

After your customer(s) have signed and dated that page then that takes you to 8th page for Section 7 (regarding your home loan customers) of this home loan application.

Section 7: Demographic Information (of the Borrower):

In the original version of 1003 form this section was titled "Information for Government Monitoring Purposes". Although the title of this Section has changed the questions that were asked are pretty much the same as what you see here.

As we discussed before, on page one of the 1003, you asked your customers their DOB and Years of Schooling: Here we are going to be checking off the boxes which are (or we believe) is the **Ethnicity and Race** of your borrowers. And, as you may have correctly guessed – these are HMDA related questions. As I understand it, we obtain this information on your borrowers because - if in the event that your company or branch office is ever audited by HUD (or one of its agencies) then they may want to be sure that you or your company does not have any (racial or other) discriminatory lending practices. And, as I said before, the government might also want to do a statistical analysis on homes bought and refinanced during a particular period by various homeowners of different Ethnicity and Race. I think you see what I mean here. Of course, the United States Government may have other reasons for monitoring this information regarding you, your mortgage company, and/or your customers but I won't go into that in this book.

In completing this Section you obtain answers to the questions regarding the **Ethnicity** and **Race** for both your Borrower. Now, I know there is a box below these rows for Ethnicity, where customers can place a check (or an "X") for: "I do not wish to furnish this information." In my opinion, that's okay. Sometimes customers you mail this application to will return it with that box checked. Sometimes when you meet with them and they will tell you this. Then check off that box. But be aware of this: There are Lenders who - when they get this loan file submitted to them and <u>that</u> little box is checked off (and none of the information is checked above it) then all loan Underwriting stops at that point.

So, if you are meeting with your customers then ask them or figure it out for yourself and then check off the appropriate proper boxes. So, make sure this Section is completed before submitting your loan to your Loan Processor and/or to your targeted Wholesale Lender. Below **Ethnicity**, it is asking for the **Sex** of your borrower. And to the right it is asking about the **Race** of the borrower. Check the appropriate box for the borrower.

Below that area of this Section are two additional areas, separated by lines, and are to be completed by you the loan originator. The first area is titled:

To be Completed by the Financial Institution (for application taken in person):

If you completed this application by actually meeting with your home loan customers then you complete this area by checking which of the three circles correctly apply to that question. The purpose of these three questions is to confirm that you answered the questions above by visually observing the loan customer and/or using their surname (e.g.

Ethnicity & Race). To property complete this section you would enter a check into either "Yes" or "No" circles for:

- Was the Ethnicity of the borrower collected on the basis of visual observation of surname?
- Was the Sex of the borrower collected on the basis of visual observation of surname?
- Was the Race of the borrower collected on the basis of visual observation of surname?

However, if you did not actually meet with this loan customer, to complete their loan application, but completed it (or had it completed) by other means (next area) then you would enter a check in these circles for "No". And, that brings us to the next and last area of this Section:

The Demographic Information was provided through:
In this area of Section 7 it is asking you how you obtained this Demographic Information on your loan customer. Check the appropriate circle that applies to you here. How did you take and complete that home loan application?

- Met with your customers? Then check the circle "**Face-to-face Interview.**" (This also includes using Electronic Media with a video Component – like skype).
- Perhaps you completed that loan application over the **Telephone**. Then enter a check within the circle for "**Telephone Interview**".
- You home loan customers may live out of your immediate area and you mailed or faxed to them an application. In that case enter a check within the circle "**Fax or Mail**".
- And finally, did you receive and/or take the application via the **Internet** or as an **Email** document? If you did, then enter a check within the circle "**Email or Internet**".

However, I would say that if you did receive the loan application over the Internet or via an email document then you most likely would be following up on that loan application by calling that prospective loan customer: To obtain more (loan) information and also to find out what their loan goals and needs are. If that is the case, then you would enter a check within the circle "**Telephone Interview**".

Once you have the answers to those questions within Section 7 - **YOU ARE ALMOST DONE ASKING QUESTIONS ON THIS 1003. Yahoo!!**

The last page of this 1003 and final Section is where you enter your loan originator information.

Section 8: Loan Originator Information:
Within Section 8 you enter all the requested and required information regarding you, as the loan originator on that home loan application, as well as the mortgage lending company you work for. To begin here, you enter:

- **Loan Originator Organization Name:** Enter the official name of the mortgage lending company you work for.
- **Address:** Enter here the physical address of the mortgage lending company you work for.
- **Loan Originator Organization NMLS ID#:** Enter NMLS ID# of the mortgage lending company you work for.
- **State License ID#:** Enter here the state license ID number assigned to the mortgage lending company you work for.
- **Loan Originator Name:** Enter here your full name: As it appears on your NMLS ID# certificate or document (if applicable).
- **Loan Originator NMLS ID#:** Enter your NMLS ID# (if applicable).
- **State License ID#:** Here you enter your state license ID number (if applicable).
- Now, in the above three questions you see where I stated (if applicable). I put that there because you may work for a bank or credit union and are legally able to originate mortgage loans under the auspices of that bank or credit union – and therefore may not be required or assigned an NMLS ID or State License number. In that case, just enter an "N/A" for those questions.
- **Email:** Enter here your working (as a loan originator) email address.
- **Phone:** Enter here your working phone number.
- **Signature:** And finally, you Sign and date that home loan application.
  Now, the question here is: When should you actually sign that 1003? That's a very important question because the date you sign that 1003 begins our so-called 'Compliance Clock' to start ticking. The answer to that question is really quite simple: The date you completed that application with your customer or when you received that completed application in the mail. And, when I said completed that application with your customer, I meant either face-to-face or completed it over the telephone. If you mailed that application to a customer, then sign it when you received it back from that customer. And, as you may recall, this is also a HMDA related question. Therefore, to summarize, you sign your name and date on that 1003 when:
  - **Face-to-Face Application**: Date application was completed with customer.
  - **Telephone Application**: Date application was completed over the Telephone.
  - **Mailed Application**: Date you received the application from your customer.

And lastly, as you previously have done, at the bottom left-hand side of this 8ᵗʰ page you enter the **Borrower's Name.**

Congratulations! We are finally done with this **URLA: Borrower Information** form. I know, that was a lot of information to take in. However, I can tell you that if you submit fully completed 1003s to your Loan Processor then this will highly and positively impact your business relationship with your Loan Processor and impress your Mortgage Manager.

Okay, having said that I do have to say that there could be reasons (and the need) to complete one or more additional URLA forms if the following comes up while completing the **URLA: Borrower Information** form (or perhaps you were aware of this before you completed this form):

- There will be a Co-borrower on that home loan
- The Borrower stated and checked off that they are Unmarried
- You needed additional space to enter related information that is on the **URLA: Borrower Information** form (or any other required URLA form).

So, let's begin here with the borrower having a Co-borrower on their home loan:

URLA: Additional Borrower:

This 1003 is very much like the Uniform Residential Loan Application for the primary Borrower who may be single. However, if the primary Borrower is filing jointly (e.g. with a Co-Borrower), whether married or not, then this 1003 (for the additional borrower) will also need to be completed on that person as well. This additional 1003 looks just like the **URLA: Borrower Information** form. However, the question that you should be asking, before completing this form (or before completing the **URLA: Borrower Information** form) is: Does the Co-borrower(s) file their financial information jointly or separately with the primary borrower? Below provides some guidance and options when addressing this question:

- **Two Borrowers with Joint Financial Information:**
  - If the Borrower initially indicates that they will have a Co-borrower on their home loan then you could combine the Borrower's and Co-borrower's Assets, Liabilities, and Real Estate information on the **URLA: Borrower Information** form. Or…
  - Complete a separate **URLA: Additional Borrower** on that Co-borrower, entering only the Co-borrower's information (that is not shown on the borrower's **URLA: Borrower Information** form). That separate and additional information will generally concern the Assets, Liabilities, and Real Estate information of the Co-borrower.

- **Two Borrowers with Separate Financial Information:**
  - Complete the **URLA: Borrower Information** form + the **URLA: Additional Borrower** on the Co-borrower. And, as above you could combine the Borrower's and Co-borrower's Assets, Liabilities, and Real Estate information on the **URLA: Borrower Information** form. If you do this then be sure not to duplicate any information regarding the Co-borrower's information that is on the **URLA: Borrower Information** form onto the **URLA: Additional Borrower** form. Or…
  - Complete a separate **URLA: Additional Borrower** on that Co-borrower, entering only the Co-borrower's information (that is not shown on the borrower's **URLA: Borrower Information** form). That separate and additional information will generally concern the Assets, Liabilities, and Real Estate information of the Co-borrower.

254

- **Three or more Borrowers:**
  - Here you have the option of using any combination of **URLA: Borrower Information** form and **URLA: Additional Borrower** form (for each Co-borrower) in accordance with the two options above.

You can download this document from Fannie Mae's website at: https://singlefamily.fanniemae.com/media/7946/display

Now, let's say that the home loan borrower stated and entered a check at "Unmarried" regarding their Marital Status on the **URLA: Borrower Information** form. In that case a **URLA: Unmarried Addendum** form would also be required to be completed.

URLA: Unmarried Addendum:

Although you would not normally complete this form for your customer(s), as a mortgage loan originator, I did want to mention it so you are at least aware of it. If needed, this optional 1-page form is normally completed by your Loan Processor. It may be used only when:

- A loan customer(s) selected "Unmarried" for Marital Status on their URLA form within Section 1a: Personal Information.

- The information on this form must be collected to determine how the State property laws (where the subject property is located) directly or indirectly affect the creditworthiness of the Borrower, including ensuring clear title of the subject property.

- A **URLA: Unmarried Addendum** may be completed for each Borrower with an unmarried status, as necessary.

This URLA for Unmarried Addendum can be downloaded in PDF format, by going to Fannie Mae's website at: https://singlefamily.fanniemae.com/media/7951/display

But, as I mentioned above, this particular URLA form, if required, is usually completed by your Loan Processor.

After the Borrower (or Co-borrower(s)) has completed their respective URLA forms then take a look at the **URLA: Continuation Sheet** form – if you have one. If you have needed this form, during the completion of any of the required URLA forms, then there will be writing on it. Those Sections, of the respective URLA, that you may have needed additional space to write all the relevant information are usually related to:

- **Section I. Employment Information**: For additional employment history.
- **Section II. Assets and Liabilities**: For additional Assets and/or Liabilities.
- **Section III. Real Estate**: For writing in additional Real Estate Owned.

URLA: Continuation Sheet:

This **URLA: Continuation Sheet** is an optional form to be used when you are completing any URLAs on your home loan customer(s) manually and you need more space to enter all the information, than what is provided within any Section on that 1003. Use as many of these **URLA: Continuation Sheets** as you may need for that home loan Borrower. However, be careful not to duplicate any information on any of the **URLA-Continuation Sheet** forms and the respective **URLA: Borrower Information** and/or **URLA: Additional Borrower** forms.

If you did use any **URLA - Continuation Sheet** forms then have your customer also sign and date this form as well. Utilization of this **URLA – Continuation Sheet** form then accompanies the respective 1003 and becomes part of the completed Uniform Residential Loan Application file for that home loan customer.

Here's Fannie Mae's website address if you wish to download this document in PDF format: https://singlefamily.fanniemae.com/media/7906/display. And, if you feel you would like to download a fillable 1003 in PDF, or wish to obtain further training on the 1003 or other Fannie Mae resources then I invite you to visit: www.FannieMae.com/URLA.

I am also happy to say that Fannie Mae has also designed a Spanish version of the 1003. This Spanish version of the 1003 can be downloaded in PDF format at: https://singlefamily.fanniemae.com/media/14216/display.

Congratulations! We are finally done with this Chapter on the Uniform Residential Loan Application. Okay, after you have rested and maybe gotten another cup of coffee then let's move on to the next chapter that discusses Mortgage Loan Disclosures.

Chapter 11

MORTGAGE LOAN DISCLOSURES

𝕸any of the Mortgage Loan Disclosures are forms that have been designed by the Federal Reserve Board. Their purpose is to protect and inform consumers and prospective borrowers who are interested in obtaining a residential mortgage loan. There are about 18 Loan Disclosures that are normally used for every mortgage loan and also a few others that are used only when applicable. The actual wording on some these Loan Disclosures may change somewhat between States. Also, some States may have state-specific Loan Disclosures in additional to those discussed in this chapter. So, check with the manager in your office to be sure what Loan Disclosures are required in your state. The importance of these Loan Disclosures, in terms of what we do as Mortgage loan originators, is that we must introduce and present these Disclosures to our prospective borrowers and loan customers. You usually do this during your first meeting with them, right after you have completed the 1003.

In presenting each different Loan Disclosure we are informing our loan customers of their rights as customers and prospective borrowers and some of the important things we do in processing their home loan as well as the features of their home loan. These Loan Disclosures also inform them of some lending options that are available to them that they may not have been aware of. After we present each Disclosure then we then ask them to sign and date each Disclosure as well. This shows (e.g. The Federal Reserve Board and/or HUD) that we have reviewed each of those signed Disclosures with our customers. One of the objectives here (with these Loan Disclosures) is to reduce as much as possible any false assumptions that our customers may have about their loan and inform them of their rights and options they are entailed to and can expect - before and during the loan process towards their loan closing.

I suggest that you get your hands on a complete set of these Loan Disclosures that your lending branch or office uses if you can. The best and ideal time to present the Loan Disclosures is right after your customers have signed the 1003. What I usually do, while my customers are signing page 4 of the 1003, is reach into my folder file that I always bring with me and pull out my set of Loan Disclosures that those customers will be signing. At this point I generally say something like, *"Now before we are done here I also need to go over these Loan Disclosures with you and have you sign these as well. These Disclosures were designed by the Federal Reserve Board to inform and protect you as consumers and borrowers in the process of obtaining a mortgage loan."*

If your borrowers are refinancing then they have seen these before. Now, what I like to achieve when I am presenting these Loan Disclosures is a nice signing operation whereby I present the important points of each Disclosure and then have them sign it. With a little practice you can develop a real rhythm going here - in terms of you presenting the various Disclosures and them signing each one.

Now let me say here that when I first became a Mortgage loan originator that I would review each one of these Loan Disclosures in (what I now call) painful detail with my customers. I did that because I really wanted to go over all the important points of each Disclosure and wanted to be sure my customers left our meeting informed and happy to be working with me on their loan. I later figured out that my customers really didn't want the Gettysburg Address rendition of each Loan Disclosure but actually would have preferred the 25 words or less explanation version of each. So that's what I do today and here's how I preface it before I begin presenting the first Loan Disclosure: *"Folks, when I was a new Mortgage loan originator I use to go into painful detail in explaining each of these Disclosures* (and they now see that there is a small stack of papers - the Disclosures in front of me). *However, over the years I have learned that a lot of my customers just wanted me to give them a 25 words or less explanation of each. I will be happy to do that - if you would like me to* (by that time they are usually nodding their heads up and down) *and I also will be happy to stop at any point in presenting these and answer any question you may have and explain any aspect or point on these Disclosures here in as much detail as you would like."* By this time they are reaching for their pens and ready to sign.

When I am presenting each Disclosure - I state the Title or Titles on each Disclosure and explain the main purpose and point of each. If I feel it is necessary (to be sure they do understand a Disclosure) I will highlight a number of points on that Disclosure. The important thing here is that your customers have a good idea of what each Loan Disclosure is all about and understand the main message or messages of each.

Let's now go over each one of these Loan Disclosures (required in Washington State). In doing this I will tell you what I generally say (*shown in italics*) as I present each Disclosure. Now over the years I have developed a certain sequence in presenting these Loan Disclosures and they are as follows:

1. Equal Credit Opportunity Act
2. Borrowers Certification and Authorization
3. Fair Credit Reporting Act / Right to Financial Privacy Act of 1978 / Flood Disaster Protection Act of 1973 => this is sometimes a 3-part form.
4. Rate Lock Agreement
5. Broker Application Disclosure
6. Servicing Transfer Disclosure Statement
7. Affidavit of Occupancy
8. Mortgage Loan Origination Agreement
9. Affiliated Business Arrangement Disclosure Statement Notice
10. Choice of Mortgage Insurance Notice
11. Mortgage Broker Compensation Agreement
12. Privacy Protection Policy Notice
13. Patriot Act Information Disclosure
14. Customer Identification Documentation Patriot Act

15. Settlement Service Provider List
16. Appraisal Disclosure
17. National Credit Score Disclosure / Notice To The Home Loan Applicant
18. Request for Copy of Transcript of Tax Form (4506)

The following Loan Disclosures must also be presented and/or sent to the loan-inquiring customer if the customer's loan contains those particular features:

1. Adjustable-Rate Mortgage Disclosure
2. Balloon Loan Disclosure
3. PMI - Initial Disclosure for Adjustable-Rate Mortgages
4. PMI - Initial Disclosure for Fixed Rate Mortgages
5. Initial Home Equity Line of Credit (HELOC) Disclosure
6. HOEPA / Section 32 Disclosure
7. Notice of Negative Amortization
8. High-Risk Mortgage Loan (HRML) Disclosure

I should mention here that the Loan Estimate is also a mortgage loan disclosure that is normally provided to the home loan customer within three business days following the completion of an applicant's 1003. I discuss the details of the Loan Estimate within Chapter 12.

All together these comprise what I refer to as a set of Loan Disclosures. Keep in mind that I am not rushing through these with my customers. However, as a convenience to them and to be as sure, as much as possible, that I have done my job here, I go over the main points of each Disclosure. And as I said, I am happy to go into as much detail on each as the customer wishes.

I have often thought that each Loan Disclosure listed above probably has a legal precedent to it - brought on by a complaint from a loan customer and/or a legal battle that subsequently ensued. I have never researched this but it just seems that might be the case. As a Mortgage loan originator, you should read all these Loan Disclosures in detail to be very familiar with each and to be able to field any questions your customers may throw at you. When you do read these Disclosures in detail you will see what I mean.

In discussing each one of these Loan Disclosures I will first state what the main purpose(s) of that Disclosure is. Then I'll state what I usually say to my customers (in italics) - if what I say is any different than what I have stated in the purpose above it. So, with that said, let's begin with our first Loan Disclosure:

1. Equal Credit Opportunity Act:
Required By: The Federal Equal Credit Opportunity Act
Purpose: This disclosure is often referred to as the ECOA Disclosure. This informs them that it is against the law for any lender to discriminate against anyone on the basis of race, color, religion, national origin, sex, marital status, and age (applicants need to be of legal age to enter into a contract - in that state). This is not news to your customers. But I

always like to begin my disclosures with this one because I believe it sets a nice tone. Please refer to ECOA for more information on this subject.

Statement: *This Disclosure informs you that it is against the law for any lender to discriminate against anyone on the basis of race, color, religion, national origin, sex, marital status, and age. If you feel you have been then there is a list of companies here that would be happy to hear from you regarding this.*

2. Borrowers Certification and Authorization:

Required By: Fair Credit Reporting Act (FACT)

Purpose: This Disclosure informs your customers: 1. That in pursuing this loan request, all the information that they provide to you (e.g. on the 1003) should be true to the best of their abilities. And, that they should not hold back (not tell us) any important and/or pertinent information that we should have regarding them and the subject property (being refinanced or purchased), and 2. Their signing of this form authorizes us to pull a Credit Report and obtain all documentation that we (normally) require in processing their loan. This is sometimes referred to as a Blanket Authorization Form. Whatever it is called the wording of it should state the following:

> I hereby authorize _____ (the "lender") to verify my past and present employment earnings records, bank accounts, stock holdings, and any other asset balances that are needed to process my mortgage loan application. I further authorize _____ (the "lender") to order a consumer credit report and verify other credit information, including past and present mortgage and landlord references. It is understood that a photocopy of this form also will serve as authorization. The information the lender obtains is only to be used in the processing of my application for a mortgage loan.

Statement: *This Disclosure authorizes us to pull a Credit Report and obtain the other things we need in processing your loan. Also, that all the information you have given me (on the 1003 which at this time has been done) is true to the best of your ability.*

3. Fair Credit Reporting Act / Right to Financial Privacy Act of 1978 / Flood Disaster Protection Act of 1973. This is normally a 3-part form.

Purpose. As you can see, in this example this is a three-part form requiring your customers to sign below each part.

Fair Credit Reporting Act: Informs your customers that if their loan request is denied, due to what we see on their Credit Report, then you or your company will inform them of this soon afterwards. Usually, by the time of credit denial (they receive a statement of denial from you or your company) your customers are also told the name, address, and telephone number of your Credit Reporting company and are entitled to receive a free Credit Report, from that Credit Reporting company, if they wish. Statement. So I don't repeat myself here, just tell them what is in the purpose stated above.

Right to Financial Privacy Act of 1978: This lets your customers know that if the Department of Housing and Urban Development or the Department of Veterans

Affairs wants to - they can access the records of your customer's loan when and if they so choose. And, they can do this without giving prior notice or obtaining further permission from those customers in doing this.

Statement: *This states that the Department of Housing and Urban Development or the Department of Veterans Affairs can review your loan file if and when they wish to without your prior consent.*

Flood Disaster Protection Act of 1973:
Purpose: This informs your customers that if their home is (or becomes) in a flood zone then they will need to carry flood insurance. Statement: I tell them exactly that.

4. Rate Lock Agreement:
This is an interest rate Lock-in Agreement and Disclosure. Normally you will not be completing this form with your customers at that first meeting time unless you are certain you can lock them in at a that requested interest rate and one that achieves the goals of the loan and makes your customers happy. At the time you do Lock-in their interest rate then this form needs to be completed (and signed by your customers) and becomes part of their loan file.

When it comes to Locking-In the rate for your customers I recommend that you always make note of your conversation with your customers (giving you permission to lock their rate) and your subsequent Lock-in actions on your Comments Sheet in that loan file. When you do Lock-in that rate with the respective Lender then note this on the Comments Sheet as well (i.e. 6/23/06 - Faxed Rate Lock-In Sheet to XYZ Lender at 11:00 am, for 7.0%, 30-Year Fixed rate loan for $125,000. Called XYZ Lender later at 11:15 am. Fax of Rate Lock-in received and Lock-in confirmed. They said they would fax us a Lock-in confirmation later today).

5. Broker Application Disclosure:
Required By: Regulation X of RESPA
Purpose: This is an extremely important Disclosure and I believe it epitomizes one of the most important aspects of the Real Estate Settlement Procedures Act. This Disclosure lets the customers know that at least 3 business days after you have met with them and completed the 1003 that they can expect from you a completed Loan Estimate, showing the amount of their loan, the interest rate, and all their loan costs. It also goes over again (and confirms) the customers' available options regarding locking or not locking their rate. Additionally, it talks about Funds Held in Trust, for third party providers (for the credit report, appraisal, etc.). And finally, whether the Lock-Fee is refundable or not (normally not, if it is required at all).

Statement: Tell your customers what is stated above in your own words.

6. Servicing Transfer Disclosure Statement:
Required By: Regulation X of RESPA
Purpose: This Disclosure basically informs them that their loan could be sold to another Lender or what we call a Mortgage Servicer (company who receives the monthly

mortgage payments). This is one of my favorite Disclosures I present to my customers and you will see why when you read my statements below.

Statement. *As you probably know, banks and lenders commonly sell their loans to other lenders or mortgage servicers - those who you send your monthly mortgage payments to* (if they are refinancing this is nothing new to them). W*e at (*your company's name*) do not service our loans so you would not make your mortgage payments to us. You would make your monthly mortgage payments to whoever is your lender or current mortgage servicer at that time. Now, if your loan is sold then this would in no way change the features of your loan. Also, regarding this, there are two main areas I wish to point out on this Disclosure.* Under the:

Transfer Practices and Requirements - (at this time my finger is pointing to this paragraph where it says 15 days) - *If your mortgage loan is sold then your current mortgage servicer must notify you of this in writing at least 15 business days prior to that transfer. And, the new mortgage servicer must inform you of this transfer within 15 business days of receiving your loan file. This is so you know where to send your next mortgage payment and (hopefully) prevent your mortgage payment from being late during this process.*

Under **Complaint Resolution** (my finger is now pointing to this paragraph, specifically where you see the 20 business days). *Here it says that if you have any questions or concerns (*I never say the word "problems") - *just put it in writing and send it to your current mortgage servicer and they must - respond to that written inquiry or request within 20 business days.* Here is where I stop and look at my customers and say: *However, as your Mortgage loan originator, if you ever have any questions or concerns regarding your loan I would like you to call me. I have been in this business long enough to know how to get answers and resolve loan concerns generally pretty quickly. I wouldn't want you to have to call up a lender or mortgage servicer and perhaps be put on hold for 15 minutes or longer. If you have any questions or concerns regarding your loan - please just call me.* Sometimes when I say this, my customers kind of look at each other in disbelief (pleasantly surprised) and then look at me, smile, and say, "Sure." They are probably saying that because no Mortgage loan originator has ever told them that before.

Remember also, that you should stay in touch with your customers after you close their loan. They may later down the road need to refinance again (for whatever reason), purchase another house, or have a referral of a friend who wants to refinance or purchase a home. And, you want them to have that friend call you so that they too can get that great lending customer service you provided them.

Servicing Transfer Estimates by Original Lender:
This section of this Disclosure informs your customers whether or not your mortgage company intends to be the servicer of their loan. In items numbered 2 and 3 here you indicate what percentage of loans closed that your mortgage company services and the percentage of those loans that have been transferred (not serviced) within the past three years. Just briefly tell your customer what you have indicated in this section.

262

I should note that this Disclosure is usually a 2-page Disclosure with this servicing transfer information on the 2nd page. However, for your convenience I have placed this Disclosure's information on only one page. As you can see at the bottom of this Disclosure there is an area for the borrowers to sign. However, according to the RESPA Reform, dated November 17, 2008 - borrowers will no longer be required to sign this Disclosure.

7. Affidavit of Occupancy:

Purpose: This Disclosure confirms what the customer's *Intent is regarding the occupancy status of the subject property.* This Disclosure provides the loan customer three available chooses here: Primary Residence, Secondary Residence, and Investment Property.

Sometimes, however, you may get a "what if" question from you customers such as, "What if it's my current intent to occupy this home as my primary residence and then my company transfers me to another location and we decide to rent this property after we move away?" The important word in the first sentence above here is "Intent." In signing this form it may be the intent of your customers to occupy their home (subject property) as their primary residence. We know things may change. But at the time of loan application and loan funding it was their intent for their home (subject property) to be owner-occupied (O/O).

8. Mortgage Loan Origination Agreement:

Required By: Regulation X of RESPA

This Disclosure discloses to the loan customer the nature of our lending relationship with them and of the loan pricing options available to them as well. It presents this information in two sections:

Section 1. Nature of Relationship

This relates to our relationship, as a loan officer to your mortgage company (generally as an independent contractor or as an employee), and to our customers for whom we are providing our services to, in assisting them in securing a home loan. Also, although your mortgage company may be approved with about 200 Wholesale Lenders, it states here that you cannot be expected to know what each of their interest rates are at any given time.

Section 2. Our Compensation:

This paragraph, in a nutshell, discloses to the home loan customer:

1. How we, as Loan Officers, get paid from a loan
2. The Buydown Option, to pay for a lower rate, and
3. The customer's option to obtain a higher interest rate thereby paying for some or all of their home loan costs.

Statement: I don't go into a whole lot of detail here but try to present the information in a concise and understandable way. Keep in mind that you will be providing them a copy of all these Loan Disclosures that they have signed. They will then have plenty of time to read every word on these Disclosures and call you if they have any questions regarding them. I have never overcharged my customers and, if anything, I have been told by other

Mortgage loan originators that I undercharge for my services. They may be right but I would rather undercharge for my services and have happy customers.

To continue here I generally say something like "*I am a Mortgage loan originator for XYZ Company and as such - work as an independent contractor in that capacity for them. As your mortgage loan originator I will try to obtain for you the very best rate and loan program I can - that will enable you to achieve the goals of your loan. As it states here there are options available to you that enable you to buydown to a lower interest rate than what might not be normally available. If you are interested in doing this then I can certainly explore the feasibility of that* (use the payback period method I discussed previously). *Also, if you wish to pay for less loan fees or no fees on your loan then this can be done, but with a higher interest rate. This higher rate is needed to pay for and offset the costs of the loan. If you are interested in exploring any of these options then please let me know and I will be happy to look into that for you.*" I then wait to see if they have any questions or wish to discuss this further. If not, then I hand them this Disclosure to sign.

9. Affiliated Business Arrangement Disclosure Statement Notice:
Required By: Regulation X of RESPA
First of all, there are two words in this Disclosure that I, as a mortgage loan originator, do not get involved in or am associated with: 1. An Affiliation, with any third-party providers, and 2. Referral fees. Note: you should know that it is against RESPA regulations for any Mortgage loan originator to accept or give Referral Fees regarding a loan (this is a bad word in the mortgage lending area). Make sure you check with your manager in your branch or office regarding this subject.

To continue: Sure, I work with third-party providers but I do not have an affiliation with them. Nor do I receive any sort of referral or benefit (financial or otherwise) from ordering a service from them. So, in addressing this I tell my customers the title of this Disclosure and that *I have no business affiliation with any third-party providers*.

Again, this Disclosure is somewhat of a duplication of the above Disclosure - Borrower's Notification and Authorization. However, instead of merely showing a range of fees, this disclosure is asking you to write in the names of those third-party providers (your company most often uses) with their range of fees charged. This isn't always possible at this point in the loan process on a loan you are working on (you may not even have had enough time or had enough information to do any research yet on this loan). In that case enter your best guess. For example, if I didn't know the name of a particular appraiser that I will use for a loan then I would just enter "Appraisal" (or whatever type of third-party provider service this form asks for) and the range of fees the customer could expect to pay for this service.

10. Choice of Mortgage Insurance Notice:
This Disclosure informs the prospective borrowers that they have the right to go with whatever Insurance Company they choose for their homeowner's insurance.

Now, if a customer asks me to recommend a homeowner's insurance company for them then what I do is give them the names of about 2 or 3 different insurance companies that I respect and inform that customer - that in the end they must decide which insurance company they wish to use.

11. Mortgage Broker Compensation Agreement:

This mortgage loan disclosures, for mortgage brokers and Mortgage loan originators become a requirement on April 1, 2008. This loan Disclosure is used to disclose to your loan customers all the compensation that you and your mortgage company will receive in originating and processing a customer's home loan. On this disclosure you show all the loan costs and fees your mortgage company earns in originating and processing your customers' loans. For example, in the middle of this Disclosure you see where it states: The total broker compensation amount from all sources for this loan will be: Then you enter that total dollar amount. The more commonly used loan fees you would include in the dollar amount you enter there would be:

- Loan Origination Fee
- Discount Fee
- Broker Fee
- Processing Fee
- Administration Fee

Do not include, in this amount, any loan fees that are paid to any third-party providers such as for the credit report and appraisal. And, if the loan changes from a fixed rate loan to an ARM or for whatever reason, your total compensation changes (on those loan cost items that must be disclosed on this disclosure) by more than $100 then you will need to re-disclose by sending that loan customer a new Mortgage Broker Compensation Agreement with the new compensation amount to be received. This is referred to as the Tolerance of Accuracy and the amount shown on the (final) Mortgage Broker Compensation Agreement must not be greater than what is shown on the final Closing Disclosure by more than $100.

And, if it is discovered after loan closing that the compensation received by the Broker, from the borrower, was greater than the amount stated on the last Mortgage Broker Compensation Agreement Disclosure given to the borrower - then that overage amount will need to be refunded to the borrower.

Unfortunately, when you first present this Disclosure to your customer you may not be certain as to what all your compensation fees and income might be with a customer's loan. That's fine. Make your best guess. However, be aware that you when you do complete that customer's Loan Estimate, and that amount you stated on the original Mortgage Broker Compensation Agreement is less by more than $100 - then you will need to re-disclose this Disclosure to that customer with an accurate amount of the compensation you and your mortgage company will be receiving. If that's the case then just include a new Mortgage Broker Compensation Agreement when sending that customer's initial Loan Estimate.

12. Privacy Protection Policy Notice:

Required By: Gramm-Leach-Bliley Act (GLB)

This disclosure also falls under the Federal Trade Commission's (FTC) Privacy Rule. This Disclosure informs your customers of the Non-Public Information (NPI) you and your mortgage company collect in providing the financial products and services they (your customers) have requested. These days I am finding customers increasingly concerned about the disclosing and sharing of their Non-Public Information, which we (normally) obtain when completing a loan application. And, that is exactly the purpose of this Disclosure: To not only inform, but to address any concerns they may have about their Non-Public (customer) Information being given to individuals or companies that are not necessary in pursuing their loan request. That is what this Disclosure states: That the customer's Non-Public Information is kept (and safeguarded) within your company and that their Non-Public Information is given to (your company's) third party providers and your targeted Lender(s) in pursuing your customer's requested loan goals. I should note also that whatever Non-Public Information you and/or your company is giving to a third-party provider (or Lender) is only the information that provider needs in providing that service to you and for your customer's loan request (i.e. Social Security number for the credit reporting service). Protection of a customer's Non-Public Information is covered in greater detail when discussing the Safeguards Rule of the Gramm-Leach Bliley Act within Chapter 25.

Opting Out:

This Disclosure also offers the customer four opportunities to "opt out" of either giving their Non-Public Information to companies (e.g. third party providers) outside of your mortgage company (non-affiliated third-parties) and of receiving information about your mortgage company's products and services. Regarding this area - the following four options are available to your loan customer:

- **Please do not share personal information about me with non-affiliated third-parties:**
  If the loan customer checks off this first option, within this section, then that customer is directing you to not share their Non-Public Information with anyone or any company outside of your firm.

- **Please do not share personal information about me with any of your affiliates except as necessary to effect, administer, process, service or enforce a transaction requested or authorized by me.**
  This is the option your loan customer should be checking because we do need to share that customer's NPI with some third-party providers who need this information in order to provide their services and enable us to satisfy the conditions of their loan (e.g. credit report, appraisal, and title report).

- **Please do not contact me with offers of products or services by mail.**
  If this option is checked off then that customer is directing you and your mortgage company to not contact or solicit him or her by mail.

- **Please do not contact me with offers of products or services by telephone.**
  If this option is checked off then that customer is directing you and your mortgage company to not contact or solicit him or her by telephone.

According to the Privacy Rule, when a customer relationship is established then you are required to provide a Privacy Protection Notice at that time. For example, if you meet with your customers to obtain information (complete an application) to do a loan then you are required to give those customers your company's Privacy Protection Notice at that time (before that meeting ends). An important question to ask here is: When is a customer relationship established? According to the Privacy Rule, a customer relationship is established at the time a customer submits (loan) application information to you. However, if you take an application over the telephone then, according to the Privacy Rule, you have a reasonable amount of time to get that Privacy Notice to that customer. My advice: Mail them two copies of your company's Privacy Protection Policy Notice as soon as you can.

Anyway, review this disclosure with your customers, have them sign two copies of it, and give them a copy of it before your meeting with them ends. The second copy of this Disclosure they signed becomes part of their loan file.

13. Patriot Act Information Disclosure:
Required By: USA Patriot Act
This Loan Disclosure became a required Disclosure as of October 3, 2003. In presenting this Disclosure just state what is on this Disclosure and then have them sign two copies of it. Also, like the Privacy Protection Notice above, leave with your customers a copy of this Disclosure - before ending your meeting with them. The second copy of this Disclosure they signed becomes part of their loan file.

14. Customer Identification Documentation Patriot Act:
This third Disclosure, relating to the Patriot Act, requires you to obtain two forms of properly identifying the primary borrower and co-borrower (if there is one). Some of the information required at the top part of this form can be taken directly from that customer's completed 1003. However, some of it is asking for detailed customer information on the borrower and co-borrower regarding their identity that is not normally asked when completing a loan application (e.g. driver's license number, its issue and expiration date, etc.). That information you would obtain during your meeting with them.

Additionally, you will most likely need to obtain a copy of a picture ID of your customers for both the borrower and co-borrower (if there is one). A copy of their driver's license will usually do the trick here. However, do check with your branch manager to see if only one picture ID is required.

At the bottom part of this form you see...

Discrepancies and Resolution:
If, in completing this form, you are having problems obtaining the required customer identification information and/or a picture ID then this should be noted in this section.

And, instead of the customer signing their name, at the bottom of this Disclosure, you (who completed this form) enter your name.

15. Settlement Service Provider List:
Purpose: This Disclosure, also named as the Loan Estimate Service Providers, provides a list of Third-Party Provider services that are either necessary to do that loan and/or may be required by the Lender. Third-Party Providers that are listed on this Disclosure are those that are usually used by your mortgage company and, as such, the fees they charge are also known. This is important when completing a Loan Estimate for your customers - for those Third-Party Provider services you will be listing, and perhaps recommending, and their fees you enter on your loan customer's LE. As will be discussed, within Chapter 12 on the Loan Estimate, if you suggest a particular Third-Party Provider that is required for that loan and that loan customer uses that particular Third-Party Provider (instead of shopping around and using another one) then your estimate of the loan cost they will incur for that provider service will usually need to be no greater than 10% of your estimate you entered on the loan customer's binding LE. The various Third-Party Providers that are listed on this Disclosure are: Settlement and Title Insurance companies, providers for Hazard and Flood Insurance, Home Inspections, Pest Inspections, and for Surveys.

In reviewing this Disclosure with your customers just briefly explain its purpose and the various Third-Party Providers that are listed. And, also tell them that your mortgage company does not assume any liability or responsibility for the accuracy, completeness of their reports, or acts or practices on the part of any service provider listed on that Disclosure. Also, that your mortgage company does not indorse any service provider listed on that Disclosure. Now, because of how the format of this Disclosure might vary, between mortgage companies, I have not included a copy of it in the Exhibits section.

16. Appraisal Disclosure:
Required By: The Equal Credit Opportunity Act
Purpose: This Disclosure informs the customers that *they have a right to receive a copy of the appraisal on the subject property* (or property that they intent to purchase or refinance) *if an appraisal is required and completed on the subject property. And, that we will send you a free copy of your appraisal, as well as any valuations, within 3 business days after we have received them.*

I should mention here that this Appraisal Disclosure came out and became effective on January 18, 2014. Please refer to CFPB's Appraisal Rule for more details regarding this within Chapter 25 on Mortgage Lending Regulations.

17. National Credit Score Disclosure / Notice To The Home Loan Applicant
This is a two-part Disclosure having on it two separate Disclosures. The top half of this Disclosure presents the:

National Credit Score Disclosure:
This is relatively new Disclosure and explains to the customer the importance of credit scores in evaluating the credit worthiness of a customer. It also states that the range of credit scores is from 300 to 850. It further states that their credit report lists key

reasons why their credit scores may be lower than perhaps 850 (When and if you explain that to your customers then that would be a good time to let them know what their credit scores are and what their middle credit score is). And, that their lender considers many factors, in addition to their credit scores, when making a decision on their loan application.

And finally, it states that you (the Mortgage loan originator) nor the Lender had anything to do with calculating their credit scores and that if they have any questions or wish to contact the consumer reporting agencies then all three are listed at the bottom part of this Disclosure. The second or bottom half of this Disclosure contains the:

Notice to the Home Loan Applicant:
Required By: Fair and Accurate Credit Transactions (FACT) Act
This Disclosure presents important points and purposes of a customer's credit report and discloses to them the main features reported on their credit report (e.g. the credit reporting bureaus shown on their credit report, their credit scores, and the factors influencing those credit scores).

Now, if prior to the meeting with your loan-inquiring customers, you had already pulled a credit report then, during your meeting with them, you would present this Disclosure to those customers. However, if you pulled a credit report on those folks after your meeting with them, then mail those folks a completed Notice To The Home Loan Applicant Disclosure within 3 business days following the date you pulled their credit report.

18. Request for Copy of Transcript of Tax Form (4506):
This form is referred to in lending as the "4506." While this is not actually a Disclosure it is a form that we oftentimes are requested, by the Lender, to be signed by the borrowers. This form, when signed, gives the Lender of that loan the right to randomly or selectively obtain (tax) records of those borrowers directly from the IRS and compare the information on those documents to what was entered on their loan application. It seems that just a few years ago it was only occasionally that a Lender would request this as a Prior-To-Doc condition. Today, however, it seems that it has become quite common for Lenders to require a signed 4506 before docs go out. Because of this I usually include it with the other Disclosures and have my borrowers sign it as well.

The additional seven loan disclosures below are also to be presented to your loan customers if they apply to their particular home loan product and type.

1. Adjustable-Rate Mortgage Disclosure:
Required By: Regulation Z of the Truth-In-Lending Act
This disclosure informs the customers that their loan has an adjustable-rate feature (it is an ARM) and that the interest can (and most likely will) increase over the life of the loan - once the adjustable rate period on that loan has begun.

2. Balloon Loan Disclosure:

Required By: Regulation Z of the Truth-In-Lending Act

This disclosure informs the customers that their loan has a Balloon feature and, as such, at the time that Balloon date arrives then the outstanding balance of that loan will become due.

3. PMI - Initial Disclosure for Adjustable-Rate Mortgages:

Required By: Regulation Z of the Truth-In-Lending Act

This disclosure, while fairly wordy, informs and discloses to the customers that their loan is an Adjustable-Rate Mortgage, which also includes Private Mortgage Insurance (PMI).

4. PMI - Initial Disclosure for Fixed Rate Mortgages:

Required By: Regulation Z of the Truth-In-Lending Act

This disclosure, also fairly wordy, informs and discloses to the customers that Private Mortgage Insurance (PMI) will be included on their Fixed Rate loan.

5. Initial Home Equity Line of Credit (HELOC) Disclosure:

Required By: Regulation Z of the Truth-In-Lending Act

This disclosure informs the customers of the features of the Line-Of-Credit that they are obtaining on their home. This Disclosure is required for HELOCs on owner-occupied as well as nonowner-occupied properties.

6. HOEPA / Section 32 Disclosure:

Required By: Home Ownership and Equity Protection Act (HOEPA)

If a home loan becomes what is referred to as a High-Cost loan and has Section 32 concerns, that "triggers" what creates a Section 32 loan, then this Disclosure is required to be presented to the home loan customers at least 3 business days prior to the closing of their loan. And, for Section 32 loans the lender must also disclose the following:

- Provide a notice to the customer containing the following statement:
  "You are not required to complete this agreement merely because you have received these disclosures or have signed a loan application. If you obtain this loan, the lender will have a mortgage on your home. You could lose your home, and any money you have put into it, if you do not meet your obligations under the loan."

- The Annual Percentage Rate on that loan

- The Amount of the Regular Monthly Payment on that loan

- For Variable Rate or ARM type of transaction: A statement that the interest rate and monthly payments may increase, and the amount of the maximum increase of their monthly payments and interest rate.

7. Notice of Negative Amortization:

Required By: Regulation Z

If you are originating a mortgage loan for a customer and there is the possibility that they could realize Negative Amortization on that loan then according to Section 226.5b of Regulation Z this must be disclosed to that customer. In past years I have rarely seen loans where negative amortization could present itself. However, recently I am seeing an increasing number of ARM loans where the customer has, in some cases, a choice of three-monthly payment options whereby choice and payment for one of those options may be lower than what is required to pay for the outstanding monthly interest on that loan. In that case, negative amortization can occur with the result of increasing the outstanding balance of that loan by that month's interest, on that loan, which was not paid.

However, I should note that this disclosure of possible Negative Amortization on their loan is required whether or not the unpaid interest is added on to their outstanding loan balance or not.

8. High-Risk Mortgage Loan (HRML) Disclosure:
Required By: Regulation Z
If you know or suspect that you will be working on a "Higher-Risk Mortgage Loan then you would also present to your home loan prospect this disclosure. Please refer to the discussion on High-Risk Mortgage Loans for more information on this.

Before leaving this area of Loan Disclosures I want to make a couple of important points regarding these: First, these Loan Disclosures are part of what we refer to as RESPA Requirements and they are required to be presented to all your customers at the time that you either meet with them to complete an application or you include these in your mailing of the application (1003) to them. Additionally, three business days after you have met with your customers and completed the 1003 (or the date you received the 1003 in the mail) you are required to send a Loan Estimate (LE) to your customers (Washington Broker Application Disclosure #6 above). Also, regarding these Disclosures, if you have not done so before that time - then include with these two forms (LE & TIL) a copy of all the Disclosures required by your state and signed by your customers. Doing so will satisfy one of RESPA's requirements here and will also provide your customers with the opportunity to review and read those Loan Disclosures (in detail) if they so choose.

Looking at these Disclosures you will notice that some of them have places for the Borrower's names and their property's address (the subject property). In preparing for my meeting with them I fill these in (beforehand) so that all my customers have to do, at the loan application meeting, is sign and date each one. This helps the meeting, with your customers, to move along smoothly and saves time.

Now, after I have gone into all the detail, on each one of the above Loan Disclosures, I should inform you that recently I have seen some banks and mortgage companies giving their loan customers (at loan application time) a Disclosure Booklet – which contains most of the main Loan Disclosures we have discussed. At that time the customer receives that Disclosure Booklet they sign an acknowledgement form - indicating that they did receive that Disclosure Booklet. This saves time, during the application meeting, and allows the customer to read, in detail, all the Loan Disclosures contained within that Disclosure Booklet later when they get home.

But for me personally, I would rather not use that Disclosure Booklet. Why? Because one of the most important things you want to develop with that new prospective customer is trust. You develop that by establishing rapport with that customer while reviewing important points and aspects of their loan request. For me, one of the ways I do that is by briefly reviewing with them all the Loan Disclosures. I enjoy doing it and I feel something positive is usually developed during that process. Not doing that, by only giving my loan customers a Disclosure Booklet, I could be missing out on developing that trust I want to establish with my customers. Besides, after the customer has signed that acknowledgement form, for receiving that Disclosure Booklet, how many folks do you think actually read that booklet (in detail) when they get home? These Loan Disclosures are very important and should either be reviewed by the Mortgage loan originator (with their customers) or read by that customer (using the Disclosure Booklet). Anyway, if you have a chance to use this Disclosure Booklet then you decide what you would rather do (if you have a choice).

Home Financing Booklets:
And finally, while we are talking about Loan Disclosures, there are also home financing booklets, which need to be given to your customers that explain the features of the particular type of home loan they are obtaining. The timing of when and how these Booklets are to be presented to your residential home loan customers matches what is required for most home mortgage Loan Disclosures previously discussed:

❖ **Face-to-face Meeting with the Customer:**
Give the customers their respective Booklet(s) after completing the loan application with them.

❖ **Complete Loan Application over the Telephone:**
Send it to the customers within three business days following completion of that application over the telephone.

❖ **Mail Loan Application to Customers:**
When mailing the loan application package to your customers include, at least, the Settlement Costs Booklet in that mailing. If it is known, at that time, that other booklets are required, because of the type of loan that customer is requesting, then include those other Booklets as well.

❖ **The Loan Program Changes during the Processing of that Loan:**
Just as we previously discussed, when talking about Loan Disclosures, sometimes things do change as we are working on a home loan. When that results in changing the type of loan (i.e. going from a fixed rate loan to an ARM) then the respective Booklet needs to be sent to that home loan customer within 3 business days of when that loan change occurred or when that Loan Officer first became aware of that change.

The following is a list of those home financing Booklets and when each is required to be given to your customers:

1. **Settlement Costs Booklet:**
    When <u>any</u> residential home loan customer is obtaining a loan then this Booklet is required to be given to them.

2. **Buying Your Home, Settlement Costs & Helpful Information:**
    If the borrowers are purchasing a home, and you are originating a purchase-money transaction loan for them, then this booklet is required to be given to them.

3. **Consumer Handbook on Adjustable-Rate Mortgages (CHARM):**
    If the borrowers are obtaining a home loan that has an adjustable-rate feature to it (an ARM) then this booklet is required to be given to them.

4. **When Your Home is on The Line: What You Should Know About Home Equity Lines of Credit**
    If your borrowers are obtaining a Home Equity Line of Credit (HELOC) type of loan (sometimes referred to as an open-end loan) or a Reverse Mortgage then this booklet must be given to those customers. This Booklet is also referred to as the Home Equity Brochure.

And, I'd like to say a few words about fully disclosing, to your loan customers, the features of their home loan. This chapter, so far, has presented those mortgage loan disclosures that must be presented to your loan customers and when those disclosures should or must be given to them. Beyond simply presenting those loan disclosures I believe it is also important sometimes to verbally present the features of the customer's loan and the impact that loan could affect them financially. For fixed rate loans this is usually pretty straightforward: Same monthly mortgage payment for the life of that loan. However, when it comes to ARM loans then things can change that could affect the loan customer's ability to service that loan, their freedom to refinance that loan when they wish, and the impact that loan might have on the outstanding balance of their loan. For example, does that loan you are suggesting and/or originating contain any of the following features?

*   A Prepayment Penalty period.
*   A low Initial Interest Rate (e.g. Teaser Rate) with a significant potential increase at its first adjustment period and/or subsequent period.
*   The potential for Negative Amortization (i.e. as in the Option ARM loan).

If it does then I believe it's also important to discuss that with your loan customer so that they fully understand the features of their loan and of the possible impact it could have on their monthly debt servicing and possibly their ability to refinance that loan sometime in the future. After you have discussed this with your loan customer and they understand the features and potential changes that could happen on their loan and they still wish to go forward with it then I think you have done everything that is expected of a mortgage loan originator in fully disclosing to your loan customers. And that's all part of being a professional mortgage loan originator who provides excellent customer service.

And finally, if a home loan application is received or completed showing two or more applicants and those applicants currently live at different addresses then each applicant must receive a complete set of Loan Disclosures.

Okay. Enough about Loan Disclosures! Now, grab your calculator, because we are ready to go on to the next chapter, which discusses another important loan form you need to be familiar with and generally requires you to do some calculations as well. I'm talking about The Loan Estimate.

Chapter 12

THE LOAN ESTIMATE

The Loan Estimate, on October 3, 2015, replaced the previous Good Faith Estimate for all close-end federally-related mortgage loans. And, because the Loan Estimate combines both the old Good Faith Estimate, designed under RESPA, and the Truth-In-Lending Statement, designed under the Truth-In-Lending Act, this Loan Estimate is also referred to as the TILA-RESPA Integrated Disclosure (TRID).

Now, the use and requirements for the Loan Estimate applies to all close-end mortgages for first and subordinate mortgage loans for purchases and refinances. However, the use and rules for the new Loan Estimate (and Closing Disclosure) do not apply to:

- Home Equity Lines of Credit (HELOCs – if open-ended)
- Reverse Mortgages
- Loans secured by mobile homes
- Loans secured by a dwelling that is not attached to the real property.

I should also mention that the TILA-RESPA Integrated Mortgage Disclosures for (e.g. Loan Estimates) are not required for:

- Loans made by a lender that makes 5 or fewer mortgage loans a years.

- Certain no-interest mortgage loans secured by subordinate liens made for the purpose of down payment or similar home buyer assistance, property rehabilitation, energy efficiency, or foreclosure avoidance or prevention

One big change that we all saw, beginning October 3, 2015, was the shift of responsibility for the delivery and accuracy of the Loan Estimate (as well as the Closing Disclosure). Those responsibilities then fell fully upon the shoulders of the lenders and creditors of close-end federally related mortgage loans. Sure, loan originators, of mortgage brokers, could and can still prepare and send out the Loan Estimates, within 3-business days of the applications, to their loan customers. But the accuracy of those Loan Estimates ultimately lies with the creditor of the home loan. This is also true with the Closing Disclosure. And, required delivery of the appraisal for a home loan (see Appraisal Rule).

The previous Good Faith Estimate, which came out in 2010, can still be used on all open-end federally-related mortgage loans. It's interesting to note that the original one-page Good Faith Estimate became effective and was required on all mortgage loans in 1974 and lasted up to 2010. The effective date for the most recent and previous Good Faith Estimate was on January 1, 2010. On that date the new 3-page GFE replaced the one-page Good Faith Estimate that had been around since 1974. The new Loan Estimate is designed to replace and combine the previous Good Faith Estimate and previously required Truth-In-

Lending Statement. Because of this combination the new Loan Estimate is also referred to the TILA-RESPA Integrated Disclosure (TRID).

The Loan Estimate documents and summarizes all the costs of a loan that the borrowers will incur and states the total loan amount, the interest rate on that loan, the Term of the loan, and what kind of loan program it is (e.g. 30-Year fixed, 2-Year ARM). It also shows the Total Estimated Settlement Charges which summaries the total costs included in the loan as well as the sum of all the accounts being paid off (including the existing mortgage or mortgages on the subject property) with that loan.

The Loan Estimate must be mailed or delivered to your customers within 3 business days after:

a. The Loan Application (1003) is completed in person or is completed by taking the information over the telephone (see Definition of an Application).

b. The day you received a completed home loan application from a customer that was either mailed to, given, or sent to them.

c. You talked with or obtain all of following six items from an inquiring loan customer. Then that would trigger a LE requirement according to RESPA:

- The Borrower's Name
- Borrower's Monthly Income
- Borrower's Social Security Number (or what is necessary to pull a credit report)
- The Subject Property Address
- The Requested or Required Loan Amount
- Estimated Value of the Subject Property

However, if you took an application, for a home loan, and it was subsequently withdrawn or denied within this three business-day period then you are not required to send that customer a Loan Estimate.

I should note that when you are counting the days, following the completion of the 1003 (or other required circumstances discussed here), that the following days are not normally counted as Business Days: Saturday and Sundays (although some lenders do count Saturdays), Federal Holidays (Washington's Birthday, Martin Luther King's Birthday, Memorial Day, Independence Day, Labor Day, Columbus Day, Veterans' Day, Thanksgiving, Christmas, and New Year's Day). However, I should also add here that RESPA defines a Business Day as a day in which a company's office is normally opened to the public in carrying out all or most of its normal business activities. Thus, if your office is normally open to the public (as defined by RESPA) on Saturdays then you would include Saturdays in counting the number of required Business Days.

I sometimes get asked if RESPA has any exemptions for which these regulations (Regulation X of RESPA) would not apply for a home loan. The answer to that is yes: Examples of these exemptions would be home loans in which the subject property is not owner-occupied, has 25 or more acres, is a temporary type of home financing (such as a bridge loan), and loans on vacant land - for which no plans currently exist to build on that land within the next two years.

And, this rule also applies if you completed a loan application over the telephone (see Definition of an Application). Also, early disclosure requires that the "final" (or revised) Loan Estimate be provided to the loan customer at least 4 business days before a customer's home loan consummation.

A concern and question by many Mortgage loan originators is – when to re-disclose a new Loan Estimate to the customer after you have presented your customers with the original Loan Estimate? That's a very good question and my answer to that is simply: When things change. And, things do often change when you are working on a home loan. The following are examples of what is sometimes referred to as a "Trigger" for re-disclosure:

- The Loan Changes from a Fixed Rate Loan to an ARM.

- The Loan Changes from an ARM to a Fixed Rate Loan.

- Circumstances change, regarding that loan, that will result in changing some of the loan costs related to that changed circumstance. This is especially true if that changed circumstance causes those related loan costs to increase.

If the above occurs then you need to re-disclose to those customers a new Loan Estimate within three business days following when you first became aware of that loan program change and/or you verbally discussed that change with your customer.

And, you should also be aware that RESPA does want you to have a darn good reason for changing (i.e. primarily increasing) the fees on a loan and/or adding on fees after you have originally disclosed a Loan Estimate to your customers. A phrase you should also be aware of is "Not Reasonably Foreseeable." This means that when you were first working on a loan, those factors on that loan that have since changed could not have been anticipated by you (the Mortgage loan originator) at the time you first disclosed that Loan Estimate to your customer.

Of course, as I mentioned above, sometimes after you have presented the original Loan Estimate to the customer then further research on that loan could result in:

- Needing to now go Non-conforming instead of the originally disclosed (and expected) Conforming loan.

- The LTV significantly changes due to the type of subject property and other factors of the borrower (that have surfaced after you originally disclosed). I hate that when that happens.

- The Interest Rate changes on that loan.
- The customer requests you to make changes on the loan program from what they originally wanted (i.e. they originally wanted a rate/term refinance loan and now want cash-out for home improvements or to take that ocean cruise vacation that they have been dreaming about).

Again, when these types of loan (program) changes occur then re-disclose to your customers a new Loan Estimate within three business days following these types of occurrences.

And finally, my suggestion here (to be on the safe side) is that if the type of loan, total loan amount, and/or loan costs change from what you originally disclosed then re-disclose to your customers.

Now, when you do complete the Loan Estimate, the costs on this disclosure should be as accurate as possible and should reflect those loan costs that your customers can expect to see at their loan closing and shown on their Closing Disclosure (which replaced the HUD-1 Settlement Statement on October 3, 2015) as well. Within this chapter I will also discuss the Tolerances (or allowed variance) of loan costs shown on the Loan Estimate (or its revised one) to the costs on the final Closing Disclosure.

This Loan Estimate is different from the previous Good Faith Estimate and yet does have some similar features:

1. They both have 3 pages.
2. As in the previous Good Faith Estimate, the HUD-1 (now Closing Disclosure) Item numbers are shown on the new Loan Estimate.
3. Some stated costs on the Loan Estimate, if increased from the allowed loan cost Tolerances from what is shown on the final Closing Disclosure from the original or revised Closing Estimate, will needed to be "cured" by the originating Broker and/or Mortgage loan originator no later than 60 calendar days after settlement.
4. Prepaid expenses, for identifying those costs in calculating the APR of the loan, are now shown on the new Loan Estimate.
5. The Loan Estimate enables you to item each loan cost feature, whereas the previous Good Faith Estimate combined and summarized the total cost of certain line items.
6. However, the Loan Estimate does not contain a list of categories informing the loan consumer of the Tolerance Levels. And finally,
7. The Loan Estimate does not contain a Tradeoff Table or Shopping Chart Comparison Tables.

Now, before I began discussing the details of each of the three pages of the new Loan Estimate I first would like to mention some important points you should be aware of when completing this loan disclosure:

- **Rounding of Loan Amounts:**
  When entering the amounts onto most sections of the Loan Estimate you should enter whole numbers that are rounded up to the nearest whole dollar. However, percentage amounts are not normally to be rounded but should be shown and entered with two to three decimals as needed.

- **Consummation of the Home Loan:**

  The CFPB wants you to know that the Consummation of a loan is different from the Closing or Settlement of a home loan. For example, Consummation occurs when the loan consumer becomes contractually obligated to the creditor on the loan and not, for example, when the loan consumer becomes contractually obligated to a seller on a real estate transaction.

  However, when a home loan consumer becomes contractually obligated to the creditor does depend on the applicable State laws where the home loan is being originated (and/or where the subject property is located – if different).

- **Definition of a Loan Application:**

  I remember years ago Mortgage loan originators discussing what constitutes having received an application that required sending out a Good Faith Estimate and Truth-In-Lending Statement (the Loan Estimate now replaces these two loan disclosures). This discussion generally centered on talking with prospective loan consumers over the telephone. According to the new rule's definition of "application" by the CFPB, having the following (six) information items - triggers the timing requirement for a Loan Estimate:

  - The Consumer's Name;
  - Their Income;
  - Social Security Number – to obtain a credit report;
  - The subject property address;
  - An estimate of the value of the subject property; and,
  - The mortgage loan amount the prospective loan customer is seeking.

  If you obtain (all of) the above information, either by you asking or the prospective loan customer telling you then a Loan Estimate is required to be sent to them.

- **Tolerances Levels of Loan Costs:**

  As you may recall, on the previously required Good Faith Estimate, the CFPB introduced three levels of loan cost tolerances for specific home loan costs (from the original or revised Good Faith Estimate to the final Good Faith Estimate at loan closing):

  1. Zero Tolerance
  2. 10% Tolerance, and
  3. Charges not Subject to a Tolerance

  So, let's go over the loan costs for each one of these three Tolerances so you are clear about what is required on this new Loan Estimate:

  1. Zero Tolerance:

  Here the loan costs shown on the final Loan Estimate must match with what is shown on the final Closing Disclosure. Any loan cost differences, if higher on the final Closing Disclosure, will need to "be cured" and paid back to the loan customer from the home loan creditor or lender (which usually means it is taken out of what you, the Mortgage loan originator, make on that loan). Zero Tolerance applies to the following loan costs:

- Origination Charges
- Charges for third-party services for which the loan consumer is not permitted to shop;
- Charges for any third-part services paid to an affiliate of the lender or mortgage broker;
- Transfer Taxes.

2. 10% Tolerance:

Here the loan costs shown on the final Loan Estimate may vary upwards to a maximum of 10% with what is shown on the final Closing Disclosure. If a loan cost item (for which this applies) is higher than 10% on the final Closing Disclosure, from the binding Loan Estimate, then the total amount greater than 10% will need to "be cured" and paid back to the loan customer by the home loan creditor or lender. This Tolerance Level applies to the following loan costs:

- Recording Fees;
- Aggregate amounts of loan costs for third-party service providers for which the loan consumer is permitted to shop for – and those third-party service providers are not affiliates of the lender or mortgage broker.

This Tolerance is also referred to as the "10% cumulative increase bucket" because the sum of charges for third-party services and recording fees, ultimately paid by or imposed on the loan consumer, does not exceed the aggregate amount of such charges disclosed on the Loan Estimate by more than 10%. In other words, the aggregate (cumulative) amount of fees subject to a particular loan category cannot increase by more than 10%.

3. Charges Not Subject to a Tolerance:

Here, there is a no loan cost Tolerance Level placed on these particular loan cost items. Therefore, what is shown on the binding Loan Estimate and any difference on the Closing Disclosure as shown - is not really considered. These include:

- Prepaid Interest (Interest Adjustment);
- Property Insurance Premiums;
- Amounts placed within an escrow, impound, reserve, or similar account;
- Loan charges to a third-party provider that is selected by the loan consumer that are not on a list provided by the lender or mortgage broker;
- Loan charges for third-party provider services that are not required by the lender.

To begin this discussion on the details of the Loan Estimate I'd like to first briefly discuss each of its three pages.

To obtain a copy of the Loan Estimate, in pdf format, please enter onto your Internet browser:https://files.consumerfinance.gov/f/201311_cfpb_kbyo_loan-estimate_blank.pdf. And, please use Google Chrome in accessing this site.

Okay, let's begin here by looking at Page One.

Page One:
The first page of the Loan Estimate shows the basic features of the home loan and at the bottom summarizes all the costs for that home loan. This first page of the Loan Estimate is composed of four subsections:

At the Top:
- Date Issued and Loan Applicants Name(s)
- Property (address) and Sales Price (or Appraised Value)
- Loan Term, Purpose, Product, and Loan Type
- Loan ID#
- Rate Lock (No or Yes); if Yes, then the date the Rate Lock ends.

Loan Term:
- Loan Amount
- Interest Rate
- Monthly Principal & Interest
- Prepayment Penalty (if any)
- Balloon Payment (if any)

Projected Payments:
- **Payment Calculation:**
  Below this heading you itemize, for the borrower, their monthly Principal + Interest, their mortgage insurance amount (if any), and their monthly Estimated Escrow amounts for their home loan.

- **Estimated Total Monthly Payment:**
  This amount represents the total of the above amounts in Payment Calculation.

- **Estimated Taxes, Insurance (homeowners), and Assessments (if any):**
  Within this subsection you enter the borrower's Estimated (property) Taxes, the amount of their homeowner's (fire) Insurance, and any other Assessment Amounts that they will be responsible for. You should know that the CFPB expects that you will present these costs as an annual amount or property cost.
  I find it interesting that the CFPB did not place this subsection before the above Estimated Total Monthly Payment subsection: Especially, since the CFPB requires all Qualified Mortgages to contain these amounts as well. However, to the right, within this subsection it states "In Escrow?" Below this statement you would enter either a "Yes" or "No" depending on whether escrow amounts will be impounded and included in that home loan.

- **Costs at Closing:**
  - **Estimated Closing Costs:**

This amount is taken from page two, subsection **J.**

- **Estimated Cash to Close:**
  This amount is also taken from page two (below subsection J) within Estimated Cash to Close.

Normally, in initially completing the Loan Estimate, you would leave these two line items blank until you have completed page two of the Loan Estimate. Having said that, let's now move on to page two of this document.

Page Two:
The second page of the Loan Estimate is where the actual itemized costs of a home loan are shown and this page is titled "Closing Cost Details". The second page of the Loan Estimate is separated into right and left sections and all total loan costs shown, within each section, are shown at the top for the total amount for that section. The sub-sections within each of the two sections are:

Loan Costs – on left-hand Section:
  A. Origination Charges
  B. Services You Cannot Shop For
  C. Services You Can Shop For
  D. Total Loan Costs (A+B+C)

Other Costs – on right-hand Section
  E. Taxes and Other Government Fees
  F. Prepaids
  G. Initial Escrow Payment at Closing
  H. Other
  I. Total Other Costs (E+F+G+H)
  J. Total Closing Costs (D+I)

Below subsection J (Total Closing Costs) is a subsection titled Calculating Cash to Close. Within this subsection you calculate all the costs of that home loan, including any deposits made by that borrower and any earnest money deposits (if it's a purchase loan) and/or any additional cost or credits to that borrower (e.g. Premium Pricing or No-cost Loan). The sum of those amounts results in the Estimated Cash to Close. That totaled amount represents the amount that the borrower will either receive at closing (e.g. cash-out refinance) or the amount that the borrower will need to bring to the closing table.

Once you have completed the bottom of this page (showing those total loan Settlement Charges) then you enter that total amount at the bottom of the Loan Estimate's 1st page.

Now, at the bottom part of this page of the Loan Estimate are two subsections that are reserved for loans whose interest, payment, and/or principal amount could change during the Term of a home loan.

- Adjustable Payment (AP) Table: at the bottom left-hand Subsection:
- Adjustable Interest Rate (AIR) Table: at the bottom right-hand Subsection

Okay, let's move on to the third and final page of the Loan Estimate.

Page Three:
Page three, of this Loan Estimate, is the page that contains much of the important information that was found on the previously required Truth-In-Lending Statement – which is no longer required for close-end home loans after October 3, 2015.

This third page is titled "Additional Information About This Loan" and, it too, is composed of four subsections:

At the Top (1ˢᵗ subsection):
Within this subsection you enter either the originating Mortgage loan originator's information of a Lender (e.g. a bank's) or Mortgage Broker:

- Lender or Mortgage Broker's name
- Lender or Mortgage Broker's NMLS licensed ID number
- Mortgage loan originator's name
- Mortgage loan originator's licensed ID number
- Mortgage loan originator's Email and Phone number

Comparisons:
This and the following subsection is where you see some of the loan features and amounts that were represented and shown on the previously required Truth-In-Lending Statement.

- **In 5 Years:**
  Entered, to the right of this, is the total PITI payment amount (plus any Assessments) that the borrower will have paid on their home loan after five years (60 months).

- **Annual Percentage Rate (APR):**
  Within this subsection, on the right, you enter the APR on that home loan for that borrower. If you are not sure how to calculate the APR on a loan then please jump ahead to Chapter 17 to the section titled "Calculating the APR of a Home Loan".

- **Total Interest Percentage (TIP):**
  The Total Interest Percentage is the total amount of interest that the loan borrower will pay over the entire Term of their home loan – expressed as a percentage of the loan amount. This is a relatively new percentage indicator that was never before shown on any of the previously required Truth-In-Lending Statements. Closely related and required on previously required Truth-In-Lending Statements was the total amount of interest paid over the entire Term of a home loan. That amount is now expressed as a percentage.

To calculate the TIP of a home loan you first take the total amount of interest the loan borrower would pay, if they kept their home loan for its entire Term, and divide that amount by the borrower's original total loan amount. Refer to and use the TIP Calculation Worksheet in Exhibit VIII to help you calculate this percentage.

For example, if the borrower's total loan amount is $300,000 and the total amount of interest to be pay over the entire Term of that home loan is $60,000 then the TIP on that home loan would be 20%.

If you are not sure how to calculate the total amount of interest over the entire Term of a home loan then you:

1. Multiply the monthly P&I of that home loan times the number of months of the Term for that loan;

2. Subtract, from the amount in #1 above, the amount of the original loan amount of that home loan.

3. Divide the amount of Interest (from #2 above) by the amount in #1 above.

Other Considerations:

Within this subsection you indicate whether the borrower's home loan contains any of those loan features and/or whether they may be required during the processing of their loan. Again, this was normally shown on the previously required Truth-In-Lending Statement.

- Appraisal
- Assumption
- Homeowner's Insurance
- Late Payment Fee
- Refinance (what it depends on)
- Servicing of that home loan

Confirm Receipt:

Within this final subsection of Page 3, the home loan customer signs and dates their Loan Estimate. I should note also, that it states "By signing, you are only confirming that that you have received this form. You do not have to accept this loan because you have signed or received this form." Thus, the prospective loan customer is not required to sign their initial Loan Estimate if they choose not to do so. However, I do want to mention that if a prospective loan customer does not sign their Loan Estimate then they must provide (to their MLO) either in oral communication, email, or written form that they do intend to proceed with their loan application. A prospective loan customer's silence is not indicative of their intent to proceed with the loan application.

Alrighty, let's now go over the details of this Loan Estimate and how to properly complete it so you are in compliance. The Loan Estimate is made up of many different subsections where you state the loan costs that you are expecting at the loan customer's home loan closing. Therefore, in this discussion I will show how each subsection looks and explain how to properly complete and enter the amount that is required for it.

Now that we have reviewed how this Loan Estimate is made up let's now use the following example to see how to complete this Loan Estimate. In completing this Loan Estimate let's make the following assumptions:

Your Borrowers are Joseph and Carol Bishop who live at 12365 Great View Drive, San Diego, California 77214. Also:

1. This is a Cash-Out Refinance loan for Home Improvements.
2. The Appraised Value (or Estimated Value) of the Subject is $337,500.
3. The Interest Rate is 5.50%.
4. This is a 30-Year Fixed Rate Loan.
5. Your Customers Want the Maximum Loan Amount they can get without PMI.
6. You charge a 1.0% Loan Origination Fee (this used to be quite common).
7. For "Reserves Deposited with the Lender" (Prepays) you estimated that: For Hazard Insurance - 4 Months will be required at $65.00 per Month, For Property Taxes - 3 Months will be required at $225.00 per Month.
8. The Outstanding Balance on the existing (and only) 1st mortgage is $200,000
9. The Loan Closing, also by the Title Company, will cost about only $300. Here I should note that the cost of Loan Closings could be more then this - because the closing agent may determine that their total closing costs are based on the total loan amount. This is especially true with purchase home loans.
10. The total cost of the Title Insurance, Title Search, and Title Settlement Fee is about $1,350. And, like I mentioned above, regarding the closing costs, the actual cost of the Title Insurance Policy is usually based on the total loan amount. So, you normally need to look up those fees.
11. Your Borrowers tell you that they need at least $60,000 in order to do the home improvements and to make the loan worthwhile (Customer's Loan Goal).
12. And finally, your customers told you that they want to keep the (new) mortgage payment (PITI) under $1,900 per month - if possible (Customer's Loan Goal).

At this point, in the processing of this home loan, you have met with your customers on November 15, 2021, and completed a 1003 on them, and plan to close their home loan by December 15, 2021. You pulled a Credit Report (we will discuss this later) and found that they have outstanding credit - so no problems there. They have good job stability (worked for their current employers for over 2 years) and it looks like their Housing and Total Debt Ratios are and will be within conforming loan guidelines. Your customers have owned and lived at the subject property for the past 5½ years - which is how old their existing mortgage is - so you know the 1st mortgage is well seasoned.

You then calculated what the maximum loan amount for this refinance loan should be to avoid having Private Mortgage Insurance (LTV of the loan will be 80% or less of the

Appraised or Estimated value of the subject property). However, since the maximum LTV for a conforming cash-out refinance loan is 80% - that will end up being the (maximum) LTV for this loan.

OK. Now, these are assumptions and/or facts that the average Mortgage loan originator could have regarding their prospective loan customer when they are ready to complete a Loan Estimate for a loan - with some fairly firm numbers. Let's now take a look at the Loan Estimate.

So, using the information for our example of Joseph and Carol Bishop - let's begin at the top of Page One of this Loan Estimate.

Page 1 of the Loan Estimate:

Top of Page One:
The upper most section of Page One shows the date the Loan Estimate was issued, the name(s) of the borrowers, the loan Term, Purpose, Type, and Rate Lock Date – if locked:

Save this Loan Estimate to compare with your Closing Disclosure

Loan Estimate

	LOAN TERM	30 Years
	PURPOSE	C/O Refinance
DATE ISSUED November 15, 2020	PRODUCT	Fixed Rate
APPLICANTS Joseph and Carol Bishop	LOAN TYPE	☒ Conventional ☐ FHA ☐ VA ☐ _____
	LOAN ID #	
	RATE LOCK	☐ NO ☒ YES, until 12/16/2020 at 5:00 p.m. PST
PROPERTY 12365 Great View Dr.; San Diego, CA 77214		Before closing, your interest rate, points, and lender credits can
SALE PRICE $337,500 (Appraised Value)		change unless you lock the interest rate. All other estimated closing costs expire on

Loan Terms:
Below the top section is the 2nd Section titled "Loan Terms" where you enter the Loan Amount, Interest Rate, the loan's P&I payment. To the right of each amount entered and shown you answer the question, "Can this amount increase after closing". Since this is a fixed-rate loan then the answer for both is "No".

And, below the P&I Payment you enter if there is any Prepayment Penalty and/or a Balloon Payment. And, you also answer the question for each, "Does the loan have these features?" For this loan the answer for both is "No".

Loan Terms		Can this amount increase after closing?
Loan Amount	$270,000	**NO**
Interest Rate	5.500%	**NO**
Monthly Principal & Interest See Projected Payments below for your Estimated Total Monthly Payment	$1,533.03	**NO**
		Does the loan have these features?
Prepayment Penalty		**NO**
Balloon Payment		**NO**

Projected Payments:

Within this section you show what the loan customer's PITI for their home loan (and any MI if included) and what is included in their monthly mortgage payment. I should also note that under the "Estimated Escrow" it states "Amount can increase over time". And, that usually occurs when either or both their homeowner's insurance and property taxes increase. At the bottom of this section it, again, shows the total monthly Escrow amount and what is included in their monthly Escrow payment.

Projected Payments				
Payment Calculation				
Principal & Interest	$1,533.03			
Mortgage Insurance	0			
Estimated Escrow Amount can increase over time	$ 290.00			
Estimated Total Monthly Payment	$1,823.03			
Estimated Taxes, Insurance & Assessments Amount can increase over time	$290	This estimate includes ☒ Property Taxes ☒ Homeowner's Insurance ☐ Other: See Section G on page 2 for escrowed property costs. You must pay for other property costs separately.	In escrow? **YES** **YES**	

Costs at Closing:

Within this last section of Page One is entered and shown the total Estimated Closing Costs and Estimated Cash to Close. These two amounts are taken from Section J, on Page Two. So, in completing the Loan Estimates you would normally leave these two areas blank until you have completed Page Two. But I already did that for you, so here it is.

Costs at Closing		
Estimated Closing Costs	$7,519	Includes $5,310 in Loan Costs + $2,209 in Other Costs − $0 in Lender Credits. See page 2 for details.
Estimated Cash to Close	− $62,481	Includes Closing Costs. See Calculating Cash to Close on page 2 for details.

As you can see above, the "Estimated Cash to Close" is shown with a minus number (-$62,481). It is shown with a minus number because that is the amount that the home loan borrower will receive from their loan. If it was a positive amount then that would be the amount the home loan customer would need to bring to the closing table (e.g. purchase loan transaction).

Okay, let's move on to Page Two of this Loan Estimate.

Page 2 of the Loan Estimate:

Closing Cost Details:
Page two of the Loan Estimate is titled "Closing Cost Details" and is made up of two parts: The first Part contains Sections A thru H which itemizes and summarizes the details of the various categories of the loan costs with Section J showing the "Total Closing Costs". And, the second part below it is titled "Other Costs" which includes Sections E thru G. I have to say that I like this Page Two over what was provided in the previous Good Faith Estimate - where loan costs, in some areas, were bundled together.

You can also see that to the right of each Section's itemized items is a column for Borrower-Paid and to right of that a column for Seller-Paid amounts. That Seller-Paid column is reserved for purchase loan transactions. The column to the right of Seller-Paid is a column for Paid by Others. This is reserved for when others are paying for any of the closing costs for the home loan borrower. In this example, we won't go into those two columns because this is a refinance home loan transaction. Okay, we begin here with Section A under the title of "Loan Costs".

Loan Costs:
Section A: Origination Charges:

Closing Cost Details	
Loan Costs	**$3,450**
A. Origination Charges	
1.00% of Loan Amount (Points)	$2.700
Underwriting Fee	$750

Section B: Services Borrower Did Not Shop For:
Within this Section you enter those third-party provider services that the loan customer would not shop for.

B. Services You Cannot Shop For	**$510**
Appraisal Fee	$400
Credit Report	$30
Flood Determination Fee	$20
Tax Service Fee	$60

Section C: Services Borrower Did Shop For:
Within this Section you enter those third-party provider services that the loan customer can shop for.

C. Services You Can Shop For	**$1,350**
Title: Insurance Binder	$700
Title: Title Search	$300
Title: Settlement Agent Fee	$350

I should mention at this point that the CFPB has also required that you provide your home loan customers with a new disclosure that provides for them a list of services that the loan customer cannot shop for and services that the borrower can shop for. That new TILA-

RESPA Integrated Disclosure can be obtained in PDF format at: http://files.consumerfinance.gov/f/201403_cfpb_mortgage-loans-transactions_cover_H27C.pdf

Section D: Total Loan Costs (Borrower Paid):
Section D is normally made up of two rows. The first row shows the total borrower paid loan cost items. This amount represents the sum of Sections A+B+C. Below that row and amount is sometimes shown the "Loan Cost Subtotals". For our refinance loan that amount would be the same as shown as the row above it. However, for purchase loan transactions the total amounts for Sections A+B+C could be different than what is shown within the first row here.

D. TOTAL LOAN COSTS (A + B + C)	$5,310

Other Costs:
Section E: Taxes and Other Government Fees:

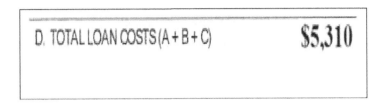

Other Costs	
E. Taxes and Other Government Fees	**$45**
Recording Fees and Other Taxes	$45
Transfer Taxes	$0

Section F: Prepaids:
Within this section you can see that the Prepaid Interest is shown for the customer's home loan. I mention this because this amount, within previous Good Faith Estimates, was shown as Interest Adjustment. Okay, here's Section F:

F. Prepaids	1,584
Homeowner's Insurance Premium (4 months)@ $65/Month	$260
Mortgage Insurance Premium (months)	
Prepaid Interest ($40.57 per day for 16 days @ 5.500%)	$649
Property Taxes (3 months) @ $225 per Month	$675

Section G: Initial Escrow Payment at Closing:

These are the required escrow amounts that will be placed in the loan customer's escrow account so that there will be adequate funds to pay for the various escrow accounts when they become due next.

G. Initial Escrow Payment at Closing						**$580**
Homeowner's Insurance	$65	per month for	2	mo.		$130
Mortgage Insurance		per month for		mo.		
Property Taxes	$225	per month for	2	mo.		$450

Section H: Other (fees):

If there are any other fees then that would be included in this loan but not shown in any of the other sections or categories then that amount would be itemized within this section.

H. Other	**$0**

Section I: Total Other Cost (Borrower Paid):

Like Section D above, Section I is sometimes made up of two rows. The first row shows the total borrower paid loan cost items. This amount represents the sum of Sections E+F+G+H. Below that row and amount is sometimes shown the "Other Cost Subtotals". For our refinance loan that amount would be the same as shown within the row above it. However, for a purchase loan transaction the total amounts for Sections E+F+G+H could be different than what is shown within the first row above it here.

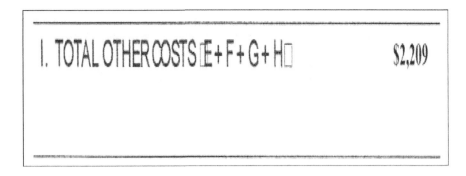

I. TOTAL OTHER COSTS (E + F + G + H) $2,209

Section J: Total Closing Costs (Borrower Paid):
The last section on Page Two shows what the loan customer's total closing costs will be. As you can see this section is made up of two subsections. The first row, within that subsection is "Closing Costs Subtotal". That amount represents the sum of Section D+I. Below that row is the row titled "Lender Credits". Entered here would be any credits that are applied (and subtracted) from the row above it. Examples of lender credits could be for premium pricing (for the interest rate) or credits for a No-Cost Loan. The results of that subtraction would be entered and shown within the top row of this Section. In our example here we have no Lender Credits and so I put a big fat zero there.

J. TOTAL CLOSING COSTS	$7,519
D + I	$7,519
Lender Credits	$0

Okay, great! We are all done with Page Two of the Loan Estimate and just need to go over Page Three which is the easiest page to complete. Page Three is made up of three parts and is titled "Additional Information About This Loan".

Page 3 of the Loan Estimate:

Top of Page Three:
The first part, at the top of this page, doesn't have a title but shows more detail regarding the Lender and/or Mortgage Broker, and the originating mortgage loan originator.

Additional Information About This Loan

LENDER		MORTGAGE BROKER	Best Rates Mortgage
NMLS/___ LICENSE ID		NMLS/___ LICENSE ID	XT 332211
LOAN OFFICER		LOAN OFFICER	Robert Gets
NMLS/___ LICENSE ID		NMLS/___ LICENSE ID	SX 998877
EMAIL		EMAIL	Gets@BestRatesMtge.com
PHONE		PHONE	609-555-4433

Comparisons:

Below the top part of this page is the section titled "Comparisons". The amounts shown here are figures that you would have normally found on the previous Truth-In-Lending Statement. Just as Regulation Z wanted customers to see, within the TIL, the APR of their loan – so they would have something to compare other prospective loans and lenders with.

I should mention that within the 3rd row of this section is entered the "Total Interest Percentage (TIP). This is a new percentage index and I wonder why they (CFPB) have included it. I say this because one of the main purposes of these new disclosures is to provide greater transparency to loan customers. In my humble opinion this new index will not provide greater transparency for loan customers but doubt and confusion. For example, when you reviewed your Loan Estimate with your loan customers you showed them the total amount of interest that they would pay on their home loan – if they held that loan for the entire loan's Term. That total interest amount was arrived at by subtracting the total P&I over the entire Term of that loan minus the original loan amount. Most loan customers I explain this to understood this (even though they didn't like what they were seeing). However, I would wager you that most every time you show and explain this new index to your loan customers - they won't get it the first time and you will need to show them the whole calculations of how you arrived at that. Just like you might have had to do when explaining the APR of their loan. Okay, I'm getting off of my soapbox. Here's the section titled "Comparisons".

Comparisons	Use these measures to compare this loan with other loans.
In 5 Years	$91,982 Total you will have paid in principal, interest, mortgage insurance, and loan costs.
	$20,356 Principal you will have paid off.
Annual Percentage Rate (APR)	5.745% Your costs over the loan term expressed as a rate. This is not your interest rate.
Total Interest Percentage (TIP)	104.40% The total amount of interest that you will pay over the loan term as a percentage of your loan amount.

Other Considerations:

This third and last part of Page Three shows the loan customers features that are or not contained within their home loan. As I mentioned within the 2nd Part of this page, every one of the items shown within this 3rd part used to be shown on the previous Truth-In-Lending Statement. These two sections of "Comparisons" and "Other Considerations" pretty much presents what was on the previous Truth-In-Lending Statement.

Other Considerations	
Appraisal	We may order an appraisal to determine the property's value and charge you for this appraisal. We will promptly give you a copy of any appraisal, even if your loan does not close. You can pay for an additional appraisal for your own use at your own cost.
Assumption	If you sell or transfer this property to another person, we ☐ will allow, under certain conditions, this person to assume this loan on the original terms. ☒ will not allow assumption of this loan on the original terms.
Homeowner's Insurance	This loan requires homeowner's insurance on the property, which you may obtain from a company of your choice that we find acceptable.
Late Payment	If your payment is more than 15 days late, we will charge a late fee of 5% of the monthly principle and interest payment.
Loan Acceptance	You do not have to accept this loan because you have received this form or signed a loan application.
Refinance	Refinancing this loan will depend on your future financial situation, the property value, and market conditions. You may not be able to refinance this loan.
Servicing	We intend ☐ to service your loan. If so, you will make your payments to us. ☒ to transfer servicing of your loan.

Alrighty. Congratulation, we are done with reviewing the new Loan Estimate. See, that wasn't so difficult. However, I should mention that when things change, as they often do, you will need to be aware of how the related individual loan costs change will impact that loan cost amount and, if that loan cost change will adversely affect the Tolerance level acceptance for that total loan amount.

Also, as I previously mentioned, the initial Loan Estimate that you provide to your home loan customers could be a binding Loan Estimate and any cost increases, shown on the final Closing Disclosure beyond whatever Tolerances are required (Zero or 10% Tolerances), from the binding Loan Estimate, will need to be "cured" and paid back to that loan customer. But, as you may know, things do change and when they do a new and revised Loan Estimate may be allowed as well as required to correctly reflect those costs and fees, of a new proposed home loan, that have changed. But when would a new Loan Estimate be allowed or required? Let's talk about that now.

Resubmitting Another Loan Estimate:

When circumstances change, regarding a home loan, which they often do in mortgage lending land, then the "Powers That Be" may require you to resubmit another subsequent revised Loan Estimate. But, in doing this you must:

1. Have a darn good reason for needing to submit to your loan customer another Loan Estimate. Some of those reasons that justify doing this are:

   - War, Acts of God, Disaster, or any other emergency.

   - The Situation has changed and/or the loan customer requested you to do another type of loan.

   - After you issued the initial Loan Estimate to your loan customer then you found out that the information they gave you was not quite accurate (i.e. their credit scores are much lower than they told you, their gross monthly income is less than what they told you, etc.). And, this would result in a change in that Loan Estimate.

2. Any loan cost changes that you make on an updated and revised Loan Estimate must be directly related to the changed circumstance(s) requiring the need to redo the initial Loan Estimate. This is really nothing new but I understand some mortgage loan originators, in mortgage lending land, may have abused this area. OK, the question is: What can change on the resubmitted Loan Estimate?

   - Only those loan costs and fees that are impacted by the changed situation or circumstance.

   - If pricing changes – due to a changed circumstance or the borrower requested a change then only the Interest Rate dependent charges and terms may change. Therefore, only changes, for dependent charges and credits, may be made for those line items and the impacted origination charges. Which brings me to my next point:

   - Fees which cannot change (e.g. origination fee) – even with a changed circumstance. However, the exception to this would be if the loan amount changes and a portion of the "Origination Charge" was a percentage of the loan amount. And, of course, if the overall loan program changes for your customer.

   - Any date changes must reflect the new information and changed circumstance.

   - Those changes resulted in an increase in the loan costs stated on the original Loan Estimate.

   - Resubmit that revised Loan Estimate to the home loan customer within three business days of the date of being revised and/or the date that revision became known and/or at least 4 business days prior to loan consummation. And, as the previous sentence states (or refers to) preparing and sending out a revised Loan Estimate could delay the home loan closing date (given that the loan customer must receive the Loan Estimate at least 4 business days prior to their home loan consummation). Of course, the loan customer could waive that 4-business day waiting period: but only for a bona fide personal financial emergency. Their waiver request will need to be in written form, with the reason for the emergency justifying that waiver, and dated and signed by all borrowers on that home loan.

However, I should mention here that creditors may not provide a revised Loan Estimate on or after the date the creditor provides the consumer with their Closing Disclosure.

And lastly, I should mention (even though I know I should not have to) that you also should keep detailed notes on your Comments Sheets that clearly demonstrate the changed circumstances that warranted redoing the initial Loan Estimate and how those changed circumstance impacted that loan customer's revised Loan Estimate that they will receive.

Preliminary written (loan) Estimates:
One question that does come up, every once in a while, is whether mortgage loan originators are still permitted to provide to loan applicants (usually at loan application time) a preliminary "written estimate" of their loan costs. The answer to that question is "Yes". However, that written Estimate must:

- Contain a specific disclosure (on it) that informs the loan applicant that this form is not a Loan Estimate.

- Must indicate on the top of the 1st page – in font no smaller than 12-point font:
  "Your actual rate, payment and costs could be higher. Get an official Loan Estimate before choosing a loan."

No Requirement to provide a Loan Estimate:
There are mainly two circumstances when the need to send to the loan applicant, their Loan Estimate within 3 business days, is not required:

- The loan applicant withdraws their loan application within that 3-business day period.

- The creditor determines, within the 3-business day period, that the consumer's application will not or cannot be approved on the terms requested by the consumer.

Document Retention of the Loan Estimate:
Creditors (lenders) must retain on file the Loan Estimate at least three years after consummation of the home loan.

Before I close this chapter on the Loan Estimate I'd also like to say a few words about initially working on a home loan for a customer. You know, sometimes when you are working on a Loan Estimate the numbers just might not come together like you would like them to. The loan costs may appear too high for the borrower. The borrower says they need more money at loan funding than you are able to come up with on their Loan Estimate. The interest rate is higher than what would make them happy. These are all considerations when preparing a Loan Estimate. But remember, there may be constraints that limit what you can do. The appraised value of the subject property may not allow the loan amount to go any higher. What you see on the Credit Report and the credit scores may limit the LTV on that loan as well as the range of interest rates you could offer that customer.

Sure, you might be able to massage some of the loan cost numbers. You might be able to lower your loan origination fee and perhaps obtain the approval of the branch manager to lower the loan-processing fee. But that's about it. Okay sure, you could waive the Credit Report fee - but who then will pay for it? You, most likely. Also, it is rare that any Lender would reduce their Underwriting (and other) fees to suit the needs of your loan customers. This is why it is so important to find out as soon as possible: What your customer's Credit (report) looks like, how much is their income, and what's the value of the subject property? This all follows from what we previously discussed in Qualifying Your Borrowers: Credit, Capacity, and Collateral.

But, it is just like anything else: The more experience you have on writing up your Loan Estimates then the more comfortable and confident you will become in doing it. I hope you can see that after going through this chapter on the Loan Estimate with you that it is not all that complicated and in no time you will be completing these with ease.

Let's now go on to another loan document that either you or your Loan Processor completes for each loan package you submit to a Wholesale Lender. I'm talking about the Transmittal Summary Report or what is more often referred to as The 1008.

Chapter 13

THE TRANSMITTAL SUMMARY

The Transmittal Summary is more formally called The Uniform Underwriting and the Transmittal Summary is a one-page form that summarizes the main features of a loan application. Like so many other loan documents - a number, the 1008, refers to this form. Whenever you are submitting a loan file to a targeted Lender you should always include a fully completed 1008 – which is usually placed on top or in front of the 1003. Like many of the other loan documents I previously discussed this one too was updated during the year 2009. To be certain you are using the most current version of this document - at the lower left-hand corner it should read as "Freddie Mac Form 1077 06/09". And, at the lower right-hand corner of this form should read as "Fannie Mae Form 1008 6/09."

The 1008 is made up of 4 Sections:

1. Borrower and Property Information
2. Mortgage Information
3. Underwriting Information
4. Seller Contract and Contact Information

The 1008 is one of the final documents you or your Loan Processor complete when submitting a loan file to a Lender. You complete this form on your mortgage company's LP (loan processing) software program after you have entered and prepared those other loan documents we previously discussed in this section: The 1003 and Loan Estimate. Once you have done that then when you are ready to prepare the 1008. Your loan processing software can take the information needed from those documents and put it into the proper areas on the 1008. This makes it easy for you. Sure, you should review the 1008 (before you print it) to be sure everything is correct. But, besides entering the appraised value of the subject (in the Borrower and Property Information Section) and making sure the Property Type is correctly shown (i.e. 1 Unit is checked for SFR) everything is generally already filled in and ready for you to print and include with your loan file you are submitting.

However, let's say for now that you do not have a loan processing software program and need to complete the 1008 by hand. With that assumption – let's now talk about how to complete the 1008 by hand - so it will be acceptable when you submit it to your targeted lender.

To obtain a copy of a Transmittal Summary form enter the following in your Google Chrome browser: https://www.fanniemae.com/content/guide_form/1008.pdf.

Let's now go over the different Sections of this form and what information most Wholesale Lenders will expect this form to contain - to be complete and acceptable to them. Before you begin completing the 1008 you should always have nearby: Your Borrower's completed 1003, the Loan Estimate, and Qualifying Analysis Worksheet (if you have completed it) - because much of the information you will enter on this form will be coming from those documents.

Let's begin at the top of the 1008:

I. BORROWER AND PROPERTY INFORMATION:
As this name implies, this Sections asks about the Borrowers (their names and social security numbers). This information is obtained from the 1003 in Section III: Borrower Information. Enter their names on the first two lines here with their respective social security numbers to the right of their names. Below their names enter the Address of the Subject Property. If the occupancy status of the subject property is owner-occupied then the address here would be the same as the Borrower's residence address. If it's a NOO loan then this address would be different then the Borrower's home address.

Property Type:
Below that and to the far left is Property Type. If the subject property is a Single-Family Residence (SFR) check "1 Unit." If you are doing a loan on a multi-unit income property then check the appropriate box below that: 2 – 4 Units. And, if the subject is a Condominium then check the box "Condominium." If the subject is a PUD (Planned Unit Development) or CO-OP then check those respective boxes. And, if the subject property is a Manufactured Home then check the appropriate size of it. If the Manufactured Home is a singlewide then check the Single Wide box. If it's a Double or Triple-wide then check the "Multi-wide" box.

Project Classification:
To the right of Property Type is Project Classification. You can see there are two lists for the type of project classification that home loan represents. Don't worry about this area. This is an area that is normally completed by your targeted lender's Underwriter. After the Underwriter reviews your loan file he or she will indicate, under either under the Freddie Mac or Fannie Mae listing what project classification is for that loan.

Occupancy Status:
To the right of that is the Occupancy Status area. Check here what the Occupancy Status is for the Subject Property. For example, if it's an owner-occupied home then you should check "Primary Residence" and so on.

Additional Property Information:
To the right of those 3 boxes representing the Occupancy Status is Additional Property Information: This area asks for the **Number of Units, Sales Price,** and **Appraised Value** (of the Subject). First, enter the Number of Units. If you are talking about a SFR then enter "1" here. If 2- 4 units then enter the appropriate number of Units. Below that it asks for the **Sales Price**. If you are doing a refinance loan then leave that line blank.

Otherwise, if you are working on a purchase loan then enter here the Sales Price of the property as stated on the Purchase and Sales Agreement. Below that it asks for the **Appraised Value** of the Subject Property. If an appraisal has been completed on the subject then enter that amount here. Usually though, you will not have ordered that appraisal yet and don't have the "official" appraised value. In that case enter what the borrower and you believe the Subject's (appraised) value will come in at.

And, below Appraised Value is **Property Rights**: You will normally check here "Fee Simple." If it's not "Fee Simple" but a Leasehold - then check that.

II. MORTGAGE INFORMATION:

In this Section you will enter information pertaining to the loan you are submitting: The type of loan, whether it's a 1st or 2nd mortgage, term of the loan, and how the PITI breaks down for the borrowers. This information can be obtained from the Loan Estimate. Looking at the upper half of this section you can see it asks for the **Loan Type, Amortization Type, Loan Purpose Type,** and **Lien Position**. Most of these are pretty self-explanatory. However, I would like to discuss two areas here. First, look at the **Amortized Type** area. Now within that column - look at the box next to the last one there – **ARM (type)**. If you are doing an ARM loan then place a check here. Also, to the right of that checked box enter the type of ARM loan you are submitting (e.g. 3/1 LIBOR ARM, 2/28, etc.). And, if the Amortization Type is an "Other" (that is not listed above) then check that box and describe what it is.

To the right of **Amortization Type** is **Loan Purpose**. Check which one of those boxes represents the purpose of that loan.

Lien Position:
Now look to the far right of the upper area where you see Lien Position. If you are doing a Second Mortgage Loan then place a check in the 2nd box for Second Mortgage. Above that, where it states **Amount of Subordinate Financing,** enter the total amount of the second mortgage loan. However, if you are doing a 1st mortgage loan and not including the existing 2nd mortgage in this loan then enter the outstanding balance of the existing 2nd mortgage loan (if any) here. And, don't forget that if you are refinancing the 1st mortgage and leaving the 2nd mortgage alone then you will need to get an approved and signed Subordination Agreement from the lien holder of the 2nd Mortgage.

Note Information:
In the lower-left part of this Section you see "Note Information." First, enter the total amount of the loan you are submitting - where it states "**Original Loan Amount**." Next, enter the Borrower's **Initial P&I Payment** with this loan. Below that, enter the **Initial Interest Rate** that is shown on the accompanying Loan Estimate (in this loan package). And, below that it is asking for the **Loan Term (in months).** For example, for a 30-year amortized loan you would enter 360 there.

Buydown:

Skip over **Mortgage Originator** and go to its right where you find **Buydown**. If your customer is Buying Down the Interest Rate then place a check in the "**Yes**" box (recall that the cost for the interest rate Buydown is shown as a Loan Discount Fee on the LE). Otherwise, enter a check in the "**No**" box. Below that is **Terms**: If your borrower is Buying Down the Rate then enter the Terms of that Buydown. For example, for a 2/1 Buydown simply enter 2/1 there.

If Second Mortgage:

To the right of Buydown it states "If Second Mortgage." This area is completed only if you are doing a stand-alone Second Mortgage. If you are then the Lender, you are submitting your loan to, will want to know what kind of existing 1st mortgage the Borrowers currently have? Is it a **Fannie Mae** or **Freddie Mac** type of loan? You will need to find this out. Or, if the existing 1st mortgage is a **Seller Contract** then you would check that respective box. Below those boxes it asks for the "**Original Loan Amount of the First Mortgage.**" Again, I don't know why it states "Original" loan. I have always entered the current outstanding balance of the existing 1st mortgage.

III. UNDERWRITING INFORMATION:

This Section is what I refer to as the Qualifying Section because in this section you are entering information that is used in calculating the Qualifying Ratios of the borrowers as well as the LTV on that loan. Most of the information you will need to complete this section can come from the 2nd page of the 1003 (Section V. Monthly Income and Combined Housing Expense Information).

First, skip over that top line item asking for **Underwriter's Name** and go to where it states "**Appraiser's Name/License#**," and to its right: **Appraisal Company Name**. If you have ordered the Appraisal or know the name of the appraiser you plan to order the Appraisal from then enter the **Appraiser's Name, their License #,** and **Appraisal Company Name**. Otherwise, leave that area blank. From there go below to where it states:

Stable Monthly Income:

Stable Monthly Income is in the upper left-hand corner of this Section. In that area where it asks for the various income sources for the Borrower and Co-borrower enter the figures exactly as shown within Section V on page 2 of 5 on the 1003.

Now jump on over to the right-hand side of this Section where it states "**Present Housing Payment**." Enter there what your Borrower's current rent or monthly housing mortgage payments are. Then below that is "**Proposed Monthly Payments** and **Borrower's Primary Residence**." You can find that information on the 2nd page of the 1003, in the lower right-hand corner of Section V, under the column titled **Proposed (Combined Monthly Housing Expenses)**. The information you enter in this area of the 1008 (monthly P&I payment, monthly hazard insurance, monthly real estate taxes, and monthly private mortgage insurance – if any) should match with what is within Section V on page

2 of 5 on the 1003 for that customer. Of course, if there are **Homeowner Association Dues** (for a condo) or any other monthly payments related to the subject (i.e. monthly rental fee for manufactured home in a park) then that too is entered here. Once you have entered all those figures - you also enter the sum of those amounts at the line item: **Total Primary Housing Expense**. This figure should also match with what you are showing on that loan customer's 1003.

Other Obligation:
Under the Total Primary Housing Expense line is "Other Obligations:" The first listed here is for **Negative Cash Flow (Subject Property)**. If this loan is on an investment property (or your borrowers have any investments properties) and the net monthly cash flow is negative (total monthly mortgage payments including monthly hazard insurance and taxes is greater than the monthly rental income) then this negative amount would be entered here. This amount is taken from page 2-3, of the 1003, in Section VI: Assets and Liabilities. Thus, if your borrowers have total monthly payments, on their investment property (including monthly taxes and hazard insurance) of $1,000 and they are receiving monthly rental payments of only $950 then they are realizing a loss (or negative cash flow) of $50.00 per month. This should be shown as such in this Section of the 1003 on the respective line for that property. Regarding the 1008, that $50.00 monthly loss should be entered here at the Negative Cash Flow line.

Now, if the borrowers have other investment properties and are realizing other losses (monthly negative cash flows) then those should also be shown on the 1003 and the total of those monthly losses would be entered here on the 1008. You enter that figure here (on the 1008) as a negative – with a minus sign in front of it. Keep in mind, though, that this area is only for monthly negative losses. If the borrowers are not realizing any monthly losses then this line would be left blank.

Below that it asks for "**All Other Monthly Payments**." This information is taken from Page 3 of 5 - of the 1003. Looking at the Liabilities Section of the 1003 - total all the remaining liabilities (excluding the mortgage to be refinanced and/or accounts to be paid off with this loan) and enter that figure here. This figure represents all of the Borrower's monthly payments (after this loan) except those related to their Housing Expenses (which were entered above).

Now total the figures in **Total Primary Housing Expense, Other Obligations** (if any), and **All Other Monthly Payments**. This represents the **Total All Monthly Payments** your Borrowers will be making after this new proposed loan. Below that is:

Borrower Funds to Close:
If that is a purchase loan transaction (or even a refinance loan) and the borrowers need to bring funds to the closing table then you enter (on the line for "**Required**") the amount of funds they will need to bring to their loan closing. And below that you see **Verified Assets**: That represents the amount of funds or Assets that have actually been verified.

Source of (those) Funds:
And below that (if this area is necessary to complete) enter the Source of (those) Funds and the **No. of Months of Reserves** – which your customers currently have. And, if your Borrowers are expecting Gift Funds or Seller Contributions then enter the actual percent of the **Interested Party Contributions**.

Now that you have entered that information - you are now ready to do some financial calculations. Look now at the upper, middle, left-hand side of this Section under the Stable Monthly Income area you previously completed where it states:

Qualifying Ratios:
Here you calculate and enter the **Housing and Total Debt Ratios** for your Borrowers. I know you don't need this but for a quick review:

- Housing Expense Ratio = Total Monthly Primary Housing Expense / Total Monthly Income of the Borrowers)
- Total Obligation/Income Ratio = Total of All Monthly Payments / Total Monthly Income of the Borrowers).

If you completed a Qualifying Analysis Worksheet on your borrowers (which I hope you did) then you need only take a look at your worksheet to get your customer's Housing and Total Debt Ratios. Those figures (on your Qualifying Analysis Worksheet) and what you have calculated on your 1008 should all match. Of course, you should have calculated those Qualifying Ratios before this and know that your borrower's Ratios are in line and within the Lender's Guidelines for that loan you are submitting for your Borrowers.

Loan-to Value Ratios:
To the right of that outlined Section is another one called "Loan-to Value Ratios." Here it asks for the loan's LTV and/or CLTV. Enter the LTV or CLTV percent of that loan here. In addition, the 1008 now provides ratios for high-end type of loans as well (HCLTV/HTLTV). After that, look below and to the left where it states

Qualifying Rate:
Enter here the Interest Rate you are showing on your customer's Loan Estimate. Unless your loan customer is doing a Step-Down Rate Loan or Buying Down the Rate - don't worry about those other boxes. Now, to the right of Qualifying Rate is:

Level of Property Review:
Here you check which box represents the type of Appraisal required for that loan and its Appraisal Form Number as well. For a Full Appraisal (**Exterior/Interior**), on a SFR, enter Appraisal Form #1004. For a Drive-By, **Exterior Only**, enter Appraisal Form# 2055. Now, looking to the far left and under Qualifying Rate is an area titled:

Risk Assessment:
First, check which box represents how that loan was underwritten. If it was manually underwritten then check the "Manual Underwriting" box. Conversely, if it was submitted

that loan via DU (and it was approved) then check whether it was submitted via **DU, LP**, or **Other**. Then below that enter what the **AUS Recommendation** was (and its Case #). Below that you enter the **DU Case ID/LP AUS Key #** and below that you enter the **LP Dcc Class (Freddie)** - if applicable. Then, below that is:

Representative Credit/Indicator Score:
And, below that you enter the **Representative Credit/Indicator Score** – if there is one.

Escrow (T&I):
To the immediate right of Risk Assessment is Escrow (T&I). Here it is asking if the loan customers are impounding their property taxes and homeowner's insurance monthly payments with their P&I payment on that loan. Check the appropriate box. Right below Escrow (T&I) you see:

Community Lending/Affordable Housing Initiative:
If your Borrowers are going that route then check the "**Yes**" box there. And, below it check off the "**Yes**" or "**No**" box asking whether the **Home Buyers/Homeownership Education Certificate** is within that loan file.

Underwriter Comments:
Once you have completed and gotten this far then you are pretty much done with the 1008. As you can see, just below the Risk Assessment area there is a lined Section for "Underwriter Comments." This area is reserved for you in case you feel there is something that the Lender's Underwriter definitely needs to be aware of before reviewing that loan file or there is something urgent regarding that file that he or she needs to know. You would enter that information here. However, if you have completed a Cover Letter or Remarks Page and included that in this loan package (which I hope you do) then that information should be included in there.

IV. SELLER CONTRACT AND CONTACT INFORMATION:
If you are submitting a home purchase loan then this is what this Section is designed for. Completing it is relatively self-explanatory and most of the information needed can be obtained from the Purchase and Sales Agreement. However, to tell you the truth, I have never filled in this Section and have never had a Wholesale Underwriter ask for this information. And, I believe, that is because they (the Underwriters) normally do not contact the Sellers: That's your job. You do that by contacting your Buyer's Real Estate Agent and letting him or her know your loan needs. The Buyer's Real Estate Agent in turn contacts the Seller's Agent - communicating what your Buyer's loan needs are. But for now, just skip over this Section.

Okay, we are all done preparing the 1008. Now put your calculator aside, grab another cup of coffee, and then let's discuss a report you can order from your local title insurance company that can be very informative and helpful when you are initially putting your loan file together. I'm talking about ordering a Property Profile or as some lending folks call it - a MetroScan. Turn now to Chapter 14 and let's see what this report can tell us.

Chapter 14

THE PROPERTY PROFILE

As soon as I get a lead, for a possible home loan, the very first thing I do is order a Property Profile. And that is one of the main reasons I put this chapter within this Section (instead of within Section IV: The Reports). Sequentially, ordering this report should be one of the first things you order and review before you start actually spending a lot of time on home loan.

A Property Profile is usually a three-page report that you can order from your favorite title insurance company and includes a MetroScan, the (latest) Deed of Trust, and a Plat Map. The MetroScan may be called by other names, in different locations or states, but whatever you call it - it has the important information we will cover shortly. I usually don't ask for a copy of the Deed of Trust unless I want a complete legal address of the subject property and/or I wish to see who the sellers were on that property. The plat map is like an aerial view of the neighborhood in which the subject property is located. Title companies usually have a pointer, placed on the plat map, showing exactly where the subject property is on that map. I have found this plat map to be quite useful at times. For instance, when I am meeting the customers at their home and having difficulty founding their place I then take out the ole' plat map and it gets me going in the right direction.

But for me, the most important part of this Property Profile is the MetroScan page or Tax Assessor's page (as some refer to it). Please go now to Exhibit IX and print out a copy of this Property Profile. After we have covered this report then I am sure you will see why I always order this as soon I begin working on a home loan file. I won't talk about every detail in this report - but will only cover those areas I feel are important to review and why I order this report.

When you receive this report there are four main areas of information regarding the subject property you should review:

1. The Ownership Information
2. Property Characteristics
3. Sales and Loan Information
4. Assessment and Tax Information

Okay. Let's go over this report starting with the first section:

I. Ownership Information:

This is one of the main reasons I order this report. First, I want to make sure who the actual owners are on the subject property. Next, I want to be sure I spell their names correctly on the 1003. Sometimes customers have unusually spelled names or you just want to be sure what they use as their legal name (Robert versus Bob). If your customers are doing a refinance loan then you should enter the names there as it is shown on this report (that is how the names are currently shown and legally recorded on title to that property).

Site:
This should confirm the address that they (the customers) gave you and identifies the street address of the subject property.

Mail:
If this is an owner-occupied property then this address should be the same as the Site address above. Otherwise, this could allude to the fact that the owners are not living there and possibly renting out that property. One of the exceptions regarding this could be that the subject property is a Second Home of the owners above.

TxpyrNam:
This shows the names of the actual Tax Payers on this subject property. Should be the same as the owners above.

TxBill Add:
This shows the address of where the Tax Bill is mailed. If an O/O property should be the same address as Site above.

Parcel #:
This number legally identifies the subject property. This property also has a legal address as well (below). If you are talking to a Title Company Person and you want them to quickly find some information on a property then just tell them the Parcel Number - if you know it. This really helps speed up their search.

Bldge #:
This shows the number of units on this property. For Single Family Residences (SFR) you will see here = 1. For a duplex = 2, and so on.

Land Use:
Here's another area I always like to check out. Remember when we discussed the Appraisal Report and I talked about the Zoning of the subject property? This shows us how this property is currently zoned. If you are working on a home loan and it states here "Res. Single Family Residence". Great. No problem, next. However, if it states "Commercial" – then you are most likely going to have a problem with the Lender. That's because most Conforming Lenders do not like to lend to single-family residences on commercially zoned properties.

Legal:

This gives you the Legal Address of this subject property. It's short but it does the trick. You can test this out and find the subject property on the plat map by matching the legal address to what is shown on the plat map.

II. Property Characteristics:

As you can see, from looking at this section, this reveals some of the amenities of the property that are considered to have an influencing factor on the actual value of the property. Shown here, for example, are the number of bedrooms, bathrooms (half or full), the total square footage of the home, if it has a basement – and the percentage of its completion.

Year Built:

This is another important piece of information and reason I order this report. It states here when that property was first built.

Quality and Condition:

This shows what the Tax Assessor's opinion was regarding the Quality of the property and its Condition. You always want to see the property described as Avg. (for average) or Good (or better). If you see a description such as "Poor" - this could indicate a problem with the subject property. If you see this then you should ask your customers if they have made any recent improvements to the property. If they have not, then the Qualify and Condition most likely has not changed and this is probably what an Appraiser will state as well on their appraisal. That can be a deal (loan) killer!

III. Sales and Loan Information:

This section tells you when this property was last sold and what the sales price was. Sometimes it also tells us what the amounts of the home purchase loans previously were. This information can be very helpful sometimes. For example, if you know that the homeowner wants to refinance their existing mortgage loan but doesn't remember what their outstanding balance is – then that piece of information (on this report) may give you a ballpark figure to begin working on that loan. Remember when we previously discussed what the homeowner thinks their property is now worth and any improvements they have made to it - in coming up with an estimate of its current value or worth?

Date Transferred:

This shows you the date when this property was last transferred (sold). This is one of those informative things I like to get too because it tells me how long they have owned the property. However, you should be aware that if the owners of this property refinanced their home, since first purchasing it, many Tax Assessor reports and MetroScans do not show this on their reports.

Sales Price:
Most of these reports will show the actual (previous) sales price of that property. However, if the Buyers of that property did not wish this information to be shown on this report, then this area may be blank. Also, there are states that have non-disclosures laws. In those states it is rare that you will see the home sales price shown here.

Prior Sales Date:
The Previous Sales Dates on that property.

Prior Sales Price:
That's right - you got it. It's the sales price on that property when sold – prior to when it was last sold.

IV. Assessment and Tax Information:

This last section deals primarily with showing the property tax information on that property. For me, this is another important reason for ordering this report. Here it tells me what the total tax assessed value of the property is as well as the current annual property taxes the owners pay (I use that information in preparing the customer's Loan Estimate).

Total:
This represents the total Tax Assessed Value of this property. Below that you see how the tax assessor breaks it down into Land and Structure (the home). Remember what I said previously: That lenders generally like a home (the actual residence) to comprise at least 65-75% of the total (appraised) value of the property. You will usually see that value distribution shown here as well. Now, one of the main reasons I look at the Total Tax Assessed value of the property is because it can give me an idea of what the appraised value will come in on that property. The Tax Assessed value of the property will usually be lower than the current market value or what an appraiser will come up with. And, this works to the benefit of the homeowners (lower taxes).

In absence of any information to the contrary, what I do is take the Total Tax Assessed Value of the property and divide that number by 80%. That should give you an idea of what an appraiser may come up with. On the other hand, if the owners purchased their property just last year then I usually divide the Total Tax Assessed value by 90%. But you need to temper this with how much they paid for the property and any improvements made since. In other words, the value you come up with should make sense.

2019 Tax:
This shows the annual taxes for the current year (or when it was last assessed). This is another good reason to order this report because you will need this information when you prepare the Loan Estimate for those folks.

IrrTax & SW Tax:
These are additional property taxes that the homeowners pay (to the city) for utility type of things: Irrigation, new roads fronting or near the property, etc. Make sure you include these annual figures (if any) with the annual total taxes above in arriving at the Total Annual Taxes on that property.

In addition to showing you what the current property taxes are on the subject property it also shows you if the property owners have been paying their taxes on time or if the property taxes are delinquent. If the property taxes are delinquent then this report will show what years have not yet been paid and are delinquent. That's an important bit of information because if the taxes are delinquent on the subject property then you can expect that those taxes will need to be brought current either prior to or at loan closing.

When you first begin working on a home loan file I recommend you order a Property Profile on the subject property. Besides giving you all the information that this report offers it also gives you information you need in preparing the 1003, for that initial meeting with your customers, and in preparing the Loan Estimate as well.

As you were reading the above, on the Property Profile, you may have been thinking, "Hey, I'm wearing my Mortgage Detective Hat now." If you did, you would be right. Looking over the Property Profile, you are looking for information that not only should match with what the customers told you but also any concerns you might encounter in doing that home loan. What your customers told you and what you see on this report should make sense. If it doesn't then you have some questions for your customers - when and if you meet with them. Using this report – you are better prepared.

If you are planning on meeting with your customers then you should prepare for that meeting by completing as many and as much of those loan application forms as possible (e.g. 1003, Loan Disclosures, and the other documents I have discussed). Doing this, your meeting with your customers should move along a lot smoother and quicker as well (that's something your customers will appreciate too). Also, when you do order a Property Profile it gives you information that you may need to be aware of (regarding that property) so you can ask those questions of any concerns showing up on this report. It also makes you look professional and prepared when the 1003 and other documents have been partially completed.

For example, your customers would, no doubt, also be impressed if during the meeting you took out the Property Profile and said something like, "I see here that you first bought this property in 1998 for $125,000. This shows them that you did your homework and that you know what you are doing. And, as I said, it also makes you look more professional. You then could ask, "What do you think your property is worth today or what would you now sell it for?" When they reply to that question and you think perhaps that there appears to be a gross disparity between the subject property's value that you see on the Property Profile and what those folks are telling you - then you should ask them if they have made any improvements to their property. Those home improvements are sometimes referred to as "Sweat Equity" and those home improvements made might definitely increase the value of their property. If that is the case, then their expressed value of their property just might be in the ballpark. I therefore recommend you always order a Property Profile on all loans you begin working on.

The next chapter that discusses a very important form you also always need to review when you are working on a home purchase loan: The Real Estate Purchase and Sales Agreement.

Chapter 15

THE REAL ESTATE
PURCHASE AND SALES AGREEMENT

When you begin working on a home purchase loan then the very first thing you need to ask your customers is: Do they have a Real Estate Purchase and Sales Agreement? Most lending folks just refer to this document as the Purchase and Sales Agreement. When you are working on a home purchase loan then you have a situation whereby your customers (the Buyers) have met with the Sellers (of a property) and have agreed upon a sales price on that property - as well as other important points of that home purchase. Their formal agreement, by the Buyers and the Sellers, is evidenced by a fully signed and completed Purchase and Sales Agreement. If you do not have a fully signed and completed Purchase and Sales Agreement then technically what you have are customers who are only thinking of buying property. In other words, they are folks looking to get pre-qualified for a home purchase loan.

When I was a new Mortgage loan originator my boss told me, "If you don't have a completed Purchase and Sales Agreement then you don't have a purchase loan. You have something else." Therefore, when customers contact you about obtaining a loan to purchase a home there are two very important questions you should first ask them: 1. Have they identified the property they want to buy, and 2. Do they have a completed Purchase and Sales Agreement? If they have not identified the property yet then you would be pre-qualifying them for a home purchase loan. If they have identified a home they wish to purchase and they say they have a Purchase and Sales Agreement – then Great. Because that is what this chapter is all about and what you will need to look for on that Purchase and Sales Agreement when you do receive it.

Before we get into the actual details of the Purchase and Sales Agreement, I first want to talk about what it is. The Purchase and Sales Agreement is a legal contract between the Sellers and the Buyers of a subject property. For this contract to be a valid contract it must be <u>fully</u> signed. That means it must be signed by All Sellers (current owners) of the subject property and by all the Buyers for that property. For example, if your customers are wanting to buy a home, currently owned by a Husband and Wife, and the Purchase and Sales Agreement is signed (in the Seller's section of that document) by the Husband only then you do not have a fully signed Purchase and Sales Agreement and that contract is not valid (or enforceable). If this is the case then you need to take steps to get that Seller's wife to sign that contract as well.

Another important point regarding a contract (between the two parties) is Consideration. Consideration is something of value. In our discussion here, of the Purchase and Sales Agreement, both parties to the contract receive and give up something of value =>

Consideration. What are the Sellers and the Buyers receiving and giving up in this type of contract? First, the Sellers are usually receiving an Earnest Money Deposit (EMD) from the Buyers (and Buyers promise to pay them for their property). This amount (the EMD) could be anything from a $1.00 to $500 or more. Also, they (the Sellers) are giving up the opportunity to accept any other offers on their home (for sale) as long as the Purchase and Sales Agreement (contract) is valid. The Buyers are giving up their Earnest Money Deposit and receiving the Purchase and Sales Agreement (the contract) which entitles them (solely) the opportunity to purchase that home as long as that contract is valid.

With that said, let's discuss those things you need to examine on all Purchase and Sales Agreements - as soon as you receive it. Doing this, you will know if you have a fully completed Purchase and Sales Agreement or that something further needs to be done in order to achieve that end. In most of these cases, the Buyers and the Sellers will be represented by their Realtor (or Real Estate Agent). If that is the case then anything that is required, regarding that Purchase and Sales Agreement (or something from the Seller, whether it is information or documents) should be obtained through your customer's Realtor. Do not "by-pass" your customer's Realtor. And, do not directly contact the Seller's Realtor as well (unless you absolutely have to). Communicate your needs through the Buyer's (your customer's) Realtor. Of course, if you have any questions or needs regarding the processing of your loan then talk to your customers directly. But when it comes to the Purchase and Sales Agreement and any needs regarding this you should communicate those needs to your customer's Realtor.

Because of this, as soon as your customers contact you and tell you that they have a completed Purchase and Sales Agreement then ask them who their Realtor is and his or her telephone and fax number. Then call that Realtor up right then, introduce yourself, and tell him or her that you are calling on behalf of your customers (their customers also) and let him or her know what your needs are. Understand, that Realtors want exactly what you want: To close that loan as soon as possible. If you have not received a Purchase and Sales Agreement by that time then ask that Realtor to email or fax you over a copy of it as soon as he or she can.

Once you have received a copy of the Purchase and Sales Agreement then below are the things you need to examine on that document to be sure it is indeed complete with the things necessary to make it a binding and valid (enforceable) contract. Because it has been my experience that different States use different formats of Purchase and Sales Agreements, I will therefore cover those aspects of this contract that should be present on each and also what you need to be aware of - that may be on this contract as well. If you currently work for a mortgage or lending company then ask them for a copy of a Real Estate Purchase and Sales Agreement. Otherwise, you should be able to obtain one at your local business office supply store.

I. DATE OF THE CONTRACT:
This states when this contract began.

II. NAMES OF THE SELLER(S):
Full names of the Sellers. Again, all owners of the subject property <u>must</u> be written here. Recall what I mentioned previously about ordering a Property Profile when you first begin doing a loan? You do that here as well. That Property Profile will tell you who the current owner or owners are on that property. This verifies to you that all owners are actually listed on that contract.

III. NAMES OF THE BUYER(S):
Again, all the names of the Buyers should be on that contract. If it is a Husband and Wife and only the Husband's name is written on it - then this would most likely not be a valid contract. Especially in a Community Property State.

IV. ADDRESS OF THE SUBJECT PROPERTY:
This is what this contract is all about - the purchase of that property. Make sure the address is correct and complete (street, city, state, zip)

V. LEGAL ADDRESS OF SUBJECT PROPERTY:
I don't think this is required to make this contract binding or valid but it's nice to see it on the contract.

VI. PURCHASE PRICE:
This is an important point and must be on this contract. What the Buyers are paying for the property (the full price). Make sure the correct sales price is shown here. Also related here, you should look for and/or inquire whether the Purchase Price includes only the real property (dwelling and surrounding land) – or it also includes equipment and/or appliances that might be located on the premises. Including those results in what is sometimes referred to as a "Package Mortgage".

VII. EARNEST MONEY DEPOSIT:
What was the amount that the Buyers (your customers) gave to the Sellers as a Deposit to purchase that subject? This should be written here. That amount will be credited to your customer's total loan costs and be shown on their Loan Estimate that you will prepare. It should also show here how that EMD was given (e.g. In cash, check, etc.).

VIII. FINANCING:
This part tends to be a multi-part paragraph on this contract. First, be aware that some Sellers do not like to have their Buyers doing an FHA, VA, or Rural Development Financing type of loan. They may prefer (and dictate) that the Buyers obtain a Conventional loan. Whatever the Sellers prefer (or agree with the Buyers regarding this) will be indicated in this area.

Also, the Sellers will usually indicate the number of days, from the signing of the contract (Date above), that the Buyers have to locate a Lender (that's through you) and submit a loan (whereby you submit a loan to one of your Wholesale Lenders). The average time I have seen here is usually about 5 days.

And, if the Seller is willing to pay for any loan and/or closing costs (Seller Contributions) that amount will be shown here also. This is also an important thing to look for because that amount should be shown on your LE - showing less funds that your borrowers will need to bring to the closing table.

And finally, Required Lender Repairs and Inspections. Recall when we discussed reviewing the Appraisal Report. Sometimes the Appraisal Report will indicate that some work needs to be done or completed on that property and perhaps the Lender subsequently (after receiving that Appraisal) wants that work to be done - as a Prior-To-Doc condition. So, who's going to pay for that? In this section it indicates whether the Seller is willing to pay for any repairs that may be required by the Lender and how much they are willing to pay. The average amount I have seen here (that Sellers are willing to pay) generally ranges from $250 - $500. If repairs are required and the amount is greater than indicated here (and the Sellers will not pay more) - then it will be up to the Buyers to come up with that amount - if they still wish to purchase that property.

IX. INSPECTION PERIOD:

This states the number of days (after contract signing) that the Buyers have - to have that home inspected. Usually there is writing on the contract stating - that after the Home Inspection the Buyers will have the option to cancel that contract if they wish to do so. This could happen if the Home Inspection Report states, in so many words, that the home is falling apart and major repairs are in order.

X. TITLE INSURER AND CLOSING AGENT:

This isn't always completed or filled in - but you do need to check this area out. If the Sellers (or the Buyers) have a preferred Title Insurance Company and/or Closing Agent stated here then this is whom you must make arrangements with for the Title Insurance and Loan Closing. I have too often seen Mortgage loan originators (myself included) not review this part and begin to order the Title Insurance and setup the Closing with a different Title Company and/or Closing Agent only to later read this section (and discover) that they had to switch things around at the last minute. So, be sure to check out this area. Also, in many areas it is a common practice for the Sellers and Buyers to split the cost of the new Title Insurance Policy and in some cases - the Closing (Escrow) Cost. How those costs are to be paid (i.e. split between the Sellers and Buyers) should be stated on this document.

XI. CLOSING AND TERMINATION DATES:

These are two dates you definitely need to check out: The first date (Closing Date) is the estimated date that the Sellers want that home loan (to purchase their house) to close and fund. Usually, this date is about 30 days from the date of signing that contract.

The second date (Termination Date) is what we affectionately refer to as "the drop-dead date" and is the date that - if the home loan (to purchase that property) does not close and fund by then – then that contract becomes null and void. This drop-dead date is usually about 1- 2 weeks after the First or Closing Date. Keep your eyes on this date as you are processing your home purchase loans. Things do come up sometimes that can cause the processing of a loan to take longer than first anticipated. Once that Termination Date has been reached (and passed) and there is no agreement by the Sellers to extend that date (what is called an Addendum to the Purchase and Sales Agreement - more on this later) then the contract becomes null and void and the Sellers can then accept other offers on their property.

XII. INITIALS OF SELLERS AND BUYERS ON EACH PAGE:

Although each State (e.g. California, Washington, Oregon, etc.) seem to have different formats of Purchase and Sales Agreements - most states have a spot at the bottom of each page of this contract for All the Sellers and Buyers to write their initials. Make sure the Sellers and Buyers have done this - if required.

XIII. SELLERS' AND BUYERS' REALTORS:

This is generally shown on the last page of the contract. It should show the names of the Realtors (or Real Estate Agents) for both the Buyers and Sellers, name of the Realtor company they both represent, their telephone and fax numbers, and sometimes email addresses. Those Realtors or Real Estate Agents should also have signed this contract.

XIV. SELLERS AND BUYERS SIGNATURES:

And finally, this area (or page) tells us whether we have a _fully signed_ Purchase and Sales Agreement. Those signatures will also usually be shown on the last page of this contract. Question: Have _All the Sellers_ signed this contract as well as _All the Buyers?_ If they have, then Great! If not, then you need to call your customer's Realtor right then and ask him or her to get that contract fully signed and to you as soon as possible. It is the Realtor's responsibility to make sure that this Purchase and Sales Agreement is complete and fully signed. This is one of the many things they learn in their training to obtain their Real Estate license. Yet, too many times when I (and other Mortgage loan originators I have known) have first received a Purchase and Sales Agreement - it was not fully signed! It can drive you crazy sometimes. And you know - you cannot do your job as a Mortgage loan originator until you do have a fully signed contract. So, if it is not fully signed then just call up your customer's Realtor as soon as you can and, as diplomatically as you can be, ask them to get a fully signed Purchase and Sales Agreement to you as soon as possible.

There are, of course, other important features to a completed Purchase and Sales Agreement but these are the main points you should check out first (and the ones that initially will most likely require your attention and follow up).

Before I leave this discussion on the Purchase and Sales Agreement let me say that as a contract it is based on the agreement between the Sellers and the Buyers. As such, all things are negotiable. In other words, if there are any subsequent changes requested and/or required on this contract and it is acceptable to both parties (Sellers and Buyers) then that change can be incorporated into this contract. However, to do that will require a fully signed (by the Sellers and Buyers) - what we call "An Addendum to the Purchase and Sales Agreement." This is a document that states the conditions (e.g. additions, changes, etc.) to the original Purchase and Sales Agreement and is signed by both parties to that contract.

For example, let's say that problems have come up with your home purchase loan and it looks like you will not be able to close that loan by the Termination (drop-dead) Date. That could be a real concern if the Seller is not willing to extend that date out for enough time for you to close that loan. If the Seller doesn't then the Buyers will then not have a valid Purchase and Sales Agreement (after the Termination Date) and you have no loan. So, in that case, you should call up your customer's Realtor and explain to them that because of those (unforeseen) problems (which they should be familiar with as well) that you will now need to get an Addendum to the Purchase and Sales Agreement extending that Termination Date out to when you feel confident that loan will close. If that Realtor does follow-up and you receive an Addendum to the Purchase and Sales Agreement extending out that Termination Date (and it is Fully Signed) then that contract is still good until that new Termination Date is reached. And, this is true with any subsequent changes to that Purchase and Sales Agreement. You will need a fully signed Addendum to that Purchase and Sales Agreement stating the conditions and changes (that have been agreed upon by the Sellers and Buyers) to the original Purchase and Sales Agreement.

And finally, try to do everything you can to keep your customer's Realtor up to date on how the loan is progressing as well as any major concerns that have come up that will need to be addressed. I know that some Realtors can drive you crazy by calling you all the time and asking you what is going on with that (their customer's) loan. If you anticipate this and call them when you can, to keep them informed, then you will most likely avoid this and perhaps impress that Realtor so much - that they may decide to refer some business to you (I talk a little about this within Chapter 27 on Marketing Your Services). But more importantly, you should look at your customer's Realtor as part of your team that is doing this home purchase loan. Keep your customer's Realtor informed and you will find this helps your home purchase loans to move along a lot smoother.

Now, what do you do if you get a call from a customer who wants to do a home loan but they live quite a distance from where you work and live or they live in another state? To find out what to do - go now to the next chapter that talks about Out-of-Town Customers.

Chapter 16

OUT-OF-TOWN CUSTOMERS

Every so often you may get a lead for a customer wanting to refinance or purchase a property that is located and lives out of your area, city, or state. Too far for you to go visit them or for them to come visit you at your office. What do you do then? The procedures that you follow, on a loan, are basically the same except at that point where you prepare for and meet with your customers. For those out-of-town customers I recommend the following:

After you have taken the call from the customer (or called them) and completed the Customer Pre-Qual Sheet on them then:

1. **Order a Property Profile** from a Title Company in the county in which that subject property is located. Some Title Companies that are "out in the sticks" may tell you that there is a charge for this service. What I do is tell them that I am planning on ordering the title insurance as well as closing the loan with them (which I intent to do). Many times when you tell them this (and you really plan on doing this too) then they may waive that fee.

2. **Prepare a 1003 and all required Disclosures** for those customers. The information on that Property Profile (that you have received) and what the customers told you, when you spoke with them, should give you ample information to complete a lot of what the 1003 is asking for.

3. **With a Yellow Highlighter Highlight and Outline** all the Sections on the 1003, and the Disclosures, you would cover with them at your meeting with them (if you were to meet with them). Also, yellow highlight all the areas requiring Initials and Signatures. Doing this (with #2 above) should make it much easier and less time consuming for your customers to review and complete these forms. You will find that when you do this then your response rate will be more favorable and timely.

   Remember also, as we previously discussed, you should not sign and date that 1003 you are mailing to those customers until you actually receive it back from them (see Signing Your Name on the 1003).

4. **Attach a Cover Letter on top of these forms**. Please refer to the Cover Letter I have included at the end of this short chapter. I have used this letter for many years and it has worked well for me. The order of these forms in your loan packet should be (from top to bottom): Cover letter with your business card attached, 1003, Loan Disclosures, and sheet stating what documents will be needed for this loan.

5. Call back your customers on the date you said you would - to answer any questions they may have. I always call them back - to not only answer any questions they may have but also to motivate them (as it often happens) to get their loan application completed and sent back to me - so I can begin working on it.

Once you receive the Loan Application Package back from your customers then that home loan is processed just like any others. The main difference here is that you need to stay in contact with those customers (as you should with all your customers) - but more so with these "type of folks" who, because of their distance from you, won't have the opportunity to actually meet with them. This can work against you because the emotional trust that could have been built up, when you have actually met with your customers, cannot happen here. So, call those customers as often as is necessary (without becoming a pest) to let them know what is going on with their loan, any documents you need from them, and their home loan's current status.

An example of a Cover Letter is on the following page.

THE COVER LETTER

June 5, 2021

Customers Names
Street Address
City, State Zip Code

Dear Customer:

Accompanying this letter is a loan application packet to refinance your property on (*name of their street*). To begin, please review, complete, and/or correct those areas where I have highlighted in yellow on these documents. Once you are done then please mail these back to me at the following address:

> Your Company's Name
> Attn. Your Name
> Street Address
> City, State Zip Code

Once I receive these documents then I can begin processing your loan application. Also, please include those documents I have checked on the Loan Application Checklist page. This will enable us to process your loan application without delay.

Moving forward on this loan I estimate we could close your loan by (*estimated time of closing*). Doing this, your next (and first) monthly mortgage payment would not be until (*Month Date and Year*) (you would skip the next month's payment).

If you wish to call me then I can be reached at (*XXX) XXX-XXXX*. I will call you this (*day of the week*) to make sure you received this loan packet and answer any questions you may have. I thank you for giving me the opportunity to be of service to you.

Sincerely

Your Name
Mortgage Loan Originator

Chapter 17

THE CLOSING DISCLOSURE

𝕴n the initial first few years of previous versions of this Loan Officer's training manual I did not include a chapter on the HUD-1 Settlement Statement. I did this because I didn't really think that most mortgage loan originators needed to know the details of the HUD-1 Settlement Statement to justify including a chapter on it. This may have been a mistake on my part. Since about 2008 I have included it within this training manual. And, since the CFPB came out with the HUD-1 Settlement Statement's replacement disclosure titled the "Closing Disclosure", that began on October 3, 2015, I have decided to take out the HUD-1 Settlement Statement in this chapter and replace it with the new Closing Disclosure since the previous 2015 edition of this training manual. I should also mention that the CFPB also refers to this disclosure form, as with the Loan Estimate, as the "Know Before You Owe" forms.

The new Closing Disclosure is a five-page home loan closing disclosure and is required to be presented to the home borrowers no later than 3 business days prior to their home loan closing. Also, if there are any changes in the information shown on the Closing Disclosure then this could "restart" that 3 business day waiting period.

And, since we're talking about a revised Closing Disclosure let's now talk about what triggers the need to reissue the Closing Disclosure according to the CFPB's new ruling:

- Increases to the APR greater than $1/8^{th}$ of a percent (or $1/4^{th}$ of a percent for loans with irregular payments or periods) that causes the disclosures to become inaccurate. However, a reissue would not be required if the changes resulted in a decrease of the APR.
- Changes to the loan product that cause the Closing Disclosure to become inaccurate.
- Adding a prepayment penalty which causes the Closing Disclosure to become inaccurate.

Of course, there could be other reasons to provide a revised Closing Disclosure to the home loan consumer, but those may not necessarily delay the closing of that home loan.

And, because the Closing Disclosure must be provided to the loan consumer no later than three business days before settlement, the consumer must also receive a revised Loan Estimate no later than 4 business days prior to the home loan consummation.

Any of the above three changes noted above could delay the closing of a home loan by an additional 3-day review waiting period. And, as I mentioned, when discussing the Loan Estimate, the loan customer could waive that 3-business day waiting period: but only for a bona fide personal financial emergency. Their waiver request will need to be in written form, with the reason for the emergency justifying that waiver, and dated and signed by all borrowers on that home loan. However, creditors are prohibited from providing home loan customers with a pre-printed waiver form.

Okay, the first two pages of the Closing Disclosure looks very much like the initial two pages of the Loan Estimate. It is not until you get to page 3 and 4 that the Closing Disclosure that it begins to look like the olé HUD-1 Settlement Statement regarding the loan costs and the loan's various loan features. The loan features and amounts, on page 5, looks much like what was on the previously required Truth-In-Lending Statement.

Now, before I begin discussing the details of each of the five pages of the Closing Disclosure I first would like to mention some important points you should be aware of when and if you complete this home loan Closing Disclosure:

- **Rounding of Loan Amounts:**
  When entering the amounts onto most sections of the Closing Disclosure you should enter whole numbers that are rounded up to the nearest whole dollar. However, if an amount is required to be rounded and is composed of rounded amounts then use the rounded amounts in calculating the total. You'll be seeing more rounding of (total) amounts shown on the Closing Disclosure than you did on the Loan Estimate.

- **Consummation of the Home Loan:**
  And, as I previously mentioned, within Chapter 12 on The Loan Estimate, the CFPB wants you to know that the Consummation of a loan is different from the Closing or Settlement of a home loan. For example, Consummation occurs when the loan consumer becomes contractually obligated to the creditor on the loan and not, for example, when the loan consumer becomes contractually obligated to a seller on a real estate transaction.

  However, when a home loan consumer becomes contractually obligated to the creditor does depend on the applicable State laws where the home loan is being originated (and/or where the subject property is located – if different).

- **Tolerances Levels of Loan Costs:**
  As you may recall, when I initially began discussing the chapter on the Loan Disclosures, I mentioned that the CFPB introduced three levels of loan cost Tolerances Levels for specific home loan costs (from the original or revised Loan Estimate to the final Closing Disclosure at loan closing):
    - Zero Tolerance
    - 10% Tolerance, and
    - Charges not Subject to a Tolerance

  The loan costs shown on the final Loan Estimate must match with what is shown on the final Closing Disclosure. If a refund is required to be "cured" by the creditor because of a Tolerance violation then two things need to happen:

1. The creditor must refund to the loan customer the full amount to "cure" the Tolerance violation no later than 60 dates after the home loan settlement.
2. The creditor must also deliver or place in the mail a corrected Closing Disclosure that reflects the refund no later than 60 dates after the home loan settlement.

However, I should mention that the above could be done either at and during the home loan settlement or after the settlement.

Now, to download this document, in PDF format, use the Google Chrome browser: https://files.consumerfinance.gov/f/201311_cfpb_kbyo_closing-disclosure_blank.pdf.

In explaining the various aspects and parts of the Closing Disclosure let's use the example we used in going over the Loan Estimate within Chapter 12: for Joseph and Carol Bishop (on page 275) who live in San Diego, California. In going over this Closing Disclosure you should also refer to the Loan Estimate that was presented in Chapter 12. And, remember what I previously said: the first two pages of the Closing Disclosure are very much (almost identical) to the Loan Estimate.

Okay, let's begin here by looking at page one of the Closing Disclosure:

Page 1 of the Closing Disclosure:

Top of Page One:
The upper most section of Page One shows the date the Closing Disclosure was issued, the name(s) of the borrowers, the loan Term, Purpose, Type, and Rate Lock Date:

Closing Disclosure

This form is a statement of final loan terms and closing costs. Compare this document with your Loan Estimate.

Closing Information		Transaction Information		Loan Information	
Date Issued	December 1, 2020	Borrower	Joseph and Carol Bishop	Loan Term	30 Years
Closing Date	December 1, 2020			Purpose	C/O Refinance
Disbursement Date	December 4, 2020			Product	Fixed Rate
Settlement Agent	Best In West Title	Seller			
File #	BRM-223344			Loan Type	☒ Conventional ☐ FHA ☐ VA ☐ _____
Property	12365 Great View Drive San Diego, CA 77214	Lender	Best Rates Mortgage	Loan ID #	123456789RF
Sale Price	$314,650 (Appraised Value)			MIC #	000456128

Loan Terms:
Below the top section is the 2ⁿᵈ Section titled "Loan Terms" where you enter the Loan Amount, Interest Rate, the loan's P&I payment. To the right of each amount entered and shown you answer the question, "Can this amount increase after closing". Since this is a fixed-rate loan the answer to that for each is "No".

And, below the P&I Payment you enter if there is any Prepayment Penalty and/or a Balloon Payment. And, you also answer the question for each, "Does the loan have these features?" For this loan the answer is "No".

Loan Terms		Can this amount increase after closing?
Loan Amount	$270,000	NO
Interest Rate	5.500%	NO
Monthly Principal & Interest See Projected Payments below for your Estimated Total Monthly Payment	$1,533.03	NO
		Does the loan have these features?
Prepayment Penalty		NO
Balloon Payment		NO

Projected Payments:

Within this section you show what the loan customer's PITI for their home loan (and any MI if included) and what is included in their monthly mortgage payment. I should also note that under the "Estimated Escrow" it states "Amount can increase over time". And, that usually occurs if either or both their homeowner's insurance and property taxes increase. At the bottom of this section it, again, shows the total monthly Escrow amount and what is included in that monthly Escrow payment.

Projected Payments				
Payment Calculation				
Principal & Interest	$1,533.03			
Mortgage Insurance	0			
Estimated Escrow Amount can increase over time	$ 290.00			
Estimated Total Monthly Payment	$1,823.03			
Estimated Taxes, Insurance & Assessments Amount can increase over time	$290	This estimate includes [X] Property Taxes [x] Homeowner's Insurance [ ] Other: See Section G on page 2 for escrowed property costs. You must pay for other property costs separately.	In escrow? YES YES	

Costs at Closing:

Within this last section of Page One is entered and shown the total Estimated Closing Costs and Estimated Cash to Close. These two amounts are taken from totals of Sections D + Section I, on Page Two. So, in initially completing the Closing Disclosure you would normally leave these two areas blank until you have completed Page Two. But, I already did that for you, so here it is.

Costs at Closing		
Estimated Closing Costs	$7,480	Includes $5,310 in Loan Costs + $2,170 in Other Costs – $0 in Lender Credits. See page 2 for details.
Estimated Cash to Close	- $62,520	Includes Closing Costs. See Calculating Cash to Close on page 3 for details.

As you can see above, the "Estimated Cash to Close" is shown with a minus number (-$62,520). It is shown with a minus number because that is the amount that Joseph and Carol Bishop will receive after the closing of their loan. If it was a positive amount then that would be the amount that the Bishops would need to bring to the closing table (e.g. purchase loan transaction).

Okay, let's move on to Page Two of this Closing Disclosure.

Page 2 of the Closing Disclosure:

Closing Cost Details:
Page two of the Closing Disclosure is titled "Closing Cost Details" and is made up of two parts: The first Part contains Sections A thru D which itemizes and summarizes the details of the various categories of the loan costs with Section D showing the "Total Loan Costs". And the second part below it is titled "Other Costs" which includes Sections E thru J.

You can also see that to the right of each Section's cost items is a column for Borrower-Paid and to right of that a column for Seller-Paid amounts. That Seller-Paid column is reserved for purchase loan transactions. The column to the right of Seller-Paid is a column for Paid by Others. This is reserved for when others are paying for any of the closing costs for the home loan borrower. In this example, we won't go into those two columns because this is a refinance home loan transaction. Okay, we begin, on the following page, with Section A under the title of "Loan Costs".

Loan Costs:
Section A: Origination Charges:

Closing Cost Details

Loan Costs		Borrower-Paid		Seller-Paid		Paid by Others
		At Closing	Before Closing	At Closing	Before Closing	
A. Origination Charges		$3,450.00				
1.00% of Loan Amount (Points)		$2,700.00				
Underwriting Fee		$750.00				

Section B: Services Borrower Did Not Shop For:
Within this Section you enter those third-party provider services that the loan customer did not shop for. Entered here are also the names of the third-party services that were used in that loan.

B. Services Borrower Did Not Shop For			$510.00			
Appraisal Fee	to Accurate Appraisals		$400.00			
Credit Report Fee	to American Credit Reporting		$30.00			
Flood Determination Fee	to Universal Surveyors		$20.00			
Tax Service Fee	to San Diego County		$60.00			

Section C: Services Borrower Did Shop For:
Within this Section you enter those third-party provider services that the loan customer did shop for. Also entered here are the name(s) of the third-party services the borrowers used for their home loan.

C. Services Borrower Did Shop For			$1,350.00			
Title: Insurance Binder	to Best In The West Title		$700.00			
Title: Title Search	to Best In The West Title		$300.00			
Title: Title Settlement Agent	to Best In The West Title		$350.00			

Section D: Total Loan Costs (Borrower Paid):
The amount within Section D represents the sum of Sections A+B+C.

D. TOTAL LOAN COSTS (Borrower-Paid)	$5,310.00	
Loan Costs Subtotals (A + B + C)	$5,310.00	

Other Costs:
The 2nd section of Page Two is titled "Other Costs". This 2nd section is made up of sub-sections E – Sub-section J.

Section E: Taxes and Other Government Fees:

Other Costs			
E. Taxes and Other Government Fees		$45.00	
Recording Fees	Deed: Mortgage: $45.00	$45.00	

Section F: Prepaids:
Within this section you can see that the Prepaids for that home loan:

F. Prepaids	$1,584.18	
Homeowner's Insurance Premium (4 mo.) to Hometown Insurance	$260.00	
Mortgage Insurance Premium (mo.)		
Prepaid Interest ($40.57 per day from 12/16/15 to 12/31/15)	$649.18	
Property Taxes (3 mo.) to San Diego County	$675.00	

Section G: Initial Escrow Payment at Closing:
These are the required escrows amount that will be placed in the loan customer's escrow account so that there will be adequate funds to pay for the various escrow accounts when they become due next.

G. Initial Escrow Payment at Closing	$580.00	
Homeowner's Insurance $65.00 per month for 2 mo.	$130.00	
Mortgage Insurance per month for mo.		
Property Taxes $225.00 per month for 2 mo.	$450.00	
Aggregate Adjustment	0.00	

I should mention that, as you can see at the bottom of this section, it states "Aggregate Adjustment". That is the amount which the closing agent comes up with (after his or her calculations) which is either a plus or minus to the escrow and loan costs. I have asked many closing agents to explain what that amount represents. When they were done explaining this is to me then I shook my head up and down and said, "thank you, I understand". But I really didn't. At your next customer's home loan closing I challenge you to ask the closing agent this same question. If you find that you do indeed understand it then please send me an email with your explanation. Okay, moving on here.

Section H: Other (fees):

If there are any other fees, that would be included in this loan but not shown in any of the other sections or categories then that amount would be itemized within this section.

H. Other	$0.00	

Section I: Total Other Cost (Borrower Paid):

Like Section D above, Section I represents the sum of Sections E+F+G+H above.

I. TOTAL OTHER COSTS (Borrower-Paid)	$2,209.18	
Other Costs Subtotals (E + F + G + H)	$2,209.18	

Section J: Total Closing Costs (Borrower Paid):

The last section on Page Two shows what the loan customer's total closing costs will be. As you can see this section is made up of two subsections. The first row, within that subsection is "Closing Costs Subtotal". That amount represents the sum of Sections D+I. Below that row is the row titled "Lender Credits". Entered here would be any credits that are applied (and subtracted) from the row above it. Examples of lender credits could be for Premium Pricing (for the interest rate) or credits for a No-Cost Loan. The results of that subtraction would be entered and shown within the top row of this Section. In our example here we have no Lender Credits so I left that row blank (which is acceptable).

J. TOTAL CLOSING COSTS (Borrower-Paid)	$7,519.18	
Closing Costs Subtotals (D + I)	$7,519.18	
Lender Credits		

Alrighty! We are done with Page Two of the Closing Disclosure and will now move on to Page Three. It is within Pages 3-5 that you will see the features and aspects of this closing loan disclosure that closely resembles what the previously required HUD-1 Settlement Statement and Truth-In-Lending disclosures contained.

Page 3 of the Closing Disclosure:

Page 3 of the Closing Disclosure is made of two sections:

Calculating Cash to Close:
This section provides an overview of the total costs, for each category and section, shown on the initial or revised Loan Estimate to those same loan costs shown on the Final (Loan Estimate). The totals for each category or section, for the Loan Estimate and Final (Loan Estimate) are displayed in columns for each. The amounts shown within the Final (Loan Estimate) column should be the same amounts displayed on the Closing Disclosure.

The amounts shown within the Loan Estimate column are rounded to the nearest dollar in order to match the corresponding amount shown on the Loan Estimate's Calculating Cash to Close Section. This rounding of amounts is also true for the amounts displayed within the Final (Loan Estimate) column.

To the right of these two columns is a column titled "Did this change?" If there are any amount changes that are displayed, between the first two columns on the left-hand side, for each section or category then you would enter the appropriate response: "Yes" or "No". If any rows, within the column "Did this change?" have a "Yes" answer then that loan cost(s) and amount(s) may need to be considered as to whether the Tolerance Level for that loan(s) cost has been exceeded.

Okay, let's take a look at what it looks like for Joseph and Carol Bishop's home loan:

Calculating Cash to Close	Use this table to see what has changed from your Loan Estimate.		
	Loan Estimate	Final	Did this change?
Total Closing Costs (J)	$7,519.18	$7,519.18	NO
Closing Costs Paid Before Closing	$0	$0	NO
Closing Costs Financed (Paid from your Loan Amount)	$7,518.18	$7,518.18	NO
Down Payment/Funds from Borrower	$0	$0	NO
Deposit	$0	$0	NO
Funds for Borrower	$70,000.00	$70,000.00	NO
Seller Credits	$0	$0	NO
Adjustments and Other Credits	$0	$0	NO
Cash to Close	-$62,481.00	-$62,481.00	NO

I should also mention here that if the home loan transaction does not contain a Seller (e.g. Refinance Loan) then the CFPB wants you or the closer to use an "Alternative Calculating Cash to Close table that has five items listed on it:

- Loan Amount
- Total Closing Costs
- Closing Costs Paid at Closing
- Total Payoffs and Payments, and
- Cash to Close.

And, below the 1st Section on Page 3 is the section titled "Summaries of Transactions".

Summaries of Transactions:

The Summaries of Transaction Section (or Table) is used to show the amounts associated with a real estate purchase transaction between the home loan borrower and the Seller. The purpose of this section is to show the amounts due from or payable to the loan borrower (purchaser) and Seller at the loan closing.

In real estate transactions that do not involve a Seller (such as a refinance transaction) then the creditor does not provide and fill-in the Seller's Transaction column within that Closing Disclosure. And, the creditor may also decide to replace the Summaries of Transaction Table with a "Payoffs and Payments Section" when the Alternative Cash to Close and Alternative Calculating Cash to Close Sections are chosen (as I mentioned in #1 above).

In our example we are using here, with Joseph and Carol Bishop's home loan, we won't be using these "alternative" options for our Closing Disclosure. And, because it is a refinance transaction – there's nothing much to show here. But, let's take a look at this Section on the following page:

Summaries of Transactions — Use this table to see a summary of your transaction.

BORROWER'S TRANSACTION

K. Due from Borrower at Closing

- Sale Price of Property
- Sale Price of Any Personal Property Included in Sale
- Closing Costs Paid at Closing (J)

Adjustments

Adjustments for Items Paid by Seller in Advance

City/Town Taxes	to	
County Taxes	to	
Assessments	to	

L. Paid Already by or on Behalf of Borrower at Closing

- Deposit
- Loan Amount
- Existing Loan(s) Assumed or Taken Subject to

- Seller Credit

Other Credits

Adjustments

Adjustments for Items Unpaid by Seller

City/Town Taxes	to	
County Taxes	to	
Assessments	to	

CALCULATION

Total Due from Borrower at Closing (K)

Total Paid Already by or on Behalf of Borrower at Closing (L)

Cash to Close ☐ From ☐ To Borrower

SELLER'S TRANSACTION

M. Due to Seller at Closing

- Sale Price of Property
- Sale Price of Any Personal Property Included in Sale

Adjustments for Items Paid by Seller in Advance

City/Town Taxes	to	
County Taxes	to	
Assessments	to	

N. Due from Seller at Closing

- Excess Deposit
- Closing Costs Paid at Closing (J)
- Existing Loan(s) Assumed or Taken Subject to
- Payoff of First Mortgage Loan
- Payoff of Second Mortgage Loan

- Seller Credit

Adjustments for Items Unpaid by Seller

City/Town Taxes	to	
County Taxes	to	
Assessments	to	

CALCULATION

Total Due to Seller at Closing (M)

Total Due from Seller at Closing (N)

Cash ☐ From ☐ To Seller

CLOSING DISCLOSURE

PAGE 3 OF 5 - LOAN ID #

Page 4 of the Closing Disclosure:

Let's now move to Page 4 of this Closing Disclosure. Much of what is displayed and disclosed on Page 4 of the Closing Disclosure was on the previously required Truth and Lending Statement (TIL). The entire Page 4 is titled "Loan Disclosures" and further presents the features of the customer's home loan. This page is split into right and left-hand sides. The next page shows what the left-hand side of this page looks like.

Left-Hand Side of Page 4:

Loan Disclosures

Assumption

If you sell or transfer this property to another person, your lender

☐ will allow, under certain conditions, this person to assume this loan on the original terms.

☒ will not allow assumption of this loan on the original terms.

Demand Feature

Your loan

☐ has a demand feature, which permits your lender to require early repayment of the loan. You should review your note for details.

☒ does not have a demand feature.

Late Payment

If your payment is more than **15** days late, your lender will charge a late fee of _____ *5% of the monthly principal and interest payment*

Negative Amortization (Increase in Loan Amount)

Under your loan terms, you

☐ are scheduled to make monthly payments that do not pay all of the interest due that month. As a result, your loan amount will increase (negatively amortize), and your loan amount will likely become larger than your original loan amount. Increases in your loan amount lower the equity you have in this property.

☐ may have monthly payments that do not pay all of the interest due that month. If you do, your loan amount will increase (negatively amortize), and, as a result, your loan amount may become larger than your original loan amount. Increases in your loan amount lower the equity you have in this property.

☒ do not have a negative amortization feature.

Partial Payments

Your lender

☒ may accept payments that are less than the full amount due (partial payments) and apply them to your loan.

☐ may hold them in a separate account until you pay the rest of the payment, and then apply the full payment to your loan.

☐ does not accept any partial payments.

If this loan is sold, your new lender may have a different policy.

Security Interest

You are granting a security interest in _____

12365 Great View Drive; San Diego, CA 77214

You may lose this property if you do not make your payments or satisfy other obligations for this loan.

Looking above, the various loan disclosures are:

Assumption:

This is a feature enabling the owner of a home and payer of a mortgage to sell their house by having a buyer assume part or all of their mortgage. With the exception of FHA and VA loans it is my understanding that the Assumption Feature on Conforming Fixed Rate Loans no longer exist. This is a loan feature that use to be quite common before the 1980's. However, during the later 1970s and early 1980s mortgage interest rates (and other rates) were going through the roof, with mortgage interest rates in the double digits - as high as 18%! I recall in 1983 I bought my first house in Southern California. Because I worked for a bank at that time, they gave me a break on the interest rate on my mortgage. As a result, my mortgage interest rate ended up being only about 12.0%! Wow, for the mortgage it was a lot of P&I!

Okay, back to Assumptions. Because many of the homes that were being sold at that time had mortgages with interest rates as low as 2.5 - 5.0% (30-year fixed rate) many home sellers (who had this Assumption feature) were selling their homes by taking a down payment (profit) with the new homebuyers assuming their existing mortgage. This was completely legal and on board. Now, as you may recall, during that unusual and crisis period of our financial history many financial institutions were "in the red." The cost of funds, for our financial institutions was high, and yet some of those mortgages that had been on their books had very low interest rates.

Now, when homeowners who had a low interest rate mortgage with a bank, for example, sold their home - this at least got that (low interest rate mortgage) off their books. However, with this Assumption feature those homeowners could sell their homes by transferring that low interest rate mortgage to a buyer by having that buyer assume all or part of their mortgage. This worked out pretty well for both the buyer and the seller. However, when this was done that bank or financial institution still had that low interest rate mortgage on their books. Anyway, since that period it is rare that you will see a Conforming Fixed Rate loan having an Assumption feature (excluding FHA & VA loans). Therefore, you will most likely be entering an "X" at "will not allow assumption of this loan on the original term." And, that's what we will enter for the Bishops' home loan.

Demand Feature:
A Demand Feature is the legal ability of the lender to demand, in full, the remaining balance of a mortgage or trust deed. This is a feature that can be exercised by the Lender if the Borrower defaults on their loan or fails to perform the conditions of the loan. Most conforming loans do not have a Demand feature.

Late Payment:
It is quite common to see entered here a late fee of 5% of the monthly payment amount if the monthly mortgage payment is received 15 days after the due date. You should know that some credit reports (and lenders) show when a borrower's monthly payment has been received. That's why I always told my home loan customers, "The monthly due date is the 1st of the month. Please don't abuse any grace periods. Plan to pay on the 1st of the month."

Negative Amortization:
Negative Amortization has a very negative connotation to it and it is unusual these days to see that this feature will be part of a conforming home loan.

Partial Payments:
This indicates whether that loan has a pre-payment feature on it. If it doesn't then the first box should be checked.

Security Interest:
Enter here the full street address of the subject property including city, state, and zip code (no P.O. Boxes please).

Okay, let's now and take a look at the right-hand side of this page, starting at the upper part of this page.

Right-Hand Side of Page 4:

As you can below, this side of the page relates to the disclosure as to whether or not their mortgage loan will have monthly Escrow Payments impounded and included with their monthly P&I payments.

Escrow Account

For now, your loan

☒ will have an escrow account (also called an "impound" or "trust" account) to pay the property costs listed below. Without an escrow account, you would pay them directly, possibly in one or two large payments a year. Your lender may be liable for penalties and interest for failing to make a payment.

Escrow		
Escrowed Property Costs over Year 1	$3,480.00	Estimated total amount over year 1 for your escrowed property costs:
Non-Escrowed Property Costs over Year 1	~~$0.00~~	Estimated total amount over year 1 for your non-escrowed property costs: You may have other property costs.
Initial Escrow Payment	$580.00	A cushion for the escrow account you pay at closing. See Section G on page 2.
Monthly Escrow Payment	$290.00	The amount included in your total monthly payment.

☐ will not have an escrow account because ☐ you declined it ☐ your lender does not offer one. You must directly pay your property costs, such as taxes and homeowner's insurance. Contact your lender to ask if your loan can have an escrow account.

No Escrow		
Estimated Property Costs over Year 1		Estimated total amount over year 1. You must pay these costs directly, possibly in one or two large payments a year.
Escrow Waiver Fee		

If the loan customer's mortgage loan includes an escrow account (as in the Bishops' loan here) then the first box would contain an "X" and below that you would enter the total (combined) Escrow costs that loan customer would incur in their first year of that loan.

Within the second row, below the above, you would enter any non-escrow costs for the first year of the customer's mortgage loan that they will incur and need to pay for themselves. In our home loan for the Bishops, we have included all of their Escrow costs.

Within the third row you enter the Prepaids that the loan customer will pay to provide a "cushion" so that they will have enough funds in their escrow account to pay for their escrow payments when they next become due. This is the total amount shown within Section G on page 2 of the Closing Disclosure.

And, within the fourth and final row you enter the amount the loan customer will pay each month with their monthly P&I payment.

Now, if the loan customer will not have included an escrow account for their home loan then you would check the second box within this subsection on Escrow Account. Most home loans you originate will have an escrow account. However, if permitted and the loan customer prefers to pay their escrow accounts (e.g. homeowner's insurance and property taxes) on their own then enter a "X" within the box just to the right at "you declined it". Also, in some cases the lender that you setup the loan customer with (most likely because you had to) may not offer escrow account servicing. In that case you would enter an "X" in "your lender does not offer one"

And, at the bottom of this subsection is titled "No Escrow". Here you would enter the total annual escrow payments that the loan customer will be responsible for paying for on their own within the first year of their home loan. And, in some cases, where the customer has chosen to not to setup an escrow account with their home loan then Lenders sometimes charge an "Escrow Waiver Fee". If that is the case then enter the total amount of that fee here.

And, below that is a paragraph titled "In the Future" which informs the loan customer of their escrow options and that the escrow payments could change (i.e. get higher) and the consequences of not making their escrow payments on time and/or of not paying their escrow payments. Here it is, take a look.

> **In the future,**
> Your property costs may change and, as a result, your escrow payment may change. You may be able to cancel your escrow account, but if you do, you must pay your property costs directly. If you fail to pay your property taxes, your state or local government may (1) impose fines and penalties or (2) place a tax lien on this property. If you fail to pay any of your property costs, your lender may (1) add the amounts to your loan balance, (2) add an escrow account to your loan, or (3) require you to pay for property insurance that the lender buys on your behalf, which likely would cost more and provide fewer benefits than what you could buy on your own.

Having discussed Page 4 of the Closing Disclosure, let's now move on its 5th and final page.

Page 5 of the Closing Disclosure:

Page 5 of the Closing Disclosure contains primarily three Sections: 1. Loan Calculations, 2. Other Disclosures, and 3. Contact Information. So, let's take a look at these three Sections.

Loan Calculations:

Within this Section you see some of the amounts and percentages shown on the 3rd page of the Loan Estimate.

Loan Calculations	
Total of Payments. Total you will have paid after you make all payments of principal, interest, mortgage insurance, and loan costs, as scheduled.	$551,890.80
Finance Charge. The dollar amount the loan will cost you.	$281,890.80
Amount Financed. The loan amount available after paying your upfront finance charge.	$270,000.00
Annual Percentage Rate (APR). Your costs over the loan term expressed as a rate. This is not your interest rate.	5.745%
Total Interest Percentage (TIP). The total amount of interest that you will pay over the loan term as a percentage of your loan amount.	104.40%

Calculating the APR of a Home Loan:

Since the Annual Percentage Rate, shown on the Loan Estimate, seems to be the most esoteric concept to explain to your loan customers, I'd like to now go over how to properly calculate the APR of a home loan so you know how to calculate it and can more easily explain it to your loan customers.

Now, before I actually begin explaining how to calculate the APR of a loan - please refer to Exhibit VII and print out a copy of it. I designed this form using parts from an old disclosure form (the Truth-In-Lending Statement) and one that I have used many times to manually calculate the APR of a proposed loan. Once I did that then I also used it to review, with my customers, the APR on their loan. Also, whenever I have trained new Mortgage loan originators and get into the subject of the APR I always like to use the ole Truth-In-Lending Statement form because of the way it was designed: It makes it easy to understand how the APR is calculated. Okay, looking at this form, the upper half of it presents and discloses loan features and the bottom half shows how the APR is calculated.

Once you have looked over a copy of this form then you should refer to your Loan Estimate. You use the Loan Estimate in calculating the APR on a loan. Before we do that though let's talk about what costs, on the Loan Estimate, are included in calculating the APR.

To begin this explanation of how to calculate the APR of a loan I would like to break from our example of the Bishops loan and use the following home loan features in this example. Now, when you look at the Loan Estimate, you see a list of all the costs of that loan. Regulation Z states that all Prepaid Finance Charges are to be considered and included in the calculation of the APR of a loan. But which costs are considered Prepaid Finance Charges? The following lists what Regulation Z considers as Prepaid Finance Charges in calculating the APR. While this list is not all-inclusive it does list those loan costs you generally will see and include and have on your Loan Estimates for residential loans.

Prepaid Finance Charges:

Origination Fee (This now includes your LO commission on the loan)
Discount Fee
Processing Fee (by Your Company)
Underwriting Fee & Other Fees by the Wholesale Lender
Tax Service (also normally charged by the Lender)
Interest Adjustment (Prepaid Interest on the new loan)
Upfront Private Mortgage Insurance Premium (if required)
Initial (Monthly) Reserves for PMI or MIP (if required)
Closing/Escrow Fee
Wire/Messenger Fees
Any Prepayment Penalty Charges Paid (needed to Refinance a Mortgage Loan)

So that we are clear on what is included in calculating the APR I am going to list those costs that are not included in calculating the APR. Again, this list is not all-inclusive but addresses those loan costs normally found on our Loan Estimates:

Non-Prepaid Finance Charges:

Credit Report Fee
Flood Certification
Appraisal
Title Insurance
Hazard (Property) Insurance
Property Taxes (paid or impounds for reserves)
Recording Fees

Okay, after saying that – I now have to mention an exception to the above: That even though the above listed Third-Party Provider fees (e.g. Appraisal) are not normally included in the APR calculation – if a Third-Party Provider is affiliated with your company then it would be included in the above (Prepaid Finance) charges. And, this holds true for any other Third-Party Provider service, affiliated with your company, and used (and charged for) in the processing of a loan.

Regulation Z also requires (and expects) that the fees and charges for those services provided and listed above (and on the LE) should be reasonable and common for that area in which the loan is being done. OK. Now that we have gone through that you should have a good idea of what costs we will be including in calculating the APR on a home loan. In doing this, please refer to the form in Exhibit VII of this manual and look at the bottom half of this form. Here is where we will do all the figuring in calculating the APR. To begin, let's use the following assumptive features and amounts of this home loan in completing this APR Worksheet:

- Loan Amount: $ 147,750.00
- Interest Rate: 5.00%
- Mortgage Product: Fixed Rate
- Loan Term: 30 Years
- Monthly P&I Payment: $ 793.15

Using "Calculating the APR Worksheet" in Exhibit VII let's begin filling in this form to calculate the APR of this home loan and later we're go over calculating the TIP of this loan. Okay, first, you enter the…

Itemization of the Loan Amount of $_____.
Enter here the total amount of the loan = $147,750. Next, below that we list all the Prepaid Finance Charges in this loan - using our list above as a guide.

Amount Paid to Others on Your Behalf:
First, we enter the actual amount of each Prepaid Finance Charge on a LE. And to the right of each amount what the name of that cost represents. Let's use the following amounts for this example. Thus:

$1,477.50	to: Origination Fee
$75.00	to: Tax Service
$300.00	to: Processing Fee
$450.00	to: Underwriting Fee
$25.00	to: Wire Transfer Fee
$325.00	to: Settlement or Closing/Escrow Fee
$423.87	to: Interest Adjustment

Okay, that looks good. Now we add all of the above costs (our Prepaid Finance Charges) and enter that amount in the space below and to the right:

Total Prepaid Finance Charge: $_____
The total amount of all Prepaid Finance Charges above should be = $3,076.37. Now take that amount and enter that figure above where it states - Prepaid Finance Charge.

$_____ Prepaid Finance Charge:
Enter $3,076.37 in this space too. I know, it looks a little redundant but you'll see the logic of this in a moment.

When you are at this point, Subtract the (total) Prepaid Finance Charge from the Total Loan Amount => ($147,750 - $3,076.37) = $144,673.63. That figure ($144,673.63) represents what is called the **Amount Financed**. Enter that amount in the space above the (total) Prepaid Finance Charges.

The Amount Financed is where it gets confusing for many customers as well as some Mortgage loan originators. According to Regulation Z, the Amount Financed represents the actual amount of the loan that borrowers are (really) paying for on their loan - after you take away all the Prepaid Finance Charges. Now, I know, this doesn't sound logical at first but keep in mind that this all has to do with coming up with the APR of that loan - which we still haven't done yet. And that's the fun part! So, let's do that now.

Now, here comes the part that most folks, who don't know how to calculate an APR, know about. Once you have determined what the "Amount Financed" is for a loan then you are ready to calculate the APR. First, obtain you financial calculator. Make sure you have cleared all registers in it. Then do the following.

APR CALCULATION:

1. Enter the figures and amounts in the calculator like you would normally do to calculate the monthly P&I on a loan. Do that for our loan here.

2. If Private Mortgage Insurance (PMI) is included within your customer's monthly mortgage payment then change the amount within the PMT key to include this. For example, if your customer's P&I payment is $700 and their monthly PMI payment is $65.00 then enter their monthly mortgage payment as $765.00. However, if there isn't any PMI on that loan (as there isn't on this loan example) then skip this step.

3. Next, enter the Amount Financed for the loan - in the PV (Present Value) Key or button on your calculator (do not change any of the other figures you previously entered above - except for this - entering the Amount Financed in PV).

4. Now press the Interest Rate Key. If your calculator presents the interest rates in monthly terms then multiply that figure by 12. If not, then there you are - The APR for your loan.

If you have correctly gone through the steps above then you should have calculated an APR of 5.19% (at least that's what I calculated). Also, remember that the APR on fixed-rate loans is always going to be higher than the Note Rate on that loan. The only exception to this would be a "No Cost" loan. Then the APR could be the same or slightly higher than the Note Rate. There is a corresponding relationship to the total Prepaid Finance Charges on a loan to the variance of the APR over the Note Rate of a loan. As the Prepaid Finance Charges increase the variance between the Note Rate and the APR on that loan increases (showing more costs are included in that loan).

The difference between the loan's Note Rate and the APR rate is where you will experience the most confusion and questions from your customers. When they ask you about this then explain to them (briefly) the purposes of the APR and the difference between their Note Rate and the APR. Also tell them that while the APR will always be higher than the Note Rate (on fixed interest rate loans) the thing to look for - is what is an acceptable range of difference between the Note Rate and the APR. I generally consider a variance of anywhere from 20 to 30 basis points for a $200,000 loan to be a pretty reasonably priced loan. Of course, there could be other considerations that may apply (i.e. total loan amount in relation to the total respective APR costs). But for a simple Conforming loan of about $200,000 I'd say that would be a reasonably priced loan.

One thing though, that I do want to mention, that is an exception to what I said above regarding the variance of the Note Rate to the APR: Is how the total amount of the loan can influence the variance between these percentages. For example, if you were working on a $100,000 loan amount (or larger amount) then I'd say you are OK. However, as the loan amount gets lower then the APR gets higher in relationship to the Note Rate. This is because most of the loan costs (on that loan) do not decrease as the loan amount decreases (or decrease slightly). For example, the cost of an appraisal is usually the same whether the home loan is $500,000 or $85,000. So, remember this when explaining the APR to your customers. Well, that's about it on the APR on the Closing Disclosure and Loan Estimate. Pretty simple huh?

Calculating the Total Interest Percentage (TIP) of a Home Loan:
The Total Interest Percentage is the total amount of interest that the loan borrower will pay over the entire Term of their home loan – expressed as a percentage of the loan amount. This is a relatively new percentage indicator that was never before shown on any of the previously required Truth-In-Lending Statements.

To calculate the TIP of a home loan you first take the total amount of interest the loan borrower would pay, if they kept their home loan for its entire Term, and divide that amount by the borrower's original total loan amount. Refer to TIP Calculation Worksheet, in Exhibit VIII to help you manually calculate this percentage.

For example, if the borrower's total loan amount is $300,000 and the total amount of interest to be pay over the entire Term of that home loan is $60,000 then the TIP on that home loan would be 20%.

If you are not sure how to calculate the total amount of interest over the entire Term of a home loan then you:

1. Multiply the monthly P&I of that home loan times the number of months of the Term for that loan;

2. Subtract, from the amount in #1 above, the amount of the original loan amount of that home loan. That gives you the Interest Amount of that loan.

3. Divide the amount of Interest Amount (from #2 above) by the amount in #1 above.

Okay, the next section on Page 5, and to the right of the Loan Calculations Section, is "Other Disclosures".

Other Disclosures:

As you can see below the first three items, within this Section are Appraisal, Contract Details, and Liability after Foreclosure.

Other Disclosures

Appraisal
If the property was appraised for your loan, your lender is required to give you a copy at no additional cost at least 3 days before closing. If you have not yet received it, please contact your lender at the information listed below.

Contract Details
See your note and security instrument for information about
- what happens if you fail to make your payments,
- what is a default on the loan,
- situations in which your lender can require early repayment of the loan, and
- the rules for making payments before they are due.

Liability after Foreclosure
If your lender forecloses on this property and the foreclosure does not cover the amount of unpaid balance on this loan,

☒ state law may protect you from liability for the unpaid balance. If you refinance or take on any additional debt on this property, you may lose this protection and have to pay any debt remaining even after foreclosure. You may want to consult a lawyer for more information.

☐ state law does not protect you from liability for the unpaid balance.

The first one is "Appraisal". You loan customer customers have seen this before when you presented (or sent them) their initial home loan disclosures. The section item "Contract Details" goes into what loan customers should check out on their home loan's Note and Security Instruction (Deed of Trust). And, the third item above is "Liability after Foreclosure". This informs them of what might be the consequences if their home ever went into foreclosure. Some States, in this great country of ours, protects the loan customer from any unpaid balance in the event their home went into foreclosure. For example, let's say the outstanding balance on their home loan was $200,000 and that home went into foreclosure and was sold for $150,000. Then (depending on the foreclosure laws in that State) the bank might have a right to go after that loan customer for the remaining balance of $50,000. Since the subject property, for the Bishop's loan, is in San Diego, California (where the Lender has no recourse) I am entering an "X" within the 1st box in this area. Remember though, this depends on the State in which the subject property is located.

The last two listed Disclosures, within this Section, are Refinance and Tax Deductions.

> **Refinance**
> Refinancing this loan will depend on your future financial situation, the property value, and market conditions. You may not be able to refinance this loan.
>
> **Tax Deductions**
> If you borrow more than this property is worth, the interest on the loan amount above this property's fair market value is not deductible from your federal income taxes. You should consult a tax advisor for more information.

Refinance:

This discloses and informs them of what is considered when and if they wish to refinance their home sometime in the future. The main point of this disclosure is that they "may not be able to refinance this loan".

Tax Deduction:

This disclosure begins to inform them of the consequences of refinancing, the current worth of their property, and whether they will be able to use their home as a deductible for their federal income taxes. However, as this item states, when customers ask you about home tax deductions, you should tell them that you are not an accountant or attorney and that they should consult with them regarding that question.

Now, just to the left of this Section on Other Disclosures is an isolated and small paragraph regarding "Questions".

> **Questions?** If you have questions about the loan terms or costs on this form, use the contact information below. To get more information or make a complaint, contact the Consumer Financial Protection Bureau at
> **www.consumerfinance.gov/mortgage-closing**

This informs the loan customer that if they have any questions about this form (Closing Disclosure) or wish to make a complaint then this website address is provided. That website address takes them to the CFPB's website. Now, I want to be clear here: This is informing them about where to go to get further information about this Closing Disclosure – not their home loan. If they have any questions about their home loan then they should contact either you (their loan originator) or their lender.

And, at the bottom of this Page is the final section titled...

Contact Information:

This final section of this page looks like what you see below:

Contact Information	Lender	Mortgage Broker	Real Estate Broker (B)	Real Estate Broker (S)	Settlement Agent
Name		Best Rates Mortgage			
Address		1235 Sunrise Drive San Diego, CA 77623			
NMLS ID					
___License ID		XT332211			
Contact		Joseph Gets			
Contact NMLS ID		SX998877			
Contact ___License ID					
Email		Gets@ BestRatesMtge.com			
Phone		609-555-4433			

I admit it; I got lazy and entered in only the information for the Mortgage Broker of the Bishops' home loan. However, you should know that the CFPB wants each Lender, Mortgage Broker, Real Estate Broker (for a purchase loan), and Settlement Agent to be listed here that is involved in that home loan. And, for each listed person, their NMLS ID number or State license ID number (as applicable), the primary contact person and their NMLS ID number, and where applicable, their email address and phone number.

Document Retention of the Closing Disclosure:

Creditors (lenders) must retain on file the Closing Disclosure as well as all documents relating to the Closing Disclosure for at least five years after consummation of the home loan.

And, if servicing of that home loan is transferred then the transfer servicer must include the Closing Disclosure within that transfer file to the new home loan servicer.

Alrighty, I know it's hard to believe, but we are all done reviewing this Closing Disclosure. See, that wasn't so painful or difficult to understand. However, as you can see, just as when we discussed the Loan Estimate, the days of merely guessing at what a customer's loan costs are - is pretty much over. As we discussed, any Line-Item amounts shown on the Loan Estimate and compared to the final Closing Disclosure, that exceed the Zero or 10% Tolerance Levels will need to be "cured" by the home loan creditor or lender. And, my experience has been, that amount refunded is usually taken out of the commissions earned by the originating mortgage loan originator. And, that can be mighty painful. So please, be careful and make sure your home loan cost estimates are as accurate as can be.

OK, having discussed the many documents involved, within this Section on The Paperwork, let's now move on to the next Section that discusses the various Reports that mortgage loan originators need to be familiar with when originating mortgage loans.

Section IV

THE REPORTS

In the previous section we talked about the loan documents that you will normally prepare when originating mortgage loans. Those loan documents, we previously discussed and that you complete in preparing a customer's loan file, provide much of what you need to know in determining what loan document needs might be required, in qualifying the customer, as well as whether or not there are any concerns regarding the customer or the subject property. But they don't provide everything you might need to know.

There are mortgage-related reports that may also need to be ordered and reviewed and that is what this Section is all about: Those Reports. Knowing what those reports are and how to properly read them is very important in originating and processing your loans. Your familiarity of these reports will also assist you in identifying what loan program(s) your customer most likely qualifies for and what additional loan documentation and/or information might be needed to further qualify the customer for their home loan.

Therefore, to achieve that goal, this section contains the following four chapters:

- ➢ Reading the Credit Reports
- ➢ Reading the Rate Sheets
- ➢ Title Insurance Reports
- ➢ Appraisal Reports

One of the first reports you will want to order and review, when initially working on a customer's loan request, is that customer's credit report. Therefore, let's begin this Section with the chapter on Reading the Credit Reports.

Chapter 18

<u>READING THE CREDIT REPORTS</u>

After you have met with your customers and completed the 1003 and had them sign the Loan Disclosures then the first thing you should do, as soon as you get back to the office, is order a Credit Report on those folks. The reason for this is because the Credit of your customers will most likely have the biggest influencing factor on what loan programs you can offer your customers. This can determine the maximum LTV on their loan and the best interest rate you can offer them with a loan program. Also, it has been my experience that Lenders are often willing to accept higher than usual housing and total debt ratios and sometimes even higher loan LTVs for those customers with excellent Credit.

I should mention at this point that if you are going to order a Credit Report on any customer then be sure you always have the permission of those folks before you do. If you have met with your customers and have a signed Borrowers Certification and Authorization Disclosure form (from them) then you have met this requirement. However, that may not always be the case. Sometimes when you are first talking to loan inquiring customers, on the telephone, they may give you their verbal permission to order a Credit Report on them (we discussed this in the chapter on Qualifying Your Borrowers). If that is the case then make sure you note this on the Credit Report Request form your branch office most likely uses to request a Credit Report on a customer. And, if you subsequently do end up preparing a loan file on that customer then make sure you also note that on the Comments Sheet in that customer's loan file (i.e. that they gave you verbal approval at that time to pull their Credit Report). And, you should also try to get a signed Borrowers Certification and Authorization Disclosure form from those folks you ordered a Credit Report on with their verbal approval - as soon as possible. Now, different mortgage companies have different policies regarding this - so make sure you check with your Branch Manager to be sure you are familiar with their required Credit Report requesting procedures.

Now, when you first met with and/or talked with your customers - they may have told you that they have good Credit. But is that true? You need to know for sure. So, before you start putting in a lot of time on a loan request make sure your customers have the Credit necessary to qualify them for that loan program you are working on and that will enable them to achieve the goals of their refinance or purchase loan. A bad Credit Report, requiring your customers to have to go with a lower LTV loan or a higher interest rate, may make that loan undoable or nullify the purpose of that loan (i.e. to lower their monthly payments). So please, order the Credit Report as soon as you can.

As a mortgage loan originator you need to be able to properly read the Credit Report and determine, from the information on it, what loan program(s) your customers qualify for. With this information you then can begin researching various loan programs of different

Lenders, with each loan program's interest rates, to find the one that will match - with what your customers qualify for as well as achieve the goals of their loan.

As I may have mentioned previously, one of the things you need to be aware of - is that Conforming Lenders are (what I call) Credit Score sensitive. By that I mean, Lenders traditionally first looked at the Credit Scores of the Borrowers, and if they do not have the minimum (middle) Credit Score they required then they won't even look at that loan. This was also true for Non-Conforming and Sub-prime lenders as well. However, as I mentioned, within the chapter titled "Loan Underwriting", today that has changed with DU and LP loan submissions. As you may recall, when you submit a loan via DU or LP then that Underwriting program determines what the minimum required credit score will be for that customer – after analyzing all their "Layers of Risk." But a customer's credit score can, in many cases, still highly influence what interest rate a Lender will offer to a customer – after considering any Adjustments to that interest rate.

Because each Credit Reporting company (that you order your Credit Reports from) will have a different format, for reporting a customer's credit information, I have not included an example of a Credit Report in this book. It used to be that Credit Reports had only about 3-4 pages. Today, it is not uncommon for Credit Reports to have 8-12 pages or more. However, I will go over what I believe is important for you to look for in reviewing your customer's Credit Report.

Please forgive me if I am repeating myself but some of what I am going to discuss below is what I previously mentioned when discussing Qualifying Your Borrowers, but it bears repeating.

When you first get a hold of your customer's Credit Report - what are you looking for? Most likely you should be looking for what the Lenders look for. Lenders look at the payment patterns of customers over a stated period - usually the last two-year period. Have they established Credit? Do they pay their bills and creditors on time and as agreed? Do they continue to pay despite temporary financial hardships (this alludes to the Character of the borrower)? Are they overextended on their Credit?

Most Conforming lenders will require that you pull a 3-bureau Credit Report on your borrowers. This is oftentimes referred to as a Tri-Merge and generally includes Credit Reporting and Credit Scores from: Experian (sometimes shown as Experian/Fair Isaac), Equifax (sometimes shown as Beacon), and TransUnion (sometimes shown as Empirica). Conforming Lenders will be most interested in what they see on this report for the last 2 years and are generally looking for at least 24 months of good credit.

Evaluating the credit worthiness of a borrower has evolved over the years whereby today Lenders are looking almost exclusively (and certainly first) at the Middle Credit Score of the primary borrower. Each credit-reporting bureau, on that Credit Report, will summarize what they calculate (and determine) as the credit worthiness of that customer translated into a Credit Score. Because each credit bureau is (seems to be) focusing and weighing the importance of different Credit aspects of borrowers differently (and the way they calculate the Credit Scores) it is rare that you will find any one of them coming up with the same Credit Score as the other. You will usually find these Credit Scores on the first or last page of the Credit Report. Conforming Lenders generally accept the middle credit score of the Primary Borrower (usually the one who makes the most income of the two).

Just a few years ago it used to be that if a borrower had a Credit Score below 680 then he or she would not qualify for a Conventional Conforming loan. The important point here is to look at the Credit Scores, identify the middle score, and compare that to the minimum required Credit Score of the Lender (and loan program) you wish to submit your loan to.

Also, Conforming Lenders want to see at least 24 months since a bankruptcy was first filed or discharged (depending on the Lender). And, they generally like to see credit re-established with perhaps 2 - 3 creditors shown and No Lates since the Bankruptcy.

Customers with less than perfect credit may not qualify for a Conforming loan or Non-Conforming loan and quite frankly you may not be able to help them at all (or get them into a loan program with an interest rate or a loan with an LTV that makes financial sense in doing that loan or one that benefits them). Less than perfect credit is a nice way of saying that they either have bad credit or there is a recent history of credit problems showing up on the Credit Report that could disqualify them from getting a Conforming loan (or most likely create a challenge in doing so).

Let's now talk about the different types of Credit Reports. Basically, there are three types of Credit Reports that you will be ordering:

1. **In-File Credit Report**:
   An in-file credit report provides credit and public record information obtained from one or more credit repositories. The report contains "as is" information, which typically has not been updated or re-verified as a result of the credit inquiry.

2. **Automated Merged Credit Report**:
   An automated merged credit report combines the in-file credit reports from multiple repositories into a single report. A joint merged credit report includes all credit repository credit data on more than one individual applicant.

3. **Residential Mortgage Credit Report**:
   A residential mortgage credit report is a detailed account of the borrower's credit, employment, and residency history, as well as public records information.

And, the Credit Report that you do order must meet the following requirements:

- The report should include all information from three different credit repositories, or two repositories, if: - that is the extent of the data available for the borrower, or - the borrower's credit information is frozen at one credit repository.

- If only one in-file credit report is available for a borrower, this is acceptable if the lender is able to obtain a credit score for the borrower and the lender requested information from three credit repositories.

- If the report does not include a reference for each significant debt reported by the borrower on the loan application, the lender must obtain a separate written verification for each unreported (or unrated) debt.

- If the report lists accounts that were not checked with the creditor within 90 days of the date of the in-file report, the lender must obtain an updated credit report or a separate written verification for those accounts.

Let's now talk about the Credit Report itself. If you have one available then I invite you to go get it now. Otherwise, bear with me as I explain the important sections (you will most likely see) and their purpose on the Credit Report. If you do not have a Credit Report available then don't worry, this will all make sense when you finally do.

Most 3-bureau Credit Reports, that I am seeing these days, have the following information within them:

1. **Consumer Information:**
   This shows the names, social security numbers, and current address of those customers you ordered the report on. This shows you what you entered (when you ordered this Credit Report) and is the basis of the report that follows.

2. **Credit Scores of Customer(s):**
   This is usually found on the first or last page of the report. Take the middle credit score of the Primary Borrower and use that for credit-qualifying your Borrower(s).

   Also, to the right or below each Credit Score will be the following:

   ➤ Name of the Borrower and/or Co-Borrower that each Credit Score represents, with their social security number.

   ➤ For each Credit Score shown – which Credit Bureau reported that.

   ➤ That Credit Bureau's reasons for arriving at that Credit Score. This is shown as: 1. Numbers that represent certain reasons for influencing that Credit Score (i.e. 00038), and 2. A Description, to the right of that number, that corresponds to that number (i.e. Serious Delinquency, Derogatory Public Record or Collection Filed). This is sometimes referred to as the Credit Reporting Factors. Fortunately, all credit-reporting bureaus appear to use the same numbers and descriptions.

3. **Open Section:**
   Open - refers to those accounts that are currently open and available to be used by those customers. Some of those accounts may have zero balances but that could change. When you are reading the accounts in this entire report you will generally see the following displayed for each:

   - **Name of Account**
   - **Account Number** (usually right below that account's name).

- **Date the Account was First Opened**. (i.e. date the loan started or credit card was first issued).

- **Date (last) Reported**. This represents the date this Credit Report last reported on this account (i.e. when payment was last received). Be aware that many Credit Reports show you the credit results (account balances) as of the previous month.

- **High Credit** (of Loan). What the original amount of that loan was or the maximum credit limit on that credit card.

- **Payment Terms**. This shows what is the minimum payment amount required or due each month. Remember that if that Credit Report doesn't show a minimum monthly amount due, then in Qualifying that customer you will need to calculate 5% of the outstanding balance on that account and use that figure in Qualifying him or her.

- **Balance**. What the current outstanding balance is on that account. Again, the actual balance may be more or less than actually shown - because this report may be looking at last month. Refer to Date of Report - as mentioned above.

- **30 60 90**. This shows you whether there are or have been any lates on this account. For example, if under the column 30 - there is a 1 – then this means there was one 30-day late payment. Many Credit Reports also show you the date(s) when those late payments occurred. Remember, we are primarily looking at what has happened in the last 2 years.

  The Credit Report that you have ordered must list the historical status of each account. This status must be presented in a "number of times past due" format and include the dates of the delinquencies. The preferred format is "0 x 30, 0 x 60, 0 x 90 days" late. The following formats are also acceptable:

  - "R1, R2, R3, …," if it also gives historical negative ratings, such as "was R3 in 6/05."

  - A consecutive numbering sequence, such as "0001000 …," provided the meaning is clear from the report. Statements such as "current," "satisfactory," or "as agreed" are not satisfactory by themselves.

- **Mo Rev**. This stands for Months Reviewed (on that account). This represents the number of payments the Credit Reporting bureaus have reviewed on that account (also alludes to how long that account has been open).

- **Account Status**. This generally states whether an account is Current and whether the borrower pays as agreed. If this were not the case then that account would most likely not be here but in another section of the Credit Report (e.g. Derogatory section or Closed section).

- **Current Rating**. Some Credit Reports have rated that customer's account, based on their payment history. For those Credit Reports I have seen – 1 stands for excellent with 9 being the lowest.

4. Closed Section:

This shows the accounts that the customers have had - but have since closed. You should review this as well because your customers may have closed some accounts that show they had lates within the past 2 years.

5. Collections Section:

This shows accounts that are currently in Collections. You will want to discuss these with your customers because perhaps those have been paid - but are still showing up with an outstanding balance. You will see this quite often.

6. Derogatory Section:

Those accounts that are not Current and have a history of Delinquent Payments and/or have been Charged-Off will be shown in this section. Again, you need to discuss what you are seeing here with your customers. An account showing as "Not Current" may have been recently brought current by your customers. An outstanding Charge-Off account may have been settled and/or paid off by your customers. You need to review these with your customers to assess whether what you are currently seeing represents the actual status of that account at this time.

7. Account Status Column:

This is usually located in the far-right column on the Credit Report page, and for each credit account shown this shows you the payment paying history of the borrower or borrowers. This column shows you whether there have been any late payments realized by each creditor and the extent of those lates if any (e.g. 30, 60, or 90-lates or greater). Credit Reports should and must summarize the number of lates and their classification (e.g. 30 or 90-day).

8. Inquiry Information Section:

This shows you if your customers have had any other companies pull a Credit Report on them. If there are a number of recent credit Inquiries here, then this could allude to the fact that the customer has been shopping around for a mortgage loan or maybe attempting to obtain additional credit (cards or loans). Lenders generally do not like to see a lot of Inquiries on the Credit Report. One of the Lender's main concerns here could be that the customers are buying more (stuff) - increasing their credit card balances and monthly payments with the result of pushing up their total debt ratios. Many Inquiries could also allude to those customers undergoing financial hardships (i.e. many inquiries from credit card companies). If a customer's Housing and Total Debt ratios are well in line and they have good credit then this normally does not become a concern. However, if your customers already have ratios that are high or bordering on that Lender's upper allowable limits then that Lender may request an explanation from the borrowers as to why all those Inquiries have occurred. Lenders generally look at (and count) the number of Inquiries within the past 90 days.

9. Public Records Section.

If there are matters of Public Records, regarding Credit of your customers, then it will be shown in this Section. Examples of those could be any history of bankruptcy, home foreclosures, liens and court judgments, child support delinquencies, and mechanics liens. And, I was surprised when I first discovered that it also could show criminal arrests and convictions.

Since I have mentioned bankruptcy, I'd like to throw in here something you should be aware of. There are folks out there who because of outstanding debts, instead of filing bankruptcy (or wishing to avoid the stigma of such), ended up talking to the Consumer Credit Counseling Services or the Debt Reduction Services (or whatever it is called in your area). Now, if your customers have gone through any of those types of services or companies that <u>reduce the outstanding balance and debt</u> on each account and then combine it all into one monthly payment - then many Conforming Lenders generally consider (and look upon) this just like a Chapter 13 Bankruptcy. It's ironic, because usually that's exactly what those folks were trying to avoid.

I have arrived at a number of (loan application) meetings with customers who were thinking that I was going to set them up with a nice Conforming loan. When they told me that they recently got their debts consolidated through a debt reduction service - I knew then that it wasn't going to happen. And, of course, you can imagine the reaction of my customers when I told them how many (Conforming) Lenders look at what I just mentioned. So be aware of this.

10. Consumer Statement Section:
If customers have had problems with their credit and want to explain the circumstances why those problems occurred then you will most likely find it in this Section.

11. Bureau Statement Section:
If your customers have used different names in the past, when obtaining credit, you will usually see their (previous) names here. Sometimes their date of birth is also shown in this section. Sometimes you may be doing a loan for a customer whose name is common and for some reason the credit bureaus get your customer's credit mixed up with another person's (credit) - whose name is the same (even though their Social Security number is different). I know, sounds screwy, but it happens sometimes. So, if your customer is complaining about this happening to him or her or there seems to be a lot (or a few) accounts showing up on her Credit Report, which she says doesn't belong to her, then check out this Section.

This section also lists the Credit Reporting Bureaus or Agencies that were involved in providing you with that customer's Credit Reporting information. You should see here the names of those Credit Reporting Bureaus, their address, and (if you are lucky) their telephone number where they can be contacted.

12. Address & Employment History Section:
As this Section's title refers to, this shows the previous addresses and employers of those customers that the credit bureaus have on record.

13. Summary Section:

This section summarizes this Credit Report into a nice snapshot of most of the important accounts in this report. It generally separates the accounts into different columns having: Mortgages, Revolving, Installment, and Other. It then shows the total outstanding balances for each lined category, the total payments, and number of 30, 60, and 90-day lates (if any) for each. And, it gives you a grand total for each column. This Summary Section, however, isn't on every type of Credit Report you will order.

At this point I would like to mention a credit related term you may not have hear of before: "Frozen Credit". If the borrower's credit information is Frozen at one of the credit repositories for borrowers who have traditional credit, the credit report is still acceptable as long as:

- The credit data is available from two repositories,
- A credit score is obtained from at least one of those two repositories, and
- The lender requested a three in-file merged report.

Loans for borrowers with credit data frozen at two or more of the credit repositories will not be eligible whether underwritten manually or in DU.

Okay, once you have reviewed the Credit Report of your customers you should have a pretty good idea of what the loan possibilities and options are for them. If you have a customer's Credit Report that you are not sure would qualify them for a particular Lender (that you wish to send it to) then call up that Lender and ask them. I do it all the time. I might say something like, "Hi, this is Steve Driscoll with XYZ Mortgage and I'm looking at this loan I'd like to submit to you but I have a question regarding this." They'll usually reply with something like, "Okay, what's your question?" "Well, I have a Cash-Out Refinance loan here with an LTV of 80% with a loan amount of $130,000. I am coming up with a "back-end" ratio at about 43%. But, I am seeing a middle credit score of 610. Is that something you folks can do?" They will tell you if they can and perhaps also advise you on how to package your loan submission file to them. Lenders are usually very helpful and happy to answer your questions - because they want your business. They're in the business of doing loans.

I would also like to mention the allowable age of credit reports and documents that Fannie Mae requires and will accept: For all mortgage loans (existing and new construction), the credit documents must be no more than four months old as shown on the Note date.
And finally, when you are reviewing a credit report, for a prospective home loan customer, and you see Past Due, Collections, and Charge-offs of non-mortgage account showing up on their credit report – here's what you can generally expect will be required prior to home closings:

- Accounts that are reported as past due (not reported as collection accounts) must be brought current.

- For one-unit, principal residence properties, borrowers are not required to pay off outstanding collections or non-mortgage charge-offs—regardless of the amount. Note: If the lender marks the collection account Paid By Close in the online loan application, DU will issue a message in the DU Underwriting Findings report stating that the collection must be paid;
- For 2 - 4 units owner-occupied and second home properties, collections and non-mortgage charge-offs totaling more than $5,000 must be paid in full prior to or at closing.
- For investment properties, individual collection and non-mortgage charge-off accounts equal to or greater than $250 and accounts that total more than $1,000 must be paid in full prior to or at closing.

Let's talk now about what is referred to in lending as Non-Traditional Credit. To give you an example of using this, let's say you are working with a young couple that wants to buy a home but haven't really established any Credit yet. You pull a Credit Report and sure enough there is nothing there and no Credit Scores either. As I have mentioned previously, there is another way of measuring Credit and that is called the Non-Traditional means of Credit. Because your customers have probably been paying rent, paying electric and heating bills, perhaps some medical bills - you have a means of determining their Credit (payment history) available to you. However, you should know that if a prospective loan customer of yours does not have any established credit (and a Non-traditional means of credit will be used) then those customers will need to be manually underwritten. Anyway, with Non-Traditional Credit, you (or the Loan Processor) can contact those utility companies, individuals leasing the property or apartment manager, and doctor and determine if your borrowers have been paying their monthly bills on time and as agreed. If they have been paying their monthly bills on time and there are four references, including where they currently rent (that you can obtain Verifications on) and you have at least a 12-month payment history on each, then this could very well satisfy a Lender's concerns and requirements about their Credit.

The current requirements for using Non-traditional Credit are:

- A minimum of three sources of non-traditional credit that have been active for at least 12 months:
    - One of the sources must be housing related, i.e., rental housing payments;
    - One of the sources must be a utility company; and
    - The remaining source may represent any reasonable service or purchase as long as the repayment terms are in writing and the borrower can provide canceled checks or money order receipts that show the creditor as the payee to document the payments;
- No history of delinquency on rental housing payments within the past 24 months (or since inception, if less than 24 months);
- Only one account, excluding rental payments, may have had a 30-day delinquency in the last 12 months;

- No collections or judgments (other than medical collections) filed within the past 24 months. Any/all judgments must be satisfied. Collection accounts (including medical) in excess of $250 per individual account or $1,000 in the aggregate must be paid in full; and

- If a borrower with no credit score has a prior bankruptcy or foreclosure in his or her credit history, he/she must have re-established credit that satisfies the requirements of waiting periods and re-establishing credit (see Foreclosure and Bankruptcy for more information).

However, as I previously mentioned, all borrowers on a Conventional Conforming purchase loan are relying solely on Non-Traditional Credit to qualify for that loan, then those borrowers will also need to complete the Pre-purchase Homebuyer Education and Counseling.

And finally, let's now talk about DU Loan Casefiles where the borrower(s) have no credit score. Lenders may submit loan casefiles to DU when no borrower has a credit score. DU will apply the following requirements:

- The property must be a one-unit, principal residence, and all borrowers must occupy the property.

- All property types are permitted, with the exception of Manufactured Housing.

- The transaction must be a purchase or limited cash-out refinance.

- The loan amount must meet the general loan limits - High-Balance Mortgage Loans are not eligible.

- The loan must be a fixed-rate mortgage.

- The maximum LTV, CLTV, and HCLTV ratios are 90%.

- The debt-to-income ratio must be less than 40%.

- Reserves may be required as determined by DU.

- A Non-traditional credit history must be documented for each borrower without a credit score.

If a loan casefile does not receive an Approve/Eligible recommendation then the loan may still be eligible for manual underwriting. The lender must determine whether the loan meets the requirements for a manually underwritten loan that includes a borrower without a credit score.

Mortgage Only Program:
Some Lenders have what is called a Mortgage Only Program in evaluating the customer's Credit worthiness. Here, the Lender is looking at only the borrower's mortgage payment history and not at the borrower's consumer credit history. This is a good way to go if the borrower's Credit Report is showing a few minor late payments and/or there are some outstanding adverse accounts with outstanding balances due - but the borrowers have always paid their mortgage payments on time. Under this credit review program, if the adverse account's balances due are not greater than $5,000 then many times these will not

have to be paid off at loan closing. With the Mortgage Only loan program Lenders usually want to see no history of foreclosure and any Bankruptcy (fully discharged) and at least 5 years discharged prior to the date of loan application.

Credit Researching:

Sometimes a customer of yours will tell you that an account showing up on their Credit Report does not belong to them. Having that account shown on their Credit Report could make a big difference in qualifying your customers and getting their loan approved. What do you do? You call that company you ordered your Credit Report from and ask them to research that account on behalf of your customer. This is one of the services that companies, who you order Credit Reports from, usually provide. Once you give them the needed (account) information they then can begin their research and normally fax or email back to you the results of their study. Be aware, however, that this may cost your customers anywhere from $10.00 or more - per account they research. So, if your customer has a lot of accounts that need researching then it could get rather pricey.

Reading Credit Reports use to be complicated and confusing. Today, the Credit Reports are a lot easier to read and understand - and that's good for us. So, when you begin as a Mortgage loan originator, get your hands on a Credit Report and look it over. Become familiar with it so you can find what you are looking for when you need to. Because when you start working on your first loan you don't want to waste your time trying to figure out then - what this Credit Report business is all about.

Before leaving this chapter on Reading the Credit Report I feel it is a good time to talk about the FACT Act. FACT stands for Fair and Accurate Credit Transactions and this Act was signed into law on December 4, 2003 and became effective on December 1, 2004. The FACT Act, I believe, is a result of the increasing concerns that consumers have regarding their privacy (of non-public information) and of identity theft. And, this is a concern of all citizens of our great nation. I also believe, that it was because of these types of concerns that Congress eliminated a state's right to enact laws related to how credit-reporting companies handle consumer credit information and enacted the FACT Act - that would establish national uniformity standards for the reporting of consumer credit information. It also increases the accuracy of consumer Credit Reports and includes requirements such as giving your loan customers their Credit Score information (see Credit Scores of Customers above). And, this is why I bring up the FACT Act at this time.

The FACT Act influences and requires of us certain responsibilities in:
1. Requesting Credit Reports on our loan-inquiring customers,
2. When we (as Mortgage loan originators) have a right or are authorized to pull a customer's Credit Report (or have the consent of a customer to do so).
3. Disclose to the customer, who you pulled a Credit Report on, the credit information you (and your company and the Lender) used in Credit Qualifying that customer.

In discussing the FACT Act I won't go into all the details of it but will focus on what, I believe, you need to know to do your jobs properly and to be **In Compliance**. Hence, I will focus only on those specific points of the FACT Act that impact what we do as Mortgage loan originators. So, let's start with number 1 above:

1. **Requesting Credit Reports on our Loan-Inquiring Customers:**
    To pull a Credit Report on a customer you need to have a valid reason to do so. For our purposes, it would be for the extension of credit (a mortgage loan) – which begins with the completion of a loan application (the 1003) and/or the need to review the Credit Report of a loan-inquiring customer.

2. **When we (as Mortgage loan originators) Have a Right or Are Authorized to pull a customer's Credit Report (or have the consent of that customer to do so).**
    When you are working on a mortgage loan request for a customer, you need to pull a Credit Report, to further see what they might qualify for. But you need to have authorization to do that. The following highlights those signed documents or other means of permission that authorizes you to do so:

    -   A signed Borrower's Certification and Authorization Disclosure and/or a Consent Form Disclosure.

    -   Signed 1003 application (page 5 of 5). I should note here: That if it is a married couple (applying for a home loan) then only one of the spouse's signatures needs to be on that application. However, if there are two single individuals (unmarried) applying for a home loan then both of their signatures need to be on that 1003 to pull both of their Credit Reports. Remember that if a couple is unmarried then you will need to pull a separate Credit Report for each loan applicant.

    -   If you completed a 1003 over the telephone then a signed 1003 is not required. But here, I would suggest you note that on that customer's Comment Sheet in that customer's loan file.

    -   If you were talking to some customers, over the telephone, and they give you Verbal Approval or Authorization to pull a Credit Report on them, then you should: 1. Note that permission was given to you on the Comments Sheet in that customer's loan file (if a loan file is indeed created), and/or 2. Complete a Verbal Authorization form – which most mortgage companies should have.

3. **Disclose to that customer, what Credit Reporting Bureau you pulled their Credit Report from.**
    Here we come to two Loan Disclosures that you need to prepare and send to your loan customer within 3 business days after pulling that customer's credit report. Those two Loan Disclosures are:

    -   National Credit Score Disclosure
    -   Notice to the Home Loan Applicant

These two Loan Disclosures, are sometimes combined on one page. And, accompanying these two Loan Disclosures that you send to your loan customers should be a copy of that customer's credit report. Years ago we were told and/or understood that we were not to give a loan customer a copy of their copy report. This has changed and now it is required that you send a copy of a customer's credit report, that you ordered and received, to them along with these two Loan Disclosures above.

If you have previously ordered a customer's credit report and are meeting with them then I suggest preparing two (of both of these two Disclosures) and have that customer sign the original and copy of each Disclosure. Give the customer the originally signed Disclosures and keep one of each for that customer's loan file.

Okay, enough about Credit Reports. Next, we'll discuss another very important report you will be using on a daily basis and is required when you begin shopping for the Lender with the best interest rates and terms for your customer's loan. I am talking about The Rate Sheets.

Chapter 19

READING THE RATE SHEETS

One of the most important things you need to quickly "get a handle on" when you are a new mortgage loan originator is how to properly read different Lender's Rate Sheets. This is because this shows you what interest rates you can offer your customers (at par) or how much your loan customer will have to pay if they wish to obtain an Interest Rate less than what is offered at par or they wish to obtain Premium Pricing to pay for some of the costs on their home loan.

I must admit, that when I first became a mortgage loan originator I was somewhat confused and overwhelmed by all the Rate Sheets from all the different Lenders as well as the information contained in each. And that is exactly why I wanted to be sure to include this chapter in this book.

Now, when you have a new loan, your initial objective should be to answer the following questions: What is the best loan program that this applicant will most likely qualify for (considering the borrower's loan goals and credit) and what's the best interest rate (at par) I can obtain for their loan. A term you hear quite often in this loan process is "Pricing." Pricing has a number of meanings - depending on how it is used - but mostly it is used in relation to mortgage interest rates and related loan programs. For example, a mortgage loan originator may ask you, "How's the pricing going on the Jones loan file?" That mortgage loan originator is asking you if you have found a loan program and selected an interest rate on it yet. Another use of this term could be in reference to the interest Rate Sheets put out by Lenders each day. For example, a mortgage loan originator may ask you, "Have you taken a look at the pricing sheets from XYZ Lender today?" Here that mortgage loan originator is asking if you have looked at the Interest Rate Sheets that came out today from that Lender. Also, much like the first example here, if someone asks you if you have priced that loan, then they are asking if you have selected an interest rate for that loan.

When you are looking over Lenders' Interest Rate Sheets - you should know that the rates are expressed as Points. In lending, Points are expressed in 8 parts or eighths of a point (when they are less than a full point). For example, an interest rate may be expressed as 5&7/8ths %. Thus, the rate here would be 5&7/8s or written as 5.875%. In written form, each eighth of a point equals 0.125 of a point. The following page breaks it down for you:

Parts of a Point:

1/8%	=	0.125	=	An Eighth of a Point
2/8%	=	0.250	=	A Quarter of a Point
3/8%	=	0.375	=	Three-Eighths of a Point
4/8%	=	0.500	=	Half a Point
5/8%	=	0.625	=	Five-Eighths of a Point
6/8%	=	0.750	=	Three-Quarters of a Point
7/8%	=	0.875	=	Seven-Eighths of a Point

As a mortgage loan originator you need to become familiar with this and comfortable in speaking in these terms. An eighth of a point can make a big difference in either: 1. What your customer would pay on his or her monthly mortgage payments, and/or 2. What options your loan customer may have to Buy-down the Interest Rate (at par) on their home loan or use Premium Pricing to pay for some of the cost on their loan. It's also important to realize that as the total amount of a loan increases then the impact of an additional $1/8^{th}$ of a point increases as well. For example, let's say you are working on a loan with an amount of $300,000 and planning on structuring it as a 30-year fixed. Based on today's rates you figure you could offer your customer a rate of 5.0% or 5.25%. What's the difference? The difference is that with 5.0% your customer's P&I payment would be $1,610.46. At 5.25% it would $1,656.61 - an increase of $46.15 per month.

However, if you are working on a loan with a loan amount of only $100,000 then for the above rates (5.0% & 5.25%) the increased difference would then be only $15.38. So, the total amount of the loan can be a real consideration in the interest rate on a loan. Get as comfortable with this as you can - because this is how Lenders will express their interest rates.

Let's get back to talking about Rate Sheets specifically. As I mentioned above, Rate Sheets are very often referred to as Pricing Sheets. These show the scale or range of interest rates with the rebates (or costs) for each and the main loan programs that that Lender offers. These days, some mortgage companies may receive these Rate Sheets on their fax machines, on a daily basis, generally from those Lenders they use most often. You, however, will most likely be viewing these on your computer. But the features mentioned are still relevant. The important features shown on a Rate Sheet are:

1. **Name of the Lender:** And their Telephone, Email Address, and Fax Numbers.

2. **Who their Wholesale Rep. Is:** This is who you can call and talk to about your loan you are working on – who represents that Lender you are thinking about submitting your loan to.

3. **Their Most Popular Loan Programs:** Generally shown in separate sections for each loan program. For example, on Conforming Lender Rate Sheets you will usually see a (separate) section for 30-Year Fixed loans, 15-Year Fixed, Jumbo 15 and 30-year fixed, and a section for govie loans (FHA & VA).

4. **Adjustments:** This is something you definitively always want to be looking out for - to see if there are any Adjustments. Adjustments can affect either the Interest Rate that is shown on that rate sheet or the Interest Rate's Rebate (or what we call "The Fee"). If an Adjustment affects the Interest Rate then usually you will see written within that Adjustment: "To the Rate." However, most Adjustments you will encounter will affect the Interest Rate's Fee. Having said that, let's now discuss how Adjustments can affect (negatively or positively) the Rebate, in relation to the interest rate you are looking at.

   For example, you look at the Rate Sheet and see the interest rate of 7.5% (on a particular loan program) with a rebate of <1.0%>. As we discussed, this means that if you locked your customer in at 7.5% for that loan program today then your loan customer could receive a credit of 1.0% of the total loan amount applied towards their loan costs. Okay, now let's say you are doing a Cash-Out Refinance Loan. Looking at the Adjustments shown in that section it shows that for Cash-Out Refinance Loans there is an Adjustment of +0.25% to the Rebate. This means that at the rate of 7.5% your customer could incur a cost of 0.25% of their total loan amount! For a $100,000 loan, that would mean $250.00 less! So look out for those Adjustments.

5. **Loan Program Requirements:** These, like Adjustments, are listed and show what the minimum requirements or parameters are for each type of loan. For example, it may say: Min. FICO => 620. What it is saying here is that the (middle) credit score of the borrower, for that type of loan program (e.g. 30-Year Fixed), needs to be 620 or greater. Another example could be: Max. C/O LTV=80%. You probably figured this one out for yourself. And that's good, because you're beginning to understand the jargon of all this. But just to be sure, this means that the maximum acceptable LTV for a Cash-Out Refinance loan is 80%. Here again, lookout for those Loan Program Requirements.

6. **What that Wholesale Lender's Fees are:** These are usually shown on the top or bottom of the first page of a Lender's Rate Sheets. Items that are usually included in the Lender's fees are: Underwriting, Tax Service, Flood Certification, and sometimes a Document and Wire Fee. The total of these fees can range from $450 to $800 (or greater). These fees do change with every Lender so make sure you are aware of what a Lender charges if you are seriously considering submitting a loan to them.

Please refer to Exhibit X now. There are two pages of Rate Sheet examples I have included here for you. Or, feel free to use any Rate Sheets available that you would prefer to use instead. I will use the Rate Sheet in Exhibit X in my discussion that follows.

I am using this rate sheet (which is actually a section of a rate sheet) as an example because it is well designed, is simple, and shows you the basic and important points we need to cover in this chapter on Reading the Rate Sheets. And, if you will look at page 2, of this rate sheet, you will see an enlarged view of the 30-Year Fixed Conforming loan program shown. This will make it easier for you to read and follow along here. Okay, let's start at the top of page one of this pricing sheet:

Lender Information:

At the top (or bottom) of most Lender's Rate Sheets is the Name of that Wholesale Lender, their address and/or addresses, and their telephone numbers (hopefully a toll-free number), email address, and their fax number(s). Many times I have found that Lenders will also list, at the top (or somewhere on the first page) the name and telephone number of their Wholesale Lender Representative (their Rep.) that you can call if you have any questions about one of their loan programs or wish to talk to them about a loan.

Lender Fees:

Lender's Fees are usually shown somewhere either at the top or bottom of the first page of a Rate Sheet. Those are all that Lender's Fees you would include on your Loan Estimate - if you plan to submit a loan to that Lender. Remember, different Lenders charge different fees (some more, some less).

Date:

When you examine a Rate Sheet, this should be the very first thing you look for: The Date on that Rate Sheet. Many a mortgage loan originator, in their rush and excitement, has picked up a rate sheet 1 or 2 days old and started working on their loan - only to find out later that they were using an old Rate Sheet. So, make sure you are looking at a current Rate Sheet for that day.

Time:

It is unusual that you will see a rate sheet with the time actually shown on it. However, I am finding these days that this information can often be quite helpful. That's because the mortgage market can change very quickly and interest rates can change at any time - and they do. And, the Lender lets you know that - at the bottom of this page "Prices Subject to Change without Notice." However, rates normally change (if they change at all) on a daily basis. When the market (affecting the mortgage interest rates) becomes very dynamic (either going up or down) then the most you will usually see is one subsequent rate change during that day - after the morning rate sheets have come out. Therefore, make sure the Rate Sheet you are looking at is the current Rate Sheet for that day. And, this is another reason why you should try to stay on top of what is going on in the financial and lending markets.

Lock-In Information:

The top of this Rate Sheet also shows you the telephone number, email address, and fax number to lock-in your customer's interest rate on their loan. After you have submitted your loan to a lender and obtained approval (on that loan) then you will be in an ideal position to lock the interest rate on your customer's loan. Up to that point you have been "Floating" the rate. When you Lock the Rate that is the interest rate that your customer's loan will have when it goes to the closing table. We will talk more about Locks below when we discuss Pricing in a moment, but for now, know that most lenders will require you to complete and either email or fax to them a "Lock-In Rate Sheet" in order to formally Lock-In an interest rate. This Lock-In Rate Sheet, when completed, will have on it important information regarding: The borrowers' names, address of the subject property, the loan type or program, loan number, the loan amount, its LTV, the interest rate locked, and lock period you are requesting.

I should note, that even though I stated the above (that you lock-in the rate after the loan is submitted) that I am finding some Lenders (these days) allowing you to lock the rate before you even submit the loan to them. I would only recommend doing this if the interest rates are changing dramatically and you have concerns about them getting worse (higher). Also, you are certain of sending that loan to that Lender and also fairly certain of obtaining approval on that borrower's loan from that Lender. Otherwise, I would wait until after you have submitted that loan. I especially recommend this procedure (waiting until after loan submission before locking the rate) for new mortgage loan originators.

Let's now jump over to the first two sections - at the top half of this sheet (Exhibit X) and look at the middle to lower half of this Rate Sheet. You should see 9 boxes (in this section) with titles at the top of each. Each one of those boxes contains a different loan program with their own interest rates and rebates - based on the Lock-In period and Adjustments shown in the lower half of each box. For our purposes here we will examine what is contained in the first box, in the upper left-hand corner, with the title of "Conforming 30 YR (AGF30)." This loan program is for a 30-Year Fixed Rate Conforming Loan. So, let's take a look at what we have here.

Now, I know and completely understand – that if you are new to this business and you start to look over some of the Lender's rate sheets that they can, at first, be somewhat confusing and perhaps intimidating. But don't worry, because after you get done with this chapter you will know how to read the rate sheets for all Lenders. Of course, the way different Lenders arrange their rate sheets will most likely be different from our example here (whether it's a Conforming, Non-conforming, or Sub-prime Lender), but that should not be a problem for you. Just do like I do: Relax, and go through those steps we are now about to go through - in looking at the Rate Sheets in our example here. Once we have gone over this - you will understand how to read the rates on the loan programs shown here (on this rate sheet) and should also be able to properly read other Lenders' rate sheets as well. To begin, please refer to the 2nd page of this exhibit for the discussion that follows.

<u>CONFORMING 30-YR FIXED:</u>
The title, at the top of this box, shows that the information contained in this box pertains to this Lender's 30-Year Fixed Rate Conforming loans. Looking again at page 1, of this Exhibit, you can see that "AGF30" is what this Lender calls this particular loan program. Or, in other words, what their program name is. If you were submitting a loan to this Lender, on their submission sheet it will ask for the program name representing that Lender's name of the loan program you are submitting it under. For this Lender and for this loan program you would enter = AGF30. OK, so let's take a look at what is contained in this box for a 30-Year Fixed Rate Conforming loan – on our Exhibit's 2nd page.

1. Range of Interest Rates:

On the Rate Sheet, for each particular loan program, Lenders will list a range of interest rates that they are offering (at that time). Looking at our example here, within the AGF30 program, the range of interest rates are (from top to bottom) 5.625% to 6.375%. We can see here that as the interest rate increases (from 5.625%) that the amount of Rebate offered increases as well - with each incremental increase being 1/8 of a point (or 0.125%) - as we discussed previously.

2. Interest Rate Lock Periods:

To the right of each interest rate shown you see three columns. At the top of each column is a number. In our example here it's: 15, 30, and 45. These represent the Number of Days that you can Lock-In one of those interest rates shown in the far-left column (for that loan program). Lenders usually have Lock-In periods of 15 and 30 days - and sometimes greater. On our 2nd Lender Rate Sheet Exhibit we will use the lock-day periods of 15, 30, and 45.

How long you should Lock-In the interest rate for your customers? The simplest answer to that question is: How long will it take to process that loan and get it to the closing table and fund? And, don't forget about the "3-Day Right of Rescission" (if it's an O/O refinance loan) before loan funding? If you are new to this business - I recommend locking in all your loans (when it is the proper time to lock) for no shorter than 30 days. I should note that it is the policy of some Lenders to not allow locking in an interest rate for 15 days or less unless that Lender is being submitted a Full Loan Package (with all supporting documentation: Paystubs, bank statements, as well as a completed Appraisal). However, if you do have all of those completed and have approval on your loan, and everything looks great to fund that loan, within the next week and a half, then by all means Lock-In the rate for 15 days. Just use common sense here in locking in your rate.

3. Rebates:

Here is where we talk about Rebates. Recall what we talked about previously, when we discussed Rebates? To repeat, a Rebate is a percentage of the total loan amount that your loan customer will have to pay or be credited for – for an Interest rate and its Rate Period. Look now at those three columns to the right of the interest rates. Each number in those three columns represents a Rebate based on the:

1. Number of Days Locked (at the top of that column)
2. As a percent (e.g. 3.375 represents 3.375%), and
3. What the interest rate is that corresponds to that Rebate (percent). Notice also that each Rebate number is expressed as a plus (e.g. +3.375) or as a negative (e.g. -3.375).

Some times you will see these Rebates when they are negative - presented in brackets as: <3.375>. The important thing here is to know the difference. If the Rebate is expressed as a plus or positive then this usually means it is a cost for the borrower, of that percentage of the total loan amount, to get that interest rate. Looking at our example here, we see that for the interest rate of 5.75%, with a lock-in period of 30 days that the Rebate is (plus) 1.000%. This means that if your customer insists on obtaining that interest rate of 5.75% then it will cost him 1.0% of the total loan amount. If that loan amount is $125,000 then it would cost that borrower $1,250. This could be the case if your loan customer wishes to Buydown the interest rate on their loan. So, Rebates expressed as a positive are costs to obtain that interest rate.

Conversely, if Rebates are expressed as a negative then that represents what your loan customer could credit and apply to their loan costs - for that corresponding interest rate and lock period (believe me, this confused me too when I first started out). This could be the case if your loan customer is considering Premium Pricing to pay for some of their loan costs. Looking at our example here, let's say you plan to lock your customer's interest rate on their loan at 6.125% for 30 days. Your loan customer's Rebate (what they could credit and apply towards their loan costs) for their loan would be -0.625 (or <0.625>). Thus, with a total loan amount of $125,000 your loan customer could apply $781.25 =($125,000 X 0.00625) towards their loan costs.

Also, looking at our example here, you can see that as the Lock-In period increases (from 15 days to 45 days) that the Rebates: 1. Increase - if it represents a <u>Cost</u> to the borrower or 2. Decrease if it represents <u>Credit</u> to your loan customer (expressed as a negative). Using this information let's look at the interest rate of 6.0%. If you lock that rate for 30 days then your loan customer could realize a credit of -0.125% (1/8 of a point). For our $125,000 loan - that would be only $156.25. Now look to the right of the 30-day lock period - the 45-day (lock) column. There you can see that if you locked that rate of 6.0% for 45 days - that it will now <u>cost</u> your loan customer $156.25 to lock-in - for that long a period. Knowing this, while looking at this rate sheet, you can understand why mortgage loan originators want to lock-in their customer's interest rate (they have chosen) for the shortest Lock-In Period. But again, use your common sense.

4. Adjustments:

Remember what I said before when we discussed these? So please, don't forget those Adjustments! And now we will talk about why. In the lower half of this box, below the columns for the interest rates and lock periods for Rebates, you see some line items (6 of them) with writing on the left with corresponding (positive percent) numbers on the right. This area is what is referred to as Adjustments. The written text on the left describes the circumstances under which each Adjustment applies. To its corresponding right - is the Adjustment to the Rebate - which you are thinking about receiving for the interest rate and lock period it corresponds to.

Just as the Rebates are a cost, when expressed as a positive (or with no sign in front of it) or as a negative or in bracket, the same is true with Adjustments. However, here we need to use a little of the algebra we learned in high school. Remember those "good old days" - if they ever existed. Now, as you may recall in algebra, if two numbers have the same sign then you add them together. If they have different signs then you subtract them. This same principle applies when applying Adjustments to your loan customer's Rebate. You can see that all the Adjustments, in our loan program here, are expressed as positives (there are no signs in front of them). For example, if you were looking at earning a Rebate (on an interest rate) of -0.75% and because of the Adjustment shown (that your loan does or does not satisfy) - there is an Adjustment to that Rebate of +0.25% - then your loan customer would actually incurred a Rebate cost of 0.50%. You see what I mean about those Adjustments? You can now begin to appreciate why it is so important to fully review these rate sheets and determine (and be certain) whether any of the Adjustments apply to your loan.

Another point to remember is that Adjustments for and on a loan program are cumulative. That is, if more than one Adjustment applies to your loan then you add up all the Adjustments that do and apply them to the respective Rebate. Let's apply this on loan for $55,000. Let's say your borrower has fairly good credit (at least it won't be a problem with this loan) but his middle credit score is 600. Okay, after you have made the Adjustment to the Rebate you then continue to read on down to see if there are any additional Adjustments that apply. You read on until you get to line six. Darn! It says here: FICO<620 and has an Adjustment of 1.000%! In other words, if the (middle) credit score (FICO) of the primary borrower is less than 620 then an adjustment (cost) of 1.0% will need to be applied. What does this mean? It means that when you apply just this Adjustment of (+1.0%) then it will be a cost to your loan customer of $550.00! That will then certainly need to be considered in structuring your customer's home loan with that loan program and with that Lender.

Okay, let me say now that Adjustments can also work in your loan customer's favor as well. For example, many Lenders will give an Adjustment (i.e. Credit shown as a negative or in brackets) to the Rebate if the loan amount is high and/or within a specified loan amount range. For example, let us say you are working on a home loan with a loan amount of $225,000. Everything looks good on this loan: Credit scores are high, income ratios well within guidelines, and no anticipated problems on this stick-built property. Your loan customer has asked you to see if you could Premium Price their loan to help pay for some of their loan costs. So, you look at the rate sheet we have here and are thinking of locking in the rate at 6.125%. For a 30-day lock the rebate will be -0.625% or $1,406.25. That's $1,406.25 that could be applied to that customer's home loan.

But wait you say. Let's be sure and check out the Adjustments. You read through the descriptions of the Adjustments and see one that applies to this loan (not actually shown on this rate sheet - just making it up) = it says: Ln Amt 200 - 250K - with an Adjustment of -0.25%. What this Adjustment is saying is that if the loan amount (for a loan program) is between $200,000 and $250,000 then an Adjustment of -0.25% will be adjusted (added) to the Rebate. So, if you locked the rate here at 6.125% with a Rebate of -0.625%, then with this adjustment, your loan customer's actual Rebate credits would be -0.875 (-0.625% + -0.25%). Hence, your loan customer would able to credit and apply $1,968.75 to their total loan costs. I'm sure your loan customer would be very happy to hear that (assuming that they are also happy with that Interest Rate). The point here is: Loan Adjustments can work for and against you in structuring a home loan for your loan customers.

5. Loan Program Requirements:

I think my previous discussion above, when I first mentioned Loan Program Requirements, pretty well sums up what this is - so I won't go into any details on this. However, let me just say that Loan Program Requirements are usually listed in the same general area as the Adjustments. Also, while the Loan Program Requirements do have a description (of its requirements) it has no corresponding Rebate adjustment (if it did then it would be an Adjustment). To show an example of a Loan Program Requirement let's look again at the Conforming 30-Yr Fixed Rate loan program on our example rate sheet. Let's say you have a customer who has a NOO home (SFR) that they rent out. Everything looks good, as far as the borrower's qualifying goes. Your customer is looking to refinance this property to obtain a better interest rate. Hence, you would be doing a Rate/Term Refinance loan here. You know from your training that the maximum LTV that you will be able to obtain for this loan will most likely be lower than you could obtain with an O/O property. So, this could be a concern and one you want to check out as soon as possible. In your initial discussion with that customer he tells you that his NOO property will (most likely) appraise at about $180,000 and that his mortgage loan has an outstanding balance of about $108,000. You take out your calculator and that comes to about 60% of the value of the subject property.

You return back to your office and look at our Rate Sheet here, to see if there are any Adjustments or Loan Program Requirements listed there. You look it over and it shows no loan Adjustments. Good. However, on the 3rd line it says "INV PROP<=75%." What it is saying here is: Investment Properties can have an LTV equal to or less than 75%. In other words, the maximum LTV on investment properties is 75% for this Lender and with that loan program. You then work out your numbers for this NOO loan of yours and figure that the total loan amount, with all the loan costs, will be about $112,000. This would result in an LTV of 70%. You are Okay. Well within the LTV constraints stated for that loan program.

Once you become fairly familiar with the loan program requirements, of the main Lenders that your company uses, for different types of loans then you will be well on your way to being a mortgage loan originator who can quickly determine which loan program a prospective borrower's home loan should go to. And, which Lenders provide the best loan programs with the best service and interest rates and rebates for that type of loan program. Knowing how to properly and fully read these Rate Sheets is a step in that direction. It's all part of becoming a knowledgeable and professional mortgage loan originator - one that you will soon become.

Let's go now to the next chapter that discusses a report you order from a title insurance company and gives you additional and important information regarding the subject property you are doing a home loan on. I'm talking about The Title Insurance Policy.

Chapter 20

TITLE INSURANCE REPORT

During the processing of your home loans you will need to order a Title Insurance Policy for your loan customers. You can expect that this will be required by the targeted Lender and will be a Prior-To-Doc condition. Because of the importance of Title Insurance and your ability to properly read this report I decided to devote an entire chapter to this subject. In this chapter I will discuss the different types of title insurance coverage, what type of title insurance policy to order, how the Preliminary Title Insurance Report is formatted, what to always review when you receive your customer's Preliminary Title Insurance report, and how these policies are generally priced.

One of the questions that many mortgage loan originators have asked me, regarding this subject, is when should a mortgage loan originator order the Preliminary Title Report or Policy for their borrowing loan customers? I suggest ordering this either when you have received an approval on your loan (i.e. a credit approval with PTD conditions) and/or you have a strong indication or feeling that your loan is going to the closing table. I suggest this because if you do order the Preliminary Title Insurance report (often referred to as the Prelim) and that loan is subsequently declined, the customers withdraw or change their minds, or whatever, and you call back that title insurance company to cancel that order on that Title Insurance then there is a good chance that you will incur a title insurance cancellation fee. This cancellation fee can be from $50.00 to $95.00 or more. If this happens then you can safely assume that your customers will not want to pay for this. Many times that means that the mortgage loan originator responsible (who ordered it) will end up paying for that cancellation fee.

This is usually avoidable. So, wait until you feel the time is right to order the Title Insurance policy. However, if you do need to cancel a Prelim Report and your company is doing a lot of business with that title insurance company then many times they will waive that cancellation fee. But try not to abuse that privilege. However, I should note here that it is my understanding that the (State) Insurance Commissioner states that they (the Title Companies) have to charge a fee on all ordered Title Insurance Policies that are subsequently cancelled. Fortunately (for us), most Title Companies that you do business with don't always enforce this policy. Now to continue: I have seen mortgage loan originators order the Preliminary Title Report as soon as they have completed the 1003. Please don't do this. Wait until it is the proper time to order it. But do keep in mind that once ordered it generally takes from 3 days to a week before you will receive a completed Preliminary Title Report from that title insurance company.

The purpose of a Title Insurance Policy is to protect and insure the homeowner and the Lender, financing the home loan (if applicable), by the title insurance company (issuing the title insurance policy) against errors or omissions in the title search. In other words, to protect the homeowner against those things (liens and rights relating to the property) that either have been recorded and are of public record during the title search (prior to preparing the Prelim Title Insurance Report and the subsequent Final Title Insurance Policy). This is sometimes referred to as protecting the homeowner against a loss due to the title being imperfect. For example, if something did present itself, that was not on the Title Insurance Report, that could challenge the ownership rights of the homeowner or impede the ability of the owner to pass clear title to a purchasing party then this is exactly what the Title Insurance Policy was designed to protect the homeowner against.

As I have mentioned, when you order a Preliminary Title Report, on a property, the title company will do what is called a Title Search. Here, the title company will review all the recorded documents relating to and affecting that subject property. Doing this will reveal: The legal owners of the property, any outstanding liens (e.g. mortgages and mechanic's liens), and any easements and encroachments. I underlined the word "recorded" in the above sentence because if a mortgage or lien is not recorded then this would most likely not be discovered by the title search folks and not shown in the resulting Preliminary Title Insurance report. For example, let us say you own a home and one day someone knocks on your door. You open the door and a man is standing there. You ask him, "Can I help you?" He asks you in return, "What are you doing in my house?" You tell him you bought the house and it's yours. He says, "No it isn't, I never sold it." This is an example of when the Title Insurance Policy would come into play and seek to protect the rights of the homeowner.

The result of this title search is a document called the Preliminary Title Insurance Report. A Preliminary Title Insurance Report (The Prelim Title Report) is like a snapshot in time - listing those owners, liens, encroachments, and easements that currently exist – and have been recorded on that subject property. This is the title document you will first receive when you order a Title Insurance policy for your customers and one that you definitely should review when you do receive it. So, let's take a look at this document and see what it tells us.

Before I get into the format of this report let me say that when you do receive the Prelim Title Report that the first things you want to verify and identify are:

- The address shown on this report (the subject) is correct
- The legal owners of the property
- That interest in the land is Fee Simple
- All outstanding mortgages and liens
- Current taxes on the property – and whether taxes are current or delinquent
- Coverage amount – should match your loan amount
- Type of Coverage (e.g. Extended)
- Cost of the Title Insurance

Although the Prelim Title Report may have about 15 pages to it, the initial 5-10 pages containing Schedules A & B are really what we are most interested in here and what you should be carefully reviewing when you first get this report - so let's talk about these. The actual way that the Prelim Title Insurance Report is formatted may be different in your state but these differences (as some Title Officers have told me) should be relatively minor.

Cover Page of the Prelim Title Report:

On the first page of the Prelim Title Report you will usually find the following:

1. The name, address, and phone number of the reporting Title Insurance company
2. The Title Officer who took the order and/or prepared this report
3. The Order or File Number for this title report
4. The Street Address of the subject property for this report
5. The Name of the Title Insurance Company that will be providing the Commitment for Title Insurance on this property (may be different from the company you ordered the title insurance from in #1 above)
6. A small paragraph stating the terms of the Commitment in this document.

Schedule A – Page Two:

Schedule A is pretty straightforward in that it states when this Prelim Title Report was first ordered, the effective date of the title search, the amount of the loan (you are doing) to purchase or refinance that property, the premium (cost) for the Final Title Insurance Policy, who is/are the current legal owner(s) on title to this property, and if a purchase – the names of the purchasers (your customers) and the legal address of the subject property. And, how the estate or interest in the land is held or described => generally as "A fee simple." Also, what type of Title Insurance Policy is being issued: 1. ALTA loan Policy, with 2. Standard Coverage, or 3. Extended Coverage. Let's talk about these for a moment. ALTA stands for American Land Title Association and is the governing body for title insurance in the United States of America. It sets the standards and regulations that title companies and those issuing title insurance must abide by. And, when it comes to the rates or fees for title insurance policies these are submitted to and enforced by the Insurance Commissioner of each state.

Reviewing Schedule A can confirm to you one of the most important things in doing a home loan for someone: That your customers are indeed who they said they are - the legal owners of the subject property. However, you might also see here that there are also other legal owners of this property that perhaps your customers didn't mention or forgot to tell you about. But that's just one of the reasons we need to review this section.

When you first order the Prelim. Title Report the Title Officer may ask you what types of coverage do you or the Lender want on that policy. There is Standard and Extended Coverage:

1. Standard Coverage: This type of Title Insurance <u>only</u> covers and protects the homeowner on what has actually been recorded.
2. Extended Coverage: This goes beyond Standard Coverage protecting the homeowner against those encroachments that Standard Coverage may not and those concerns that have not been recorded. You will find that most Conforming

Lenders require Extended Coverage. True, it cost more than Standard Coverage but makes up for it in the additional coverage and protection it provides.

If you are working on a purchase loan then Schedule A will also show the names of those purchasing the subject property (your loan customers). When you order the Prelim Title Report make sure you tell the person who is taking your order – your customer's full legal name or names. For example, if your customer says his name is Bob Jones but his legal name is Robert B. Jones then this is the name you should give to that title person. I should also note that the legal names of your loan customers should also be shown on the first page of the URLA: Borrower Information. Therefore, make sure the names of your borrowers are shown as their legal names and that those names match to what will be shown on the Title Insurance Report. This is how those names will be shown on the Deed of Trust when it is recorded.

Because this is a legal document (and has plenty of legal wording on it) there are a couple of terms I'd like to define that you may see on this report:

Beneficiary: This is the Name of the Lender of the home loan.
Trustor/Grantor: The name(s) of the Borrowers (your loan customers)
Trustee: This is the Title Company, Lawyer, or Bank – that has the power to reconvey Title to that subject property.

The Note: The Note on the loan states the Terms of the loan, and
Deed of Trust: The Deed of Trust secures that Note

Legal Description: This is the legal description of the subject property as originally developed by a government survey and is shown on this Title Report exactly as it appeared on the previous Title Commitment. One of the things that make legal descriptions so important is because they (usually) do not change. Names of streets or street addresses may change but not the legal address of a property.

Schedule B:
Schedule B is generally made up of three sections: Section I – Requirements, Section II – Exceptions and, Section III - Informational Notes.

Section I: Requirements:
This lists those requirements that must be met before the title insurance company will issue the Final Title Insurance Policy. For example, to payoff the existing mortgage lien(s) on the subject property. These may be the mortgage loans being refinanced or in a purchase - the outstanding balance of the Seller's mortgage loan(s). Also, that the premium and fees for the Title Insurance Policy will be paid – before the policy becomes effective.

Section II: Exceptions:

This Section lists those liens, easements, restrictions, and covenants that have been recorded and encumber the subject property. These are called Exceptions to the Title Insurance Policy because the Title Insurance Policy will insure this property Except for those items that are listed here. However, those items listed are usually paid off (with the proposed loan) or in some way are resolved before the new Final Title Insurance Policy is issued and becomes effective. These liens and/or easements, for example, are often referred to as "clouds." You hear this sometimes when people are talking about title. They'll say something like, "there's a cloud on title to that property." Many times these "clouds on title" will need to be cleared up (e.g. paid off) prior to or at loan closing. Once that is done then "clear title" is then passed on to the home purchasers or existing homeowner. Now back to Section II. In this Section, for example, you could find listed here:

1. Delinquent Taxes on the property, going back to the year when those taxes first became delinquent.
2. Existing Mortgage Liens on the property. The name of the Lender (Beneficiary) and the original loan amount. The date the Deed of Trust on the loan was recorded and who closed the loan (Trustee). And, the legal name(s) on that Deed of Trust (Trustor).
3. A legal Judgment that has not yet been paid.
4. An outstanding Mechanic's Lien.
5. An Easement by the local utilities company.
6. An Easement (i.e. for the neighbors to have the right of access to cross this property - necessary so they can get to their property).

While this list is not all-inclusive it does give you an idea of what you could expect to see in this Section. Because of what it does contain you definitely will want to review this section to make sure: 1. There are no other outstanding mortgages on the property other than what your customers told you about when you completed the 1003. Unfortunately, this will not always be the case. Sometimes you will find another mortgage securing the subject property that your customers forgot to tell you about or didn't know existed. I know that sounds strange but it does happen. Also, this can tell you if an existing mortgage is seasoned.

It also will tell you whether the property taxes are current and if there are any outstanding liens on the subject property. If there are then those will most likely need to be paid off prior to or at loan closing. All these factors can affect the total loan amount necessary to achieve the loan goals of your customers and, of course, the LTV on that loan. And, that can be a real consideration in qualifying your borrowers and being able to do their loan.

Section II: Informational Notes:

This Section has some helpful notes. When I have reviewed the Prelim Title Report it is rare that I have found anything of material significance here relating to the loan I have been working on. I give this area a quick glance and if nothing there jumps out at me then I move on.

I should note here that the Final Title Insurance Policy is not actually prepared and recorded until the new Deed of Trust has been recorded. Once the Deed of Trust has been recorded and the title company reviews all related documents then the Final Title Insurance Policy is prepared and mailed to the Lender of that home loan, with the homeowners receiving their homeowner's policy of the Final Title Insurance policy. When I was a new mortgage loan originator this was something I was never aware of - because I never saw this Final Title Insurance Policy. But this is one of the reasons your initial order is called a Prelim Title Insurance Report. That report states the existing conditions on title and the requirements for a new title insurance policy. Once those conditions have been met then the Final Title Insurance Policy is prepared, recorded, and mailed to the legal owners (the Lender and your loan customers) of that subject property.

After you have reviewed the Prelim Title Report then you should have a good idea of the actual mortgages on that subject property and any outstanding liens, easements, or encroachments that will need to be addressed and possibly paid off. And, this is another reason why you definitely want to review this report as soon as you can. There's nothing worse than submitting a loan to a Lender, getting approval, and later finding out that there is another mortgage or lien on that property that you were previously unaware of – that will need to be paid off with your customer's loan. The need to now payoff that outstanding mortgage or lien could perhaps significantly change the LTV on that loan, the interest rate you could offer, and your pricing. Worst-case scenario you now cannot do that loan. So please, thoroughly check out this report as soon as you receive it.

Changes to the Title Report:

As you work on a loan things may change – as they so often do. For example, you are doing a cash-out refinance loan. You have submitted that loan and obtained loan approval. You then ordered the Title Report and the Appraisal. A week later you received the completed appraisal, on the subject property, and find that its value came in larger than you and your borrower expected. After reviewing that Appraisal then you call up your borrower and tell him or her the good news. Since the appraisal came in at a higher amount than they anticipated they then ask you if they could increase the loan amount on their loan. You explore that possibility and you find that you can. You call back that customer and agree on a new loan amount. In going forward, on requesting a new loan amount for your customer, you can expect to submit to that Lender a new 1008, 1003, and LE. However, you will also need to request an update on that borrower's Title Report (that you previously ordered). To do that, simply call that title company you ordered the Title Report from and inform them that you are increasing (or changing) the loan amount on that loan. They will then update that Title Report and fax (or email) to you that revised section (e.g. Schedule A). When you receive that revised section, of that Title Report, you then, in turn, fax or email that to the Lender on that loan. And, you do this with any subsequent changes to a borrower's loan that may impact how the information on their Title Report is reflected.

Title Insurance Fees and Costs:

Let's now talk about the fees and costs for Title Insurance. It has been my experience that the cost of Title Insurance is a function of the total loan amount – that will be shown on the title report. Thus, as the total loan amount increases - the cost of the title insurance increases in some proportion to that loan amount. Most title insurance companies, you will be working with, will have a fee sheet or schedule that lists the Basic Fees for title insurance. Any additional coverage or endorsements would be added on to this basic fee.

On a matrix sheet showing those fees you will generally find four columns. The far-left column showing different (and increasing) loan amounts with three columns to its right containing corresponding title insurance fees – based on the type of title insurance needed. For example, to the right of the **Total Loan Amount** column you will generally find the: **General Rate** (Cost to the Seller – for a purchase loan), the **Simultaneous Rate** (Cost to the Buyer – for a purchase loan), and the **Reorganization Rate** (Refinance Rate).

To give you an example of what I am talking about, please look at the matrix below:

AMOUNT UP TO	GENERAL RATE	SIMULT. RATE	REORGANIZATION
$90,000	$435	$181	$218
95,000	450	185	225
100,000	465	190	233
105,000	475	193	238

Purchase Loans:
If you are working on a purchase loan and want to determine what the Title Insurance cost would be for your borrowers then you would first find the line that has the **Amount Up To** (of your total loan amount) and match that to the cost in the **Simult. Rate** column. Thus, if the total loan amount were $100,000 then the basic Title Insurance fee would be $190.00. Now, let's say you will include the Extended Coverage on that policy and this costs an additional $35.00. This now adds up to $225.00. Also, keep in mind that the sales tax, of the state where the subject property is located, is usually added on to this figure. Therefore, if the sales tax were 8.0% then the total Title Insurance fee would add up to $243.00.

Refinance Loans:
Based on the total refinance loan amount - match that figure to the **Reorganization Rate** in the far-right column. Thus, if the total loan amount were $100,000 then the basic rate would be $233. And, as above with Extended Coverage added on, this basic rate would then be increased by $35.00 for a total of $268.00. And, don't forget the sales tax! Using a sales tax of 8.0% would then increase that Title Insurance fee to $289.44.

And finally, because many title companies also provide the closing of the loan let's take a quick look at the closing costs of closing a home loan or what is also referred to as The Escrow. Depending on where and with whom you close your customer's loan will determine the total Escrow or Closing fee. Although some Escrow companies have a flat fee to perform this service many use a sliding scale, like we saw in calculating the title insurance fee. In other words, as the total loan amount increases the Escrow fee increases as well. For example, here in Washington some title companies may use the following formula:

Flat fee of $35.00 + $3.00 per $1,000 of the total loan amount

Thus, if the total loan amount were $110,000 then the total Escrow or Closing fee would be $365.00.

Knowing how to calculate the costs for the Title Insurance and Loan Closing is important because this information is entered on your customer's Loan Estimate and the amounts you enter on that Loan Estimate should be as accurate as possible. I know, it's a good faith estimate but we should try to be as close as possible to what will actually be realized at loan closing when we first present the LE to our customers.

And finally, I find it is always a good idea to send to your loan closer a memo that tells them exactly how and to whom you wish those funds to be disbursed - that are going to any third-party providers (that you wish to be paid directly out of the funding) and your company's fees as well. This is what we call Escrow Instructions. On the following page is an example of an Escrow Instruction letter I have used quite often:

TO: Excellent Loan Closings
            Attn. Loan Closer

FROM: Your Name
            Mortgage Loan Originator

DATE: April 10, 2021

RE: Escrow Instructions for the James Smith's Refinance Loan.

At time of funding for James Smith's refinance 1st and 2nd mortgages I request that you pay all third-party providers directly from the funding from Best Rates Home Lenders. These third-party providers are:

1. Always Correct Title for the Title Insurance policies (2) for the 1st and 2nd mortgages.
2. Joseph Jones, the appraiser, who performed the appraisal on this subject property. (I have included a copy of Joseph Jone's appraisal invoice).

And please, pay the loan processing fee, credit report fee, and loan origination fee (combined) directly to *Your Company's Name* at:

Your Company's Name
Attn. Check Processor
Address, City State Zip

If you have any questions regarding this then please feel free to call me at (XXX) XXX_XXXX or fax me at (XXX) XXX_XXXX. I thank you.

<u>Warranty Deed:</u>
Also, before I leave this chapter on Title Insurance I felt it would not be complete without talking about the Warranty Deed. A Warranty Deed comes into play whenever there is a home or property purchase. It is sometimes referred to as The Seller's Warranty Deed because with this deed the Seller is warranting title to the Buyer. Now, what does that mean? It means that the Sellers are stating that they are the actual owners of the property, that they are giving Clear Title to the buyers, and that they will defend that title (on the subject property) they are passing (selling) to the buyers against any liens, encumbrances, or persons who may subsequently make a claim on title to that property. Doing this, creates what is also sometimes referred to as passing title that is free from encumbrances enabling the new purchasers to have "Quiet Enjoyment" of title to their new property.

Now, as mortgage loan originators, you and I normally do not get involved in the ordering of the Warranty Deed nor is this something we reflect on the LE on a purchase loan. However, you should know about the Warranty Deed and that at loan closing this is a cost (for the Warranty Deed) that the sellers will incur. In home purchase transactions, whereby the home is bought without a home loan (e.g. paid by cash), then usually this is the only Deed that is passed on to the homebuyer. This is because - without a home purchase loan there is not a Note or Deed of Trust. So, the Warranty Deed is very important to the homebuyers, in this type of home or property purchase. Because of its importance you would think that the Warranty Deed is required on all home purchase transactions. However, as one Title Officer recently told me, there are some States (of our great country) that do not require Warranty Deeds for home purchase transactions. Go figure?

And, I should also note that on home purchase loans that the homebuyers will need to obtain their own title insurance policy. Title insurance folks generally refer to these as the Lender's Title Insurance Policy and you can expect that the Buyers, on that home loan you are preparing, to have to purchase and pay for this. And, this cost would also be shown on your Loan Estimate you send to your home loan purchase customers. Fortunately, the cost of this policy is about half of what the Seller's (Warranty) title insurance policy costs. And while I am talking about the Loan Estimate, know that the total closing costs charged by your closing agent (title insurance company, attorney, etc.) is usually split between the home Seller and the Buyer. The exception to this would be, for example, if the Purchase and Sales Agreement stated otherwise. Therefore, if the total Closing Cost is $400.00 then you would normally show your purchasing home customers paying $200.00 of this.

In closing on this chapter of Title Insurance I've like to say that some title insurance companies (who may also do home loan closings) sometimes give free presentations on title insurance policies to title insurance people and mortgage loan professionals. If you are interested in attending one of these then I suggest discussing this with you Branch Manager and/or one of your Title Insurance companies within your area.

Okay. Now that you have a pretty good idea of what the Title Insurance Report is all about and what to look for when reviewing this document let's now move on and discuss another very important report that should also be reviewed when you first receive it – The Appraisal Report.

Chapter 21

THE APPRAISAL REPORT

Whether it is a residential refinance or purchase loan you will most likely need to order an Appraisal on the subject property to obtain an estimate of its current market value. In this chapter we are going to talk about what an Appraisal is as well as what you should look for in reviewing the Appraisal, once it is completed and delivered to you. Remember what I said about reviewing all documents and reports received on your home loans - whether it relates to your borrowers or to the subject property? The Appraisal is no exception. It can be one of the most influencing factors on your loan. This is because the appraised value of the subject property will most likely determine the maximum LTV that your borrowers will be able to have on their loan (within the limits of the loan program you are setting them up on).

Most mortgage loan originators I have worked with merely look at their Appraisal to see what the appraiser came up with, in terms of the total market value of that subject property. If the subject property "came in at value" (to what he or she expected or needed to make that loan work) then sometimes I see them raise their arms (as in a sign of victory) and hear them yell out, "Wahoo" (just like Homer Simpson). They then put the Appraisal aside and look at it no further. Yet, even though the Appraisal did come in "at value" there could be something written in this report, by that appraiser, that could be a concern for your prospective Lender. So we need to look further into this report - beyond just the appraised value of the subject property.

The Consumer Financial Protection Bureau (CFPB) amended Regulation B, which implements the Equal Credit Opportunity Act (ECOA). This amendment revised Regulation B and implemented the Appraisal Rule which, part of, concerns requiring creditors to now provide to home loan applicants free copies of all appraisals and other written valuations that were required and provided in connection with a home loan secured by a 1st lien on a dwelling. This Rule also requires creditors to notify applicants in writing that copies of their appraisal will be provided to them promptly (recall the Appraisal Disclosure. However, you can't charge a home loan customer a fee to provide to them a copy of their home appraisal). Although you cannot charge an upfront fee for the appraisal you can, of course, charge a reasonable fee to your home loan applicants for their home appraisal (normally within the Loan Estimate as a loan cost). And, you now will need to provide home loan applicants a free copy of their appraisal at least 3 business days after you received it or before home loan closing.

I never charged a home loan customer for their copy of their home appraisal. Generally, what I would do is request that the Appraiser send me three copies of the appraisal: One for the creditor, one for that (our) customer's home loan file, and one for the home loan customer. And, I would hand deliver that appraisal to the home loan borrower when I attended their home loan closing (or mailed it to them if they were an out-of-town customers). So, this Rule does change things regarding the time requirements as to when home loan customers must receive their appraisal(s). This Appraisal Rule went into effect January 18, 2014.

According to CFPB's Appraisal Rule lenders (Creditors) are required to:

- Tell their home loan customers, within business three days of receiving their mortgage loan application (1003), that they will receive a copy of their appraisal.

- Tell their home loan customers that they will also receive a free copy of any additional home valuations that were required and made: For example, an automated valuation model report, or a broker price opinion.

- Must provide these free copies to the home loan applicant either promptly after these reports have been completed and received or within three business days before their home loan closes. However, creditors are permitted to charge loan applicants reasonable fees for the costs of appraisals or other written valuations unless applicable law provides otherwise.

And, just as with some of the requirements of the Loan Estimate and Closing Disclosure it is ultimately the creditor's responsibilities to satisfy the above and delivery on the requirements of the Appraisal Rule.

In amending the Equal Credit Opportunity Act the CFPB also wanted to make it easier to know whether unlawful discrimination may have taken place during a customer's home loan process. There are two lists of federal Protected Class Members: Under the Equal Credit Opportunity Act and the Fair Housing Act. And, according to this Rule lenders cannot discriminate against a home loan borrower because they are a member of a Protected Class. Nor consider the fact that a home loan borrower is a member of a Protected Class in any aspect of doing a home loan. I should also mention here that the Equal Credit Opportunity Act has special rules restricting when lenders may consider Age and Receipt of Public Assistance (two Protected Classes under the ECOA).

Now, those that provide Appraisal services (real estate appraisers) should have an appraisal license issued by that state they are appraising real estate in. Also, you want to be sure that the appraiser is licensed in the state in which the subject property (to be appraised) is located. When you first talk to an appraiser, about doing an Appraisal, also find out if they carry Errors and Omissions (E & O) Insurance. Many Lenders require appraisers to have this type of insurance coverage.

It used to be that when an appraiser was doing a full tilt-boogey Appraisal, on a 1 - 4 family unit (regardless of what type of home it was) then that appraiser would use the ole Uniform Residential Appraisal Report (URAR) Form 1004. Like our 1003, this is the number that you will find on the lower right-hand corner of the appraisal form. However, since November 1, 2005 that has changed. Fannie Mae came out with a new version of the Appraisal Form 1004 and requires this form to be used only on one-unit SFR properties.

And, that's for a full Appraisal. If an Appraisal is a Drive-By (or only requires an exterior inspection) then another type of Appraisal form is required. And, if that wasn't enough, if the subject property is anything other than a one-unit SFR then a different type of Appraisal form is required for each. The following list the various types of Appraisal forms and what they are required for:

FORM NUMBER	PURPOSE OF APPRAISAL
1004	Full Appraisal for a One-Unit SFR
1004C	Manufactured Home Appraisal Report
1004MC	Market Conditions Addendum
1004D	Appraisal Update / Completion Report
1073	Full Appraisal for a Condo
1075	Exterior Inspection for a Condo
2055	Exterior Inspection for a One-Unit SFR
2090	Full Appraisal for a Co-op
2095	Exterior Inspection for Co-op
1025	Full Appraisal for a 2-4 Multi-Family Unit

In addition to requiring these new Appraisal forms, depending on the type of subject property, Fannie Mae has also changed the format of the URAR 1004, and in many cases the wording in it as well. It appears that Fannie Mae has done this to eliminate (or reduce) as much as possible any subjectivity by the appraiser: Thereby instilling an acceptable level of consistency within these new Appraisals. For example, in the previous Appraisal forms there were areas where the appraiser could state their subjective opinion regarding that area of inspection. With these new Appraisal forms, most of those areas have been replaced with a "Yes" or "No" response. In doing this, one of Fannie Mae's goals is for appraisers (and Lenders) to be held to an enforceable level of accountability. And, of course, eliminate or reduce any areas on an Appraisal where there could be fraud, resulting in misrepresenting the subject property and/or inflating the actual value of a property.

As you can see, from the above list, an Appraisal is either a Full Appraisal or an Exterior Inspection. Now, what does that mean? Well, to summarize:

1. **The Full Residential Appraisal:**
    This is the one you will usually order and is required by Lenders for most home loans you will work on. It requires an inspection, by the appraiser, of the interior and exterior areas of the subject property.

2. **Exterior Inspection:**
    This is what is often referred to as a Limited or Drive-by Appraisal. Some loans will be such that the Lender will require only an Exterior or Drive-by Appraisal. As the name implies, the appraiser doesn't need to inspect the interior of the property but only examines the exterior of the property from the street as well as the other features he or she normally analyzes in completing an Appraisal of that type.

Most Appraisals that you will be ordering, I believe, will be for a one-unit SFR. Therefore, for our purposes here, we will be reviewing the details of the new URAR 1004. The average URAR 1004 Appraisal has about 12 pages to it and generally has the following in estimating the value of the subject property:

1. The first 3 pages of an Appraisal has written text, which describes the subject property and compares the features of that subject property to 3 - 4 other homes with similar features. Those other homes (the subject is compared to) are called Comps: That's short for Comparable Sales. Also, you will see that the first 3 pages have eleven sections.

2. Next are 3 more pages of text and at the bottom of the 6th page is what we have all been waiting for: "Appraised Value of the Subject Property."

3. Following that are 2 pages displaying pictures of the subject property taken by the Appraiser. Shown are pictures of the front and back of the home and the interior of the home. Also included is what is called a "Street View." This is a picture showing one side of the street as viewed while standing in the middle of it - in front of the subject property.

4. A Page showing the Frontal (viewed) pictures of those homes used as Comps.

5. Then a page showing a sketch of the Floor Plan of the subject property.

6. The next page shows a Location Map pointing to where the subject property is located and also pointing to where each Comp is located as well. This visually shows the location and distance of the Comps to the subject property.

7. The next page is what is called a Plat Map, which gives you a closer view of property lines, dimensions, and possible easements of the subject and also shows how the Legal Description of that property was determined.

8. And finally, the last 2 pages of the Appraisal are composed of text by the appraiser that you generally see on all Appraisals.

While it's true that either you (the Mortgage Loan Originator) or your Loan Processor will order the Appraisal on the subject property it is now ultimately the Lender that is responsible for ensuring that the subject property provides adequate collateral for the mortgage loan. For most loans, Fannie Mae requires that the Lender obtain a signed and complete appraisal report that accurately reflects the market value, condition, and marketability of the property. However, some loans may be eligible for an appraisal waiver. And, an appraisal is not required if the lender exercises the waiver and complies with the related requirements.

If an Appraisal is obtained then the Lender is responsible for:
- Compliance with the Appraiser Independence Requirements,
- Selection of the Appraiser,
- Compliance with the Uniform Appraisal Dataset (UAD),
- Ensuring the Appraiser has utilized sound reasoning and provided evidence to support the methodology chosen to develop the value opinion, particularly in cases that are not covered by Fannie Mae policy,

- Successful submission of the Appraisal through the UCDP prior to delivery, and
- Continually evaluating the Appraiser's work through the quality control process.

Before we get into the details of reviewing the new 1004 Appraisal let me go over some important points you should know about Appraisals. A common confusion among customers, as well as some Mortgage loan originators, is: Who does the Appraisal belong to? True, the customer will ultimately pay for it and get a copy of it, so it just makes sense that it belongs to them. Right? I'm afraid not. The Appraisal belongs to whoever ordered that Appraisal. This is true even if the customer (and/or borrower) paid the Appraiser directly. If you ordered the Appraisal, on behalf of your customer, to move towards completion of processing that loan then that Appraisal (when done) belongs to your company. On the very front page of that Appraisal the appraiser types: The address of the subject property, the date completed, prepared by (the appraiser), and who that Appraisal was prepared for (this will show your company's name and address). That is whom the Appraisal belongs to.

So, what does this mean? It means that your company has the rights and privileges of the use of that Appraisal. In other words, no one else (or another company) can use that Appraisal without your permission (in writing). This will become increasingly clear to you after you have submitted a loan to a Lender, with an Appraisal (you ordered) included. For example, if your loan is approved then one of the Prior-To-Doc conditions might be for you to Assign that Appraisal to that Lender. In other words, to transfer your rights and uses of that Appraisal to that Lender. Otherwise, that Lender may not be able to legally use that Appraisal as part of their Underwriting process for that loan and after the loan is completed - for it to become a part of that Lender's loan file. That request, by a Lender to assign your rights (to them) on an Appraisal, is quite common. To do this, you could type a letter to that Lender, on your company's letterhead, saying something like the following:

> I, Joseph Smith of XYZ Mortgage, assign my rights and uses of the Appraisal on the Billy Bob Gator's property, located at: 1215 East 4th Swampland Way and completed by Jeffrey Higgins of Higgins Appraisals, Inc., on January 18, 2019, to Best Darn Loans, Inc.

Once you have sent this to the Lender then they have the (legal) rights to that Appraisal and can fully use it in underwriting, approving, and funding that loan.

And, while I am talking about ownership of an Appraisal I feel that this is the proper time to also talk about a another appraisal ruling, under the Uniform Standards of Professional Appraisal Practice (USPAP). Whew! That's a long-winded title. This Appraisal ruling that came into effect January 1, 2005 impacts and changes when a new Appraisal is required (to be ordered) for a mortgage loan. Under this ruling, if a home loan buyer or home loan borrower wishes to refinance or purchase a property then a new Appraisal is required. This departs from the past when Lenders and mortgage companies could transfer their rights (of an Appraisal) from one Lender or mortgage company to another and use that Appraisal (as it was or have it re-inspected) to determine whether there have been any significant changes since that Appraisal was originally done.

Let me give you an example of how this new appraisal ruling applies:

Your new loan customers meet with you because they were not pleased with the service they received at XYZ Mortgage. They previously met with XYZ mortgage, to refinance their home, about 1 month ago. They were approved and an appraisal was ordered and completed. They now want to do the loan with you and want to use that same appraisal (which they paid for). Remember that whoever orders the appraisal owns the rights of that appraisal - regardless of who paid for that appraisal directly. Also, secondary markets will not accept appraisals ordered by borrowers. If a borrower pays directly, also known as COD, it is merely an arranged payment for appraisal services between the borrower and the lender; the borrower has no claim to that appraisal - except that they are entitled to receive a copy of the appraisal from the lender if they request a copy in writing within ninety days of application for their loan.

Under this new ruling they would not be able to use that appraisal in their new loan with you. However, you could contact and ask the appraiser, who did that appraisal, if they would reappraise that property. And, because of the recent age of that appraisal also ask them if they could give you a discount on the cost of that appraisal. That, of course, would be up to them. But most appraisers I have met are fair and have been willing to consider giving a discount on completing an appraisal of that type. However, my feeling is that the further away you get from the original appraisal's effective date then the less of a discount you can expect.

But my main point here is: Whenever a borrower goes to another lender then a new Appraisal is now required. So, when a new loan (with a new lender) is begun then a new Appraisal is required – regardless of how old (or recent) that previous Appraisal, on the subject property, was done.

Now, is a new Appraisal required for all subsequent home loan transactions? The answer to that is "Yes" and "No". Here's what I mean by that: Fannie Mae will allow the use of an Origination Appraisal for a subsequent transaction if the following requirements are met:

- The subsequent transaction may only be a Limited Cash-Out Refinance,
- The Appraisal Report must not be more than 12 months old on the Note date of the subsequent transaction.
- If the Appraisal Report is greater than 4 months old on the date of the Note and Mortgage then an Appraisal Update is required (See below).
- The Lender must ensure that the property has not undergone any significant remodeling, renovation, or deterioration to the extent that the improvement or deterioration of the property would materially affect the Market Value of the subject property, and
- The borrower and the Lender/Client must be the same on the original and subsequent transaction.

Continuing along, with the above, I'd like to now talk about the Age of the Appraisal the requirements for updating an Appraisal. Now, when an appraisal is obtained then the property must be appraised within the 12 months that precede the date of the Note and Mortgage.

When an Appraisal Report is more than four months old, on the date of the Note and Mortgage, then regardless of whether the property was Appraised as proposed or existing construction, the Appraiser must inspect the exterior of the property and review the current market data to determine whether the property has declined in value since the date of the original Appraisal. This inspection and results of the analysis must be reported on the Appraisal Update and/or Completion Report (Form 1004D). When an Appraiser does complete a Form 1004D then:

- If the appraiser indicates on the Form 1004D that the property value has declined, then the lender must obtain a new appraisal for the property.

- If the appraiser indicates on the Form 1004D that the Property Value has not declined then the Lender may proceed with the loan in process without requiring any additional fieldwork.

Below are a couple more points, I would like to mention, regarding completion of the 1004D:

- The Appraisal update must occur within the four months that precede the date of the Note and Mortgage,

- The Original Appraiser should complete the Appraisal Update. However, Lenders are allowed to use Substitute Appraisers,

- When updates are completed by Substitute Appraisers then the Substitute Appraiser must review the Original Appraisal and express an opinion about whether the Original Appraiser's opinion of market value was reasonable on the date of the Original Appraisal Report, and

- The lender must note in the file why the Original Appraiser was not used.

Now, when should you order the Appraisal? I usually do not order the Appraisal until I have approval on that loan and/or I can see that the loan has an excellent chance of going to the closing table. I have seen mortgage loan originators order the Appraisal as soon as they obtain a completed 1003. I don't recommend this. If the Appraisal gets completed and the loan is subsequently declined or there are problems that (you later discover) prevent that loan from being doable - who's going to pay for that Appraisal? Most likely, not the customer but the mortgage loan originator who ordered it. So, wait until you are fairly certain you have a doable loan before you order the Appraisal. This doesn't mean wait until the last minute: No, I am not saying that. An Appraisal can take from 1 to 2 weeks (or longer in some cases) - depending on where the subject property is located and how busy the Appraisers are at that time. However, you do want to order the Appraisal as soon as you think it wise - just don't jump the gun on it.

Let's now take a look at a URAR 1004 Appraisal and at those areas that I suggest you review when you first receive your Appraisal. For our discussion here, if you have a full 1004 Appraisal available to you then please get it now. Otherwise, please obtain this report in pdf format by going to Fannie Mae's site. And, please use Google Chrome in doing this: https://www.fanniemae.com/content/guide_form/1004.pdf

In reviewing the Appraisal Report I will discuss pages 1, 2, 3, and 6. Now, looking at these first three pages you can see that they are separated into different Sections. Each section focuses on a different aspect of the subject property. Below, I'll list those Sections in the order that they are presented on the Appraisal Report and suggest what you should be checking out within each Section.

Page 1:

Subject:

This Section identifies the street address, legal description of the subject property, its parcel number, and its annual property taxes. You will also find here the Borrower's Name and the name of the Owner of Public Record. This item "Owner of Public Record" is new. This is an area you definitely should check out. The Borrower's Name and Owner of Public Record, on an O/O refinance loan, should be the same. This area is used to detect any fraudulent transactions and/or to prevent flipping sales. Below that, the appraiser indicates whether that transaction (which requires this Appraisal) is a purchase, refinance, or other.

And lastly, another new item that has been added onto this Appraisal asks the appraiser, "Is the subject property currently offered for sale or has it been for sale in the twelve months prior to the effective date of this Appraisal?" If this is marked "Yes" then that could be a problem for your loan customers (and your Lender) if they are now wishing to do a refinance loan. Just look this area over quickly.

Contract:

This Section is reserved for those home purchase loan transactions. Two areas you definitely want to check out here are: 1. In the right-hand side of this Section it asks, "Is the property seller the owner of public record," and 2. In the lower half of this Section it also asks if there is any financial assistance (loan charges, sale concessions, gift, or down-payment assistance, etc.) to be paid by any party on behalf of the borrower. If the appraiser marked a "Yes" then that appraiser will also, below that, write its dollar amount worth. This is important, because if that appraiser did mark a "Yes" then that could impact the total loan amount for your customer (i.e. sales concessions).

Neighborhood:

Now, here is a Section you should always check out. The upper part of this Section describes some common characteristics of the neighborhood and alludes to the condition of that neighborhood as well. Always check out which boxes the Appraiser entered an "X" in - where it states Location. You want that "X" to be in either Urban or Suburban. Because some Lenders just Do Not lend to properties in Rural areas. Also, check out Growth Rate (below Built-Up). Lenders like to see a Neighborhood, of the subject property, experiencing a Rapid or Stable growth rate with Property Values Increasing and/or Stable (over time). If the appraiser placed an "X" in the box indicating that the Property Values are Slow then you may have a concern here. If there are any adverse conditions or considerations then it will be noted in the middle part of this Section. Appraisers will then state the Boundaries and a Description of that Neighborhood. Following that, appraisers will make a few comments about the Market Conditions of that Neighborhood – that supports their conclusions stated above. What you are looking for is anything negative about the neighborhood or the market conditions of that neighboring area.

Site:

This section has a number of different but important subjects worth checking out. One very important area I always like to check out (because I have been burned once or twice here) is: What classification of Zoning is the subject located in. Look at the second line in the upper left-hand corner where it states "Specific Zoning Classification and Zoning Description." Our question here is: Is the subject (a residential home) located in a Residentially Zoned area? This is important because if the home is located in a Commercially Zoned area (which happens sometimes) this could be a problem with your Lender. For a residential home loan, you want that (appraiser) to state something like R-1 Single Family Residential. If it does then great. However, if you have done your homework and previously ordered a Property Profile (as suggested in this book) then you should already know what the Zoning is on that subject property. Also, look in the upper area of this Section where it states, "Highest & best use as improved." Did the appraiser put an "X" in Present Use? If he did then good. Otherwise, if he put an "X" in "Other Use" then make sure you read his comments at the bottom of this Section.

The bottom half of this Section addresses the Utilities available to the subject and whether they are Public or Private. Look for anything here out of the ordinary. For example: a private well or septic sewer system. If a private well is shown here then does that well need to be inspected? If the subject uses a septic sewer system then when was the last time it was pumped? Of particular interest here (that you want to check out) are the line items regarding FEMA (Federal Emergency Management Agency). Is the subject Not in a Flood Zone? Good. Then your customers don't have to carry Flood Insurance.

Improvements:

Improvements in Appraisal jargon basically mean immovable objects that have become attached to the land. Improvements can be "to" or "on" the land. This Section describes or states improvements "on" the land. Most often it's referring to the home and outbuildings.

The upper-half of this Section has four categories: 1. General Description, 2. Foundation, 3. Exterior Description (materials/conditions), and 4. Interior (materials/conditions). Look this area over carefully. What did the appraiser write here? Are all the improvements, to the subject property, completed? If not, then what yet needs to be done and does that impact the appraised value of that property?

In the bottom half of this Section also review what that appraiser stated regarding the condition of the property and whether it conforms to the neighborhood it is located in.

Again, what you are looking for here are any negative statements about the subject property.

Page 2:

Sales Comparison Approach:

This Section shows the results of using the Sales Comparison Analysis approach. What the appraiser is doing here is comparing features and amenities of the subject property (listed on the far left of this Section) to at least three - sometimes four other comparable properties (that are called Comps). Those Comps are properties that are comparable to the subject's main features, amenities, and structure - that are located within a radius of no farther than: 10 blocks within a town, 1 mile in a suburban area, and 10 miles of a home with acreage - from the subject <u>and</u> has been sold within the last 12 months (that's why they call it Sales Comparison). You can see here that each Comp, located in a separate column, is compared to the subject's features listed on the far-left column. Differences between the Comps and the Subject, for each lined feature, are shown in each Comps' column under the heading + (-) $ Adjustments.

What you should look for (and what Lenders look at) is any <u>significant</u> variances (on the Comps) from the subject. If a variance on any of the lined items here is greater than 10% or 15% total net adjustment and/or 25% gross adjustment - then that appraiser will need to comment on that and explain why this is so. If there are a lot of significant variances on the Comps, shown on that Appraisal, then the Lender may have concerns regarding the validity of that Appraisal. Also, look at the bottom of the columns for each Comp. On the bottom right-hand side is the adjusted Sales price that Comp sold for. Just below that figure shows the Net: and Gross: Adjustments on that Comp. Does each Comp show a Net Adjustment of less than 15% of the Comparable Sales Price? If it does then good. Remember that those Comps must support the value of the subject property.

And finally, in the bottom-half of this Section, the appraiser comments on their research of the subject and addresses whether this property has been sold within the three years prior to this Appraisal. At the bottom of this Section the appraiser also states the Indicated Value of the subject property - by the Sales Comparison Approach.

Reconciliation:

In this Section the appraiser states the Indicated Value, of the subject property, by the Sales Comparison Approach. Here, the appraiser also states what the Indicated Value is using the Cost Approach and Income Approach - if used in that Appraisal. In this Section the appraiser reconciles those approaches used to estimate the value of the subject property. That is, the appraiser is basically weighting the approaches to value according to their relevance. In theory, if the Sales Comparison Approach was $102,000, Cost Approach value was $100,000, and the Income Approach was $102,000 then the appraiser could reconcile the value (of the subject property) to be $101,000. However, in practice, the value is almost always reconciled to the value estimated in the Sales Comparison Approach in regards to residential property.

When you first look at this Section make sure you check out the area in the middle left-hand side stating "This Appraisal is made" and see if the Appraiser placed an "X" in the "As Is" box. If he did then good. Otherwise, if he checked the other available boxes there (to the right of it) then the Appraisal is based on those changes taking place (which the Appraiser will comment on in this report as well). That means that the actual Value of the subject here is contingent on those changes, alternations or whatever, occurring or to be done before the actual Appraised Value (as stated) is realized. So, be sure to check out this area.

At the bottom of this Section the Appraiser then states the Market Value of the subject property. Here I would like to say that it is generally considered that Market Value is the most probable price that a property should bring in during a competitive and open market under all conditions requisite to a fair sale, the buyer and seller, each acting prudently, knowledgeably and assuming the price is not affected by undue stimulus.

Implicit in the above definition is the consummation of a sale as of a specified date and the passing of Title from a seller to a buyer under conditions whereby:

- Buyer and Seller are typically motivated;

- Both parties are well informed or well advised, and each acting in what he or she considers his/her own best interest;

- A reasonable time is allowed for exposure in the open market;

- Payment is made in terms of cash in U.S. dollars or in terms of financial arrangements comparable thereto; and

- The price represents the normal consideration for the property sold unaffected by special or creative financing or Sales Concessions granted by anyone associated with the sale.

Page 3:

Additional Comments:
This is another area you definitely want to have a look at. If the appraiser has any concerns about the condition of the subject it will be noted here. For example, if the paint on the back of the home is peeling off and exposing the wood underneath then this might be a concern and noted as such. If you see this on the Appraisal then this could mean that the owners of that house may need to get that side of the house painted before that home loan closes.

Cost Analysis:
I should note here that there are actually three approaches that an appraiser could use to estimate the value of the subject property: 1. Sales Comparison Analysis: Also referred to as the Market Sales Comparison Approach, 2. Cost Analysis Approach, and 3. Income Analysis Approach (this is used on income-producing properties). This Section reveals the appraiser's findings using the Cost Analysis Approach (i.e. Indicated Value by Cost Approach). The most commonly relied on approach, in residential appraising, is the Sales

Comparison Approach. Rarely are the Cost and Income Approaches relied on in residential appraising. However, any approach that could be considered applicable should be considered by the appraiser. Then a final opinion of value is rendered only after reconciling all applicable approaches to value.

The data, for the Cost Approach, is obtained from several different means: Such as published cost tables and local data obtained directly from builders. Appraisers may use the Cost Approach as additional support to the value indicated in the Sales Comparison Approach.

Income Approach:

As I mentioned above, when discussing the Cost Analysis Approach, the new URAR 1004 does not require the appraiser to use the Income Approach in determining the value of the subject property (for a one-unit SFR). Therefore, unless it is a NOO property you could expect this Section to be blank.

However, if you are doing a loan on a Non-Owner Occupied (rental) property then this is an approach that the Lender will require as well. If the subject property is rented then the appraiser should estimate a rental amount per month and a monthly rent multiplier to estimate a market value of the subject property, based on the Income Approach. Again, if it is a NOO property then what does that figure state? Is there is much difference between that figure and the final Appraised Value of the subject found on page six?

PUD Information:

This stands for Planned Unit Development. This is somewhat like a condominium. There may or may not be a borrower's association there. These types of developments allow for flexibility in zoning and/or have commonly held amenities, such as a swimming pool. If you are doing a home loan on a PUD then be sure to check out this area and see if all requirements for doing a PUD loan, with your Lender, are satisfied here. For example, your Lender may require that a minimum number of units be available and/or occupied in that PUD. Do you see that here? Also, do you see that there is a Homeowner's Association, with that PUD, requiring monthly and/or annual dues? This is important because this is information you will use in qualifying that customer and becomes a part of their PITI monthly payment on their new home loan. However, if this Appraisal were not for a PUD then this Section would be blank.

Page 6:

And finally, on page 6 of the Appraisal and at the bottom of that page is the all-important figure that you have been patiently (and perhaps anxiously) waiting for: The Appraised Value of the Subject Property. Why Fannie Mae decided to put that on page 6, I just cannot figure out. In my opinion it should be on page 1 of this Appraisal. It's what we have all been waiting for.

It's kind of like writing a formal report to the CEO (Chief Executive Officer) of a company. The first page, of that report, should summarize the results of that study, and the rest of that report presents the various approaches used in that study: The findings, any concerns, recommendations for improvements, and the benefits of implementing those recommendations. You write it that way because most CEOs don't have the time to leaf through a report to get to the bottom line. They will read the summary on the front page and, if they wish to, they can (later) read the supporting documentation. Just like this, I would like to see the Appraised value of the subject property stated on page one on this new Appraisal form, with two boxes below it: "As Is" and "Subject To." The appraiser would check one of those boxes. And, if the "Subject To" box was checked then, certainly, I would review that Appraisal Report in greater detail to determine why and what work, on that home, yet needs to be done (if any) to make that loan happen.

It just takes a few minutes for you to go over and review the important points of the Appraisal I have discussed above. If you do this then you will have a much better handle on what is going on with your loan and if there are any concerns here you think need following up on. The timing of doing this is important as well. You should review your Appraisal Report as soon as you get it and definitely before it is sent to your targeted Lender. Doing this should give you ample time to anticipate any possible (Lender) concerns and request any changes on that Appraisal, if necessary (and of course whether the appraiser is able to make that change). For example, the frontal picture of the subject property may have been taken during a snowstorm and is not clearly as visible as you would like it. You might then request another photo from that appraiser.

If you do review your Appraisals, as I have suggested here, then you are doing what every successful and professional Mortgage loan originator does: Anticipating the needs and requirements of the Lender you are sending your loans to.

I would also like to mention at this point that if you know (or suspect) that you will be or are originating a 'High Risk Mortgage' then you can anticipate that you will need two home appraisals on the subject property. Please see High-Risk Mortgages for more information on this subject.

Before I leave this chapter on Appraisals let me mention another term you may hear every once in a while: a 442. A 442 is a Certificate of Completion that is completed by an appraiser (usually the original or last one) that certifies that the work on the subject property has been finished and that the value is as stated in the original Appraisal (previously completed). You will see the need for these when working on construction home loans and when further improvements need to be done to the subject property such as in an Escrow Holdbacks (see Escrow Holdbacks). Again, the 442 confirms that the work and/or improvements have been completed and that the appraised value (afterwards) came in (hopefully) as originally appraised.

If your vision is getting a little blurry from looking at those Appraisal Report forms – I understand. Just grab another cup of coffee or tea and move on to next Section that discusses Loan Processing.

Section V

LOAN PROCESSING

This section of the book is appropriately titled "Loan Processing" because in this section we are going to apply everything you have learned into what Mortgage loan originators actually do in processing, submitting, and preparing for the closing of their mortgage loans. So, for me this is the fun section of this book because here we're going to put it all together and build on everything you have previously read and learned. Within this section you will also find a chapter that contains those mortgage lending regulations and laws you need to be familiar with and employ, when originating and processing mortgage loans, so that you and your loans are In Compliance.

The final chapter, of this Section, contains a checklist or flowchart to assist you when you first begin originating and processing your loans. After you have originated loans for a while then most of what is on that flowchart will become "second nature" to you.

To address these subjects - this section contains the following five chapters:

- ➢ Processing Your Loans
- ➢ The Remarks Page
- ➢ Loan File Stacking Order
- ➢ Mortgage Lending Regulations
- ➢ Putting It All together

Okay, grab another cup of coffee or tea and let's get started with that loan phase Mortgage loan originators normally go through after they have completed the initial paperwork on a loan file: Processing Your Loans.

Chapter 22

PROCESSING YOUR LOANS

In this chapter on Processing Your Loans I am not referring to what your Loan Processor will be doing on your loans but what most Mortgage loan originators need to be aware of, as well as do, in processing their loan files. Although many times there tends to exist some crossover of what the Loan Processor normally does and what the Mortgage loan originator will do. With that said, let us begin this chapter.

At this point in the loan process let's say you have met with your customers and have a completed and fully signed 1003 with signed Loan Disclosures. You have returned back to your office and are looking over this loan file to determine what additional supporting documents you anticipate the Lender of this loan may require. Remember when we discussed qualifying your borrowers and the three main things that you (and the Lenders) look at in qualifying and approving borrowers are: Credit, Capacity (income), and Collateral? In this chapter we will look at what are the common document needs that most Conforming Lenders will ask for when encountering the following:

I. CREDIT:

You will most likely need to order a 3-bureau Credit Report for starters here. If you have any questions, at this time, regarding reading this report then please refer to Chapter 18 on Reading the Credit Report. Now, if any of the following that is listed below relates to what you are seeing on the Credit Report then I have listed those documents and/or information that you will most likely need to obtain.

1. Recent Previous Bankruptcy:
* Copy of the Full Bankruptcy papers.
* Sometimes Lenders like a letter of explanation stating what happened (that caused that Bankruptcy).

2. Derogatory Information:
* 30-days or more late payments showing. Call your customer and ask them about these.
* If any accounts shown as late are actually current - documents proving this.
* Collection Accounts: Were those settled and paid off? If so then documents showing that.

3. Child Support or Alimony Payments Being Made:
* Copy of complete Divorce Decree and/or Separation Settlement Agreement.
* Statement showing payments made and received for the past 1 to 2 years.

4. Accounts Show up on the Credit Report that Do Not Belong to Borrower:
- Call the Credit Reporting company (that you ordered the Credit Report from) and have them do a research on the account or accounts. There is usually a fee per account researched.

5. Many Inquires (e.g. over 6 Inquires) Shown on the Credit Report:
- Call customer and ask them about these.
- The Lender may request a letter, from the borrower, explaining why those Inquires are shown and (hopefully) for them to state that they have not obtained additional credit (and debt) since beginning their loan application.

In your meeting with your customers you found out what their Gross Monthly Income is (now entered on the 1003) and now with the Credit Report you have a more accurate picture (and list) of all the borrower's monthly debts. Also, you now know what their Credit Scores are. It's an excellent time to do a qualifying analysis on your customers. And, based on your best guess (at this time) of the loan program you are considering or might suggest you can determine what the Housing and Total Debts Ratios might look like. This gives you your first and important clue as to what type of loan your borrowers will most likely qualify for. Hopefully, it is the one that will exactly match the goals of their loan that they spoke to you earlier about.

II. CAPACITY (INCOME):
When you met with your customers and completed the 1003 you listed all the income sources of your borrowers. Your Lender will most likely require documentation showing that your borrowers actually earn and/or receive the income that they told you about (and is on that 1003).

1. Works for an Employer - Salary:
- Current Paystub covering a full 30-day period with Year-To-Date figures
- Last 2-years W2's.

2. Is a Commissioned Employee:
- Current Paystub covering a full 30-day period with Year-To-Date figures
- Last 2 Years (full) Tax Returns. Lenders will generally take the average of the commissioned income over the last 2 years. And sometimes, those Lenders may also include the YTD income figures, on that customer's paystub, in averaging out their monthly commission income.

3. Retirement Income or Disabled Income:
- Document Showing Individual is Retired or Disabled
- Retirement and/or Disabled Annual Award letter.

4. Social Security Income:

- Annual Award Letter from the Social Security Administration. These Annual Award Letters are usually received, by the recipients, during the months of January and February.

Remember that we can usually "Gross-Up" this type of non-taxed income. Check with your targeted Lender on what percentage they will allow.

5. Investment Income (Stocks, Mutual Funds, Trust Estate, Etc.):

- Stock Certificate and/or Document showing current value of Investment.
- Document showing owner or recipient (your customers) are receiving what they told you - and at what time they receive it. Statement from the Investment Company and/or their Bank Statements confirming those amounts are being or have been deposited into their checking and/or savings accounts.

6. Child Support Payments and/or Alimony Payments Received:

- Copy of complete Divorce Decree and/or Separation Settlement Agreement.
- Copy of recent bank statements showing deposits of payments received.
- Copies of canceled checks of payments received for the past 24 months.

Remember that most Conforming Lenders require that Child Support income needs to continue for the next 3 years in order to include that in qualifying them. Be sure to ask how long those payments will continue (or what are the ages of the children).

7. Rental Income from O/O and/or NOO Property:

- Document showing how many years the customer has been renting this property (shows time of experience as a Landlord).
- Copy of the current and signed Lease Agreement from the Renters.

Using Rental Income for Qualifying Purposes:

I would also like to add the following current FNMA policy requirements to determine the amount of Rental Income from the subject property that can be used for qualifying purposes - when the borrower is purchasing a 2 – 4 unit Principal Residence or 1 - 4 unit Investment Property, then the Lender must consider the following:

A. Rental Income Qualifying Purposes:

- If the borrower currently owns a Principal Residence (or has a current housing expense), and...
- Has at least a one-year history of receiving Rental Income or documented property management experience...

Then, there is No Restriction on the amount of Rental Income that can be used.

B. Rental Income Qualifying Purposes:
- If the borrower currently owns a Principal Residence (or has a current housing expense), and…
- Has less than one-year history of receiving rental income or documented property management experience…

Then, for a Principal Residence, rental income in an amount not exceeding the PITIA of the subject property can be added to the borrower's gross income. Or, for an Investment Property, rental income can only be used to offset the PITIA of the subject property.

C. Rental Income Qualifying Purposes:
- If the borrower currently does not own a Principal Residence, and…
- Does not have a current Housing Expense.

Then, Rental Income from the subject property cannot be used.

However, I would also like to mention that this policy does not apply to HomeReady Loans with Rental Income from an accessory unit. And, the above policies apply to both DU and Manually Underwritten loans.

8. Self-Employed:
- Copy of Business License.
- Year-To-Date (YTD) Income Statement.
- Last 2 Years (Complete) Tax Returns.
- Contracts & other documents showing business is a viable and ongoing concern.

9. Gaps Between Jobs of Greater than 30 days - Within the Last Two Years:
- Letter of Explanation stating reason for the extended time between Jobs – having an Employment Gap of 30 days or more between jobs.

10. College or Course of Study Related to Current Employment Position:
Here your borrower may have been in his or her current position for less than 2 years with no prior related working experience. However, they previously attended a college or took courses that directly relates to their current employment. Their time spent at that college or time in those courses could be applied to this 2-year work experience requirement.
- Copy of Diploma and/or Transcripts.

When it comes to qualifying your customers based on their income sources - be prepared to ask for documentation that substantiates what your customers told you. If you cannot show documentation for an income source (to that Lender) you may not be able to use that income source in qualifying your customers.

III. COLLATERAL - THE SUBJECT PROPERTY

This may seem pretty straightforward. You know you are most likely going to have to order an appraisal on the subject property in order to obtain a firm number on its value. However, for review, there are some questions you should have asked when first talking to your customers about doing their loan:

1. **What Kind of Property Is It?**
   - Stick Built
   - Manufactured Home. If yes, what year was it built and what size is it?
   - Modular Home
   - Farm Property

2. **How Many Units does it Have?**
   - Single Family Residence (SFR)
   - Duplex, 3, or 4 Units?

3. **If it Owner-Occupied (O/O)?**

4. **What Kind of Condition is the Property In?**

5. **Where is the Subject Property Located?**
   - Urban, Suburbs, or Rural area?

6. **What is the Subject Property Worth?**
   - What's the Tax Assessor's Value? Recall how we calculated the value of the home based on the tax assessor's value? If you're not sure then please refer to the Chapter 14 titled "The Property Profile".

Answers to the above questions, regarding the Collateral, will assist you in determining what is the best Lender to send this loan to, what the maximum LTV will most likely be available with this loan, and what questions you need to ask your customers when you meet with them or afterwards.

LOCK THE INTEREST RATE ON A LOAN:

Sometime during the loan process you will need to lock the interest rate on that loan. Depending on how interest rates are behaving - will most likely have the most influencing factor as to when to do this. You could wait until just before it's time to send the Lender the Broker Demand Statement (see below). That, of course, is up to you. However, if you are going to lock the rate make sure you call your customers first and obtain their approval to do so at the interest rate you intend to lock at. And, always make sure that when you do obtain verbal approval from your customers, to lock an interest rate, that you make note of this on the Comments Sheet in that loan file.

I should not have to mention this (but I will) – that if your customers told you to lock the rate at a certain time then make sure that you do. I know there are Mortgage loan originators who sometimes try to play the market to get the best rate for their customers

- but be very careful when doing that. Too many Mortgage loan originators have waited until it was too late - with the result that they either: Are making much less than they expected and/or the interest rates went up to the point whereby that customer is no longer interested in doing that loan (financial benefit no longer exist). So don't get greedy. When you get into this business then you will see what I mean. And also, don't ever, ever, ever, tell your customers that you locked-in the rate - when you actually didn't. Not only is this lying to your customers but also could have very serious (and negative) consequences for you and your company. So please, don't ever do that.

COMMENTS SHEET:
As your loan progresses along make sure you keep a "diary" of what is going on with that loan. By diary, I mean that you make notes of what is happening on that loan on the Comments Sheet in that loan file or in the Notes Section, for that loan file, within your LOS program. Whenever you do something on your loan - note it (e.g. ordered title insurance with order number 12345. Should receive this within 2 days). Every time you talk with your customers make sure you that you note that conversation on the Comments Sheet. If something important comes up on the file - note it. In other words, ask yourself: If something happened to me whereby another Mortgage loan originator would need to continue on with this loan would they be able to easily pick up where I left off by going through this loan file and reading the Comments Sheets? Your answer to this question should be, "Yes."

Another reason for the Comments Sheet is to help your memory regarding a loan file and any others you may be working on. When you first start out in this business you may be working on only about 1 or 2 loans. You can probably remember what has been done and what still needs to be done on each one and when those things need to be done. However, when you start working on 3-5 or more loans - things start to get blurry and the average mind of a Mortgage loan originator begins to confuse one loan with the other. You may forget that you still need to do something on one or more of your loans. You may forget what you have done on a loan. Believe me. When you start to get busy processing 3 or more loans you will be happy you got into the (good) habit of keeping your Comments Sheets complete and current on all your loans.

And there's another important reason to maintain an up-to-date diary on the progress of your loans: A completed and up-to-date Comments sheet can also put you in a strong legal position (if it ever came to that). For example, with your customer's verbal permission you locked the interest rate on their loan (just as that customer requested). Following your conversation with that customer you noted this in the Comments Sheet in that customer's loan file (noting the time and what your customer said). After locking in that interest rate (as requested) you again noted the time, date, and interest rate locked. However, later on your customer complains that he told you to lock-in at a lower interest rate or cannot recall giving you permission to lock that interest rate. However, your written remarks on that Comments Sheet tells a different story. Here, your Comments Sheet could weigh very heavily in your favor if the customer took you to court regarding this. So please, maintain a completed and up-to-date Comments Sheet on all your loans.

PRIOR-TO-DOC CONDITIONS:

Prior-To-Doc (PTD) conditions are documents or whatever the Lender is requiring (that they receive or to be done) before the closing loan documents will be prepared and sent out to the Closing Agent (title company, Attorney, or escrow & closing company). Many of those PTD conditions will relate to the credit, income, and/or the subject property itself (e.g. the Appraisal). In addition to those relating to the credit, income, and collateral the following is what you could (normally) also expect as PTD conditions. This will be completed either by you or the Loan Processor:

1. **New Title Report:**

   Each time a property is purchased or refinanced then a new Title Insurance policy will usually be required. To do this, first call a title insurance company - located in the same county in which the subject property is located. Tell them you wish to order a title policy for a home (or whatever) that is being refinanced or purchased. The title officer will ask you for: The names of the current and/or new owners, the amount of the loan, who the new lender will be, and when will this new title policy begin. He or she will also ask you what type of policy do you want (Standard, Extended, and with Endorsements). Of course, the type of title insurance policy you will need on that loan will usually depend on what that Lender requires and/or what your customer has requested. Another added service, that the Title Officer provides, is to obtain the Payoff Amount on the existing mortgage and any other liens on the subject property that will be paid off with that new loan. Now don't wait until the last minute to do this because it can take a title insurance company anywhere from 2 days to a week (or more) before they fax you a copy of the new title insurance policy with the payoff amount on that existing mortgage (being refinanced).

2. **Hazard insurance: New Loss Payee or Mortgagee:**

   Because there will be a new Lender on that loan, on the subject property, this needs to be reflected on the homeowner's insurance policy (hazard insurance). To do this, call the borrower's insurance agent, introduce yourself and tell them what you are doing (e.g. refinancing their customer's existing mortgage loan). Tell them you need a new Declaration Page or Binder of the borrower's hazard insurance policy showing the New Lender, on that home loan, as the Loss Payee or Mortgagee. First, the Declaration Page is the first page of the homeowner's hazard insurance policy, which shows most of the important facts regarding that policy (customers' names, annual premium, total amount of coverage, etc.). It also shows the name of the current Loss Payee on that policy. The Loss Payee is the name of the lending company (if there is a mortgage loan on that property) that will receive the financial benefit of that insurance policy in the event of a major loss (e.g. fire) to the subject property. So, the new Lender's name and address needs to be on that policy before that Lender will send docs out. When you call and ask for this the insurance agent will know what you are talking about.

   When you do request this, from an insurance agent or company, be aware that they may ask you to fax to them a written (typed) request with a copy of the borrower's signed Borrowers Certification and Authorization Disclosure.

3. Broker Demand Statement:

This is called by a number of names (e.g. Document Request, Broker Pricing Sheet, etc.) but they all basically state the same thing. The Broker Demand Statement is used to tell your targeted Lender how much your mortgage company will get paid for originating the loan (based on what interest rate you locked at) and the various fees that will be paid through the escrow company – out of the closing funds of the loan (e.g. the appraisal, your company's processing fee, administrative fee, etc.). This is usually the final document you fax to the Lender before they prepare the loan documents to be sent to the closing and/or escrow office – where the closing will take place. On this form you will also list:

- **Borrower's Names and Subject Property:**
  Also, the loan program and interest rate you have locked for this loan as well as the other features regarding this loan (e.g. O/O, Full Doc loan, Prepayment Penalty feature, etc.).

- **What Fees You and Your Company are Charging on That Loan**:
  Appraisal fee, Credit Report fee, and Processing fee you expect to receive (as per the Lock Confirmation from that Lender).

- **Escrow and Closing Company Information:**
  They will need information about what and who will be closing that loan: Name of the title or closing company, their address, their telephone and fax number, name of the person doing the closing, and their (escrow company's) email address. They need this information in order to properly send out the closing docs without delay.

PRIOR-TO-FUNDING CONDITIONS:

These are conditions required by the Lender that must be satisfied before the Lender will fund the loan. These Prior-To-Funding (PTF) conditions are listed on the same sheet as the PTD conditions. Be sure you are aware of these as well. I don't like to want until the last minute to start addressing the PTF conditions, so I try to take care of these at the same time as the PTD conditions and I recommend you do the same.

SCHEDULE AND ORCHESTRATE THE CLOSING OF THE LOAN:

Once you receive the title insurance policy for your borrower's loan then you may be in a position whereby you can see when that loan will most likely go to docs and when it will close. This is an ideal time to talk to the Escrow Officer (of the title company) or Closing Agent (or Attorney) to make arrangements for the closing. They will have some simple questions, regarding that loan and its Lender, for you to answer as well as when you wish to close that loan.

Also, be aware that if you are planning on closing your loan around the end of the month that it can get rather crazy for Lenders as well as title and closing companies at that time. Their closing schedules are filling up at the month-end period. So here again, don't wait until the last minute to schedule the closing of your loan. Also, don't forget about the Three-Day Right of Rescission - it can impact when (what month) that loan actually funds (which also affects when you will get paid on that loan).

PLAN ON ATTENDING YOUR LOAN'S CLOSING:

Since I was a new Mortgage loan originator I have tried to attend all of my customers' loan closings. Of course, if the loan closing is taking place more than 80 miles away - then I generally will not attend it. But I will be available by the telephone if something comes up during the closing and/or the closing agent needs to ask me a question or solve a problem regarding that loan. And, this is one of the main reasons you always want to attend your loan closings - if you can. Because, on rare occasions, things do come up and/or there is a problem with the loan docs that the closing agent cannot correct or address on her own.

You should understand that it is the closing agent's responsibility to do and follow up on what he or she has been instructed to do by that Lender (on the closing documents). The Closing Agent has the legal responsibility to perform the loan closing in accordance with the laws of that state. But the Closing Agent is not privy to all the details of the loan just as you are and if a problem comes up (i.e. Docs say interest rate is 4.25% although you locked the rate at 4.0%) he or she won't know or might not recognize this mistake. Your customers will most likely recognize it and mention it to that closing agent. But that is not their job to know that. When this (or things like that) happen then you can thank your lucky stars for having the wisdom to attend that loan's closing. Remember, if the loan doesn't close and fund then you don't get paid.

Another reason you should attend your loan closings is to provide that level of excellent customer service you pride yourself on providing to your customers. And, of course, the referrals that can come from providing that high level of customer service. If you intend to be in this business for many years (which I hope you do) you will want to build up your (previous) customer base and referrals. When you are with your loan customers from the beginning (application) to the end (loan closing) you are providing your customers a level of customer service that is not common out there in mortgage lending land. And, if your customers are refinancing (and they have done mortgage loans before) then they will appreciate it as well. When I tell my customers I will be with them from the beginning to the end - right up to the loan closing, many of them just can't believe it. Your customers will appreciate you being there with them at their closing. And, you can expect that if they need another loan in the future or have friends who need a mortgage loan then there is a very good chance that they will either call or refer you for that loan. So attend all of your loan closings when you can. It's another way of taking care of your customers, your business, and your future as a Mortgage loan originator.

PREPARE AND MAINTAIN A LOAN SHADOW FILE:

Now sooner or later you may be required to prepare your loan file to be passed over to the Loan Processor, who will do what she does to move that loan file along towards loan closing. Once you have passed your loan files over to the Loan Processor what do you have to use - to stay on top of your loans? That's right: A Shadow File. A Shadow File should contain a copy of the original 1003, the LE, the TIL, comments sheets, and copies of any loan documents you need to pursue the progress of that loan (without bothering the Loan Processor - who has the full and original loan file now). I have heard of some Mortgage loan originators who copy the entire loan file that they are preparing to give to the Loan Processor for their Shadow Files. This is not necessary, a waste of good paper, and I don't recommend it. Just keep it simple with what you absolutely need and you will have a decent Loan Shadow File.

Processing your loan is an ongoing stage in the life of a loan that fulfills all the informational and documents needs required by your targeted Lender to move that loan file towards "Docs" whereby the loan closing documents are delivered to the closing agent, the docs are signed by your customers, and loan funding takes place. When loan funding takes place then you and your company get paid. Your goal in processing your loan file should be to anticipate the needs of your loan file, obtain all information and documents required as soon as possible, maintain your loan (shadow) file, and keep your loan customers informed as to the status of their loan. Also, I cannot over-emphasize how important it is to continually communicate with your Loan Processor, on the loan file, as your loan progresses towards completion and loan closing.

SHOPPING YOUR LOANS:

Shopping your loans is a term used in our business that refers to researching the lending market for Lenders who will do that type of loan (you are working on) - with the best rates and terms for your borrowers. Usually the (mortgage) company you work for will have established lending relationships with Conforming, Non-Conforming, and Sub-prime Lenders who provide good service, competitive rates, and loan programs. When you first begin as a Mortgage loan originator and are in doubt as to where to submit your loans to or analyze the possibilities of doing the loan with a particular Lender then I recommend you discuss that loan with your Branch Manager or one of the more experienced Mortgage loan originators in your office. However, before you go asking your Manager or another Mortgage loan originator about their suggestion (or suggestions) of a lender for your loan make sure you can provide them with the following information regarding that loan. These are questions you could expect them to ask you:

1. **CREDIT OF THE BORROWERS:**
   You have pulled a tri-merge Credit Report on your borrowers. What is the middle credit score of the primary borrower? How does their overall Credit Report look? Is there anything showing in the Public Records section (e.g. bankruptcy, foreclosure, collections)? How many Inquiries are you seeing within the past 90 days?

2. **TYPE OF SUBJECT PROPERTY (COLLATERAL):**
   What kind of property are we looking at? A stick-built house, manufactured home, condo, 4-plex, or bare land?

3. **AMOUNT OF THE LOAN:**
   What is the total loan amount that will enable your customers to achieve the goals of their loan? Are we talking about a Conforming loan amount or Jumbo loan amount?

4. THE LOAN-TO-VALUE (LTV):

Based on the above (amount of the loan) in relation to the estimated value of that subject property - what is the LTV on that loan?

5. HOUSING AND TOTAL DEBT RATIOS (CAPACITY):

Based on the (possible) monthly mortgage payments of the new proposed loan and the borrower's other outstanding monthly debts, in relation to their total gross monthly income, you should be able to calculate (or estimate) their Housing and Total Debt Ratios. Now, this can be a slippery one because you most likely have not yet identified a targeted Lender and have a firm interest rate in mind. In that case make your best guess as to whether (at this point) you feel this is a Conforming, Non-Conforming, or Sub-prime loan. And, based on your best guess, estimate an interest rate on their loan and their new monthly mortgage payment.

6. TIME OF OWNERSHIP OF THE SUBJECT PROPERTY:

How long have your customers owned the subject property (if a refinance loan)? Is their existing mortgage loan Seasoned?

7. TYPE OF EXISTING MORTGAGE LOAN(S):

What type of existing mortgage loan do your customers have? Do they have a 2nd mortgage? If they do then do they wish to consolidate both – or refinance only the 1st mortgage? If they wish to refinance and/or consolidate a HELOC is it Seasoned?

8. FINANCIAL GOALS OF YOUR CUSTOMERS:

And, of course, always keep in the back of your mind the financial goals that your customers have expressed to achieve with their loan. Are they looking for a better interest rate (aren't they all) with a lower monthly mortgage payment, payoff some or all of their credit card debts, and/or want the very lowest interest rate possible, and/or plan to sell their home in the next four years? Are they looking for a 30-year fixed rate loan program or willing to look at various ARM programs? Your customer's financial goals and the loan programs that are available to them (based on the above) should determine how you will structure this new loan and what Lender you can and should submit it to.

Shopping your loans can be one of the most time-consuming phases of processing your loans. Although looking for the best interest rates and terms for your borrower's loan will usually be your prime objective, sometimes we are looking for just about any Lender that will do that loan. This is especially true with Non-conforming (and Sub-prime) loans and properties that have unusual characteristics. This is when you really have to roll up your shirtsleeves and research the lending market. Although not all-inclusive the following are some resources you might take a look at in identifying some lenders for your more difficult loans:

- The Scottsman
- Origination News
- Broker (magazine)
- Mortgage Originator (magazine)

While the above resources may help you to identify a lender for your loan, they also offer excellent reading articles that can keep you up to date on what's happening in the lending market and sometimes offer advice on processing your loans and marketing your services as a Mortgage loan originator.

The Internet also can provide many resources for you as well – in looking for a lender for a tough loan you may be working on

If you are a new Mortgage loan originator then Shopping Your Loans, by researching the lending market for the best rates and terms for your customers' loan, is a skill you will want to fully develop. It is this skill that can contribute towards becoming a more successful Mortgage loan originator and one of the main reasons we get paid as we do.

SUBMITTING YOUR LOAN FILE TO A LENDER:

After you have completed your research on a loan file and identified a Lender who you believe will be able to do that loan, with a loan program, interest rate, and term that will enable your borrowers to achieve the goals of their loan, you then can submit that loan to that Lender. At this point - what you are usually looking for is a Credit Approval on that loan. In other words, whether that Lender can and will approve your loan as you are planning on submitting it (i.e. based on the loan's LTV, customer's credit, income, property type, etc.). Also, at this point in time, you most likely have not ordered the Title Insurance Policy or Appraisal.

You can generally submit a loan for credit approval one of two ways:

1. By directly entering that loan's information into your mortgage company's Loan Origination System (LOS) and submitting it online. For example, most conforming Lenders allow you to submit your conforming loans into Fannie Mae's DU or Freddie Mac's LP Underwriting program through your company's computer. Also, I am increasingly seeing Sub-prime lenders offer this type of direct loan submission option as well. Or:

2. By submitting (via fax or mail) the minimum required loan documents to the targeted Lender's Underwriter. There are some Wholesale Lenders that have you do it this way, even though they themselves may subsequently submit your loan through an Automated Underwriting approach (e.g. Fannie Mae's DU or Freddie Mac's LP) once they have received your submitted loan docs.

If you are submitting your loan file using #1 above it has been my experience that most mortgage companies and offices prefer (or require) that this be done by your Loan Processor. Hence, you would need to pass on to that Loan Processor all the necessary documents he or she needs to (directly) submit that loan file for you.

However, if you are submitting your loan using the #2 approach above then the following lists those (completed) loan documents that will usually be initially required. Again, depending on the required policies of the mortgage company you work for, it may be the Loan Processor who is only authorized to submit loans to Lenders.

Also, the Stacking Order in which you submit your loan file, either by mail or being emailed or faxed, is normally listed as below (see Loan File Stacking Order):

1. Completed Loan Submission Form – For that Particular Lender (Usually Handwritten).
2. Although not required, I always include a Remarks Page with an attached Qualifying Analysis Worksheet on the borrowers - behind the Submission Form (refer to Chapter 23 on the Remarks Page).
3. A Completed 1008.
4. A Fully Completed 1003.
5. 3-Bureau Credit Report on Your Borrower or Borrowers.
6. Signed Borrower's Authorization Disclosure (copy).

If at the time you are submitting your loan file for a Credit Approval and have some supporting income documents (e.g. recent paystubs, annual award letter, etc.) then go ahead and include those in your loan submission package. Although not normally required for a Credit Approval, if the loan is subsequently approved then having placed those documents in your loan submission package will result in less needed PTD conditions shown on your Approval Sheet.

I should also mention that the information on those documents listed above (with the exception of the Submission Form) should be in printed form using your office's loan originating software (e.g. Calyx Point, Genesis, etc.) Please do not submit your loans with those documents (e.g. 1008 and 1003) handwritten. This is unprofessional and can possibly cause delays in fully reviewing your loan file by the Lender's Underwriter. And, submitting handwritten loan documents will (most likely) not create that motivation and sense of urgency you want that loan Underwriter to have - to review your loan file as soon as possible.

For example, let's just say that it is about 4:30 pm on Friday afternoon. The Underwriter looks at the wall clock and sees that she has about 30 more minutes before she starts her weekend. She thinks, "Ok, I have about 30 more minutes to go until I am free for the weekend. That should give me enough time to review one more loan file." She looks on her desk and sees two loan files to be reviewed. Which one will she choose? She looks at the loan file on the left and sees that the loan docs are nicely printed and look there - it even has a Remarks Page that explains what that Mortgage loan originator wants to do with their loan file and even explains some of things that are showing up on the Credit Report. She says to herself, "Hmmm, very impressive." She then looks to her right. The loan file is handwritten, hard to read, and doesn't appear to be in any particular order. She thinks, "It looks like this one is going to take a few minutes - just to figure out exactly what this Mortgage loan originator wants me to do with this loan file." So, which one of those loan files do you think that Underwriter will choose to review before she leaves for the day and begins enjoying her weekend?

My point here is: Submit your loan files with documents (fully) completed and printed using your office's loan processing software (if you can). Remember what we (or most of us) were told when we were kids: Neatness counts. And, as the above story exemplifies, submitting a completed and orderly loan file sometimes results in the Lender's Underwriter reviewing you loan file sooner. And that is something all Mortgage loan originators want.

After the Lender's Underwriter has reviewed and approved your loan file and you've received the Approval Sheet from them, then here is what you should do next:

1. Thoroughly review that Loan Approval Sheet, looking for any PTD and PTF conditions that may still exist.

2. Call your customers and tell them the good news and inform them of any needed PTD conditions and/or documents you may still need from them.

3. Prepare a Shadow File (as we previously discussed) on your loan file and prepare and package a new loan folder (with this loan's original loan documents) to be passed on to your Loan Processor (if you have not previously done this).

However, if the Underwriter did not approve that loan then here is when you have more work to do on that loan (then if it had been approved). You will then need to review that Underwriter's comments or reasons why that loan was not approved. Was the LTV or Total Debt to Income (DTI) ratio too high, credit scores too low, or too many lates showing up on the Credit Report? Would restructuring that loan (i.e. by lowering the LTV) result in getting this loan approved (with this Lender) and still achieve the customer's goals for the loan? Would submitting this loan to another (Conforming) Lender possibly enable you to obtain loan approval on this loan? If you think so, then return again to Shopping Your Loans.

Whatever the reason(s), for the loan being declined, sometimes it is at that point when you have to ask yourself - whether this customer's loan is not the type of loan you first thought it was (e.g. Conforming) or hoped it would qualify for. In other words, instead of being a Conforming loan - are you really looking at a Non-Conforming or Sub-prime type of loan? If that's the case then would restructuring that loan differently, with those types of loan programs, make that loan doable? And if so, would it still enable your customers to achieve the goals of their loan? Or, on the other hand, will it nullify the benefits of doing that loan (i.e. interest rate would then be too high or the LTV will be too low)?

If you believe that the loan is still doable, even though you are now restructuring it under a different Type of Loan Program (e.g. Non-Conforming or Sub-prime) then start Shopping the Loan again by looking at those Lenders who provide those types of loan programs you are looking for. I know, it can be a lot of work researching a loan and trying to find the right Lender with the right loan program with interest rates and terms that can make it all happen and come together - whereby your customers are happy with the loan and it reaches the closing table. But hey, that's why we make the big bucks! Right?

Sometimes, however, we just can't make all the pieces come together. The customer's credit scores are too low for the LTV they want and need. Or, the customer's credit scores are too low to allow them to obtain any Conforming interest rates at this time. Whatever it is, it is preventing you from obtaining a loan for your customers that could not only benefit them but also enable them to achieve the goals of their loan. It's a reality: Sometimes we just can't find a Lender who will do a loan. Or, a Lender that would provide an interest rate and/or LTV that would make the loan doable. In that case, call up your customer and explain to him or her that, unfortunately, you cannot help them at this time and tell them why. Also, if you have any suggestions for them that could possibly result in them obtaining approval on a loan of theirs (sometime in the future) then certainly advise them of that as well. Because that's what most folks want to know anyway: Where they stand and what their options are. So, if your customer's loan is declined and/or you cannot find a Lender who will approve a loan for them - with all the loan features that would make your customers happy and benefit them then:

1. Call your customers right then and explain to them that the loan cannot be done (as they would like and intended) and why.

2. If they don't wish to explore other lending options (e.g. Sub-prime loan) then thank them and mail them a decline letter with the reason(s) why you could not help them (e.g. credit reason, not enough equity, income, etc.).

Once you have done that then you can now spend your time more productively on a loan application that, hopefully, will go to the closing table.

COMPENSATING FACTORS:

Compensating Factors are those characteristics, of prospective borrowers and/or their property, which can reflect a (more) positive light on their loan file package - which you are working on. In some cases it can be the Compensating Factor or Factors that result in the Lender's Underwriter deciding to approve a loan exception you requested and in some cases to do the loan at all or as you have submitted it.

It has been my experience that most Mortgage loan originators I have worked with either do not know what Compensating Factors are and/or do not mention those (when they do exist) in their customer's loan file. Because of the importance of knowing what Compensating Factors are and how they can improve the quality of a submitted loan file let's now go over some of the more well-known Compensating Factors.
In listing these Compensating Factors I have separated them into two groups: 1. Characteristics of the subject property, and 2. Characteristics of the borrowing customers. While this list may not contain all the Compensating Factors (that exist) it should give you an idea of the more important and commonly known ones.

I. The Subject Property:
*   Stable Market for that type of Property (versus a declining market).
*   The Property Value is well established and maintained (gives credibility to appraised value of property - especially high-end value homes).
*   Value of Subject Property has increased over the years (this can tie-in to the Compensating Factor mentioned immediately above).

II. The Borrowers:

- Borrowers have demonstrated good money management and savings ability.
- Borrowers are purchasing a property (who were previously renting) and either will not be experiencing Payment Shock or Payment Shock will be minimal.
- They have substantial Net Worth.
- Borrowers have strong (financial) Reserves after loan closing.
- Currently or after the proposed loan there is or will be Substantial Discretionary Income. Although different, this can relate to the Compensating Factor previously mentioned.
- Low Loan-To-Value on proposed loan with large Equity Interest in the Subject Property.
- Sizable Down Payment on a Purchased Loan with resulting low Loan-To-Value.
- Borrowers have demonstrated doing previous loans or obligations having high (or similar) monthly payments - which they have paid on time and as agreed.
- Borrower has been with current employer for many years and shows good job stability.
- Credit Report shows minimal credit usage and/or minimal liabilities. This can tie-in with Compensating Factors regarding Reserves and Discretionary Income.
- Borrowers have other income sources, which do not qualify to be included in qualifying your borrowers (part-time income, child support which ends in next 2 years, etc.). This should be mentioned as a Compensating Factor.
- Very Low Housing and Total Debt Ratios before and (most importantly) after the proposed loan.

You may have noticed that I have not mentioned excellent credit as a Compensating Factor. This is because, as my first mortgage loan manager used to say, "Excellent credit on Conforming loans is expected." However, if your customer has a perfect credit history with credit scores higher than you have ever seen before (e.g. over 800) I probably would mention it.

I have to admit that I don't always mention existing Compensating Factors when submitting a loan. However, if there is a real or perceived weakness in the loan file or I know I will be asking for some sort of exception on a loan then I always look for and mention any existing Compensating Factor or Factors on those borrowers. Thus, using and mentioning Compensating Factors will only strengthen the qualifying position of your borrower's submitted loan. Also, the Wholesale Lender's Underwriter may not see everything regarding your customers and their loan. Mentioning existing Compensating Factors about your customers may bring attention to an area that the Underwriter may not have seen or realized. This could make the difference in the Underwriter finally approving your loan and/or granting you that loan exception you requested. Therefore, I suggest that when you perceive any qualifying weaknesses in your customer's loan file then look for Compensating Factors and if there are any - mention them. The ideal place to mention your customer's Compensating Factors is on the Remarks Page - included in your loan file package.

PROTECTING CUSTOMERS' PRIVATE AND NON-PUBLIC INFORMATION:
Before I end this chapter on Processing Your Loans I'd like to talk about obtaining, maintaining, and disposing of your customers' sensitive, private, and non-public information. With the implementation of the Gramm-Leach-Bliley Act (GLBA) and the issuance of its Safeguards Rule by the Federal Trade Commission it is incumbent upon every financial institution and mortgage company today to have a security plan, with the appropriate systems and procedures in place that protects and safeguards the confidentiality of their customers' personal, private, and non-public information. This security plan and its systems and procedures must satisfy the requirements of GLBA's Safeguards Rule.

I mention this here because when originating and processing a customer's loan – Mortgage loan originators and Loan Processors (and any employee of a financial institution and mortgage company) must be vigilant and careful to be sure that whenever they are accessing, working on, transferring (mailing or emailing), storing, and/or disposing of a customer's loan file (or any material containing a customer's sensitive, private, and non-public information) that their procedures satisfy the requirements of the GLBA's Safeguards Rule. This is not an option but a requirement of all of us who handle any materials or information containing a customer's personal, private, and non-public information.

For example, if you are a mortgage loan originator and wish to email some material either back to your customer and/or a third-party provider (a title company) and that material contains some sensitive, personal, and non-public information then that transmission must be encrypted. Also, where you store your customers' information: Is it secure? Before leaving for the day, do you file away loan documents and files and lock up the file cabinet that contains all the loan files you are working on? That's good. Or, do you leave them on your desk – in an unlocked office room or open working area? If you do then that is a violation of the Safeguards Rule. Also, is your computer password protected - so only you (and other authorized persons – like your Loan Processor) can access your customers' information? Do you have a firewall, anti-virus, and anti-spyware setup on your computer to prevent (as much as possible) any unauthorized access to your computer containing your customers' information? If you do then that's good. If not, then you could be in violation of the Safeguards Rule.

Therefore, it is imperative that your mortgage company (that you work for) and you do everything reasonably possible to protect your customers' information as required by the Safeguards Rule. Because of the importance of this subject I discuss the Gramm-Leach-Bliley Act and its Safeguards Rule in more detail within Chapter 25 titled "Mortgage Lending Regulations".

With that said, let us go now to the next chapter that talks about preparing The Remarks Page - which you can prepare for your Loan Processor and/or targeted Lender.

Chapter 23

THE REMARKS PAGE

When I was in banking many years ago I recall when I met with Branch Managers and mortgage loan originators that they would tell me about how they were packaging their loans. A common requirement of those packaged loans was to have a "Remarks Page." This was sometimes referred to as the comments sheet (not to be confused with our loan Comments Sheet). Whatever they called it, this Remarks Page was written by the originating mortgage loan originator and highlighted the important points and features of their loan. Shortly after I became a mortgage loan originator I too began preparing and including a Remarks Page with all of my loan submissions. I found that when I did this I received fewer questions from the Loan Processor as well as the Wholesale Lender's Underwriter regarding my loan files I submitted to them. Another added benefit was that in preparing this Remarks Page I found that it forced me to review all the important points on that loan. On more than one occasion, just doing this prevented me from overlooking an important aspect of that loan that I, beforehand, had missed or forgot to examine. So, I prepare a Remarks Page for all my loan file submissions.

This Remarks Page is certainly not a required thing in processing your loans. However, if you decide that you do want to complete and have one of these on top of your loan files then you will find that most Loan Processors will really appreciate it (half the time it seems they're just trying to figure out what the mortgage loan originators want them to do with their loans). The Remarks Page summarizes all the important points regarding a loan. It includes the following in text form:

I. First Paragraph:
Names of the Borrowers and the Subject Property's address. Goals of the loan. How long the Borrowers have owned their property (if a refinance loan) and who the current mortgage lien holder or lien holders are.

II. Second Paragraph:
Employment Information, regarding the Borrower and Co-Borrower, and their Gross Monthly Income.

III. Third Paragraph:
Comments regarding their credit, noting the primary Borrower's middle credit score. If there is anything negative that is showing up on their Credit Report - I address it. Usually by this time I have talked with the borrowers about it and have an explanation for what is showing up there. I then state how many Inquiries are showing up and if there are any records showing within the Public Records Section.

IV. Fourth Paragraph:

How I have structured that loan, regarding the type of loan program, loan amount, interest rate, term, and LTV - based on the Appraised (or estimated) value of the subject property.

V. Fifth Paragraph:

Here I refer to my Qualifying Analysis worksheet and show that loan's impact on the customer's Housing and Total Debt Ratios. If there is anything that I think would be helpful to the Loan Processor or Lender's Underwriter (that would not be obvious from the loan docs) I mention it here.

VI. Sixth Paragraph:

Here I sign out and leave my telephone and fax number.

Below is a copy of one of my Remarks Page - to give you some idea of what this looks like. Again, as I mentioned, this is not required. But in preparing a Remarks Page for your loans you will find Loan Processors asking you fewer questions regarding those loans and it will make you look much more professional. An example of a Remarks Page is on the next page.

TO: Best Rates Bankers
            Attn. Underwriting

FROM: Steven Driscoll
            Senior Mortgage Loan Originator

DATE: May 16, 2021

RE: Rate/Term Refinance Loan for Joseph and Natalie Smith.

Joseph and Natalie Smith wish to refinance their existing mortgage and obtain a better interest rate with a lower monthly mortgage payment. The address of the subject property is: 123 Sunnyside Avenue, Spokane, Washington 99208. They first purchased this property in 1998 for $170,000. The existing Lien Holder on their mortgage is Gotcha Bank.

Joseph Smith works for Windmill Worlds as a Rubber Band Maintenance Advisor and has worked for this company for the past 20 years. His gross monthly income is about $5,000. Natalie Smith is a Homemaker.

Regarding credit, the Smiths have outstanding credit with Joseph's middle credit score being 726 (Empirica). There is a collection shown with Eyes Closed Eyewear for $525. I talked with Joseph regarding this and he said this is an additional result of when he was victimized by fraud - whereby a blind man posed as someone with excellent vision. Joseph said that he has talked with Eyes Closed Eyewear and they told him that they had zeroed out this account for him. I told him we would probably need documentation showing this. Joseph is in the process of obtaining that. Under the Consumer Statement Section we can see here that these folks were victims of credit card fraud. There are two Inquires, within the past 90 days, and no Public Records showing.

I have structured this loan as a Rate/Term Refinance loan with a loan amount of $130,000, 30-Year Fixed @ 4.50%. Based on an appraised value of $180,000 the LTV on this loan is about 72%.

Looking at the attached Qualifying Analysis worksheet you can see that this new loan would result in the housing and total debt ratios improving slightly from 25%/32% to 22%/30% respectively with a monthly savings of about $125.00.

If you have any questions then please call me at (509) 123-4567 or fax me at (509) 765-4321. I thank you and look forward to doing business with you again.

Let's now move on to the next chapter that your Loan Processor will be very happy that you are aware of this when you first start passing your home loan files to him or her. I'm talking about the Loan File Stacking Order.

Chapter 24

LOAN FILE STACKING ORDER

𝕷oan Stacking Order usually refers to the order in which loan documents are placed in a legal sized file folder. But it can also refer to the order in which loan documents are electronically transmitted and submitted, from you or your Loan Processor, to the targeted Lender on a loan. When I say placed in a legal file folder, I mean that the loan documents are secured to the file folder with prong paper fasteners on both sides of that file folder. Stacking Orders are great for loan files because this gives you (or the Loan Processor) a pretty good idea where to look in a file when you are searching for a particular loan document. This beats looking all through the loan file folder for it. And believe me, it gets mighty messy (as well as aggravating) when we need to do that.

Preparing your loan file in the Stacking Order requested by your Loan Processor usually takes place after you have obtained a completed and signed 1003, signed Disclosures, and most of the supporting income documentation. Once you have reached that point then it is the usual policy of most mortgage branches I have worked in and seen that the Loan File is then passed on to the Loan Processor - who then does what Loan Processors do on loans (e.g. order verifications, submit the loan to the lender you have selected, etc.).

In additional to preparing that loan file in the proper Loan Stacking Order you should write the loan customer's information on a file folder label – attached to that loan folder. An example of what should be written on a file folder label is:

James and Vicki Smith 8510 Golden Road San Francisco, California 86205   Refi. C/O

The name(s) on the above label are the borrowers. The address below the names is the address of the subject property (this could differ from their residence address – as in a purchase transaction). And, to the right of the zip code is the type of loan transaction. In this case it is a Refinance Cash-Out loan.

Okay, you now know what a Loan Stacking Order is, but what is the order to stack the loan docs by? Your Loan Processor will no doubt make that clear to you. However, to give you an idea of a Loan Stacking Order, below is a Loan Stacking Order I developed for mortgage loan originators years ago, when I was a mortgage branch manager. I have placed this Stacking Order on the next page so you can see the entire stacking order at a glance. This should give you an idea of what folks are talking about when they mention Stacking Order of a loan file.

LOAN FILE STACKING ORDER

I. LEFT SIDE OF THE FILE - FROM TOP TO BOTTOM:
- File Information Sheet
- Approval Sheet from Lender
- Lock Confirmation
- Copy of Lender's Rate Sheet (for that Lock-In Rate)
- Comments Sheet
- Originally Signed Loan Application (1003)
- Initial Loan Estimate (LE)
- Copy of Deposit Checks (If Any)

II. RIGHT SIDE OF FILE - FROM TOP TO BOTTOM:
- Final Loan Application (1003)
- Final Loan Estimate (LE)
- Credit Report
- Credit Explanations (from customer)
- Filed Divorce Decree
- All Income Documentation:
    - Paystubs: Recent Paystub with YTD figures or Paystub for last 30 days
    - Last 2 years W2's
    - Last 2 years Tax Returns
    - Copy of Complete Bankruptcy Papers
    - YTD Profit and Loss Statement - for Self-Employed
- Assets Owned by the Borrowers – Stocks, Bonds, IRAs, Etc.
- All Verifications
- Title Insurance
- Hazard Insurance
- Purchase and Sales Agreement
- Appraisal
- Property Profile
- All Required Loan Disclosures (Signed)

III. FILE LABELS:
All file folders normally will have the proper colored labels on them and have written on these: the Borrower's names, the Subject Property Address, and the Type of Loan being done. Also, based on the type of loan, please use the following colored labels:

- **Refinance Loans** => Green Colored Labels
- **Purchase Loans** => Red Colored Labels

Chapter 25

MORTGAGE LENDING REGULATIONS

As a new Mortgage loan originator or even an experienced loan officer you should be familiar with those regulations and laws that dictate what we, as mortgage loan originators, can and cannot do, and perhaps more importantly must do when providing our services to mortgage loan customers and be "In Compliance". I gave quite a bit of thought as to how I would present this needed chapter. My thinking was that on the one hand I could present you with all the major written regulations and laws affecting the mortgage lending area, oftentimes written in legal jargon that is difficult to understand. Or, I could those lending regulations and laws in alphabetical order and translate how those lending regulations and Laws impact on us in our day-to-day activities as a mortgage loan originator. I thought about this and decided on the latter. So, let's begin with our first regulation.

ABILITY-TO-REPAY RULES (ATR):
The effective date for the Ability-To-Repay Rule was January 10, 2014. According to the Ability-To-Repay Rule a creditor shall not make a loan unless the creditor makes a reasonable and good faith determination at or before loan consummation that the home loan consumer will have a reasonable ability to repay their loan according to the terms of that loan. The basis for determining a consumer's ability to repay their loan should be based upon:

- Current or reasonably expected income
- Current employment status
- Monthly mortgage payment
- Monthly payment on any simultaneous loans
- Monthly payment for mortgage-related obligations
- Current debt obligations (e.g. alimony and child-support)
- Monthly debt-to-income ratio or residual income
- Credit History

The Ability-to-Repay Rule applies to almost all closed-end consumer credit transactions that are secured by a dwelling – including any real property attached to the dwelling such as 1-4 units, condominiums, and co-ops. And, unlike some other mortgage types, the ATR is not limited to 1st liens or to loans on primary residences. I previously discussed in detail the subject of the Ability-To-Repay Rules within Chapter 6.

APPRAISAL RULE:
The current home appraisal requirements are summed up in CFPB's Appraisal Rule, went into effect on January 10, 2014. According to the Consumer Financial Protection Bureau's Appraisal Rule creditors (lenders) are now required to:

- Tell their home loan customers, within business three days of receiving their mortgage loan application (1003), that they will receive a free copy of their appraisal.

- Tell their home loan customers that they will also receive a free copy of any additional home valuations that were required and made: For example, an automated valuation model report, or a broker price opinion.

- Must provide these free copies to the home loan applicant either promptly after these reports have been completed and received (by the creditor or mortgage broker) or three business days before their home loan closes, whichever is earlier (My guess is that means that they'll need to receive it shortly after you have received it).

- Creditors may request home loan customers to waive this deadline, to receive their appraisal, so that they receive their free copy of it at their home loan closing. This is optional.

- If an appraisal is completed and received by the creditor (or mortgage broker) and their customer's home loan does not close then that home loan applicant must still be provided with a free copy of their appraisal.

DO-NOT-CALL REGISTRY AND RULES:
Since October 1, 2003 there is an established regulation that radically and dramatically changed how you and I, as mortgage loan originators, can market our services when using the telephone: It's called the National Do-Not-Call (DNC) Rules and was established by the Federal Communication Commission (FCC).

These days, it seems, consumers are becoming increasingly concerned about protecting their privacy and rights. And, this is another result of protecting those rights. Under the DNC Rules, consumers can request to be free from telemarketing calls. They can request this from calls from a specific company or from any telemarketer. Now, you might ask, "How does that affect me? I am not a telemarketer; I am a mortgage Loan officer?" But guess what? If you are calling customers to sell them something then the FCC considers you to be a telemarketer.

Now, under the DNC Rules, if a consumer has registered to be on the National Do-Not-Call Registry then you, as a loan officer, must honor that request within 30 days, of them registering, and honor that request for the next five years. The DNC Registry is managed by the Federal Trade Commission (FTC), but it's actually the FCC that enforces it. And, because this is a national regulation, if a consumer is on that DNC Registry then it doesn't matter whether they are in or out-of-state of your business location.

Under the FCC's national Do-Not-Call Rules, the following highlights some of the main Rules you need to be familiar with and practice as a mortgage loan originator:

1. If a consumer is listed on the Do-Not-Call Registry and you don't have an expressed and written consent to call them then - you do not call them. This also applies to loan customers that you may have done a home loan with in the past. If they are now on that DNC list and you don't have any documented permission to call them - then don't call them. You would need to contact them by other means.

2. Whether a consumer is on this DNC list or not, all consumers are to be freed from telemarketing calls between 9:00 P.M. and 8:00 A.M.

Since the DNC rules first became effective I have seen a few mortgage loan originators (and some branch managers) have a cavalier attitude about this ruling and thought that they could continue to call prospective or past loan customers without any research and with impunity. However, I must tell you that the FCC takes the DNC rules very seriously and has setup a Do-Not Call Team or Task Force of attorneys and investigators to enforce these DNC rules. And, if a consumer has registered on the DNC list and is called by a telemarketer, they could then make a formal complaint with the FCC by either calling them at their toll-free number (888-CALL-FCC), emailing them (https://www.donotcall@fcc.gov), or sending the FCC a letter. And if they did make a formal compliant then you can be certain that the FCC will be more than happy to follow up on that compliant.

I should also mention that the consequences of being in violation of the DNC rules can also be very serious and expensive. For example, years ago a fairly large mortgage company was found to be in violation of the DNC rules and was fined $770,000! And, if you are a mortgage loan originator and found to be in violation, of the DNC rules, on just one phone call then it could perhaps cost you around $11,000. Thus, I think you would agree with me that these are serious consequences.

Okay, after saying all of this, on the DNC rulings, how can we protect ourselves and be 'In Compliance' – according to the Do-Not Call rules? As a mortgage company and/or a Mortgage loan originator the following is the minimum of what you must do to be In Compliance:

1. Every call that you make, to a prospective home loan customer, to solicit business, must first be researched to be absolutely certain that they are not on a DNC list. And, I should note here that, even though you may have purchased a mortgage lead list that was "scrubbed" (to be sure that no one on that list is registered on the DNC list) you are still ultimately responsible to be sure that no one on that list is registered on a DNC list. And, that DNC registry needs to be reviewed at least every 31 days. If someone is on the DNC Registry and you call him or her and he or she subsequently makes a format complaint, then the FCC will be looking for you – not the company that sold you that list. And that's because it was you that made that call.

2. If you are making telemarketing (or making any outbound soliciting calls) then you must get a Subscription Account Number (SAN) from the government.

3. You also must have in writing a DNC compliance policy, for your company or yourself, on how to comply with the DNC rulings and laws.

4. A procedure and/or system needs to be setup that you always follow, when calling customers, that demonstrates (and documents) that the customers you have called (or plan to call) are not on the Do-Not Call Registry. And, I should further add here that there are federal and state Do-Not Call registries or lists. So, to be sure, I recommend you check them both.

5. And, when you do make a telemarketing call (after doing all the above) then you need to identify, to that person on the phone, who you are and the company you represent as well the telephone number (or address) of your company (if they wish to subsequently contact you or your company).

Therefore, the first thing you need to do here, as a Mortgage loan originator, is obtain a Subscription Account Number (SAN) because calling (new and existing) customers is what we do in our business. Now, if you are calling customers, on behalf of your mortgage company, then you could use your company's SAN number. However, if you are calling on your own (representing yourself) then you will need to have your own SAN number. Before obtaining a SAN number you should first select the area codes you wish to make calls in. And that's because the first five area codes you select are free. However, after more than five area codes the annual fee is $62.00 - with a maximum annual fee of $17,050 for the entire U.S. database. To begin the process of obtaining the detailed information you need to know, regarding the DNC Rulings and its Registry, and of obtaining a SAN number for yourself– please go to: http://www.fcc.gov/cgb/donotcall.

Secondly, you need to meet with your mortgage branch manager and obtain the training you need to know (either in-house or through a seminar) that demonstrates you have received the training you are required to have regarding the DNC rules. And thirdly, you need to setup a special file system that shows that those customers you have called were previously researched and not found to be on any Do-Not Call registry.

EQUAL CREDIT OPPORTUNITY ACT (ECOA):
The Equal Credit Opportunity Act, or Regulation B, seeks to provide the availability of credit to all loan applicants, who are creditworthy, regardless of their race, national origin, age, sex, religion, marital status, and color. The ECOA also seeks to prevent any prejudices toward granting of credit (for a loan) because all or part of their income is from a government or public assistance program. It also seems to have been originally written to prevent lenders from not granting credit to women because they were or could have children (possibly resulting in them temporarily or no longer working). And, as you might expect, if after reviewing all the credit information on a customer and a lender decides to not approve their loan then that lender must send to that customer an Adverse Action Notice with the reason(s) why they were not approved.

While the above seems to be fairly well known amongst lending folks you might be unaware that the ECOA also impacts virtually all steps of loan processing such as:

- Interviewing loan-inquiring customers
- Making the credit decision on loan applications, and

- Requires lenders to:
    1. Inform their loan applicants of the action taken on their application.
    2. Retain records of those loan applications that were taken.
    3. During the application process – to obtain certain personal information regarding the applicant as well as their race (this is also required by HMDA).
    4. If an appraisal was ordered and completed – to provide those loan applicants with a copy of that appraisal (see also FDIC Improvement Act of 1991).
    5. Inform their loan applicants of the status of their loan within 30 days after they have completed a loan application. This includes pre-qualification (pre-quals) and pre-approval requests.

- And, it also addresses the way in which a mortgage company (or lender) presents their advertisements and the wording used in each. In this case it is primarily focusing on any advertisements, which could be interpreted as discriminatory, and/or discouraging any applicant from applying for a home loan because they are a member of a Protected Class.

I also would like to mention that Regulation B was amended to the Equal Credit Opportunity Act on April 15, 2003. According to Regulation B, when a married or unmarried couple completes a loan application jointly it is incumbent upon the lender to:

1. Determine that both applicants do (or did) intend to file jointly.

2. Evaluate each applicant independently and based on each applicant's noted information on the 1003,

3. Apply uniform standards of credit qualifying for married and unmarried couples filing jointly, and,

4. If any loan applicants' request is denied then, under Regulation B as of April 15, 2004, an Adverse Action Notice is to be sent to those home loan customers with the reason(s) for their home loan denial and any follow-up options that may be available to them.

FAIR AND ACCURATE CREDIT TRANSACTIONS ACT (FACT):
The Fair and Accurate Credit Transactions Act, an amendment of the Fair Credit Report Act (discussed above), was signed into law in 2003 and became effective on December 4, 2004. The FACT Act, I believe, is a result of the increasing concerns that consumers have regarding their privacy (of nonpublic information) and of identity theft. And, this is a concern of all citizens of our great nation. I also believe that it was because of these types of concerns that Congress eliminated a state's right to enact laws related to how credit-reporting companies handle consumer credit information and enacted the FACT Act - that would establish national uniformity standards for the reporting of consumer credit information. It also increases the accuracy of consumer credit reports and includes requirements such as giving your loan customers their credit score information.

The FACT Act is very broad in nature and has what are called Titles for each area of concern under the FACT Act. For example:

Title I: Identity Theft, Prevention, and Credit History Restoration
Title II: Improvements in Use of Consumer Access to Credit Information
Title III: Enhancing the Accuracy of Consumer Report Information
Title IV: Limiting the Use and Sharing of Medical Infor. in the Financial System
Title V: Financial Literacy and Education Improvement
Title VI: Protecting Employee Misconduct Investigations
Title VII: Relations to State Laws
Title VIII: Miscellaneous

For us, within mortgage lending, the FACT Act influences and requires of us certain responsibilities in:

- Requesting Credit Reports on our loan-inquiring customers,
- When we, as loan officers, have the right or are authorized to pull a customer's credit report or have the consent of a customer to do so.
- Disclose to the customer, on whom you pulled a credit report, the credit information you and the Lender used in credit qualifying that customer.

In discussing the FACT Act, I won't go into all the details of it but will focus on what, I believe, you need to know as loan originators, to be "In Compliance". Hence, I will focus only on those specific points of the FACT Act that impact what we do as mortgage loan originators. So, let's start with number 1 above:

1. **Requesting Credit Reports on your Loan-Inquiring Customers:**
   To pull a credit report on a customer you need to have a valid reason to do so. For our purposes, it would be for the extension of credit (a mortgage loan) – which begins with the completion of a loan application (the 1003) and/or the need to review the credit report of a loan-inquiring customer.

2. **When we, as Loan officers, have a right or are authorized to pull a customer's Credit Report:**
   When you are working on a mortgage loan request for a customer, you need to pull a Credit Report, to further identify what they may qualify for. But you need to have authorization to do that. The following highlights those signed documents or other means of permission that authorizes you to do so:
   a. A signed Borrower's Certification and Authorization Disclosure and/or a Consent Form Disclosure.
   b. Signed 1003 application (page 4 of 5). I should note here: That if it is a married couple (applying for a home loan) then only one of the spouse's signatures needs to be on that application. However, if there are two single individuals (unmarried) applying for a home loan then both of their signatures need to be on that 1003 to pull both of their Credit Reports. Remember, that if a couple is unmarried then you will need to pull a separate credit report for each loan applicant.

c. If you completed a 1003 over the telephone then a signed 1003 is not required. But here, I would suggest you note that on that customer's Comment Sheet in that customer's loan file.

d. Now, if you are talking to some customers, over the telephone, and they give you verbal approval or authorization to order their Credit Report, then you should: 1.) Note that permission given to you on the Comments Sheet within that customer's loan file (if a loan file is indeed created), and/or 2.) Complete a verbal authorization form (which most mortgage companies should have), and finally, 3.) Obtain a signed Consent Form from those customers as soon as possible.

3. **Disclose to that Customer: Which Credit Reporting Bureau you pulled their Credit Report from, and the Credit information that the Lender used in Credit Qualifying that Customer:**
As required by the FACT Act, all consumers who have their Credit Report pulled, for the purposes of obtaining credit (e.g. a mortgage loan), are to receive a completed Notice To The Home Loan Applicant disclosure within 3 business days following the date that credit report was pulled. This form is sometimes referred to as the "Credit Score Information Disclosure."

FAIR CREDIT REPORTING ACT (FCRA):
The Fair Credit Reporting Act, which was enacted in 1970, is also referred to as Regulation V. Under the Fair Credit Reporting Act loan officers must obtain the permission of their customers before ordering a credit report on their behalf. This consent, to order a credit report on their behalf, can be given either verbally and/or by signing a consent form. If permission is given verbally then the loan officer should obtain a signed consent form shortly thereafter.

In addition to the mortgage lending folks, FCRA also seeks to promote accuracy, fairness, and of course, privacy of any personal information that is obtained by the credit reporting agencies or bureaus.

Ordering a credit report on behalf of a customer, without their consent and/or using false pretenses (or as stated in the FACT Act below), can also have very negative consequences: Fines of up to $1,000 and/or imprisonment of up to two years.

The Fair Credit Reporting Act also requires, that if a home Loan application or credit request is denied or rejected for whatever reason, after three business-days of taking or receiving that home loan application, then that home loan customer must be sent a completed Adverse Action Notice with the reasons for that credit denial(s) as well as any follow-up options that may be available to them. For more information on ordering a credit report please refer to Chapter 18 titled *Reading the Credit Reports*.

FDIC IMPROVEMENT ACT OF 1991:
Just to be sure you know: FDIC is an acronym that stands for the Federal Deposit Insurance Corporation. This Act amended the Equal Credit Opportunity Act and allows loan applicants, who are obtaining a loan secured by their residential property, the right to receive a copy of the Appraisal Report used in obtaining that loan. According to this Act, customers are entitled to receive a copy of their Appraisal Report, within 30 days of their lender's receipt of a written request on their loan. However, these days, it seems it is customary for customers to receive their Appraisal Report prior to or at loan closing.

If those loan applicants have already paid for that appraisal or been charged for that appraisal then the lender cannot charge a fee in providing that appraisal report to their loan customers. This includes any photocopying costs necessary to provide customers with a copy of their Appraisal Report.

FINANCIAL INSTITUTIONS REFORM, RECOVERY, AND ENFORCEMENT ACT OF 1989 (FIRREA):
Whew, now that is a long-winded name of an Act. Anyway, not to take away from its importance, for our purposes here, FIRREA provided amendments to the Home Mortgage Disclosure Act (HMDA) and expanded its coverage to include independent non-depository mortgage lenders. See HMDA below for a more detailed discussion of the requirements of HMDA.

FLOOD DISASTER PROTECTION ACT (FDPA):
The Flood Disaster Protection Act first presented itself in 1973 and is an offshoot of The National Flood Insurance Act of 1968 (sometimes referred to as Title XIII of HUD). The National Flood Insurance Act of 1968 made flood insurance programs available to the private sector and the subsequent Flood Disaster Protection Act of 1973 made it mandatory, for lenders, to determine and/or require flood insurance on any loan secured by improved real estate or a mobile home. And to clarify, this requirement includes residential real estate and commercial property.

Therefore, if a residential or commercial property was found to be located within a flood zone, as determined by a Flood Hazard Boundary Map or Flood Insurance Rate Map, then flood insurance would be required on that loan. In that case, a copy of their flood insurance binder would need to be sent to the Lender (on that loan) prior to the loan docs being sent to the closer on that loan.

There are no exceptions to this ruling as far as requiring that a determination be made as to whether the subject property is located in a flood zone. And, according to this ruling, there are no exceptions to requiring flood insurance - if the subject property is located in a flood zone. However, I will note that one time I was doing a small commercial loan and that subject property was shown to be in a flood zone. The business owners couldn't believe it and weren't about to pay for any flood insurance. I didn't want to lose that loan so I researched this further and found that because the last flood in that area occurred about 78 years ago, it had been classified as a flood zone. However, no floods, in that area, had occurred since. And, that river, located not too far away from the subject property, was now hardly a stream. Through the efforts of the appraiser, on that property, and the cooperation of the city we were able to reclassify (or perhaps rezone is a better word) to show that the subject property is currently not located in a flood zone. Doing this, however, can be a long process and sometimes "The Powers that Be" just may not want to change their flood zone boundaries.

Since I'm talking about Flood Zones I would also like to mention the **Special Flood Hazard Area (SFHA)**. This identifies land(s) that are in a flood plain within a community having at least a 1% chance of flooding in any given year, as designed by FEMA.

GRAMM-LEACH-BLILEY ACT (GLBA):
The Gramm-Leach-Bliley Act (GLBA) was passed by Congress in November 1999 and last amended in July 2016. It is also referred to as Regulation P. I should also mention that the Gramm-Leach-Bliley Act is also known as the Financial Services Modernization Act. It is a United States federal law that requires financial institutions to explain how they share and protect their customers' private information.

Quite a few "Powers that Be" came together to write the GLBA: The Federal Reserve, the Federal Deposit Insurance Corporation, the Office of the Comptroller, the Federal Trade Commission, and the Office of Thrift Supervision. The Gramm-Leach-Bliley Act contains within it provisions regarding the privacy of customers' Nonpublic Personal Information (NPI) as well as the safeguarding of their personal financial information. Under the first part of this (regarding privacy practices) financial institutions (and mortgage companies) are required to disclose to their loan-inquiring customers a notice (e.g. The Privacy Protection Policy Notice) stating their information collection and sharing practices. For example, for mortgage companies some of a loan customer's NPI may need to be shared with third-party providers in the pursuance of processing their home loan request towards the closing table. Now, according to the Gramm-Leach-Bliley Act customers are to be given an option to "opt out" if they don't want their NPI shared with any third-party provider (e.g. credit reporting bureaus or appraisal services). That option to "opt out" would be provided on the privacy notice given to any loan applicants.

However, it should be noted that the Gramm-Leach-Bliley Act also provides specific exceptions under which financial institutions and mortgage companies can share their customers' information with third party providers and whereby the customer may not "opt out." According to Section 313.13, regarding the Exception to Opt-Out Requirements, financial institutions and mortgage companies must provide the Notice of Privacy, but not offer that customer the right to "opt out" when it is providing NPI to those third party providers - necessary to complete the loan transaction requested by that customer (i.e. ordering credit reports, appraisals, title insurance).

The second important part of the Gramm-Leach-Bliley Act is its Safeguards Rule. The Safeguards Rule (17 C.F.R. 248.30), as referred to as Regulation S-P, relates to the security requirements of this Act and requires financial institutions and mortgage companies to have policies, procedures, and systems setup to ensure the security and confidentiality of all of their customers' information. If you are a mortgage broker of a branch or owner of a mortgage company then you need to be aware of this and have in place a security plan that satisfies the requirements of the Safeguards Rule. And, if you are a loan officer then you need to also be aware of GLBA's Safeguards Rule and how it impacts what you are required to do in storing, organizing, and maintaining your customers' sensitive and non-public information. Therefore, this discussion that follows will cover the main aspects of the Safeguards Rule that every mortgage broker should know about and implement and what every loan officer should be familiar with as well.

To satisfy the requirements of the Safeguards Rule, financial institutions and mortgage companies must implement a formal and written security program that presents how their security program works and the importance of protecting all their customers' information. Additionally, all employees are to be trained on GLBA's Safeguards Rules and the systems, procedures, and plan setup, within that company, to satisfy the requirements of the Safeguards Rule. I should also mention that it is a requirement that all financial institutions and mortgage brokers must have had their (security) plan in place to protect their customers' information, which satisfies the requirements of the Safeguards Rule, by May 23, 2003. Please note that this is not an option but a requirement.

As part of this security and customer protection program, it is required that:

1. At least one employee be assigned to oversee this security program;
2. To conduct a risk assessment, of the company's security systems and procedures, to determine what is needed to properly and fully protect this information;
3. Implement safeguards to protect against those identified risks. This should also be followed up with continued monitoring and testing to ensure that all customers' information is indeed protected.
4. Those third-party providers, who provide their services to the financial institution and mortgage brokers must acknowledge their awareness and willingness to protect the personal information of their customers that is provided to them, by signing a contract stating exactly that.
5. Employees and loan officers will be fully informed and trained on the Safeguards Rule, of the Gramm-Leach-Bliley Act, as well as the security systems, procedures, and expectations setup within that organization.
6. Any sensitive, NPI, and/or private customer information that is electronically transmitted outside the company's network (e.g. emailed) needs to be encrypted. Therefore, if you are a loan officer (or any employee of a financial institution or mortgage company) and are emailing sensitive data or data which contains private and non-public customer information online (e.g. emailed) then that transmission must be encrypted.
7. If credit cards or any other sensitive financial data is collected online (for loan application purposes) then use a Secure Socket Layer (SSL) or some other type of secure connection.

8. Disseminate customers' information on a "need to know" basis and dispose of customers' information and files in a secure manner.

9. Financial institutions and mortgage companies are to continually monitor and test their security systems and procedures to determine if their security program is working well, as required and expected, and update it as the case may be or requires.

According to the Safeguards Rule there are three areas that are important in providing the required and expected security of customers' information:

I. Employee Management and Training:

The basis of this first part is that the success of any security program and plan really rests upon the employees who implement and use it. The following are some suggestions by the Federal Trade Commission (FTC) on how to fulfill the expectations of this area:

- Checking references and doing background checks before hiring employees who will have access to customers' information.
- Limiting customer information access on a "need to know" basis.
- Using "strong" password protection when accessing customer's information on a company's computer and online.
- Training employees what to do to maintain the security, confidentiality, and integrity of their security systems. This includes encrypting sensitive customer information when it is being electronically transmitted (e.g. emailed) outside the company's network.
- Taking the proper steps to prevent terminated employees from subsequently accessing customer information from the company's files and online network.

II. Information Systems:

Information Systems relates to the company's computer and online network, software design, and information processing, storage, transmission, retrieval, and disposal. The following are some of the suggestions, by the FTC, on how to maintain the security of a company's Information Systems:

- Managers and their employees should know where their customer's sensitive information is located and stored and ensure that it is stored safe and securely. This includes protecting that information from hazards like fire and floods, and locking rooms or cabinets that store that information, when it is unattended. This also includes regularly backing up your computer records and storing archive data off-line and in a physically secure area.
- Sensitive customer information that is either electronically transmitted and/or collected online should be secured by either encrypting the transmission of that information or using a Secure Sockets Layer or other secure connection.

- Disposing of customers' information in a secure manner as well as disposing of the software, disks, hardware, and transmission devices that contained customer information.

III. Detecting and Managing System Failures:

This area deals with continually monitoring and detecting the soundness and security of a company's security systems and detecting and defending against any possible breaches of the company's security systems. The following are some suggestions to achieve this:

- Staying up-to-date and current regarding news of existing and emerging threats and available defenses to your company's security systems and its various software programs.

- Setting up and maintaining appropriate programs and controls to prevent unauthorized access to customers' information.

- Continually oversee and audit internal systems to prevent and detect any improper disclosure or theft of customer information.

- Setting up, communicating, and training employees on how to maintain the soundness and integrity of the existing security systems and what to do if and when a breach occurs.

- Who to contact if and when a breach, of a security system, does occur (e.g. related customers, law enforcement, credit bureaus, and any others that may be affected by the breach).

In closing, on this discussion on the Safeguards Rule, of the Gramm-Leach-Bliley Act, I would like to mention again that all financial institutions and mortgage brokers must have had a plan in place to protect their customers' information that satisfies the requirements of the Safeguards Rule as of May 23, 2003. In other words, every financial institution and mortgage company today must have an existing security plan and program in place that satisfies the requirements of GLBA's Safeguards Rule.

HOME MORTGAGE DISCLOSURE ACT (HMDA):

The Home Mortgage Disclosure Act, oftentimes referred to as HMDA (that's pronounced like HOMDA – like Honda but with an "M" in there), was first enacted by Congress in 1975 and was updated and expanded in 1989. The Home Mortgage Disclosure Act is also referred to as Regulation C. The main purpose of HMDA is to provide additional and required information and data entered on a mortgage loan application (the 1003): Characteristics of your loan applicants, location of the subject property, and it also relates to the types of loan applications received by your mortgage company and the final credit decisions made on each.

HMDA also focuses on detecting lending discrimination by home mortgage lenders. These are what I refer to as Government Monitoring questions. Therefore, when you are completing the 1003 with your borrowers and get to an area on that form that asks about personal characteristics of your borrowers, the location of the subject property, and some features of the loan for those borrowers, then it is a good chance that you asking questions relating to HMDA. Loan originations that are covered under HMDA are home purchase, improvement, and refinance loans. Therefore, from a loan officer's standpoint, it's the information on the 1003 that HMDA is mainly focusing on.

HOME OWNERSHIP AND EQUITY PROTECTION ACT (HOEPA):
Home Ownership and Equity Protection Act (HOEPA) first came into being in 1994 and is a part of Regulation Z within Section 226.32. The Home Ownership and Equity Protection Act is often referred to as Section 32. And, during December of 2001, the Federal Reserve Board approved the issuance of another ruling that amended Section 32, of Regulation Z, in which compliance became mandatory for us on October 1, 2002.

Now, because of the complexities, in the calculations for determining if a loan has Section 32 concerns, I hesitated as to whether or not to include it in this chapter. However, because of the Federal Reserve Board's and the CFPB's continuing efforts to curb Predatory Lending (which I applaud them on) I felt that the subject of HOEPA would not be complete without discussing Section 32. Therefore, please consider this discussion on Section 32 a brief and incomplete presentation of it. Its main purpose is to introduce you to its existence and alert you to when you might have a Section 32 concern on a loan you are be working on, and to research further if you suspect that you do.

Now, as the acronym HOEPA implies, Section 32 applies to owner-occupied and currently owned properties. It, therefore, is focusing on refinance type of loans and not purchase or home construction type of loans. Broadly speaking, Section 32 dictates what are the maximum loan fees and points, as a percent of the total loan amount, that a loan may contain as well as the maximum APR on that type of loan. Thus, there are primarily two tests in determining if a loan has Section 32 concerns, whereby that loan could then be covered under HOEPA:

1. The percent of the total loan fees and points, in relation to the total amount of that home loan
2. The APR on that home loan.

If you are originating refinance home loans with the loan amounts around $100,000 then you most likely would not encounter any Section 32 concerns. However, if you are originating a small 1st mortgage loan (around $30,000 or less) and/or a 2nd mortgage loan with the same loan amount (or less) then Section 32 could come into play here and be a real concern. When this happens then you need to know how to calculate the various loan costs to determine if you are within the loan cost limits stipulated by Section 226.32.

The Home Ownership and Equity Protection Act came about, I believe, because of the increasing concerns, of the "Powers That Be", of the perceived increase in predatory lending practices within the mortgage-lending arena. It was also believed that predatory lending practices have been an influencing factor in the increase of home foreclosures within certain communities. Now, currently HOEPA covers only closed-end loans. However, the "Powers That Be" have been and are seriously looking at including open-end loans under the coverage of HOEPA as well. So, be prepared for this when it happens. Now, when I say "Predatory Lending practices" what am I referring to? The following lists four of the more common "Predatory Lending practices":

1. **High-Cost Loans:**

   While there may be a number of definitions as to what a "High-Cost" loan is, HOEPA has laid out some very specific descriptions of what this is, and what "Triggers" cause a loan to be covered under HOEPA. As you may recall, there are two tests that a mortgage loan is given that can Trigger a loan being covered under HOEPA. And, according to the CFPB, under the High-Cost Mortgage Rule (which started in January 2014) the maximum points and fees as well as the maximum APR also depends on whether the home loan is a 1st or 2nd mortgage. For example, for:

   First Mortgage Loans:

   - The APR exceeds 6.5 percentage points higher than the Average Prime Offer Rate (APOR).

   - However, if the home loan is less than $50,000, for a personal property dwelling (e.g. Manufactured home) then the APR exceeds 8.5 percentage points higher than the APOR.

   Second or Junior Mortgages:

   - The APR exceeds 8.5 percentage points higher than the Average Prime Offer Rate (APOR) for a similar second mortgage.

   - However, is that home loan is $20,000 or more and the total points and fees exceed 5% of the total home loan amount then it is a High-Cost Mortgage Loan. Or,

   - If the home loan amount is less than $20,000 and the total points and fees exceed the lesser of 8% of the loan or $1,000 then it becomes a High-Cost Mortgage Loan.

2. **Refinancing `Troubled' Loans into Another High-Cost Loan:**

   When loan customers are having problems paying on their existing mortgage (which may already be defined as a "High-Cost" loan) then this is the practice of some lenders of encouraging those loan customers to refinance into another loan, which may contain high-fees. Doing this, results in increasing the new loan amount owed over their previous loan, and reduces the equity that those customers had in their home. This practice of steering loan customers into another unaffordable loan that further decreases the equity in their home is referred to as "loan flipping" or "equity stripping." Oftentimes, this new refinance loan is not any more affordable, for those customers, than their previous one and this takes us back to #2 above.

3. Repayment Ability:

This concerns a lender's practice of making mortgage loans to consumers, primarily based on the equity in their property, with little or no regard to that consumer's ability to repay or make payments on that new home loan. Their repayment ability should include that consumer's current and expected income, current obligations, and their employment status. This information enables us to calculate the qualifying ratios for a home loan customer.

This could also fall under what is referred to as "Discounted Introductory Rates" or "Teaser Rates," whereby that customer's loan is set at an initial low interest rate and that rate is later adjusted higher. The question here is: When that interest rate adjusts, or let us say increases, up to the maximum interim interest rate cap - causing an increase in their monthly mortgage payments, will that loan customer then be able to afford and pay those newly adjusted monthly mortgage payments? This generally should not occur if you have qualified that home loan customer according to the Ability-to-Repay and Qualified Mortgage Rules.

4. Structuring a Close-End Loan as an Open-End Loan:

Creditors, in order to avoid the restrictions placed on those loans covered under HOEPA, may encourage and/or steer some loan customers toward an open-end type of loan. In doing this, that creditor then need not worry about those Triggers of HOEPA. And, that creditor may have done this solely for the purpose of avoiding those restrictions of HOEPA, without any regards to what is in the best financial interest of a loan customer.

However, creditors who do this should be aware that if a loan is documented as an open-end loan but the features and terms, of that loan, show that it does not meet the definition of an open-end loan then that loan is subject to the rules for a closed-end loan. At that point it could also be covered under HOEPA – if the rate (APR) and/or fee Trigger is met.

Section 32 Mortgages:

And finally, I want to talk about another federal lending regulation I mentioned above that you should be aware of. It is referred to and called Section 32 in our profession and also is covered under HOEPA. It first came into being in 1994 and is a part of Regulation Z in Section 226.32. And, during December of 2001 the Federal Reserve Board approved the issuance of another ruling that amended Section 32, of Regulation Z, and in which compliance became mandatory for us on October 3, 2002.

Because of the complexities, in the calculations for determining if a loan has Section 32 concerns I hesitated as to whether to include it in this chapter on Mortgage Lending Regulations. However, because of the Federal Reserve Board's continuing efforts to curb Predatory Lending (which I applaud them on) I felt that this chapter on Mortgage Lending Regulations would not be complete without discussing this subject. Therefore, please consider this discussion on

Section 32 a brief and incomplete presentation of it. Its main purpose is to introduce you to its existence and alert you to when you might have a Section 32 concern on a loan you are working on and to research further if you suspect that you do.

As the acronym HOEPA implies, Section 32 applies to owner-occupied and currently owned properties. It is therefore focusing on refinance type of loans and not purchase or home construction type of loans. Broadly speaking, Section 32 dictates what are the maximum loan fees and points, as a percent of the total loan amount, that a loan may contain as well as the maximum APR on that (type of) loan. Thus, there are primarily two tests in determining if a loan has Section 32 concerns, whereby it would then be covered under HOEPA: 1. Percent of total loan fees and points, in relation to the total loan amount, and 2. The APR on that loan. For greater detail on what those maximum fees and points, as well as the maximum APR, for Section 32 mortgages please refer to the discussion on High-Priced loans below under the topic of predatory lending.

If you are doing a small mortgage loan and exceeding the percent (costs) limits of Section 32 then you will need to have your customers signed a Section 32 Disclosure form at least 3 business days prior to that loan's closing (and I understand that there could be other Loan Disclosures that those customers might now need to be presented with as well). I personally feel, that with all the legal suits and concerns taking place today regarding Predatory Lending, that the legal protection (for you and your company) of the borrowers signing this Disclosure form is suspect. I therefore recommend you do everything you can to keep your total loan costs (and APR rate) on your loans within the acceptable Section 32 limits. On the Wholesale Lending side I am increasingly seeing Lenders today refusing to do <u>any</u> Section 32 loans (loans that exceed Section 32 limits). Section 32 is another subject I recommend you should discuss with your branch manager when covering the important subject of Lending Regulations. And certainly, if you suspect you are working on a loan that just might have a Section 32 concern then please discuss this with your manager.

HOMEOWNER'S PROTECTION ACT OF 1998:
The Homeowner's Protection Act of 1998, also referred to as the PMI Act, addresses the issue of Private Mortgage Insurance and when PMI can be eliminated from a homeowner's monthly payments. Essentially, within this Act, it states three situations in which a borrower's PMI may be cancelled:

1. **By Request:** When the LTV on a customer's home loan reaches 80% or less, through a combination of reduction of their outstanding loan balance and/or appreciation of the value of their home, then that customer can request their Lender to cancel the PMI on their loan. It has been my experience that when this option is used then the Lender will generally require a minimum of a drive-by appraisal - to verify the current value of that home.

2. **Automatic:** When the LTV on their home loan reaches 78%. This would be due to the reduction of their outstanding loan balance through the borrower's monthly mortgage payments. Here, the Lender would automatically cancel their PMI when the borrowers' equity position reaches at least 22%.

3. **Final Termination:** If the PMI on a mortgage has not been terminated through numbers 1 and 2 above, then it is required by this Act, that following the first day of the month immediately following the date that is the midpoint of the amortization period of that loan – that the PMI be eliminated from that homeowner's monthly mortgage payments.

I should also mention here that in order for a homeowner to eliminate the PMI on their mortgage, either through options 1, 2, or 3 above, the homeowner's monthly mortgage payments must be current at that time, according to the terms of that mortgage.

And, I should further note that the above PMI Act relates only to those home loans - which originated after July 29, 1999. However, I believe you will find that even for those loans older than that most Lenders would be agreeable to eliminating the borrower's PMI if those conditions as stated in numbers 1 & 2 above are or could be realized.

LOAN ORIGINATOR RULE:
First, a little history: on August 16, 2010, the Federal Reserve Board amended Regulation Z, of the Truth-In-Lending Act that included new provisions regarding Loan Originator Compensation and what is permissible in structuring mortgage home loans. Those new rulings, regarding loan originator's compensation, applied to all mortgage loans received by the Creditor (the lender on the loan) on or after April 1, 2011. That ruling profoundly changed how mortgage loan originators were paid for originating mortgage loans – especially because it eliminated mortgage loan originators from being paid on the 'back-end' of a mortgage loan via yield spread premiums. Those regulations were later re-codified, by the CFPB, in December 2011 to further restrict certain loan originator compensations.

Then, following this earlier loan originator compensation ruling, the CFPB implemented new loan originator regulations for the purposes of implementing the related rules from the Dodd-Frank Act. Those revised regulations, for loan originator compensation, were officially referred to as the Bureau's Loan Originator Rule. However, today, we simply refer to it as the Loan Originator Rule. I should mention that the CFPB had planned to fully implement the regulations of the Loan Originator Rule on June 1, 2013. However, implementation of the new Loan Originator Rule took place on January 10, 2014.

After reviewing the regulations of the Loan Originator Rule I could see that it maintains many of the prior Loan Originator Compensation rules while making some additional and new ones. Especially those regulations relating to mortgage loan originators that must be licensed and registered, if required, under the SAFE Act or other state or federal law.

Compensation, as it is used in the CFPB's rulings, includes commissions, salaries, any financial or otherwise incentives, periodic or annual bonuses, and any awards of merchandise, services, prizes, or trips. I should also mention that compensation to a loan originator is any amount(s) that is received by and retained by a loan originator. The key word in that sentence is "retained".

The provisions of the Loan Originator Rule pertain to anyone who could be defined as a "Loan Originator". According to the Loan Originator Rule, that includes individuals and entities that perform loan origination activities for compensation, such as taking an application, offering credit terms, negotiating credit terms on behalf of a consumer, obtaining an extension of credit for a consumer, or referring a consumer to a loan originator or creditor. A "loan originator" could be either an individual or an organization. For example:

- **Individual Loan Originators**: Are natural persons, such as individuals who perform loan origination activities and work for mortgage brokerage firms or creditors.

- **Loan Originator Organizations**: Are generally loan originators that are not natural persons, such as mortgage brokerage firms or sole proprietorships.

Therefore, if you can be defined as a "loan originator" then, for purposes of compensation provisions, you generally may not receive compensation that is based upon:

- A *term* of a single transaction
- The *terms* of multiple transactions conducted by you.
- The *terms* of multiple transactions conducted by multiple loan originators, taken in the aggregate (such as most profits-based compensations plans).

Having said that, allow me now to define what a Transaction Term is according to the Loan Originator Rule. A Transaction Term is any right or obligation of the parties to a credit transaction, except for the amount of credit (e.g. the amount of the loan).

Now, before I go into the details of the Loan Originator Rules let me say that I have heard a number of Mortgage loan originators, out there in mortgage lending land, say that some of these rulings are very confusing to work with in structuring a home loan for a prospective home loan customer. I know that when I first read the amended Truth-In-Lending Act containing these LO Compensation rulings I too was somewhat confused

So, in response to this, apparently a HUD official attended a local NAMB meeting and explained how to easily understand the Loan Originator Rules and how to properly input this information on the Loan Estimate. On the following page is a picture of that HUD representative presenting his explanation of the CFPB new rulings on the chalk board behind him. A mortgage loan originator friend of mine sent me this picture (below) and I'm sure you'll find it amusing as well.

HUD Official going over the "Loan Originator Compensation Rules"

I hope you got a few chuckles and laughs out of this picture as I did. And, I also hope the CFPB and HUD will forgive me for having a little fun at their expense. But seriously though, the new Loan Originator Rules are not that difficult to understand and apply – once someone clearly explains how to do this. And, that's what I am going to do now.

Okay, while there could, and most likely are, numerous reasons for the development of the 'old' rulings on Loan Originator Compensation, that began on April 1, 2011, and the new Loan Originator Rule, I believe it would be safe to say that it was and is to prevent fraud and predatory lending, provide a level playing field between mortgage bankers and mortgage brokers, provide consistency in structuring mortgage loans, and also provide transparency to home loan borrowers.

I should also note that the CFPB previous rulings, that began on April 1, 2011, and the new Loan Originator Rule that went into effect on January 10, 2014, applies to (all) individuals who participate in originating mortgage loans.

- Mortgage loan originators (employed by mortgage companies & depository financial institutions, as well as other Lenders).

- Mortgage Brokers (and any companies that employ them).

- Creditors (Lenders, those providing funding for the loan).

The Loan Originator Rule applies to all closed-end loans secured by real property or a dwelling and with first and subordinate liens. And, it also includes reverse mortgages as well. However, these new rulings currently do not apply to HELOC loans and timeshares.

According to the CFPB, as it impacts loan originator's compensation, the following three prohibitions which began on, April 1, 2011, continue on today under the Loan Originator Rule:

1. **Payments (Compensation) to any Loan Originator that are based upon the Terms and Conditions of a mortgage loan.**

   Therefore, mortgage loan originators cannot be allowed to be compensated based upon the Terms and Conditions of a loan, such as:

   - Interest Rate
   - Loan-To-Value (LTV)
   - Credit Score of the Primary Borrower
   - Debt-To-Income Ratio (DTI)
   - Annual Percentage Rate (APR)
   - Any Prepayment Penalty on the loan, and
   - The Loan Product selected

   OK. Conversely, let's now take a look at some examples of compensation, to a loan originator (LO), that is not based upon loan Terms and Conditions:

   - The quality of loan files submitted and/or loan performance over time.
   - Overall loan volume.
   - Hourly Rate of Pay – to compensate the LO for hours worked.
   - A legitimate business expense.
   - Payments that are fixed in advance for every loan submitted and/or closed.
   - The percentage of loan applications to a Creditor or Lender that closed.

2. **Compensation Directly from Loan Customers.**

   Before I get into this ruling, first allow me to define what is considered to be a direct and indirect payment by a loan customer – according to the amended TIL.

   - **Direct**: Payments to a loan originator made from out of the loan proceeds are considered Compensation received directly from the consumer.

   - **Indirect**: Payments to a loan originator that are derived from an increased interest rate (Premium Pricing) or Points paid on the loan (to the Creditor or Lender) (Discount Points) are not considered Compensation received directly from the consumer (hence, received Indirectly)

   Now, in the past, prior to the April 1st ruling, loan originators could receive compensation on a home loan through the origination fee charged and the YSP paid by the Creditor or Lender on that loan. Since April 1, 2011 this has not been permitted. All compensation that is received by the loan originator, for a home loan, today, and under the Loan Originator Rule must be:

   - Received either directly from the consumer – as shown within "Origination Charge" at the top of page two of the Loan Estimate. Therefore, in fulfilling this ruling, Compensation to a loan originator made out of the customer's loan proceeds that is considered Compensation received directly from the consumer or loan customer. Or,

- Indirectly, if the loan customer pays points (e.g. Discount Points) to the Creditor and Lender then this is not considered loan originator compensation from the consumer or loan borrower. The percent and amount of these Points would be shown on page two of the Loan Estimate, under Section J within the "Calculating Cash to Close" section. Within this last section of Page Two you would include any:
    - Premium Pricing
    - Discount Points

The Loan Originator Rule continues, as with the previous rulings, that states that all loan originators may receive compensation from only one source. For example, if the loan customer pays the origination fee on their loan to the Lender or Creditor and the Lender then compensates the loan originator – then the loan originator is not permitted to also receive Compensation directly or indirectly from that loan customer or any other person. Another example could be in structuring a "No-Cost" loan: If all costs of a "No-Cost" loan (including the mortgage loan originator's Compensation) are included within the Discount Points then that loan originator may not also be paid through an Origination Fee, or by any other payment source.

According to the Truth-In-Lending Act - any person who knows that a consumer has paid Compensation to a loan originator on any loan transaction then that person will be prohibited from additionally paying any Compensation (directly or indirectly) to that loan originator in connection with that home loan transaction. I should further add here, that if a person was unaware of any Compensation paid to the loan originator then I'd say that the responsibility would then fall upon that loan originator to inform that person of their Compensation to be received (or has been received) for that loan transaction (and refuse any additional Compensation).

And, within Compensation Paid, the compensation paid to an individual loan originator may not exceed, in aggregate, 10% of the individual loan originator's total compensation corresponding to the time period for which the compensation under the non-deferred profits-based compensation plan is paid.

Modification of Loan Terms:
According to the existing loan originator's compensation rules a loan originator's Compensation can neither be increased nor decreased based upon a loan's Terms and Conditions. For example, if a loan customer requested a lower interest rate and that was accepted by the Creditor then that Creditor is not permitted to reduce the amount it pays to the loan originator – based on the change in loan terms. Similarly, any reduction in Origination Points paid by a consumer would then be a cost paid by the Creditor.

However, the Loan Originator Rule does have an exception to this that does allow a loan originator to lower their compensation. And, that is when there are unforeseen increases in the settlement cost. The key word here is "unforeseen". For example, let's say that the loan customer locked in their interest rate and because of unavoidable delays, caused by the title company, that the loan customer lost their rate lock. In that case, if the loan customer needed or wanted to keep that rate (at perhaps a cost to extend it) then the originating mortgage loan originator is permitted to lower their compensation in order to pay for that interest rate extension. Again, keep in mind, that the circumstances permitting this exception must be unforeseen.

Now that I've covered some of the regulations of what is prohibited, according to the Loan Originator Rule, I'd like to also go over some loan originator compensation rules that the Loan Originator Rule does allow:

- **Compensation That Varies from One Loan Originator to Another:**
  Creditor and Lenders may compensate their own mortgage loan originators differently than mortgage brokers they do business with. For instance, this is to account for mortgage brokers that incur certain fixed overhead costs associated with loan originations. A Creditor may therefore pay mortgage brokers more than its own retail mortgage loan originators.

- **Compensation based on Loan Volume**:
  The Loan Originator Rule also does not prohibit a Creditor or Lender from basing compensation on an originator's loan volume, whether by the total dollar amount of credit extended or the total number of loans originated over a given time period. This ruling also goes on to add that Creditors, in following this ruling, must ensure that their incentive compensation arrangements comply with the current requirements of TILA.

- **Compensation that differs based on Geography**:
  Payment of compensation to a loan originator that differs by geographical area is allowed, under the Loan Originator Rule, provided that such compensation arrangements also complied with other applicable laws – such as the Equal Credit Opportunity Act and Fair Housing Act. Here, it appears that the CFPB decided that the differences in compensation, paid to a loan originator, and based upon geography would be allowed – provided that the differences (in compensation) would account for the costs of origination – such as fixed overhead costs (in that area).

- **Periodic changes in Loan Originator Compensation:**
  A Creditor may periodically revise the compensation they pay a loan originator as long as the revised compensation arrangement is not based on the Terms or Conditions of a (single) transaction. Thus, a Creditor may periodically review factors, of a loan originator, such as loan performance, loan volume, and current market conditions for determining and revising a loan originator's compensation. And, prospectively revise the compensation the Creditor will pay the loan originator based on future loan transactions.

- **Compensation that is based on the Amount of Credit Extended on a Loan:**
  This last item seems to be where a lot of misunderstanding resides – so let's talk about it. While it's true that a loan originator's compensation could be based on

the total loan amount (credit extended), there are certain conditions that apply to this:

1. Compensation paid to loan originators that is based upon the amount of credit extended (the total loan amount) is permitted as long as the percentage is fixed and does not vary with the total amount of credit extended. Thus, a Creditor or Lender could pay a loan originator 1% of the total credit extended for each loan – but no less than $1,000 and no more than $5,000. For example, $1,000 on a $50,000 loan and no more than $5,000 on a $900,000 loan.

2. However, a Creditor or Lender may <u>not</u> pay compensation to a loan originator that is based upon a leveled or tier scale of the amount of credit extended. Applying this, and as an example, it is not permitted to pay a loan originator 1% of the total amount of credit extended for loans having a total amount of $300,000 or more; 2% of the total amount of credit extended for total loan amounts of $200,000 to 299,000; and 3% of the total amount of credit extended for loan amounts of $199,000 or less.

   The important point, of this last item, is that any compensation that is paid to a loan originator, by a Creditor or Lender, must be fixed and agreed upon in advance and is in no way is related to the Terms or Conditions of any one mortgage loan.

Safe Harbor Compensation Methods:
The Loan Originator Rule does recognize 7 acceptable compensation methods with respect to payment of salary, commissions, and other compensation. However, these methods are not based on transaction terms (or proxies for transaction terms). Those seven compensation methods are:

- The loan originator's overall dollar volume (total dollar amount or total of loan transactions) delivered to the creditor.

- The long-term performance of the originator's loans.

- An hourly pay rate based on the actual number of hours worked.

- Loans made to new customers versus loans to existing customers.

- A payment that is fixed in advance for every loan the originator arranges for the creditor.

- The percentage of the loan originator's applications that close.

- The quality of the loan originator's loan files. For example, the accuracy and completeness of the loan documentation that is submitted to the creditor.

Other compensation methods may also be used, and still provide the Safe Harbor stated above, as long as those methods comply with the Loan Originator Rule.

Steering a Customer towards a Loan with a Higher Compensation:
A Loan Originator may not suggest, advise, or counsel a prospective loan customer to accept a loan transaction that would increase the Loan Originator's compensation but yet would not be in that customer's best interest and/or a loan with less favorable Terms. As I previously mentioned, in the discussion on predatory lending, this type of "Steering" victimizes loan borrowers and creates a higher monthly P&I mortgage payment, for that mortgage loan borrower, and puts additional and undo pressure on a homeowner's total monthly debt servicing. And, can cause erosion of a homeowner's equity. All these factors can and have contributed towards an increase in mortgage delinquencies, defaults, and foreclosures.

Safe Harbor:
However, as a Loan Originator, it is your job to counsel and advise your prospective home loan customers on what mortgage loan product(s) you believe would best meet their expressed financial interest, need, and goals. So, what can you do? If you are not sure or certain of what loan product, Terms, and Conditions to suggest to any home loan customer then a "Safe Harbor" is provided for Loan Originators, in complying with this anti-steering rule (To be on the safe side I also suggest always doing this). No violation of this anti-steering rule would occur if:

- Under certain circumstances, the consumer was presented with at least three loan options for each type of transaction the consumer expressed an interest in and would qualify for.

- Present to your loan customer those loan offers, for each type of loan transaction, in which that loan customer qualifies and has expressed their interest in (e.g. FRM, ARM, 2nd Mortgage, or a Reverse Mortgage):

  - The lowest interest rate for which that loan customer qualifies, and

  - The lowest dollar amount for Origination Points and Fees and Discount Points for each presented loan offer. And,

  - Presented the lowest interest rate that the loan customer qualifies for without any "Risky Loan Features" such as:
    - ➤ Prepayment Penalty
    - ➤ Negative Amortization
    - ➤ A Demand Feature
    - ➤ Balloon Payment – within the first seven years
    - ➤ With Shared Equity or Shared Appreciation
    - ➤ For Reverse Mortgages: No prepayment Penalty, Shared Equity or Shared Appreciation.

- If the Loan Originator regularly does business with fewer than three Lenders or Creditors then the Mortgage loan originator is considered compliant by obtaining and presenting to their loan customers loan offers from all the Lenders he or she regularly does business with and for which the customer qualifies. However, if the Loan Originator regularly does business with a significant number of Creditor or Lenders (more than three) then it is not expected that the Mortgage loan originator needs to obtain loan offers from all of them.

As a follow-up to the above, a Loan Originator is considered regularly doing business with a Creditor or Lender if:

- There is a written agreement between the originator and a Creditor governing the originator's submission of mortgage loan applications to that Creditor.

- The Creditor has extended credit, secured by a dwelling, to one or more consumers during the current or previous calendar month based on an application submitted by the Loan Originator; or

- The Creditor has extended credit, secured by a dwelling, twenty-five or more times during the previous twelve calendar months based on applications submitted by the Loan Originator. For this purpose, the previous twelve calendar months begin with the calendar month that precedes the month in which the Loan Originator accepted the loan customer's application.

- However, if the Loan Originator presents more than three loan options, that the customer has expressed interest in and qualifies for, then the Loan Originator must highlight the three loans that satisfy the requirements of the Safe Harbor (as stated above).

Home Loans with Variable Interest Rate Features:
If an offered loan product (e.g. ARM) has an initial fixed rate for the first five years then Loan Originators must use that initial interest rate in structuring their customer's loan and final loan disclosures. However, if that loan product's interest rate could adjust within the first five years then the following is required:

- If a loan's Interest Rate can vary and is based upon changes to an index then the Loan Originator must use the fully-indexed rate that would be in effect at loan closing – without regards to any discount or premium.

- If the loan is a Step-rate loan then the Loan Originator must use the highest interest rate that could apply during the first five years of that loan.

Required Loan Originator Information on the Loan Documents:
If you are a loan originator organization for home loan transactions then you must provide the following information on specified loan documents (according to the SAFE Rule):

- Your name and NMLSR ID number (if the NMLS has provided you with an NMLSR ID number).

- The name of the individual loan originator (as the name appears in the NMLSR) who had primary responsibility for the home loan origination and his NMLSR ID number, if he has one.

Those home loan documents that must contain the loan originator's name and NMLSR ID number are:

- The Credit Application (e.g. the 1003).

- The Note or Loan Contract, and
- Loan Estimate
- Closing Disclosure
- The Security Instrument.

I should also mention here, that in doing the above, you do not need to include this information more than once on each of the above specified loan documents (i.e. no need to put that information on every page of each document).

And finally, after stating the above, regarding the new rulings on Loan Originator Compensation, I'd like to list a couple of items you might also be interested in knowing since January 10, 2014 rolled around:

- Lender's Rate Sheets are not expected to change.

- Yield Spread Premiums may still be changed to the borrower. However, instead of being "back-end" income to a Mortgage loan originator the YSP is now applied as a credit to the customer's home loan costs (e.g. Premium Pricing).

- Lenders, Creditors, Mortgage Brokers, and any other persons that compensate Loan Originators must retain records for at least three years after the consummation of the loan transaction. My experience has shown me that different states have had different record retention requirements: Some states require retaining records up to five years or more. This new ruling, at least, sets a minimum time of record retention.

MORTGAGE ACTS AND PRACTICES RULE (MAPS):
On July 19, 2011, the Federal Trade Commission (FTC) issued a final rule banning deceptive mortgage advertising. That ruling is called the Mortgage Acts and Practices - Advertising Rule (The MAPS Rule). Although the Federal Trade Commission was the first regulator of MAPS it is now enforced by the CFPB. The Mortgage Acts and Practices Rule applies only to non-deposit mortgage lenders, state-chartered credit unions, and entities that market and advertise mortgage products.

And, as you will see below, RESPA, Regulation X, under 12 CFR 1024.14 and Regulation Z also gets involved in the advertising practices for mortgage loan originators.

According to the Mortgage Acts and Practices Rule (16 C.F.R. Part 321), Regulation N (Section 1014), it considers advertising as "any written or oral statement, illustration, or depiction . . . that is designed to effect a sale or create interest in purchasing goods or services, whether it appears on or in (various media), such as:

- Newspapers, magazines, brochures, leaflets, or pamphlets
- Radio, television, or cable television-Internet or cellular network-Letter or insert
- Poster, billboard, or public transit card
- Audio program transmitted over a telephone system, telemarketing script, or on-hold script.

So, let's begin with the first example of advertising on the above MAPS Rule's List. And, as you will see, what restrictions apply to one type of media advertising pretty much applies to all others.

I. Advertising in Newspapers, Periodicals, Poster and Flyers, and on a Billboard:

According to Regulation Z, whenever you advertise your services, in a newspaper, magazine, poster or flyer, and/or on a billboard (to name a few) and quote an interest rate and/or closing costs and/or loan fees (what are called the Cost of Credit) then you need to also state, on that advertisement, the APR on that loan and/or quoted interest rate. And, I should note that the size of the print, for that stated APR, needs to be prominent (i.e. the same size as the interest rate shown) and not made up of some tiny print located way at the bottom of the page, as on some I have seen in the past.

Some time ago I completed compliance reports for some of the states in which a nation-wide mortgage company was approved. During my research I found that some states have some very specific regulations they required of loan originators when advertising their services. My point of mentioning the advertising requirements of different States is to alert you to the fact that the state in which you are advertising may have very additional and specific advertising requirements peculiar to it. So, check it out and make sure you are doing what you need to do to be "In Compliance" with not only the national and federal regulations but also what is required in your state.

Advertising with Realtors:

Now, according to MAPS it is all right for a mortgage loan officer or broker and a real estate agent to jointly advertise in a brochure or newspaper as long both participants are equally paying in this advertising endeavor. However, if one of those participants is paying less than a pro-rata share of the total cost then this could be a MAPS violation.

Trigger Terms in Advertisements:

The wording that you use in your advertisements is also important. According to MAPS, if there are certain words or phrases, called Triggering Terms, that are used in your advertisements then additional disclosure(s) are required - to clarify what those Triggering Terms mean. For example:

➢ **Down-payment Required**:
  If an actual down payment is required then this statement needs to be qualified, for example:
  - Only 10% Down Required
  - Move In with As little as $200

➢ **Payment Period**:
  If you state a Payment Period in your advertising then this too needs to be clarified, for example:
  - 30-Year Mortgage
  - Repayment in 40 monthly installments

> **Payment Amount**:
>
>   As above, with payment period, if you state a Payment Amount in your advertising then this needs to be clarified, for example:
>   - Monthly payments of only $300.00
>   - Weekly payments of only $200.00

> **Finance Charge**:
>
>   If you state a Finance Charge(s) in your advertising then this needs to be clarified as well, for example:
>   - Total Cost of Credit is Only $800.00
>   - $100,000 mortgages with Only 1.0 point to the borrower

And, before I leave this discussion on Triggering Terms let me say that if you use any of these triggering terms in your oral solicitations, such as talking to a prospective loan customer on the telephone, then you must also clarify those terms as shown above.

Guaranteed Terms:

MAPS seems to be concerned with not only what is actually stated, on your advertisements, but also what might not be stated. For example, if you advertise a promotional loan product and any customer, who wishes to take advantage of that promotional offer, must contact you within the next 30 days, then this must be stated on that advertisement. Thus, if a lender wishes to not guarantee any terms of a loan in their advertisements, then that lender needs to also state when and what terms are subject to change, and what terms are not.

On the other hand, if an advertisement states specific credit terms of a loan, then that lender needs to also state, in that advertisement, those terms that are actually offered and/or will be arranged by that lender.

II. Working with Real Estate Agents and other Service Providers:

Restriction and violations that fall under this area can also be found within RESPA, Regulation X, under 12 CFR 1024.14. Now, it has been my experience that many successful mortgage brokers and loan officers have developed a working relationship with one or more realtors and some may have also established working relationships with home contractors, attorneys, and financial consultants (to name a few). Doing this can provide excellent referral sources of folks who are interested in obtaining a mortgage loan. In the field of business it is a common practice that when someone does something for you – you in turn reciprocate and do something for them. Many times this is referred to as "Tit-for-Tat." or "Quid Pro Quo". However, it's that very thing (reciprocating a referral) that can cause loan originators to cross the line and either knowingly or inadvertently do something that is not "In Compliance" with mortgage lending regulations. And, Frank Torch and I have found that this is the area that has the most "myths" about what are acceptable and legal practices between business-referring relationships.

For example, below are some myths, I have heard, regarding working with real estate realtors:

1. It's all right to give a gift to a referring source, like a realtor, as long as the gift is not greater than $50.00.
2. It's not a violation to bring donuts to the realtor's office or take them out to lunch every once in a while.
3. It's okay to treat a realtor (hopefully someone who is sending you a good amount of business) to a game of golf.
4. There's no wrong doing in giving a small referral fee to anyone who has referred and/or sent a borrower to you – as long as it is under $50.00.

Have you heard any of these myths before? Perhaps you may have done one or more of the above in the past, thinking that it was all right and no harm was done. Now let me tell you the truth regarding the above. First, let me say that one of the purposes of enacting the Real Estate Settlement Procedures in 1974 was to eliminate kickbacks and/or referral fees that tend to increase unnecessarily the costs of certain settlement services. When mortgage folks are talking about this area of RESPA, they usually refer to it as Section 8 of RESPA.

Now what does that mean? That means that anything of value, such as a gift, money, discounts, commissions, or movie tickets that are given as a result of loan referral(s), received and/or to be received, falls under what could be considered a kickback or a referral fee. It's what Regulation X of RESPA, defines as a "Thing of Value". And, that's a violation of RESPA. Therefore, when you look at the list above, I think you can see that each one of those four myths listed is a violation of RESPA.

And, since I am talking about kickbacks and referral fees, I'd like to also talk about another closely related subject regarding this – sometimes referred to as commission fee splits or splits fees. This also falls under Section 8(b) of RESPA. This Section prohibits the giving and/or receiving of a split fee except for those services that were actually performed (otherwise it could be considered a kickback or referral fee). For example, let's say a customer comes to you for a home loan. You complete the 1003 on them and come to the conclusion that you and your mortgage company cannot do that loan for them. However, you know that Louie Mortgage, that is located around the corner, can. You then call up a loan officer of Louie Mortgage, explain the details of that loan, and he says he can do it. You completed the 1003 on that customer so you believe you deserve something for that. You, therefore, talk with that loan officer about this and you both agreed on a split fee in doing that loan. Is this okay? No, it is a violation of Section 8(b) and is also considered a referral fee. Why? Because you haven't done enough work on that loan to be paid on "services that have actually been done".

Therefore, my advice is: If you cannot do the loan for a loan customer, then perhaps suggest to that customer one or two mortgage companies or banks that might be able to do that loan for them. And, who knows, maybe that mortgage company or bank may one day reciprocate and send you some business that they are unable to do. But the bottom line here is: Avoid anything that could be construed as a kickback, referral fee, and/or a commission split.

III. Advertising on the Internet:

Many years ago it used to be that there were not any lending regulations that addressed mortgage loan originators advertising on the Internet. However, since the Dodd-Frank Act and the creation of the Consumer Financial Protections Bureau (CFPB) all that has changed. As you saw at the beginning of this chapter, advertising on the Internet is viewed by the Truth-In-Lending Act (Regulation Z) and the Mortgage Acts and Practices (MAPS) Rule (Regulation N) the same as any of the other means of advertising and those restriction that apply to those others also apply to advertising on the Internet.

IV. Calling Prospective Loan Customers on the Telephone:

I hate to have to repeat myself, but what I stated above regarding Section 1026.26 of Regulation Z and also Title XII of the Dodd-Frank Act applies when you are talking to prospective loan customers on the telephone. If you are talking to them and quote them an interest rate or state the closing costs or fees on a loan then you need to also tell them, immediately afterwards, the APR on that loan. This is an area, I am afraid, where many loan originators drop the ball: They either willingly or feel forced by the customer to quote them an interest rate for a loan and yet don't follow that up with the APR for that quoted interest rate. There are, however, options when the APR cannot be determined in advance: You could quote a comparable APR for that interest rate. For more information on quoting the APR on open-end and closed-end loans, please refer to:

https://www.consumerfinance.gov/policy-compliance/rulemaking/regulations/1026/26/

And, for information on how to manually calculate the APR of a loan please go to Chapter 12.

Also, as discussed above, when you are talking to a prospective loan customer, on the telephone, and you mention any Triggering Terms then those 'Terms' need to be clarified with that customer as well.

PATRIOT ACT (THE USA):

The USA Patriot Act was first signed into law by President Bush, on October 26, 2001 and is an amendment to the Bank Secrecy Act. The purpose of this Act, sometimes referred to as Section 326, is to prevent, detect, and prosecute those who may be money laundering and financing terrorism in our country. And, as a result of the USA Patriot Act, on October 1, 2003 it became a requirement for mortgage loan originators to further confirm the identity of all those we complete a loan application on. As loan officers, our primary job here, in satisfying the requirements of this Act, is to obtain specific information regarding the identity of those who wish to obtain a mortgage loan. In satisfying the requirements of the USA Patriot Act, we must:

1. Present and disclose the Patriot Act Information Disclosure, and
2. Complete the Patriot Act Information Form

The purpose of completing the Patriot Act Information Form is to obtain additional and specific information on prospective borrowing customers (borrowers and co-borrowers) regarding their identities. Much of the information needed to complete this form should be available on that customer's completed 1003. I also expect that you will need to obtain one to two means of identification for each borrower and co-borrower, with at least one of those being a photo ID (e.g. driver's license).

QUALIFED MORTGAGE RULE (QM)::

First, let's define what a Qualified Mortgage is. According to the CFPB a Qualified Mortgage is one that (the originating loan officer) has complied with the ATR requirements for that type of mortgage. And, the protection afforded that MLO is based on what type of Qualified Mortgage they originated. Now, as you recall, I previously presented in detail the subject of Qualified Mortgages within Chapter 6.

REAL ESTATE SETTLEMENT PROCEDURES ACT (RESPA):

The Real Estate Settlement Procedures Act is what we, within the mortgage lending business, affectionately refer to as RESPA. Congress first enacted RESPA in 1974 and it was the responsibility of HUD (now the CFPB) to enforce the Rules, Regulations, and Laws stipulated in RESPA. Many of the rules and regulations that we, within the mortgage lending business, must abide fall under what is referred to as Regulation X of RESPA.

Now, the essence of RESPA is that it is mainly focusing on the origination and closing costs and settlement procedures of owner-occupied, home mortgage loans. And, the purposes of RESPA are:

1. Enable mortgage home loan borrowers to be better shoppers when considering purchasing and/or refinancing their homes. In other words, to have the information they need, in a timely manner, to be able to contact other lenders and find out what their rates and fees are. Ideally, this should enable them to obtain the lowest and best interest rate and terms for their home loans.

2. Addresses those areas of concern that can unnecessarily increase the costs of the settlement services of a loan. This includes, for example, kickbacks, referral fees, and for services charged that were not actually performed.

3. Reduce the amount of funds, for homebuyers that are required to be placed in escrow for homeowner's insurance and property taxes on a home loan.

As I mentioned above, the rules and regulations of RESPA primarily focus on what are called "settlement costs for Federally Related Mortgage Loans." Now what does that mean? Well first, the term "settlement costs" means all services and their costs provided in a real estate settlement or mortgage loan. Essentially, it means services and costs that are part of mortgage loan transactions – and shown on the Loan Estimate. When I first heard the term "Federally Related Mortgage Loans," I have to admit it, I had to look that one up to be sure of it myself. But basically, Federally Related Mortgage Loans means purchase and refinance mortgage loans on 1-4 family units that are owner-occupied properties. Coverage of RESPA, however, does not include the following types of loans:

- A loan on property of 25 acres or more.
- Business, Commercial, and Agricultural loans.
- Temporary Financing, such as an interim construction type of loan. The exception to this would be if the lender, that is providing this Temporary Financing, would also be the lender for the Permanent (Take-Out) loan, then it is covered by RESPA.
- Vacant Land
- Assumption without Lender Approval: If a Federally Related Mortgage Loan contains an Assumption Feature and does not allow the lender the right to approve the subsequent borrower on that loan then it would not be covered under RESPA.

And, RESPA's requirements mainly relate to loan settlement costs, mortgage loan disclosures, the timeliness of those disclosures, and the Loan Estimate (also considered a loan disclosure).

The coverage of RESPA is quite vast, as it relates to the processing of mortgage loans as defined above. And, this creates quite a challenge in terms of covering it as completely as possible. It is for this reason I have presented and broken down the various aspects of RESPA, into its many parts and regulations, throughout this book.

SECTION 8 of RESPA:
Sooner or later you knew that I was going to talk about kickbacks and/or referral fees. Well, you were right, and this is the Section that addresses just that. Section 8, under RESPA, states that Referral Fees, Kickbacks, and Origination Fee Splits (i.e. between a mortgage broker and any other person) is strictly prohibited. Also prohibited, under Section 8, is what are called Unearned Fees. Unearned Fees are fees being charged for services that have not actually been performed. This, also, falls under part of Regulation X of RESPA. It's interesting, but Section 8 of RESPA seems to be the area where there is the most misinformation and myths and perhaps the main reason why there are so many violations involving this subject. I will talk about more about referral fees, kickbacks, and origination fee splits when we get to Section II of this book.

SECURE AND FAIR ENFORCEMENT FOR MORTGAGE LICENSING ACT: (SAFE ACT):
The President of the United States, during July 2008, signed into law the Housing and Economic Recovery Act of 2008 (HERA). Title V of HERA entitled The Secure and Fair Enforcement for Mortgage Licensing Act of 2008 (S.A.F.E Mortgage Licensing Act with

the purpose of enhancing consumer protection and reduce fraud by requiring all mortgage loan originators to be either state-licensed or federally licensed.

Under the S.A.F.E. Mortgage Licensing Act all states must implement a Mortgage loan originator (MLO) licensing process that meets certain standards through the Nationwide Mortgage Licensing System & Registry (NMLS). This Act requires all MLOs seeking state-licensure, or currently holding a state license, to pass the NMLS-developed S.A.F.E. Mortgage loan originator Test. That test includes both state and national components and those taking the test must obtain a score of 75% or better on each component.

If you are a loan originator organization for home loan transactions then you must provide the following information on specified loan documents (I'll list those below):

- Your name and NMLSR ID number (if the NMLS has provided you with an NMLSR ID number).

- The name of the individual loan originator (as the name appears in the NMLSR) who had primary responsibility for the home loan origination and his NMLSR ID number, if he has one.

Those home loan documents that must contain the loan originator's name and NMLSR ID number are:

- The Credit Application (e.g. the 1003).
- The Note or Loan Contract, and
- Loan Estimate
- Closing Disclosure
- The Security Instrument.

I should also mention here, that in doing the above, you do not need to include this information more than once on each of the above specified loan documents (i.e. no need to put that information on every page of each document).

And finally, since the passing of the Secure and Fair Enforcement for Mortgage Licensing Act of 2008 the days of simply reading a few mortgage regulations and then meeting with prospective home loan consumers is gone.

- Loan originators must be registered and licensed in accordance with the SAFE Act and State SAFE implementing law.

- Loan originator organizations must ensure that each loan originator who works for their organization is registered or licensed in accordance with the above law.

- All applicable NMLS requirements: Which includes completion of annual continuing education hours (depending on the State one originates loans in).

However, I do want to mention the exception to the above regarding screening and training requirements for mortgage loan originators as a result of this amendment to Regulation Z that became effective on November 24, 2019. According this amendment to Regulation Z, if a mortgage loan originator's organization employs an individual loan originator who is not licensed and is not required to be licensed, Regulation Z requires the loan originator organization to perform specific screening of that individual before permitting the individual to act as a loan originator and to provide certain ongoing training.

This interpretive Rule concludes that a mortgage loan originator's organization is not required to comply with certain screening and training requirements under Regulation Z if that individual loan originator employee is authorized to act as a loan originator pursuant to the temporary authority described in the SAFE Act.

To obtain information, guidance, and assistance on state participation, testing, pre-licensing, continuing education, and system updates visit the Nationwide Mortgage Licensing System & Registry's online resource center at:
http://mortgage.nationwidelicensingsystem.org/Pages/default.aspx

TILA-RESPA INTEGRATED MORTGAGE DISCLOSURES RULE:

Prior to this rule there was the Good Faith Estimate (GFE) and the Truth-In-Lending Statement (TIL) disclosures that were prepared (by you) and presented to your home loan customers. However, under the TILA-RESPA Integrated Mortgage Disclosures (TRID) rule, which came into effect on October 3, 2015, the Good Faith Estimate and Truth-In-Lending Statement were combined into one disclosure called the Loan Estimate. I should also mention that this Loan Estimate is also referred to as the TILA-RESPA Integrated Disclosure (TRID).

It's interesting to note that the previous Good Faith Estimate was originally designed under RESPA and the Truth-In-Lending Statement was designed under the Truth-In-Lending Act.

Now, the use and requirements for the Loan Estimate applies to all close-end mortgages for first and subordinate mortgage loans for purchases and refinances. However, the use and rules for the new Loan Estimate (and Closing Disclosure) do not apply to:

- Home Equity Lines of Credit (HELOCs – if open-ended)
- Reverse Mortgages
- Loans secured by mobile homes
- Loans secured by a dwelling that is not attached to the real property.

I should also mention that the TILA-RESPA Integrated Mortgage Disclosures for (e.g. the Loan Estimate) are not required for:

- Loans made by a lender that makes 5 or fewer mortgage loans a years.

- Certain no-interest mortgage loans secured by subordinate liens made for the purpose of down payment or similar home buyer assistance, property rehabilitation, energy efficiency, or foreclosure avoidance or prevention

One big change that we all saw, beginning October 3, 2015, was the shift of responsibility for the delivery and accuracy of the Loan Estimate (as well as the Closing Disclosure). Those responsibilities then fell fully upon the shoulders of the lenders and creditors of close-end federally related mortgage loans. Sure, loan originators, of mortgage brokers, could and can still prepare and send out the Loan Estimates, within 3-business days of the applications, to their loan customers. But the accuracy of those Loan Estimates ultimately lies with the creditor of the home loan. This is also true with the Closing Disclosure. And, the required delivery of the appraisal for a home loan.

The previous Good Faith Estimate, which came out in 2010, can still be used on all open-end federally-related mortgage loans. It's interesting to note that the original one-page Good Faith Estimate became effective and was required on all mortgage loans in 1974 and lasted up to 2010. The new Loan Estimate is designed to replace and combine the previous Good Faith Estimate and previously required Truth-In-Lending Statement. Because of this combination the new Loan Estimate is also referred to the TILA-RESPA Integrated Disclosure (TRID).

The Loan Estimate documents and summarizes all the costs of a loan that the borrowers will incur and states the total loan amount, the interest rate on that loan, the Term of the loan, and what kind of loan program it is (e.g. 30-Year fixed, 2-Year ARM). It also shows the Total Estimated Settlement Charges which summaries the total costs included in the loan as well as the sum of all the accounts being paid off (including the existing mortgage or mortgages on the subject property) with that loan.

The Loan Estimate is be prepared and sent to your borrowing customers within 3 business days after you have met with them and completed an application (1003) or received a completed 1003 in the mail from your customers. And, this rule also applies if you completed a loan application over the telephone. Also, early disclosure requires that the "final" (or revised) Loan Estimate be provided to the loan customer at least 4 business days before a customer's home loan consummation.

Now, when you do complete the Loan Estimate, the costs on this disclosure should be as accurate as possible and should reflect those loan costs that your customers can expect to see at their loan closing and shown on their Closing Disclosure (which replaced the HUD-1 Settlement Statement on October 3, 2015) as well. Within this section I will also discuss the Tolerances (or allowed variance) of loan costs shown on the Loan Estimate (or its revised one) to the costs on the final Closing Disclosure.

This Loan Estimate is different from the previous Good Faith Estimate and yet does have some similar features:

- They both have 3 pages.
- Some stated costs on the Loan Estimate, if increased from the allowed loan cost Tolerances from what is shown on the final Closing Disclosure from the original or revised Closing Estimate, will needed to be "cured" by the originating Broker and/or Mortgage loan originator no later than 60 calendar days after settlement.

- Prepaid expenses, for identifying those costs in calculating the APR of the loan, are now shown on the new Loan Estimate.

- The Loan Estimate enables you to item each loan cost feature, whereas the previous Good Faith Estimate combined and summarized the total cost of certain line items.

- However, the Loan Estimate does not contain a list of categories informing the loan consumer of the Tolerance Levels. And finally,

- The Loan Estimate does not contain a Tradeoff Table or Shopping Chart Comparison Tables.

I now would like to mention, on the following page, some important points you should be aware of when completing the Loan Estimate:

- **Definition of a Loan Application:**
  I remember years ago mortgage loan originators discussing what constitutes having received an application that required sending out a Good Faith Estimate and Truth-In-Lending Statement (the Loan Estimate now replaces these two loan disclosures). This discussion generally centered on talking with prospective loan consumers over the telephone. According to the new rule's definition of "application" by the CFPB, having the following (six) information items - triggers the timing requirement for a Loan Estimate:

  1. The Consumer's Name;
  2. Their Income;
  3. Social Security Number – to obtain a credit report;
  4. The subject property address;
  5. An estimate of the value of the subject property; and,
  6. The mortgage loan amount the prospective loan customer is seeking.

  If you obtain (all of) the above information, either by you asking or the prospective loan customer telling you then a Loan Estimate is required to be sent to them.

- **Rounding of Loan Amounts:**
  When entering the amounts onto most sections of the Loan Estimate you should enter whole numbers that are rounded up to the nearest whole dollar. However, percentage amounts are not normally to be rounded but should be shown and entered with two to three decimals as needed.

- **Consummation of the Home Loan:**
  The CFPB wants you to know that the Consummation of a loan is different from the Closing or Settlement of a home loan. For example, Consummation occurs when the loan consumer becomes contractually obligated to the creditor on the loan and not, for example, when the loan consumer becomes contractually obligated to a seller on a real estate transaction.

However, when a home loan consumer becomes contractually obligated to the creditor does depend on the applicable State laws where the home loan is being originated (and/or where the subject property is located – if different).

- **Tolerances Levels of Home Loan Costs:**
  As you may recall, on the previously required Good Faith Estimate, the CFPB introduced three levels of loan cost Tolerances for specific home loan costs (from the original or revised Good Faith Estimate to the final Good Faith Estimate at loan closing). These loan cost Tolerance are still required on the currently required Loan Estimate.

  1. Zero Tolerance
  2. 10% Tolerance, and
  3. Charges not Subject to a Tolerance

  So, let's go over the loan costs for each one of these three Tolerances so you are clear about what is required on this new Loan Estimate:

  1. **Zero Tolerance:**
     Here the loan costs shown on the final Loan Estimate must match with what is shown on the final Closing Disclosure. Any loan cost differences, if higher on the final Closing Disclosure, will need to "be cured" and paid back to the loan customer from the home loan creditor or lender (which usually means it is taken out of what you, the mortgage loan originator, make on that loan). Zero Tolerance applies to the following loan costs:

     - Origination Charges
     - Charges for third-party services for which the loan consumer is not permitted to shop;
     - Charges for any third-part services paid to an affiliate of the lender or mortgage broker;
     - Transfer Taxes.

  2. **10% Tolerance:**
     Here the loan costs shown on the final Loan Estimate may vary upwards to a maximum of 10% with what is shown on the final Closing Disclosure. If a loan cost item (for which this applies) is higher than 10% on the final Closing Disclosure, from the binding Loan Estimate, then the total amount greater than 10% will need to "be cured" and paid back to the loan customer by the home loan creditor or lender. This Tolerance Level applies to the following loan costs:

     - Recording Fees;
     - Aggregate amounts of loan costs for third-party service providers for which the loan consumer is permitted to shop for – and those third-party service providers are not affiliates of the lender or mortgage broker.

This Tolerance is also referred to as the "10% cumulative increase bucket" because the sum of charges for third-party services and recording fees, ultimately paid by or imposed on the loan consumer, does not exceed the aggregate amount of such charges disclosed on the Loan Estimate by more than 10%. In other words, the aggregate (cumulative) amount of fees subject to a particular loan category cannot increase by more than 10%.

3. **Charges Not Subject to a Tolerance:**
   Here, there is a no loan cost Tolerance Level placed on these particular loan cost items. Therefore, what is shown on the binding Loan Estimate and any difference on the Closing Disclosure as shown - is not really considered. These include:

   - Prepaid Interest (Interest Adjustment);
   - Property Insurance Premiums;
   - Amounts placed within an escrow, impound, reserve, or similar account;
   - Loan charges to a third-party provider that is selected by the loan consumer that are not on a list provided by the lender or mortgage broker;
   - Loan charges for third-party provider services that are not required by the lender.

As I mentioned above, the specific home loan costs shown on the final Loan Estimate must match with what is shown on the final Closing Disclosure – which is presented to the loan customer at their home loan closing. However, any loan costs that are higher than what is allowed for that listed Tolerance level (either Zero Tolerance or 10% Tolerance) then those costs (higher than what is allowed) will need to be what is call "cured". If a refund amount is required to be "cured" by the creditor, because of a Tolerance violation, then two things need to happen:

1. The creditor must refund to the loan customer the full amount to "cure" the tolerance violation no later than 60 dates after the home loan settlement.
2. The creditor must also deliver or place in the mail a corrected Closing Disclosure that reflects the refund no later than 60 dates after the home loan settlement.

However, I should mention that the above could be done either at and during the home loan settlement or after the settlement.

TRUTH-IN-LENDING ACT (TILA):
The Truth-In-Lending Act (12 CFR Part 1026) was enacted by Congress in 1968 and was most recently amended, by the CFPB, on April 1, 2019. It is affectionately referred to as TILA and/or as Regulation Z. Regulation Z represents those Regulations issued by the Board of Governors of the Federal Reserve System to implement the Truth-In-Lending Act. Regulation Z, as a part of TILA, addresses loan disclosure forms required on home mortgage loans, how the Annual Percentage Rate (APR) of a loan is calculated, and how the Truth-In-Lending Statement was to be prepared (much of the information within the

TIL is now presented within the Loan Estimate). While we're talking about the APR of a loan, it's important to remember that one of the main purposes of the APR is to translate specific costs of a loan (what are referred to as Prepaid Finance Charges) into a percentage and enable prospective mortgage loan borrowers to shop around and obtain that loan which offers them the best interest rate with the lowest loan costs. Now, here's an example I have used at first-time homebuyer seminars that illustrates the purpose of the APR - as the Federal Reserve Board, I believe, intended:

Let us say a woman decides that she wants a mortgage loan. She knows three lenders who she wouldn't mind doing business with to obtain a mortgage loan from. She also knows that each one of those three lenders provides excellent customer service - so she is indifferent as to which one she obtains her home loan with. She, therefore, is only interested in finding out which one of them has the loan she wants with the best interest rate and the lowest loan costs.

She begins her loan-inquiring quest and calls those three lenders and asks each one - what their best interest rate is for her home loan. The first one says 7.0%. The second one says 7.0%. And, the third also replies 7.0%. The woman says to herself, "Hmmm, those do sound like good rates, but who has the lowest loan costs?" In other words Who has the lowest APR? She then calls back each one of those lenders and asks, "Okay, you said the interest rate was 7.0% but what is the APR on that loan?" The first lender says, "7.25%." The second replies, "7.20%." And, the third tells her, "7.38%." So, which one should she go with? The quote with the lowest APR: The lender with the APR of 7.20%.

This is really the main purpose of the APR: To provide prospective borrowers with a means to compare rates and fees between different lenders and mortgage brokers as well. And, this is made possible because all lenders and mortgage companies should be calculating the APR the same way as dictated by the Federal Reserve Board.

Also, Section 1026.26 of Regulation Z contains guidelines and restrictions as to when you quote interest rates to loan-inquiring customers and advertise your mortgage company and/or your mortgage loan products. For example, as required by Regulation Z, whenever you discuss a possible loan with an inquiring loan customer and quote them an interest rate and/or closing costs and/or loan fees (what we call the Cost of Credit) or advertise an interest rate or rates, then you need to also quote (them) the APR for that loan and/or quoted interest rate. To clarify, let me give you a couple of examples:

1. A customer calls in and discusses a loan with you. You discuss with him or her your loan fees and/or quote them an interest rate. Then, you must also calculate and quote them (at that time) the respective APR for that loan and quoted interest rate – or a comparable APR for that quoted interest rate.
2. You mail out flyers to prospective customers with an interest rate you can offer them. You must also quote an APR for that interest rate shown on your flyer.
3. Your mortgage company has a billboard and quotes an interest rate for that day (for example). That billboard will also need to state the APR accompanying that displayed interest rate.

In other words, whenever you discuss the cost of credit on a loan and/or offer an interest rate to a prospective home loan customer then you must immediately follow that up with the cost of credit on that loan and/or with that quoted interest rate – the APR. I know this can be cumbersome and time consuming sometimes but this is what is required of us as loan officers in order to be "In Compliance". Failure to do just this could result in very serious consequences for you and the mortgage/lending company you work for. For more information regarding what is required when quoting interest rates to prospective home loan customers please refer to TILA's discussion on 'Oral Disclosures' at:
https://www.consumerfinance.gov/policy-compliance/rulemaking/regulations/1026/26/

UNIFORM STANDARDS OF PROFESSIONAL APPRAISAL PRACTICE:

There is a ruling under the Uniform Standards of Professional Appraisal Practice (USPAP) that came into effect January 1, 2005 and impacts and changed when a new appraisal is required to be ordered for a mortgage loan. Under this new ruling, if a home loan buyer or home loan borrower wishes to refinance or purchase a property then a new appraisal is required. This departs from the past, when lenders could transfer their rights of an appraisal from one lender to another and use that appraisal (as it was or have it re-inspected) to determine whether there have been any significant changes since that appraisal was originally done.

Let me give you an example as to how this new appraisal ruling applies:

Your new loan customers meet with you because they were not pleased with the service they received at XYZ Mortgage. They previously met with XYZ mortgage, to refinance their home, about one month ago. They were approved, and an appraisal was ordered and completed. They now want to do the loan with you and want to use that same appraisal (which they paid for). Remember, that whoever orders the appraisal owns the appraisal regardless of who paid for that appraisal directly. Secondary markets will not accept appraisals ordered by borrowers. If borrowers pay directly, also known as COD, it is merely an arranged payment for appraisal services between the borrowers and the lender; the borrowers have no claim to that appraisal - except that they are entitled to a copy of the appraisal from the lender if they request a copy in writing within ninety days of application for their loan.

Under this ruling, however, they would not be able to use that appraisal in their new loan with you. However, you could contact and ask the appraiser, who did that appraisal, if they would reappraise that property. And, because of the recent age of that appraisal also ask them if they could give you a discount on the cost of that appraisal. That, of course, would be up to them. But most appraisers I have met are fair and have been willing to consider giving a discount on completing an appraisal of that type.

But my main point here is: Whenever a borrower goes to another lender then a new appraisal is now required. So, when a new loan with a new lender is begun, then a new appraisal is required, regardless of when that previous appraisal, on the subject property, was done.

Now, if borrowers are not changing their lender but doing a new loan, and their appraisal is relatively recent, then that lender still, at least, needs to re-inspect that subject property and certify that there have been no changes, since their previous appraisal was done, either to the subject property or in the market, that would yield a lower appraised value.

In closing this chapter on Mortgage lending Regulations and Laws I'd like to say that just within the last 10 years we've seen a lot of changes in how we, as mortgage loan originators, are to originate and process mortgage loans:

- The new and previous Good Faith Estimate (2010)
- Dodd-Frank Wall Street Reform and Consumer Protection Act (signed into law 2010)
- Ability-To-Repay/Qualified Mortgage Rule (2014)
- High-Cost Mortgage Rule (2014)
- The Loan Origination Compensation Rule (2014)
- Appraisal Rule (January 18, 2014)
- The Loan Estimate (replaced both the Good Faith Estimate and Truth-In-Lending Statement in 2015)
- The Closing Disclosure (replaced the HUD-1 Settlement Statement in 2015)
- The Appraisal Rule (2015)
- The previously revised Uniform Residential Loan Application (2018)
- The new and currently required Uniform Residential Loan Application (2020)
- New home loan underwriting guidelines from Fannie Mae's *Eligibility Matrix* and *Selling Guide* (may significantly change from year-to-year).
- Maximum Loan Limits: for General and High-Cost areas (sometimes changes annually).

These new revisions and changes, by the CFPB and the "Powers That Be", to the mortgage lending process are a result of the continuing and increased concerns of predatory lending and to make the mortgage lending process as "transparent" and understandable as possible to prospective home loan borrowers. The area of mortgage lending is dynamic and I expect to see additional new regulations and laws as well as amendments to the existing mortgage regulations and laws.

As I mentioned above, in being a mortgage loan originator you need to be familiar with and originate your home loans according to what is currently required. And, you should also make every effort to ensure that you do follow the requirements of the above rules and regulations so that you and your home loans are "In Compliance". I know, it's not always easy but I know you can do it. Knowing what is required to stay "In Compliance" is the first step towards achieving that end. Also, in following the requirements of the above rules and regulations you are providing your customers with a level of customer service and lending professionalism that you can be proud of. Besides having a positive impact on your reputation as a mortgage loan originator this can also lead to loan referrals (from your loan customers) which in turn can contribute towards building up your mortgage loan originator business. And, that's a good thing.

Okay, enough about Mortgage Lending Regulations. The next chapter is titled *"Putting It All Together"* and it does exactly that: It summarizes all you have learned in this training manual into a kind of flowchart that you can use when originating and processing your mortgage loans.

Chapter 26

PUTTING IT ALL TOGETHER

In this chapter I are going to summarize what we have previously discussed into a sort of game plan that you can envision and follow whenever you are working on a home loan. Once you become more experienced in being a mortgage loan originator then this will become second nature to you. I recall when I was a new loan officer that I had to often think to myself, "OK, I did that, now let me see, I believe I now need to do this" and so on. To make it easier for you to conceptualize originating and processing of home loans, from beginning to end, I have put together the main steps that mortgage loan originators normally follow in processing their loans. I have separated each main step into what I call "Phases" with elemental sub-steps that are normally done in each phase.

Now, I would like to mention here that when I first wrote this loan officer training manual in 2004 there wasn't available many of the features that loan processing softwares offer today. In those days most loan officers prepared a loan file, for each prospective home loan customer, within a legal folder, and prepared and completed their 1003s, loan disclosures, and other supporting loan documents by hand. Later, the information for many of those loan documents were entered into a loan processing software (e.g. Genesis). Today, this has changed. With the advances that various loan processing softwares offer today most loan officers circumvent the previous need of preparing loan paper documents and prepare and maintain the origination and processing of their home loans on their computer. Thus, instead of creating a paper home loan file – all that information, regarding their home loan files, is now entered and shown within that loan officer's loan processing software. Now, while this is true, those steps you read below in the "Phases to process a home loan" are still relevant and need to be completed. So, please keep this in mind as you go through the Phases to Process a Home Loan.

If you are new to being a mortgage loan originator and want to be sure you haven't forgotten a loan processing step then I suggest making a copy of these Phases listed below and check-off each sub-step (in the arrows) for each task required and completed for that particular loan. Here then is the list of Phases to process a mortgage loan:

I. PHASE ONE: LOAN ORIGINATION:
⇨ Obtain the loan lead
⇨ Complete the Customer Pre-Qual Sheet
⇨ Setup a Meeting Time with your Loan Customer

II. PHASE TWO: MEETING PREPARATIONS:
⇨ Create (Preliminary) File Folder for your Loan Prospect
⇨ Order a Property Profile
⇨ Prepare a Preliminary 1003 (preferably on your LP Software)
⇨ Prepare Disclosures
⇨ Review (Anticipated) List of Loan Document Needs for this loan
⇨ Research Feasibility & Possible Direction of Loan based on Loan Goals expressed by those Customers:
  o Maximum LTV for that type of loan
  o Maximum Loan Amount based on Information so Far.
  o Possible Lender(s) for this Loan
  o Questions to ask (Based on information known)
⇨ If it's an Out-of-Town Customer – then Mail that customer a Loan Application Packet as discussed within Chapter 16 titled Out of Town Customers.

III. PHASE THREE: MEETING WITH LOAN CUSTOMERS:
⇨ Confirm Objective and Loan Goals of your Customers
⇨ Complete the 1003
⇨ Review & Complete Disclosures (For them to sign)
⇨ Review with Customers Needed Documents for their Loan
⇨ Review with Customers the Loan Process => What to expect
⇨ Give Customers Your Business Card and means of contacting you.
⇨ If it's an Out-of-Town Customer – Review the completed Loan Documents signed and returned to you. Also, call those loan customers then to let them know you have received their loan application. And, ask them any questions that they may not have answered on their home loan application.

IV. PHASE FOUR: RESEARCH LOAN:
⇨ Enter the new 1003 information into your LP Software - from your meeting with the customer, or based on the information on the returned (mailed) docs to you.
⇨ Order their Credit Report
⇨ Verify & Enter all Outstanding debts on 1003 in LP Software
⇨ Prepare an Initial Qualifying Analysis Worksheet on Your Customers
⇨ Research Loan:
  o Loan Options based on the Customer's Credit Scores and Monthly Income and Type of Collateral (e.g. Stick built house, Manufactured home, etc.).
  o Identify Type of Loan (Conforming, Non-Conforming, or Govie).
  o Most likely maximum LTV and Interest Rate based on Customer's Information.
  o Question: Can their Goals of the Loan be achieved? Is their home loan Doable? If Yes, then;
⇨ Research Pricing (Rate) Sheets of Prospective Lenders:

o   Identify (1-2) Lenders - Who can do those types of loans with the best Interest Rates and Service.
⇨   Call Prospective Lenders, if necessary, to answer any questions regarding them doing the loan and what their requirements are (minimum credit scores, maximum LTVs, maximum Ratios, types of acceptable Collateral).
⇨   Prepare Initial Loan Estimate to further determine loan feasibility (different loan amounts, LTVs, and range of interest rates). Remember to satisfy all requirements of the Safe Harbor Rule.
⇨   Decide on Most Likely (Loan) Numbers (loan amount, LTV, and interest rate)
⇨   Complete the Qualifying Analysis Worksheet. Do the numbers look acceptable for that loan?
⇨   Call Customer and discuss Findings. If OK with them then continue below. If Not OK, but loan is still feasible (requiring changes) then go back to:
⇨   Research Loan of Phase IV.

V. PHASE FIVE: PREPARE LOAN DOCUMENTS:

⇨   Prepare, Print, and Review the Loan Estimate.
⇨   Print Updated 1003
⇨   Prepare a Remarks Page discussing that Loan (optional).
⇨   Review all documentation on that loan. Question: Have you satisfactorily considered all 8 Ability-to-Repay underwriting factors? If not, then complete that factor or factors that requires reviewing. If yes, then go on to the next step.
⇨   Mail Customers the Loan Estimate, copy of signed Disclosures, with a Cover Letter (within 3 business days following your meeting with them or receiving the completed Loan Application Packet from that customer).
⇨   Obtain (Additional) Needed Loan Documents from Your Customers.
⇨   Submit Your Loan to a Targeted Lender for a Credit or Full Approval or have this done by the Loan Processor – after you have passed the loan file to her.
⇨   Maintain Your Comments Sheet, for your loan customer, throughout the Processing of that Loan.

VI. PREPARE TO PASS THE LOAN FILE TO THE LOAN PROCESSOR:

I should mention here that the purpose of a loan officer having a "Shadow File" is to store all supporting documents on that home loan customer.

⇨   Prepare a Shadow File on that loan.
⇨   Obtain and prepare a new loan file folder.
⇨   Place and attach all original documents of that loan into the new loan file folder according to your Branch's and/or your Loan Processor's preferred Loan Stacking Order.
⇨   Pass Loan File Folder with supporting documents received to the Loan Processor. However, this step may be circumvented if your Loan Processor is able to access that customer's home loan file, on your computer, via her loan processing software.

⇨ Coordinate with the Loan Processor what she will do and what she further expects you to do on that loan - regarding obtaining any additionally needed loan documents and/or information.

NOTES REGARDING THE LOAN PROCESSOR:

When the Loan File is passed onto the Loan Processor they will usually follow up with:

1. Contacting your Customers for any additionally needed documents (not yet received) and/or information needed.

2. Submits the loan file to the Lender you have selected with the program, interest rate, and terms you decided on (if you have not previously submitted that loan).

3. Assuming => The Loan is Approved! She receives the Approval sheet with all PTD and PTF conditions listed.

4. She reviews the Approval Sheet with you and you both decide who will do what and when - to satisfy the PTD and PTF conditions.

5. Orders all Lender requested Verifications.

6. Sends out the Loan Estimate to the customers (within the 3 business days) - if this has not already been done.

7. With your customer's (and your) permission she could lock the interest rate, on that loan, if you haven't already done so.

8. She or he orders the new Title Report.

9. Orders the Appraisal on the subject property.

10. Faxes or mails (if the Lender requires the originals) any Loan Verifications, documents received, and the Title Insurance Report to the Lender.

11. Confirms all PTD & PTF Conditions are satisfied and that the loan is ready to go to Docs.

12. If the Loan Processor feels that the loan is ready to go to docs then the Loan Processor will prepare and fax a Broker Demand Sheet to the Lender. This form lists all the important information regarding that loan plus information regarding the Closing Agent for your loan.

As you can see the Loan Processor can make your job a lot easier. As I mentioned before - there can exist crossovers as to who does what. So, it is very important that you both clearly understand who is going to do what and when - and then do it. When I have worked for mortgage companies in the past, that had a Loan Processor, I always tried to make a special effort to meet with my assigned Loan Processor at least once a week to review all my loan files with her. Doing this helped me to stay informed, in a timely manner, as to the current status of my loans, what yet needed to be done, and whether there were any problems or concerns regarding any of my loans. When you do this you generally are on top of all your loans. And, this is to be expected. I recommend you try to do this as well.

VII. COMPLETE ALL PRIOR-TO-DOC CONDITIONS:

⇨ Order the Appraisal (after loan approval) - if you have not yet done so.

⇨ Obtain any remaining needed documents and reports - to satisfy the PTD and PTF conditions.

⇨ Stay in touch with the Lender of this loan. Are interest rates changing? Should you lock the rate or wait. What rate does the customer want or what do you need to make this loan happen?

⇨ Once the Appraisal is received then make sure you review it. Then Fax, Email, or mail the Appraisal to the targeted Lender.

⇨ Once the Prelim. Title Report is received then make sure you also review it. Then Fax, Email, or mail that Prelim. Title Report to the targeted Lender.

⇨ Call that customer's Hazard Insurance Agent and request a new Binder and/or Declaration Page - which includes the new Loss Payee (new Lender on the loan).

⇨ Once the above is ordered (homeowner's insurance) and the Declaration Page is received then fax this to the Lender.

VIII. COORDINATE AND SCHEDULE THE LOAN CLOSING:

⇨ Prepare and email to the Lender – the Broker Demand (Pricing) Statement.

⇨ Call that Lender and find out when Loan Docs will or can be sent out.

⇨ Make sure the home loan customer receives their Appraisal 3 business days before home loan closing.

⇨ Contact the Closing Agent and determine available times they have to close that loan.

⇨ Call your Customers to coordinate a convenient time for them to sign docs and inform them of anything they need to bring to their closing (down payment funds, any documents, etc.).

⇨ Call back Closing Agent to Confirm Closing Time that is convenient with your Customers.

⇨ Prepare any loan documents you need to bring to the closing and/or documents that need to be signed by the customers (e.g. final 1003).

⇨ Show up to Your Customer's Loan Closing. And, bring a copy of their Appraisal, so after they have signed the Closing Documents then briefly review their Appraisal with them - if they would like you to.

Throughout these Loan Phases it should be your goal to contact your customers at least once each week to update them on the status of their loan or just to say hello. Customers can get "squirrelly" on you sometimes if they don't hear from you in a while and may start to call other lenders, banks, or mortgage companies (for their rates, fees, etc.). Don't let this happen to you. Stay in touch with your customers. It's all part of providing that level of excellent customer service that you said you would be giving them as their mortgage loan originator.

IX. AFTER FUNDING OF THE LOAN:

⇒ Give all original documents that may be in your Shadow File to the Loan Processor.

⇒ Prepare and mail a Thank You card or letter to your Customers.

⇒ Later => Mail your Customers a Christmas card or whatever to let them know that you have not forgotten about them (and hopefully they have not forgotten about you).

⇒ Make a (card) file of your customers with a note to remind you when to call them or send them a letter sometime in the future - letting them know you are alive and well and hope they are too. And, letting them know that you are (still) there - if they have any questions or financial needs whereby you can be of service them.

Remember, things change and your customers may later decide to purchase another home or may want or need to refinance their existing home for whatever reason. When and if that occurs then you want them to think of you. This is one way of building your future business.

In closing this chapter on 'Putting It All Together' I felt this might be an excellent time to discuss, on the following page, what I call here "The Golden Rules":

THE GOLDEN RULES

While these are not necessarily official rules, I feel that if you follow these suggestions then your life, within your mortgage office, will go a lot smoother and will enhance your chances of success as a mortgage loan originator.

> ➤ Return all calls and messages as soon as possible - at least within 24 hours.

> ➤ You should make every effort to call your loan customers at least once a week. If for nothing else - to say hello to them and let them know what's currently going on with their loan. Remember, 'Communication is Key' in our business.

> ➤ Do not interfere with another mortgage loan originator's relationship with their borrower. This includes discussing a loan with a borrower – who is working with another mortgage loan originator.

> ➤ Follow-up to be certain your electronic messages sent are received. This one trips up a lot of folks. After you have faxed or emailed (or however you sent) a document or documents then follow-up with a telephone call to be sure those documents were actually received.

> ➤ When you take a message, for another person in your office, always try to write down, on a message pad, all the other important stuff regarding that message: Date and time received, caller's name and phone number, and your initials or name (so they know who took that message).

> ➤ Do not ever lie to a customer. This includes telling a customer you locked their interest rate when you didn't or the loan has been approved when it hasn't (yet). Or, saying things like, "I guarantee you we can do that loan." Or, "Rates are going down" (you don't know that for sure). You get my point here: Not only is this unethical but it could also result in serious and negative consequences for you and your mortgage office.

> ➤ If your customers have given you instructions and permission to lock an interest rate now - then do it right then. Don't wait.

> ➤ Always be honest with your customers. If the prospective loan doesn't make financial sense to do or you cannot do it then tell them so and why.

As I have told new mortgage loan originators in the past, always try to be as ethical and the very best you can be, because after you have been in this business for a while you will develop a reputation as a mortgage loan originator. This will happen no matter what you do. So, protect your reputation. You want others, that know you or have heard of you, to see you as a mortgage loan originator who is honest, ethical, good to work with (a team player), takes care of their customers, and knows the loan products.

Let's go now to the final section of this book which contains a chapter that talks about a subject many new and experienced mortgage loan originators may and should be thinking about: Marketing Your Services.

Section VI

<u>MARKETING</u>

The final section of this book begins with a chapter on various marketing techniques that many mortgage loan originators have and still do to get the phones ringing and obtain loan leads and referrals. Following that I've included a chapter that contains some suggestions on how to be successful in your career as a mortgage loan originator.

This final Section, of the book, presents these subjects in the following two chapters:

➢ Marketing Your Services
➢ Closing Thoughts

So, let's begin this final Section with the chapter on Marketing Your Services.

Chapter 27

MARKETING YOUR SERVICES

𝕴 originally wasn't planning on having a chapter on marketing in this book because there are so many books you can find on marketing at your local bookstores and libraries. For many of these marketing books, the entire focus of them is on marketing and sales. And I can tell you that I have read quite a few of those books. However, as I said in the Introduction of this book, this book is primarily intended for those new to mortgage lending as well as providing a reference guide for new and experienced mortgage loan originators. And, just as there are few, if any, books on the shelves out there that specifically focus on the needs of the mortgage loan originator there are also few, if any, books that narrowly focus and address the many ways of marketing your services as a mortgage loan originator. But my main concern here was whether you would receive any training on sales and *Marketing Your Services* in the branch office where you start out your career as a mortgage loan originator.

With that thought in mind I decided to have a short chapter on marketing that would discuss some of the marketing activities that I personally, as a mortgage loan originator, have done and/or have seen other mortgage loan originators do. As mortgage loan originators, we are in the field of sales. Therefore, I strongly suggest you read as many books as you can on sales and marketing. I am not endorsing any particular author or books but I liked those I have read by Zig Ziglar, John Hopkins, Tom Peters, and Jay Levinson. As a professional, in the field of lending, you should try to be well read on books on lending, sales, and on providing excellent customer service.

Okay, let's say you are a new mortgage loan originator (but you have read this book) so you should be feeling fairly comfortable about your general knowledge of what mortgage loan originators do and how they process their loans. The thing is - if you don't have a loan lead then you have nothing to work on. Unless the telephone is ringing, from loan-inquiring customers, then you most likely will need to rustle up some business on your own. This is what I call *Marketing Your Services*. You should want to look upon what you do, as a mortgage loan originator, as your own business. And, as a business owner, one of the most important things you must consider, in order to ensure that your business will prosper and be an ongoing and viable concern, is how to *Market Your Services* as a mortgage loan originator. With that said, there is an acronym I recall hearing that I feel is appropriate here - and it is "**ABS**". Now, that doesn't mean anything nuclear, it means **Always Be Selling**.

Always be selling. Have you ever been to a party where there was a real estate agent who passed out business cards to everyone he or she talked to? That's an example of what I mean. That ties in with another rule to follow called: The 3-Foot Rule. If someone is within 3 feet of you (i.e. at a social gathering) you should introduce yourself and give him or her your business card. Believe me, if you religiously do this then you will be getting calls, every once in a while, from someone you gave a business card to who now has a need for that service you offer. It happens. When I was a new mortgage loan originator I tried to follow those two rules as much as I possibly could. I am not shy so this is not a problem for me. For example, my family and I were at the Silverwood Fair Grounds, during one summer about ten years ago (there you pay one fee and can get on all the rides and see all the shows). The place was fairly crowded and I was trying to talk my Brother into riding the roller coaster one more time. I looked over to my left and saw a nice-looking young couple sitting on a bench. I recall seeing those young folks before that day. I stopped trying to persuade my Brother, excused myself, and walked over to that couple. I introduced myself, asked them if they owned a home, and if not, to be sure to give me a call when they are ready to buy one. They were very nice and took my business card.

Now, I don't recall ever hearing back from that couple but that doesn't matter. The point here is: You have to let people out there know that you offer a service and for them to call you if and when they are thinking of refinancing or purchasing a home. And, you should do this to everyone you know. You never know when they or someone they know will have a need for what you have to offer. So, get your name out there. You will, no doubt, learn this lesson the hard way, as all of us have: You bump into a friend or someone you know but haven't talked with since you became a mortgage loan originator. They tell you that they just bought a house and are really excited about it (or just refinanced their home). You ask them, "How come you didn't call me?" They reply, "I didn't know you were in the business or a mortgage loan originator." So, try to minimize these types of (negative) experiences: Get Your Name Out There!

In *Marketing Your Services* as a mortgage loan originator that is the really the main objective: Getting your name out there so folks who have a need for your services will (hopefully) call you when they do. Having gone through that long preface, here is a list of things you might consider doing in *Marketing Your Services* and getting your name out there:

- ➢ Business Cards
- ➢ Farming Lists
- ➢ Meeting Bankers and other Mortgage loan originators
- ➢ Attorneys
- ➢ Real Estate Agents
- ➢ Newspaper Advertising
- ➢ Chamber of Commerce
- ➢ Internet Leads
- ➢ Internet Website
- ➢ For Sales By Owner (FSBO)
- ➢ Posters and Flyers

I. BUSINESS CARDS:

Having Business Cards is one of the least expensive and yet productive ways of advertising yourself and what you have to offer. It's also the easiest and quickest way to "get your name out there." Many businesspersons think that Business Cards are just small rectangular pieces of paper that have on them their basic information, like their name and contact information, and should always hand them out at every opportunity. Although some of that is true there is so much more to be aware of when preparing and giving out your Business Cards.

The Design and Type of Business Cards:

When first designing your Business Cards you should consider what information you want presented on the front of your cards. Information that is commonly printed on Business Cards is your name, business position (e.g. Mortgage loan originator), office and cell number, email address, website address (if you have one), and your mortgage company's street address and logo. Most professional looking Business Cards have this information printed with Black ink on white paper with a colored company logo.

The printed information on a Business Card could also be printed on "raised ink" giving it a more impressive appearance and feel as well on a textured paper and/or within a raised frame. These aspects of Business Cards are not necessary but can give your Business Cards a more professional and impressive appearance and sometimes it's that little bit of difference that can determine whether the person you gave that card to keeps it or not.

Because Business Cards are and can be an important part of your overall marketing plan you should consider having a statement or saying on your Business Card that might encourage that person, who received your Business Card to keep it and possibly follow up on it and later contact you. For example, you could have the following stated on your Business Cards:

- Call Me for a Free Home Loan Quote
- Residential and Commercial Loans
- Great Credit, Bad Credit, We do It All

Also, the back of your Business Cards could contain additional marketing and promotional information as well as information that could be useful to that person. For example, on the back of your Business Cards (for mortgage loan originators) you could list the various supporting documents prospective loan customers need to provide and/or bring when you meet with them to complete a loan application. Having that information, on the back of your Business Cards, can also be very useful for you when an interested prospect calls your telephone number shown on the front of that card. After you have talked with that customer and setup an appointment to meet with them to complete an application you can tell to please have those items listed on the back of your Business Card with them when you meet with them. That also saves the time you might otherwise spend in telling them what documents to obtain while they are writing down all those documents. So, consider what additional important, marketing, and useful information you could have on the back of your Business Cards. Most Business Cards are blank on the back and in putting important and useful information on the back of your cards will set you apart from the rest who don't.

In additional to those Business Cards that are commonly used and known there are also the folded Business Cards – that are also referred to as Tent Business Cards or Mini-Brochures. These types of Business Cards are folded cards that provide you with twice as much space to present your business and marketing information to prospective clients. These types of folded Business Cards are the same size as conventional Business Cards but have four sides to it. If you have a lot of information you would like to present to your prospects then this could be the way to go regarding the type of Business Card to choose. Additionally, folded Business Cards can be used like a mini-brochure to further promote your mortgage loan originator services and/or offer a special promotion. Taking this concept further, folded Business Cards could also be used as a small portable flyer for your products and services.

II. FARMING LISTS:

This is a common term used in our business that refers to obtaining a list of folks (usually homeowners) - with their names and addresses and, if you are lucky, their telephone numbers. This Farming List can usually be obtained from your local title insurance company. Just call up your local and favorite title insurance company and ask to talk to a Title Officer. When that person answers the phone then introduce yourself and tell them you are new to the business and work for a mortgage company and would like to meet with them to discuss developing a Farming List of homes for refinancing purposes (or for whatever your marketing goals are). They will know what you are talking about and some of those Title Officers (especially the more experienced ones) can be very helpful - not only in helping you develop your Farming List but also in other ways to market your services.

The Title Officer, in preparing a Farming List for you, will need to know what information or criteria you want to use in developing your Farming List: 1. What price range (of homes) are you looking for, 2. How far back do you want to go, as far as home ownership (i.e. 2-3 years since purchasing their home), 3. Any particular neighborhood or home building additions, and 4. How many homes do you want on that list? If you are not sure about the answers to any of these - don't worry. Listen to the Title Officer, ask for their suggestions, consider it, and then decide what you want.

Understand, that even though there is usually no charge for the title insurance company to provide you with this Farming List - they do usually expect something in return. They expect that for any loans you develop, from that Farming List, that you will order the title insurance policy and close the loan with them (if they provide that service). That's fair. It's Tit-for-Tat.

Once you get that Farming List you can send a letter or flyer to each address on that list. I have done both and I suggest you send a nice flyer telling them what you can offer them. Research I have read on this subject seems to suggest that one method (writing letters) is not much better than the other (one-page flyers). I have done both and prefer mailing flyers (with nice bright colors!). When you send out those flyers most marketers will tell you that you will be lucky if you get a 5% response rate. You should expect a 1% response rate. But hey, what's 1% of 250 flyers? That's almost 3 possible loans. When you are creating your flyers then those flyers should always address and attempt to answer two questions. And, you can expect that those two questions will be on the minds of those folks receiving your flyers: 1. What's in it for me? And 2. So What? If your flyer answers those questions then you most likely have created a very good flyer and one that will succeed over others that don't. In addressing those two questions, your flyers should contain the following (which your customers will most likely be asking themselves as well):

1. **What is it you are offering?**
   Various loan products, quick turnaround time, competitive rates and fees, and your excellent customer service.

2. **What is the benefit they will realize?**
   Translate the above features you offer into benefits they will realize.

3. **What is their motivation?**
   Again, translate what you have to offer into what would motivate them to take action NOW (e.g. Lower interest rates, no-appraisal fee, etc.). Always try to create a sense of urgency in your flyers for your customers to take action NOW. You see this all the time and this is one of the keys to successful marketing. For example, you may have seen a TV commercial whereby someone is selling the latest kitchen knives or whatever for ONLY $19.99. And then they throw in that phrase that creates that sense of urgency, "But Wait, if you call now within the next 10 minutes, we will include in this amazing offer...blah, blah, blah." You see what I mean?

4. **How does your flyer satisfy your customer's need or needs?**
   This need is oftentimes referred to as their "self-serving need" and can be the main reason they are compelled to follow up on your flyer.

Here's another thing you can do that few mortgage loan originators do - but has proven to increase the response rate on their flyers (sometimes by quite a bit): Call those customers on your Farming List about a week (or less) after you mailed them that flyer. I know, you may not like telemarketing but this can really work for you if you give it a try. And, of course, don't forget what we previously discussed regarding the DNC Rules. So, Farming Lists can be a good thing. Try to do at least one Farming List every other month.

Before I leave this section on Farming Lists I'd like to mention another marketing source where you can obtain Farming Lists. There are marketing companies out there that sell Farming Lists to lenders, mortgage companies, and mortgage loan originators just like you and me. Many times these marketing companies can provide for you Farming Lists containing names and addresses of homeowners that are located not only in your local area but in other states as well. Of course, here we are talking about some money needed – to pay for these types of Farming Lists. However, many times those lists can contain additional (marketing) criteria that are not available through a title insurance company's Farming Lists. This very thing enables you to more (narrowly) focus your target market - versus what we call shot-gunning the market. And, that could make a big difference in your response rate. For example, instead of marketing to Conforming type of Borrowers you may wish to focus instead on Non-Conforming and/or Sub-prime type of Borrowers and loans. Most of those marketing (list) companies can then generally provide for you a list of homeowners having those types of characteristics. But of course, this option needs to be considered from a cost/benefit standpoint. In other words, what is the cost (to purchase a Farming List) to the (possible) financial benefits of using that marketing company's Farming List? So, check out this (other) optional source of obtaining Farming Lists and see if it's something you'd like to explore and include in your marketing efforts.

III. MEETING BANKERS AND OTHER LOAN BROKERS:

If the mortgage company you work for provides what we call "Full Service" then this means you can do the full spectrum of loans: Conforming, Govies, Non-Conforming, and Sub-prime. Banks, by their nature, usually don't do Sub-prime loans. So where do they send their customers to who want to do a home loan but that they cannot help? Therein could be an opportunity. Also, not all mortgage companies are Full-Service Providers (although this is becoming increasingly rare these days). If you know some who are not Full Service then where are they sending their customers they cannot help? Also, Finance Companies could be worth checking out as well. Just use your imagination.

What you do here is: 1. Develop a professional looking flyer that shows all the various types of loans that your company offers (that this other company doesn't offer), 2. Get dressed in what is considered professional in your part of the country, and 3. Walk right into those places, introduce yourself, ask for just a few minutes of their time (and take only that), give them your flyer, tell them what you can do for them, and leave. When I have done this, going to banks for example, I never call beforehand: I walk right in and ask for the Branch Manager. If he or she is not there I then ask for the lead mortgage loan originator. Just be professional and they will usually be quite accommodating. And, following your visit to that company write them a nice follow-up letter thanking them for taking the time to meet with you and that you look forward to doing business with them.

IV. ATTORNEYS:

When it comes to these types of folks then I do suggest you give them some notice first. What I do is write them a short letter explaining our services (and how it could benefit some of their clients). And, at the close of that letter - let them know that you will be calling them on a certain date - to setup an appointment. Then call them on that date. If they are not interested in meeting with you then you can expect their secretary or receptionist to let you know this. No problem. Next. Just go on to the next Attorney call.

You know, it's kind of funny, but I have had the best success doing this with bankruptcy Attorneys. The irony is my services might enable their clients to avoid bankruptcy. However, there are some good Attorneys out there who are really looking out for the best interests of their clients. And, if some of their clients can avoid bankruptcy by refinancing their home and/or consolidating their debts then they may be happy to refer them to you. I have received, on more than one occasion, a call from an Attorney's client - asking if they could meet with me to discuss home refinancing to avoid bankruptcy. So, check this out and see if it works for you.

V. REAL ESTATE AGENTS:

I have found that most mortgage loan originators do not like to go out and try to develop relationships with Realtors (or Real Estate Agents). I understand them completely. However, I do suggest you at least give this a try. If you are planning on making this business a career of yours then you definitely want to do what you can to develop some Realtor relationships. But how do you do this and how should you approach them? First of all you should understand what a Realtor (realistically) wants from a lender or mortgage broker: 1. The ability to do difficult as well as easy loans, 2. To be periodically informed of the status of their customers' loans, 3. If a problem comes up then let them know about it right away, 4. To go the extra mile for your (their) customers to make it easy for them to complete the loan application and to obtain all the other required loan documents, and 5. That your loan costs are competitive. If you can do all those things and you tell that Realtor that you are with your customers from the beginning to the end because you attend all your customer's loan closings, then you might just have a chance with that Realtor.

Whenever I am interested in developing new realtor relationships - I don't call on the most experienced and highest selling Realtors. I have found that those Realtors have already established their lender relationships. You'd be wishful thinking - that you could steer them away from that lender relationship. You can try it. But for myself I wouldn't waste my time. What I do is call the Realtors who just started out in the business and/or recently relocated here. Those folks usually haven't had time to establish any lender relationships and, in many cases, they will be very happy to meet with you and see what you have to offer. They know that having a good mortgage loan originator that they can depend on and refer their customers to can help their business as well.

When you do meet with a Realtor dress professionally for that area (i.e. dress like they dress) and bring a professionally designed flyer with you to give them. Don't forget your business cards either. Do what I do when I have met with Realtors for the first time. After we have sat down and got settled in I look at them and ask, "Tell me (their first name) what is it that you look for and want in your lender relationships?" After asking that question - be quiet and listen to what they have to say. You will find that most Realtors are looking for those very things you are about to tell them that you have to offer them (and that we previously discussed above). They may also be surprised that you are beginning that meeting by asking them a question (of what they want) - instead of starting off by selling yourself and your company. Don't do that. Ask them what they want and need (in a lender relationship). Then tell and show them what you can do and then ask for the opportunity to serve them. And then leave. Try not to take any more than about 20 minutes to do this. Realtors are busy folks too and will appreciate your meeting being fairly short.

Also, during the meeting impress upon that Realtor all the points I covered above (1-5) and let them know you are always available to be reached on your cell phone. If you can (and are open to it) let that Realtor know that you are available to meet with customers and/or answer any lending questions that Realtor may have anytime, including the weekends (if you are). Since most Realtors work on the weekends, they will appreciate that and might even be very impressed by it. After your meeting, when you return back to your office, write and mail that Realtor a nice "thank you" letter for taking the time to meet with you and end it with something like, "I look forward to working with you." And, after your initial meeting with a Realtor continue to call or visit them every week thereafter to ask them how things are going with them and if there are any home purchase customers (or flyers, open house events, etc.) that you could help them with. There's the ole marketing "5-7 times" rule: Customers need to be contacted 5-7 times before they remember, follow-up, and/or purchase a product or service. So, follow this "5-7 times" rule with those Realtors you are working on. And, be persistent and consistent in your Realtor follow-up efforts.

When you are first starting out try to setup a meeting with a new Realtor about once a week. Remember, all you need is about 1-2 Realtors who refer to you some new (loan) business. Any more than that and you are in referral heaven!

VI. NEWSPAPER ADVERTISING:

I am not referring here to your city or town's main newspaper but those smaller shopping type of periodicals such as the Penny Saver and Nickel's Worth. Of course, we are again talking about some money needed to do this. But for an ad that costs perhaps $35.00 - $75.00 for a week - that's not too bad. Especially, if you can get at least one loan out of it (per month) and make about $1,000 - $2,000 from a home loan from that source. So, if you have a few bucks to spend on advertising then the Cost/Benefit of doing this just might be worth exploring.

VII. YOUR LOCAL CHAMBER OF COMMERCE:

About once a month most Chamber of Commerce organizations have a networking meeting, after working hours, whereby business owners, Chamber of Commerce members, and folks like you and me come together to meet, have fun, and network. These meetings are usually scheduled from 5:00pm to 7:00pm. I have always enjoyed attending these and sometimes I left with an appointment to later talk to a customer about a home loan. Of course, I am the kind of person that when I show up to these types of things that, before I leave, I have usually introduced myself to everyone there and left my business card with them as well. It's something I learned while in banking and watching the CEOs (Chief Executive Officers) do when they attended any of the bank's social or formal gatherings. The CEO would make his entrance - usually after most of the bank folks had already arrived. Once he made his grand entrance he would start moving to his left (from the door) and shake hands and chat with those folks he met as he moved around the room. Once he had made a complete circle of the room then he had pretty much met with most of the (important) folks there and had, during that time, a single drink (if it was proper to have one at that occasion). After making a complete circle of the room - if an important announcement was to be made, he would make it then. Afterwards, he would stick around (for a short while) to answer any questions and then would leave.

That is an example of what could be called "working the room." It seems that today, without thinking about it, that's how I operate when I attend business gatherings. I work the room - starting on the left as I enter the room. It's fun, I enjoy it, and before I leave I have had the opportunity to meet just about everyone there. Anyway, call your local Chamber of Commerce and found out when their next networking meeting is – and work the room. It could lead to some loans.

VIII. INTERNET LEADS:

I remember that over 14 years ago a mortgage professional was telling me that in about six years that the Internet would replace us as mortgage loan originators. He said that the Internet would offer homebuyers and homeowners the lending options we do today and that those folks could then shop the Internet market and get the best rates themselves. They would then no longer need us little ole starving mortgage loan originators. I begged to differ with that gentleman and told him the main reason why I didn't think that was going to happen. My reason: People still like to talk to people - eyeball to eyeball, belly-to-belly. That, however, may not be the only reason you and others still have a job as a mortgage loan originator - even though I still feel that it's a valid reason. The important thing here is: It is many years later and I don't have any concerns now or in the near future about your job, as a mortgage loan originator, being stolen or taken by the Internet.

However, the Internet does have many websites available today whereby individuals can shop for a loan and request for a mortgage loan originator to contact them to discuss a mortgage loan. And, this is the reason for including it here. There are also a number of Internet marketing companies that sell loan leads, which they receive on a daily basis (via their website on the Internet) from customers all over the USA who are interested in talking to a mortgage loan originator about doing a mortgage loan. They (the Internet marketing companies) in turn sell those loan leads to mortgage companies and people like you and me. As of today, some of those Internet marketing companies may require you to buy a minimum number of leads - with each lead costing a certain amount. Just a couple of years ago each lead was rather expensive. Today, I am finding that the price of the per-lead cost coming down to a point whereby it is quite reasonably priced. For example, about seven years ago one Internet marketing company I know quoted a fee of $525.00 for 15 non-exclusive leads ($35.00 per lead) or $875 for 25 leads. Now, out of say 15 leads my thinking was that I should be able to get at least 3 of those to the closing table. If I did, then that's about 20% of total leads purchased that would go to the closing table. That's a pretty good return on my investment don't you think? About that same time I contacted another Internet marketing company and paid them $675.00 for only 7 exclusive leads. Of those, I took 3 to the closing table (with a closing percentage of about 40% of total leads purchased).

However, today I am finding that things have changed in purchasing these Internet leads.

1. First, as I mentioned above, the price of these leads has come down quite a bit – whereby each non-exclusive lead now cost from $10.00 to about $25.00 – depending on which Internet marketing company you purchase the lead from. That cost represents current leads for that day. As leads get older (2 days or more) then the Internet marketing companies generally lower the cost of those leads as they age or get older. That's good.

2. Most Internet marketing companies that sell these (non-exclusive) leads will sell each lead only up to three times. Once a lead has been sold three times then it no longer is sold. That too is good.

3. Mortgage leads are sold as either exclusive or non-exclusive. If a lead is exclusive then that Internet marketing company may be selling that lead only to you. Of course, exclusive leads are more expensive – say about $45.00 or more. But the quality is much better and the chances of contacting the customer of that lead and taking it to the closing table is greater too.

4. Okay, now here comes the bad news. Non-exclusive leads are exactly that: They are sold to whoever purchases them and chances are those non-exclusive leads are also being sold by other Internet marketing companies as well. As a result, even though an Internet marketing company might sell each lead only three times there are other Internet marketing companies that may also be selling that lead. Therefore, (and I speak from personal experience here) by the time you do finally contact that customer (of that non-exclusive lead) that customer may have already talked to five other mortgage loan originators (who also purchased that lead). This can make it very confusing and sometimes overwhelming for a (lead) customer.

    And, this very fact probably explains why I was unable to contact, by telephone, less than 50% of those non-exclusive leads that I recently purchased from an Internet marketing company.

5. And, because of number 4 above, that probably explains why the generally accepted percent of total non-exclusive leads that go to the closing table averages around 10%. Exclusive leads have a higher expected percentage of total leads purchased going to the closing table - of about 15 – 20% or more – depending on the exclusivity and quality of that lead. For example, some Internet marketing

companies, for their exclusive leads, actually talk to their lead customers and obtain more qualifying information than you would normally obtain on non-exclusive leads. To me this means a lot: For a customer to take the time and effort to talk with a representative (of an Internet marketing company) is a tacit signal that that customer is serious and not just shopping around or testing the waters. That very fact can greatly contribute towards actually making contact with that customer and having the opportunity to offer them your services as well.

6. Some Internet marketing companies require you to deposit with them a minimum amount of funds before you can purchase leads from them. For non-exclusive leads the average amount I am seeing these days is about $100.00. However, when you get into exclusive leads then the Internet marketing companies, who sell these, usually require you to deposit with them an amount representing their minimum number of exclusive leads to be purchased. For example, if each one of their exclusive leads cost $45.00 and they require you to purchase a minimum of 25 leads then we are talking about an upfront deposit of $1,125.

I realize that $1,125 can be a lot of money. However, if you can come up with that amount of money then you should be able to recoup your investment after the first loan closing. And, after that - it's all gravy.

To assist you in appraising the quality of the leads that an Internet marketing company may offer, the following are some questions you should ask them when exploring this option:

1. Where and how do they obtain their leads?
2. How exclusive are their leads?
3. What information (on the lead customer) is shown when selecting a lead from their website?
4. What information (on the lead customer) is provided on each lead purchased?
5. If the lead customer wishes to do a Rate/Term refinance loan, to better their interest rate, is their current interest rate shown?
6. If the lead customer wishes to obtain a home purchase loan do they ask if the customer has identified the property they want to purchase?
7. Does the Internet marketing company charge more for each criteria (what they call filters) you select (e.g. no manufactured homes, minimum loan amount of $100,000, no 2nd mortgages)? If they do then this can tend to increase the amount you actually end up paying for each lead.

So, what does all this mean? Well, as a legal term so appropriately states it: Caveat Emptor (let the buyer beware). And, this especially applies if you are purchasing non-exclusive leads. And, don't forget the ole saying, "You get what you pay for." I have found this to be so especially true when purchasing Internet mortgage leads. My opinion on this is: Even though you may pay more for exclusive leads you will spend less time (and aggravation) following up on and trying to contact and speak with that lead customer (than you would with non-exclusive leads). And, your chances of taking those purchased exclusive leads to the closing table are better too.

So, explore this lead generating option and see if it's for you. If you can afford it then I do suggest you at least use it as one of your marketing sources of loan leads.

IX. INTERNET WEBSITE:

One way of advertising and marketing your services, as a mortgage loan originator, is by having your own Internet website. The Internet today is commonly used by homeowners and homebuyers when they are initially thinking about obtaining a mortgage loan. For this reason alone, it makes sense to be available to these prospective loan customers when they go shopping on the "net" for a loan. And, having a professional website you are available to them 24/7. What better way to start the day then to see on your website's email site that you have one or more prospective loan customers who have visited your website and would like you to call them to do a home loan?

Also, having your own website creates a sense of credibility in the eyes of those who are thinking about refinancing their home or buying a home and use the Internet to begin investigating what is happening or available in the mortgage market. If prospective home loan customers, who know you or have heard of you, cannot find you or your mortgage company (that may also list you) on the Internet then this could create doubt in the mind of that prospective customer - in terms of who you are and the mortgage company you work for. Many people, prior to working with or purchasing a major item from a company, will first investigate that company on the Internet. If that company does not have their own website or is not listed on the Internet then that tends to create suspicion and doubt of that company's actual existence, viability, and performance.

Just as it was with the cost of cell phones, the start-up and ongoing costs for a website today has come down considerably, making it quite affordable for virtually anyone to have a professional looking website of their own. And, many mortgage companies these days either have their own main website and list their mortgage loan originators on that website or offer their mortgage loan originators the opportunity to obtain a website provided by that mortgage company. If it's the latter then usually there is a nominal monthly fee of around $35.00 or more. But with these everything is setup for you. All you have to do is fill-in certain areas on your website: Like inserting a short "bio" and perhaps a picture of yourself. These company websites also usually offer visitors the opportunity to explore various loan products (provided by that mortgage company), shows what the interest rates are for that day, as well as provide links that enable them to request a mortgage loan originator on that site to later contact them to discuss the possibility of doing a home loan. And that's where the marketing advantages come from having a website: Receiving "warm leads" of prospective home loan customers who wish you to contact them to discuss the possibility of doing a mortgage loan.

However, if the mortgage company you work for doesn't provide a website for you then you should consider getting your own. If this is the case then the following are some important points you should consider:

➤ The Domain Name or URL of your website

➤ What company will Host your website

➤ Whether you design the website yourself or have an outside source do that

➤ What Information and options you want available on your website?

➤ How will you market your website?

Of course, how much money you have to invest and/or budget for your website has a lot to do with what website options you choose. If you have around $1,200 - $5,000 to spend on setting up and creating your own website then this can become a fairly easy project for you. You could then just contact and hire a website creating company and they will take care of all this for you. Just tell them how you want your website to appear and what to have within it. Sometimes these website companies can also provide Internet marketing services for your website – to help increase the number of visitors to your website.

On the other hand, if you have a tight budget that allows you a minimum amount of investment for your website then the following are some important points to consider:

1. Website Building Services:

If you want to build a personal website then virtually any website building company, on the Internet, can do the job for you. These types of Internet website building companies enable you to build your own website. Most of them offer over a hundred different website templates and formats that you can use to create your website. Once you've selected a template and format for your website then you simply enter the text and any pictures you wish to have on your website. At that point it's pretty much a "cut and paste" and "drag and drop" operation.

However, when it comes to a professional website, with the purpose of providing information and services to those interested in obtaining a mortgage loan, then you are looking to have a website that does more than just present information about loan products and what you can offer your website visitors. Here, you would want to also provide links on your website that provide choices for your website visitors and, most importantly, an opportunity for them to complete a short loan application with the purpose of requesting you to later contact them to discuss the possibility of doing a home loan. These types of website features are not normally offered by most website building service companies on the Internet. I therefore suggest you do some research on the Internet for those website building services that do offer what you are looking for and compare their prices.

For example, I recently researched this, by typing "Mortgage loan originator websites" on my Internet browser and up came a list of about 5 Internet companies that offer websites that are designed for those in the mortgage lending business. One of those Internet listed website building companies offered some of the following features to those interested in obtaining a website with them:

➤ Many Templates and Formats to choose from.

➤ Customer Rate Sheets that can integrate with your rate ticker.

➤ A Link that enables visitors to complete a mini or complete 1003.

- ➢ Hosting can be provided and included with your website.
- ➢ Provides up to 48 pages on your website.
- ➢ Has a Mortgage Glossary.
- ➢ Calculator options enabling website visitors to:
  - Calculate Monthly Payments with an amortization schedule
  - Determine the amount needed to borrow
  - Do a Rent vs. Own comparison calculation
- ➢ A News Ticker that is updated several times during the day.
- ➢ Ability to import into your LOS (e.g. Calyx Point, Encompass, Genesis). This saves you time if a visitor completed a mini 1003.
- ➢ Different pricing plans depending upon how many features you want on your website. For those above features, for one mortgage loan originator, this website builder company has a setup fee of $25.00 with a monthly fee of $19.99. Or, you could pay an initial and annual fee of $199.00, which would include your initial setup fee of $25.00 as well as your monthly fee of $19.99 (for that year).

And, with their Premium Plan (which appears more suited for a mortgage company) they also offer Instant Messenger Service, or as most of us refer to it as - Online Chatting. Of course, with that service you or someone would always need to be standing by a computer ready to chat with an online visitor to your website.

With the website features provided above I believe you can see that the benefits of getting your website setup with an Internet website building service that caters to and specializes in providing websites for those in the mortgage lending business.

2. **Domain Name or URL:**
Regardless of which way you go, in terms of selecting how you will setup and design your own website, one of the very first things you need to do is decide on the domain name of your website: What is commonly referred to as your website's URL. Your domain name or URL is the Internet address of your website. For example, a URL could read as: http://www.WeDoLoansFast.com.

There are a number of Internet service companies that provide this service for you. Some examples that come to mind are www.Register.com and www.GoDaddy.com. Once you have decided on a domain name for your website then Google the domain name you wish to purchase for your website. It will then research that domain name to be sure no one else is currently using or owns that domain name. If no one else is using or owns that domain name then you are good to go. If not then you might need to think of some variations of that domain name. The upfront fee for a domain name is usually its annual fee and those fees do change based upon what Internet company you setup your domain name with. For example, with GoDaddy.com it is only about $12.00 a year. However, there is a difference in cost for website domain names. As always, it's best to get on the Internet and shop around.

And finally, the name of your website domain or URL should be carefully considered. Most Internet experts will tell you that your domain name should match the purpose of a website - as those words could be the "keywords" that are often entered into the Internet browser when folks are searching for what you have to offer – within your website. That will more enable Internet searchers to find your website. Your domain name should also contain a word or words that are also within your website as well. This helps in listing your website on the various search engines like Google.com and Yahoo.com. For example, the domain name above of "WeDoLoansFast.com" clearly states the purpose of that website as well as contains a word within it (loans) that is most likely used many times within that website. After you've gotten your domain name setup then each year you will need to pay an annual fee to your URL service provider to keep that domain name. Otherwise, if you don't pay your annual fee before the annual due date then that domain name becomes available for someone else to purchase and own.

3. Advertise Your Website:

Once your website is setup and running then you need to make sure that every form of advertising you send out has all of your contact information on it including your website address. And, that includes your Business Cards, Marketing Flyers, Postcards, and Letters and within any promotional media like newspapers or periodicals. Also, if you do email marketing then you can also direct those prospective customers, who receive your email, to your website.

And, because it is a website you also should purchase the services of an Internet service provider that offers website traffic services. These companies list your website on some of the main Internet listing companies like Google, Yahoo, Vista, and many others. These Internet service providers, that offer Internet traffic services, normally charge a monthly fee from about $39.00 and up. So again, it pays to shop around and find out and compare what a company charges and what you get for their services. But regardless of which company you choose to obtain Internet traffic services from or you choose to do it on your own - you must advertise your website on the Internet if you intend to get a reasonable amount of Internet visitors to your website.

Having a website of your own is another way of advertising your mortgage loan originator services with the goal of increasing your loan pipeline. And, when you consider and compare the costs to implement other forms of advertising, within this chapter, then the costs for your own website can appear pretty reasonable.

X. FOR SALE BY OWNER:

For Sale by Owner are home sellers who are selling their home on their own - without the assistance and cost of a Realtor. The term "For Sale by Owner" is usually referred to as FSBO (pronounced FIS-BO). FSBOs can be a real opportunity for loans if you do it right. Just as with all the above marketing activities and suggestions I have discussed, you should also apply the same concepts with FSBOs. If you are offering your services as a mortgage loan originator to a FSBO and/or asking them to refer business to you then before you walk through the door to talk to those folks - you should have prepared to address the question that will be paramount on their minds => What's in it for me? If, in your presentation to them, you can reasonably answer this question (to their satisfaction) then you are more than halfway there and most likely they will do what they can to assist you - which benefits them in return.

In talking about FSBOs, you as a mortgage loan originator can offer them (your) services that can make selling their home a lot easier. You can prepare sales flyers for their home (that is for sale). You can be available on the weekends to assist anyone interested in obtaining a home loan to buy his or her property, to answer any homebuyer's lending questions, and/or complete a loan application for a prospective homebuyer. And that's what you want - to get the referrals of those who are interested in buying that house or are in the market to buy a house. Think of all the ways you can help that FSBO sell their house as quickly as possible. That's what they really want. If you can help them achieve that then most times they will be happy to listen to what you have to say and offer.

When it comes to the subject of FSBOs I always make sure I mention this little caveat about the Purchase and Sales Agreement (contract to purchase the subject property between the Sellers and the Buyers). Do be aware and know that when the time comes for the interested homebuyers to buy a home (from the home sellers) that you cannot assist and/or advise them (the home sellers and/or buyers) regarding the completion of the Residential Purchase and Sales Agreement. You would need a Realtor's (Real Estate) license to do this. They have had the training and have <u>legal</u> capacity to advise in these matters and in completing the Purchase and Sales Agreement. So don't get involved in this. If your FSBO does need a Purchase and Sales Agreement contract you could suggest he get one at the local business supply store. They usually carry copies of those.

XI. POSTERS AND FLYERS:

Here is a marketing approach I have not seen many mortgage loan originators use: Preparing and putting up Posters and Flyers at local merchants' business locations. For example, have you ever gone into your local supermarket and seen those flyers hanging on the board (as you first enter the store) that are selling something or offering you a service? Many of those flyers have small strips at the bottom of them - which have the telephone number of who to call if you are interested in buying that product or obtaining more information regarding that service. Using this approach you could create a flyer that tells all those folks, entering that establishment, about all the mortgage loan options available to them (that they may not be aware of), the great interest rates you can offer them, and how easy you can make it for them to meet with you and explore the options of:

- Purchasing the home of their dreams.

- Reducing their monthly mortgage payments by refinancing <u>Now</u> – when interest rates are as great as they currently are, and

- Reducing their monthly debt servicing by consolidating some or all of their outstanding debts.

And don't forget, if you are quoting an interest rate or stating loan fees (Cost of Credit) on your posters and/or flyers you will also need to display the appropriate APR for that quoted interest rate or stated loan fees (refer to MAPS Rule within Chapter 25 on Mortgage Lending Regulations).

There is a mortgage loan originator I know who uses this approach as one of the ways of Marketing her services. She prepares her flyers and attaches them to the announcement boards at the entrances of the local supermarkets, libraries, and wherever she thinks there is good customer traffic. And, she tells me that she gets calls every week from folks who saw her flyer, pulled off the tab with her telephone number on it, and called her. Some of those calls, she says, do turn into loans and go to the closing table. So, checkout this option and see if it works for you.

XII. ASK FOR THE SALE:

Although this is not a marketing or promotional technique to Get Your Name Out There - this process is so important to being a successful mortgage loan originator and salesperson that I believe it deserves mentioning. To be successful in sales (and as mortgage loan originators we are in a sales position) you need to ask the closing question, "Let's setup a time to get together to get started on this (the loan and the completion of the application). Would Monday or Tuesday be best for you?" I could give you a number of examples but I think you get my point. You <u>must</u> ask the customer for the sale. And, by the sale I mean (for example): 1. A meeting time, 2. A loan program you believe will achieve the goals of their loan, and 3. To lock in a rate that you believe will enable your customers to meet their financial and loan goals (and yours as well).

Whenever I have trained mortgage loan originators and get to this point, where I am talking about 'Asking for the Sale', I like to tell them a story about when I was a manager of an electronics and computer store many years ago. This story begins when one day I was assigned a new manager trainee - to train him on the business of store managing and how to sell high-end priced products (like computers) if he didn't already know. He was just starting out but Wow, what a salesperson. He really hustled and customers liked him. He was doing very well in sales but wasn't selling many computers. One day he came into my office and said, "Steve, I just don't understand it, I can't seem to sell as many computers as I would like. Just now I was talking to some customers about a computer, that I thought would be perfect for them, but they didn't buy. I took them through all the parts of the presentation - just like you showed me, but they didn't buy. What's up?" I listened very intently and then I asked him, "So you qualified the customers and took them to a computer that matched their particular current and future needs?" He replied yes. I then asked, "And you presented all the features and benefits of that computer - that we have gone over in the past?" He again replied yes. Hmmm.

I thought about this for a short while and then I asked him, "Did you ask them for the sale?" He then asked, "What do you mean?" I then asked him, "Did you ask them if they would like to buy that today or looks like this computer will do the job for you, or, why don't we get that today?" His reply was "NO".

We talked about this for a minute and it seemed to me that he was having a problem that a lot of salespersons suffer from: Fear of getting a No or rejection. So, this is what I told him, "Look, before you met with those customers you didn't have a (computer) sale and after you spent time with them you still had no computer sale. So, nothing has changed. Your sales are great but you have got to get over this hurdle and Ask for the Sale. Once you do this then your sales are going to go through the roof. Now, here is what I want you to do at your next computer sales presentation. When you are making your next sales presentation on a computer, that you think those customers might be interested in purchasing, I want you to be thinking to yourself, "I don't care if these folks want a computer or not. I didn't have a computer sale when these folks walked in and I probably don't have one now. But I am going to ask them the question to buy and if they don't, then it's OK, I won't care, I'll just go on to the next customer." The idea here was for him to not care about the outcome but just to do it - to ask the question and to Ask for the Sale. Before he left my office, he said he would give it a try and seemed excited about this approach as well.

This story has a happy ending. Two days later he came running into my office all excited and told he just sold two of our best and highest priced computers in our store! He said, "Steve, I did just like you said. I didn't even care what their response might be. And then after I was finished with the presentation and thought it was the right time to ask I just asked them if they would like to pick that up today. I'll tell you I was pretty relaxed about it because if they didn't buy, then it would be all right with me. I expected they weren't going to buy anyway. But what happened was the wife (of the couple) said that she not only wanted one computer for herself, but also would like to purchase one for her son, who is going through his first year of college. So, I rang up the sale of those two computers for that couple and they were very happy to buy those computers too. I can't believe, it really works - what you said." Well, the end of this story is that that management trainee shortly thereafter became the highest selling salesperson (in total sales dollars) in our district and also one of the management trainees who continually sold more computers in our district than most of the other management trainees. I should also note that it didn't take that guy long before he got his own store and became a manager himself. The point of all this is that once he learned how to ask the question (or questions) necessary to close the sale then his sales took off like crazy. Remember this when you are out there talking to customers or clients or a person (like an Attorney) who can refer loan customers to you: **Ask for the Sale**.

Chapter 28

CLOSING THOUGHTS

I sincerely hope that you've enjoyed reading this book and that it has achieved its main purpose: To provide you with the basic tools and information you need to begin your career as a mortgage loan originator. If you are an experienced mortgage loan originator then I also hope you found this book informative and will use it as a reference guide as well.

After having read this book one could ask, "Okay, now that I have the product knowledge of being a mortgage loan originator, what does it take to not only do well but to really succeed in this business?" That's a very good question. Unfortunately, I don't think there is any one answer to that question. Believe me, I have searched for the "Holy Grail" answer to that question. There are mortgage loan originators out there that are making annual incomes in the six-figure level. What are they doing differently that other mortgage loan originators are not? I don't know of any research that has actually been done to answer this question but I can tell you what you definitely need to do - to be successful in this business:

I. Know your loan products:
This includes not only knowing all the various types of loan products but how to properly and efficiently process and package the loan file so it progresses towards the closing table without delay.

II. Familiarize yourself with the current Lending Regulations:
I am referring, of course, to the regulations of the Real Estate Settlement Procedures Act (RESPA) and TILA as well as the current and latest required mortgage loan regulations from the CFPB. And, do everything you possible can to ensure your loans are "In Compliance".

III. Make every effort you can to provide the highest level of Customer Service:
I know we discussed this previously but this is so important. Communicate with your loan customers throughout the processing of their home loan. When they show up to their loan closing - there should be no surprises. You being there at loan closing will make sure this happens - right up to the end of their loan.

IV. Actively Market Your Services:
When it comes to marketing - you need to be pro-active here. Follow some of my suggestions, within Chapter 27 on *Marketing Your Services*, and any others you can come up with. And, don't forget about ABS and the 3-Foot Rule.

V. Stay in Contact with All Your Past Customers:

This is an area where I would say a lot of the mortgage loan originators out there drop the ball. They don't stay in contact with their past customers. What do I mean by past customers? Let me tell you a story that clearly exemplifies this point. After I had been a mortgage loan originator for almost two years, I decided I was ready to move on to the next level, for myself, and see what I could do differently that might result in being more successful and, of course, make more money. I remember what my Father used to say: He'd say, "Son, if you want to know how to be more successful then talk to those who are." So, I began asking around - who was the most successful and highest paid mortgage loan originator (in our area)? Some of the more experienced mortgage loan originators referred to this one guy to me who had been a mortgage loan originator for only about five years but pretty much did all his loan business on referrals (from past customers) and made about $150,000 a year (good income at that time). That sounded impressive to me so I called up that mortgage loan originator (let's call him John). I told him, "John, I've been in the mortgage business, as a mortgage loan originator, for about two years now and I understand you are one of the top guns around these parts. Would you have time to meet with me and tell me a little about what you do or have done to be so successful?" John chuckled and said, "Well, I don't know what I can tell you but sure, how does this Wednesday morning at 10:00 am in my office sound?"

I guess I don't have to tell you that not only was that time okay but I was there at 9:50 am - ready to hear what it takes to go on to the next level. At 10:00 am sharp John came out and greeted me and then led me into his office. We sat down and began to chat. Finally, I asked him, "John, can you tell me what you think you do differently that separates you from what other mortgage loan originators do and makes you more successful?" John scratched the back of his head and replied, "You know Steve, I am not sure if this is what you're asking for but quite simply - I take care of my customers and stay in contact with them." While saying that, he pulled opened one of his desk drawers and took out three plastic (3 x 5 inch) card file boxes and placed each one on his desk in front of me. Then he said to me, "These are my boxes of gold. The first box here - contains card files of all my customers I have done loans on, with the dates of their birthdays, marriage anniversary, and other important dates in their lives."

"The second box here contains the names of those customers I have talked with and/or met with but which their loan was subsequently denied - for whatever reason. I note that denial reason on their card, with the expectation that when that denial reason no longer exists then I will call them back."

"And, the third box here, this contains customers who I have talked with but either told them to hold off on doing their home loan then and/or recommended that they do it sometime in the future. Could be that they filed bankruptcy only 8 months ago or for whatever reason doing a home loan at that time did not make financial sense or would really benefit them. I note that on each customer's card and when it would be a good time to follow up and contact him or her. When that reason may no longer exists then I call them back."

"Now, the important thing" as he continued, "Is to stay in contact with these customers of mine. I send them birthday cards, anniversary cards, son and/or daughter graduation cards, Christmas or special religious holiday cards. Even those customers of mine that were denied or I could not help at that time I do the same. After a while, of doing this, these customers know me by my first name and when any of them are thinking of doing a home loan - who do you think they will call? Or, when I do finally call these customers of mine, who were previously denied or I recommended that they hold off for a while, do you think they will remember who I am? You bet they will. You see Steve, it's all about customer service. After you have been in this business for a while it's really about the level of customer service that you provide that separates you from the pack. Any mortgage loan originator that has been in this business for two or more years could be at a point whereby they are receiving referrals during every month of the year - instead of constantly looking for new business. That's really about it. Take care of your customers and your customers will take care of you."

I left that meeting with a new perspective on marketing myself. Now, I cannot say that I have followed the same method that John has. But how many mortgage loan originators out there even do a fraction of what he does? The point here is: Stay in contact with your past customers.

I have really enjoyed the time I have spent writing and rewriting this book and, in a way, it has been a fulfillment of a dream of mine that I have had for some time: To put together a training book and manual for mortgage loan originators that would truly be informative and instrumental in learning the fundamentals of being a mortgage loan originator. If you bought this book for that purpose and it achieved that for you then I have reached my goal as well. If you have any comments and/or suggestions on how I could improve this book then I very much would like to hear from you. Please email me your comments at: StevenD@MortgageTrainingLibrary.com and I will return your email as soon as I can.

Also, if your mortgage company, bank, or lending company has a need for a mortgage loan originator training guide or manual I would be happy to discuss that with them. Simply email me the name of your company's representative, with their telephone number, and I will call them promptly.

And, if you would like a copy of the Exhibits, within this manual in PDF format, then just email me your request at: StevenD@MortgageTrainingLibrary.com and I will get that to you straight away.

Again, I thank you for purchasing this training manual and wish you all good luck, success, and prosperity in your career as a mortgage loan originator.

BIBLIOGRAPHIC NOTE

Chapter 1:

John T. Molloy. *Dress for Success*. Warner Books. August 1978.

John T. Molloy. *Live for Success*. William Morrow. 1981.

EXHIBIT I

Name: _____

~ WEEKLY LOAN STATUS REPORT ~

FOR WEEK BEGINNING: _____

BORROWER'S NAME	TEL. NO. #	TARGETED LENDER	LOAN AMOUNT	LOAN TYPE	RATE	INT. LOCK ENDS	LOAN NEEDS	CUSTOMER'S RESPONSE
			$		%	/ /		
			$		%	/ /		
			$		%	/ /		
			$		%	/ /		
			$		%	/ /		
			$		%	/ /		
			$		%	/ /		
			$		%	/ /		
			$		%	/ /		
			$		%	/ /		

485

EXHIBIT II

Date: ____/____/____

CUSTOMER PRE-QUAL WORKSHEET

BORROWER: _____ HM PH: _____

WK PH: _____

CO-BORROWER: _____ HM PH: _____

ADDRESS: _____

_____

HOW DID THEY HEAR ABOUT US?
    RADIO   NEWSPAPER   FLYER   OTHER: _____

PURPOSE:
    REFI/CO   REFI/RATE TERM   LOWER RATE   REMODEL   PURCHASE
        CONVERT TO FIXED   BALLOON DUE   SECOND MORTGAGE

PURCHASE:
    SALES PRICE: $_____   DN PAY. AMT: $_____
    ADDRESS: _____

REFINANCE:
    CURRENT O/S 1ST MTGE BAL: $_____   MO. PAYMENT: $_____
    O/S 2nd MTG BAL: $_____   MO. PAYMENT: $_____
    VALUE OF PROP.: $_____   REQ.CASH-OUT AMT: $_____

PREPAYMENT PENALTY? YES: _____   NO: _____
    IF YES, THEN HOW MUCH TO PAYOFF THAT LOAN? $ _____

PROPERTY TYPE:
    SFR   O/O   NOO   UNITS: _____   COMMERCIAL
    STICK BUILT   MANUFACTURED HOME - SW DW TW / YR BLT: _____

CREDIT RATING:
    1 2 3 4 5 6 7 8 9 10 => TEN BEING EXCELLENT!
    REMARKS: _____

_____

    BANKRUPTCY? YES NO / TYPE? 7 13 / MO/YR DISCHARGED _____

EMPLOYMENT:
    BORROWER EMPLOYER: _____
    YEARS THERE: _____   YEARS IN PROFESSION: _____
    GROSS MONTHLY INCOME: $ _____   OTHER MO. INC.: $_____

    CO-BORROWER EMPLOYER: _____
    YEARS THERE: _____   YEARS IN PROFESSION: _____
    GROSS MONTHLY INCOME: $ _____   OTHER MO. INC.: $_____
    TOTAL MONTHLY PAYMENTS TO CREDITORS: $_____

SSN: BORROWER: _____ - _____ - _____   CO-BORR.: _____ - _____ - _____

EXHIBIT III

TO: John Smith

FROM: Steven Driscoll
             Senior Mortgage Loan Originator

RE: Some Comments on Your Home Purchase Loan.

On my last memo that I sent with your loan application packet, I stated that even though the interest rate is 9.50%, for a 30-Year Fixed Rate loan, that I felt we did pretty well here. I'd like to explain why I said that and put some perspective on the subject of interest rates.

Lenders primarily price or charge interest rates on their loans - based on the borrower's credit, the loan-to-value (LTV), and the property being purchased. Quite simply, it's the relationship of risk to benefit. From a lender's standpoint, as the LTV on a loan goes up (especially when it goes over 80%) then the risk on that loan is perceived to be greater, and so the interest rate is increased in some proportion to this increased perceived risk. Applying this risk philosophy to the borrower's credit, as their credit moves away from having excellent or very good credit then, this too, is perceived as increased risk and the interest rate is increased to accommodate this. Single-family residences that are occupied by their homeowners, are perceived by Lenders as having the least amount of risk of all property (investments) and therefore are generally offered the best interest rates - comparatively speaking.

Now, in applying the above to your home loan I will only look at comparing your loan at 9.50%, with an LTV of 95%, and with no mortgage insurance to a more conventional type of loan with an LTV of 95% with mortgage insurance.

Looking at the Loan Estimate I recently mailed you, with an interest rate of 9.50%, the principal and interest (P&I) on that loan is $2,795.42. Now most (conventional) lenders charge mortgage insurance when the LTV is greater than 80%. The higher the LTV (above 80%) the more mortgage insurance is required. At an LTV of 95% the annual mortgage insurance is usually about 1.15% - 1.20% of the total loan amount or outstanding balance. This total amount of mortgage insurance per year is broken down into 12 monthly payments. If we applied this to your loan and conservatively use the mortgage insurance percent of 1.15% then that translates into an annual amount of $3,823.18 or a monthly mortgage insurance payment of $318.60.

Now if we subtract this monthly mortgage insurance amount from your (current) P&I payment of $2,795.42 that results in a net P&I mortgage payment of $2,476.82. With a monthly P&I mortgage payment of $2,476.82, for a 30-Year Fixed Rate Loan, that translates into an interest rate of 8.16%! This rate is actually better than what we initially discussed at about 8.25% - 8.50% that would have included mortgage insurance. If you focus on the total monthly mortgage payment instead of the interest rate I hope you can begin to see that we have indeed done pretty well here.

I should also like to note that as borrowers move away from conventional type of loans that lenders generally set up their loans to have a prepayment penalty period of 2 - 3 years. To eliminate this prepayment penalty usually cost the borrower from one to three points of the total loan amount. Your loan has no prepayment penalty and gives you the liberty to refinance in the future, at the proper time, and get into a conventional type of loan with a much better interest rate.

I apologize if my explanation here is long winded. However, I hope this has been informative and you have a better feel and understanding of your loan. Please feel free to call me if you have any questions or concerns regarding your loan. I thank you.

EXHIBIT IV

<u>LOAN APPLICATION NEEDS</u>

Your Home Loan Application Package Contains the Following Documents:

    O Residential Home Loan Application
    O Completed Loan Estimate
    O Loan Disclosures

Please review, complete, and/or correct those areas where I have highlighted in yellow on those documents. When you are done then please return these loan documents with copies (preferably) or originals of those documents listed below where I have placed a check.

    O Last 2 Years W-2's
    O Last 2 Years Tax Returns
    O Current Profit & Loss Statement
    O Paycheck Stubs (Covering Last 30-day period)
    O Last ___ Months (full) Bank Statements
    O Pension 401K Mutual Funds and IRA's Statements
    O Divorce Decree and/or Property Settlement Statement
    O Full Bankruptcy Papers
    O Landlords' Name Address and Phone Number (for last 2 years)
    O Other: _____

If you have any questions and/or wish to contact me then please call me at (XXX) XXX-XXXX. I thank you for the opportunity to be of service to you.

Your Name
Mortgage Loan Originator

EXHIBIT V

TEMPORARY LEAVE INCOME WORKSHEET

I. **Month Temporary Leave Income:** $_____
    (That she will be receiving from her employer)

II. **Available Liquid Assets per Month:**

    Total Liquid Assets of Borrower: $_____

    Closing Costs of Loan: (-) $_____

    Available Net Liquid Assets: (=) $_____

    Total Months on Temporary Leave: (÷) #_____
    (Divide Available Net Liquid Assets by
    the Total Months on Temporary Leave

    Available Liquid Assets per Month: (=) $_____
         (+) $_____

III. **Qualifying Temporary Leave Income per Month:** $_____
    (Add Mo. Temp. Leave Income + Available Liquid Assets per Month)

Fannie Mae Underwriting Notes:
The combination of these two incomes (equaling the Qualifying Temporary Leave Income per Month) may not exceed the borrower's Regular Monthly Employment Income.

The Lender must reduce the amount of the borrower's Total Liquid Assets by the amount of Reserves used to supplement the Temporary Income. Thereby, avoiding the borrower's Reserves being used for both Income and Assets.

EXHIBIT VI

FIXED 30-YEAR
CALCULATING PRIVATE MORTGAGE INSURANCE

LTV	Coverage	Exposure	30-Year Loans	15-Year Loans
95.01% - 100%	40%	60%	109%	98%
	35%	65%	96%	85%
	30%	70%	84%	73%
	25%	75%	71%	60%
	20%	80%	59%	48%
90.01 - 95%	35%	62%	90%	79%
	30%	67%	78%	67%
	27%	70%	71%	60%
	25%	72%	67%	56%
	22%	75%	63%	52%
85.01 - 90%	22%	71%	47%	36%
	17%	75%	39%	28%
	12%	80%	34%	23%
85% and below	25%	64%	43%	32%
	20%	68%	39%	28%
	17%	71%	37%	26%
	12%	75%	32%	21%
	6%	80%	27%	16%

I have used the above PMI matrix to explain how to calculate the monthly PMI payment for your customers. Conforming lenders today using Fannie Mae guidelines will generally use the following Coverage requirements for their fixed rate loans as shown below:

	~ Coverage Required ~	
LTV	15 Year Fixed	30-Year Fixed
90.01 - 95%	25%	30%
85.01 - 90%	12%	25%
80.01 - 85%	6%	12%

Adjustments to PMI Annualized Rates

Rate and Term Refinances:	Subtract 0.05% from Rates Shown Above
Cash-Out Refinances:	Add 0.10% to the Rates for LTVs > 80%
Second Homes:	Add 0.14% to the Rates Shown Above
Investment Properties:	Add 0.38% to the Rates Shown Above

NOTE:
This is shown for exercise purposes only and does not necessarily reflect current PMI rates and percentages.

EXHIBIT VII
APR Calculation Worksheet

I. Home Loan Features:
- **Loan Amount:** $ _____
- **Interest Rate:** _____%
- **Mortgage Product:** _____
- **Loan Term:** _____ Years
- **Monthly P&I Payment:** $ _____

Number of Payments	Amount of Monthly Payments

Finance Charge: The dollar amount the credit will cost you.	Amount Financed: The amount of credit provided to you.	Total of Payments: The amount you will have paid after you've made all payments.
$ _____	$ _____	$ _____

Itemization of the Loan Amount of $ _____

$ _____ Amount Financed
$ _____ Prepaid Finance

Charge

Amount paid to others on your behalf:

$ _____ To: _____
$ _____ To: _____
$ _____ To: _____
$ _____ To: _____
$ _____ To: _____
$ _____ To: _____
$ _____ To: _____
$ _____ To: _____
$ _____ To: _____
$ _____ To: _____

Total Prepaid Finance Charge: $ _____

Annual Percentage Rate (APR):
Take the above amounts and numbers and calculate the APR of the loan as shown on Calculation of the APR on page 335: _____%

EXHIBIT VIII
TIP Calculation Worksheet

I. Home Loan Features:
- **Loan Amount: $ _____**
- **Monthly P&I Payment: $ _____**
- **Loan Term (Months) : _____**

Amount of Monthly Payments	Term of Loan (Months)
$_____	#_____

Loan Amount: The amount of credit provided to you.	Total Finance (Interest) Amount: The dollar amount the credit will cost you.
$_____	$_____

Calculation of the TIP of a Home Loan:

1. Multiply the monthly P&I of that home loan times the number of months of the Term for that loan;

2. Subtract, from the amount in #1 above, the amount of the original loan amount of that home loan. That gives you the Interest Amount of that loan.

3. Divide the amount of Interest Amount (from #2 above) by the amount in #1 above.

Total Interest Percentage (TIP): _____%

EXHIBIT IX
PROPERTY PROFILE

OWNERSHIP INFORMATION

Owner	John and Jane Smith
Co-Owner	
Site	123 E. Anywhere Avenue, Coolsville, USA 99555
Mail	123 E. Anywhere Avenue, Coolsville, USA 99555
TxpyrNam:	John and Jane Smith
TxBillAdd:	123 E. Anywhere Avenue, Coolsville, USA 99555
Parcel #:	54321 123 Bldg # 1 of 1
Land Use:	Res. Single Family Residence
Legal:	Lot 1 Block 2 GREATVIEW ADDITION

PROPERTY CHARACTERISTICS

BedRms:	2	**Heating:** Forced		**Year Built:**	1980	**Ext. Wall:** Plywood	
TotlBaths: 2.5		**Fireplace:**	Yes	**Living SF:**	1514	**Interior:** Drywall	
HalfBaths:	1	**DishWshr:**		**Bldg SF:**	1514	**Foundatn:** Concrete	
FullBaths:	2	**GarbgDisp:**	Yes	**Bsmt %:**	79	**Garage:** Attached	
DiningRm:		**Pool:**		**Attic:**	No	**Garage SF:** 648	
Utility:		**Patio:**		**Condition:**	Good	**Deck:**	
InterCom:		**Stories:**	1	**RoofShape:** Gable		**MiscImpv:** Miscell	

SALES AND LOAN INFORMATION

Date Transferred:	09/03/1999	**Loan Amount:**	$127,600
Sales Price:	$159,950 Full	**Prior Sales Price:**	09/02/1993
Deed Type:	Warranty	**Prior Sales Date:**	$131,750

ASSESSMENT AND TAX INFORMATION

Total:	$139,300	**Tax Dist:**	Central Valley
Land:	$ 24,000	**2020 Tax:**	$2,198.07
Structure:	$ 115,300	**IrrTax:**	
Other:		**SWTax:**	
% Imprvd:	83%	**TaxRate:**	01561640001
Exempt:		**School:**	Central Valley
Exempt Type:			

EXHIBIT X   Page 1 of 2

EXHIBIT X

LENDER RATE SHEET

Best Rates in the Universe Lender
1000 Light Years Avenue
San Francisco CA 94100

Telephone: 800-765-1000
Fax: 800-765-1100
Gotcha@BestRatesUniverse.com

Rate Lock Desk
Tel: 800-765-1200
Fax: 800-765-1300
RateLock@BestRatesUniverse.com
Cut-Off Time: 2:00 pm

FEES:

Document Preparation	$70.00
Flood Certification	$25.00
Assignment Fee	$10.00
Tax Service	$75.00
Underwriting Fee:	$450.00

Date: 06/01/2021
Time: 8:00 am PST

CONFORMING 30-YEAR (AFG30)

	15	30	45
5.625	3.375	3.625	3.875
5.750	0.750	1.000	1.250
5.875	0.000	0.250	0.500
6.000	-0.375	-0.125	0.125
6.125	-0.875	-0.625	-0.375

See ALTAF30 for Other Adjs.

Pur & R/T Stated/FICO>700	0.250
Inv. Property-Max LTV <=75%	
25K – 59,999	0.500
60K – 99,999 (No Impounds)	0.250
FICO < 620	1.000

ALT A 30-YEAR (ALTAF30)

	15	30	45
6.125	-0.875	-0.625	-0.375
6.250	-1.350	-1.125	-0.875
6.375	-1.750	-1.500	-1.250
6.500	-2.375	-2.125	-1.875
6.625	-2.750	-2.500	-2.250

All Other AGF30 Adj. Apply

2 Unit 90.01-95% (Pur & R/T)	0.500
Cashout 80.01-85%	0.500
Cashout 75.01-80%	0.250
80/15/5	0.250
N/O/O 75.01-80%	2.000

CONFORMING 15-YEAR (AGF15)

	15	30	45
5.625	-1.125	-0.875	-0.625
5.750	-1.500	-1.250	-1.000
5.875	-1.875	-1.625	-1.375
6.000	-2.375	-2.125	-1.875
6.125	-2.750	-2.500	-2.250

See ALTAF15 For Other Adjustments.

Inv. Property <= 75%	1.500
Pur & R/T Stated /FICO>700	0.250
80K – 99,999 / No Impounds	0.250
FICO < 620	1.000
25K – 59,999	0.500

JUMBO 30-YEAR (JLF30)

	15	30	45
6.250	-0.250	-0.125	0.000
6.375	-0.875	-0.750	-0.625
6.500	-1.375	-1.250	-1.125
6.625	-1.875	-1.750	-1.625
6.750	-2.125	-2.000	-1.875

2nd Home / 2Units / Low-Combo	0.500
C/O FICO – 660-679/LTV>=90%	0.250
LP /DU Accept Required	
LTV <=70.0% / FICO >= 720	-0.250
LTV>90%/HI-Condo	1.000
Max L/A=650K/Min FICO=640	

JUMBO 15-YEAR (JLF30)

	15	30	45
5.750	-0.125	0.000	0.125
5.875	-0.750	-0.625	-0.500
6.000	-1.375	-1.250	-1.125
6.125	-2.000	-1.875	-1.750
6.250	-2.125	-2.000	-1.875

2nd Home / 2Units / Low-Combo	0.500
C/O FICO – 660-679/LTV>=90%	0.250
FICO >=720% / LTV<=70%	-0.250
LP /DU Accept Required	
LTV>90%/HI-Condo	1.000
Max L/A=650K/Min FICO=640	

JUMBO 5/1 ARM (JLT5C1)

Margin: 2.75 Index: 1.880 CAPS: 5.0/2.0/5.0

	15	30	45
4.375	1.250	1.375	1.500
4.500	0.875	1.000	1.125
4.625	0.500	0.625	0.750
4.750	0.000	0.125	0.250
4.875	-0.375	-0.250	-0.125

Condo <= 4 Units	0.250
Second Homes	0.500
LTV/CLTV Cannot Exceed 90%	
Call for FICO/LTF Adjustments	
No Impounds	0.250
Cashout Up to 75%	0.250

40-YEAR TERM 5/1 ARM (JLF40)

Margin: 2.75 Index: 1.880 CAPS: 2.0/2.0/6.0

	15	30	45
5.000	1.000	1.125	1.500
5.125	0.500	0.750	1.000
5.250	0.000	0.250	0.500
5.375	-0.500	-0.250	0.000

Max 80% to 750K / 90% to 500K

750K – 1 Million	0.375
Max Rebates Apply-Please Call	
No Impounds (Primary Only)	0.250
California Properties	0.250
Max. LTV 75% to $1 Million	

A-MINUS (AMINF30)

	15	30	45
6.875	0.875	1.125	1.375
7.000	0.750	1.000	1.250
7.125	0.500	0.750	1.000
7.250	0.250	0.500	0.750
7.375	-0.375	-0.125	0.125

80K – 99,999, C/O 75.01 – 80.0	0.250
75/20/5, 80/10/10	0.500
25K – 59,999, C/O 80.01-85%	0.500
80/15/5, C/O 85.01-90.0%LTV	0.750
N/O/O <= 75.0	1.500

GOVT. 30-YEAR (FHA30)

	15	30	45
6.000	-1.000	-0.750	-0.625
6.125	-0.875	-0.625	-0.500
6.250	-1.750	-1.500	-1.375
6.375	-1.875	-1.625	-1.500
6.500	-3.000	-2.750	-2.625

25K – 59,999/ HUD REPO	0.500
N/O/O (2.0 For HUD REPO)	1.500
Ln Amt. 60K -74,999 /FICO < 550	0.250
Loan Amount 75K – 99,999	0.125
20 Year	0.375

PRICES SUBJECT TO CHANGE WITHOUT NOTICE

EXHIBIT X

Page 2 of 2

THE LENDER'S RATE SHEET

CONFORMING 30-YR FIXED (AGF30)

	<u>15</u>	<u>30</u>	<u>45</u>
5.625	3.375	3.625	3.875
5.75	0.750	1.000	1.250
5.875	0.000	0.250	0.500
6.000	-0.375	-0.125	0.125
6.125	-0.875	-0.625	-0.375
6.250	-1.375	-1.125	-0.875
6.375	-1.750	-1.500	-1.250

PUR & R/T STATED>700 FICO (.5) > 730 FICO	0.250
INV. PROP <=75%	1.500
25K – 59,999	0.500
60K – 99,999 / NO IMPOUNDS	0.250
FICO < 620	1.000

Index

ABOUT THE AUTHOR

Steven W. Driscoll has been in the mortgage lending business for over eighteen years and currently lives in Spokane, Washington. Since entering the mortgage lending business in 1995 he has been a mortgage loan originator, branch manager, trainer, and has given live and online presentations on residential mortgage loan products and services. Prior to mortgage lending, he was an internal consultant for banks in the San Francisco and San Diego, California areas where he gave training seminars on operations analysis and productivity improvement. He received his Bachelors of Science degree, from San Francisco State University in Banking, and MBA in Organizational Development, from National University in San Diego, California. Training and helping individuals improve their job performance is something that Steven has always enjoyed and finds personal satisfaction in doing. He is also the author of six mortgage training books:

- The Loan Officer's Handbook for Success
- Trainer's Guide for The Loan Officer's Handbook for Success
- Organizing Your Mortgage Branch for Success
- The Mortgage Loan Originator's FHA Loan Manual
- The Complete Loan Processor's Handbook
- Mortgage Lending Regulations and Laws
  (Co-authored with Frank Torch)

If you wish to contact Steven Driscoll then email him at:
StevenD@MortgageTrainingLibrary.com

Made in the USA
Middletown, DE
19 July 2021